Soc   Social Cognition

Social Identity and Social Cognition

Edited by

Dominic Abrams and Michael A. Hogg

Copyright © Blackwell Publishers 1999

First published 1999
Reprinted 2000

Blackwell Publishers Ltd
108 Cowley Road
Oxford OX4 1JF
UK

Blackwell Publishers Inc.
350 Main Street
Malden, Massachusetts 02148
USA

British Library Cataloguing in Publication Data

A CIP catalogue record for this book is available from the British Library.

Library of Congress Cataloging-in-Publication Data

Social identity and social cognition / edited by Dominic Abrams
and Michael A. Hogg.
    p.   cm.
Includes bibliographical references and index.
ISBN 0–631–20642–6 (alk. paper). – ISBN 0–631–20643–4 (pbk.: alk.paper)
    1. Group identity. 2. Social perception. 3. Social groups.
I. Abrams, Dominic, 1958– . II. Hogg, Michael A., 1954–
HM131.S5843   1999
302.4–dc21   98–29202   CIP

Typeset in 10 on 12.5 pt Sabon
By Puretech India Ltd, Pondicherry, India
http://www.puretech.com
Printed in Great Britain by MPG Books Ltd, Bodmin, Cornwall

This book is printed on acid-free paper

Contents

Figures

Tables

Contributors

Dominic Abrams is Professor of Social Psychology and director of the Centre for the Study of Group Processes at the University of Kent at Canterbury, UK. He obtained his BA from Manchester University, his MSc from the London School of Economics, and his PhD from the University of Kent. He held lectureships at Bristol University (1983) and Dundee University (1985) before returning to Kent in 1989. His primary research interests are social identity, group decision processes, and the role of norms in social behavior. In addition to numerous articles and chapters, he has published three books with Michael Hogg, *Social Identifications*, *Social Identity Theory*, and *Group Motivation*, and is co-editor of a quarterly journal, *Group Processes and Intergroup Relations*.

Mahzarin R. Banaji took her PhD from Ohio State University, completed postdoctoral work at the University of Washington, and is currently Professor of Psychology at Yale University. Her research interests focus on unconscious processes in social judgment and the emergence of self in social context. She has served as Associate Editor of the *Journal of Experimental Social Psychology* and *Psychological Review*. She received Yale's Lex Hixon Prize for teaching excellence and, recently, a fellowship from the Guggenheim Foundation.

Rupert Brown is Professor of Social Psychology at the University of Kent. He graduated from the University of Edinburgh and obtained his PhD from the University of Bristol. His primary research interests are in group processes, especially intergroup relations and prejudice. He is the author of *Group Processes* (1988) and *Prejudice* (1995).

Richard J. Crisp received his PhD from the University of Cardiff, where he is currently a postdoctoral research associate. His research interests are the antecedents, processes, and social consequences of multiple categorization; multiple stereotype formation and use; and the effects of majorities and minorities on perceived group variability.

Julie M. Duck is a lecturer in the School of Psychology at the University of Queensland. She received a BA and PhD from the University of New England, and after positions as lecturer at the Australian National University and as a postdoctoral research fellow at the University of Queensland, she accepted a lecturing position at this university in 1996. Her primary research interests are group processes and intergroup relations, especially in the context of use and responses to the mass media. She has published more than 20 journal articles and book chapters, and has served on the Editorial Board of *Human Communication Research*.

Shelly D. Farnham is a doctoral student at the University of Washington, having received her undergraduate degree at Georgetown University. Her primary research interests are self-esteem, self-concept, and social identity, and interactions among the three.

Susan T. Fiske, Distinguished University Professor of Psychology, joined the University of Massachusetts at Amherst faculty in 1986. A 1978 Harvard PhD, she has authored over 100 journal articles and book chapters; she currently edits, with Gilbert and Lindzey, *The Handbook of Social Psychology* and, with Schacter and Zahn-Waxler, the *Annual Review of Psychology*. Her federally funded social cognition research focuses on social structure, motivation, and stereotyping. Fiske won the American Psychological Association Award for Distinguished Contributions to Psychology in the Public Interest, Early Career. She also won, with Glick, the Gordon Allport Intergroup Relations Prize from the Society for the Psychological Study of Social Issues for work on ambivalent sexism.

Anthony G. Greenwald is Professor of Psychology at the University of Washington in Seattle. He received an AB degree at Yale University, and AM and PhD degrees from Harvard University, and taught at Ohio State University from 1965 to 1986. His primary current research interests concern unconscious cognition generally, and unconscious influences on social behavior specifically. He is a recent recipient of a Research Scientist Award from the National Institute of Mental Health of the US Public Health Service.

David L. Hamilton is Professor of Psychology at the University of California, Santa Barbara. He received his PhD from the University of Illinois and previously was on the faculty of Yale University. His research investigates a variety of issues in social perception, including stereotyping and group perception, impression formation, and attribution processes. He has edited or co-edited four volumes concerned with social cognition.

S. Alexander Haslam is a senior lecturer in psychology at the Australian National University. He obtained his MA Hons from St Andrews and his PhD from Macquarie. His research is primarily focused on social identity and self-categorization processes in group and organizational contexts. He is a co-author of *Stereotyping and Social Reality* (1994) and *Doing Psychology: An Introduction to Research Methodology and Statistics* (1998), and co-editor of *The Social Psychology of Stereotyping and Group Life* (1997) and *The Message of Social Psychology: Perspectives on Mind in Society* (1997).

Miles Hewstone obtained his doctorate from Oxford University and is now Professor of Psychology at Cardiff University. He has published widely on the topics of attribution theory, social cognition, stereotyping, and intergroup relations. His current research focuses on stereotype change and the reduction of intergroup discrimination. He is co-founding editor of the *European Review of Social Psychology* and a former editor of the *British Journal of Social Psychology*.

Michael A. Hogg is Professor of Social Psychology and Director of the Centre for Research on Group Processes at the University of Queensland, Brisbane. He graduated from the University of Birmingham, UK, obtained his PhD from Bristol University, and was a postdoctoral research fellow at Macquarie University, Sydney. His other past appointments have been at Bristol University and Melbourne University, and he has held visiting positions at UCLA and UC, Santa Cruz. Most recently he was visiting professor of social psychology at Princeton University. He has published widely on group processes, intergroup relations, and social cognition, and has been closely associated for 20 years with the development of social identity theory and self-categorization theory – his books *Social Identifications* (with Dominic Abrams) and *Rediscovering the Social Group* (with John Turner and others) are landmark publications in this area. He is founding editor with Dominic Abrams of the journal *Group Processes and Intergroup Relations*.

Sarah B. Hunter is a PhD candidate in social psychology at the University of California, Santa Barbara. She received her BA in psychology as a University Scholar at New York University. She is currently working on her dissertation, which examines the impact of cardiovascular challenge and threat on cognitive processing. Her primary research interests are social influence, intergroup relations, and physiological and cognitive responses to social stressors. She is also interested in applications of social psychology to public policy and has consulted for the RAND Corporation.

Lorella Lepore is a lecturer in the Department of Psychology at University College, London, UK. She was co-principal and principal investigator on two grants from the Economic and Social Research Council of Great Britain while at the University of Kent at Canterbury (UK). After receiving her PhD from the University of Kent in 1996, she moved to the University of Maryland, where she was a postdoctoral research associate until 1998. In 1997 she was awarded the Society for Experimental Social Psychology Dissertation Award. Her research interests include automatic cognitive processes, stereotyping and prejudice, and motivated social cognition.

Amy C. Lewis is a graduate research assistant at Indiana University, Bloomington. She graduated from Arizona State University and is currently in the PhD program at Indiana University. Her research interests are perceptions of individuals and groups, group membership, and judgment and decision-making.

Vance Locke completed his undergraduate education at Murdoch University and his doctoral research at the University of Western Australia, where he is now a lecturer. His main interests are in the relationship between prejudice and stereotypes, and the interplay between automatic processes and processing goals in stereotype activation.

Diane M. Mackie is Professor of Psychology and Communication and Associate Dean of the Graduate Division at the University of California, Santa Barbara. She received a PhD in social psychology from Princeton University after gaining her undergraduate degree at the University of Auckland, New Zealand. Her research focuses on the interplay of the affective, cognitive, and motivational processes that shape social influence and intergroup relations. The recipient of several research and teaching awards, Dr Mackie is the co-author (with Eliot Smith) of an introductory textbook, *Social Psychology*, as well as author of numerous articles and chapters on social psychological topics.

Barbara-A. Mullin graduated from the Australian National University and obtained her PhD from the University of Queensland. She has published a number of journal articles and has given conference presentations on the role of uncertainty reduction in social identification and intergroup discrimination. While at the University of Queensland she was a co-convenor of the annual Brisbane Social Identity Conference and a member of the Centre for Research on Group Processes. She is currently a freelance researcher and educator in psychology.

Penelope J. Oakes is a reader in social psychology at the Australian National University. She obtained her BSc and her PhD from Bristol University. Her main research interests are in areas of stereotyping, group processes, and intergroup relations. She is a co-author of *Stereotyping and Social Reality* (1994) and *Rediscovering the Social Group: A Self-Categorization Theory* (1987), and co-editor of *The Social Psychology of Stereotyping and Group Life* (1997).

Don Operario received his PhD in social psychology from the University of Massachusetts at Amherst. His dissertation focused on the intersection between social identity and social cognition, examining how members of stigmatized groups perceive and react to discrimination depending on the strength of their stigmatized-group identity. His current work, at the University of California at San Francisco, investigates how these social identity and social cognition processes impact the stress levels and health outcomes of members of stigmatized groups.

Katherine J. Reynolds is a postdoctoral research officer in the Division of Psychology at the Australian National University. She received her BA and her P. Grad. Dip. Psych. from the University of Queensland, and her PhD from the Australian National University. Her PhD examined the social psychology of impression formation, and she is currently pursuing interests in areas of stereotyping and intergroup discrimination. She is the co-editor (with Martha Augoustinos) of an upcoming volume on prejudice and intergroup conflict.

J. Mark Rubin is in the third year of his PhD at the University of Cardiff, where he is studying the social psychological processes underlying intergroup discrimination.

Steven J. Sherman is Professor of Psychology at Indiana University, Bloomington. He graduated from Harvard University and received his PhD from the University of Michigan. His areas of interest are judgment and decision-making, perceptions of individuals and groups, and counterfactual thinking.

Eliot R. Smith is Professor of Psychological Sciences at Purdue University in West Lafayette, Indiana. He obtained his AB and PhD degrees from Harvard University and served on the faculty at the University of California, Riverside, before coming to Purdue in 1982. His research interests are in social cognition, particularly implicit memory, stereotyping and intergroup relations, and the self. He is also interested in applying connectionist models of mental representation and process in social psychology. With Diane M. Mackie, he is co-author of a textbook, *Social Psychology*.

Deborah J. Terry is an Associate Professor in the School of Psychology at the University of Queensland. She received a BA and PhD from the Australian National University, and after a one-year postdoctoral fellowship in the School of Psychology at the University of Queensland, accepted a lecturing position at this university in 1991. Her primary research interests are attitudes, social influence, persuasion, group processes, and intergroup relations. She also has applied research interests in organizational and health psychology. She has published more than 70 journal articles and book chapters, and two edited books: *The Theory of Reasoned Action: Its Application to AIDS-Preventive Behaviour* (1993) and *Attitudes, Behavior, and Social Context: The Role of Group Norms and Group Membership* (1998, with Mike Hogg). She is on the Editorial Boards of the *European Journal of Social Psychology* and *Group Processes and Intergroup Relations*.

Daan van Knippenberg is a senior lecturer of organizational psychology at the University of Amsterdam, The Netherlands. He graduated from the University of Groningen and obtained his PhD from Leiden University. After his PhD he worked at Leiden University, first as a researcher at the Centre for Energy and Environmental Research, then as a lecturer of social and organizational psychology. His current research interest is in social identity processes in organizational contexts.

Theresa K. Vescio received her PhD from the University of Kansas and is currently a postdoctoral researcher at the University of California, Berkeley. Her research focuses on how various perceiver attributes (intergroup attributions, value endorsement, perceived outgroup variability) and target attributes (individuating characteristics, multiple group memberships) influence stereotype activation, contrastive and assimilative stereotype use, and the revision of stereo-typic beliefs.

Iain Walker is a senior lecturer in social psychology at Murdoch University in Perth, Western Australia. His education is the responsibility of the University of Adelaide, Flinders University, and the University of California at Santa Cruz. His primary research interests are in stereotyping and prejudice, relative deprivation, and the psychosocial issues involved in medically assisted reproduction and organ donation. He is co-author with Martha Augoustinos of *Social Cognition* (1995), and is co-editor with Heather Smith of *Relative Deprivation Theory: Specification, Development, and Integration* (forthcoming).

Preface and Acknowledgments

Ten years ago, in 1988, we published a book describing social identity theory. In that book we reflected the traditional European concern that social cognition was too fixated at the level of individual cognition to be of much help in understanding the behavior of people in groups. We argued that social identity theory was better suited to the analysis of groups because it integrated cognitive, interactive, social, and societal levels of explanation, and the specification and integration of these levels was essential to a proper social psychology of group phenomena. However, even then we felt concern and sadness about the scientifically deleterious effects of polarized opposition between largely North American social cognition and largely European social identity theory. Indeed we, along with many colleagues in Europe and North America, have spent the last ten years working towards a rapprochement – it became increasingly obvious to us and our North American and European colleagues that both "sides" could learn from one another, and indeed were learning from one another.

This development has gathered momentum in recent years, and it was very late at night in a bar in Washington in September 1995 that we realized that the time had come to try to capture this integrative theme in a book. Quite appropriately, the occasion was the joint meeting of the European Association of Experimental Social Psychology (EAESP) and the Society of Experimental Social Psychology (SESP). We finalized the plan at the EAESP meeting in Gmunden, Austria, in July 1996 and at the International Congress of Psychology in Montreal, Canada, in August 1996. We then invited contributors, concentrating on researchers who had been strongly identified with one of the two traditions, and gave them a brief to relate the perspective within which they had worked to the other perspective. Social cognition researchers were asked to consider explicitly how their research relates to the social identity approach. Social identity researchers were asked to examine the way their work links to social cognition research. Since battle lines had been well drawn in the past we were slightly apprehensive about the likely responses to our invitations. In the event we were delighted that all the contributors accepted our invitations and approached the task with relish – we saw this as further evidence of the mutual respect that had now developed between these two traditions.

This book represents a notable milestone in the progress of research in group processes and intergroup relations. The battle lines are redrawn as social psychologists build on the strengths of both social cognition and social identity approaches to ask new questions and provide new answers. The same underlying problem faces social psychology – how to understand the relationship between mental or psychological processes and social processes. But now there is a recognition that tackling the problem requires a theoretical framework that encompasses both rather than waging a battle for the supremacy of any particular level of analysis. That framework clearly emerges through the chapters in this book. We hope that, if not convinced already, readers will feel persuaded that this is the way forward for the social psychology of group processes and intergroup relations.

For their direct and indirect guidance, thoughtful advice, patience, and interest in this project, we would like to thank Marilynn Brewer, Diane Houston, and Barbara Masser. We are also very grateful to Martin Davies, our editor at Blackwell, for his responsive and supportive involvement in the project, and to Alison Mudditt, who initially signed us on. Michael Hogg would also like to acknowledge more than ten years of continuous grant support from the Australian Research Council, which has made it possible for him to travel regularly to Europe and North America, and therefore be able to undertake enterprises such as this book.

Dominic Abrams and Michael A. Hogg
Canterbury and Princeton

1

Social Identity and Social Cognition: Historical Background and Current Trends

Michael A. Hogg and Dominic Abrams

As we move into the twenty-first century, social psychologists are taking a new and revitalized interest in the study of group processes and intergroup relations. This development has received significant impetus from approaches, concepts, and methods in the study of social identity and of social cognition. Initially these approaches were starkly separated by the Atlantic Ocean – they represented different metatheories, scientific discourse, research communities, and national/cultural perspectives and agendas. In the early days, there was even a relatively frosty if not hostile relationship, particularly from the European side of the ocean. In recent years, however, this has changed as the two perspectives have mutually recognized each other's strengths and found common ground on which to grow together – there has been a remarkable and continuing integration that has contributed to the revival of group and intergroup research. While these developments should be applauded as they clearly advance scientific understanding, it is also perhaps the case that too much metatheoretical and scientific homogeneity may not be such a good thing as it removes some of the benefits of diversity. The latter is not, in our opinion, a real danger – social psychology embraces different levels of explanations (individual, interpersonal, intragroup, and intergroup/societal – cf. Doise, 1986) which automatically provide scientific diversity.

The purpose of this book is to document ways in which social identity and social cognition have grown together, and how such integration has led to developments in our understanding of group and intergroup phenomena. Differences in perspective and level of explanation still exist, but rather than viewing this as a pretext for metatheoretical imperialism, we consider this a positive source of scientifically constructive diversity. The chapters represent an excellent sample of the range of areas across which social identity and social cognition researchers are integrating aspects of each other's research, and we have been honored to have contributions from leading figures in the field. In this chapter we briefly overview the contributions, with the aim of identifying both common and unique themes in order to discuss future directions. However, before looking to the future, we look back at where social identity and social cognition have come from, how each has influenced the other, and how they have jointly influenced social psychology.

Resurrection of the Group

Histories of social psychology (e.g., Farr, 1996; Jones, 1998) tell us that the discipline was born out of an interest in collective phenomena such as culture and society, was quickly converted to a focus on the individual in the 1920s (e.g., Allport, 1924), but refocused on interaction in groups and the dynamics of groups in the 1930s through 1950s (largely through the influence of Kurt Lewin and his students – see Cartwright and Zander, 1953). We also know that there was a dramatic decline, or what McGrath (1997) calls a "system crash," in interest in group dynamics during the 1960s and 1970s. This has been well documented by Steiner's classic set of increasingly pessimistic declarations about the state and prospects of groups research in social psychology (Steiner, 1974, 1983, 1986). Although social psychologists appeared to lose interest in group dynamics as a "hot" topic, the torch was not extinguished. Rather, traditional groups topics were "annexed" by social psychologically oriented researchers in the field of industrial and organizational psychology (see Levine and Moreland, 1990, 1995; McGrath, 1997; Sanna and Parks, 1997), and the fields of education, health care, and international relations (Tindale and Anderson, 1998). Furthermore, Steiner's lament was very much about American social psychology and its waning interest in small interactive groups. Outside America, particularly in Europe, the picture was quite different. Here the postwar reconstruction of social psychology was intricately tied to a focus on intergroup relations and large-scale collective phenomena, but we will return to this below when we discuss the historical development of European social psychology.

In addition to Steiner, there has been a large number of other commentaries on the state of groups research in social psychology, for example Abrams and Hogg, 1998; Bettenhausen, 1991; Davis, 1996; Hogg and Moreland, 1995; Jones, 1998; Kaplan, 1993; Levine and Moreland, 1990, 1995; McGrath, 1978, 1997; McGrath and Altman, 1966; McGrath and Kravitz, 1982; Manstead, 1990; Moreland, Hogg, and Hains, 1994; Sanna and Parks, 1997; Simpson and Wood, 1992; Tindale and Anderson, 1998; Zander, 1979. Among and in addition to these, there are now quantitative analyses of research trends in social psychology that provide very specific information on the trajectory of groups research.

In 1982, Fisch and Daniel published an analysis of topic trends in research published in the *Journal of Experimental Social Psychology* (*JESP*), the

European Journal of Social Psychology (*EJSP*) and *Zeitschrift für Sozialpsychologie* for the period 1971 through 1980. They used 21 broad categories (devised and used in an earlier project – Daniel and Fisch, 1978) to classify articles by topic. They found that the *EJSP* (which they characterized as mainly European because most work came from Belgium, Britain, France, and Germany) specialized in intergroup relations, social influence, cross-cultural research, and socialization. Furthermore, these topics, in particular intergroup relations and social influence, were twice as popular in Europe (*EJSP*) than North America (*JESP*).

Manstead (1990) conducted an ad hoc comparison of topics which appeared in 1981–2 and 1987–9 in the *European Journal of Social Psychology* and the *British Journal of Social Psychology*, and concluded that there had been an increase in publication of intergroup relations research and a decrease in publication of social perception research. Manstead predicted that during the 1990s there would be a continuing increase in popularity of intergroup relations research, and that this would now be accompanied by an upward trend in research on intragroup processes.

Vala, Lima, and Caetano (1996) used the tenth general meeting, in Lisbon in 1993, of the European Association of Experimental Social Psychology as an opportunity to investigate the relative profile and popularity of different topics in European social psychology. This meeting had 364 delegates (91 percent from Europe). Vala and associates identified, from authors' keywords, 249 distinct keywords that occurred 870 times across the 339 papers that were presented. The two most frequently used keywords were "social identity" (4.9 percent) and "stereotypes" (4.2 percent), followed by "emotion" (3.9 percent), but then in fourth through seventh position were "intergroup relations" (3.6 percent), "self" (3.4 percent), "groups" (2.7 percent), and "social representations" (2.5 percent). Just taking these six "group" topics that were most frequently mentioned, groups were used as keywords 21.3 percent of the time. Vala et al. conclude that intergroup behavior remains the most important topic in European social psychology, but that the study of intragroup processes (including the study of norms) is experiencing a revival.

Moreland et al. (1994) conducted a systematic archival analysis of publication trends in groups research over the period 1975 through 1993 in the three major American social psychology journals – *Journal of Experimental Social Psychology*, *Journal of Personality and Social Psychology*, and *Personality and Social Psychology Bulletin*. They identified articles on groups, and, for each year, formed an index of interest in groups by dividing the total number of pages occupied by articles on groups by the total number of journal pages. In addition, articles on groups were coded on a number of dimensions, including method used, topic researched, and whether or not the article had been influenced by social cognition or by European research. They reported a curvilinear pattern in which interest in groups fell during the late 1970s, remained low during most of the 1980s, and then rose again during the 1990s. In 1975, on average 14 percent of journal pages concerned groups. This fell to about 10 percent in the mid-1980s and then rose to about 19 percent in 1993. From their analyses, Moreland et al. were able to attribute much of the revival of research on groups to theoretical developments and approaches originating in social cognition and European social psychology. Research on groups in the 1990s is revitalized, but is different in emphasis and topics to research on groups in the 1970s.

Hogg and Moreland (1995) applied the same methodology to investigate trends from 1975 through 1994 in the two main English-language European journals – *European Journal of Social Psychology* and *British Journal of Social Psychology*. They found a linear upward trend from 28 percent of pages in 1975 to almost 50 percent of pages in 1994. The most popular groups topics were intergroup relations and conflict in groups (53 percent and 21 percent, respectively, of pages in groups articles). Traditional small-group topics, such as group performance and group structure (9 percent and 7 percent, respectively, of groups pages) were less popular. There was a strong upward trend in intergroup research, from a low of 10 percent of groups pages in 1975 to a plateau of about 55 percent in the mid-1980s and then a new surge to 74 percent in 1994. There was a corresponding, but less marked, downward trend in intragroup research.

Sanna and Parks (1997) used Moreland et al.'s criteria and methods to analyze trends in publication of groups research from 1975 through 1994 in the principal three organizational psychology journals – *Journal of Applied Psychology, Organizational Behavior and Human Decision Processes,* and *Academy of Management Journal*. Like Moreland et al., they found a drop from about 14 percent of pages in 1975 to about 9 percent in the mid-1980s and then a rise to about 18 percent in 1994. They also found that by far the most popular group topics were the intragroup topics of group performance, which showed a declining trend over time, and intragroup conflict, which showed an increasing trend. One notable statistic is that only 2 percent of organizational articles concerned intergroup relations, whereas Moreland et al. found that 38 percent of social psychology articles concerned intergroup relations.

Most recently, Abrams and Hogg (1998) conducted a computer-based (PSYCH-LIT) search, based on group/intergroup keywords, of all journals relevant to social psychology published from 1974 through 1996. In 1974 approximately 5.5 percent of articles related to groups. This dropped to 4 percent during the early 1980s, but then has shown continuous growth to 7.5 percent in 1996. A more restricted sample of just the ten or so principal social psychology journals revealed a similar but even stronger revival. In 1974 approximately 6 percent of articles related to groups. This flattened out to about 4.5 percent during the early 1980s, but then has shown strong growth to about 16 percent in 1996.

Taken together, these quantitative analyses of publication trends support the narrative commentaries. There has been a growing revitalization of research on groups. Traditional intragroup topics have grown in popularity, but outside social psychology – they are now largely investigated by organizational social psychologists. Within social psychology, European perspectives and American social cognition have provided impetus for significant growth in research into intergroup relations, stereotyping, social categories, social identity, and the self-concept. The new social psychology of groups is actually a social psychology of group processes and intergroup relations that embraces the analysis of basic social cognitive processes and structures as well as the study of interaction among group members, and the sociohistorical and organizational contexts of groups. Social identity theory, in conjunction with social cognition, has been an important contributor to this revival.

Social Cognition

Social psychology has always been cognitive (Zajonc, 1980), but the cognitive emphasis within social psychology has waxed and waned (Jones, 1998; Taylor, 1998). Although early empirical psychology drew heavily on cognitive processes (e.g., Wundt, 1897), this emphasis fell into disfavor as psychology abandoned introspection in favor of operationalism and the study of observable behavior. Although social psychologists resisted radical behaviorism, they did embrace a generally behaviorist approach which held sway for many years. During this period the flame of a cognitive perspective within social psychology was kept alive by, for example, Lewin's notion of the "life space" (Lewin, 1936), Sherif's research on norms (1936), and Asch's research on impression formation (Asch, 1946, 1952). Heider's notion of naive psychology, and the publication of his influential 1958 book, set the scene for a marked reemphasis on cognition in social psychology – there was a subsequent explosion of research on attribution which dominated the late 1960s and the 1970s (e.g., Jones and Davis, 1965; Kelley, 1967 – see Hewstone, 1989; Smith, 1994). Accumulation of evidence for biases and errors in the attribution process (e.g., Nisbett and Ross, 1980), in conjunction with a deliberate attempt to bring cognitive and social psychology closer together (Carroll and Payne, 1976), produced what we recognize as contemporary social cognition (e.g., Fiske and Taylor, 1984, 1991; Hastie, Ostrom, Ebbesen, Wyer, Hamilton, and Carlston, 1980).

Heider's naive scientist model of people was replaced by a cognitive miser model (Fiske and Taylor, 1984), and more recently by a motivated tactician model (Fiske and Taylor, 1991). During the 1980s there was a breathtaking expansion of research on social cognition, to the extent that it now dominates social psychology – Taylor (1998) observes that during its heyday 85 percent of submissions to the *Journal of Personality and Social Psychology* were social cognition articles. Social cognition is still extremely healthy and vibrant as a perspective on the explanation of social behavior (e.g., Gollwitzer and Bargh, 1996; Moskowitz, forthcoming; Wyer, 1998). It has taught us a great deal about how we process and store information about people, and how this affects the way we perceive and interact with people. It has also taught us a whole range of new methods and techniques for conducting social psychological research – methods and techniques borrowed from cognitive psychology and then refined for social psychological use. It has had an enormous impact on social psychology (Devine, Hamilton, and Ostrom, 1994).

However, critics of social cognition worry that there is very little "social" in social cognition, and that the focus on cognitive processes and structures has distracted attention from the study of human interaction, to produce a markedly reductionist and asocial account of human behavior (e.g., Augoustinos and Walker, 1995; Kraut and Higgins, 1984; Markus and Zajonc, 1985; Moscovici, 1982; Zajonc, 1989). Some recent approaches to social cognition have tried to redress the balance by attempting to locate social cognitive processes in the social context of human interaction (e.g., Levine, Resnick, and Higgins, 1993; Nye and Brower, 1996; Wyer and Gruenfeld, 1995). Indeed, social cognition is increasingly attending to wider social contextual dimensions of cognition. Although early social cognition largely disregarded language and communication, the role of affect, and the articulation of basic cognitive processes and structures with interpersonal, group, and societal processes, many of these limitations are now being addressed. Higgins and associates (e.g., Higgins, 1992; McCann and Higgins, 1990) have explored the role of social cognition in communication, Maass and Arcuri (1996) have explored the role of social cognition in language and stereotyping, and recent developments in the intergroup study of language point towards an emphasis on social cognitive processes (see overview by Hogg, 1996a). Affect, mood, and emotion have now all become important foci for social cognition research (e.g., Fiske and Taylor, 1991; Forgas, 1995), the group basis of cognition is developing as a research focus (e.g., Nye and Brower, 1996), and the study of prejudice, stereotyping, and intergroup behavior is a lively field for social cognitive research (e.g., Leyens, Yzerbyt and Schadron, 1994; Spears, Oakes, Ellemers, and Haslam, 1997; Zanna and Olson, 1994).

Social identity theory, and the broader social identity perspective, has played an important role in the socializing of social cognition, particularly through a shared focus on stereotyping and prejudice. The reason why this has happened is that social identity theory is a theory of the dynamic and generative interdependence of self-concept and intergroup relations. It is a true social cognitive theory, which specifies cognitive and social processes and structures and their interrelationship, and which therefore encourages dialogue between researchers operating at different levels of explanation. The rapid development of this integration is the rationale for this book, and can also be detected in embryonic form in two earlier books, by Leyens, Yzerbyt, and Schadron (1994), and Spears, Oakes, Ellemers, and Haslam (1997).

European Social Psychology

Social identity theory is a product of postwar European social psychology, and so its development cannot properly be understood without knowing something about the development of European social psychology. (For historical accounts of European social psychology see Doise, 1982; Jaspars, 1980, 1986; Tajfel, 1972; also Hogg and Vaughan, 1998, pp. 32–4.)

European fascism and its culmination in World War II and the holocaust decimated intellectual and academic life in Europe, so that by 1945 very little European social psychology remained. During the 1940s and 1950s the United States financed western European reconstruction – not only material and military reconstruction but also education and research. In the latter case the motive was partly scientific, but also part of a Cold War strategy to develop an intellectual climate to combat the feared encroachment of communism. During this period, centers of social psychology were gradually established in western Europe, but these centers were more closely linked to the United States than they were to one another. European social psychology was principally a set of isolated outposts of American social psychology, in terms of both research activity and ideas, and academic links and loyalties.

Gradually, European social psychologists became conscious of the hegemony of American ideas, their isolation from one another, and of intellectual, cultural, and historical differences between Europe and America. They sought "independence" from the United States and a distinct scientific identity. A series of meetings/conferences beginning in Sorrento in 1963 culminated in the establishment of the European Association of Experimental Social Psychology at Royaumont in 1966, and in the launching of the *European Journal of Social Psychology* in 1971. Europe now had its own independent scientific infrastructure for social psychology. The 1970s and part of the 1980s was very much a period of consolidation for European social psychology. During this time – precisely the period when social identity theory developed in Bristol – it is fair to say that European social psychology set itself up in scientific, metatheoretical, and ideological opposition to American social psychology, a stance that was often frosty and sometimes hostile (e.g., Plon's 1974 critique of American social psychology, specifically the work of Deutsch, in the *European Journal of Social Psychology*, 4 (4)). American social cognition seemed to embody much of what European social psychology was distancing itself from – many critiques of social cognition came from European social psychologists (e.g., Moscovici, 1982).

As the 1980s drew to a close, relations were improving – a process that has gathered momentum ever since. This was partly a natural occurrence stemming from greater self-confidence in European social psychology and greater accessibility to Americans of European research (especially work on social identity and on minority influence), and partly a deliberate attempt by individuals and organizations on both "sides" to break down scientific barriers. In particular, Europeans are now involved in social cognition research, and Americans in social identity research. This is not to say, however, that the critical and relatively isolationist tradition of the 1970s has entirely disappeared, nor that European social psychology is identical to American social psychology. There is still a critical orientation in Europe that often targets American social psychology, and European social psychological priorities are different to those in America (e.g., the study of discourse in Britain, and social representations in continental Europe). But what exactly was/is European social psychology?

Against a continuing background of diversity, European social psychologists gradually discovered, in the 1960s, that they had a common and distinctive European perspective, emphasis, or agenda in social psychology, which focused on the "wider social context" of social behavior. For instance, Jaspars believed that "social psychology in Europe is moving in the direction of studying more and more social behavior in relation to a wider social context and in a theoretically meaningful way to real social issues" (1980, p. 427). This European emphasis is nowhere more evident than in Tajfel's (1984) two-volume, 700-page edited collection, *The Social Dimension: European developments in social psychology*, intended to capture the essence of a distinctive European social psychology over the 20 years since the early 1960s (i.e., since the "birth" of postwar European social psychology). There were 33 chapters by 41 authors from almost all countries in Europe – Americans were conspicuous by their absence. In their introduction to Volume 1, Tajfel, Jaspars, and Fraser noted that, amidst the diversity of European social psychology,

> there seems to exist a very general common denominator: in a phrase, it can be referred to as *the social dimension* of European social psychology. This is simply described: in much of the work – whatever its background, interests, theoretical approach or research direction – there has been a constant stress on the social and interactive aspects of our subject. Social psychology in Europe is today much more *social* than it was 20 years ago. (Tajfel, Jaspars, and Fraser, 1984, p. 1)

Later, they defined the social dimension as a "view that social psychology can and must include in its theoretical and research preoccupations a direct concern with the relationship between human psychological functioning and the large-scale social processes and events which shape this functioning and are shaped by it" (ibid., p. 3).

This emphasis and orientation in social psychology has sponsored a strong interest among European social psychologists in groups, but in particular large-scale intergroup relations (e.g., Moscovici and Doise, 1994). Manstead (1990) argued that intergroup relations is closely linked to a general European perspective on social psychology, which focuses on people's interaction with one another not as unique individuals but as members of social groups. The study of group processes, and in particular intergroup relations, has a relatively high profile in

European social psychology – it occupies significant space in European journals (see Fisch and Daniel, 1982; Hogg and Moreland, 1995) and the two major recent European social psychology textbooks (Hogg and Vaughan, 1998; Hewstone, Stroebe, and Stephenson, 1996). Social identity theory deliberately followed the European metatheoretical agenda to focus on the social dimension – its genealogy is distinctly European.

Social Identity

Social identity theory has its roots in Tajfel's early work on categorization and social perception, his research on intergroup behavior, and his lifelong pursuit of a properly *social* psychological (in the European sense described above) understanding of the causes of prejudice and intergroup conflict (see Turner, 1996, for an historical overview of Tajfel's work, and Tajfel, 1981a, for Tajfel's own selection of some of his important work).

The earliest step was Tajfel's perceptual research that led to his elaboration of the accentuation principle (e.g., Tajfel, 1957, 1959; Tajfel and Wilkes, 1963) – the categorization of stimuli produces a perceptual accentuation effect in which intracategory similarities among stimuli and intercategory differences among stimuli are accentuated on dimensions believed to be correlated with the categorization. Furthermore, the effect is enhanced when the categorization or the correlated dimension is important to the perceiver. Tajfel quite explicitly believed that this effect characterized both physical and social perception, but that in the perception of people the effect is stronger because self is involved – the perceiver usually falls within one category and social comparative dimensions (the correlated dimensions) have implications for self. He also believed that in the social realm the belief that a dimension was correlated with a categorization was a stereotype. In this early work Tajfel was effectively exploring the cognitive aspects of stereotyping and prejudice – he was developing a cognitive theory of stereotyping (e.g., Tajfel, 1969a, 1969b).

In this respect Tajfel can be considered to have pioneered the cognitive approach to stereotyping that became dominant in North American social cognition in the 1980s (e.g., Hamilton, 1981) – see Taylor, Fiske, Etcoff, and Ruderman's (1978) rediscovery of the accentuation effect, and Hamilton's (Hamilton and Gifford, 1976) analysis of stereotypes as beliefs in the correlation between attributes and categories. Tajfel, however, believed that a purely cognitive analysis was an incomplete and socially decontextualized explanation of stereotyping (see Tajfel, 1981b). In keeping with the European social psychological agenda, he believed that a complete analysis should also consider social functions of stereotypes, such as justification, causal attribution, and social differentiation. He reminded us that stereotypes are widely *shared* images of social groups, and therefore that any analysis of stereotyping needed to conceptualize their shared nature, and that in order to do this their analysis needed to be grounded in a wider analysis of intergroup relations and self definition as a group member – i.e., social identity.

Building on his categorization research, but now concerned with intergroup behavior rather than just stereotyping, Tajfel and his colleagues at Bristol were able to show that social categorization *per se* was sufficient to generate inter-group discrimination (Tajfel, 1970; Tajfel, Billig, Bundy, and Flament, 1971). The paradigm developed to demonstrate this effect, the minimal group para-digm, has now become a classic paradigm in social psychology (Bourhis, Sach-dev, and Gagnon, 1994). It seemed that there was a discontinuity between how people behaved when they related to others on an intergroup basis as opposed to an interpersonal or individual basis, and that the discontinuity rested upon whether people were socially categorized or not. This behavioral discontinuity mapped onto a self-conceptual discontinuity between social identity and perso-nal identity – only the former was associated with group and intergroup behav-iors. In intergroup contexts people strive for positive distinctiveness – they try to differentiate their own group from the outgroup in an evaluatively positive manner because, in so doing, the positive connotations of ingroup membership become positive connotations of self. In the rarefied atmosphere of a minimal group study, ingroup favoritism in point allocation is about the only way that this can be achieved.

Intergroup behavior was not, however, a mechanical reflection of positive distinctiveness motives and categorization-based accentuation effects. If was influenced by people's beliefs about the nature of intergroup relations, in part-icular beliefs about status relations and their stability and legitimacy, and about intergroup permeability (Tajfel, 1974a, 1974b; Tajfel and Turner, 1979). This macrosocial dimension of social identity theory has spawned a truly prodigious amount of research, and in many quarters is equated with social identity theory. In many ways it is this aspect that most strikingly distinguishes social identity theory from American social cognition and assimilates it to classic European metatheoretical concerns. It is also this aspect that fueled the phenomenal development of an entire field of the social psychology of language in the 1970s.

By the early 1980s social identity theory was a social cognitive theory of the social group that integrated self-definitional processes related to social identity and people's need for self-esteem and positive intergroup distinctiveness (Turner, 1982) with macrosocial analyses of social belief structures (Tajfel and Turner, 1979). Bristol was the center of this research, and almost all the research was conducted by British and European social psychologists who had Bristol connec-tions, mainly as students and associates of Tajfel. This work was distributed across journal articles and edited books (Tajfel, 1978, 1982, 1984; Turner and Giles, 1981), and very little indeed appeared in American journals. However, it was not until 1988 that a comprehensive, detailed, and integrated account of theory and research in social identity theory was published (Hogg and Abrams, 1988).

With the death of Tajfel in 1982, the impact of the Thatcher administration's higher education policy, the emergence of discourse analysis in the UK, and the new dominance of American social cognition, the Bristol focus rapidly disintegrated in the early 1980s. With the concomitant diaspora, social identity research was now becoming more diverse, and was gaining popularity across Europe and also in Australia and North America. The most far-reaching conceptual advance at this stage was self-categorization theory, which was developed by Turner and his students while they were still at Bristol in the late 1970s and early 1980s (Turner, 1985; Turner, Hogg, Oakes, Reicher, and Wetherell, 1987). Self-categorization theory represented a refocus of attention on the cognitive underpinnings of social identity processes. Although still contextualized by social identity theory, self-categorization theory was strongly cognitive in its focus on the categorization process rather than self-esteem motivation and social belief structures – indeed, some social psychologists felt this represented a "sell-out" to American social cognition (see Farr, 1996). The core notion of self-categorization theory was that social categorization produces distinct and polarized ingroup-and outgroup-defining prototypes that assimilate relevant group members – this depersonalization process (i.e., people as embodiments of group prototypes rather than as distinct biographical entities), when applied to self (i.e., self-categorization), transforms one's self-representation, perceptions, cognitions, feelings, and behavior so that they are governed by the ingroup prototype. The far-reaching consequences of this process include conformity and group influence (Turner, 1991), cohesion and solidarity (Hogg, 1992), and stereotyping (Oakes, Haslam, and Turner, 1994). There are different perspectives on the relationship between social identity theory and self-categorization theory – the one that we adhere to is that self-categorization theory is that aspect of social identity theory that specifies in detail the cognitive underpinnings of social identity processes (see Abrams and Hogg, in press; Hogg, 1996b; Hogg and Abrams, 1988, in press; Hogg and McGarty, 1990).

The 1990s have witnessed an explosion of interest in social identity theory; as discussed earlier, it has been very influential in the recent revival of groups research in social psychology. The theory has been applied and developed, with varying degrees of conceptual strictness, in a broad range of relevant areas (e.g., Abrams and Hogg, 1990a; Hogg and Abrams, 1993; Robinson, 1996): for example, cohesion and solidarity (e.g., Hogg, 1992; 1993); conformity, norms, and group influence (Abrams and Hogg, 1990b; Hogg and Turner, 1987; Turner, 1991); stereotyping (Oakes, Haslam, and Turner, 1994; Leyens, Yzerbyt, and Schadron, 1994; Macrae, Stangor, and Hewstone, 1996; Spears, Oakes, Ellemers and Haslam, 1997); prejudice (Brown, 1995); delinquency and adolescent reputation (Emler and Reicher, 1995); marginal and threatened identities (Breakwell, 1986); crowd behavior (Reicher, 1987); attitudinal phenomena and group norms (Terry and Hogg, 1999); identity salience (Oakes, 1987); small group processes (Hogg, 1996b, 1996c); organizational contexts (Hogg and Terry, 1998); group motivation (Hogg and Abrams, 1993); self-concept (Abrams,

1994, 1996; Brewer, 1991; Deaux, 1996); role theory and microsociology (Hogg, Terry, and White, 1995); and large-scale intergroup relations (Taylor and Moghaddam, 1994).

The self-categorization emphasis within contemporary social identity theory provides an obvious interface for social identity and social cognition perspectives. In recent years this interface has been particularly active in the study of stereotyping (e.g., Oakes, Haslam, and Turner, 1994; Leyens, Yzerbyt, and Schadron, 1994; Macrae, Stangor, and Hewstone, 1996; Spears, Oakes, Ellemers, and Haslam, 1997), self-perception and self-conceptualization (e.g., Abrams, 1994, 1996; Brewer, 1991; Deaux, 1996), group motivational processes (Hogg and Abrams, 1993), and norms, attitudes, and influence (Terry and Hogg, 1999; Turner, 1991). This book brings together these strands under one cover, in order to take stock of the current state of the relationship between social identity and social cognition research, and to identify directions for the next century.

The Chapters

This chapter, and chapter 2 by Don Operario and Susan T. Fiske, provide an historical and intellectual context for the relationship between social identity and social cognition – they discuss the historical and current relationship between social identity and social cognition research and make prognoses for the future. Although we come from a European social identity background, and Operario and Fiske are writing from an American social cognition background, it is quite remarkable how similar our analyses are. Operario and Fiske consider social cognition and social identity to be two different resolutions of the late 1960s crisis of confidence in social psychology. The micro- and macrosocial emphases of these two different approaches were confounded with geographical isolation to produce accentuated hostility – our own analysis adds a more strategic ideological intergroup dimension. Operario and Fiske argue that metatheoretical differences are largely to do with level of analysis differences, and that theoretical rivalry between social cognition and social identity works against articulation of levels of analysis and subsequent disciplinary advances. It is the articulation of individual and social levels of analysis that provides the way forward for further integration of social identity and social cognition. They also argue that social cognition and social identity are metatheoretically more alike than often thought – they share an assumption that people have pragmatic goals in the service of a need to act adaptively, and an assumption that individual behavior can only be understood within the wider cultural context of human existence.

Chapters 3 through 7 deal with how people perceive and judge groups. In chapter 3, Penelope J. Oakes, S. Alexander Haslam, and Katherine J. Reynolds discuss stereotyping and stereotype change, and believe that there are "major points of divergence" between social identity and social cognition perspectives. For Oakes et al. the critical difference is that self-categorization theory views stereotypes as *entirely* context dependent because the categorization process that produces stereotyping is absolutely context dependent, whereas social cognition views stereotypes at least to some extent as cognitive structures that are stored in memory. From their social constructionist interpretation of self-categorization theory, Oakes et al. reject the notion that stereotypes or social identities have cognitive traces – they are transitory reflections of cognitive organization of the immediate social context (cf. chapters 9 and 11 for alternative perspectives). The practical implication of this analysis is that stereotype change is not a matter of cognitive reorganization or generalization from, for example, favorable equal status intergroup contact, but a matter of real enduring material change in intergroup relations.

Steven J. Sherman, David L. Hamilton, and Amy C. Lewis, in chapter 4, adopt a more integrationist approach in pursuing an integrative understanding of the relationship between social identity and the social cognition notion of entitativity. As the perceived entitativity (i.e., unity, coherence, consistency) of an individual or an aggregate of people increases, information processing and impression formation become more *integrative* (i.e., on-line, encoding based, inconsistency resolving) and less *retrospective* (i.e., memory and retrieval based, inconsistency ignoring). Drawing on social identity theory, self-categorization theory, and optimal distinctiveness theory, Sherman et al. identify a dimension of *social identity value*, which refers to the self-esteem, self-understanding, and optimal distinctiveness benefits derived by a person from membership in a specific group. Although the relationship between these two dimensions is complex (there are many moderating factors), Sherman et al. argue that entitativity and social identity value are generally positively related (the greater the value of an ingroup, the greater its entitativity), and that ingroups generally have greater entitativity than outgroups (a view that conflicts with the outgroup homogeneity effect). The effects of entitativity and identity value are discussed.

Theresa K. Vescio, Miles Hewstone, Richard J. Crisp, and J. Mark Rubin (chapter 5) remind us that a person may be categorized in many different ways, such that a person may simultaneously be an ingroup member on some dimensions and an outgroup member on other dimensions. Vescio et al. argue that a proper understanding of these crossed-categorization phenomena requires an integration of social identity and social cognition research. On the basis of a detailed critical review of these research literatures, Vescio et al. are able to propose testable hypotheses for a number of different crossed-categorization effects. In a crossed-categorization setting: (1) if both categorization dimensions are equally salient then double outgroups are rated more negatively than single outgroups (category differentiation predictions); (2) if cognitive representations of subgroups exist then double and single outgroups are rated equally negatively relative to ingroups (category conjunction predictions); (3) if only one

categorization dimension is salient then outgroup ratings depend on that dimension (category dominance predictions); and (4) if one categorization dimension is
more salient than the other then outgroup ratings are dominated by that dimension to produce additive outgroup rating effects (hierarchy predictions).

The next two chapters, chapters 6 and 7, both focus on stereotype activation,
and can both be considered in some respects to be reactions to Devine (1989).
Lorella Lepore and Rupert Brown, in chapter 6, contest what they believe is the
dominant view of both social identity and social cognition research, that stereotype activation is an inevitable and automatic consequence of categorization.
They review research to conclude that prejudice is not an automatic consequence
of stereotyping, and stereotyping is not an automatic consequence of categorization. To support this conclusion they report their own research, which shows
that nonprejudiced people can control prejudice – i.e. stereotyping is not an
automatic response to categorization. Lepore and Brown propose a "functionalist view of stereotyping in which stereotypes are . . . useful tools, automatically
activated when it is appropriate . . . to do so," and go on to relate this to recent
developments in social identity theory.

In chapter 7, Vance Locke and Iain Walker suggest that Devine's (1989)
stereotype activation model is the most widely accepted social cognition model
of how stereotypes and prejudice are related – stereotypes are automatically
activated by social categorization because they are internalized cognitive structures (learned through socialization), but low-prejudiced people are able to exert
some control over the expression of automatically activated stereotypes. Locke
and Walker go on to present a systematic criticism of this model, primarily on
empirical grounds. They then describe their own recent research in order to
make their main point, that not only the expression but also the activation of
stereotypes is based upon proximal or distal context-dependent "processing
goals" (cf. Bargh, 1994). Locke and Walker rest their analysis on the "motivated
tactician" rather than "cognitive miser" model of social cognition – people
activate and use stereotypes when it is pragmatic to do so. They suggest that
social cognition cannot readily specify the sorts of contexts that provide goals
which encourage or inhibit stereotyping, but that social identity theory can. For
instance, social identity theory predicts that conditions of real or imagined social
identity threat are precisely those conditions where the goal is to "judge" the
outgroup, and it is this goal that Locke and Walker have shown to be associated
with automatic stereotype activation and expression.

Chapters 8 and 9 change perspective – they focus more on how people
perceive and judge themselves. Eliot R. Smith, in chapter 8, describes a new
conceptualization of prejudice that follows from the social identity idea that the
group becomes part of the self, and from social cognition ideas and methods
relating to emotions (specifically, appraisal theories of emotion). In contrast to
much prejudice research, which focuses on stereotypes and attitudes, Smith
emphasizes the emotional dimension of prejudice. The core idea is that specific
emotions are aroused when people perceive objects or events as affecting the self.

If the object or event threatens self, then negative emotions such as fear will be experienced and will motivate appropriate actions directed at the object. In contexts where a group is part of the self (i.e., self is defined in group terms – social identity) then the entire dynamic is an intergroup dynamic – appraisals of an outgroup relative to self are *stereotypes* that produce *prejudice* (a set of specific group-based emotions, e.g., fear, disgust, resentment, envy), which are expressed as *discrimination* (a constellation of emotion-based actions). Smith describes this model and shows how it differs from a range of other models of prejudice, and reviews research, including his own, that provides some support. The worst excesses of prejudice are violent and hate-filled – prejudice is an emotional issue. This dimension is underplayed by much recent social identity and social cognition research, which focuses mainly on perception, memory, and evaluation. Smith provides an important shift in emphasis.

Self-conceptualization is also at the heart of Dominic Abrams's chapter (chapter 9). In contrast to Oakes et al. (chapter 3), but consistent with other chapters (e.g., Lepore and Brown, chapter 6; Locke and Walker, chapter 7; Hogg and Mullin, chapter 11), Abrams proposes that a context-based analysis of social identity must deal with underlying stabilities in social and cognitive processes and structures. He reviews research demonstrating that social comparative context can affect intergroup and self-perceptions by shifting the self-categorization that defines social identity. Logically and empirically, the content of self-conception is highly flexible and malleable. However, a purely contextualist interpretation of social identity leaves the person as an unanchored entity. Whereas some theorists characterize self primarily as a partitioned structure (e.g., collective vs. private), Abrams develops a self-categorization theory approach to argue that self is a continuous process that gives rise to structure-like properties in the organization of knowledge about self and others. He proposes that psychological continuity in the self-concept is sustained by two further psychological processes: (1) over time, particular cognitive constructs and knowledge structures become differentially accessible in memory, and thus influence the way people relate events in the social world to themselves; (2) conscious and nonconscious self-regulatory processes create and sustain stability and continuity both in people's own behavior and in their ability to coordinate with others' perceptions and actions – self-regulation relates the product of the self-process to one's knowledge about social and personal norms. In contrast to models proposing that the self acts to control or inhibit stereotypical images of groups (see Lepore and Brown, chapter 6; and Locke and Walker, chapter 7, for review), Abrams proposes that shared normative stereotypes do not form the primary perceptual input for judging category members. Rather, idiosyncratic (personal) stereotypes are generated first, and normative stereotypes are used as a reference point against which to judge personal stereotypes. According to Abrams, the relative stability of social environments and social norms combines with self-categorization and self-regulation to confer both continuity *and* flexibility in self-conception and behavior in terms of social category membership.

Abrams argues that this self-process model and self-categorization principles are consistent with other social–cognitive approaches such as parallel constraint satisfaction models, which emphasize a process-push towards optimally meaningful interpretations of social stimuli (see Hogg and Mullin's uncertainty resolution model, chapter 11).

Motivation is the focus of chapters 10 and 11. In chapter 10, Shelly D. Farnham, Anthony G. Greenwald, and Mahzarin R. Banaji focus on the motivation for self-esteem – a motivation that has long lain at the heart of social identity theory, in so far as ingroup favoritism is believed ultimately to be motivated by a need for self-esteem. Farnham et al. believe that one reason why the empirical relationship between self-esteem and ingroup favoritism or group stigmatization is not clearly established is that self-report measures of self-esteem are unreliable. Farnham et al. provide a detailed discussion of issues in the measurement of self-esteem, and conclude that self-report measures of self-esteem are significantly influenced by self-presentation motives and thus do not correspond well to the underlying construct. A similar problem also plagues the measurement of attitudes relating to prejudice – solutions to which may provide some help in measuring self-esteem. Farnham et al. advocate indirect cognitive measures of self-esteem that take advantage of "automatic activation" and the "spread of activation" among related constructs – people respond more quickly to words that are affectively related than unrelated to a primed construct. Thus, high self-esteem should be associated with faster reaction times to self-positive than self-negative pairings, whereas the opposite should obtain for low self-esteem. Farnham et al. describe and evaluate a methodology for measuring self-esteem in this way, called the implicit association test.

Like Farnham et al., Hogg and Mullin, chapter 11, also focus on self-esteem motivation, but in this case it is a stepping stone to a reexamination of the motivational bases of social identity processes. Social identity theory has placed much of its motivational emphasis on positive distinctiveness and an underlying human need for self-esteem. Although this has proved a useful idea for understanding intergroup relations, research on the specific relationship between self-esteem and social identity has been strangely inconclusive. Drawing on early suggestions by Tajfel and the more recent cognitive emphasis within social identity theory, Hogg and Mullin propose that resolution of subjective uncertainty may be an important human motivation that is rather well satisfied by social identity and self-categorization processes. They summarize a series of minimal group-type experiments that robustly demonstrate that social identification and group behavior is produced when people are explicitly categorized under conditions of subjective uncertainty, particularly uncertainty that has nontrivial consequences for self. Implications for and support from analyses of large-scale intergroup phenomena are discussed, as are similarities to and differences from related motivational analyses in the wider social psychological literature.

The final three chapters address issues revolving around attitudes, norms, and social influence. Chapter 12, by Deborah J. Terry, Michael A. Hogg, and Julie

M. Duck, explores the role of social identity-contingent group norms upon attitude–behavior correspondence and the perception of the impact of persuasive communications. Building on a critical overview of attitude–behavior research, Terry et al. develop a social identity perspective that predicts that attitudes and behavior should be more closely associated when the attitude (and behavior) is highly normative of an important self-inclusive group which contributes to social identity and is contextually salient. In addition, it is suggested that the impact of normative information under high group salience should be most marked when people have adequate resources to process that information – i.e., when the mode of behavioral decision-making is deliberative. A series of studies supporting these analyses is described. Terry et al.'s chapter also focuses on people's perceptions of how much they and others have been influenced by persuasive messages. The general prediction, which is supported by a series of studies reported in this chapter, is that the general third-person effect, in which self is seen to be less vulnerable than others to persuasive communications, is moderated by the contextually salient relationship between self and other and by the extent to which being persuaded is considered desirable in that context – where persuasibility is undesirable, ingroup others are seen to be less vulnerable than outgroup others or individuals; and where persuasibility is desirable, then the opposite occurs.

Chapter 13, by Daan van Knippenberg, and chapter 14, by Diane M. Mackie and Sarah B. Hunter, both focus on social influence and persuasion. Van Knippenberg argues that contemporary social cognitive approaches to persuasion and attitude change which draw a general distinction between heuristic or peripheral processing and systematic or central processing tend to neglect the social context of group memberships. Traditional approaches that do focus on social context have drawn a related distinction between normative compliance-based influence and informational conformity-based influence, but tend to neglect underlying cognitive processes. Social identity theory, which places group membership center-stage in the influence process, has integrated normative and informational aspects into a single group membership-based influence process in which ingroup norms define subjective reality in a specific context and thus the influence process is both normative and informational. Van Knippenberg integrates social identity theory and the dual-process social cognition models of influence to propose that although ingroup messages can be processed heuristically/peripherally, there is a motivation to process them systematically/centrally if resources are available to do so (see Terry et al., chapter 12). He describes research, including his own research with Wilke, that provides some support for this idea.

Mackie and Hunter, chapter 14, also focus on dual processes of social influence and persuasion, but in this case applied to the distinction between majority and minority influence. The original idea that majority influence involves heuristic/peripheral route processing and minority influence systematic/central route processing has become more complicated – for example, counterattitudinal majority messages can be systematically influenced and proattitudinal minority messages can be heuristically processed. Mackie and Hunter explore a further complication which comes from a focus on how persuasive messages are stored, rather than how they are processed. Drawing on the social cognition finding that group representations become more differentiated and less prototype-based with increasing group size, and the persuasion finding that messages from independent sources are more persuasive than messages from nonindependent sources, Mackie and Hunter suggest that majorities are generally more persuasive than minorities because majority messages are stored at the level of the individual and minority messages at the level of the group. Two new experiments are described to support this analysis.

Themes and Directions

The chapters in this book confirm our belief not only that in a number of areas social cognition and social identity processes are being integrated, but that such integration is generally a good thing that leads to exciting conceptual advances in the understanding of group and intergroup phenomena. Almost all authors enthusiastically promote this integration.

A number of specific themes and foci emerge. One theme is that social cognition and social identity approaches emphasize different levels of explanation, which stem partly from the different historical origins of these approaches. In the past this issue has been divisive, but now there is clear recognition that the integration or articulation of different levels of explanation is a powerful force for conceptual advance – see this chapter, and chapter 2 by Operario and Fiske, and contrast with chapter 3 by Oakes et al. A second theme is the degree to which stereotypes and the self-concept are context dependent – Oakes et al. (chapter 3) adopt a strong social constructionist perspective, while most other chapters (e.g., chapter 9, by Abrams) adopt an interactionist perspective where contextual factors influence but do not wholly *determine* stereotypic beliefs and self-conceptualization. A third focus is on the way in which groups are represented in memory or in the self-concept – for example, chapter 4 by Sherman et al., chapter 5 by Vescio et al., chapter 9 by Abrams, and chapter 14 by Mackie and Hunter.

A fourth focus is on the motivational dimension of social identification and group behavior, specifically the role of self-esteem and of uncertainty resolution – chapters 10 and 11 by Farnham et al. and by Hogg and Mullin (also see chapter 4 by Sherman et al.). Obliquely related to motivational issues is the general theme of affect in intergroup relations and prejudice – this theme is represented by chapter 8, by Smith. A sixth focus is on the automatic and controlled aspects of stereotyping and prejudice – are stereotypes automatically activated by categorization and subsequently controlled by individuals, or is activation itself a function of context-based and social identity-contingent goals (see chapter 6 by Lepore and Brown, chapter 7 by Locke and Walker, and chapter 9 by Abrams)? A final focus is on the cognitive processing mechanisms involved in persuasion, influence, and other normative phenomena – for example chapter 12 by Terry et al., chapter 13 by van Knippenberg, and chapter 14 by Mackie and Hunter.

We anticipate that these themes and foci will fuel future developments in the articulation of social identity and social cognition approaches and processes, helping to further socialize social cognition and to provide a cognitive basis of social identity theory. However, we should not lose sight of the macrosocial dimension of social identity theory that addresses the societal context of social identity and intergroup relations.

References

Abrams, D. (1994). Social self-regulation. *Personality and Social Psychology Bulletin*, 20, 473–83.

Abrams, D. (1996). Social identity, self as structure and self as process. In W.P. Robinson (ed.), *Social Groups and Identities: Developing the legacy of Henri Tajfel*. Oxford: Butterworth-Heinemann, pp. 143–67.

Abrams, D. and Hogg, M.A. (eds) (1990a). *Social Identity Theory: Constructive and critical advances*. London: Harvester Wheatsheaf.

Abrams, D. and Hogg, M.A. (1990b). Social identification, self-categorization and social influence. *European Review of Social Psychology*, 1, 195–228.

Abrams, D. and Hogg, M.A. (1998). Prospects for research in group processes and intergroup relations. *Group Processes and Intergroup Relations*, 1, 7–20.

Abrams, D. and Hogg, M.A. (in press). Self, group and identity: A dynamic model. In M.A. Hogg and R.S. Tindale (eds), *Blackwell Handbook in Social Psychology*, Vol. 3, *Group Processes*. Oxford: Blackwell.

Allport, F.H. (1924). *Social Psychology*. Boston: Houghton Mifflin.

Asch, S.E. (1946). Forming impressions of personality. *Journal of Abnormal and Social Psychology*, 41, 258–90.

Asch, S.E. (1952). *Social Psychology*. New York: Prentice-Hall.

Augoustinos, M. and Walker, I. (1995). *Social Cognition: An integrated introduction*. London: Sage.

Bargh, J.A. (1994). The four horsemen of automaticity: Awareness, intention, efficiency, and control in social cognition. In R.S. Wyer, Jr and T.K. Srull (eds), *Handbook of Social Cognition*, 2nd edn, Vol. 1. Hillsdale, NJ: Erlbaum, pp. 1–40.

Bettenhausen, K.L. (1991). Five years of groups research: What we have learned and what needs to be addressed. *Journal of Management*, 17, 345–81.

Bourhis, R.Y., Sachdev, I., and Gagnon, A. (1994). Intergroup research with the Tajfel matrices: Methodological notes. In M. Zanna and J. Olson (eds), *The Psychology of Prejudice: The Ontario symposium*, Vol. 7. Hillsdale, NJ: Erlbaum, pp. 209–22.

Breakwell, G. (1986). *Coping with Threatened Identities*. London: Methuen.

Brewer, M.B. (1991). The social self: On being the same and different at the same time. *Personality and Social Psychology Bulletin*, 17, 475–82.

Brown, R.J. (1995). *Prejudice: Its social psychology*. Oxford: Blackwell.

Carroll, J.S. and Payne, J.W. (1976). *Cognition and Social Behavior*. Hillsdale, NJ: Erlbaum.

Cartwright, D. and Zander, D. (eds) (1953). *Group Dynamics: Research and theory*. New York: Harper and Row.

Daniel, H.-D. and Fisch, R. (1978). Forschungstrends in der Sozialpsychologie: Themenanalyse der *Zeitschrift für Sozialpsychologie*. *Zeitschrift für Sozialpsychologie*, 9, 265–80.

Davis, J.H. (1996). Small group research and the Steiner question: The once and future thing. In E. Witte and J.H. Davis (eds), *Understanding Group Behavior*, Vol. 1. Mahwah, NJ: Erlbaum, pp. 4–16.

Deaux, K. (1996). Social identification. In E.T. Higgins and A.W. Kruglanski (eds), *Social Psychology: Handbook of basic principles*. New York: Guilford, pp. 777–98.

Devine, P.G. (1989). Stereotypes and prejudice: Their automatic and controlled components. *Journal of Personality and Social Psychology*, 56, 5–18.

Devine, P.G., Hamilton, D.L., and Ostrom, T.M. (eds) (1994). *Social Cognition: Impact on social psychology*. San Diego: Academic Press.

Doise, W. (1982). Report on the European Association of Experimental Social Psychology. *European Journal of Social Psychology*, 12, 105–11.

Doise, W. (1986). *Levels of Explanation in Social Psychology*. Cambridge: Cambridge University Press.

Emler, N. and Reicher, S.D. (1995). *Adolescence and Delinquency: The collective management of reputation*. Oxford: Blackwell.

Farr, R.M. (1996). *The Roots of Modern Social Psychology: 1872–1954*. Oxford: Blackwell.

Fisch, R. and Daniel, H.-D. (1982). Research and publication trends in experimental social psychology: 1971–1980 – A thematic analysis of the *Journal of Experimental Social Psychology*, the *European Journal of Social Psychology*, and the *Zeitschrift für Sozial Psychologie*. *European Journal of Social Psychology*, 12, 395–412.

Fiske, S.T. and Taylor, S.E. (1984). *Social Cognition*. New York: Random House.

Fiske, S.T. and Taylor, S.E. (1991). *Social Cognition*, 2nd edn. New York: McGraw-Hill.

Forgas, J.P. (1995). Mood and judgment: The affect infusion model. *Psychological Bulletin*, 117, 39–66.

Gollwitzer, P.M. and Bargh, J.A. (eds) (1996). *The Psychology of Action: Linking cognition and motivation to behavior*. New York: Guilford.

Hamilton, D.L. (ed.) (1981). *Cognitive Processes in Stereotyping and Intergroup Behavior*. Hillsdale, NJ: Erlbaum.

Hamilton, D.L. and Gifford, R.K. (1976). Illusory correlation in interpersonal personal perception: A cognitive basis of stereotypic judgments. *Journal of Experimental Social Psychology*, 12, 392–407.

Hastie, R., Ostrom, T.M., Ebbesen, E.B., Wyer, R.S., Jr, Hamilton, D.L., and Carlston, D.E. (eds) (1980). *Person Memory: The cognitive basis of social perception*. Hillsdale, NJ: Erlbaum.

Heider, F. (1958). *The Psychology of Interpersonal Relations*. New York: Wiley.

Hewstone, M.R.C. (1989). *Causal Attribution: From cognitive processes to collective beliefs*. Oxford: Blackwell.

Hewstone, M.R.C., Stroebe, W. and Stephenson, G.M. (eds) (1996). *Introduction to Social Psychology*, 2nd edn. Oxford: Blackwell.

Higgins, E.T. (1992). Achieving "shared realities" in the communication game: A social action that creates meaning. *Journal of Language and Social Psychology*, 11, 107–31.

Hogg, M.A. (1992). *The Social Psychology of Group Cohesiveness: From attraction to social identity*. Hemel Hempstead and New York: Harvester Wheatsheaf and New York University Press.

Hogg, M.A. (1993). Group cohesiveness: A critical review and some new directions. *European Review of Social Psychology*, 4, 85–111.

Hogg, M.A. (1996a). Identity, cognition, and language in intergroup context. *Journal of Language and Social Psychology*, 15, 372–84.

Hogg, M.A. (1996b). Intragroup processes, group structure and social identity. In W.P. Robinson (ed.), *Social Groups and Identities: Developing the legacy of Henri Tajfel*. Oxford: Butterworth-Heinemann, pp. 65–93.

Hogg, M.A. (1996c). Social identity, self-categorization, and the small group. In E.H. Witte and J.H. Davis (eds), *Understanding Group Behavior*, Vol. 2, *Small Group Processes and Interpersonal Relations*. Mahwah, NJ: Erlbaum, pp. 227–53.

Hogg, M.A. and Abrams, D. (1988). *Social Identifications: A social psychology of intergroup relations and group processes*. London: Routledge.

Hogg, M.A. and Abrams, D. (eds) (1993). *Group Motivation: Social psychological perspectives*. Hemel Hempstead and New York: Harvester Wheatsheaf and Prentice-Hall.

Hogg, M.A. and Abrams, D. (in press). Social categorization, depersonalization and group behavior. In M.A. Hogg and R.S. Tindale (eds), *Blackwell Handbook in Social Psychology*, Vol. 3, *Group Processes*. Oxford: Blackwell.

Hogg, M.A. and McGarty, C. (1990). Self-categorization and social identity. In D. Abrams and M.A. Hogg (eds), *Social Identity Theory: Constructive and critical advances*. Hemel Hempstead and New York: Harvester Wheatsheaf and Springer-Verlag, pp. 10–27.

Hogg, M.A. and Moreland, R.L. (1995). European and American Influences on small group research. Invited paper presented at the Small Groups Preconference of the joint meeting of the European Association of Experimental Social Psychology and the Society for Experimental Social Psychology, Washington, DC, October.

Hogg, M.A. and Terry, D.J. (1998). Organizational identification: Social identity and self-categorization processes in organizational contexts. Manuscript under editorial review.

Hogg, M.A., Terry, D.J. and White, K.M. (1995). A tale of two theories: A critical comparison of identity theory with social identity theory. *Social Psychology Quarterly*, 58, 255–69.

Hogg, M.A. and Turner, J.C. (1987). Social identity and conformity: A theory of referent informational influence. In W. Doise and S. Moscovici (eds), *Current Issues in European Social Psychology*, Vol. 2. Cambridge and Paris: Cambridge University Press and Editions de la Maison des Sciences de l'Homme, pp. 139–82.

Hogg, M.A. and Vaughan, G.M. (1998). *Social Psychology*, 2nd edn. Hemel Hempstead: Prentice-Hall.

Jaspars, J.M.F. (1980). The coming of age of social psychology in Europe. *European Journal of Social Psychology*, 10, 421–8.

Jaspars, J.M.F. (1986). Forum and focus: A personal view of European social psychology. *European Journal of Social Psychology*, 16, 3–15.

Jones, E.E. (1998). Major developments in five decades of social psychology. In D.T. Gilbert, S.T. Fiske, and G. Lindzey (eds), *The Handbook of Social Psychology*, 4th edn, Vol. 1. New York: McGraw-Hill, pp. 3–57.

Jones, E.E. and Davis, K.E. (1965). From acts to dispositions: The attribution process in person perception. In L. Berkowitz (ed.), *Advances in Experimental Social Psychology*, Vol. 2. New York: Academic Press, pp. 219–66.

Kaplan, M.F. (1993). Group decisions are cognitive and social events. Paper presented at the meetings of the Midwestern Psychological Association, Chicago.

Kelley, H.H. (1967). Attribution theory in social psychology. In D. Levine (ed.), *Nebraska Symposium on Motivation*. Lincoln, NB: University of Nebraska Press, pp. 192–238.

Kraut, R.E. and Higgins, E.T. (1984). Communication and social cognition. In R.S. Wyer, Jr and T.K. Srull (eds), *Handbook of Social Cognition*, Vol. 3. Hillsdale, NJ: Erlbaum, pp. 87–127.

Levine, J.M. and Moreland, R.L. (1990). Progress in small group research. *Annual Review of Psychology*, 41, 585–634.

Levine, J.M. and Moreland, R.L. (1995). Group processes. In A. Tesser (ed.), *Advanced Social Psychology*. New York: McGraw-Hill, pp. 419–65.

Levine, J.M., Resnick, L.B., and Higgins, E.T. (1993). Social foundations of cognition. *Annual Review of Psychology*, 44, 585–612.

Lewin, K. (1936). *Principles of Topological Psychology*. New York: McGraw-Hill.

Leyens, J.-P., Yzerbyt, V., and Schadron, G. (1994). *Stereotypes and Social Cognition*. London: Sage.

Maass, A. and Arcuri, L. (1996). Language and stereotyping. In C.N. Macrae, C. Stangor, and M. Hewstone (eds), *Stereotypes and Stereotyping*. New York: Guilford, pp. 193–226.

McCann, C.D. and Higgins, E.T. (1990). Social cognition and communication. In H. Giles and W.P. Robinson (eds), *Handbook of Language and Social Psychology*. Chichester: Wiley, pp. 13–32.

Macrae, C.N., Stangor, C., and Hewstone, M. (eds) (1996). *Stereotypes and Stereotyping*. New York: Guilford.

McGrath, J.E. (1978). Small group research. *American Behavioral Scientist*, 21, 651–74.

McGrath, J.E. (1997). Small group research, that once and future field: An interpretation of the past with an eye to the future. *Group Dynamics: Theory, Research, and Practice*, 1, 7–27.

McGrath, J.E. and Altman, I. (1966). *Small Group Research: A synthesis and critique of the field*. New York: Holt, Rinehart, and Winston.

McGrath, J.E. and Kravitz, D. (1982). Group research. *Annual Review of Psychology*, 33, 195–230.

Manstead, A.S.R. (1990). Developments to be expected in European social psychology in the 1990s. In P.J.D. Drenth, J.A. Sergeant, and R.J. Takens (eds), *European Perspectives in Psychology*, Vol. 3. Chichester: Wiley, pp. 183–203.

Markus, H. and Zajonc, R.B. (1985). The cognitive perspective in social psychology. In G. Lindzey and E. Aronson (eds), *The Handbook of Social Psychology*, 3rd edn, Vol. 1. New York: Random House, pp. 137–230.

Moreland, R.L., Hogg, M.A., and Hains, S.C. (1994). Back to the future: Social psychological research on groups. *Journal of Experimental Social Psychology*, 30, 527–55.

Moscovici, S. (1982). The coming era of representations. In J.-P. Codol and J.-P. Leyens (eds), *Cognitive Analysis of Social Behaviour*. The Hague: Martinus Nijhoff, pp. 115–50.

Moscovici, S. and Doise, W. (1994). *Conflict and Consensus: A general theory of collective decisions*. London: Sage.

Moskowitz, G. (ed.) (forthcoming). *Future Directions in Social Cognition*. New York: Cambridge University Press.

Nisbett, R.E. and Ross, L. (1980). *Human Inference: Strategies and shortcomings of social judgment*. Englewood Cliffs, NJ: Prentice-Hall.

Nye, J.L. and Brower, A.M. (eds) (1996). *What's Social about Social Cognition: Research on socially shared cognition in small groups*. Thousand Oaks, CA: Sage.

Oakes, P.J. (1987). The salience of social categories. In J.C. Turner, M.A. Hogg, P.J. Oakes, S.D. Reicher, and M.S. Wetherell, *Rediscovering the Social Group: A self-categorization theory*. Oxford: Blackwell, pp. 117–41.

Oakes, P.J., Haslam, S.A., and Turner, J.C. (1994). *Stereotyping and Social Reality*. Oxford: Blackwell.

Reicher, S.D. (1987). Crowd behaviour as social action. In J.C. Turner, M.A. Hogg, P.J. Oakes, S.D. Reicher, and M.S. Wetherell, *Rediscovering the Social Group: A self-categorization theory*. Oxford: Blackwell, pp. 171–202.

Robinson, W.P. (ed.) (1996). *Social Groups and Identities: Developing the legacy of Henri Tajfel*. Oxford: Butterworth-Heinemann.

Sanna, L.J. and Parks, C.D. (1997). Group research trends in social and organizational psychology: Whatever happened to intragroup research? *Psychological Science*, 8, 261–7.

Sherif, M. (1936). *The Psychology of Social Norms*. New York: Harper Bros.

Simpson, J.A. and Wood, W. (1992). Introduction: Where is the group in social psychology? An historical overview. In S. Worchel, W. Wood, and J.A. Simpson (eds), *Group Process and Productivity*. Newbury Park, CA: Sage, pp. 1–10.

Smith, E.R. (1994). Social cognition contributions to attribution theory and research. In P.G. Devine, D.L. Hamilton, and T.M. Ostrom (eds), *Social Cognition: Impact on social psychology*. San Diego: Academic Press, pp. 77–108.

Spears, R., Oakes, P.J., Ellemers, N., and Haslam, S.A. (eds) (1997). *The Social Psychology of Stereotyping and Group Life*. Oxford: Blackwell.

Steiner, I.D. (1974). Whatever happened to the group in social psychology? *Journal of Experimental Social Psychology*, 10, 1467–78.

Steiner, I.D. (1983). Whatever happened to the touted revival of the group? In H. Blumberg, A. Hare, V. Kent, and M. Davies (eds), *Small Groups and Social Interaction*, Vol. 2. New York: Wiley, pp. 539–48.

Steiner, I.D. (1986). Paradigms and groups. *Advances in Experimental Social Psychology*, 19, 251–89.

Tajfel, H. (1957). Value and the perceptual judgement of magnitude. *Psychological Review*, 64, 192–204.

Tajfel, H. (1959). Quantitative judgement in social perception. *British Journal of Psychology*, 50, 16–29.

Tajfel, H. (1969a). Social and cultural factors in perception. In G. Lindzey and E. Aronson (eds), *The Handbook of Social Psychology*, Vol. 3. Reading, MA: Addison-Wesley, pp. 315–94.

Tajfel, H. (1969b). Cognitive aspects of prejudice. *Journal of Social Issues*, 25, 79–97.

Tajfel, H. (1970). Experiments in intergroup discrimination. *Scientific American*, 223, 96–102.

Tajfel, H. (1972). Some developments in European social psychology. *European Journal of Social Psychology*, 2, 307–22.

Tajfel, H. (1974a). Social identity and intergroup behaviour. *Social Science Information*, 13, 65–93.

Tajfel H. (1974b). Intergroup behaviour, social comparison and social change. Unpublished Katz-Newcomb Lectures, University of Michigan, Ann Arbor.

Tajfel, H. (ed.) (1978). *Differentiation between Social Groups: Studies in the social psychology of intergroup relations*. London: Academic Press.

Tajfel, H. (1981a). *Human Groups and Social Categories: Studies in social psychology*. Cambridge: Cambridge University Press.

Tajfel, H. (1981b). Social stereotypes and social groups. In J.C. Turner and H. Giles (eds), *Intergroup Behaviour*. Oxford: Blackwell, pp. 144–67.

Tajfel, H. (ed.) (1982). *Social Identity and Intergroup Relations*. Cambridge: Cambridge University Press.

Tajfel, H. (ed.) (1984). *The Social Dimension: European developments in social psychology*, 2 vols. Cambridge: Cambridge University Press.

Tajfel, H., Billig, M., Bundy, R.P., and Flament, C. (1971). Social categorization and intergroup behaviour. *European Journal of Social Psychology*, 1, 149–77.

Tajfel, H., Jaspars, J.M.F., and Fraser, C. (1984). The social dimension in European social psychology. In H. Tajfel (ed.), *The Social Dimension: European developments in social psychology*, Vol. 1. Cambridge: Cambridge University Press, pp. 1–5.

Tajfel, H. and Turner, J.C. (1979). An integrative theory of intergroup conflict. In W.G. Austin and S. Worchel (eds), *The Social Psychology of Intergroup Relations*. Monterey, CA: Brooks-Cole, pp. 33–47.

Tajfel, H. and Wilkes, A.L. (1963). Classification and quantitative judgement. *British Journal of Psychology*, 54, 101–14.

Taylor, D.M. and Moghaddam, F.M. (1994). *Theories of Intergroup Relations*. Westport, CT: Praeger.

Taylor, S.E. (1998). The social being in social psychology. In D.T. Gilbert, S.T. Fiske, and G. Lindzey (eds), *The Handbook of Social Psychology*, 4th edn, Vol. 1. New York: McGraw-Hill, pp. 58–95.

Taylor, S.E., Fiske, S.T., Etcoff, N.L., and Ruderman, A.J. (1978). Categorical and contextual bases of person memory and stereotyping. *Journal of Personality and Social Psychology*, 36, 778–93.

Terry, D.J. and Hogg, M.A. (eds) (1999). *Attitudes, Behavior, and Social Context: The role of norms and group membership*. Mahwah, NJ: Erlbaum.

Tindale, R.S. and Anderson, E.M. (1998). Small group research and applied social psychology: An introduction. In R.S. Tindale, L. Heath, J. Edwards, E.J. Posavac, F.B. Bryant, Y. Suarez-Balcazar, E. Henderson-King, and J. Myer (eds), *Social Psychological*

Applications to Social Issues: Theory and research on small groups, Vol. 4. New York: Plenum Press, pp. 1–8.

Turner, J.C. (1982). Towards a cognitive redefinition of the social group. In H. Tajfel (ed.), *Social Identity and Intergroup Relations*. Cambridge: Cambridge University Press, pp. 15–40.

Turner, J.C. (1985). Social categorization and the self-concept: A social cognitive theory of group behaviour. In E.J. Lawler (ed.), *Advances in Group Processes: Theory and research*, Vol. 2. Greenwich, CT: JAI Press, pp. 77–122.

Turner, J.C. (1991). *Social Influence*. Buckingham: Open University Press.

Turner, J.C. (1996). Henri Tajfel: An introduction. In W.P. Robinson (ed.), *Social Groups and Identities: Developing the legacy of Henri Tajfel*. Oxford: Butterworth-Heinemann, pp. 1–23.

Turner, J.C. and Giles, H. (eds) (1981). *Intergroup Behaviour*. Oxford: Blackwell.

Turner, J.C., Hogg, M.A., Oakes, P.J., Reicher, S.D., and Wetherell, M.S. (1987). *Rediscovering the Social Group: A self-categorization theory*. Oxford: Blackwell.

Vala, J., Lima, M.L., and Caetano, A. (1996). Mapping European social psychology: Co-word analysis of the communications at the 10th general meeting of the EAESP. *European Journal of Social Psychology*, 26, 845–50.

Wundt, W. (1897). *Outlines of Psychology*, trans. 1907. New York: Stechert.

Wyer, R.S. (1998). *Stereotype Activation and Inhibition: Advances in social cognition*, Vol. 11. Hillsdale, NJ: Erlbaum.

Wyer, R.S., Jr, and Gruenfeld, D.H. (1995). Information processing in social contexts: Implications for social memory and judgement. In L. Berkowitz (ed.), *Advances in Experimental Social Psychology*, Vol. 27. New York: Academic Press, pp. 49–91.

Zajonc, R.B. (1980). Cognition and social cognition: A historical perspective. In L. Festinger (ed.), *Retrospections on Social Psychology*. New York: Oxford University Press, pp. 180–204.

Zajonc, R.B. (1989). Styles of explanation in social psychology. *European Journal of Social Psychology*, 19, 345–68.

Zander, A. (1979). The psychology of small group processes. *Annual Review of Psychology*, 30, 417–51.

Zanna, M.P. and Olson, J.M. (eds) (1994). *The Psychology of Prejudice: The Ontario symposium*, Vol. 7. Hillsdale, NJ: Erlbaum.

2

Integrating Social Identity and Social Cognition: A Framework for Bridging Diverse Perspectives

DON OPERARIO AND SUSAN T. FISKE

As the field celebrates the end of its first century, significant insight into human behavior should provide social psychologists cause for collective pride. However, recurrent perceptions of disunity and inconsistency between research areas have led to sweeping criticism and internal rivalry (e.g., Elms, 1975; Gergen, 1973; Pepitone, 1981; Sampson, 1977; Steiner, 1974; see also Jones, 1985; Taylor, 1998, for reviews). Differing metatheoretical and theoretical perspectives lie at the heart of social psychology's supposed conflict. As discussed in the previous chapter, the divergent approaches of social identity and social cognition have contributed to this intradisciplinary tension. But rather than conceding to speculations of internal conflict, this chapter argues that social psychology truly has much to rejoice.

Social identity and social cognition researchers in particular should celebrate one another's progress. In this chapter we will see why, by tracing back to the roots of both approaches, reviewing the (perhaps unnecessary) tension between the two, and exploring areas of mutual agreement and integration. We will argue throughout that the social identity and social cognition approaches are not only compatible with one another, but that each depends on the other for theoretical and empirical viability. Furthermore, we argue that both approaches together are vital for the field's continued growth and prosperity.

Four related sections will guide our discussion of the compatibility and interdependence between social identity and social cognition. First, the chapter posits that implicit collaboration between social identity and social cognition researchers helped deliver the field from the 1970s "crisis" of confidence. Second, the

Preparation of this chapter was supported by NIMH Research Training Grant MH 15742 (administered by the American Psychological Association) to the first author, and NIMH Grant MH 41801 to the second author.

The authors wish to thank Dominic Abrams and Michael Hogg for helpful comments on previous drafts. Special thanks to Michael Berg and John Bickford for valuable input.

chapter suggests that two overarching themes, namely pragmatism and cultural competence, unite social identity and social cognition approaches into a coherent integrative framework within social psychology. Third, the chapter argues that confusion between metatheory and theory underlies the perceived tension between social identity and social cognition approaches; by distinguishing between levels of analysis, both approaches appear completely congruous. Fourth, the chapter advocates for more explicit collaboration and exchange between the two research approaches, which together can advance social psychology toward an integrated, internally consistent, and thriving discipline.

Historical Context: A Glance Back and a Step Forward

The tension between social identity and social cognition approaches is deep-seated, reflecting the disciplinary tension whence the two traditions emerged. We will see, however, that this conflict is highly overstated and even unnecessary. Both approaches met critical needs in social psychology's evolution, and both are vital to its continued growth.

The crisis of confidence and its resolution

The late 1960s and early 1970s represented a pinnacle of social psychology's collective self-criticism. Journal articles and conference symposia abounded with declarations of the field's shortcomings: scientific identity, empirical innovation, methodological validity, ecological applicability, and historical generality were questioned by members and nonmembers of the field alike. Juxtaposed with the unsympathetic experimental psychology backdrop of behaviorism, social psychology's "fuzzy" scientific topics were held suspect by outsiders, and its hypothesis-testing procedures were considered inadequate even among insiders (see Gergen, 1997; Jones, 1985; Parker, 1989, for reviews).

Elaborated discussion of this crisis era is not appropriate for this chapter, but suffice it to say that social psychology at that time was simply in need of *more*: more theory, more precision, more variety, more generalizability, more applicability, and more cumulative findings. Indeed, the field was ready for a pendulum swing, but the direction of that swing seemed uncertain.

Instead of swinging in a new direction, the pendulum exploded, and research momentum moved toward several foci simultaneously. Thus commenced the resolution of the crisis, as multiple research programs became embedded in the field. In true Kuhnian tradition, intellectual tension and self-criticism during the 1960s and 1970s facilitated the flourishing of manifold research topics, including applications to health, gender, close relationships, the environment, and politics. Propelled by these new programs, the decades following social psychology's crisis witnessed an unprecedented surge in scientific enthusiasm and productivity. The sheer amount of post-crisis empirical articles and text-books published, grants obtained, and applications made to other disciplines and to society at large (see Berscheid, 1992; Jones, 1985; Reis and Stiller, 1992) attests to the field's amazing recovery of enthusiasm.

Two approaches in particular emerged at the forefront of social psychology's empirical agenda. Social cognition and social identity gained wide popularity by providing rich ongoing research programs, addressing the need for increased theory, precision, and applicability.

Enter the social cognition approach

Social cognition bloomed in the years following the crisis, but its roots predated even the first hint of disciplinary tension. Since its inception, social psychology has almost always emphasized the cognitive underpinnings of human behavior (see Zajonc, 1980). Unfortunately, most other areas of psychology had not shared this enthusiasm; as mentioned, the behaviorist milieu of the mid-century placed little regard on mental processes. The later rise in cognitivism, heralded by the publication of Neisser's (1967) *Cognitive Psychology*, generated a dis-ciplinary atmosphere that welcomed the study of internal processes guiding social behavior. Enterprising social psychologists profited from this new methodological vogue; they continued to investigate the same issues as before the cognitive revolution (e.g., impressions, attitudes, stereotypes), only now received new ideas and methods from the broader scientific community. Thus commenced the social cognition boom, and thus ended social psychology's crisis.

The social cognition approach met the demands of critics seeking increased precision, empirical innovation, and theoretical viability. Rather than employ "showy demonstrations" of social behavior characterizing, and to some extent enervating, much early research (see Fiske and Leyens, 1997), the social cogni-tion approach looked within the individual, using tightly controlled studies for understanding intrapsychic processes. High drama, such as mock prisons or shock administrations, had offered inadequate ongoing methodologies for "get-ting inside the head" of research participants; these earlier studies provided provocative descriptive data yet lacked integrative theory and cumulative findings regarding individual-level phenomena. Cognitive social psychologists turned their attention away from demonstrating the power of situations, focusing instead on the internal processes mediating people's responses to their situations.

Social cognition research profited greatly from scientific discoveries occurring outside the field. Technological advances, largely in computer sciences, allowed fine-grained analysis of mental phenomena (e.g., subliminal priming and milli-second reaction times), and psychological researchers were able to look inside people's minds for clean answers to complex questions. The computer metaphor, borrowed from cognitive science, provided a unique and fruitful framework for understanding human thinking. Statistical advances allowed mediational analysis via path modeling, and psychological researchers were able to propose cognitive process theories for integrating discrete findings.

We will review the specific metatheoretical and theoretical contributions of this approach shortly, but emphasize here the historical need for social cognition's empirical precision, theoretical innovation, technological skill, and above all, scientific vigor (see Devine, Hamilton, and Ostrom, 1994, for a collection of accolades). Although early social cognition research deemphasized ecological applicability for the sake of internal validity, we will see in later sections that an emphatically *social* cognition characterizes more recent research.

Enter the social identity approach

Just as social psychology has always been cognitive, so too has it always emphasized the group (e.g., early works by Le Bon, 1896; McDougall, 1920). But similar to the rocky beginnings of social cognition approaches, group research was stunted by the experimental hegemony in psychology during the 1950s and 1960s. Researchers of group behavior found themselves caught at the crossroads of psychological social psychology and sociological social psychology. In the United States in particular, researchers with a strong individual-level orientation emerged as the vanguard of social psychology's theory-building. Their ideological focus on individuals resonated with North American cultural sentiment (Sampson, 1977; Steiner, 1974), and the cognitive approach predominated in North American social psychology laboratories and journals. Critics reacted to North America's emphasis on the individual, claiming that group research had disappeared.

The social identity approach emerged as a compromise between individual-level and group-level explanations. Developed by Tajfel and his European colleagues, social identity research stressed the fluidity between individuals and groups, thereby ushering in a new enthusiasm for the scientific study of group behavior. Drawing from several other social sciences, including political science, sociology, and economics, social identity addressed the macro-level contextual issues mediating human behavior.

Research under this tradition replied to the crisis-induced question, "Whatever happened to the group in social psychology?" (Steiner, 1974) with an insistent "It never left, it just went intergroup." Topics altogether dismissed by psychology's individual emphasis became valid areas of empirical study: group formation and interaction, social change, status, and conflict.

Practical implications of their findings, particularly for social intervention, enhanced researchers' confidence regarding the field's value and its overall direction (see Hogg and Abrams, 1988, for a review). Hence, the social identity approach helped resolve social psychology's crisis of confidence by keeping in mind the unarguably social nature of individual processes and the societal roots of human behavior.

Crisis redux?

Despite their joint roles in delivering the field from intellectual and scientific despair, rivalry between social cognition and social identity soon followed. Members of the field perceived the microemphasis of social cognition at odds with the macroemphasis of social identity; accordingly, mental processes and societal structure were perceived to have nothing to do with each other. Geographic isolation exacerbated this perceived opposition, as social cognition has thrived primarily in North America and social identity has thrived primarily in Europe and Australasia.

Accounts of this divide pervade the field. For example, at a recent conference, one of us was approached by a graduate student from a large American university, who stated, "I can't wait for this social cognition stuff to end. Who do they [social cognition researchers] think they're fooling anyway? It's all just a pretension to hard science." Although a glimpse at this student's poster title made clear that he resided within the social identity camp, closer inspection of his research revealed an operational focus on social categorization and intergroup stereotyping – that is, the cognitive properties of group behavior. At another conference, where a social cognition meeting followed a groups meeting, some disgruntled wag left behind the diagonally bisected circle (international symbol for prohibition) superimposed on "social cognition."

Indeed, most criticism has been directed at the social cognition approach, often coming from members of the social identity camp and their "group approach" allies (e.g., Stroebe and Insko, 1989; Turner and Oakes, 1986). Critics claimed that social cognition overemphasized the individual and completely neglected societal context. Social cognition's emphasis on mental processes appeared too reductionistic, computational, and prescriptive. Allegedly, social cognition's findings reflected life in a vacuum – the experimental laboratory – rather than life in the complex world (see Fiske and Leyens, 1997). In this vein, social cognition's messages were seen as contributing little insight into the human condition.

Research under the social identity banner similarly received a fair amount of reproof. Critics argued that empirical data did not support the basic postulates of Tajfel and colleagues' original theorizing; contradictory findings brought social identity's message into question (see Brewer and Brown, 1998). The self-esteem predictions of the theory, discussed later in the chapter, did not hold up well (Abrams and Hogg, 1988; Fiske and Taylor, 1991; Hogg and Abrams, 1990; Long, Spears, and Manstead, 1994). Others suggested that this approach inappropriately treated "the group" as an objective and static variable, rather than as a subjective or fluid conception (Turner, Hogg, Oakes, Reicher, and Wetherell, 1987). Moreover, some argued that social identity research merely reflected instrumental behavior aimed at maximizing self-gain, that economic utility models explained social identity research findings equally well (Rabbie, Schot, and Visser, 1989).

At first glance, such criticism directed at two of social psychology's strongest areas might evoke alarm, portraying a disjointed discipline in a state similar to its earlier crisis period. But although every criticism echoes with some truth, we feel neither alarm nor pessimism. Neither social cognition nor social identity researchers are oblivious to the weaknesses of their approach. Indeed, many researchers would agree with the criticism directed at their work, and some have offered the same criticism themselves. For example, even during its infancy, cognitive-oriented researchers were aware of the limitations of a purely mentalistic approach to social phenomena (Fiske and Linville, 1980; Higgins, Kuiper, and Olson, 1981; Neisser, 1976; Nisbett and Wilson, 1977; Zajonc, 1980). Likewise, social identity researchers have been continually conscious of the tenuous fit between theory and data (see Hogg and Abrams, 1990); as reviewed later, self-categorization theory developed for precisely this reason.

Rather than suggesting disciplinary despair, we argue that the ongoing debates between social identity and social cognition approaches signify a natural and even healthy byproduct of scientific advancement. Social psychology has gained much from its internal squabbles. Social cognition and social identity researchers in particular have advanced their programs with the help of one another's criticism.

Summary

Social cognition and social identity approaches both emerged out of a disciplinary context in need of increased theory, scientific validity, and programmatic viability. Both traditions satisfied these needs, through taking distinct methodological approaches. Now that the field stands safe from full-blown crisis, lingering skepticism should serve as a reminder to consider a more sophisticated agenda, a bigger picture, for social psychology. Social cognition's microemphasis and social identity's macroemphasis are both integral for advancing this more comprehensive picture – one that embraces multiple levels of analysis and multiple methodological approaches (see also Fiske and Leyens, 1997).

We argue that the time is ripe for considering integrative themes that can bridge historically separated areas – e.g., social cognition vs. social identity, the micro vs. the macro, the person vs. the situation. Frequent consideration of social psychology's bigger, integrated picture is vital to the field's continued prosperity.

Integration and Confluence of Social Identity and Social Cognition

Comprehensive and integrative themes are fully evident in the works of social psychology's earlier thinkers, such as James's (1890) *The Principles of Psychology*, Asch's (1952) *Social Psychology*, Lewin's (1952) *Field Theory in Social Science*, and Heider's (1958b) *The Psychology of Interpersonal Relations*. Although drawing heavily from these classic texts, more recent work has tended to shy away from the grand styles of explanations reminiscent of our intellectual forebears.

Contemporary researchers have opted for more focused styles, taking piece-meal, phenomenon-focused approaches to scientific inquiry. Indeed, significant empirical advances in the last few decades owe considerable debt to the piece-meal approach of investigators, particularly social identity and social cognition researchers. However, some reminders of the field's integrative messages are necessary for maintaining disciplinary cohesion and crosstalk.

Integrative themes

We suggest that two basic themes, evident throughout many earlier writings and implicit in contemporary research, bridge the historically separate social identity and social cognition approaches, as well as other distinct research areas. From James's classic discussion of consciousness to Lewin's discourse on "life spaces" to Bruner's essays on construction of meaning to Heider's attribution models, one can see careful emphasis on both (1) the pragmatic nature of psychological processes, and (2) the cultural competence of human agents. Reconsideration of these themes can redirect social psychology's attention, from intertheoretical rivalry to disciplinary advance.

Pragmatism

Pragmatism refers to the goal-oriented and functional nature of basic social psychological processes. Recent reviews (Fiske, 1992, 1993) have examined the role of pragmatism in social cognition research, arguing that social psychologists all along have emphasized the motivational and intentional bases of perception and cognition (e.g., Bruner, 1957; Heider, 1958a; James, 1890). Cognitive processes stem from people's pragmatic goals, which themselves derive from multiple sources, including person-level variables, situational constraints, societal structure, and evolutionary mechanisms. Simply put, "thinking is for doing," a message from James (1890) positing that cognition follows from people's goals, which vary according to their social situation. Research guided by this pragmatic principle justly deserves the rubric *social* cognition.

Pragmatism and human agency have similarly guided group research, though this emphasis has been less explicit. Collective forms of behavior arguably derive from people's pragmatic goals, such as self-enhancement (e.g., Tajfel and Turner, 1979), belonging (Baumeister and Leary, 1995), and social survival (Caporael and Brewer, 1995). Thus, social identity research suggests that human agency and intent, rather than passivity and biological determinism, guide social behavior in groups; pragmatic motivation underlies group formation, personal identification, social comparisons, and social change.

Cultural competence

Cultural competence refers to individual behavior as situated and adaptive within a larger societal–cultural context (Markus, Kitayama, and Heiman, 1996). According to this view, social psychological processes derive largely from cultural–societal pressures and standards. Cultural social psychologists remind the field that a larger level of analysis, far beyond the mere individual level, underlies the field's topics of study (e.g., Markus and Kitayama, 1991; Moghaddam, Taylor, and Wright, 1993; Schweder, 1991; Triandis, 1989).

An emphasis on culture dates back to the beginnings of social psychological thought, though appears absent from much empirical work. Many of the same early works that underscored individual-level pragmatism also addressed cultural influences, standards, and practices (Asch, 1952; Bruner, 1957; Lewin, 1952). For example, Asch (1952) reminded us that "The material and social conditions with which each society surrounds its members are obviously far more than objects of reflection . . . Each need and capacity, however fundamental, takes form in the course of interaction with a particular physical and social environment . . . These reach into every detail of psychological activity, into modes of striving, feeling, and thinking" (p. 364).

Empirical investigations into the cultural basis of human behavior have recently come to the forefront of experimental social psychology's agenda (Fiske, Kitayama, Markus, and Nisbett, 1998). Within the past decade, social cognition and social identity researchers have returned to their theoretical roots, embracing the notion that culture directs how human agents think, feel, and act – both individually and collectively.

Thematic confluence

We posit that pragmatism and cultural competence underlie and unite both the social identity and social cognition approaches, directing researchers' study of socially adaptive (and maladaptive) behavior. Together, these themes remind us of lessons from our evolutionary past, that the psychological processes we study serve a grander purpose. This purpose revolves around social survival and interdependence among social beings (see also Caporael, 1997; Stevens and

Fiske, 1995). We consider this idea anew by examining an earlier incarnation stressing pragmatism and cultural competence, Campbell's (1974) theory of downward causation.

Social survival and downward causation

Downward causation is an evolutionary-based perspective on social behavior. This idea posits that all social systems are hierarchically organized, such that all adaptive biological and psychological phenomena survive based on their fit within higher-order processes (see also Brewer, 1997; Caporael, 1997).

The biological level of analysis reflects this notion thus: genetic processes must function adaptively within larger cellular processes or risk extermination; cells must themselves function within tissues, tissues within organ systems, organs within individuals, individuals within communities, and so on. Accordingly, the most microscopic biological processes answer inevitably to environmental constraints, as higher-order units select for the most optimally functioning lower-order processes (Campbell, 1974).

All social psychological processes, from micro-level neurological processes to mid-range cognitive–motivational processes to macro-level interpersonal and intergroup processes, must likewise function adaptively within higher-order units or risk extermination. Just as environmental systems select for the most adaptive biological processes through downward causation, cultural systems determine the most adaptive social psychological processes that promote social survival. *Cultural* topography and its downward effect on psychological processes parallels *environmental* topography and its downward effect on biological processes.

Social psychological adaptations to the cultural environment manifest themselves in harmonious community living, cognitive energy-saving tactics, interdependence among members, socially shared cognitions, normative influences, and intergroup behavior – all functional and pragmatic facets of group life and all topics of study within social identity and social cognition theories. Thus, applications of evolutionary principles to social psychology need not be limited to reproductive strategies (e.g., Buss and Schmidt, 1993; Kenrick, Groth, Trost, and Sadalla, 1993). More important than mating patterns, *human social and cultural networks* determine the range of individual and socially pragmatic survival skills through the process of downward causation (Campbell, 1983; Caporael, 1997; Caporael and Brewer, 1991), thereby providing a larger picture for framing discrete social psychology research areas. People are made to live competently in group culture.

Summary

Pragmatism and cultural competence represent thematic trademarks of a truly *social* psychology. The pragmatist emphasis on goals complements the cultural emphasis on coordinated social living, both of which point to the defining role of social survival and its implications for people's social cognitions and social identities. These themes guided both social cognition and social identity research since their respective onsets, but remained at the implicit level during social psychology's post-crisis experimental boom. Within the past decade, both pragmatism and culture have reemerged as valid areas of experimental study.

These themes, pragmatism and cultural competence, are fully evident at the metatheoretical levels of the social cognition and social identity approaches, but less so at their respective theoretical levels. Thus we will see that the metatheoretical levels of both areas are in mutual agreement with one another.

Distinguishing Level of Analysis, from Metatheory to Theory

Intradisciplinary tension between social cognition and social identity often stems from confusion between levels of discourse. We will argue that the compatibility between the two areas is fully evident by distinguishing levels of discourse, from metatheory to theory. By unpacking these levels, we will see that both approaches focus on human agents as (1) pragmatic and (2) culturally competent – both vital skills for social survival and coordinated coexistence.

These themes are most evident at the level of metatheory, wherein each offers broad perspectives on human thinking processes and human group processes. Turning to the level of theory, wherein each perspective makes specific predictions, individual-level process and cultural context admittedly do not balance. However, the discussion will argue that theories from both research traditions rely on pragmatism and cultural competence, fully evident at the meta-level, in guiding their predictions.

Let us now attempt to disentangle theory from metatheory in both approaches. Conflict between the two areas can resolve by considering the integrative roles of pragmatism and cultural competence across all levels of analysis, pronounced most strongly at the metatheoretical level.

Social cognition as metatheory

Social cognition is foremost a metatheoretical approach to studying social behavior. Its metatheoretical focus is on the mental processes that guide social interaction. One previous definition posits that social cognition researchers study "how ordinary people think about people and how they think they think about people" (Fiske and Taylor, 1991, p. 1). Unlike basic theory, social cognition metatheory does not advance an interrelated set of hypotheses bearing on one singular conceptual domain. Instead, social cognition research spans the breadth of social psychological topics, including impression formation, attitudes, social influence, attributions, self-concept, and relationships (Devine, Hamilton, and Ostrom, 1994).

Social cognition researchers apply basic concepts from cognitive psychology to each of these diverse topics, illuminating the internal mechanisms that guide complicated social phenomena. These cognitive concepts include memory, atten-tion, automaticity, schemas, categories, and associative networks, to name but a few (see Fiske and Taylor, 1991; Higgins, Herman, and Zanna, 1981; Wyer and Srull, 1994, for comprehensive reviews). Popularized in the 1970s, related cog-nitive techniques allow social psychologists to measure what was once consid-ered unmeasurable, namely, internal processes. A neophyte would be hard pressed to imagine a social psychology now neglecting basic cognitive principles and devoid of its vocabulary, yet empirical sophistication about cognition in social phenomena is relatively recent.

As mentioned earlier, social psychology has always taken a cognitive approach to examine human behavior (e.g., Allport, 1954; Bruner, 1957; Heider, 1958b; Lewin, 1952), but general psychology's mid-century restriction to observable phenomena undercut explicit cognitive analysis. The cognitive boom of the 1970s generated a new scientific milieu, equipped with advanced technological skills, that supported the unabashed study of mentalism and brought social psychology out of its doldrums (see Carroll and Payne, 1981, for a collection of representative social psychological essays).

The first wave of social cognition research was marked by heavy borrowing of cognitive methodologies without substantial alterations; many research pro-grams simply tweaked certain variables from basic cognition research into social versions. Perception became person perception, memory became person memory, and categorization became person categorization. This purely cognitive analysis of social phenomena engendered various metatheoretical metaphors for human thought processes, two of which gained wide popularity – the person as "infor-mation processor" and the person as "cognitive miser" (see Fiske and Taylor, 1991; Taylor, 1982, for reviews).

The information processor metaphor adopted a computer analogy to describe human thinkers. According to this metaphor, both people and computers take in information automatically (i.e., encoding), perform various mental permutations on cognitive data (i.e., assimilation and inference), and produce output (i.e., judgment). Research guided by this machine metaphor depicted person percei-vers as cold, imperfect thinkers. This orientation emphasized accuracy and bias, both theoretically and prescriptively, viewing deviations from normative rules as processing error (e.g., Nisbett and Ross, 1980).

In contrast, the cognitive miser metaphor adopted a cognitive economy ana-logy, depicting people as thinkers whose mental strategies lay chronically vulner-able to cognitive scarcity. Researchers viewed cognitive energy as a limited commodity that people frugally conserve. Consequently, human thinkers use convenient shortcuts (heuristics, schemas, scripts, and stereotypes) in place of effortful thought. Cognitive frugality urges people to compromise accuracy for efficiency.

These metaphors swept the field during the 1970s and 1980s, influencing and often limiting researchers' metatheoretical views about human thinkers. Drawing epistemological backing from other disciplines, such as computer science, early social cognition perspectives overlooked the individual's social motivations and contextual constraints, instead emphasizing prescriptive norms and (in)accuracy. Consider, for example, the first Ontario symposium on personality and social psychology, which focused on the then-emerging social cognition *Zeitgeist* (see Higgins, Herman, and Zanna, 1981). Throughout talks on diverse areas of interest, researchers portrayed people as asocial perceivers chronically susceptible to cognitive blunders. Common dependent measures across these early papers included memory distortions, schematic errors in perception, and attribution biases. The emphasis on human shortcomings was not subtle.

Hundreds of studies later, after much introspection and well-taken criticism, social cognition became more social again (for an overview, see Fiske, 1992). Circa the early 1990s, theory and research started to deemphasize objectivity and (in)accuracy, focusing instead on the individual's goals and social context. That is, pragmatism and cultural competence emerged at the cutting edge of social cognition's metatheoretical agenda.

Researchers abandoned the information processor and cognitive miser metaphors, and a new metaphor for social perceivers took their place. The "motivated tactician" described people not as machines or mindless automatons, but as fully engaged thinkers with multiple cognitive strategies available (Fiske and Taylor, 1991). According to this metatheoretical view, people choose among a wide range of pragmatic cognitive tactics, from the effortless heuristic processes of the cognitive miser, to the effortful thorough processes of the motivated thinker, based on their goals, motives, and needs as determined by the power of the situation (see Chaiken and Trope, in press; Fiske and Taylor, 1991, for reviews).

The motivated tactician metaphor responded to earlier criticisms by emphasizing the undeniably pragmatic and flexible nature of mental activity. Empirical research turned to the roles of affect, motivation, and situational constraints in guiding thought and behavior (see Gollwitzer and Bargh, 1996; Higgins and Sorrentino, 1990; Sorrentino and Higgins, 1986, for reviews). Research that previously might address "schematic biases in impression formation" would reframe its approach under this new paradigm, possibly referring to "motivated impressions shaped by social situations." Note the important distinction: schema-based perception now follows from people's context-driven goals, not merely from human cognitive shortcomings. Context-driven subjectivity has indeed emerged at the core of this new wave of social cognition, the motivated tactician paradigm (Fiske and Leyens, 1997).

Looking back, it would be a mistake to assume that social cognition metatheory by nature overlooks the role of societal context and the notion of pragmatic subjectivity. The extreme reductionism of the 1970s and early 1980s reflected enthusiasm over new methodologies for studying basic mechanisms; it was only a matter of time for interest to return to its original social course.

Indeed, context and subjectivity have always been at the heart of social cognition's agenda. For example, Lewinian field theory embodies both principles, as people's fields and life space (i.e., societal context) determine interpretation and perception (i.e., subjectivity). Going back even further, emphasis on context and pragmatic subjectivity can be found in James's (1890) early discourse on reasoning:

> The essence of a thing is that one of its properties which is so *important for my interests* that in comparison with it I may neglect the rest. Amongst those other things which have this important property I class it, after this property I name it, as a thing endowed with this property I conceive it; and whilst so classing, naming, and conceiving it, all other truth about it becomes to me as naught. The properties which are important vary from man to man and from hour to hour. (James, 1890/ 1950, pp. 335, italics in original)

To summarize, social cognition has turned full circle at the level of metatheory. Pragmatic ("good-enough") subjectivity and societal context were central concepts to early preexperimental analysis. Much later, fueled by collective enthusiasm for cognitive methodologies, the first empirical wave of social cognition research largely neglected these issues, instead testing the limits of a purely mentalistic approach. Although criticized for its extremism, this period was integral for opening up the black box for theory-building and empirical analysis. Resting on growing knowledge of cognitive properties, social cognition research has returned once again to pragmatics and context, examining the roles of motivation, goals, situational constraints, and more recently culture, on intrapsychic phenomena. Thus, just as social psychology has always emphasized cognitive processes, social cognitive metatheory has almost always emphasized pragmatic, goal-oriented subjectivity and societal–contextual forces. At the level of metatheory, social cognition resonates with the macro approach advocated by social identity researchers (discussed shortly), which similarly stresses pragmatism and cultural context.

Social cognition as theory

Numerous social cognitive theories correspond with the metatheoretical framework provided by the "motivated tactician" metaphor. These theoretical models traverse the breadth of social psychological topics, offering specific predictions for multiple social phenomena, including impression formation (e.g., Brewer, 1988; Fiske and Neuberg, 1990), persuasion and attitude change (Chaiken, 1987; Petty and Cacioppo, 1986), stereotyping and prejudice (Banaji and Green-

wald, 1993; Devine, 1989), political judgment (Kinder and Sears, 1985), personality (Epstein and Pacini, in press), and others (see Chaiken and Trope, in press,
for a comprehensive collection). Although expansive in their domains of empirical prediction, common processes link these theoretical models when framed
within the motivated tactician metaphor.

First, much theory-driven social cognition research posits that two coacting
subsystems underlie social thought (Abelson, 1994; Fiske and Taylor, 1991).
These subsystems reflect distinct cognitive processes operating in parallel,
which together guide people's thinking strategies toward the fulfillment of
their cognitive goals. Such dual-process models specify that a low-effort, spontaneous channel trades off against a high-effort, deliberate channel to direct
social cognitive activity. For example, researchers posit that impression
formation operates via category-based vs. piecemeal channels (Brewer, 1988;
Fiske and Neuberg, 1990), persuasion operates via heuristic-peripheral vs. sys-
tematic-central channels (Chaiken, 1987; Petty and Cacioppo, 1986), and stereotyping operates via automatic-implicit vs. controlled-explicit channels (Banaji
and Greenwald, 1993; Devine, 1989). In tandem, these parallel subsystems
regulate encoding, attention, memory, and judgment (see Chaiken and Trope,
in press, for a collection).

Second, social cognition models postulate that cognitive activity proceeds
from an initial automatic response, potentially extending with effort to more
controlled, complex processes (see Bargh, 1997, for review). The automatic
response typically occurs instantaneously, and a fair amount of research depicts
this default cognitive tendency as less than ideal (e.g., Banaji and Hardin, 1996;
Chaiken and Maheswaran, 1994; Devine, 1989; Gilbert and Hixon, 1991;
Langer, 1989; Macrae, Bodenhausen, Milne, and Jetten, 1994). Progression
from reflexive response to detailed elaboration depends largely on perceivers'
cognitive resources, including capacity, awareness, intentionality, and
mental control (cf. Bargh, 1994). Culture interacts with this process, determining
the culturally pragmatic forms of automatic cognition. Recent cross-cultural data
indicate that the *nature* of people's spontaneous inferences, in the absence or
inactivation of cognitive effort, may not be universal. Findings suggest that
cultural orientation determines the type or quality of people's initial judgment,
such that individualists form dispositional inferences more readily whereas col-
lectivists form situational inferences more readily (e.g., Miller, 1984; Morris and
Peng, 1994). Despite cultural differences in the specific forms that automatic
cognitions take, social cognitive models of the *processes* underlying people's
judgments (i.e., automatic vs. controlled subsystems) remain valid vehicles of
explanation.

A third common thread among social cognition theories holds that most
significant cognitive activity results from motivation. People think for the purpose of satisfying their pragmatic motives, and tend to think with less effort
when their knowledge goals are satisfied (Fiske, 1992, 1993). Subjective accuracy thus follows from a "good-enough" criterion level: under most conditions,

people's cognitive strategies proceed only to the minimal adequate level of understanding. Heuristic strategies characterize human thought because most situations do not necessitate piecemeal, detailed information processing (Fiske and Neuberg, 1990). Subjective understanding guides social cognitive processes, mediated by people's internalized needs (e.g., self-concept-related values) or situation-based motives, and guided by cultural standards of good-enough accuracy (cf. Judd and Park, 1993; Leyens, Yzerbyt, and Schadron, 1992).

Hence, the motivated tactician resides within a social–cultural context that determines (1) the pragmatic cognitive strategies requisite for (2) good-enough or functional levels of accuracy, as derived from (3) situational goals and cultural standards. As discussed, the core motives that guide the tactician's thinking strategies derive ultimately from social survival needs (see Stevens and Fiske, 1995).

To summarize, recent social cognitive theories guided by the motivated tactician paradigm equally emphasize cognitive process, societal context, and the functional relation between the two (see Caporael, 1997, for an excellent theoretical discussion). This reconfigured framework solidifies the bond between social cognition and social identity, blending the two perspectives into one that underscores the interaction between pragmatism and cultural competence.

Social identity as metatheory

The work of Henri Tajfel set the tone for contemporary studies of intergroup behavior (see Robinson, 1996, for a celebration of Tajfel's legacy). Unlike the social cognition literature, the original writings on social identity advanced a set of theory-based hypotheses regarding one specific issue, intergroup relations (Tajfel, 1969; Tajfel and Turner, 1979). However, the data in support of the original social identity model have produced equivocal results, calling its basic premises under question (see Brewer and Brown, 1998, for a review). Thus, we argue that the original form of social identity may work best at the level of metatheory, as a backdrop for framing more specific theories of intergroup behavior, reviewed shortly.

As discussed earlier, the social identity tradition emerged out of the need to address social behavior and societal phenomena in nonreductionistic terms. Social identity researchers refuted the traditional emphasis on individualism espoused by most psychological theories (see Pepitone, 1981; Sampson, 1977; Steiner, 1974, for commentaries). Instead, social identity stressed that individual behavior reflects the individual's larger societal unit. Cultural competence lies at the heart of this metatheory, as collective group membership influences and sometimes determines individuals' thoughts and behaviors. Viewed thus, the individual is not a self-contained unit of psychological analysis to which researchers should limit their scope. Social psychologists must constantly consider the overarching societal structures that guide internal structures and processes, including groups, organizations, cultures, and most importantly the individual's identification with these collective units (cf. Markus, Kitayama, and Heiman, 1996). The parallel between social identity's metatheoretical message since the 1970s and cultural social psychology's more recent message (e.g., Markus and Kitayama, 1991; Schweder, 1991; Triandis, 1989) is striking.

Although these ideas have a solid foundation in social psychology, relatively less empirical work has addressed social identity and group membership in North American social psychology journals, compared with the enthusiasm directed towards social cognition research (Brewer and Brown, 1998). Early in the field's history, however, even American social psychologists stressed group behavior and the structural foundations of individual thought and action (e.g., Asch, 1952; Lewin, 1952; Sherif, 1936). These views presaged the social representations and discourse analysis movements popular in contemporary social psychology, suggesting that societal–cultural norms and values determine people's perceptions of reality, thereby treating accuracy and objectivity as fluid constructions based on one's collective frame of reference (Oakes, Haslam, and Turner, 1994, provide an excellent review).

While American social psychologists turned their attention away from these issues, focusing instead on individual-level processes, the work of Tajfel and colleagues kept group behavior at the forefront of European social psychology's empirical agenda. Their approach answered others' doubts regarding the feasibility of groups research by focusing on the individual *qua* group member, rather than treating the group as the primary unit of analysis. The social identity metatheoretical approach advocated that people sometimes think, feel, and act as unique individuals (as advanced by traditional American social psychology), but most of the time people think, feel, and act as members of collective groups, institutions, and cultures. European researchers argued that these collective variables are amenable to scientific investigation simply by focusing on the behavior of individuals who identify within the larger unit.

In addition to its ideological resemblance to cultural social psychology, social identity's metatheoretical message rests on basic concepts from social cognition. Internal cognitive processes are central to social identity's metatheoretical treatise on the self and intergroup behavior. According to Tajfel's original discussion of social identity, the self-concept derives meaning from the categorization of self and other within larger social units or groups, and social comparisons within and between groups motivate people's attitudes, appraisals, and judgments (Tajfel, 1969). Note the strong reliance on cognitive principles (e.g., self-concept, categorization, social comparison, attitudes, and judgments) in this summary of Tajfel's argument. Social identity metatheory describes intergroup relations as the product of basic social cognition principles operating within the context of intergroup dynamics.

The social identity approach reinforces the idea that people's social cognitions are socially constructed, depending on their group or collective frame of reference. Stemming from this framework, specific social identity research programs deemphasized the roles of accuracy and objectivity, turning instead to how people-as-group-members interpret and make sense of their environments. Social constructionism thus thrives in social identity metatheory.

To summarize, this metatheoretical approach has been invaluable to social psychology's progression. The social identity movement advocated the departure from socially ungrounded cognitive processes – the staple of social cognition's first wave of research – bringing societal context and group membership to the forefront of empirical study. Researchers emphasized the fluidity between individual and society, advancing the notion that all human behavior is resolutely social behavior, determined by the synergetic interaction between person and societal–cultural context (Tajfel, 1979).

Social identity as theory

As originally formulated, social identity theory sought to explain intergroup relations in general, and social conflict in particular. Its basic argument included three main points: (1) people are motivated to maintain a positive self-concept; (2) the self-concept derives largely from group identification (in addition to personal identification, as stressed by American social psychologists); and thus (3) people establish positive social identities by comparing the ingroup favorably against outgroups. As such, this model assumed that internal psychological processes drive intergroup conflict, even in the absence of explicit rivalry or competition between groups. Structural variables, such as power, hierarchy, and resource scarcity, increase the baseline proclivity to perceive the ingroup more favorably than the outgroup (but see Rabbie and Horwitz, 1969, 1988).

The diverse and complex array of findings yielded by social identity research attests to the conceptual value of the theory. Despite inconsistencies in some of the findings, the overall message of the theory engendered several more specific theories regarding the individual–society link. Much like the specific social cognition theories discussed previously, theories of social identity and group behavior share several implicit underlying themes. Again, the roles of pragmatism and cultural competence stand out among these themes.

Self-categorization theory (Turner, Hogg, Oakes, Reicher, and Wetherell, 1987) emerged as a direct outgrowth of Tajfel's earlier work, advancing an analysis of group behavior predicated on individual-level cognitive processes and omitting the empirically tenuous role of self-esteem. Self-categorization theory argued that social contexts create meaningful group boundaries, and social identities are socially constructed categories that shift depending on situational pragmatics. The salience of social categories (via numerosity, common fate, interdependence, overt conflict, etc.) provides perceptual filters for organizing ingroups and outgroups (e.g., Brewer and Kramer, 1986; Wilder and Shapiro, 1984). Strong personal identification with a particular group leads to "depersonalization," whereby individuals view themselves and each other as interchangeable representatives of their category (e.g., Simon and Hamilton, 1994). Cognitive processes exacerbate the perception of group boundaries, such as the "meta-contrast" principle, which is the tendency for individuals to minimize the perceived variance among members of the same group and maximize the variance between members of different groups (Turner, Oakes, Haslam, and McGarty, 1994). The outgroup homogeneity effect soon takes hold, blurring distinctions among outgroup members (Mullen and Hu, 1989; Ostrom and Sedikides, 1992, provide meta-analysis and reviews). Thus, situational factors guide cognitive processes, leading to the perceived "entitativity" of social categories (Campbell, 1958). Self-categorization theory suggests that these pragmatic cognitive processes form the basis for ensuing intergroup interaction, such as prejudice and conflict, which stems from cultural standards, such as egalitarianism and social harmony or antipathy.

Optimal distinctiveness theory (Brewer, 1991) is a close relative to self-categorization theory. This conceptualization of group behavior and identity provides a motivational counterpart to the cognitive analysis advanced by Turner and colleagues' work. According to this view, social identifications are guided by two core human motives, the need to be unique (e.g., Snyder and Fromkin, 1980) and the need to belong (e.g., Baumeister and Leary, 1995). Having a social identity (e.g., ethnic, religious, or national) satisfies individuals' simultaneous needs for inclusion and differentiation, meanwhile contributing to the robust ingroup bias phenomena for which social identity research is famous (Brewer and Brown, 1998).

Realistic group conflict theory has historically rivaled social identity theory in the group behavior literature (e.g., Rabbie, Schot, and Visser, 1989). However, reframed within the social identity metatheory discussed previously, realistic conflict theory corroborates the cognitive analysis of self-categorization theory and the self-concept themes provided by Tajfel's original work. Realistic group conflict refers to the structural conditions that determine hostile intergroup relations, including resource scarcity, competition, and power (LeVine and Campbell, 1972; Sherif, 1966). According to this view, group competition stems from the perceived zero-sum principle – that outgroup prosperity leads to ingroup misfortune (and vice versa). This theory does, however, advance a more optimistic potential for intergroup relations. Cooperative interdependence between groups can undercut perceived competition and hostility, as overarching goals elicit feelings of common fate and unity between ingroup and outgroup members (Brown and Abrams, 1986; Worchel, Andreoli, and Folger, 1977). Cultural context, such as intergroup harmony standards, determines people's pragmatic cognitive strategies, thereby enhancing or minimizing perceived group differences.

A recent heir of social identity metatheory, and sibling to realistic group conflict theory, is social dominance theory (Sidanius, 1993). This theory posits that all social institutions and cultures involve some form of hierarchy. Unlike most other social identity theories that focus on situational explanations, this theory of intergroup relations rests on individual differences in social dominance. Individual orientations toward social dominance are pragmatic insofar as hierarchies are functional for the collective unit, facilitating the distribution of labor or (im)balance of resources. Social hierarchies are validated through social consensus; cultural ideologies sustain the legitimacy and centrality of hierarchy within the larger society (Pratto, Sidanius, Stallworth, and Malle, 1994; Sidanius, Pratto, and Bobo, 1994). This theory accounts for large-scale examples of group dominance that occur in the absence of overt conflict, such as ethnic or gender oppression. Social dominance theory differs in form from the cognitive and motivational analysis of self-categorization and optimal distinctiveness theories, stressing across cultures both the inevitability and functionality of consensual hierarchies, such as legitimized class distinctions and gender roles, as a function of individual differences (Sidanius and Pratto, 1993).

In summary, pragmatism and cultural competence are central to the theories of intergroup behavior summarized here, though their acknowledgment remains theoretically implicit. Framed within social identity metatheory, these specific theories (self-categorization, optimal distinctiveness, realistic conflict, and social dominance) promote diverse models of social survival and group life, yet converge to suggest that psychological processes operate in the service of functional existence within a collective network. The specific predictions offered by these social identity theories argue convincingly that individual processes derive from and determine societal context, and the two are irreducibly interdependent.

Summary

Principles of pragmatism and cultural competence guide and unite the social cognition and social identity approaches. The compatibility between approaches is most evident at the level of metatheory, as the assumptions of one rest firmly on basic principles borrowed from the other. Both metatheoretical perspectives consider individual-level pragmatics and their interaction with cultural–societal processes.

The theoretical topics covered by both perspectives resonate with their respective metatheoretical focus on pragmatism and culture. For example, stereotyping, one of the staple topics of social cognition, persists because it facilitates economic functioning of the cognitive system, meeting good-enough accuracy standards set by the cultural system (Fiske, 1993). Likewise, self-categorization satisfies people's basic motivational needs to identify within the parameters of larger social categories (e.g., race, region, gender, or religion), which are constructed by the overarching cultural system (see Operario and Fiske, 1998, for more discussion).

Various facets of human thought and behavior, as studied separately by social identity and social cognition researchers, function from the intersection between pragmatism and culture. Downward causation propels both individual and group-level processes, selecting and reinforcing the psychological phenomena best suited for social survival. Empirical findings from social identity and social cognition research traditions truly converge within this integrative backdrop.

Further Directions for Social Identity and Social Cognition

From metatheory to theory, this analysis of social cognition and social identity highlights the compatibility between the two research traditions. The messages of one approach resonate and rest securely on the messages of the other: social cognitions derive from our social identities, and vice versa. As reviewed, tension between the two approaches stems from (1) ideological incongruency, attributable to the historical conditions surrounding their respective origins; and (2) confusion between level of analysis, wherein specific theories are mistaken for metatheories.

Social cognition and social identity converge (1) at the level of metatheory, where they provide overarching principles – pragmatism and cultural competence – for framing knowledge, and (2) at the level of theory, where they provide testable hypotheses for understanding specific events or circumstances. Their respective explanatory foci differ, but do not contradict. The social cognition approach brings scientific inquiry into the head by examining mental structures and processes, and the social identity approach brings scientific inquiry out into the field by examining social structures and processes. Yet why the sustained perception of incompatibility between the two approaches?

Beyond disciplinary meta-contrast: Bridging the two perspectives

The principle of meta-contrast, acting on geographically dispersed social psychologists, along with the tendency to perceive outgroup members as a unified entity, may themselves perpetuate doubt regarding the incompatibility between social identity and social cognition. Many researchers inappropriately frame cognitive processes and group processes along a unidimensional continuum. Categorized as such, researchers may tend to augment perceptually the difference between approaches, and concomitantly perceive each approach as a homogeneous entity (not to mention favoring the ingroup's approach over the outgroup's approach). The preceding review of the two traditions-as-theory suggests the ample diversity *within* as well as between each approach. Moreover, both traditions-as-metatheory are more similar than they are different, contrary to meta-contrast perceptual tendencies. But to assuage persistent rumors of incompatibility and competition, we now offer a few superordinate goals for both research traditions.

Orthogonal dimensions of research

The future of an integrated social psychological agenda relies on acknowledging the orthogonality of dimensions often mistaken to be dichotomous. The (mis)perception of social cognition and social identity as dichotomous dimensions reflects the ongoing (mis)perception that individual vs. situational explanations are mutually exclusive. Decades ago, Allport (1961) questioned researchers' tendency to perceive these dimensions at odds, often favoring one over the other: "If there is no personality apart from the situation, it is equally true that there is no situation apart from personality" (p. 181). Social psychological explanations cannot reduce their explanations to merely one dimension.

The present discussion counters historical dichotomies by positing that the two approaches, the individual and the situation (or more specifically, social cognition and social identity), are *stylistically* at odds, but not diametrically opposed. Those who view these approaches as diametrically opposed inappropriately place person-centered vs. context-centered research along a unidimensional continuum; research is thus viewed as either one or the other. Instead, we suggest that these dimensions lie orthogonally to one another (see figure 2.1). In keeping with its cross-disciplinary lineage, social psychology varies simultaneously along two independent axes that consider individual-level processes (high vs. low emphasis) and societal context (high vs. low emphasis).

By viewing research thus, each cell of this schematic diagram corresponds to varying brands of social science investigation in general, and social psychology

Figure 2.1 Individual-level processes and societal context lie along orthogonal dimensions of research.

research in particular. Pre-"crisis" social psychology tended to be low on both dimensions, describing social phenomena in the *immediate* social context (Fiske and Leyens, 1997) without systematically probing the micro intrapsychic or macro societal–cultural processes guiding these phenomena. Pure cognition research emphasizes individual-level process but neglects societal context and immediate social context. Conversely, sociological and anthropological research tend to operate in the opposite manner, investigating societal context without adequately stressing individual-level processes. An integrated social psychology must sufficiently consider both dimensions, the person and the societal–cultural environment.

Pragmatism and cultural competence, respectively, parallel these two dimensions. Again, pragmatism refers to people's functional skills for satisfying individual-level goals (parallel with axis I), whereas cultural competence refers to functional skills for societal and cultural survival (parallel with axis II). Keeping in mind the roles of pragmatism and culture, social cognition and social identity research converge harmoniously, both addressing individual-level processes and societal context equally well.

Increasing methodological collaboration

Upon appreciating the converging themes that integrate, rather than separate, social cognition and social identity, researchers have now the task of building a mutually collaborative body of empirical work. Keeping in mind the lessons learned from one another's approach, scientists can now draw upon fresh perspectives to advance existing knowledge.

Social cognition researchers who study the cognitive processes underlying stereotyping, the self-concept, and persuasion must remember the basic metatheoretical message of social identity – that society comprises social groups that stand in status and power relations to one another. Thus, the basic processes examined by many social cognition researchers may not be so basic after all, depending on the individual's cultural–societal frame of reference. Societal structure can get inside people's heads, influencing their mental processes (see Operario, Goodwin, and Fiske, 1998, for more discussion specific to the stereotyping literature). By incorporating societal variables such as power and hierarchy into their models, social cognition research can more closely approximate the *social* processes they set out to understand (e.g., Ellemers, Doosje, van Knippenberg, and Wilke, 1992; Sachdev and Bourhis, 1991). Further tests of the "universality" of existing cognitive models are necessary; given the current efforts to quantify societal and cultural context effects, universal models may change significantly. Only the data can tell.

Social identity researchers can similarly learn from social cognition's approach. Tighter manipulations and measurements of their variables – hallmarks of the social cognition approach – can only enhance social identity's theoretical strength (e.g., schema accessibility, normative vs. informational fit, personal vs. social identifications). In addition, we suggest that social identity researchers place an empirical focus back on the person, rather than solely on the situation. Just as social identity researchers attempted to emphasize the "social" in social cognition, we urge social identity researchers to remember the "self" in self-categorization. Most such research, particularly studies on meta-contrast, explain group identification as a function of situational variance. Cultural social psychologists argue that for some individuals, the group becomes part of the self, hence provides a chronically accessible frame of social perception. Individuals who have internalized their group may display even more pronounced social identity effects (e.g., ingroup bias) than individuals who situationally perceive their ingroup status as more contingent on the situation. Other personality variables, such as need for cognition or dominance, may likewise moderate the predictions of social identity theories. This suggestion implies using ideographic measures of identity, along with situational manipulations, to refine social identity theoretical models.

Concluding remarks

Social psychology is in its prime. Despite temporary periods of self-doubt and recurrent claims of inadequacy, the field stands ready for a new century of empirical discovery. Guided by the integrative themes of social identity and social cognition, social psychologists can continue to advance their insight into human behavior.

In this chapter, we have tried to keep in mind the benefits derived from previous accounts of disciplinary tension. This tension has kept social psychologists on their toes, reinforced a multi-pronged approach to the scientific investigation of human social relations. Social identity and social cognition are two of the most noteworthy approaches. We have reviewed the disciplinary context whence these approaches derived, arguing that their initial extremism and concomitant tension reflected newfound enthusiasm over recent discoveries. Their youthful zeal has subsided, due in part to each other's ongoing criticism, as each returns to social psychology's earlier agenda, set by forebears such as James, Asch, Lewin, Heider, and others. This agenda involves inquiry into the processes guiding social survival and coordinated collective existence, with particular emphasis on pragmatism and cultural competence.

Social cognition and social identity still have much to learn from one another. Social cognition researchers must continue to remember the significance of society, and its implications for internal processes; social identity must continue to remember the significance of the self, and the internal states that moderate reactions to one's context. Specific effort should focus on collaborative methodological techniques, refining the translation of conceptual theory into operational test.

Indeed, social psychology has much to celebrate, and social identity and social cognition researchers should rejoice in their own and each others' accomplishments. Together, their collaborative efforts will bring social psychology into a new century of discovery about the human social condition.

References

Abelson, R.P. (1994). A personal perspective on social cognition. In P.G. Devine, D.L. Hamilton, T.M. Ostrom (eds), *Social Cognition: Impact on social psychology*. San Diego: Academic Press, pp. 15–37.

Abrams, D. and Hogg, M. (1988). Comments on the motivational status of self-esteem in social identity and intergroup discrimination. *European Journal of Social Psychology*, 18, 317–34.

Allport, G.W. (1954). *The Nature of Prejudice*. Cambridge, MA: Addison-Wesley.

Allport, G.W. (1961). *Pattern and Growth in Personality*. New York: Holt, Rinehart, and Winston.

Asch, S.E. (1952). *Social Psychology*. Englewood Cliffs, NJ: Prentice-Hall.

Banaji, M.R. and Greenwald, A.G. (1993). Implicit stereotyping and prejudice. In M.P. Zanna and J.M. Olson (eds), *The Psychology of Prejudice: The Ontario symposium*, Vol. 7. Hillsdale, NJ: Erlbaum, pp. 55–76.

Banaji, M. and Hardin, C. (1996). Automatic stereotyping. *Psychological Science*, 7, 136–41.

Bargh, J.A. (1994). The four horsemen of automaticity: Awareness, intention, efficiency, and control in social cognition. In R.S. Wyer, Jr, and T.K. Srull (eds), *Handbook of Social Cognition*, 2nd edn, Vol. 1. Hillsdale, NJ: Erlbaum, pp. 1–40.

Bargh, J.A. (1997). The automaticity of everyday life. In R.S. Wyer (ed.), *Advances in Social Cognition*, Vol. 10. Mahwah, NJ: Erlbaum, pp. 1–61.

Baumeister, R.F. and Leary, M.R. (1995). The need to belong: Desire for interpersonal attachments as a fundamental human motivation. *Psychological Bulletin*, 117, 497–529.

Berscheid, E. (1992). A glance back at a quarter century of social psychology. *Journal of Personality and Social Psychology*, 63, 525–33.

Brewer, M.B. (1988). A dual process model of impression formation. In T.K. Srull and R.S. Wyer, Jr (eds), *Advances in Social Cognition*, Vol. 1. Hillsdale, NJ: Erlbaum, pp. 1–36.

Brewer, M.B. (1991). The social self: On being the same and different at the same time. *Personality and Social Psychology Bulletin*, 17, 475–82.

Brewer, M.B. (1997). On the social origins of human nature. In C. McGarty and S.A. Haslam (eds), *The Message of Social Psychology*. Cambridge, MA: Blackwell, pp. 54–62.

Brewer, M.B. and Brown, R.J. (1998). Intergroup relations. In D.T. Gilbert, S.T. Fiske, and G. Lindzey (eds), *The Handbook of Social Psychology*, 4th edn. New York: McGraw-Hill, pp. 554–94.

Brewer, M.B. and Kramer, R.M. (1986). Choice behavior in social dilemmas: Effects of social identity, group size, and decision framing. *Journal of Personality and Social Psychology*, 50, 543–9.

Brown, R.J. and Abrams, D. (1986). The effects of intergroup similarity and goal inter-dependence on intergroup attitudes and task performance. *Journal of Experimental Social Psychology*, 22, 78–92.

Bruner, J.S. (1957). On perceptual readiness. *Psychological Review*, 64, 123–52.

Buss, D.M. and Schmidt, D.P. (1993). Sexual Strategies Theory: A contextual evolutionary analysis of human mating. *Psychological Review*, 100, 204–32.

Campbell, D.T. (1958). Common Fate, Similarity, and other indices of the status of aggregates of persons as social entities. *Behavioral Science*, 3, 14–25.

Campbell, D.T. (1974). "Downward causation" in hierarchically organized biological systems. In F. Ayala and T. Dobzhansky (eds), *Studies in the Philosophy of Biology*. London: Macmillan, pp. 179–86.

Campbell, D.T. (1983). Two distinct routes beyond kin selection to ultrasociality: Implications for the humanities and social sciences. In D. Bridgeman (ed.), *The Nature of Prosocial Development: Theories and strategies*. New York: Academic Press, pp. 11–41.

Caporael, L.R. (1997). The evolution of truly social cognition: The core configurations model. *Personality and Social Psychology Review*, 1, 276–98.

Caporael, L.R. and Brewer, M.B. (1991). Reviving evolutionary psychology: Biology meets society. *Journal of Social Issues*, 47, 187–95.

Caporael, L.R. and Brewer, M.B. (1995). Hierarchical evolutionary theory: There is an alternative, and it's not creationism. *Psychological Inquiry*, 6, 31–4.

Carroll, J.S. and Payne, J.W. (eds) (1981). *Cognition and Social Behavior*. Hillsdale, NJ: Erlbaum.

Chaiken, S. (1987). The heuristic model of persuasion. In M.P. Zanna, J.M. Olson, and C.P. Herman (eds), *Social Influence: The Ontario symposium*, Vol. 5. Hillsdale, NJ: Erlbaum, pp. 3–39.

Chaiken, S. and Maheswaran, D. (1994). Heuristic processing can bias systematic proces-sing: Effects of source credibility, argument ambiguity, and task importance on attitude judgment. *Journal of Personality and Social Psychology*, 66, 460–73.

Chaiken, S. and Trope, Y. (eds) (in press). *Dual Process Theories in Social Psychology*. New York: Guilford.

Devine, P.G. (1989). Stereotypes and prejudice: Their automatic and controlled compon-ents. *Journal of Personality and Social Psychology*, 56, 5–18.

Devine, P.G., Hamilton, D.L. and Ostrom, T.M. (eds) (1994). *Social Cognition: Impact on social psychology*. San Diego: Academic Press.

Ellemers, N., Doosje, B.J., van Knippenberg, A., and Wilke, J. (1992). Status protection in high status minority groups. *European Journal of Social Psychology*, 22, 123–40.

Elms, A.C. (1975). The crisis of confidence in social psychology. *American Psychologist*, 30, 967–76.

Epstein, S. and Pacini, R.E. (in press). Some basic issues regarding dual-process theories from the perspective of cognitive-experiential self-theory. In S. Chaiken and Y. Trope (eds), *Dual Process Theories in Social Psychology*. New York: Guilford.

Fiske, A.P., Kitayama, S., Markus, H.R., and Nisbett, R.E. (1998). The cultural matrix of social psychology. In D.T. Gilbert, S.T. Fiske, and G. Lindzey (eds), *The Handbook of Social Psychology*, 4th edn. New York: McGraw-Hill, pp. 915–81.

Fiske, S.T. (1992). Thinking is for doing: Portraits of social cognition from daguerreotype to laserphoto. *Journal of Personality and Social Psychology*, 63, 877–89.

Fiske, S.T. (1993). Social cognition and social perception. In M.R. Rosenzweig and L.W. Porter (eds), *Annual Review of Psychology*, Vol. 44. Palo Alto, CA: Annual Reviews Inc., pp. 155–94.

Fiske, S.T. and Leyens, J.-Ph. (1997). Let social psychology be faddish or, at least, heterogeneous. In C. McGarty and S.A. Haslam (eds), *The Message of Social Psychology*. Cambridge, MA: Blackwell, pp. 92–112.

Fiske, S.T. and Linville, P.W. (1980). What does the schema concept buy us? *Personality and Social Psychology Bulletin*, 6, 543–57.

Fiske, S.T. and Neuberg, S.L. (1990). A continuum of impression formation, from category-based to individuating processes: Influences of information and motivation on attention and interpretation. In M.P. Zanna (ed.), *Advances in Experimental Social Psychology*, Vol. 23. San Diego: Academic Press, pp. 1–74.

Fiske, S.T. and Taylor, S.E. (1991). *Social Cognition*, 2nd edn. New York: McGraw-Hill.

Gergen, K.J. (1973). Social psychology as history. *Journal of Personality and Social Psychology*, 26, 309–20.

Gergen, K.J. (1997). Social psychology as social construction: The emerging vision. In C. McGarty and S.A. Haslam (eds), *The Message of Social Psychology*. Cambridge, MA: Blackwell, pp. 113–28.

Gilbert, D.T. and Hixon, J.G. (1991). The trouble of thinking: Activation and application of stereotypic beliefs. *Journal of Personality and Social Psychology*, 60, 509–17.

Gollwitzer, P.M. and Bargh, J.A. (eds) (1996). *The Psychology of Action: Linking cognition and motivation to behavior*. New York: Guilford.

Heider, F. (1958a). Perceiving the other person. In R. Tagiuri and L. Petrullo (eds), *Person Perception and Interpersonal Behavior*. Palo Alto, CA: Stanford University Press, pp. 22–6.

Heider, F. (1958b). *The Psychology of Interpersonal Relations*. New York: Wiley.

Higgins, E.T., Herman, P.C., and Zanna, M.P. (eds) (1981). *Social Cognition: The Ontario symposium*. Hillsdale, NJ: Erlbaum.

Higgins, E.T., Kuiper, N.A., and Olson, J.M. (1981). Social cognition: The need to get personal. In E.T. Higgins, P.C. Herman, and M.P. Zanna (eds), *Social Cognition: The Ontario symposium*, Vol. 1. Hillsdale, NJ: Erlbaum, pp. 395–420.

Higgins, E.T. and Sorrentino, R.M. (eds) (1990). *Handbook of Motivation and Cognition: Foundations of social behavior*, 2 vols. New York: Guilford.

Hogg, M.A. and Abrams, D. (1988). *Social Identifications*. London and New York: Routledge and Kegan Paul.

Hogg, M. and Abrams, D. (1990). Social motivation, self-esteem, and social identity. In D. Abrams and M. Hogg (eds), *Social Identity Theory: Constructive and critical advances*. Hemel Hempstead: Harvester Wheatsheaf, pp. 28–47.

James, W. (1890). *The Principles of Psychology*. Cambridge, MA: Harvard University Press (repr. 1950, New York: Dover Publications).

James, W. (1907). *Popular Lectures on Philosophy*. New York: Longmans, Green, and Co., pp. 43–81.

Jones, E.E. (1985). Major developments in social psychology during the past five decades. In G. Lindzey and E. Aronson (eds), *The Handbook of Social Psychology*, 3rd edn. New York: McGraw-Hill, pp. 47–108.

Judd, C.M. and Park, B. (1993). Definition and assessment of accuracy in social stereotypes. *Psychological Review*, 100, 109–28.

Kenrick, D.T., Groth, G.E., Trost, M.R., and Sadalla, E.K. (1993). Integrating evolutionary and social exchange perspectives on relationships: Effects of gender, self-appraisal,
and involvement on level of mate selection. *Journal of Personality and Social Psychology*, 64, 951–69.

Kinder, D.R. and Sears, D.O. (1985). Public opinion and political action. In G. Lindzey
and E. Aronson (eds), *Handbook of Political Psychology*, 3rd edn. New York: Random
House, pp. 659–741.

Langer, E.J. (1989). Minding matters. In L. Berkowitz (ed.), *Advances in Experimental
Social Psychology*, Vol. 22. New York: Academic Press, pp. 137–73.

Le Bon, G. (1896). *The Crowd: A study of the popular mind*. London: Unwin.

LeVine, R.A. and Campbell, D.T. (1972). *Ethnocentrism: Theories of conflict, ethnic
attitudes, and group behavior*. New York: Wiley.

Lewin, K. (1952). *Field Theory in Social Science*. New York: Harper and Row.

Leyens, J.-Ph., Yzerbyt, V., and Schadron, G. (1992). The social judgeability approach to
stereotypes. *European Review of Social Psychology*, 45, 92–120.

Long, K.M., Spears, R., and Manstead, A.S.R. (1994). The influence of personal and
collective self-esteem on strategies of social differentiation. *British Journal of Social
Psychology*, 23, 313–29.

McDougall, W. (1920). *The Group Mind*. Cambridge: Cambridge University Press.

Macrae, C.N., Bodenhausen, G.V., Milne, A.B., and Jetten, J. (1994). Out of mind but
back in sight: Stereotypes on the rebound. *Journal of Personality and Social Psychology*,
67, 37–47.

Markus, H.R. and Kitayama, S. (1991). Culture and the self: Implications for cognition,
emotion, and motivation. *Psychological Review*, 98, 224–53.

Markus, H.R., Kitayama, S., and Heiman, R.J. (1996). Culture and "basic" psychological
principles. In E.T. Higgins and A.W. Kruglanski (eds), *Social Psychology: Handbook of
basic principles*. New York: Guilford, pp. 857–913.

Miller, J. (1984). Culture and the development of everyday social explanation. *Journal of
Personality and Social Psychology*, 46, 961–78.

Moghaddam, F.M., Taylor, D.M., and Wright, S.C. (1993). *Social Psychology in Cross-
cultural Perspective*. New York: Freeman.

Morris, M.W. and Peng, K. (1994). Culture and cause: American and Chinese attributions
for social and physical events. *Journal of Personality and Social Psychology*, 67, 949–71.

Mullen, B. and Hu, L. (1989). Perceptions of ingroup and outgroup variability: A meta-
analysis integration. *Basic and Applied Social Psychology*, 10, 233–52.

Neisser, U. (1967). *Cognitive Psychology*. New York: Appleton-Century-Crofts.

Neisser, U. (1976). *Cognition and Reality*. San Francisco: W.H. Freeman.

Nisbett, R.E. and Ross, L. (1980). *Human Inference: Strategies and shortcomings of
social judgment*. Englewood Cliffs, NJ: Prentice-Hall.

Nisbett, R.E. and Wilson, T.D. (1977). Telling more than we can know: Verbal reports on
mental processes. *Psychological Review*, 84, 231–59.

Oakes, P.J., Haslam, S.A., and Turner, J.C. (1994). *Stereotyping and Social Reality*.
Oxford: Blackwell.

Operario, D. and Fiske, S.T. (1998). Racism equals power plus prejudice: A social
psychological equation for racial oppression. In J.L. Eberhardt and S.T. Fiske (eds),
Confronting Racism: The problem and the response. Thousand Oaks, CA: Sage, pp.
33–53.

Operario, D., Goodwin, S.A., and Fiske, S.T. (1998). Power is everywhere: Social control and personal control both operate at stereotype activation, interpretation, and response. In R.S. Wyer (ed.), *Advances in Social Cognition*, Vol. 11. Mahwah, NJ: Erlbaum, pp. 163–75.

Ostrom, T.M. and Sedikides, C. (1992). Out-group homogeneity effects in natural and minimal groups. *Psychological Bulletin*, 112, 536–52.

Parker, I. (1989). *The Crisis in Social Psychology – and How to End It*. New York: Routledge.

Pepitone, A. (1981). Lessons from the history of social psychology. *American Psychologist*, 36, 972–85.

Petty, R.E. and Cacioppo, J.T. (1986). The elaboration likelihood model of persuasion. In L. Berkowitz (ed.), *Advances in Experimental Social Psychology*, Vol. 19. San Diego: Academic Press, pp. 123–205.

Pratto, F., Sidanius, J., Stallworth, L.M., and Malle, B.F. (1994). Social dominance orientation: A personality variable predicting social and political attitudes. *Journal of Personality and Social Psychology*, 67, 741–63.

Rabbie, J.M. and Horwitz, M. (1969). Arousal of ingroup–outgroup bias by a chance win or loss. *Journal of Personality and Social Psychology*, 13, 269–77.

Rabbie, J.M. and Horwitz, M. (1988). Categories versus groups as explanatory concepts in intergroup relations. *European Journal of Social Psychology*, 18, 117–23.

Rabbie, J.M., Schot, J.C., and Visser, L. (1989). Social identity theory: A conceptual and empirical critique from the perspective of a behavioral interaction model. *European Journal of Social Psychology*, 19, 171–202.

Reis, H.T. and Stiller, J. (1992). Publication trends in JPSP: A three-decade review. *Personality and Social Psychology Bulletin*, 18, 465–72.

Robinson, W.P. (ed.) (1996). *Social Groups and Identities: Developing the legacy of Henri Tajfel*. Oxford: Butterworth-Heinemann.

Sachdev, I. and Bourhis, R.Y. (1991). Power and status differentials in minority and majority group relations. *European Journal of Social Psychology*, 21, 1–24.

Sampson, E.E. (1977). Psychology and the American ideal. *Journal of Personality and Social Psychology*, 35, 767–82.

Schweder, R.A. (1991). *Thinking through Cultures: Expeditions in cultural psychology*. Cambridge, MA: Harvard University Press.

Sherif, M. (1936). *The Psychology of Social Norms*. New York: Harper and Row.

Sherif, M. (1966). *Group Conflict and Co-operation: Their social psychology*. London: Routledge and Kegan Paul.

Sidanius, J. (1993). The psychology of group conflict and the dynamics of social oppression: A social dominance perspective. In S. Iyengar and W. McGuire (eds), *Explorations in Political Psychology*. Durham, NC: Duke University Press, pp. 183–219.

Sidanius, J. and Pratto, F. (1993). The inevitability of oppression and the dynamics of social dominance. In P. Sniderman and P. Tetlock (eds), *Prejudice, Politics, and the American Dilemma*. Stanford, CA: Stanford University Press, pp. 173–211.

Sidanius, J., Pratto, F., and Bobo, L. (1994). Social dominance orientation and the political psychology of gender: A case of invariance? *Journal of Personality and Social Psychology*, 67, 998–1011.

Simon, B. and Hamilton, D.L. (1994). Self-stereotyping and social context: The effects of relative in-group size and in-group status. *Journal of Personality and Social Psychology*, 66, 699–711.

Snyder, C.R. and Fromkin, H.L. (1980). *Uniqueness: The human pursuit of difference.* New York: Plenum.

Sorrentino, R.M. and Higgins, E.T. (eds) (1986). *Handbook of Motivation and Cognition: Foundations of social behavior*, Vol. 1. New York: Guilford.

Steiner, I.D. (1974). Whatever happened to the group in social psychology? *Journal of Experimental Social Psychology*, 10, 94–108.

Stevens, L.A. and Fiske, S.T. (1995). Motivation and cognition in social life: A social survival perspective. *Social Cognition*, 13, 189–214.

Stroebe, W. and Insko, C.A. (1989). Stereotypes, prejudice, and discrimination: Changing conceptions in theory and research. In D. Bar-Tal, C.F. Graumann, A.W. Kruglanski, and W. Stroebe (eds), *Stereotypes and Prejudice: Changing conceptions*. New York: Springer-Verlag, pp. 3–34.

Tajfel, H. (1969). Cognitive aspects of prejudice. *Journal of Social Issues*, 25, 79–97.

Tajfel, H. (1979). Individuals and groups in social psychology. *British Journal of Social Psychology*, 18, 183–90.

Tajfel, H. and Turner, J.C. (1979). An integrative theory of intergroup conflict. In S. Worchel and W.G. Austin (eds), *Psychology of Intergroup Relations*, 2nd edn. Chicago: Nelson-Hall, pp. 7–24.

Taylor, S.E. (1982). The interface of cognitive and social psychology. In J.H. Harvey (ed.), *Cognition, Social Behavior, and the Environment*. Hillsdale, NJ: Erlbaum, pp. 189–211.

Taylor, S.E. (1998). The social being in social psychology. In D.T. Gilbert, S.T. Fiske, and G. Lindzey (eds), *The Handbook of Social Psychology*, 4th edn. New York: McGraw-Hill, pp. 58–95.

Triandis, H.C. (1989). The self and social behavior in differing cultural contexts. *Psychological Review*, 93, 506–20.

Turner, J.C., Hogg, M., Oakes, P.J., Reicher, S.D., and Wetherell, M.S. (1987). *Rediscovering the Social Group: A self-categorization theory*. Oxford: Blackwell.

Turner, J.C. and Oakes, P.J. (1986). The significance of the social identity concept for social psychology with reference to individualism, interactionism, and social influence. *British Journal of Social Psychology*, 25, 237–52.

Turner, J.C., Oakes, P.J., Haslam, S.A., and McGarty, C. (1994). Self and collective: Cognition and social context. *Personality and Social Psychology Bulletin*, 20, 454–63.

Wilder, D.A. and Shapiro, P.N. (1984). Role of outgroup cues in determining social identity. *Journal of Personality and Social Psychology*, 47, 342–8.

Worchel, S., Andreoli, V.A., and Folger, R. (1977). Intergroup cooperation and intergroup attraction: The effect of previous interaction and outcome of combined effort. *Journal of Experimental Social Psychology*, 13, 131–40.

Wyer, R.S., Jr and Srull, T.K. (1994). *Handbook of Social Cognition*, 2nd edn. Hillsdale, NJ: Erlbaum.

Zajonc, R.B. (1980). Cognition and social cognition: A historical perspective. In L. Festinger (ed.), *Retrospections on Social Cognition*. New York: Oxford University Press, pp. 180–240.

3

Social Categorization and Social Context: Is Stereotype Change a Matter of Information or of Meaning?

PENELOPE J. OAKES, S. ALEXANDER HASLAM, AND KATHERINE J. REYNOLDS

Introduction

Interest in social stereotyping has been one of the constants in modern social psychology, a discipline which can seem somewhat "faddish" at times (Fiske and Leyens, 1997). There has been more or less uninterrupted effort directed at our understanding of the "general structure and function" (Tajfel, 1969, p. 82) of stereotypes since Tajfel's watershed analysis of the issue in 1969, and the two approaches discussed in this volume – social identity and social cognition – have been major players in this research area (Hamilton, 1981; Leyens, Yzerbyt, and Schadron, 1994; Macrae, Stangor, and Hewstone, 1996; Oakes, Haslam, and Turner, 1994; Spears, Oakes, Ellemers, and Haslam, 1997).

The treatments of stereotyping offered by the two approaches appear to occupy a fair degree of common ground. Both have emphasized the value of drawing a clear distinction between individual uniqueness and categorical homogenization, between the perception of people as individual personalities and their characterization in stereotypical terms. Indeed, researchers from both traditions have recruited the idea of a theoretical continuum to underline the importance of distinguishing between individual variation and stereotypical homogeneity (Fiske and Neuberg, 1990; Tajfel, 1978). Further, in both areas, the categorization process – its nature, functions, and effects – has been of crucial explanatory significance.

In fact, these apparent commonalities may be somewhat chimerical, because the nature of the distinction between individuated and stereotypical perception, and the role of categorization in that distinction, define major points of divergence

Grateful thanks to Andrew Dempster, Rachael Eggins, Mark Nolan, and Janet Tweedie for their invaluable contributions to all aspects of the empirical research reported in this chapter. The research was supported by a Large Grant from the Australian Research Council.

between the two approaches. This should not surprise us. The two approaches emerge from different starting points, with different metatheoretical underpinnings (Fiske and Leyens, 1997; Turner and Oakes, 1997). Social identity research (but not social cognition research) is guided by a principle we can refer to as the *discontinuity hypothesis*, the recognition of a qualitative distinction between intergroup and interpersonal behavior. One major aim of social identity work is to detail the processes that provide the distinctive social psychological underpinnings of *group life*. For social cognition, on the other hand, the focus has tended to be on types of processing *per se*, such as piecemeal vs. category based, which may underlie variations in perception, judgment, inference, and hence behavior. The drive to solve that "essential problem" (Asch, 1952, p. 256; see also Allport, 1962) of social psychology – the psychological nature of the group – which contributed to the genesis of the social identity perspective has not powered social cognition research. Indeed, social cognition researchers tend to treat the individual–group relationship as nonproblematic from the outset by defining both social and psychological reality in terms of the *individual* information processor, and suggesting that this reality is vulnerable to *distortion* through the influence of group phenomena (see Oakes, 1996, for a detailed discussion; see also Oakes and Reynolds, 1997; Oakes and Turner, 1990; Oakes et al., 1994; Turner and Oakes, 1986, 1997).

Ultimately, however, we all want to explain the same things – stereotyping, prejudice, intergroup discrimination, impression formation, etc. – and hence the value of a volume of this kind, in which the shared and differentiating assumptions and findings of each tradition of work can be juxtaposed. In this chapter, we explore the implications of the view of the categorization process developed in self-categorization theory (Turner, 1985; Turner, Hogg, Oakes, Reicher, and Wetherell, 1987; Turner, Oakes, Haslam, and McGarty, 1994) for the cognitive analysis of stereotype change. In particular, the "prototype subtyping" (Hewstone, 1996, p. 340) model of change is juxtaposed with self-categorization theory's emphasis on the context dependence of the categorization process, and the consequent variability of category form and content. Two studies testing the usefulness of self-categorization ideas for our understanding of the change process are briefly outlined. We begin by uncovering some of the roots of the self-categorization analysis in work on social identity.

Social Identity: The Interpersonal–Intergroup Discontinuity

As well as the development of theory and its testing through empirical research, the social identity tradition has made an important and explicit contribution at the level of metatheory (e.g., Tajfel, 1978, 1979; Turner and Oakes, 1986, 1997). Building on the contributions of Asch (1952) and Sherif (1936, 1967), and beginning with Tajfel's rejection of individualistic approaches to group behavior, there has been a consistent emphasis on the qualitative distinctiveness of group phenomena, on the need for critical examination of analyses which attempt straightforwardly to extrapolate principles of interpersonal behavior to inter-group contexts (e.g., Billig, 1976; Brown and Turner, 1981), and on the conscious development of theory consistent with interactionist, anti-individualistic metatheory.

One early idea which expressed this metatheoretical commitment was Tajfel's suggestion that interpersonal and intergroup behavior might represent the extremes of a bipolar continuum upon which all instances of social behavior could be placed (see Tajfel, 1978, ch. 2). At the "intergroup" extreme all of the behavior of two or more individuals towards each other would be determined by their membership of different social groups or categories (i.e., by group affiliations and loyalties to the exclusion of individual characteristics and interpersonal relationships). The "interpersonal" extreme referred to any social encounter in which all the interaction that took place was determined by the personal relationships between the individuals and their individual characteristics (i.e., idiosyncratic personal qualities were the overriding causal influences). More formally, the two extremes were distinguished in terms of the presence or absence of social categorizations and the degree of uniformity or variability in intra-and intergroup behavior.

In essence, the continuum described the distinction between an intergroup social reality and an interpersonal social reality. It represented a persuasive argument against individualism in theories of group behavior, and was put to good use in several research areas (e.g., Brown and Turner, 1981; Hewstone and Brown, 1986; Hogg, 1992), but it was basically descriptive in character. Later work attempted to develop a causal analysis of variation between the interpersonal and the intergroup, and it was here that the categorization process, and especially the role that it plays in the definition of the *self*, came to the fore. The concept of *social identity* – the group-related aspects of the self-concept; see Tajfel (1978), p. 63 – became an important foundation of *social identity theory*, Tajfel and Turner's (1979, 1986) influential account of intergroup relations. However, Tajfel was quite aware that he had presented only a partial, limited exploration of the role of categorization in the self-process. The more comprehensive exposition of just how categorization might function in self-definition, and in turn regulate the form (interpersonal vs. intergroup) of social interaction, has been the subject of *self-categorization theory*, initially developed by John Turner in the early 1980s (Turner, 1982, 1984, 1985; Turner et al., 1987, 1994; Turner and Oakes, 1989).

Self-categorization Theory: Categorization and Context

A major aim of self-categorization theory was to develop an explicitly interactionist explanation of the psychological basis of the social group, an explanation that would encompass both psychological process and the social reality of group life. Building on Tajfel's argument that categorization was the psychological basis of "self-definition in a social context" (1978, p. 61), Turner elaborated a view of (self-) categorization as the pivotal process through which the individual and the social interact (Turner et al., 1994). In self-categorization theory, categorization works to *align the person with the realities of the social context*, to produce dynamic, context-specific definitions of self and others which both reflect and make possible the almost infinitely variable pattern of human social relations. In particular, variability in self-categorization underlies and can contribute to the explanation of the emergence of *collective, group phenomena* such as social stereotyping (Oakes et al., 1994), social influence (David and Turner, 1996; Turner, 1991), crowd behavior (Reicher, 1996), social movement participation (Kelly, 1993; Simon, 1998), prejudice and intergroup conflict (Duckitt, 1992; Turner and Bourhis, 1996), social cooperation (Morrison, 1997), and so forth. The fact that the theory began as an attempt to explain the psychological underpinnings of these manifestations of collective, group life provides the indispensable context within which its analysis of categorization needs to be understood.

It is unnecessary to present a detailed account of the theory here (see Turner, 1985; Turner et al., 1987, 1994). Rather, we shall focus on the categorization process, as discussed in the theory, and its role in the context-specific, relational definition of self and others. The theory argues that self-conception reflects a variable process of self-categorization, the cognitive grouping of the self as identical to some class of stimuli in contrast to some other class of stimuli. As is the case with all systems of natural categories (Rosch, 1978), self-categorizations can exist at different *levels of abstraction* related by *class inclusion*. That is, a given self-category (e.g., "scientist") is seen as more abstract than another (e.g., "biologist") to the extent that it can contain the other, but the other cannot contain it: all biologists are scientists, but not all scientists are biologists. Going-beyond the parameters of Tajfel's original interpersonal–intergroup continuum, self-categories both more and less abstract than personal and social identity are envisaged, but for purposes of theoretical exposition three levels of abstraction of self-categories are distinguished: the interpersonal (subordinate level of abstraction, personal identity, self as an individual person), intergroup (intermediate level of abstraction, social identity, self as a group member), and interspecies (superordinate level of abstraction, self as a human being).

The theory regards categorization, including self-categorization, as a dynamic, context-dependent process, determined by *comparative relations within a given context*. To predict categorization, therefore, the entire range of stimuli under consideration, rather than isolated stimulus characteristics, must be taken into account. This point is formalized in the principle of *meta-contrast*, which predicts that a given set of items is more likely to be categorized as a single entity *to the degree that differences within that set of items are less than the differences between that set and others within the comparative context*. The meta-contrast principle draws upon but also extends the classic idea that categories form on the basis of intraclass similarities and interclass differences (cf. Campbell, 1958; Rosch, 1978; Tajfel, 1969; Tversky, 1977). In meta-contrast, the similarities and differences involved are not independent and additive, but mutually defined in terms of currently salient comparisons (cf. Medin, 1989; see below). Thus, the meta-contrast principle is explicit that categorization is *relative to the frame of reference*, to the contrasts available within the perceiver's salient stimulus field. It depends not just on similarities between stimuli but on *relative similarities*, the perception that there is more similarity between certain stimuli than between others. The meta-contrast principle has been slightly vulnerable to misunderstanding, in part because of the precise quantitative role it has played in explanations of some social influence and social judgmental phenomena (e.g., group polarization, perceptual accentuation effects; see Haslam and Turner, 1992; McGarty, Turner, Hogg, David, and Wetherell, 1992). By far its most important, and perhaps most controversial, implication is the absolute context dependence of categorization, the rejection of social categories (and of the self-concept) as prestored mental entities or stable cognitive representations:

the meta-contrast principle is explicit that categorizing is inherently comparative and hence is intrinsically variable, fluid, and relative to a frame of reference. It is always context dependent. Self-categories do not represent fixed, absolute properties of the perceiver but relative, varying, context-dependent properties. (Turner et al., 1994, p. 456)

In fact, meta-contrast provides only a partial account of the context dependence of categorization. It describes the *comparative relations* between stimuli which lead them to be represented by a category, but it is also important to take into account the *social meaning* of differences between people in terms of the normative and behavioral *content* of their actions, and the relative accessibility of particular categorizations (Oakes, 1987; Oakes, Turner, and Haslam, 1991). In general terms, the theory explains the salience of any given category as a function of an interaction between its relative accessibility (the "readiness" of a perceiver to use a particular categorization) and the "fit" between the category and reality. Meta-contrast is the theory's principle of "comparative fit" (the match between category and the comparative properties of stimuli), but "normative fit" (the match between the content properties of stimuli and general "background theories," normative beliefs about the substantive social meaning of the category) is also always inseparably at work (for relevant evidence see Haslam, Oakes, Turner, and McGarty, 1996; Nolan, Haslam, Spears, and Oakes, 1997; Oakes, 1994; Oakes et al., 1991; Simon, Hastedt, and Aufderheide, in press; van Knippenberg, van Twuyver, and Pepels, 1994).

This emphasis on categorization as highly variable and context dependent produces a concomitant emphasis on the context dependence of perceived similarity and difference, the major outcome of categorization. People who are categorized and perceived as different in one context (e.g., "biologists" and "physicists" within a science faculty) can be recategorized and perceived as similar in another context (e.g., as "scientists" rather than "social scientists" within a university) without any actual change in their own positions (Gaertner, Mann, Murrell, and Dovidio, 1989). This is the essence of categorization: it is a cognitive grouping process that transforms differences into similarities, and vice versa. Are physicists and biologists similar or different? Arising from the comparisons specified in the meta-contrast principle, categorization subjectively defines currently relevant similarities and differences, and from perceived similarities and differences flow, amongst other things, perceptions of attraction and dislike, agreement and disagreement, cooperation and conflict. In sum, categorization underlies and defines our social orientation towards others. Within the science faculty, physicists might reject and deride biologists, claiming they aren't "real scientists," but in comparison with social scientists the two groups may present as inseparable allies.

Of particular relevance for our present discussion, as changes in the comparative context produce changes in ingroup–outgroup relationships, they also affect *intra*category structure. The meta-contrast principle can be used to define the relative prototypicality of members within a group (see Turner and Oakes, 1989, pp. 259–65). In general terms, the more a group member differs from outgroup members and the less he or she differs from other ingroup members (i.e., the more this person exemplifies what ingroup members share and what they do not share with the outgroup), the more that individual will be perceived as prototypical of the group. So, for example, individuals wishing to be perceived as prototypical members of the New Labour Party in Britain must differ in politics from members of more conservative parties, but they must not be so left-wing, so "old Labour" that they begin to differ significantly from other New Labourites – prototypicality depends upon both inter-and intragroup comparisons. One important point is that, because relative prototypicality depends on (amongst other things) intergroup comparisons, *it will vary along with variation in the intergroup context in which judgments are made.* For example, the prototypical member of New Labour in a comparative context including socialists will be *different* from the prototypical member as compared with the Conservative Party. Self-categorization theory thus agrees with Rosch (1978) that fixed prototypes are "fictions," and emphasizes context-dependent *judgments of prototypicality* rather than fixed prototypical images which represent groups as constants across changing contexts (see Haslam, Oakes, McGarty, Turner, and Onorato, 1995; Hogg, 1996; Hogg, Hardie, and Reynolds, 1995; Oakes, Haslam, and Turner, 1998; cf. Brewer, 1988; Brewer, Dull, and Lui, 1981; see below).

There are further aspects of the analysis of categorization presented within the theory (e.g., the relationship between the different levels of abstraction, the dependence of comparison and categorization upon identity at a higher level of abstraction), but these issues are not central to our current discussion and are covered elsewhere (e.g., Oakes et al., 1994; Turner and Oakes, 1989). The major point to emphasize here is the dynamic and variable nature of the categorization process, a process designed to give perceivers access to the *context-dependent meaning* of stimuli – meaning which is only given through appreciation of the way in which individual stimuli *relate to each other* in the present context. Both the level (inclusiveness) and the content (including the prototypical position) of categorization are, as a consequence, sensitive to and vary with variations in comparative and normative aspects of context.

Social Cognition: Category Content and Stereotype Change

How can we change stereotypes? Given the common association between stereotyped beliefs and prejudiced, discriminatory intergroup attitudes, the question of change has always been at the forefront of research in the area. From the earliest investigations of the contact hypothesis to the most recent analyses of relevant cognitive processes, the assumption has been that stereotype content misrepresents groups, and that we need to find ways in which to replace that distorted content with less damaging information.

In his excellent recent overview of stereotype change research, Miles Hewstone comments that a "focus on *information processing* is the hallmark of cognitive analyses of intergroup relations" (1996, p. 338; emphasis added). One manifestation of this focus is an approach to stereotype change which emphasizes *the processing of disconfirming information*, the management of data inconsistent with cognitively represented stereotypical expectations (Hewstone, 1989, 1994). Translating the "generalization" problem from the contact hypothesis literature (see Brown and Turner, 1981; Hewstone and Brown, 1986), the aim of cognitive research into stereotype change has been to specify the conditions under which disconfirming information can gain entry to the cognitive representation of the category as a whole, producing generalized change rather than localized awareness of "exceptions."

Of three potential models of the processing and effects of disconfirming information, the most consistently supported has been what Hewstone terms the "prototype subtyping" model (1996, p. 340). This develops Rothbart and John's (1985) prototype analysis of categorization, in which they suggest that it is goodness of fit to a category prototype, "the degree to which the individual's attributes match those of the category" (1985, p. 90), that determines categorization (cf. the fit hypothesis in self-categorization theory; see above). By definition, an exemplar carrying category-disconfirming information is not highly prototypical, may not be securely categorized as a member of the category it disconfirms, and may not, therefore, have any impact on the representation of that category.

Building on these ideas, and on the work of Weber and Crocker (1983), Hewstone and his colleagues argue that stereotypes are "hierarchical structures" (1996, p. 339) which can respond to disconfirming information by becoming more internally differentiated. Specifically, subtypes develop within the higher-level category (e.g., black lawyers; aggressive women) such that disconfirming information is assimilated without revision of the overall stereotype (of lawyers as white, of women as gentle).

Support for this model comes from a series of studies in which a constant amount of stereotype-disconfirming information is presented to subjects in varying patterns (e.g., Hewstone, Hopkins, and Routh, 1992; Johnston and Hewstone, 1992; see Hewstone, 1994, for a review). For example, in the first study reported by Johnston and Hewstone (1992) subjects (psychology students) were presented with both confirming and disconfirming information about members of an outgroup, physics students. The patterning of the information across outgroup members was varied, such that it was either *concentrated* in two out of the eight members presented, *dispersed* across six members or, in an *intermediate* condition, dispersed across four members. We shall focus on the dispersed and concentrated conditions, which are described in table 3.1 (adapted from Johnston and Hewstone, 1992, table 2). The confirming information described physics students as interested in new technology and hardworking, whereas the disconfirming information referred to their fashion consciousness and involvement in student politics. Johnston and Hewstone predicted more stereotype

Table 3.1   Distribution of behavioral information in the disconfirming-information paradigm

Condition	Group member							
	1	2	3	4	5	6	7	8
Concentrated	I	I	C	C	C	C	C	C
	I	I	C	C	C	C	C	C
	I	I	R	R	R	R	R	R
	I	I	R	R	R	R	R	R
	I	I	R	R	R	R	R	R
	I	I	R	R	R	R	R	R
Dispersed	I	I	I	I	I	I	C	C
	I	I	I	I	I	I	C	C
	C	C	C	C	C	C	C	C
	R	R	R	R	R	R	R	R
	R	R	R	R	R	R	R	R
	R	R	R	R	R	R	R	R

I = Inconsistent, stereotype-*disconfirming* information.
C = Consistent, stereotype-*confirming* information.
R = Stereotype-*irrelevant* information.

Adapted from Johnton and Hewstone (1992), table 2.

change under dispersed than concentrated conditions because disconfirming stimulus group members were more prototypical when disconfirming information was dispersed. They were, therefore, more likely to be categorized as "physics students," and to import their disconfirming attributes into that category. This prediction was confirmed, and the authors conclude that dispersal of disconfirming information enhances stereotype change *because* dispersed disconfirmers are more prototypical, and they are more prototypical *because* "prototypicality... is determined by the amounts of confirming and disconfirming information used to describe a member" (Hewstone, 1994, p. 81).

These findings are consistent with the notion of subtyping as a cognitive response to category disconfirmation. Furthermore, mediational analyses indicate that change does depend on the perceived typicality of the stereotype disconfirmer (Hantzi, 1995; Johnston and Hewstone, 1992), and both card-sorts and "Who said what?" memory tasks have been used in an attempt to render the hypothesized subtyping process more transparent (Hantzi, 1995; Hewstone et al., 1992; Johnston, Hewstone, Pendry, and Frankish, 1994). These latter studies have shown that concentrated disconfirmers are especially likely to be represented as separate from other stimulus individuals, a finding which has been interpreted as evidence of subtyping.

There is no doubt that Hewstone's analysis of stereotype change is well supported by data. Clearly, the categorization process does become active in the face of disconfirming, inconsistent information – the parameters of perceived similarity and difference shift to accommodate observed patterns. Consistent with the prevailing social cognitive view of categories and stereotypes as cognitive structures (e.g., see Fiske and Taylor, 1991, for a discussion of stereotypes and categories as cognitive schemas), Hewstone interprets both observed change and observed stability as reflections of the state of the relevant cognitive structure – the overall category has assimilated some new information (change), or (more often) a subtype has been constructed to accommodate the new information, perhaps with the deliberate intent of preserving the established meaning and value connotations of the overall category (stability; see Hewstone, 1996, p. 340; and Yzerbyt, Rocher, and Coull, 1996). Hewstone comments that, because subtyping is such an ever-ready response to stereotype disconfirmation, the model is "more a model of non-change... than change" (1994, p. 73), and he feels that his studies add up to "depressing support for the view that the persistence of stereotypes is cognitively overdetermined" (ibid., p. 101).

Self-categorization theory suggests a different view of this research, a view that leads us to question both the extent to which stereotypes really are "persistent," and the extent to which the persistence we do observe can be considered "*cognitively* overdetermined." In the next section we reconsider Hewstone's findings from a self-categorization perspective, and conclude that they may be more consistent with the operations of a context-dependent, variable categorization process of the kind envisaged in self-categorization theory than with change-resistant hierarchical cognitive structures.

Stereotype Change as Categorization-in-Context

It has been a mainstay of stereotyping research that stereotypical beliefs are rigid, unresponsive to reality, and generally resistant to change. This was the view long before the cognitive analysis was developed (e.g., Fishman, 1956; Kerr, 1943; Lippmann, 1922), and perhaps contributed to the construal of stereotypes as cognitive structures with built-in processing defenses against disconfirmation. Importantly, the view of stereotypes as cognitive structures, as relatively stable cognitive entities, has meant that attempts at stereotype change have usually taken the form of assaults on those structures, on the content of the relevant cognitive representations. Thus, we present perceivers with *information* (content) that allegedly applies to a member of a given category, and then examine the receptiveness of that category to that (allegedly) relevant content.

In contrast, and as we have outlined above, self-categorization theory rejects the idea of categories as preformed, waiting-to-be-activated cognitive structures in favor of an emphasis on the categorization *process* as a context-dependent, variable means of representing current stimulus relationships (see Oakes et al., 1994, pp. 197–9). In rejecting the notion of preformed categories, our analysis necessarily recasts the nature of the categorization process itself. Rather than being a matter of referring the attributes of each stimulus to a cognitive representation, and membership decisions following from calculation of the "hits" and "misses" by confirming and disconfirming attributes respectively, we argue that categorization involves interpreting, with reference to background theories and expectations, the *pattern of similarities and differences between stimuli across the context as a whole* (see Haslam and Turner, 1992, 1995; Haslam et al., 1996b). This process is specified in the fit hypothesis discussed above. We might also note that influential recent discussions of categorization within cognitive psychology have been highly critical of approaches (including both prototype and exemplar-based theories) which treat categorization as the outcome of attribute-matching similarity judgments (e.g., see Medin, 1989; Medin, Goldstone, and Gentner, 1993).

The cognitive subtyping account of stereotype change in the disconfirming information paradigm rests heavily on an attribute-matching view of categorization. It argues that change is mediated by the relative typicality of the disconfirmers under dispersed and concentrated conditions, and that relative typicality depends on "the degree to which the individual's attributes match those of the category" (Rothbart and John, 1985, p. 90). Given that we have presented an alternative to this view of categorization, what does our analysis imply for the process of stereotype change? We shall discuss implications both for the specific interpretation of results in the disconfirming information paradigm and for the general issue of stereotype stability and change.

Let us return to the first study reported by Johnston and Hewstone (1992), outlined above, in which psychology students read both confirming (interested in new technology, hardworking) and disconfirming (fashion conscious, involved in student politics) information about physics students, presented under concentrated or dispersed conditions (table 3.1). As predicted, Johnston and Hewstone found more stereotype change under dispersed than concentrated conditions. They attributed this finding to the comparatively strong prototypicality of dispersed disconfirmers, commenting that "prototypicality...is determined by the amounts of confirming and disconfirming information used to describe a member" (Hewstone, 1994, p. 81).

Recall, however, that self-categorization theory defines prototypicality in a way which goes beyond this attribute-matching approach. We assume that the nature of relevant comparison outgroups plays a major role in defining prototypicality, which means that the prototypical physics student in one particular intergroup context may be far less prototypical in a different intergroup context. Interestingly, a close reading of Johnston and Hewstone's paper reveals that their procedure involved presentation of the physics student stimulus group in *explicit comparison* with drama students. In effect, then, a specific *inter*group context was defined in the study, the categorization in action was *physics students as compared to drama students*, and the *prototypical* physics student was the sartorially challenged, apolitical, hardworking technologist who best represented this *contrast* between physics and drama. But what if computer science or engineering majors rather than drama students had been introduced into the comparative context? According to self-categorization theory, this should affect the definition, including the prototype, of the "physics student" category, perhaps even to the extent of physics students being defined as *comparatively* politically aware and well dressed (this argument is represented schematically in figure 3.1). In other words, it might be misleading to think of "fashion conscious" as a piece of "information" with a constant (disconfirming) relationship to the category "physics student." Rather, the *meaning* of the attribute, the meaning of the category, and the relationship between them, may have been implicitly but crucially specific to the comparative context made salient in the study. This may, in turn, have contributed to the relative impact of dispersed vs. concentrated disconfirmation on subjects' reported stereotypes. Perhaps, as suggested in figure 3.1, there are comparative contexts in which Johnston and Hewstone's well-dressed concentrated disconfirmers would actually gain in perceived typicality over the hardworking dispersed disconfirmers, and the usual dispersed/concentrated effect might be reversed under these conditions.

We have tested this possibility in a program of studies in which manipulations of the comparative context are introduced into the dispersed/concentrated disconfirmation paradigm (Oakes and Dempster, 1996; Oakes, Haslam, Reynolds, Nolan, Eggins, Dempster, and Tweedie, 1997). In the first of these, the target group was students attending the Australian Catholic University (ACU), a former teacher-training institution with a local campus. These Catholic students were

				Prototypicality		
				P_1	P_2	P_3
Case 1		P_1 P_2 P_3 D D D		++	++	+
Case 2	CS CS CS	P_1 P_2 P_3		+	++	++

Underlying
comparative "geekish" ———————————— trendy
dimension

Case 1 = Physics students compared with Drama students (cf. Johnston and Hewstone, 1992)

Case 2 = Physics students compared with Computer Scientists

Note: P_1 (the most "geeky" physicist) is more prototypical of physics students than P_3 (the most trendy physicist) in Case 1 and therefore the whole physics student category is defined as more "geekish." This is because in this case P_1 makes a greater contribution to the intercategory difference component of meta–contrast. This situation is reversed in Case 2.

Figure 3.1   The contextual basis of prototypicality and category definition.

generally perceived by our subjects (students at the Australian National University; ANU) as conservative, conventional, and tradition-loving. The manipulation of comparative context involved either presenting the ACU group alone (*restricted* context), or leading subjects to believe that they would also be reading about members of the Call to Australia (Fred Nile) Party (*extended* context). The Call to Australia Party (CTA) is a right-wing religious group led by the Reverend Fred Nile. It is extremely conservative and campaigns vigorously on moral issues, declaiming what it sees as the evils of homosexuality, abortion, and prostitution. In its campaign material for the 1996 Australian Federal Election, CTA described itself as "pro-God," "pro-family," and "pro-moral," and its slogan was "For God and the Family." Thus, the salient comparative dimension within the experimental context was *conservatism*, with the three groups involved in the study – the ANU student subjects, the ACU stimulus group, and the CTA comparison group – varying along this dimension such that the ANU subjects were towards the nonconservative extreme, the CTA highly conservative, and the ACU group in between.

Subjects read about six students attending the Australian Catholic University, each of whom was described in terms of six attributes. Stereotype-disconfirming attributes, which portrayed them as progressive, frivolous, and rebellious, were either concentrated in the descriptions of three group members or dispersed across all six (see table 3.2). Control subjects did not receive any information, and simply described the stimulus group under either restricted or extended comparison conditions.

Table 3.2 Experiment 1: Distribution of information describing students at the Australian Catholic University across concentrated and dispersed conditions

Condition	Group member					
	1	2	3	4	5	6
Concentrated	I	I	I	C	C	C
	I	I	I	C	C	C
	I	I	I	C	C	C
	I	I	I	C	C	C
	R	R	R	R	R	R
	R	R	R	R	R	R
Dispersed	I	I	I	I	I	I
	I	I	I	I	I	I
	C	C	C	C	C	C
	C	C	C	C	C	C
	R	R	R	R	R	R
	R	R	R	R	R	R

C = Confirming information, e.g., conservative, religious, loyal to family, traditional.
I = Disconfirming information, e.g., progressive, irreligious, life of the party.
R = Stereotype-irrelevant information.

Following the meta-contrast principle outlined above, and in particular the relevant work by Haslam and colleagues (Haslam and Turner, 1992, 1995; Haslam, Turner, Oakes, McGarty, and Hayes, 1992), we expected that the introduction of the extremely conservative CTA group into the comparative context would affect the overall comparative relations between the groups. Specifically, the relative positions of the ingroup (ANU) and the Catholic students should be affected such that under restricted conditions the Catholic students would be contrasted from the ANU and seen as highly conservative, but in the extended context they would be contrasted from the CTA (and assimilated to the ANU) and seen as significantly less conservative. As part of this process of context-specific category definition, the *prototype* of Catholic students should shift away from the conservative extreme under extended conditions, creating the possibility that the less conservative *concentrated* disconfirmers could have more impact on judgments of the category as a whole than the relatively conservative dispersed disconfirmers under these conditions. In short, we predicted a reversal of the usual dispersed/concentrated effect under extended comparison conditions.

Experimental subjects read the descriptions of the six Catholic students, with extended subjects expecting subsequent presentation of CTA members. All subjects completed a series of dependent measures, with control subjects completing only those items which referred to ACU students in general rather than the stimulus group itself. Stereotyping of the ACU group was assessed in two ways – subjects selected the five traits they felt were "most descriptive" of a typical student at the ACU from a modified Katz–Braly checklist (after Katz and Braly,

1933), and rated ACU students in general on a series of bipolar trait scales including both stereotype-consistent and inconsistent items.

The Katz–Braly trait selections are presented in table 3.3. Qualitative consideration of these frequencies provides some initial support for our prediction. Within the restricted range conditions, dispersed disconfirmation clearly had more impact on stereotype content, relative to restricted/control, than did concentrated disconfirmation (e.g., see frequencies for religious, conservative, conventional). In contrast, the extension of the frame of reference to include Call to Australia greatly reduced the impact of dispersed disconfirmation, whereas there is evidence of significant change in the extended/concentrated condition (see again, religious, conservative, conventional). To quantify the stereotypicality of checklist responses we carried out a log linear analysis on the frequency with

Table 3.3   Percentage of participants assigning listed traits to students of the Australian Catholic University

Frame	Control		Information dispersed		Concentrated	
Restricted	religious	62	religious	37	religious	62
	conservative	56	multifaceted	37	conservative	56
	conventional	56	intelligent	37	conventional	50
	tradition-loving	50	conservative	37	loyal to family	44
	loyal to family	37	conventional	37	tradition-loving	37
	neat	37	courteous	31	honest	37
	quiet	31	honest	31	courteous	31
	honest	25	tradition-loving	31	intelligent	31
	straightforward	19	loyal to family	25	neat	31
	practical	19	neat	19	multifaceted	25
	multifaceted	19				
	methodical	19				
	courteous	19				
Extended	conservative	50	conservative	50	religious	37
	honest	50	conventional	37	multifaceted	37
	loyal to family	50	multifaceted	37	conservative	37
	religious	44	religious	31	intelligent	37
	tradition-loving	37	tradition-loving	31	loyal to family	37
	conventional	37	neat	31	progressive	37
	courteous	37	intelligent	31	conventional	31
	straightforward	31	honest	31	honest	31
	progressive	25	courteous	25	practical	25
	practical	25	loyal to family	25	courteous	25
	intelligent	25	rebellious	25	complex	19
	neat	19	straightforward	19	straightforward	19
			irreligious	19		
			complex	19		

Table only includes traits assigned by 19 percent of subjects in a particular condition.

which the four most stereotypically consistent and four most inconsistent traits (as identified in pretesting) were selected as descriptive of a typical ACU student. For each condition we calculated a relative stereotyping score by subtracting the inconsistent frequency from the consistent frequency, and the resulting pattern is presented in figure 3.2. As predicted, we observed the usual impact of dispersed but not concentrated disconfirming information under restricted comparison conditions. However, the extension of the comparative context in itself produced the expected shift away from conservatism (see results under control conditions) and consequent impact of the concentrated disconfirmers in the extended context. Planned comparisons indicated that, under restricted conditions, dispersed but not concentrated disconfirmation produced a significant shift from the stereotype expressed by control subjects. For extended context subjects, the control-concentrated comparison was significant, but not the control-dispersed comparison. A very similar pattern of findings emerged from analysis of the rating scales, as can be seen in figure 3.3.

Briefly, a second study in this program involved a very similar design, but varied the stimulus and comparison groups. This time, subjects (students) were presented with short written extracts allegedly taken from interviews in which volunteer bushfire fighters outlined their reasons for going to fight devastating bushfires in and around Sydney in January 1994. Each extract was accompanied by a photograph of the interviewee. Subjects expected to read about either the group of firefighters alone, or the firefighters followed by a group of World

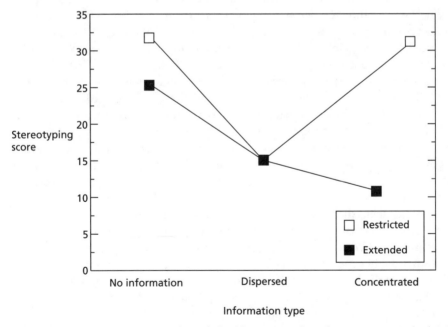

Figure 3.2 Relative stereotypicality of checklist traits selected as "most typical of ACU students."

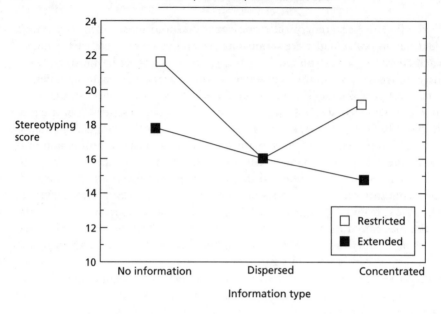

Figure 3.3   Ratings of ACU students in general on stereotypical trait dimensions.

Vision volunteers. Disconfirming information was either concentrated in three of the six firefighters presented, or dispersed across all six. The relevant comparative dimension was selflessness, with the student subjects towards the selfish pole, World Vision volunteers defining the selfless extreme, and bushfire fighters in between. Stereotype-confirming information described the firefighters as brave, dedicated, selfless, helpful, while the inconsistent information portrayed them as apathetic, irresponsible, and selfish. As in the first study, we expected the introduction of the extremely selfless World Vision group to shift the definition of the firefighter category, and the prototypical firefighter, towards apathy and selfishness, relative to the restricted condition. This, in turn, was expected to enhance the influence of the relatively selfish concentrated disconfirmers under extended conditions, while the usual effectiveness of dispersed disconfirmation was expected in restricted conditions. These predictions were confirmed on both checklist and stereotypic trait-rating assessments of subjects' stereotypes of "bushfire fighters in general" (see Oakes et al., 1997, for details).

   It appears, then, that dispersed disconfirmers do not have any privileged status in the stereotype change process. Hewstone's conclusion that it is "the amounts of confirming and disconfirming information used to describe a member" (1994, p. 81) that defines their effectiveness as change agents clearly does not give us a full picture of the relevant factors in stereotype variation of the kind observed in both his studies and our own. In our experiments, the combination of an extended comparative context and the presentation of some extremely "disconfirming" group members produced as much stereotype change as did the presentation of only slightly "disconfirming" group members in the restricted context. Relative "amounts of confirming and disconfirming information" characterizing given group members could not account for emergent stereotypes in isolation from the context in which that information was given meaning.

The information-processing approach to categorization tends to assume that attributes are rather concrete, absolute aspects of stimulus reality, that they are also represented in categories, and that categorization is a matter of the relevant stimulus attributes triggering the relevant cognitive category (e.g., see the role of consistent and inconsistent attributes in Fiske and Neuberg's (1990) continuum model). The attribute–category relationship is fixed and predictable in this view, producing the straightforward definition of some attributes as "confirming" (consistent) for a given category, and others as "disconfirming" (inconsistent). Our findings suggest, however, that *the comparative context can alter the category–attribute relationship,* that the categories were not defined in the same way across context conditions, even in the absence of any new or "disconfirming" information (see results for control subjects in figures 3.2 and 3.3; see also Haslam et al., 1992). This suggests to us that the idea of "confirming" and "disconfirming" attributes as definable in any abstract, acontextual manner may need to be reconsidered (Reynolds, 1996). Was "progressive," for example, disconfirming or confirming for the Catholic student category in our first study? Apparently, it could be either depending on context (see table 3.3) – it was selected as one of five traits "most descriptive" of ACU students by 25 percent of subjects in the extended-control condition, and by 37 percent in the extended-concentrated condition, but by no subjects at all in the restricted-context conditions. We would argue that category definition is always *relative,* and therefore that there is no fixed relationship between certain categories and certain attributes.

It should be noted, moreover, that the conservative/progressive dimension would generally be considered an absolutely core aspect of the categorization examined in our first study, so the contextual variation we are proposing is not a matter of core stability and peripheral change, such that relatively enduring representations are somehow adjusted for contextual purposes (see also Haslam, Oakes, McGarty, Turner, Reynolds, and Eggins, 1996). Rather, we would argue that *both categories and attributes are context-specific, mutually defining outcomes of the categorization process,* a process in which the range of current stimuli is interpreted and made meaningful through the application of theoretical knowledge and stored expectations represented at a more abstract, generalized level than categories – ideologies, values, general theories about the way our world works, the type of cognitive repositories that Medin (1989) calls "background theories" (cf. problems with the attribute/category distinction in other work, e.g., Fiske and Neuberg, 1990, pp. 9–12).

Of course, any argument for this degree of context dependence immediately confronts the manifest stability of many stereotypes – as we noted above, rigidity and insensitivity to context have long been considered defining features of social stereotypes. Although evidence contradicting this view has been available since the earliest days of stereotyping research (e.g., Buchanan, 1951; Diab, 1963; see Oakes et al., 1994, ch. 2), it is nonetheless obvious that relative stability characterizes many stereotypes. But stability is not evidence against context dependence. Stable contexts, in particular stable intergroup realities and stable explanatory theories about what those realities mean, produce stable emergent categories and stereotypes. It is when the material conditions and/or the social interpretation of intergroup relations change that stereotypes change.

We have recently found some evidence of this process occurring in our own research into the effects of manipulations of the comparative context on stereotype content and perceived group homogeneity (see Haslam et al., 1996b, for an overview). During the course of this work, we have assessed Australian students' national self-stereotypes under single-group conditions (i.e., without explicit manipulation of the comparative context) on five occasions across a time period of six years. As can be seen from table 3.4, the stereotypes elicited in four different studies between 1992 and 1996 were remarkably stable in terms of their favorableness, uniformity, consensuality, and substantive content. There is every reason to believe that aspects of group life related to national identity were

Table 3.4   Data from control studies of introductory psychology students' Australian self-stereotypes (1992–7)

Year (N)	Study	Favorableness (-5 to $+5$)	Uniformity (U: $max = 2.5$)	Consensus (P_a)	Content* P_a	%
1992 (16)	Homog. (Exp. 1) BJSP (1995)	1.94	7.00	.21	happy-go-lucky straightforward sportsmanlike reserved talkative	56 50 44 31 31
1994 (20)	Influence and consensus BJSP (1996)	2.00	7.25	.21	happy-go-lucky sportsmanlike pleasure-loving straightforward talkative	50 50 45 35 31
1995 (20)	Consensualization (Exp. 1) EJSP (1998)	1.70	8.00	.21	sportsmanlike happy-go-lucky straightforward pleasure-loving	65 35 35 30
1996 (46)	Consensualization (Exp. 3) EJSP (1998)	2.01	8.28	.20	sportsmanlike straightforward pleasure-loving	54 43 39
1997 (20)	Control	1.20	9.00	.15	happy-go-lucky pleasure-loving straightforward	40 40 40

* Table only contains traits assigned by at least 30 percent of subjects.

also relatively stable for this population over this time (cf. Meenes, 1943; Seago, 1947; Sinha and Upadhyaya, 1960).

In the 1997 data, however, there is a clearly discernible shift in all aspects of the stereotype. In terms of substantive content, the usually strongly endorsed "sportsmanlike" (which refers in part to a belief in an egalitarian, sporting sense of fair-mindedness and all playing by the same rules) has disappeared, and there are significant changes in favorableness (the stereotype is less favorable), uniformity (the stereotype is more complex), and consensuality (there is less agreement between subjects) – these students' national self-stereotype has become more negative, and there is more disagreement, more uncertainty, about what it means to be Australian.

To explore these findings further, we presented the data (in graphical form) relating to favorableness and consensus to a group of the students who had taken part in some of our stereotyping research in 1997, and asked them to "list any and all factors that you feel may be responsible for the less positive and less consensual view of Australians that emerged this year." Many of the students' responses made reference to events following the Australian federal election of March 1996, in which the party of government changed for the first time in 13 years (from Labor to Liberal, i.e., "conservative"), and several explicitly racist candidates, including Pauline Hanson, an Independent from Queensland, were elected to the federal parliament. This change of political direction provoked unprecedented questioning of Australians' capacity for tolerance and acceptance of diversity – salient and valued aspects of the national self-image. Subsequent events relating, in particular, to Aboriginal Australians (e.g., conflict between Aboriginals and farmers over land rights; debate over compensation for the forced adoption of Aboriginal children), together with expressions of concern from some overseas leaders about increasingly overt racism in Australia, contributed to a sense of deteriorating intergroup relations, both within the country and between Australia and its international neighbors. Approximately 60 percent of our subjects' responses alluded to these factors as responsible for the observed impact on the favorableness and consensuality of the national self-stereotype (52 percent mentioned Hanson explicitly). The following statements are typical:

"The fact that John Howard is Prime Minister and Pauline Hanson is a member of One Nation Party states that there isn't much to be proud of about our country. We are seen as racist and a joke. A lot of us see ourselves (the country) this way as well. How can we have a positive outlook of [sic] Australia with people like this ruling us?"

"People are not as 'proud' of being Australian due to Pauline Hanson and Howard government's portrayal overseas as Australians being backward economically, environmentally, socially (racist and human rights)."

Australian society has undoubtedly become more divided since the 1993 federal election, and it seems that this has changed the way in which some

citizens are able to define (to stereotype) themselves as "Australian." Important-
antly, this is happening despite consistent official political messages ("information") to the contrary – the government's rhetoric is of national unity (the
Liberals' election slogan was "For all of us"), and Hanson's party is called
"One Nation." But it appears that this does not count as "information" with
any validity for the student population taking part in our studies. The reduced
favorableness and consensuality of their national self-stereotypes can be seen as
an attempt to communicate their rejection of this rhetoric, to comment on the
political and social realities of national life as they experience them, and as those
they identify with interpret and evaluate them (see Haslam, 1997; Haslam et al.,
1996a). And, of course, we would expect the very same national political shifts
to have quite different effects on national self-stereotyping for those who identify
with the government agenda and the monocultural vision of Hanson and her
followers.

Conclusion

Intergroup images play a crucial role in almost all aspects of social and political
life, and there are frequently very good reasons for trying to change some of
them. Just as Sherif argued thirty years ago, our point has been to emphasize that
"attitudes towards other groups and images of them are *products* of particular
relationships between groups, *not their original cause*" (Sherif, 1967, p. 25,
emphasis added; see also Rothbart, 1981, p. 177). Much stereotype change
research seems to be motivated by the belief that changing the way groups
stereotype each other will change the way they relate to each other. We suspect
that the reverse process is far more prevalent and powerful, and that it is
changing intergroup realities, and the available ideological interpretations of
those realities, that effects changes in the process of social stereotyping.

We have moved a long way from the idea that stereotyping involves the
activation of a stable, prestored cognitive category that can be changed with
"information," and without reference to the context-specific, motivated, sense-
making processes through which, we would argue, "information" is transformed
into meaningful knowledge. Perhaps it is time for those who hope to influence
intergroup images, both inside and outside the laboratory, to at least consider the
possibility that stereotype change does not take place in a cognitive structure that
represents the category, but in the data (the intergroup reality), or the theory
used to make sense of that data, or in both of these elements that interact to
produce emergent categorical judgments.

References

Allport, F.H. (1962). A structuronomic conception of behaviour: Individual and collective. *Journal of Abnormal and Social Psychology*, 64, 3–30.

Asch, S.E. (1952). *Social Psychology*. New York: Prentice-Hall.

Billig, M. (1976). *Social Psychology and Intergroup Relations*. London: Academic Press.

Brewer, M.B. (1988). A dual-process model of impression formation. In T.K. Srull and R.S. Wyer (eds), *Advances in Social Cognition*, Vol. 1. Hillsdale, NJ: Erlbaum, pp. 1–36.

Brewer, M.B., Dull, V., and Lui, L. (1981). Perceptions of the elderly: Stereotypes as prototypes. *Journal of Personality and Social Psychology*, 41, 656–70.

Brown, R.J. and Turner, J.C. (1981). Interpersonal and intergroup behaviour. In J.C. Turner and H. Giles (eds), *Intergroup Behaviour*. Oxford and Chicago: Blackwell and University of Chicago Press, pp. 33–65.

Buchanan, W. (1951). Stereotypes and tensions as revealed by the UNESCO International Poll. *International Social Science Bulletin*, 3, 515–28.

Campbell, D.T. (1958). Common fate, similarity, and other indices of the status of aggregates of persons as social entities. *Behavioural Science*, 3, 14–25.

David, B. and Turner, J.C. (1996). Studies on self-categorization and minority conversion: Is being a member of the out-group an advantage? *British Journal of Social Psychology*, 35, 179–99.

Diab, L.N. (1963). Factors determining group stereotypes. *Journal of Social Psychology*, 61, 3–10.

Duckitt, J.H. (1992). *The Social Psychology of Prejudice*. New York: Praeger.

Fishman, J.A. (1956). An examination of the process and function of social stereotyping. *Journal of Personality and Social Psychology*, 43, 27–64.

Fiske, S.T. and Leyens, J.-P. (1997). Let social psychology be faddish or, at least, heterogeneous. In C. McGarty and S.A. Haslam (eds), *The Message of Social Psychology*. Oxford: Blackwell, pp. 92–112.

Fiske, S.T. and Neuberg, S.L. (1990). A continuum of impression formation, from category-based to individuating processes: Influences of information and motivation on attention and interpretation. In M.P. Zanna (ed.), *Advances in Experimental Social Psychology*, Vol. 23. New York: Random House, pp. 1–73.

Fiske, S.T. and Taylor, S.E. (1991). *Social Cognition*. New York: McGraw-Hill.

Gaertner, S.L., Mann, J., Murrell, A., and Dovidio, J.F. (1989). Reducing intergroup bias: The benefits of recategorization. *Journal of Personality and Social Psychology*, 57, 239–49.

Hamilton, D.L. (ed.) (1981). *Cognitive Processes in Stereotyping and Intergroup Behaviour*. Hillsdale, NJ: Erlbaum.

Hantzi, A. (1995). Change in stereotypic perceptions of familiar and unfamiliar groups: The pervasiveness of the subtyping model. *British Journal of Social Psychology*, 34, 463–77.

Haslam, S.A. (1997). Stereotyping and social influence: Foundations of stereotype sharedness. In R. Spears, P.J. Oakes, N. Ellemers, and S.A. Haslam (eds), *The Social Psychology of Stereotyping and Group Life*. Oxford and Cambridge, MA: Blackwell, pp. 119–43.

Haslam, S.A., Oakes, P.J., McGarty, C., Turner, J.C., and Onorato, R. (1995). Contextual changes in the prototypicality of extreme and moderate outgroup members. *European Journal of Social Psychology*, 25, 509–30.

Haslam, S.A., Oakes, P.J., McGarty, C., Turner, J.C., Reynolds, K., and Eggins, R. (1996a). Stereotyping and social influence: The mediation of stereotype applicability and sharedness by the views of ingroup and outgroup members. *British Journal of Social Psychology*, 35, 369–97.

Haslam, S.A., Oakes, P.J., Turner, J.C., and McGarty, C. (1996b). Social identity, self-categorization and the perceived homogeneity of ingroups and outgroups: The interaction between social motivation and cognition. In R.M. Sorrentino and E.T. Higgins (eds), *Handbook of Motivation and Cognition*, Vol. 3, *The Interpersonal Context*. New York: Guilford, pp. 182–222.

Haslam, S.A. and Turner, J.C. (1992). Context-dependent variation in social stereotyping 2: The relationship between frame of reference, self-categorization and accentuation. *European Journal of Social Psychology*, 22, 251–77.

Haslam, S.A. and Turner, J.C. (1995). Extremism as a self-categorical basis for polarized judgement. *European Journal of Social Psychology*, 25, 341–71.

Haslam, S.A., Turner, J.C., Oakes, P.J., McGarty, C.A., and Hayes, B.K. (1992). Context-dependent variation in social stereotyping 1: The effects of intergroup relations as mediated by social change and frame of reference. *European Journal of Social Psychology*, 22, 3–20.

Hewstone, M. (1989). Changing stereotypes with disconfirming information. In D. Bar-Tal, C.F. Graumann, A. Kruglanski, and W. Stroebe (eds), *Stereotyping and Prejudice: Changing conceptions*. New York and London: Springer-Verlag, pp. 207–23.

Hewstone, M. (1994). Revision and change of stereotypic beliefs: In search of the elusive sub-typing model. In W. Stroebe and M. Hewstone (eds), *European Review of Social Psychology*, Vol. 5. Chichester: John Wiley and Sons, pp. 69–109.

Hewstone, M. (1996). Contact and categorization: Social-psychological interventions to change intergroup relations. In C.N. Macrae, C. Stangor, and M. Hewstone (eds), *Foundations of Stereotypes and Stereotyping*. New York: Guilford, pp. 323–68.

Hewstone, M. and Brown, R.J. (eds) (1986). *Contact and Conflict in Intergroup Encounters*. Oxford: Blackwell.

Hewstone, M., Hopkins, N., and Routh, D.A. (1992). Cognitive models of stereotype change: (1) Generalization and subtyping in young people's views of the police. *European Journal of Social Psychology*, 22, 219–34.

Hogg, M.A. (1992). *The Social Psychology of Group Cohesiveness*. Hemel Hempstead: Harvester Wheatsheaf.

Hogg, M.A. (1996). Intragroup processes, group structure and social identity. In W.P. Robinson (ed.), *Social Groups and Identities: Developing the legacy of Henri Tajfel*. Oxford: Butterworth-Heinemann, pp. 65–93.

Hogg, M.A., Hardie, E.A., and Reynolds, K.J. (1995). Prototypical similarity, self-categorization, and depersonalized attraction: A perspective on group cohesiveness. *European Journal of Social Psychology*, 25, 159–77.

Johnston, L. and Hewstone, M. (1992). Cognitive models of stereotype change: (3) Subtyping and the perceived typicality of disconfirming group members. *Journal of Experimental Social Psychology*, 28, 360–86.

Johnston, L., Hewstone, M., Pendry, I.., and Frankish, C. (1994). Cognitive models of stereotype change: (4) Motivational and cognitive influences. *European Journal of Social Psychology*, 24, 237–65.

Katz, D. and Braly, K. (1933). Racial stereotypes of one hundred college students. *Journal of Abnormal and Social Psychology*, 28, 280–90.

Kelly, C. (1993). Group identification, intergroup perceptions and collective action. *European Review of Social Psychology*, 4, 59–83.

Kerr, M. (1943). An experimental investigation of national stereotypes. *Sociological Review*, 35, 37–43.

Leyens, J.-P., Yzerbyt, V., and Schadron, G. (1994). *Stereotypes and Social Cognition*. London: Sage.

Lippmann, W. (1922). *Public Opinion*. New York: Harcourt Brace Jovanovich.

McGarty, C., Turner, J.C., Hogg, M.A., David, B., and Wetherell, M.S. (1992). Group polarization as conformity to the most prototypical group member. *British Journal of Social Psychology*, 31, 1–20.

Macrae, C.N., Stangor, C., and Hewstone, M. (eds) (1996). *Foundations of Stereotypes and Stereotyping*. New York: Guilford.

Medin, D.L. (1989). Concepts and conceptual structure. *American Psychologist*, 44, 1469–81.

Medin, D.L., Goldstone, R.L., and Gentner, D. (1993). Respects for similarity. *Psychological Review*, 100, 254–78.

Meenes, M. (1943). A comparison of racial stereotypes of 1935 and 1942. *Journal of Social Psychology*, 17, 327–36.

Morrison, B.E. (1997). Social co-operation: Redefining the self in self-interest. Unpublished Ph.D. thesis, The Australian National University, Canberra.

Nolan, M.A., Haslam, S.A., Spears, R., and Oakes, P.J. (1997). Testing between resource-based and fit-based theories of stereotyping. Manuscript submitted for publication.

Oakes, P.J. (1987). The salience of social categories. In J.C. Turner, M.A. Hogg, P.J. Oakes, S.D. Reicher, and M.S. Wetherell, *Rediscovering the Social Group: A self-categorization theory*. Oxford and New York: Blackwell, pp. 117–41.

Oakes, P.J. (1994). The effects of fit versus novelty on the salience of social categories: A response to Biernat and Vescio (1993). *Journal of Experimental Social Psychology*, 30, 390–8.

Oakes, P.J. (1996). The categorization process: Cognition and the group in the social psychology of stereotyping. In W.P. Robinson (ed.), *Social Groups and Identity: Developing the legacy of Henri Tajfel*. Oxford: Butterworth-Heinemann, pp. 95–120.

Oakes, P.J. and Dempster, A.A. (1996). Views of the categorization process, with an example from stereotype change. Paper presented at the General Meeting of the European Association of Experimental Social Psychology, Gmunden, Austria, July.

Oakes, P.J., Haslam, S.A., Reynolds, K.J., Nolan, M.A., Eggins, R.A., Dempster, A.A., and Tweedie, J. (1997). Relative prototypicality and stereotype change: Effects of comparative context. Manuscript submitted for publication.

Oakes, P.J., Haslam, S.A., and Turner, J.C. (1994). *Stereotyping and Social Reality*. Oxford and Cambridge, MA: Blackwell.

Oakes, P.J., Haslam, S.A., and Turner, J.C. (1998). The role of prototypicality in group influence and cohesion: Contextual variation in the graded structure of social categories. In S. Worchel, J.F. Morales, and D. Paez (eds), *Social Identity: International perspectives*. London: Sage, pp. 75–92.

Oakes, P.J. and Reynolds, K.J. (1997). Asking the accuracy question: Is measurement the answer? In R. Spears, P.J. Oakes, N. Ellemers, and S.A. Haslam (eds), *The Social Psychology of Stereotyping and Group Life*. Oxford and Cambridge, MA: Blackwell, pp. 51–71.

Oakes, P.J. and Turner, J.C. (1990). Is limited information processing the cause of social stereotyping? In W. Stroebe and M. Hewstone (eds), *European Review of Social Psychology*, Vol. 1. Chichester: Wiley, pp. 111–35.

Oakes, P.J., Turner, J.C., and Haslam, S.A. (1991). Perceiving people as group members: The role of fit in the salience of social categorizations. *British Journal of Social Psychology*, 30, 125–44.

Reicher, S.D. (1996). "The Battle of Westminster": Developing the social identity model of crowd behaviour in order to explain the initiation and development of collective conflict. *European Journal of Social Psychology*, 26, 115–34.

Reynolds, K.J. (1996). Beyond the information given: Capacity, context and the categorization process in impression formation. Unpublished Ph.D. thesis, The Australian National University, Canberra.

Rosch, E. (1978). Principles of categorization. In E. Rosch and B.B. Lloyd (eds), *Cognition and Categorization*. Hillsdale, NJ: Erlbaum, pp. 28–49.

Rothbart, M. (1981). Memory processes and social beliefs. In D.L. Hamilton (ed.), *Cognitive Processes in Stereotyping and Intergroup Behaviour*. Hillsdale, NJ: Erlbaum, pp. 145–81.

Rothbart, M. and John, O.P. (1985). Social categorization and behavioural episodes: A cognitive analysis of the effects of intergroup contact. *Journal of Social Issues*, 41, 81–104.

Seago, D.W. (1947). Stereotypes: Before Pearl Harbour and after. *Journal of Social Psychology*, 23, 55–63.

Sherif, M. (1936). *The Psychology of Social Norms*. New York: Harper.

Sherif, M. (1967). *Group Conflict and Co-operation: Their social psychology*. London: Routledge and Kegan Paul.

Simon, B. (1998). Individuals, groups, and social change: On the relationship between individual and collective self-interpretations and collective action. In C. Sedikides, J. Schopler, and C. Insko (eds), *Intergroup Cognition and Intergroup Behaviour*. Hillsdale, NJ: Erlbaum, pp. 257–82.

Simon, B., Hastedt, C., and Aufderheide, B. (in press). When self-categorization makes sense: The role of meaningful social categorization in minority and majority members' self-perception. *Journal of Personality and Social Psychology*.

Sinha, A.K.P. and Upadhyaya, O.P. (1960). Change and persistence in the stereotypes of university students toward different ethnic groups during the Sino-Indian border dispute. *Journal of Social Psychology*, 52, 31–9.

Spears, R., Oakes, P.J., Ellemers, N., and Haslam, S.A. (eds) (1997). *The Social Psychology of Stereotyping and Group Life*. Oxford and Cambridge, MA: Blackwell.

Tajfel, H. (1969). Cognitive aspects of prejudice. *Journal of Social Issues*, 25, 79–97.

Tajfel, H. (ed.) (1978). *Differentiation Between Social Groups: Studies in the social psychology of intergroup relations*. London: Academic Press.

Tajfel, H. (1979). Individuals and groups in social psychology. *British Journal of Social and Clinical Psychology*, 18, 183–90.

Tajfel, H. and Turner, J.C. (1979). An integrative theory of intergroup conflict. In W.G. Austin and S. Worschel (eds), *The Social Psychology of Intergroup Relations*. Monterey, CA: Brooks-Cole, pp. 33–47.

Tajfel, H. and Turner, J.C. (1986). The social identity theory of intergroup behaviour. In S. Worschel and W.G. Austin (eds), *Psychology of Intergroup Relations*, 2nd edn., Chicago: Nelson-Hall, pp. 7–24.

Turner, J.C. (1982). Towards a cognitive redefinition of the social group. In H. Tajfel (ed.), *Social Identity and Group Relations*. Cambridge: Cambridge University Press, pp. 15–40.

Turner, J.C. (1984). Social identification and psychological group formation. In H. Tajfel (ed.), *The Social Dimension: European developments in social psychology*. Cambridge: Cambridge University Press, pp. 518–38.

Turner, J.C. (1985). Social categorization and the self-concept: A social-cognitive theory of group behaviour. In E.J. Lawler (ed.), *Advances in Group Processes*, Vol. 2. Greenwich, CT: JAI Press, pp. 77–122.

Turner, J.C. (1991). *Social Influence*. Milton Keynes: Open University Press.

Turner, J.C. and Bourhis, R. (1996). Social identity, interdependence and the social group: A reply to Rabbie et al. In W.P. Robinson (ed.), *Social Groups and Identity: Developing the legacy of Henri Tajfel*. Oxford: Butterworth-Heinemann, pp. 25–64.

Turner, J.C., Hogg, M.A., Oakes, P.J., Reicher, S.D., and Wetherell, M.S. (1987). *Rediscovering the Social Group: A self-categorization theory*. Oxford and New York: Blackwell.

Turner, J.C. and Oakes, P.J. (1986). The significance of the social identity concept for social psychology with reference to individualism, interactionism and social influence. *British Journal of Social Psychology*, 25, 237–52.

Turner, J.C. and Oakes, P.J. (1989). Self-categorization theory and social influence. In P.B. Paulus (ed.), *The Psychology of Group Influence*. Hillsdale, NJ: Erlbaum, pp. 233–75.

Turner, J.C. and Oakes, P.J. (1997). The socially structured mind. In C. McGarty and S.A. Haslam (eds), *The Message of Social Psychology*. Oxford: Blackwell, pp. 353–73.

Turner, J.C., Oakes, P.J., Haslam, S.A., and McGarty, C.M. (1994). Self and collective: Cognition and social context. *Personality and Social Psychology Bulletin*, 20, 454–63.

Tversky, A. (1977). Features of similarity. *Psychological Review*, 84, 327–52.

van Knippenberg, A., van Twuyver, M., and Pepels, J. (1994). Factors affecting social categorization processes in memory. *British Journal of Social Psychology*, 33, 419–31.

Weber, R. and Crocker, J. (1983). Cognitive processes in the revision of stereotypic beliefs. *Journal of Personality and Social Psychology*, 45, 961–77.

Yzerbyt, V., Rocher, S., and Coull, A. (1996). What saves the stereotype? The role of cognitive resources in stereotype maintenance. Paper presented at the General Meeting of the European Association of Experimental Social Psychology, Gmunden, Austria, July.

4

Perceived Entitativity and the Social Identity Value of Group Memberships

STEVEN J. SHERMAN, DAVID L. HAMILTON, AND
AMY C. LEWIS

This chapter is concerned with two concepts that have been historically important in social psychology: entitativity and social identity. One of these concepts, entitativity, has been developed primarily within a social cognition tradition as it has tried to understand the nature of group impressions and the processing of information about social targets. The other concept, social identity, was developed primarily within the intergroup tradition and has been used in understanding the role of group membership in self-identity.

Both entitativity and social identity have been used to help understand the perception of social groups, but they have done so in somewhat different ways. On the one hand, work on entitativity has tended to focus on understanding the formation of group stereotypes, typically without reference to the perceiver's own group memberships. On the other hand, social identity research has been primarily concerned with the differentiation between ingroups and outgroups and its various ramifications. Despite their differing historical roots and their different points of emphasis, both of these concepts have important relevance for our understanding of social perception, impressions of groups, interaction both within and between groups, feelings about the self, and social information processing. The purpose of this chapter is to outline these two concepts and to develop an integrative understanding of the relationship between them.

Preparation of this chapter was supported in part by NIMH Grant NH-40058. The authors appreciate helpful comments provided by Dominic Abrams, John Jost, and Diane Mackie on a preliminary draft of the chapter. We also benefited from discussions of our ideas with Brian Lickel and Toni Schmader.

Perceiving Entitativity

One emerging theme in recent social cognition work has been an analysis of the importance of the degree to which a collection of persons is perceived as a unified group. Campbell (1958) used the term *entitativity* to refer to this aspect of group perception. After a long period of dormancy, this concept has recently gained renewed theoretical interest (Abelson, Dasgupta, Park, and Banaji, 1994; Brewer and Harasty, 1996; Hamilton and Sherman, 1996; Hamilton, Sherman, and Lickel, 1998; Hamilton, Sherman, and Maddox, in press; Rothbart and Taylor, 1992; Yzerbyt, Rocher, and Schadron, 1997), as well as research attention (Brewer, Weber, and Carini, 1995; Dasgupta, Banaji, and Abelson, 1997; McConnell, Sherman, and Hamilton, 1994, 1997; McGarty, Haslam, Hutchinson, and Grace, 1995).

Our own work on entitativity began with our interest in investigating and explaining differences in perceptions of individual and group targets. We had noticed important differences in the way information is processed and impressions are formed for individual and group targets. For example, people make more extreme judgments, and they make those judgments faster and with more confidence for individual than for group targets (Susskind, Maurer, Thakkar, Hamilton, and Sherman, in press). They remember more information about individuals than about groups (McConnell et al., 1994, 1997; Srull, 1981; Stern, Marrs, Millar, and Cole, 1984; Wyer, Bodenhausen, and Srull, 1984). They work more at resolving inconsistencies for individuals than for group targets (Susskind et al., in press). Finally, perceivers form distinctiveness-based illusory correlations between targets and attributes if these targets are groups, but not if they are individuals (McConnell et al., 1994, 1997; Sanbonmatsu, Sherman, and Hamilton, 1987). In sum, impression formation seems to involve different processes and outcomes as a function of whether the target of perception is an individual or a group. We (Hamilton et al., in press) have referred to these differences in terms of a distinction between *integrative processing* (characterized by on-line judgments and inferences, organization of information during encoding, and resolution of inconsistencies as information is acquired) vs. *retrospective processing* (characterized by memory-based judgments, organization of information during retrieval (if at all), and lessened concern with resolving informational inconsistencies).

In order to account for these findings, Hamilton and Sherman (1996) proposed that, for social perception, the key difference between individual and group targets is the degree of expected and perceived unity or entitativity of those targets. Specifically, people expect individuals to have unity, coherence, and consistency, in that individuals are perceived as organized units (Asch, 1946) and are viewed as the causes of their own behavior (Heider, 1958; Ross, 1977). Because individuals are basic-level units, perceivers try to extract this unity or essence in forming impressions of individuals (Rothbart and Taylor, 1992). In contrast, groups are not assumed to have as much coherence and consistency, in that group members are distinct individuals and one member's behavior is not necessarily constrained by that of other members. Therefore, social perceivers are less likely to process information about group targets with the goal of discovering the bases of the group's unity and coherence. We used this difference in expectations of entitativity for individual and group targets to account for the processing and outcome differences obtained in research findings.

To empirically test the role of entitativity in the perception of social targets, we manipulated the type of processing engaged (integrative vs. retrospective) and the degree of entitativity expected about both individual and group targets. In one set of studies (McConnell et al., 1994), some subjects were encouraged to form integrated impressions of either individual or group targets on the basis of behavioral information. This instruction would induce integrative processing for both types of targets. In another condition, subjects were asked to judge whether the behavioral information would be comprehensible to a four-year-old child. These instructions were designed to eliminate concerns about the nature of the social target and thus to inhibit integrative processing for both individual and group targets. Finally, some subjects were given nondirective processing instructions. The results strongly supported our hypotheses. Specifically, when integrative processing was induced through impression formation instructions, both the individual and group target conditions manifested results typical of the individual target conditions of the studies cited earlier. In contrast, when integrative processing was inhibited by comprehension-set instructions, neither the individual nor group target condition manifested these effects, and the results indicated retrospective processing for both types of targets. Only when no directive processing instructions were provided did we observe differences in processing between individual and group targets (in terms of recall, illusory correlation, etc.). These results strongly supported Hamilton and Sherman's (1996) contention that it is not the target type *per se* that produces differences in processing and impressions, but rather the nature of the processing engaged that is the critical factor.

In a second set of studies (McConnell et al., 1997), we directly manipulated the degree of entitativity that was expected for either individual or group targets. In one condition, targets (both individual and group) were described as coherent and consistent; in another condition, targets (both individual and group) were described as lacking coherence and consistency; and, in a third condition, individual and group targets were not specifically characterized in either of these ways. With expectations for high entitativity, subjects engaged in integrative processing for both individual and group targets. That is, they recalled a high proportion of the stimulus behaviors (particularly those that were presented early), and their evaluative judgments were uncorrelated with the items recalled. In contrast, with expectations for low entitativity, subjects did not engage in integrative processing for either individual or group targets, and judgments were based on retrospective processing. That is, they had poor overall recall, no primacy effect in recall, and high recall–judgment correlations. Again, only in the baseline "no information" condition did subjects' processing for individual and group targets differ.

These findings demonstrate that, although *a priori* there will be greater expectations of entitativity for individual than for group targets, it is the degree of perceived entitativity for any target that makes the difference for the processing of target-relevant information. Therefore, we (Hamilton et al., 1998) have emphasized the importance of the Entitativity Continuum for understanding the processing of information about social targets and the impressions formed of these targets.

Antecedents of perceived entitativity

If this is so, then it becomes important to understand the antecedents of perceived entitativity. That is, how do perceivers "know" whether a group is high or low in entitativity? A number of possible answers have been suggested by various authors. Indeed, in the original formulation of perceived entitativity, Campbell's (1958) purpose was to identify perceptual cues that the perceiver might use in inferring entitativity in an aggregate of individuals. Drawing on Gestalt perception research, he emphasized the role of the proximity and similarity of individuals, and their sharing a common fate and collective movement, as determinants of perceived entitativity.

Other authors have emphasized the importance of other variables. Hamilton et al. (1998) proposed that one key cue to entitativity is the extent to which a group is organized. That is, groups that are structured, have clear leadership functions, have differentiation of roles and task assignments, have shared norms, etc., will be perceived as entitative more than will groups that lack these characteristics.

Brewer and Harasty (1996) conceive of differences in perceived entitativity in terms of the difference between prototype and exemplar models of category representation. They propose that social targets with high entitativity are represented as prototypes, whereas low-entitativity targets are more likely to be represented by exemplars. Thus, according to Brewer and Harasty (1996), high- and low-entitativity targets may be differentiated not only on the basis of initial expectancies of unity and coherence, but also in terms of the types of cognitive representations. Yzerbyt et al. (1997) link the concept of entitativity to the idea that social categories must have a basically essentialistic representation. That is, social groups must be seen as having some core nature or common features that interconnect the members and bind them together (Rothbart and Taylor, 1992). This kind of group perception is embodied in the concept of entitativity, and the function of such perception is to help the social perceiver understand and stabilize the current state of social affairs with respect to group relations, differential statuses, etc.

McGarty et al. (1995) investigated the role of four factors in group entitativity judgments: intragroup variability, group size, and the diversity and extremity of group members. In their analysis, variability refers to the overall degree of spread of group members on some dimension; diversity refers to the number of distinct positions held by different group members on that dimension, which they describe as a measure of the richness and variety of group membership. They found no impact of extremity on perceived entitativity, but found that perceived entitativity increased as variability and diversity decreased. Interestingly, they found that, once diversity is held constant, entitativity increased with group size. This result contradicts previous work suggesting that smaller groups should be more entitative (Mullen, 1991; Simon and Hamilton, 1994). McGarty et al. (1995) also suggested that groups will be perceived as more entitative when the ratio of differences between groups to differences within groups is high. This analysis implies an important correspondence between entitativity and self-categorization, given that the meta-contrast ratio is also a key element of self-categorization (see below).

In addition to these group characteristics, other perceiver variables can also contribute to the perception of group entitativity. In particular, Brewer and Harasty (1996) point to the role of the perceiver's momentary goals and mood states on the perception of groupness. For example, research suggests that the perceiver's processing goals can influence the type of representation formed (Park, DeKay, and Kraus, 1994; Seta and Hayes, 1994) and that individuals may differ in their need to form simplified or differentiated representations of groups (Roney and Sorrentino, 1987).

Varieties of groups

Another important consideration in understanding entitativity is that the perception of entitativity may be based on different factors for different types of groups. As already noted, we (Hamilton et al., 1998) have proposed that groups vary along an Entitativity Continuum. However, considering the variety of types of groups that we encounter in everyday life, it is important to recognize that more complex differentiations among types of groups may also be important (for other discussions of different types of groups, see Deaux, Reid, Mizrahi, and Ethier, 1995; Prentice, Miller, and Lightdale, 1994; Wilder and Simon, 1998). For example, groups may differ in the properties that help to define them as groups, that lend them their characteristic degree of perceived entitativity. Some of our recent research supports this contention (Lickel, Hamilton, Wieczor-kowska, Lewis, Sherman, and Uhles, 1998). We had subjects rate 40 different groups on a scale measuring perceived entitativity; more precisely, they rated the extent to which they considered that each of 40 descriptions "qualifies as a group." They also rated each group on a variety of scales pertinent to entitativity, such as similarity among members, proximity, the extent of interaction, the degree of common goals and common fate, the importance of the group to the members, group size, etc.

Analyses of these ratings led to the identification of several types of groups that differed in the extent to which these properties described them. For example, one category consisted largely of goal-oriented or task-oriented groups (airplane flight crew, jury, cast of a play, employees of a restaurant), which were rated as having a high degree of interaction and as sharing common goals. Another category consisted of close, intimate groups (family, friends who do things together, a romantic relationship), which also were rated as high in interaction but in addition were rated as unusually high in importance to the members. A third distinct type of group consisted of broad social categories (blacks, women, teachers, Jews), which were differentiated from the other types of groups primarily by their size and the length of their history. A fourth type of group was characterized by weak associations among its members, such as people living in the same neighborhood, working in the same factory, or liking classical music. These groups were rated similarly to social categories in some respects (e.g., they are large), but differently in others (e.g., one can easily join or leave such groups). Thus, we can distinguish among several meaningfully different types of groups. Moreover, ratings on the entitativity scale indicated that the first two categories of groups were rated as higher on this dimension than were the latter two types of groups. Thus, some types of groups are more "groupy" than other types, and there are specifiable profiles of features or properties that differentiate among them.

An important implication of distinguishing among these different types of groups is that there should be different cues or antecedent conditions that serve as indicators of entitativity for the different types of groups. For task-oriented groups, factors involving group structure and group dynamics (e.g., shared goals, role differentiation, organization, amount of interaction) should be the most important determinants of perceived entitativity. For intimacy groups, group attraction factors (e.g., cohesiveness, permeability, quality of interaction) should be the strongest cues to perceived entitativity. For social categories, on the other hand, surface-level cues (e.g., physical similarity, proximity, group size, length of the group's existence) should be the especially strong indicators of perceived entitativity.

In most of the research considered thus far, perceivers learned information about groups to which they did not belong. To date, far less consideration has been given to variations in entitativity for groups to which social perceivers belong. Interestingly, the second major approach to studying group perception, social identity theory, has focused primarily on the role of own-group memberships on group perceptions, emphasizing the importance of ingroup–outgroup differentiations. We turn now to a consideration of three approaches that derive from a focus on social identity. We then explore the interface between the social cognition-based entitativity approach and the social identity approach, with particular regard to the implications of our own work on perceived group entitativity for understanding social identities.

Theories of Ingroup Identification

In general, social identity approaches emphasize the importance of people's group memberships for their own self-conceptions of who they are, what they are like, and how they differ from others. Thus, an individual's self-concept and self-understanding are not simply a function of his or her own experiences and accomplishments, but are also a function of the groups to which that individual belongs. As a basis for our subsequent theoretical development, we now briefly summarize and differentiate three theoretical positions reflecting the social identity approach.

Social identity theory

Social identity theory (Tajfel, 1978; Tajfel and Turner, 1986) grew out of Tajfel's (cf. Tajfel, 1969, 1970) early research on the role of the categorization process in intergroup perceptions. In an important series of experiments, Tajfel and his colleagues (Billig and Tajfel, 1973; Tajfel, Flament, Billig, and Bundy, 1971) demonstrated that rather arbitrary categorizations of individuals into ingroups and outgroups reliably produced a number of impressive outcomes, such as the exaggeration of between-group differences, the attenuation of within-group differences, the differential allocation of resources favoring the ingroup, and evaluative preferences for ingroup members. The categorization process by itself was sufficient to account for some of these findings, such as between-group contrast and within-group assimilation. However, given the evaluative neutrality of the categorization process, something more was needed to account for the ingroup bias evidenced in allocations and evaluations, which are particularly robust findings in intergroup perceptions (Brewer, 1979). As an answer, Tajfel (1978; Tajfel and Turner, 1979) introduced the idea that people attain part of their self-esteem from their group memberships, and because people are motivated to attain and maintain positive self-esteem, they are simultaneously motivated to perceive their ingroups in favorable terms. In other words, people strive to have a positive social identity.

One basis for feelings of satisfaction derived from group membership emanates from the actual positively valued experiences that one has through one's association with that group. Thus, when the group as a whole attains some goal, experiences success, receives praise, etc., members share in this positive outcome and thereby experience enhanced feelings of self-worth. These positive feelings from group success may derive from one's actual participation in and contribution to the group's achievements, or they may be the consequence of one's identification with the group, even though one had no direct role in its success (as in basking in reflected glory (BIRGING): Cialdini, Borden, Thorne, Walker, Freeman, and Sloan, 1976).

Evaluations of groups, however, are typically subjective; they lack an objective standard. Therefore, Tajfel argued, perceivers compare their own group to another group. This comparison process, being subjective, is open to bias, and in particular can be biased in the direction of ingroup favoritism, which then bolsters self-esteem. One can seemingly enhance the stature of the ingroup through derogation of the outgroup, even if it requires selectively focusing on ingroup-favoring dimensions of comparison. Thus, this motivated bias in group perceptions produces the ingroup favoritism so robustly obtained in experimental research. Moreover, the individual group member derives an enhancement in self-esteem through this process of intergroup differentiation.

Given its central role in social identity theory, there has not been sufficient research directly investigating the self-esteem hypothesis (Abrams and Hogg, 1988). Moreover, what evidence exists provides only mixed support (for reviews, see Abrams and Hogg, 1988; Crocker and Luhtanen, 1990; Deaux, 1996; Hogg and Abrams, 1990; Long and Spears, 1996; Messick and Mackie, 1989). As Hogg and Abrams (1990, p. 39) observed, "A need for self-esteem may be involved, but it may not have the status of ultimate cause or primal mover ... Intergroup behavior is quite likely to be multiply caused." We shall later return to this notion of multiple factors underlying group identification and the benefits that derive from it.

Self-categorization theory

Like social identity theory, self-categorization theory (Turner, Hogg, Oakes, Reicher, and Wetherell, 1987; Turner and Oakes, 1989) focuses on the categorization process and on its role in determining one's self-concept. Self-categorization theory emphasizes the extent to which the self-concept reflects the categorization of the self into some social grouping. An analysis of this self-categorization process is therefore at the heart of self-categorization theory.

Any individual has many group memberships, which provide multiple potential bases for self-categorizations at any given time. According to the theory, the self-definition that is adopted at the moment is largely context dependent, and involves a dynamic process. The categorization of any stimulus, including the categorization of the self into a social group, depends on the range and the salience of stimuli that are present at the current moment. What determines which self-identity is adopted at the moment? A major determinant in answering this question is the set of alternative social categories that is present and salient in the immediate situation. This idea is captured in the meta-contrast principle, which states that "a given set of items is more likely to be characterized as a single entity to the degree that differences within that set of items are less than the differences between that set and others within the comparative context" (Oakes, Haslam, and Turner, 1994, p. 96). In other words, categorization assures that the differences between currently perceived categories are larger than differences within these categories. In addition to the meta-contrast principle, self-categorization depends on the accessibility of any self-category and normative fit, the degree to which the content of the specific instance matches the general category specifications (Turner, Oakes, Haslam, and McGarty, 1994).

Once self-categorization has occurred, the individual comes to perceive him or herself as indistinguishable from and interchangeable with other members of the category (and increasingly different from members of contrasting categories). Through this depersonalization process, the importance of the individual's *personal* identity is diminished, and the importance of the person's *social* identity is increased. The consequence is self-stereotyping, in which the individual takes on the properties and attitudes that are characteristic of the group. That is, the person assumes that the attributes stereotypic of the group are also characteristic of the self. An important consequence of such context-dependent self-categorization is that one's self-perceptions can change depending on the particular self-categorization that is evoked.

A central element in this argument is that group identification leads to depersonalization and self-stereotyping, and through this process the individual gains self-understanding of his or her own attributes. Perhaps the best evidence in support of this argument is a study by Smith and Henry (1996), in which the response latencies of participants' self-judgments on a number of traits were assessed. When the trait being judged was part of the stereotype of the person's ingroup, self-descriptive responses were made faster and with fewer errors than when the attribute did not match the group stereotype. Thus, attributes characteristic of the ingroup had become associated with the self.

Self-categorization theory and social identity theory share many assumptions and foci of emphasis (Turner, 1987). Indeed, both theories are primarily concerned with the relationship between people's group memberships and their social identities. However, the theories differ in important ways. For example, an important element of social identity theory is the motive to enhance one's positive social identity – an important component of one's self-esteem – through comparison of ingroup and outgroup. Thus, although the categorization process has an important role in social identity theory, it is the motivation for positive social identity that drives the process by which one's self-esteem is produced and maintained. This motive is much less central in self-categorization theory, which is primarily a cognitive theory of how self-categorizations occur. Therefore, (1) one's self-categorization is viewed as temporally and contextually determined, and consequently is in continual flux, and (2) the nature of one's self-concept is a product of this cognitive categorization process through application of the meta-contrast ratio. One interesting implication of this theory is that if, through self-categorization, one (at least momentarily) identifies with a negatively valued group, the consequent self-stereotyping will produce a negative impact on one's current level of self-esteem. Any corrective motivation to alter this consequence is not centrally developed in self-categorization theory.

Optimal distinctiveness theory

Like the other two theories, optimal distinctiveness theory (Brewer, 1991; Brewer and Gardner, 1996; Brewer and Pickett, in press) begins with the assumption that individuals define themselves as much in terms of their group memberships as in terms of their individual achievements. As we have seen, self-categorization theory is a cognitively based model of self-identity, emphasizing the role of situational determinants of the categorization applied to the self as a function of the salience of that category in any given context. Although Brewer sees this self-categorization process as important, she believes that social identity has important motivational as well as cognitive determinants. Thus, optimal distinctiveness theory was developed to account for the motivational principles by which individuals identify with different social groups at different times, and to explain how such social identification helps to achieve and maintain a stable self-concept.

Brewer's (1991) view is that an individual's sense of self is shaped by two opposing needs: the need for assimilation (group identity) and the need for differentiation (self-identity). That is, people need to feel a part of some larger social entity, while at the same time they need to feel unique and individuated. Too much of either feeling arouses the opposing motivation, is associated with negative affect, and instigates efforts to change the current level of social identification. Thus, when in a situation that casts a person as an anonymous member of a very large group, that individual feels the need to differentiate him or herself from others and to emphasize his or her own unique properties. In contrast, when isolated from or feeling extremely different from others, the need for commonality with others is enhanced and the individual will seek greater identification with (larger) social groups. In sum, the organism seeks a homeostatic balance between the opposing needs.

Consistent with the predictions of optimal distinctiveness theory, Brewer and Weber (1994) found that, when people were assigned to a distinctive minority (said to comprise only 20 percent of the population), they showed assimilation toward their ingroup. On the other hand, when assigned to a majority group (said to comprise 80 percent of the population), people needed to differentiate themselves in some way from this inclusive group, and thus exhibited contrast away from their ingroup. Additionally, Brewer and her colleagues have manipulated the need for differentiation (Brewer, Manzi, and Shaw, 1993). People in the depersonalized condition were given instructions worded to increase their inclusion in the group "college student." Raising the need for differentiation led people to identify more with another available ingroup when this ingroup was

a distinctive minority (again, 20 percent of the population) than when it was a
majority (again 80 percent of the population).

The tension between the two motives will thus determine the level of social
categorization that an individual seeks at any given point in time. In addition,
any individual differences in these two motives, as well as any situationally
determined changes in the motives, will affect the level of social categorization
that is adopted and the group with which one identifies. In any case, social
identity level will be chosen in order to balance the opposing motives of assimilation and differentiation and to achieve an optimal level of distinctiveness. It is
this motivation for an optimal distinctiveness level, rather than the motivation
for positive self-esteem of social identity theory, that drives the level of social
identification, according to Brewer. In fact, she is quite clear (Brewer and Pickett,
in press) that this motivation for an optimal level of distinctiveness is independent of positive evaluation needs, and thus even identification with negatively
evaluated groups can be used to achieve the optimal balance of the needs for
assimilation and differentiation.

Social Identification and Social Identity Value

The three theories discussed in the preceding section have common roots and
share many assumptions. At the heart of all three is the assumption that our
group memberships play a central role in our understanding of who we are, of
what we are like, and of how we are similar to and different from others. In
other words, all three are theories of *social* identity and therefore focus on how
our self-concepts reflect our memberships in social groups.

The benefits of social identification

All three theories also assume that individuals derive meaningful psychological
benefits from their identification with the groups to which they belong. However, they differ in precisely what those benefits are. What do these three theories
say about the psychological benefits of group membership?

In social identity theory, one of the important underlying motivations for
social categorization is the enhancement of self-esteem (Tajfel and Turner,
1979). Gains in self-esteem are achieved through group identification and differentiation of one's own group from other groups in such a way that the ingroup is
favorably evaluated. Thus, for social identity theory, this esteem-enhancement
motive is one of the central mechanisms driving the whole system.

In self-categorization theory, identification with a particular group at a given
time is the result of the application of the meta-contrast principle – one identifies
with that ingroup that maximizes the ratio of the average intercategory differ-

ence to the average intracategory difference. These differences are a function of salient or distinctive features of the groups in the particular context; esteem enhancement plays little or no role in this process. Once self-categorization has occurred, the person may become depersonalized, perceive the self as an interchangeable member of the group, engage in self-stereotyping, and thereby take on the prototypic attributes of the group. An important benefit deriving from this process is self-understanding, gaining knowledge of one's own attributes through group identification.

In optimal distinctiveness theory, self-categorization is based on motivational rather than cognitive principles. Unlike social identity theory, however, the motive is not esteem enhancement; rather, self-categorization depends on the degree of satisfaction of two opposing needs, inclusion and differentiation. Thus, optimal distinctiveness theory is essentially a model based on homeostasis. Achieving an optimal level of distinctiveness provides the benefit of balancing the opposing needs (or restoring homeostasis). This benefit, however, derives specifically from achieving homeostasis and is therefore different from and independent of any self-enhancement associated with the group identification. One important implication of this view is that identification with a negatively valued ingroup could have positive value if such identification helped to restore homeostasis, that is, if it led to attaining a greater balance of the two opposing needs for assimilation and differentiation. Brewer et al. (1993) offered support for this proposition when they pitted the need for positive self-identity against the need for an optimal level of distinctiveness. They found that subjects preferred an optimal level of distinctiveness to increases in social identity and esteem.

Thus, all three theories highlight the psychological benefits of group membership, but they emphasize different aspects of those benefits: self-esteem, self-understanding, and optimal distinctiveness. We believe that all three of these factors can be important benefits that contribute to the importance attached to one's membership in a given group. Let us use the term *social identity value* to refer to those benefits that derive from group membership. That is, at any given moment, a group's social identity value for the individual may be based on the positive feelings of self-worth associated with that group membership, it may be based on the self-understanding achieved through adopting group characteristics through self-categorization, or it may be based on the balance of needs for inclusion and differentiation afforded by defining oneself in terms of that group. Thus, we view social identity value to be multiply determined. Moreover, we believe that a group's social identity value for the individual is reflected in the *importance* to that individual of his or her membership in the group.

Contextual and chronic categorizations

As we have discussed, theories representing the social identity approach (especially self-categorization theory and optimal distinctiveness theory) account for social identifications in terms of context-based factors that are operative at the moment. Consequently, these theories emphasize the transitory, shifting, and malleable nature of people's group identifications, and they provide mechanisms that account for those contextually based categorizations.

The fact that group identifications and self-categorizations are fluid, transitory, and context dependent means that, according to these theories, the self cannot be considered a completely stable and static mental structure. Rather, the self is the outcome of a process of activation, categorization, and social judgment. Although there may be a stable core aspect of the self, there are also a number of different selves, the activation of which depends upon the immediate context. This idea that the self does not exist as a completely stable mental structure is compatible with Barsalou's (1987) proposal that categories in general are not stored as stable structures, but rather are generated in a context-dependent manner. Other views of the self-concept (Bem, 1967; Markus and Wurf, 1987; Stryker and Statham, 1985) also assume a self that varies with the situation and conceive of a hierarchy of different selves.

While acknowledging the importance of recognizing the flexibility of group identifications and self-categorizations, we believe that these context-based determinants do not provide the whole story. In particular, with its emphasis on temporal determinants of social identification, contemporary theorizing has, perhaps inadvertently, lost sight of the stability with which we hold many of our group identities. In our view, people have *chronic* group identifications that are always potentially accessible, always "right there when needed." For African-Americans, their "blackness" is never too far from affecting their mental processes; Jews are Jews in most social situations; for many people, their professional identification is a central element of their self-definition in many contexts. These group memberships would function much like the chronically accessible trait constructs researched by Higgins, King, and Mavin (1982) and others. As such, these chronically accessible group identifications would be particularly likely to influence momentary self-categorizations in any given situation, and because of their ongoing importance to the individual, the social identity values associated with these group memberships seem likely to be continually important for the individual's self-conception. In other words, we believe that group memberships that are high in social identity value exert stable influences on people's social identifications across many, though of course not all, situations.

We can carry this analysis one step further. As the theories discussed earlier have clearly delineated, properties of the immediate context can be powerful determinants of the individual's momentary group identification. In addition, however, we suggest that, even in these circumstances, certain chronic social identifications can exert a secondary influence on one's immediate experience. A ballplayer on the playing field will obviously self-categorize in terms of that athletic category, but may also think of himself as "a black ballplayer." A physician will self-categorize as a member of the medical profession, but if female, may often think of herself as "the woman doctor." Thus, we suggest that there may be interesting *joint* influences of contextual and chronic self-categorizations that together can influence one's social identity value associated with those categorizations.

Variations in social identity value

Every person has multiple group memberships. Those groups have varying social identity values for the individual. Thus, there is likely to be a whole spectrum of social identity values associated with a person's group memberships. In any given context, one or another of these social identities may predominate and thereby influence the person's momentary self-definition, and therefore the social identity benefits experienced by the individual can vary considerably as groups of varying importance become the basis for self-categorization.

Thus, we conceive of the spectrum of a person's group memberships as providing a range of social identity values that may be evoked and have bearing on the person's self-definition. The social identity theories discussed earlier have addressed the importance of alternative self-categorizations and they have implicitly emphasized different benefits associated with different self-categorizations. We have argued that these different benefits can all contribute to the social identity value of a group membership and that the social identity values associated with different group memberships can be chronically accessible, as well as activated by contextual determinants. We believe these ideas offer useful extensions to current conceptions of social identity.

Entitativity and Social Identity Value

We have now discussed two important concepts regarding group perceptions, entitativity and social identity value. We have argued that both of them can be conceptualized as varying along a continuum and that different groups possess these attributes to varying degrees. We have further pointed out that both entitativity and social identity value can have important implications for perceptions and impressions of groups. We now turn to the important question of the relation between these two concepts. How are they similar and how are they different? How do they affect one another? What are the consequences of each?

The answers to these questions are not immediately obvious because these two concepts have their origins in different aspects of group perception. As we noted earlier, the question of perceived entitativity of groups developed out of work analyzing when and how perceivers come to comprehend that a collection of persons constitutes a group (Campbell, 1958; Hamilton et al., 1998). Thus, entitativity has been discussed as something we see in "other" groups. In contrast, notions of social identity have developed from analyses of ingroup–

outgroup differentiation (Tajfel, 1978; Tajfel and Turner, 1979). In particular, the concept of social identity value, as we have developed it, is something that the individual gains from his or her membership in a particular group; generally speaking, we do not get social identity value from "other" groups (at least not directly). We suspect that these different origins account in part for the fact that the two concepts have never been considered in relation to each other.

Despite this disparity, the two concepts have obvious bearing on each other. It seems likely that there is variation among our ingroups not only in their value for us but also in the extent to which we see them as tight, entitative units. In fact, some of our recent findings support this line of reasoning. Earlier we described research by Lickel et al. (1998) in which participants rated a variety of groups with regard to their "groupness," along with a number of other features. In an extension of that work, Lickel et al. (1998, Study 3) followed the same procedures in having participants rate a number of their ingroups. Specifically, they were asked to list 12 groups to which they belong. When the assessed variables were correlated with ratings of entitativity (groupness), the most highly correlated variable was the participants' ratings of the importance of their own membership in those groups. The own-membership importance is highly similar to our notions of social identity value of group membership. Thus, at least correlationally, there is a substantial relationship between these two concepts, perceived entitativity and social identity value.

Despite this strong association, we believe that there are also some important differences between these concepts. In this section, then, we consider a variety of questions regarding the relationship between entitativity and social identity value of groups. In the absence of prior research on these questions, our discussion is necessarily speculative. Our hope is that the issues raised here will spawn the needed research for more thorough answers.

Cognitive and motivational aspects

One way that the concepts of entitativity and social identity value differ is in the relative emphasis on their cognitive as opposed to motivational aspects in various conceptual analyses of these concepts. Campbell's (1958) original analysis of entitativity rested on Gestalt principles of object perception (e.g., the similarity and proximity of elements), highlighting the role of properties that had little emotional involvement of the perceiver. More recent discussions of this concept (Abelson et al., 1994; Brewer and Harasty, 1996; Hamilton et al., 1998; Yzerbyt et al., 1997) have also focused on perceptions of groups "out there," without involving the role of own-group memberships of the perceiver on the perception of groupness in a set of individuals. Such a focus further reinforces the role of cognitive rather than motivational factors in perceptions of entitativity. Conversely, the concept of social identity value has its roots in the theorizing of Tajfel (1969, 1978; Tajfel and Turner, 1986), who emphasized the role of self-esteem enhancement as underlying social identity and intergroup differentiation. This theoretical tradition has thus highlighted the role of motivational processes in generating ingroup favoritism, intergroup discrimination, and the like.

Despite this historical difference, more recent developments have moved the two traditions closer to each other. For example, among entitativity theorists, Brewer and Harasty (1996) emphasize the functional aspects of perceiving entitativity. These authors have discussed the possible roles of individual differences in perceiver needs (e.g., cognitive complexity, certainty orientation) as well as temporary, situation-based motivational factors, such as processing goals, expectancies, and mood. Within the social identity tradition, Turner's self-categorization theory (Turner et al., 1987; Turner and Oakes, 1989) offers a much more heavily cognitive analysis of the processes underlying self-categorization and identification with alternate group memberships. Thus, the difference in emphasis on the role of cognitive and motivational mechanisms is one of degree, and that difference appears to be narrowing.

Ingroup–outgroup differences

Obviously, the distinction between ingroups and outgroups is central to discussions of social identity value. We derive social identity value from our ingroup memberships. Nevertheless, we have argued, ingroups vary in their social identity value for the individual. In addition to the factors already discussed, we suggest that, other things being equal, greater identity value will be derived from ingroups to the extent that perceived entitativity is high. That is, value and benefits that are gained from ingroup membership should be greater when those groups are highly entitative – that is, characterized by high interaction, shared goals, common outcomes, etc. (Lickel et al., 1998).

The case of perception of entitativity for ingroups and outgroups is not so clear. We have already referred to an Entitativity Continuum along which groups are perceived as varying, a notion based on our earlier analyses of perception of entitativity in "other" groups. It seems likely that ingroups and outgroups differ in the extent to which they fall along the full range of this dimension of perceived entitativity. It is easy to think of outgroups spanning this entire dimension. We can think of outgroups that are high in entitativity (perhaps those that pose a particular threat to the ingroup; Abelson et al., 1994), and other outgroups that would not be characterized by this property (e.g., groups that have little self-relevance). For ingroups, however, we suspect that the range is more restricted. Specifically, it seems to us that people believe that the groups to which they belong are "real" groups and, as a consequence, see them as having at least moderate amounts of essence, stability, and coherence. Surely even our ingroups would vary in the extent to which this is true, such that some ingroups are considered very tight and solid entities, whereas other ingroups are more loosely formed. However, we venture the opinion that the very nature of "ingroup" means that there is some degree of entitativity defining the group, such that ingroups do not fully extend to the lower end of the Entitativity Continuum, as outgroups can. This analysis posits a main effect such that, overall, ingroups are perceived as having more entitativity than outgroups. Perhaps a more interesting way of stating this point is that, for any given group, group members will perceive that group as possessing more entitativity than will nonmembers. Thus, one of the consequences of becoming a member of a group should be an increase in the perception of that group's level of entitativity. Interestingly, this proposition is in contrast to that of Brewer and Harasty (1996) and of McGarty et al. (1995), who suggest that ingroups (having exemplar-based representations) will be less entitative than outgroups (which generally have prototype representations).

A further implication of our proposition (cf. Hamilton and Sherman, 1996) is that, conceptually, entitativity is distinct from a seemingly related concept, homogeneity. Perceived homogeneity refers to the perceived similarity of the group's members. This notion seems relevant to entitativity because, as Campbell (1958) noted, similarity among members is one cue from which entitativity might be inferred. However, an often-replicated result in the literature on intergroup perception is the outgroup homogeneity effect (Linville and Fischer, 1993; Linville and Jones, 1980; Park, Ryan, and Judd, 1992), the finding that outgroup members are perceived as being similar to each other relative to ingroup members, who are viewed as representing considerable diversity. If perceived entitativity is strongly tied to similarity, then the outgroup homogeneity effect implies that outgroups should be perceived as more entitative than ingroups – the opposite of what we have just proposed. Note, however, that similarity is only one of many cues to entitativity, and in our view (Hamilton et al., 1998), not the most diagnostic cue. Moreover, there have now been a number of demonstrations of greater *ingroup* homogeneity (e.g., Simon, 1992; Simon and Hamilton, 1994), and these effects have occurred under conditions that would enhance perceptions of entitativity of the ingroup (minority group, high status, etc.). Thus, in our view, the relationship between perceived homogeneity and perceived entitativity of ingroups and outgroups is likely to be complex.

In fact, the relationship between entitativity and homogeneity may be particularly interesting. Ryan and Bogart (1997) reported a longitudinal study of the development of the perceptions of ingroup and outgroup members. Interestingly, they found that, at the beginning of group membership, ingroups were perceived as more homogeneous than outgroups. Only after a longer period of membership did the typical outgroup homogeneity effect emerge. We would account for this finding in the following way. When one joins a new group, this group is perceived as highly entitative. One seeks out the defining attributes of this group, trying to construct a simplified representation of the group and trying to identify the common attributes of group members. This would explain Ryan and Bogart's finding that initially there is an ingroup homogeneity effect. Once such a unified representation has been established, one can begin to appreciate the diversity of the group's members and begin to differentiate oneself from the other members – processes unlikely to occur for outgroups. Thus, over time, the outgroup homogeneity effect begins to emerge.

Varieties of ingroups

Earlier we described Lickel et al.'s (1998) studies in which four different types of groups were identified, based on structural analyses of participants' ratings of 40 groups on a variety of characteristics. Comparable analyses were conducted in Lickel et al.'s follow-up study of perceivers' judgments of their ingroups. Did perceivers "see" the same types of groups among their ingroups as did perceivers of groups to which they did not belong? To an impressive degree, they did. Specifically, structural analyses again revealed that perceivers categorized these groups into intimacy groups, task-oriented groups, social categories, and loosely associated groups. Thus, it appears that perceivers make much the same kinds of broad distinctions among groups, regardless of their membership in those groups.

Do these different types of groups also differ in the degree of social identity value that they provide for their members, and if so, how? If we consider the participants' ratings of the importance of their memberships in the groups they listed as a measure of the social identity value of those groups, then we can begin to answer this question. Specifically, the high-intimacy groups (e.g., family, friendship groups) were rated highest in social identity value, followed by task-oriented groups, social categories, and finally, the loose associations. These findings parallel participants' ratings of these types of groups on perceived entitativity.

Complementing these similarities, it seems to us that there are at least two ways in which groups differ that have implications for both their degree of perceived entitativity and for their social identity value: relative size and status. Some authors (e.g., Brewer and Harasty, 1996; Mullen, 1991) have argued that minority groups are higher in perceived entitativity than are majority groups. If so, then information about majority and minority groups should be processed differently. Consistent with this view, Brewer et al. (1995) found that recognition errors in the Taylor (1981) matching paradigm (i.e., recognizing which person said what in a discussion, where each person is a member of one of two groups) were biased toward intracategory confusions for minority groups. However, for information generated by majority group members, intracategory and intercategory errors were equivalent. This result suggests that information about the majority group may be represented at the individual member level. Minority groups, on the other hand, because of their high degree of perceived entitativity, are represented at the category level, and it is thus difficult to distinguish among the different individual members of a group.

Consistent with these findings, Simon and Hamilton (1994) found that minority group members were more likely to stereotype themselves than were majority members. Minority group members saw themselves more in terms of group membership and rated themselves higher on attributes characteristic of the group. It seems quite plausible that this tendency is related to the greater degree of entitativity involved in the perception of small as opposed to large groups.

Although minority status seems clearly related to high levels of perceived entitativity, it is less clear how minority status relates to social identity value. This ambiguity is in part due to the multiple possible bases of social identity value, as discussed earlier. And the relationship of valence to social identity value of minority vs. majority group membership is not as direct as one might expect. For example, in the Simon and Hamilton (1994) research, minority members stereotyped themselves more than did majority members, regardless of the degree to which the stereotypic attributes were positive or negative. Minority and majority groups should also differ in value of group membership based on the extent to which the group identification provides an optimal level of distinctiveness. Brewer (1991, p. 479) states that, because large majorities "are not sufficiently differentiated to constitute meaningful social groups," optimal distinctiveness is more likely to be achieved by minority groups than by groups in a relative numerical majority. Findings reported by Simon and his colleagues (Simon and Brown, 1987; Simon and Pettigrew, 1990) are consistent with this view.

These considerations are further complicated by a second important factor for both entitativity and social identity value, namely, the relative status of the membership group. Because status usually bestows importance, one derives more social identity value from membership in high- than in low-status groups. However, as just noted, high-status groups may often not provide an appropriate level of optimal distinctiveness. Thus, one may satisfy positive evaluation needs in high-status groups and may adopt the attributes characteristic of the group, but at the expense of achieving a less than optimal level of distinctiveness.

In support of derivations from optimal distinctiveness theory for effects of group size and status on ingroup favoritism, Brewer et al. (1993) assigned subjects to categories of "overestimator" or "underestimator." Some were told that this was the category of most college students (majority condition), and others were told that it was a minority category. In addition, prior to categorization, some subjects were made to feel depersonalized. Finally, based on feedback about performance, subjects were told that their group was either high or low in status. The outcome variable was degree of group identification. As expected, without depersonalization, both high status and majority size contributed to positive evaluations of the ingroup. However, given depersonalization, and thus a need for uniqueness, subjects valued minority group membership more than majority group membership, and no effects of group status were observed.

Other findings indicate that these relationships are likely to be complex. It might be predicted that high-status groups will lead to enhanced self-stereotyping, and thus to increased perceptions of entitativity. However, Simon and Hamilton (1994) found that this was true only for minority groups; high- and low-status majority groups did not differ in the extent of self-stereotyping.

As we have noted, the social identity value of group membership can derive from a variety of factors (needs for self-esteem, self-understanding, optimal distinctiveness), and these bases of social identity value may not always function in concert or have equal impact in any given circumstance. Therefore, analyses of social identity value should give attention to the nature of the benefits afforded by membership in a particular group, as recognition of those bases of social identity value is likely to provide insight into the specific effects and relations to be expected.

Consequences of perceived entitativity and social identity value

Both entitativity and social identity value are properties of groups as perceived by the individual. Nevertheless, research in recent years has begun to document that both of these perceptions have important consequences for other effects and processes. Moreover, despite similarities, those consequences differ somewhat for the two concepts. In this section we discuss the consequences that follow from the perception of each of these properties in groups.

Entitativity

Most evidence regarding the consequences of perceived entitativity comes from studies that have compared individual and group targets, rather than by comparing groups that vary in entitativity (see Hamilton and Sherman, 1996). The differences obtained in these studies have been summarized by Hamilton et al. (in press) as reflecting differences in integrative processing, that is, the extent to which information about a social target is carefully processed and developed into a coherent impression at the time it is received. Hamilton et al. (in press) argue that there are several markers of integrative processing, including: more extreme and faster judgments, efforts to explain inconsistencies in information, better recall, primacy in recall, lower degrees of memory–judgment correlations, and reduced evidence of distinctiveness-based illusory correlations (an outcome that depends largely on memory-based judgments). These effects have been shown to be more characteristic of processing information about a high-entitativity target (an individual) than a low-entitativity target (an undefined group). More relevant to present considerations, McConnell et al. (1997) have recently manipulated the degree of perceived entitativity of target groups by providing information regarding their coherence and consistency. When participants were led to believe that the target groups were high in entitativity, strong evidence of integrative processing emerged. For groups perceived as low in entitativity, integrative processing was not evoked, and judgments and impressions of these groups were based on information retrieved at the time of judgment.

When a group is perceived as having entitativity, it is assumed to be a meaningful and a predictable unit, as well as an entity that has purpose and coherence. Therefore, it seems to us that greater perceived entitativity implies that the group has greater solidity and less penetrable boundaries. Findings consistent with this notion were reported by Knowles and Bassett (1976), who found that the barriers around a group high in entitativity were less likely to be penetrated than the barriers around a group low in entitativity. This was suggested by results showing that pedestrians walked further away from a group of persons engaged in group discussion than from a group of persons looking at the same stimulus.

Abelson et al. (1994) investigated a different consequence of perceived entitativity: the degree to which a group is viewed as threatening. Subjects were presented with images of groups of five humanoid creatures. In the low-entitativity condition, these creatures were scattered randomly and were dissimilar in color and appearance. In the high-entitativity condition, the five creatures were in close proximity to each other and shared highly similar features. Subjects judged these groups in terms of both positive and negative actions in which the groups might engage. The main finding was that higher entitativity increased the perceived potential of the group for negative actions toward other groups. It did not, however, decrease the likelihood of positive actions toward other groups. Abelson et al. (1994) concluded that an important effect of perceived entitativity (in nonmembership groups) is to experience feelings of threat from such groups – an increase in the perception that these groups are capable of hurtful actions.

We suggest an alternative possibility: that increased perceptions of entitativity result in more polarized perceptions of such groups, either in the positive or negative direction. The basis for this prediction is our assumption that the perception of high entitativity of an outgroup will lead to greater perceived *potency* of the group, where potency implies the capacity to do either good or bad things. Entitativity enables a group to be ready and able to act collectively and thus to be impactful. Some groups, such as those that one admires or to which one aspires, would be perceived as having greater potential for doing good as perceived entitativity increases. Other groups, such as enemies and competitors, would be perceived as having greater potential for inflicting harm as perceived entitativity increases.

The idea that highly entitative targets will be perceived in more polarized ways than low-entitativity targets is supported by recent work comparing impressions of individual vs. group targets. We have argued that, in general, individuals are seen as more entitative units than are groups (Hamilton and Sherman, 1996). Consistent with the above reasoning, Susskind et al. (in press) found that people make more extreme (positive or negative) dispositional inferences about individual than group targets, and those inferences are made more quickly and with greater confidence for individuals than for groups. Similarly, Welbourne, Harasty, and Brewer (1997) reported that individual targets were rated more negatively than group targets when the targets engaged in immoral behaviors, but individuals were rated more positively than groups for ability behaviors. In each case, the individual was rated as more extreme. These findings, then, provide support for the notion that perceptions of entitativity will lead to perceptions of extremity and potency.

Moreover, in addition to perceived extremity effects of increased entitativity, we suggest that more entitative social targets are processed more schematically than less entitative targets. That is, more well-developed schematic representations should exist for targets high in entitativity, and these schemata should be used as information about the targets is assimilated and integrated (Coovert and Reeder, 1990). In support of this argument, Welbourne et al. (1997) reported greater schematic processing for individual than for group targets, and they attributed this difference to the greater perceived unity and entitativity of individual targets. Thus, information about highly entitative targets was processed typologically in terms of the schematic, interactive relations among traits (Anderson and Sedikides, 1991). Information about less entitative targets was processed by simply averaging the evaluations of the traits. The greater schematic processing for entitative targets is consistent with our proposal of greater extremity for entitative targets, in that typological impression formation will generally lead to more extreme impressions than averaging or associationistic processes. We expect that these differences in processing associated with individual vs. group targets would also be evident in processing information about high- vs. low-entitativity groups.

These considerations suggest that the perceived entitativity of groups has implications for stereotyping of those groups. In fact, for both Brewer and Harasty (1996) and Yzerbyt et al. (1997), entitativity is intimately related to stereotypes. For Brewer and Harasty, high levels of entitativity are related to prototype representation, and prototype representation is related to the degree to which a stereotype is invoked. Thus, groups that are perceived as highly entitative will be stereotyped more, and the members of that group will be perceived as having the attributes associated with the stereotype. In addition, the behavior of members of highly entitative groups will be assimilated to the group stereotype (Hilton and von Hippel, 1990). For Yzerbyt et al. (1997), stereotypes help achieve an essentialism for social categories, and this entitative view of groups is necessary in order to help maintain the current social structure. Stereotypes thus help rationalize existing conditions and account for existing social circumstances (see also Jost and Banaji, 1994).

Finally, we suggest that the differential (and biased) processing of information about ingroups as opposed to outgroups is mediated, at least in part, by differences in perceived entitativity. To date, there has been little consideration of the consequences of differing levels of perceived *ingroup* entitativity. However, we can speculate on some of the consequences that might follow from perceiving one's own group as being relatively high or low in entitativity. Some of these consequences will be perceptual in nature. For example, we would predict that members of highly entitative groups will perceive greater differentiation from outgroups, and thus show a greater degree of ingroup bias in the perceptions and interpretations of events. Relatedly, in accounting for the performance of the group or of its members, members of highly entitative groups should show a greater degree of ingroup linguistic bias, where good outcomes or behaviors of the ingroup are described by general terms, and bad outcomes or behaviors are described by concrete terms (Maass and Arcuri, 1992; Maass, Salvi, Arcuri, and Semin, 1989).

In addition, just as for outgroups, perceptions of higher entitativity should lead to impressions of greater potency of the ingroup. However, given the positive evaluative bias toward ingroups (Brewer, 1979), these impressions should tend to be more positive. That is, entitative ingroups should be seen as having more power to do good things and to achieve positive goals, in contrast to the increased negative potential that Abelson et al. (1994) demonstrated for nonmembership groups. In fact, recent research supports the prediction that highly entitative ingroups are viewed as having greater potential for positive achievements (Dasgupta et al., 1997).

Other possible consequences of perceived entitativity of the ingroup would be behavioral in nature. We suggest that highly entitative groups are more likely to develop clear group norms, and that members of such groups should be more subject to social influence and conformity pressures by other group members. Such a proposal is consistent with research on the behavioral effects of group cohesiveness, a concept closely related to entitativity. Schachter, Ellertson, McBride, and Gregory (1951) found that high-cohesive groups induced individual members to be either highly productive or quite unproductive, compared to low-cohesive groups, for which induction attempts were significantly less effective. In other words, the between-group variability in performance was much higher for high-cohesive groups. An interesting question concerns whether perceivers are sensitive to these differences in actual group performance (Hamilton et al., 1998). If so, then perceptions of groups high and low in entitativity may show polarizations in judgments parallel to these actual differences in performance levels. In addition, perceptions of entitativity by group members should render the group more susceptible to change from internal sources and more resistant to change from external sources.

Social identity value

Just as there are important perceptual and behavior consequences of perceived entitativity for group members, there are also important consequences of social identity value. And many of these consequences are similar to those discussed for entitativity. The literature documenting the effects of ingroup membership on differential perceptions of and behavior toward ingroup and outgroup members is, of course, voluminous. The general prediction we are making is that these effects will be stronger when the ingroup is one to which the individual attaches considerable importance, that is, one that provides high social identity value for the individual. For example, for such groups there should be a greater differentiation from outgroups, as well as a greater degree of ingroup bias (Brewer, 1979), as indicated by the kinds of interpretations made of group events and outcomes. Evidence for the "ultimate attribution error" (Pettigrew, 1979), whereby positive and negative acts by ingroup and outgroup members are differentially attributed to internal vs. external causes (Hewstone, 1989), should be enhanced for high social identity value ingroups. In addition, ingroup linguistic bias (Maass and Arcuri, 1992; Maass et al., 1989) should be more evident for groups that have a high social identity value. With regard to social influence and conformity, we suggest, as with entitativity, that members of high social identity value groups will be more influenced by such groups and will conform more to the norms of these groups.

Moreover, groups that provide high social identity value should be more susceptible to changes from internal sources and should show greater resistance to change from outside pressures. In support of this last suggestion, a recent study by Spears, Doosje, and Ellemers (1997) investigated the effects of threats to the group on members who showed high or low identification with the group. Across several studies, these investigators found that members who had what we would call low social identity value were likely to set themselves apart from the group and to show dissociation from other group members when there were threats to the value of the group. On the other hand, members who strongly identified with the group reacted to these same levels of threat by enhancing their degree of solidarity with group members and by increasing their degree of association with the group. In other words, high social identity value rendered the group more stable and more resistant to change from outside pressures.

Another interesting consequence of social identity value is seen in reactions to positive outcomes by groups. When a group to which one belongs achieves a success, as when a university football team wins an important game, group members (students of the university) increase their level of public identification with the group. This increased identification has been called BIRGING (Cialdini et al., 1976), and it increases for all members of the group. However, such behavior is probably more likely to occur for those members who strongly identify with the group in the first place. In addition, Cialdini et al. reported that BIRGING is more likely to occur for those who need a boost in self-esteem (e.g., those who have recently had a failure experience) and can derive such a boost from group identification. Thus, BIRGING is likely to be both an antecedent of social identity value as well as a consequence. This is no doubt true for other factors that have already been discussed such as influenceability, stability, etc.

In general, the predominant effect of a group's high level of social identity value will be to increase levels of self-stereotyping. That is, those members who identify most strongly with the group, who attach considerable importance to their membership in the group, are likely to define themselves in terms of the prototypic properties of the group, properties that are represented in the group's stereotype.

Conclusions

We have explored two important concepts, entitativity and social identity value. Although these concepts have different historical roots, one stemming from social cognition principles and the other stemming from principles of intergroup relations, we have identified several parallels in the way in which both factors can have impact on the perceptions and impressions of groups, on the processing of information about those groups, on the types of interactions that result both within groups and between groups, and on feelings about the self and the self's relationship to the group.

We have indicated that the entitativity concept was historically grounded in principles of cold cognitive processing, with little attention paid to motivational factors or self-esteem needs, and with little attention given to the role of group membership. Social identity, on the other hand, was initially conceived in terms of the self-concept and the need for positive and stable feelings about the self. Importantly, in recent years these concepts have moved toward each other, with consideration of the functional aspects that are involved in perceptions of entitativity and with consideration of the cognitive processing factors that are involved in self-categorization. These changes in focus have allowed us to see the interrelationships between social identity and entitativity, and the ways in which both concepts involve cognitive and motivational factors.

Thus, we conceive of entitativity and social identity value as two important aspects of social groups that influence our perceptions of these groups and their members as well as our behavior within those groups. Both entitativity and social identity value affect information processing about ingroups and outgroups, as they impact the amount and direction of attention given to information, the interpretation of that information, and memory for information. Both concepts play a role in the biases in perceptions of ingroups and outgroups. And we pointed out that both concepts affect group judgments, impressions, and behaviors on the basis of both cognitive and motivational processes. It is likely, however, that entitativity and social identity value play their roles under somewhat different circumstances and for different purposes. The goal now will be to further specify exactly when and how these two concepts, separately and in interaction, guide group impression formation as well as intragroup and intergroup behavior.

Finally, it is important to recognize the bidirectional causality between these concepts: each can influence the other. On the one hand, perceiving that a group is of high social identity value will cause us to perceive that group as being high in entitativity. Ingroups with high social identity value are important to us, and such importance implies that the group is a meaningful, coherent, ongoing entity. Such perceptions of entitativity bestow predictability, controllability, stability to these groups, and these are properties that we would want in our highly valued groups. When we see value in membership, we want this group to continue, to have stability and permanence, and to be resistant to change and intrusion. These properties are provided through increased perceptions of entitativity. On the other hand, perceiving an ingroup to be high in entitativity may lend importance to that group and therefore add to its social identity value. Highly entitative groups can involve commitment, permanence, and investment, and these are features that lead us to see the value of our membership in those groups.

Although many of our observations have the character of suggestions and speculations rather than tested or proven facts, we hope that these suggestions will stimulate further thinking about entitativity and social identity value, and about the relationships between these concepts. We believe that there is much to learn about group dynamics, group impression formation, self-concept, and self-esteem by a continued inquiry into the roles of perceived entitativity and social identity in these processes.

References

Abelson, R.P., Dasgupta, N., Park, J., and Banaji, M.R. (1994). Ingroup perceptions of the collective other. Paper presented at American Psychological Society.

Abrams, D. and Hogg, M. (1988). Comments on the motivational status of self-esteem in social identity and intergroup discrimination. *European Journal of Social Psychology*, 18, 317–34.

Anderson, C.A. and Sedikides, C. (1991). Thinking about people: Contributions of a typological alternative to associationistic and dimensional models of person perception. *Journal of Personality and Social Psychology*, 60, 203–17.

Asch, S.E. (1946). Forming impressions of personality. *Journal of Abnormal and Social Psychology*, 49, 258–90.

Barsalou, L.W. (1987). The instability of graded structure: Implications for the nature of concepts. In U. Neisser (ed.), *Concepts and Conceptual Development: Ecological and intellectual factors in categorization*. Cambridge: Cambridge University Press, pp. 101–40.

Bem, D.J. (1967). Self-perception: An alternative interpretation of cognitive dissonance phenomena. *Psychological Review*, 74, 183–200.

Billig, M. and Tajfel, H. (1973). Social categorization and similarity in intergroup behavior. *European Journal of Social Psychology*, 3, 27–52.

Brewer, M.B. (1979). Ingroup bias in the minimal intergroup situation: A cognitive motivational analysis. *Psychological Bulletin*, 86, 307–24.

Brewer, M.B. (1991). The social self: On being the same and different at the same time. *Personality and Social Psychology Bulletin*, 17, 475–82.

Brewer, M.B. and Gardner, W. (1996). Who is this "we"? Levels of collective identity self representations. *Journal of Personality and Social Psychology*, 71, 83–93.

Brewer, M.B. and Harasty, A.S. (1996). Seeing groups as entities: The role of perceiver motivation. In R. Sorrentino and E.T. Higgins (eds), *Handbook of Motivation and Cognition*, Vol. 3, *The Interpersonal Context*. New York: Guilford, pp. 347–70.

Brewer, M.B., Manzi, J.M., and Shaw, J.S. (1993). In-group identification as a function of depersonalization, distinctiveness, and status. *Psychological Science*, 4, 88–92.

Brewer, M.B. and Pickett, C.L. (in press). Distinctiveness motives as a source of the social self. In T. Tyler, R. Kramer, and O. John (eds), *The Psychology of the Social Self*. Hillsdale, NJ: Erlbaum.

Brewer, M.B. and Weber, J.G. (1994). Self-evaluation effects of interpersonal versus intergroup social comparison. *Journal of Personality and Social Psychology*, 66, 268–75.

Brewer, M.B., Weber, J.G., and Carini, B. (1995). Person memory in intergroup contexts: Categorization versus individuation. *Journal of Personality and Social Psychology*, 69, 29–40.

Campbell, D.T. (1958). Common fate, similarity, and other indices of the status of aggregates of persons as social entities. *Behavioral Science*, 3, 14–25.

Cialdini, R.B., Borden, R.J., Thorne, A., Walker, M.R., Freeman, S., and Sloan, L.R. (1976). Basking in reflected glory: Three (football) field studies. *Journal of Personality and Social Psychology*, 34, 366–75.

Coovert, M.D. and Reeder, G.D. (1990). Negativity effects in impression formation: The role of unit formation and schematic expectations. *Journal of Experimental Social Psychology*, 26, 49–62.

Crocker, J. and Luhtanen, R. (1990). Collective self-esteem and ingroup bias. *Journal of Personality and Social Psychology*, 58, 60–7.

Dasgupta, N., Banaji, M.R., and Abelson, R.P. (1997). Beliefs and attitudes toward cohesive groups. Paper presented at Midwest Psychological Association, Chicago.

Deaux, K. (1996). Social identification. In E.T. Higgins and A.W. Kruglanski (eds), *Social Psychology: Handbook of basic principles*. New York: Guilford, pp. 777–98.

Deaux, K., Reid, A., Mizrahi, K., and Ethier, K.A. (1995). Parameters of social identity. *Journal of Personality and Social Psychology*, 68, 280–91.

Hamilton, D.L. and Sherman, S.J. (1996). Perceiving persons and groups. *Psychological Review*, 103, 336–55.

Hamilton, D.L., Sherman, S.J., and Lickel, B. (1998). Perceiving social groups: The importance of the Entitativity Continuum. In C. Sedikides, J. Schopler, and C.A. Insko (eds), *Intergroup Cognition and Intergroup Behavior*. Mahwah, NJ: Erlbaum, pp. 47–74.

Hamilton, D.L., Sherman, S.J., and Maddox, K.B. (in press). Dualities and continua: Implications for understanding perceptions of persons and groups. In S. Chaiken and Y. Trope (eds), *Dual Process Theories in Social Psychology*. New York: Guilford.

Heider, F. (1958). *The Psychology of Interpersonal Relations*. New York: Wiley.

Hewstone, M. (1989). *Causal Attribution: From cognitive processes to cognitive beliefs*. Oxford: Blackwell.

Higgins, E.T., King, G.A., and Mavin, G.H. (1982). Individual construct accessibility and subjective impressions and recall. *Journal of Personality and Social Psychology*, 43, 35–47.

Hilton, J.L. and von Hippel, W. (1990). The role of consistency in the judgment of stereotype-relevant behaviors. *Personality and Social Psychology Bulletin*, 16, 430–48.

Hogg, M.A. and Abrams, D. (1990). Social motivation, self-esteem and social identity. In D. Abrams and M.A. Hogg (eds), *Social Identity Theory: Constructive and critical advances*. New York: Springer-Verlag, pp. 28–47.

Jost, J.T. and Banaji, M.R. (1994). The role of stereotyping in system-justification and the production of false consciousness. *British Journal of Social Psychology*, 33, 1–27.

Knowles, E.S. and Bassett, R.L. (1976). Groups and crowds as social entities: Effects of activity size, and member similarity on nonmembers. *Journal of Personality and Social Psychology*, 34, 773–83.

Lickel, B., Hamilton, D.L., Wieczorkowska, G., Lewis, A., Sherman, S.J., and Uhles, A.N. (1998). Varieties of social groups: Differing bases of perceived entitativity. Unpublished manuscript, University of California, Santa Barbara.

Linville, P.W. and Fischer, G.W. (1993). Exemplar and abstraction models of perceived group variability and stereotypicality. *Social Cognition*, 11, 92–125.

Linville, P.W. and Jones, E.E. (1980). Polarized appraisals of outgroup members. *Journal of Personality and Social Psychology*, 38, 689–703.

Long, K. and Spears, R. (1996). The self-esteem hypothesis revisited: Differentiation and the disaffected. In R. Spears, P.J. Oakes, N. Ellemers, and S.A. Haslam (eds), *The Social Psychology of Stereotyping and Group Life*. Oxford: Blackwell, pp. 296–317.

Maass, A. and Arcuri, L. (1992). The role of language in the persistence of stereotypes. In G. Semin and K. Fiedler (eds), *Language, Interaction, and Social Cognition*. London: Sage, pp. 129–43.

Maass, A., Salvi, D., Arcuri, L., and Semin, G. (1989). Language use in intergroup contexts: The linguistic intergroup bias. *Journal of Personality and Social Psychology*, 57, 981–93.

McConnell, A.R., Sherman, S.J., and Hamilton, D.L. (1994). The on-line and memory-based aspects of individual and group target judgments. *Journal of Personality and Social Psychology*, 67, 173–85.

McConnell, A.R., Sherman, S.J., and Hamilton, D.L. (1997). Target cohesiveness: Implications for information processing about individual and group targets. *Journal of Personality and Social Psychology*, 72, 750–62.

McGarty, C., Haslam, S.A., Hutchinson, K.J., and Grace, D.M. (1995). Determinants of perceived consistency: The relationship between group entitativity and the meaningfulness of categories. *British Journal of Social Psychology*, 34, 237–56.

Markus, H. and Wurf, E. (1987). The dynamic self-concept: A social psychological perspective. *Annual Review of Psychology*, 38, 299–337.

Medin, D.L. (1989). Concepts and conceptual structure. *American Psychologist*, 44, 1469–81.

Medin, D.L., Goldstone, R.L., and Gentner, D. (1993). Respects for similarity. *Psychological Review*, 100, 254–78.

Messick, D.M. and Mackie, D.M. (1989). Intergroup relations. *Annual Review of Psychology*, 40, 45–51.

Mullen, B. (1991). Group composition, salience, and cognitive representations: The phenomenology of being in a group. *Journal of Experimental Social Psychology*, 27, 297–323.

Oakes, P.J., Haslam, S.A., and Turner, J.C. (1994). *Stereotyping and Social Reality*. London: Blackwell.

Park, B., DeKay, M., and Kraus, S. (1994). Aggregating social behavior into person models: Perceiver-induced consistency. *Journal of Personality and Social Psychology*, 66, 437–59.

Park, B., Ryan, C.S., and Judd, C.M. (1992). Role of meaningful subgroups in explaining differences in perceived variability for ingroups and outgroups. *Journal of Personality and Social Psychology*, 63, 553–67.

Pettigrew, T.F. (1979). The ultimate attribution error: Extending Allport's cognitive analysis of prejudice. *Personality and Social Psychology Bulletin*, 5, 461–76.

Prentice, D.A., Miller, D.T., and Lightdale, J.R. (1994). Asymmetries in attachments to groups and to their members: Distinguishing between common-identity and common-bond groups. *Personality and Social Psychology Bulletin*, 20, 484–93.

Roney, C. and Sorrentino, R.M. (1987). Uncertainty orientation and person perception: Individual differences in categorization. *Social Cognition*, 5, 369–82.

Ross, L.D. (1977). The intuitive psychologist and his shortcomings: Distortions in the attribution process. In L. Berkowitz (ed), *Advances in Experimental Social Psychology*, Vol. 10. New York: Academic Press, pp. 173–220.

Rothbart, M. and Taylor, M. (1992). Category labels and social reality: Do we view social categories as natural kinds? In G. Semin and K. Fiedller (eds), *Language, Interaction, and Social Cognition*. London: Sage, pp. 11–36.

Ryan, C.S. and Bogart, L.M. (1997). Development of new group members' ingroup and outgroup stereotypes: Changes in perceived group variability and ethnocentrism. *Journal of Personality and Social Psychology*, 73, 719–32.

Sanbonmatsu, D.M., Sherman, S.J., and Hamilton, D.M. (1987). Illusory correlation in the perception of individuals and groups. *Social Cognition*, 5, 1–25.

Schachter, S., Ellertson, N., McBride, D., and Gregory, D. (1951). An experimental study of cohesiveness and productivity. *Human Relations*, 4, 229–38.

Seta, C.E. and Hayes, N. (1994). The influence of impression formation goals on the accuracy of social memory. *Personality and Social Psychology Bulletin*, 20, 93–101.

Simon, B. (1992). The perception of ingroup and outgroup homogeneity: Reintroducing the intergroup context. In W. Stroebe and M. Hewstone (eds), *European Review of Social Psychology*, Vol. 3. Chichester: Wiley, pp. 1–30.

Simon, B. and Brown, R.J. (1987). Perceived intragroup homogeneity in minority–majority contexts. *Journal of Personality and Social Psychology*, 53, 703–11.

Simon, B. and Hamilton, D.L. (1994). Self-stereotyping and social context: The effects of relative in-group size and in-group status. *Journal of Personality and Social Psychology*, 66, 699–711.

Simon, B. and Pettigrew, T.F. (1990). Social identity and perceived group homogeneity: Evidence for the ingroup homogeneity effect. *European Journal of Social Psychology*, 20, 269–86.

Smith, E.R. and Henry, S. (1996). An ingroup becomes part of the self: Response time evidence. *Personality and Social Psychology Bulletin*, 22, 635–42.

Spears, R., Doosje, B., and Ellemers, N. (1997). Self-stereotyping in the face of threats to group status and distinctiveness: The role of group identification. *Personality and Social Psychology Bulletin*, 23, 538–53.

Srull, T.K. (1981). Person memory: Some tests of associative storage and retrieval models. *Journal of Experimental Psychology: Human Learning and Memory*, 7, 440–62.

Stern, L.D., Marrs, S., Millar, M.G., and Cole, E. (1984). Processing time and the recall of inconsistent and consistent behaviors of individuals and groups. *Journal of Personality and Social Psychology*, 47, 253–62.

Stryker, S. and Statham, A. (1985). Symbolic interaction and role theory. In G. Lindzey and E. Aronson (eds), *The Handbook of Social Psychology*, 3rd edn, Vol. 1. New York: Random House, pp. 311–78.

Susskind, J., Maurer, K., Thakkar, V., Hamilton, D.L., and Sherman, J.W. (in press). Perceiving individuals and groups: Expectancies, dispositional inferences, and causal attributions. *Journal of Personality and Social Psychology*.

Tajfel, H. (1969). Cognitive aspects of prejudices. *Journal of Social Issues*, 25, 79–97.

Tajfel, H. (1970). Experiments in intergroup discrimination. *Scientific American*, 223, 96–102.

Tajfel, H. (1978). *Differentiation between Social Groups: Studies in the social psychology of intergroup relations*. London: Academic Press.

Tajfel, H., Flament, C., Billig, M.G., and Bundy, R.F. (1971). Social categorization and intergroup behaviour. *European Journal of Social Psychology*, 1, 149–77.

Tajfel, H. and Turner, J.C. (1979). An integrative theory of intergroup conflict. In W.G. Austin and S. Worchel (eds), *The Social Psychology of Intergroup Relations*. Monterey, CA: Brooks-Cole, pp. 33–47.

Tajfel, H. and Turner, J.C. (1986). The social identity theory of intergroup behaviour. In S. Worchel and W.G. Austin (eds), *Psychology of Intergroup Relations*, 2nd edn. Chicago: Nelson-Hall, pp. 7–24.

Taylor, S.E. (1981). A categorization approach to stereotyping. In D.L. Hamilton (ed.), *Cognitive Processes in Stereotyping and Intergroup Behavior*. Hillsdale, NJ: Erlbaum, pp. 88–114.

Turner, J.C. (1987). Rediscovering the social group. In J.C. Turner, M.A. Hogg, P.J. Oakes, S.D. Reicher, and M.S. Wetherell, *Rediscovering the Social Group: A self-categorization theory*. Oxford: Blackwell, pp. 19–41.

Turner, J.C., Hogg, M.A., Oakes, P.J., Reicher, S.D., and Wetherell, M.S. (1987). *Rediscovering the Social Group: A self-categorization theory*. Oxford: Blackwell.

Turner, J.C. and Oakes, P.J. (1989). Self-categorization theory and social influence. In P.B. Paulus (ed.), *The Psychology of Group Influence*. Hillsdale, NJ: Erlbaum, pp. 233–75.

Turner, J.C., Oakes, P.J., Haslam, S.A., and McGarty, C. (1994). Self and collective: Cognition and social context. *Personality and Social Psychology Bulletin*, 20, 454–63.

Welbourne, J.L., Harasty, A.S., and Brewer, M.B. (1997). The impact of kindness and intelligence information on extremity ratings of groups and individuals. Paper presented at Midwest Psychological Association, Chicago.

Wilder, D. and Simon, A.F. (1998). Categorical and dynamic groups: Implications for social perceptions and intergroup behavior. In C. Sedikides, J. Schopler, and C.A. Insko (eds), *Intergroup Cognition and Intergroup Behavior*. Mahwah, NJ: Erlbaum, pp. 27–44.

Wyer, R.S., Bodenhausen, G.V., and Srull, T.K. (1984). The cognitive representation of persons and groups and its effect on recall and recognition memory. *Journal of Experimental Social Psychology*, 20, 445–69.

Yzerbyt, V.Y., Rocher, S.J., and Schadron, G. (1997). Stereotypes as explanations: A subjective essentialistic view of group perception. In R. Spears, P. Oakes, N. Ellemers, and S.A. Haslam (eds), *The Psychology of Stereotyping and Group Life*. Oxford: Blackwell, pp. 20–50.

5

Perceiving and Responding to Multiply Categorizable Individuals: Cognitive Processes and Affective Intergroup Bias

THERESA K. VESCIO, MILES HEWSTONE,
RICHARD J. CRISP, AND J. MARK RUBIN

Any given individual presents multiple possibilities for categorization. For example, a person may simultaneously be black, American, female, a doctor, a mother, and an athlete. Each category membership may provide a useful basis for categorization in that it can be used as a guide for one's own behavior toward the target and a standard against which their behavior can be interpreted. The questions of interest are (1) which categories become activated, and hence are used as a basis of categorization, and (2) what are the consequences of category activation.

Initial interest in the issue of multiple categorization stemmed from anthropological observations of reduced conflict in cultures containing crossed-societal structures (e.g., Brewer and Campbell, 1976; Evans-Pritchard, 1940; LeVine and Campbell, 1972; Murphy, 1957; Simmel, 1908). For example, intergroup conflict between villages was reduced when individuals in different villages shared family ancestry (Murphy, 1957); in other words, individuals were simultaneously ingroup members on one dimension and outgroup members on another.

Creating an analogous experimental intergroup situation, crossed-categorization researchers (e.g., Deschamps and Doise, 1978) have compared patterns of intergroup bias in situations involving a single categorization dimension (e.g., gender, called simple categorization conditions) and crossed conditions. In crossed conditions two categorization dimensions (e.g., race and gender) are orthogonally arrayed such that individuals can be classified according to four-

This work was supported by a Cardiff Research Initiative grant awarded to Miles Hewstone and Romin Tafarodi. We would like to thank Charles Judd, Monica Biernat, and Michael Hogg for helpful comments on an earlier version of this chapter.

	Race	
Gender	Black	White
Female	Black females	White females
Male	Black males	White males

Figure 5.1 The crossed-categorization design

subgroupings (e.g., black females, black males, white females, white males). The relationship between various individuals in crossed contexts differs, such that individuals either (1) share ingroup status on both categorization dimensions (i.e., double ingroups), (2) share ingroup status according to one dimension but not the other (i.e., partial outgroups), or (3) do not share ingroup status (i.e., double outgroups). Given the example depicted in figure 5.1, a black female shares double ingroup status with other black females (i.e., according to race and gender), shares partial ingroup status with white females (according to gender) and black males (according to race), and is a double outgroup member to white males (i.e., outgroup according to race and gender).

Extending Doise's (1978; based on Tajfel, 1959) category differentiation model, Deschamps and Doise (1978; Deschamps, 1977) suggested that category accentuation processes underlie intergroup bias effects and operate differently in simple vs. crossed conditions. In simple conditions, categorization presumably produces intergroup discrimination via the simultaneous accentuation of similarities within groups (e.g., women are viewed as more similar to one another) and differences between groups (e.g., men and women are viewed as increasingly different from one another; Doise, 1978; see also Doise, Deschamps, and Meyer, 1978). However, in crossed conditions the simultaneous accentuation of within-category similarities (i.e., convergence) and between-category differences (i.e., divergence) operating across conflicting categorization dimensions cancel each other out. Because groups defined by one dimension (e.g., racial groups) are composed of two subcategories based on the other dimension (e.g., males and females), the accentuation of within-category similarities is counteracted by the accentuation of differences between the subparts. Similarly, the accentuation of differences between categories (e.g., blacks and whites) is counteracted by the accentuation of similarities within the cross-cutting categories (e.g., gender). Processes of convergence and divergence operating across competing dimensions in crossed conditions, then, nullify category accentuation processes. Without the accentuation of similarities within and differences between categories, discrimination against outgroups (both partial and double) should be eliminated (Deschamps and Doise, 1978).

Consistent with their discrimination elimination predictions, Deschamps and Doise (1978) found that when participant sex was crossed with an experimentally created categorization (e.g., red and blue groups determined by pen color), as compared to simple conditions (e.g., sex only dimension available), there was an elimination of intergroup bias as assessed by general evaluations. In addition, Deschamps (1977) found that the accentuation of differences between classes of physical stimuli (i.e., intercategory differentiation) varied as predicted across categorization conditions. As compared to simple conditions (i.e., squares belonged to A or B groups based on size), intercategory differentiation was *reduced* when categorization dimensions were *crossed* (e.g., smallest A and B squares were blue and largest were green) and *enhanced* when dimensions were *superimposed* (e.g., A and B squares also green and blue, respectively).

Thus, in the original tests of category differentiation predictions Deschamps and Doise (1978; Deschamps, 1977) focused on empirical examinations of both (1) the underlying *categorization processes* involved in the *perception* of targets in crossed-categorization contexts, and (2) the predicted *consequences* of categorization processes for *responding*. These findings (and this theorizing) inspired a great deal of work. For example, researchers were quick to note methodological flaws in Deschamps and Doise's (1978) work (see Brown and Turner, 1979) and point out that patterns of intergroup discrimination in crossed conditions do not generally support the predictions of Deschamps and Doise (see Hewstone, Islam, and Judd, 1993; Migdal, Hewstone, and Mullen, 1998; Vanbeselaere, 1991). As a result, several additional perspectives on crossed categorization have been introduced. As we will discuss briefly, these perspectives vary in terms of the patterns of intergroup biases predicted and the mediating mechanisms hypothesized.

Unfortunately, however, attempts to test the viability of various perspectives have been hindered by the fact that subsequent researchers have been interested in testing discriminatory responding in crossed conditions, while neglecting to address mediational questions. Only one study has tested the generalizability of Deschamps's (1977) categorization findings to social contexts (Arcuri, 1982). And, although all crossed-categorization theorists assume the importance of underlying categorization processes (either as contributors or sole determinants of intergroup biases), not one has included measures intended to assess both these processes and presumed consequences. Rather, it has been assumed that categorization processes (and, for some researchers, social identity motives) similarly influence ingroup–outgroup responding along a host of dependent measures (e.g., liking, trait ratings, point allocations, social distance, perceived group variability); the operation of these mechanisms is inferred from emergent patterns of bias.

We raise two specific concerns with respect to this general approach. First, in the absence of research that demonstrates *both* the predicted intergroup bias effects and their mediation by critical theoretical variables, the viability of crossed-categorization perspectives cannot be critically tested. Second, the variety of dependent variables that have been used to assess intergroup bias may differ in their relationship to categorization processes. Some dependent variables may even be better conceptualized as mediating mechanisms. For example, Hewstone et al. (1993) included variability measures to test Tajfel's (1982) hypothesis that crossed conditions would result in a breakdown of the perceived homogeneity of outgroups. But perceived variability was treated as a form of intergroup bias, rather than as a mechanism which might produce this bias. This failure to distinguish between underlying mechanisms and their consequences is problematic for attempts to identify critical theoretical mechanisms.

Given the lack of attention to categorization processes, as well as the confusion added by the lack of clearly conceptualized dependent variables, it would not be an exaggeration to say that we are no more knowledgeable regarding the categorization processes underlying intergroup bias effects in crossed-categorization contexts today than we were following the publication of Deschamps and Doise's (1978; Deschamps, 1977) original research. Our primary goal in this chapter is to redirect attention to a consideration of both (1) the *categorization processes* involved in the perception of individuals who belong to multiple groups, and (2) the *potential consequences* of these processes. Attending to both categorization processes and consequential intergroup responding can be aided by a consideration of two areas of research: crossed-categorization research, which has strong social identity roots, and research that has used the name-matching paradigm (Taylor, Fiske, Etcoff, and Ruderman, 1978) to assess categorization of outcomes. Whereas crossed-categorization research has been primarily focused on intergroup bias as an outcome of manipulating categorization contexts, the name-matching paradigm has been used to examine how people categorize particular individuals who belong to multiple groups (e.g. Arcuri, 1982; Stangor, Lynch, Duan, and Glass, 1992). We suggest that a consideration of relevant name-matching paradigm findings can contribute to our understanding of the categorization processes that operate in crossed-categorization contexts, and aid attempts to assess both the viability and compatibility of crossed-categorization perspectives. Although crossed-categorization predictions have frequently been conceptualized as competing models (e.g., Hewstone et al., 1993; Migdal et al., 1998), we move away from this conceptualization and focus on the situations to which predictions speak and the compatibility among sets of predictions. In particular, we review relevant name-matching paradigm findings in the context of crossed-categorization theorizing to generate testable hypotheses regarding *when* (in what situations) and *how* (via what cognitive mechanisms) various patterns of intergroup bias emerge in crossed contexts. In the service of these broader aims, the following sections of this chapter (1) more clearly conceptualize the dependent variables, (2) review crossed-categorization perspectives and findings, and (3) consider relevant social cognition findings within the context of crossed-categorization theorizing.

Conceptualizing Dependent Variables

Since all of the theoretical perspectives we will review suggest that categorization processes drive or contribute to the perception of multiply categorizable individuals, one type of dependent variable in crossed-categorization research is *cognitive* in nature. Most basically, by cognitive measures we refer generally to assessments of the representations people have of ingroups and outgroups. As previously noted, categorization involves the simultaneous accentuation of within-category similarities and between-category differences (Doise, 1978; Tajfel, 1959). Therefore, measures that tap these accentuation processes are cognitive measures (e.g., intracategory similarity vs. intercategory differentiation, Arcuri, 1982; Stangor et al., 1992; intercategory differentiation, Deschamps, 1977; intracategory similarity, Hewstone et al., 1993). Of course, categorization also involves the heightened accessibility of relevant categories and corresponding categorical content. Therefore, response latency measures of category salience or accessibility (e.g., speed with which targets are categorized; Stroessner, 1996; Zarate and Sandoval, 1995; Zarate and Smith, 1990) and speed of responses to relevant stereotype content (e.g., Macrae, Bodenhausen, and Milne, 1995; Pendry and Macrae, 1996), provide additional cognitive measures of category activation and use.

Like other researchers (Brewer and Kramer, 1985; Brewer and Silver, 1978; Messick and Mackie, 1989; Vanbeselaere, 1991), we also distinguish between *behavioral* and *affective* (or evaluative) measures of intergroup bias. Behavioral measures are considered to be assessments of how people behave toward targets, and affective measures assess how positively or negatively one feels toward ingroups and outgroups. Though seemingly straightforward, this distinction requires two points of elaboration. First, we use affective in the most common social psychological sense to refer to the general positivity or negativity of one's feelings toward a target, which is distinct from emotional states (e.g., anger, pride; Hewstone et al., 1993; Islam and Hewstone, 1993) resulting from particular actions, outcomes, or attributions (e.g., Batson, Shaw, and Oleson, 1992).

Second, the distinction between affective and behavioral measures of intergroup bias is not based on the consequences of perceivers' responses for the targets. Although Vanbeselaere (1991) suggests that evaluative responses that have consequences for targets are similar to behaviors, we contend that such a conceptualization is based on the erroneous assumption that behaviors are impactful and affective responses (or evaluations) are not. Just as biases in affective (or evaluative) responses may vary in terms of the consequences they have for targets (for a discussion see Vanbeselaere, 1991), biases in behavioral responses may also vary in terms of the consequences they have for targets. For example, gender biases in the verbal praise directed toward female vs. male employees may have fewer or less meaningful consequences for female targets than biases in the allocation of resources (e.g., job assignments and pay), but both kinds of responding represent instances of behavioral discrimination (Biernat, Vescio, and Manis, 1998). Therefore, we suggest that the important defining feature of behaviors is that they are visibly linked to a source; behaviors are observable, whereas affective responses are not. If evaluative measures are to be used as proxy measures of behavioral discrimination, then they must involve a visible link between the evaluation and the evaluator (or at least the belief that such a link exists).

Behavioral measures of bias assess how people behave toward ingroups and outgroups (e.g., point allocations, helping, chair distance). In contrast, typical measures of intergroup bias in crossed-categorization research, which are the focus of this chapter, tend to be affective in nature. These include ingroup–outgroup comparisons along general adjective ratings (e.g., Eurich-Fulcer and Schofield, 1995; Hagendoorn and Henke, 1991; Hewstone et al., 1993), performance evaluations (Eurich-Fulcer and Schofield, 1995; Vanbeselaere, 1987, 1991), liking and social distance measures (Brewer, Ho, Lee, and Miller, 1987; Vanbeselaere, 1987, 1991) and measures of perceived self–group similarity (Brewer et al., 1987; Marcus-Newhall, Miller, Holtz, and Brewer, 1993; Vanbeselaere, 1991). Although these measures have typically been conceptualized as indices of discrimination, as Abrams and Hogg (1988) note, "experiments which have reported ingroup bias in terms of trait adjective ratings, affective ratings and performance evaluations . . . are, in effect, directly tapping the relative esteem in which subjects hold their own group" (p. 323). In other words, evaluative measures of intergroup bias are affective, not behavioral, in nature.

Crossed-categorization Predictions and Findings

As noted, Deschamps and Doise's (1978; Deschamps, 1977) original theorizing and research suggested the complete elimination of bias toward outgroups (both partial and double) in crossed-categorization conditions, but the majority of later findings have not supported these predictions (see Hewstone et al., 1993; Migdal et al., 1998; Vanbeselaere, 1991). Therefore, these predictions will not be rearticulated and we turn our attention to alternative predictions.

Crossed-categorization predictions

Social identity predictions

Whereas Deschamps and Doise's (1978) original theorizing represents a purely cognitive model of intergroup bias, social identity predictions posit more motivational bases of intergroup discrimination. Given two categories of equal salience and relevance to one's social identity, Brown and Turner (1979) suggest that the self-esteem-enhancing need to positively distinguish one's ingroup from outgroups will result in discrimination toward all outgroups (both partial and double outgroups). The same motivational processes that operate in simple categorization situations are expected to persist in crossed-categorization situations, but in an additive fashion. Brown and Turner argue that if categorization along a single dimension results in the positive evaluation of ingroups (+1) and the negative evaluation of outgroups (−1), then "the most parsimonious hypothesis is to assume that the effects of each single categorization combine additively" (1979, p. 373). Consistent with this notion, as table 5.1 indicates, Brown and Turner predict that individuals who are ingroup members along both dimensions will be evaluated positively (+1+1 = +2), individuals who are ingroup

Table 5.1 Theoretical models of intergroup bias effects in crossed-categorization contexts

Model	Mechanisms	Contrast weight			
		in–in	*in–out*	*out–in*	*out–out*
Social identity	Category differentiation and social identity motives. Outcome expected when dimensions are equally salient identity relevant.	+1 +1	+1 −1	−1 +1	−1 −1
		+2	0	0	−2
Category differentiation (elimination)	Cancellation of accentuation effects. Dimensions must be equal in terms of psychological significance.	+1	+1	+1	−3
Category differentiation (reduction)	Cancellation of accentuation effects. Dimensions must be equal in terms of psychological significance.	+2	0	0	−2
Category conjunction	Identity threat moderates conjunction effects.				
(dissimilarity) (similarity)	High identity threat Low identity threat	+3 +1	−1 +1	−1 +1	−1 −3
Category dominance	Relative difference in category salience.	+1	+1	−1	−1
Hierarchical ordering	Migdal et al. (1998) suggest that the relative difference in category salience and social identity threat mediate effects.	+4	0	−2	−2

In–in refers to double ingroup and out–out refers to the double outgroup. In–out and out–in refer to the partial outgroups and specify which dimensions are shared and nonshared. Category dominance and hierarchical predictions are presented such that category dominance occurs on the first dimension (for complete presentation of contrasts, see Hewstone et al., 1993; Migdal et al., 1998).

members along one dimension $(+1)$ and outgroup members along another (-1) dimension will be evaluated neutrally $(+1-1 = 0)$, and individuals who are outgroup members along both dimensions will be evaluated negatively $(-1-1 = -2)$. In other words, double ingroups will be rated more positively than partial outgroups, who are rated more positively than double outgroups (also called additive predictions, Brewer et al., 1987).

In the original statement of social identity predictions, Brown and Turner (1979) stated that "minimal intergroup discrimination has primarily a motivational and not cognitive basis" (p. 373; see also Turner, 1975). However, social identity theorists have since clearly articulated the importance of both categorization processes and social identity motives in producing intergroup bias (see Hogg and Abrams, 1988). As Turner (1981) states, category differentiation processes are a fundamental component of a social identity analysis and intergroup bias is assumed to be a result of *both* category differentiation processes and self-esteem-enhancing motives to positively differentiate ingroups from outgroups. Consistent with this notion, Oakes, Haslam, and Turner (1994) have noted that the following cognitive and emotional factors influence intergroup bias:

(1) the degree to which subjects identified with the relevant ingroup and (2) the salience of the relevant social categorization in the setting, (3) the importance and relevance of the comparative dimensions to ingroup identity, (4) the degree to which the groups were comparable on that dimensions (similar, close, ambiguously different), including, in particular, (5) the ingroup's relative status and the character of the perceived status differences between the groups. (p. 83)

These factors presumably determine the salience and social identity relevance of particular categories and hence influence motives to positively differentiate ingroups from outgroups in attempts to enhance self-esteem. Considering these factors in the context of Brown and Turner's (1979) theorizing, social identity-based intergroup bias effects are dependent on the *equivalence* of available categories along these dimensions; when categories are equivalent in terms of cognitive and emotional salience, they will contribute additively to intergroup bias (see table 5.1).

Modified category differentiation predictions

Category differentiation (elimination) predictions. Like Deschamps and Doise's (1978) original statement of category differentiation predictions, Vanbeselaere (1991) contends that (1) category accentuation processes drive intergroup biases, and (2) crossed-categorization conditions result in the elimination of intergroup biases because accentuation processes operating across competing dimensions cancel one another out. However, whereas Deschamps and Doise (1978) predicted the elimination of bias toward all outgroups (both partial and double), Vanbeselaere's modified version of the category differentiation (elimination) predictions suggests that accentuation processes operating across competing dimensions are in conflict (and cancel one another out) only in the perception of partial outgroups (i.e., adjacent subgroups). Given the four subgroups created by crossing categorization dimensions (e.g., figure 5.1), convergence among subgroups is expected when ingroup membership is shared and divergence between subgroups is expected when ingroup membership is not shared. In the perception of partial outgroup members (e.g., black females perceiving white females), convergence of similarities between subgroups is expected on the dimension in which ingroup membership is shared (i.e., accentuation of similarities within gender), and divergence between subgroups is expected on the nonshared dimension (i.e., accentuation of differences between blacks and whites). These competing processes cancel each other out, resulting in less differentiation between adjacent or partial outgroups and, hence, the elimination of bias toward partial outgroups. However, when perceiving diagonally opposing or double outgroups (e.g., black females perceiving white males), only processes of divergence operate and increased discrimination is expected. As table 5.1 indicates, the elimination of bias toward partial outgroups and increased bias toward double outgroups is expected.

Although category accentuation processes are assumed to be the sole mechanism underlying intergroup bias, additional factors may influence patterns of intergroup bias via their effect on category accentuation processes. For example, it can be inferred from Vanbeselaere's (1991) discussion of Diehl's (1989, 1990) work that categories may have to be of "equal psychological significance" for processes of convergence and divergence to cancel one another out. Equal psychological significance influences the operation of accentuation processes, which in turn produces biases in intergroup evaluations. Unfortunately, because Vanbeselaere mentions psychological significance only in passing and the meaning of the term is not clearly articulated, we cannot speak to the specific conditions under which intergroup bias effects would be expected to be strongest according to the category differentiation (elimination) perspective.

Category differentiation (reduction) predictions. Because Vanbeselaere (1991) interprets evidence of both the elimination and reduction of bias toward partial outgroups as consistent with predictions, Hewstone et al. (1993) have distinguished between strong and weak versions of category differentiation predictions. As table 5.1 indicates, the weaker category differentiation (reduction) predictions suggest the reduction, rather than the elimination, of bias toward partial outgroups and result in the same pattern of bias predicted by the social identity perspective.

Category conjunction predictions

Whereas the social identity perspective predicts that ingroup–outgroup categorization along equally salient dimensions combine additively, the category conjunction perspective suggests that categorization on available dimensions combine interactively. Individuals would be expected to be classified as ingroup members only if they are ingroup members according to both dimensions (Brewer et al., 1987; see table 5.1). Ingroup–outgroup definition at the subgroup level results in typical ingroup–outgroup biases; ingroups (i.e., double ingroups) are rated more positively than all outgroups (i.e., partial and double outgroups). We suggest that categorization of targets at the subgroup level may provide the basis for such intergroup biases. However, social identity-related motives may importantly determine the specific patterns of bias (for a discussion of the cognitive and motivational bases of intergroup bias, see Hogg and Abrams, 1988; Turner, 1981; Vanbeselaere, 1991; van Knippenberg, 1984). Speaking to the motivational bases of category conjunction patterns of intergroup bias, Miller and his colleagues (Miller, 1992; Vanman and Miller, 1992, as cited in Hewstone et al., 1993) have differentiated between category conjunction effects based on a consideration of identity threat. In identity-threatening situations, the predictions of Brewer et al. (1987) are expected to hold. Partial outgroups are discriminated against as much as double outgroups, referred to as the category conjunction (dissimilarity) predictions. According to Miller and his colleagues, self-esteem-enhancing needs to positively differentiate ingroups from outgroups are aroused and the dissimilarity, rather than similarity, of groups along categorization dimensions is more influential in judgments. In contrast, under conditions of low identity threat, Miller and his colleagues presented category conjunction (similarity) predictions, which suggest that partial outgroups will be rated as positively as double ingroups, but double outgroups will be rated negatively. Presumably, when identities are not threatened similarities along dimensions have greater impressional importance. As table 5.1 indicates, category conjunction (similarity) and category differentiation (elimination) perspectives predict the same pattern of intergroup biases.

Category dominance predictions

Whereas the previously outlined perspectives address crossed situations involving dimensions that are equivalent in terms of salience, when dimensions differ in terms of salience the dominant dimension may provide the sole basis for classification (Brewer et al., 1987). Ingroup–outgroup categorization, then, would be expected on the dominant (or salient) dimension, with nondominant dimensions being ignored. Specifically, when *situational cues* heighten the salience of one category distinction over the other a main effect of the dominant dimension would be expected. Dominant-category ingroups should be rated more positively than dominant-category outgroups (see table 5.1). However, when *individual differences* determine salience an interaction between perceiver attributes and categorization dimensions should emerge, the nature of which depends on the specific perceiver attributes and categorization criteria.

Hierarchical ordering predictions

Brewer et al. (1987) also introduced hierarchical ordering predictions, which suggest that multiple categories may be meaningful, but also differ in terms of impressional importance. According to hierarchical predictions, ingroup–outgroup classification according to one dimension is dependent upon prior categorization along the other dimension. Specifically, ingroup–outgroup differentiation on a second dimension would be greater among individuals classified as ingroups on the first dimension than for those classified as outgroups on that dimension (e.g., Brewer et al., 1987). For example, if race and gender are crossed (see figure 5.1), with race being relatively more salient, black females would rate other black females (i.e., double ingroup members) more favorably than black males (i.e., same-race partial outgroup), who are rated more positively than both white females (i.e., other-race partial outgroup) and white males (i.e., double outgroup). No differences in the evaluation of white females and white males should emerge (see table 5.1).

Brewer et al. (1987) did not discuss the theoretical mechanisms underlying these effects. However, Hewstone et al. (1993) suggested that the hierarchical predictions combine two previous perspectives. Hierarchical predictions imply (1) category dominance in that one dimension is relatively more salient, and (2) category conjunction in that the double ingroup is rated more positively than all other subgroups. Extrapolating from this suggestion, Migdal et al. (1998) suggested that hierarchical effects should be mediated by both differences in the relative salience of dimensions (i.e., mediator of the category dominance perspective) and social identity threat (i.e., mediator of the category conjunction perspectives). Although hierarchical predictions do imply differences in the relative salience of available dimensions, they do not suggest a category dominance effect *per se*; a single dimension does not provide the sole basis for responding. Therefore, while reviewing relevant social cognition findings we will be attentive to the categorization processes that could provide a basis for hierarchical patterns of intergroup bias. Namely, the categorization processes that characterize situations in which both available dimensions are salient, but also differ in terms of relative salience (e.g., situational salience).

Crossed-categorization findings: Affective intergroup bias effects

Migdal et al. (1998) meta-analyzed crossed-categorization findings that speak to key predictions[1] and found that five of the crossed-categorization perspectives provided highly significant accounts of emergent intergroup bias effects. These included: (1) the social identity and category differentiation (reduction) perspectives, which predict the same patterns of intergroup bias; (2) the category conjunction (dissimilarity) perspective; (3) the category dominance perspective; and (4) hierarchical ordering perspective. Pitting models against one another, Migdal and his colleagues further attempted to tease apart the viability of competing perspectives via attention to mediational factors. *Potency* (i.e., the ability of a categorization dimension to exert impact on the lives of group members), *ego-involvement* (or self-relevance, i.e., the capacity of a categorization dimension to involve or implicate the self of group members), *identity threat* (i.e., the capacity of a categorization dimension to evoke needs to discriminate against outgroups), and *similarity* (defined in terms of equivalence of available categorization dimensions along the prior three factors) indexes were compiled for each study based on the ratings of two independent judges. Mediational analyses revealed that similarity was the only factor that influenced the strength of predicted effects. As the similarity between dimensions increased in terms of salience, ego-involvement, and identity threat, there was an increase in the magnitude of category differentiation (reduction) and social identity-predicted patterns of intergroup bias (i.e., double ingroups rated positively, partial outgroups rated moderately, and double outgroups rated negatively). Migdal et al. interpreted these findings as support for the category differentiation (reduction) perspective, which they argued provided the most compelling account for the data.

However, we suggest that this conclusion is premature for two reasons. First, their interpretation of the mediational findings can be questioned in the presence of an alternative plausible explanation. According to Migdal et al. (1998), the tendency for double ingroups to be rated positively, partial outgroups moderately, and double outgroups negatively seems "to be driven by perceptual, cognitive mechanisms of the category differentiation (reduction) model, and not the more motivational mechanisms like ego-involvement...or identity threat" (p. 23). In other words, they contend that an index (i.e., similarity) comprised largely of social identity-related motivational factors (i.e., ego-involvement, identity threat) mediated the cognitive category differentiation (reduction) model. This conclusion requires both (1) speculation regarding the meaning of the term "psychological significance," which has not been clearly defined (see Vanbeselaere, 1991), and (2) assumptions that motivational factors directly influence accentuation processes, which are presumably the sole determinants of intergroup bias. In contrast, social identity theorists have suggested that category salience (e.g., Brown and Turner, 1979; Turner, 1981), social identity threat (e.g., Sachdev and Bourhis, 1984), and self-relevance (e.g., Brown and Turner, 1979; see also Oakes et al., 1994) importantly influence intergroup bias. Furthermore, social identity patterns of intergroup bias would only be expected to hold when categorization dimensions are equivalent on these factors (e.g., equal cognitive and emotional significance, see Brown and Turner, 1979).

Therefore, findings that social identity and category differentiation (reduction) predictive effects were strongest when dimensions were equivalent in terms of salience, identity threat, and ego-involvement also support social identity predictions.

Second, more generally, we question the extent to which Migdal et al.'s (1998) mediational analyses speak to critical questions regarding the mechanisms that drive intergroup bias effects in crossed-categorization contexts. Given the lack of direct assessments of theoretical mechanisms in original research, mediational tests were based on inferences regarding the likely factors that were operating in particular experiments. Although there was consensus among raters regarding the factors that appeared to be operating in specific studies, a consensual perception is not necessarily indicative of reality. For example, Arcuri (1982) crossed gender and academic status (faculty or student) to investigate whether categorization would ensue based on the less salient academic status dimension, as well as the salient gender dimension. Given societal gender stereotypes and the physical visibility of gender cues, many would agree with Arcuri's assumption that gender would be relatively more salient than academic status (see Brewer, 1988; Fiske and Neuberg, 1990). However, contrary to expectations, academic status was salient and used as the sole basis of categorization. Such counterintuitive findings point to the need for direct assessments of cognitive processes, as well as motivational factors, in mediational inquiries.

In sum, rather than illuminating our understanding of the mechanisms driving intergroup bias effects in crossed conditions, Migdal et al.'s (1998) work highlights the importance of including direct assessments of proposed cognitive mediators in original research. This would avoid the interpretational difficulty created when others must infer the likely factors that were operating in any given experiment. Given the ambiguous meaning of the mediational findings, we contend that Migdal et al.'s conclusion that the category differentiation (reduction) perspective provides the most compelling account for crossed-categorization effects is premature. Rather, we more conservatively suggest that the strongest conclusion that can be reached on the basis of the meta-analytic findings is that several perspectives rendered predictive effects of moderate size and provided highly significant accounts of the intergroup bias effects, and, hence, are plausible. These perspectives include: (1) the social identity and category differentiation (reduction) perspectives, which predict the pattern of intergroup bias; (2) the category dominance perspective; (3) the category conjunction (dissimilarity) perspective; and (4) the hierarchical ordering perspective.

Name-matching Paradigm Findings: Categorization Effects

In response to findings that rendered support for different crossed-categorization perspectives, Hewstone et al. (1993) suggested that "it would seem more appropriate, in present theorizing and future research, to concentrate on when (i.e., in which particular intergroup contexts) and how (i.e., by what processes) specific models operate, rather than on which model is correct" (p. 789). Consistent with both this suggestion and findings that several perspectives predict crossed-categorization effects (Migdal et al., 1998), we turn attention to relevant social cognition findings in attempts to generate hypotheses regarding when and how particular intergroup bias effects emerge in crossed contexts. Of particular interest are findings emerging from the name-matching paradigm (Taylor et al., 1978).

In the name-matching paradigm participants are presented with a group discussion in which each individual makes particular contributions. Based on the presence of physical cues, targets can be categorized according to single (e.g., gender) or multiple (e.g., gender and race) group memberships. After viewing the group discussion participants are presented with a recognition task requiring that they match statements made during the course of the discussion with the targets who made them. Based on Tajfel's (1959; Deschamps and Doise, 1978; Doise, 1978) accentuation principle, information that is stored according to a categorization criterion should be influenced by simultaneous processes of convergence and divergence (Taylor et al., 1978). As a result, when perceivers are later asked to match information presented in the context of the group discussion with the source of the contribution, more within-than between-category confusions are expected. For example, if targets are categorized according to gender, contributions made by a woman are more likely to be misattributed to another woman (i.e., intracategory error) than a man (i.e., intercategory error). Intra- and intercategory errors, then, provide a measure of category differentiation, analogous to Deschamps's (1977) interclass ratios.

Although analogous to crossed-categorization research, name-matching paradigm research has not investigated the influence of ingroup status on perception. Therefore, when reviewing name-matching findings, we will not refer to double ingroups, partial outgroups, and double outgroups, which are defined in relation to the perceivers' ingroup membership. Rather, we talk in terms of differentiation between adjacent subgroups, which share ingroup status on one but not the other dimension (e.g., within row or column comparisons, such as black women and white women; see figure 5.1), or diagonally opposite subgroups, which are outgroups to one another on both dimensions (e.g., black women and white men). Despite the lack of focus on perceiver ingroup status, a consideration of relevant findings from the name-matching paradigm is informative to crossed-categorization theorizing. As noted, all crossed-categorization perspectives assume important underlying category differentiation processes, which involve the accentuation of similarities within and differences between groups. Regardless of ingroup membership, if perceivers categorize targets according to a dimension (e.g., sex), similarities among members of both ingroups and outgroups, as well as differences between groups, should be exaggerated. Therefore, a consideration of the relative fit between categorization outcomes emerging from name-matching research and intergroup biases emerging from crossed-categorization research is straightforward and informative to crossed-categorization theorizing.

Category dominance

Arcuri (1982) manipulated academic status (student or teacher) and target sex in the name-matching paradigm to create simple (i.e., sex only available dimension), superimposed (e.g., all women teachers and all men students), and crossed (i.e., male teachers, female teachers, male students, female students) conditions. In part, he was interested in whether category differentiation would occur on the basis of a less salient (i.e., academic status), as well as a salient (i.e., target sex), dimension. Arcuri (1982) found that perceivers did categorize targets on the basis of the relatively less salient academic status dimension. When academic status and sex covaried (i.e., superimposed condition), category differentiation was greater (e.g., more intra-than intercategory confusions) than in situations in which only target sex was available (i.e., simple condition). There was also evidence that categories were differentiated on the basis of academic status in crossed conditions (i.e., more intra-than interacademic status confusions). Contrary to expectations, however, there was no evidence that targets were categorized on the basis of sex.

Multiple salient dimensions that differ in terms of relative salience: Dominance and inhibition

Although initially surprising, Arcuri's (1982) findings are consistent with recent models of category activation and inhibition (e.g., Bodenhausen and Macrae, in press; Macrae et al., 1995; see also Stroessner, 1996). According to Bodenhausen and Macrae, when multiple salient dimensions are mutually incompatible (i.e., in competition for limited attentional resources), both excitatory and inhibitory mechanisms operate. One dimension dominates categorization processes, whereas the other is inhibited. For example, Macrae et al. (1995) found that when perceivers were presented with an Asian woman, who could potentially be categorized on two salient dimensions (sex and/or ethnicity), the relatively more salient (i.e., primed or situationally relevant) dimension was activated and the competing dimension was inhibited. Specifically, using a lexical decision task, people were faster to verify stereotypic words associated with the dominant category (indicative of activation) and slower to verify stereotypic words associated with the nondominant category (indicative of inhibition) than under control conditions of nonactivation.

The simultaneous arousal of excitatory and inhibitory mechanisms appears to be particularly likely in situations in which experimental manipulations or demands (1) heighten the relevance of one salient categorization dimension over another (e.g., Macrae et al., 1995) or (2) require attention to a nonsalient (or less salient) dimension in the presence of a competing salient dimension (Stroessner, 1996). Responding in such situations requires both a focusing of attention to the situationally relevant dimension and inhibition of the competing attention-grabbing dimension (Stroessner, 1996; for a discussion of category salience see also Zarate and Sandoval, 1995; Zarate and Smith, 1990). As Arcuri (1982) notes, his experimental context presented perceivers with a situation in which cues (i.e., group discussion about academic issues) heightened the relevance of a less salient dimension (i.e., academic status) over a salient dimension (i.e., target sex). Consistent with the notion that such situations arouse both excitatory and inhibitory mechanisms, Arcuri found weak categorization effects on the basis of the situationally relevant academic status dimension (compared to the strong categorization effects on the salient dimension in simple conditions). The competing salient sex dimension also appears to have been inhibited. There was both (1) less categorization according to target sex in crossed as compared to simple conditions and (2) a reversal of the expected pattern of intra-vs. intersex errors (i.e., fewer intra-than intercategory errors than in conditions of nonactivation). Both the weaker category differentiation according to academic status (see Stroessner, 1996) and the reversal of expected category differentiation patterns on the sex dimension are consistent with a category activation–inhibition interpretation rather than the category differentiation perspective (cf. Arcuri, 1982), which suggests that accentuation processes operating across competing dimensions cancel one another to produce less differentiation along each dimension.

A single salient categorization dimension: Dominance (without corresponding inhibition)

Whereas dominance effects involve the arousal of both excitatory and inhibitory mechanisms when multiple dimensions are salient, categorization on the basis of a dominant dimension does not require the simultaneous inhibition of competing dimensions when a single dimension is salient (e.g., Stroessner, 1996). For example, Stangor et al. (1992) crossed salient target race or sex (Study 4, no goal conditions, and Study 5, respectively) with trivial clothing cues (e.g., shirt color) and found that categorization occurred on salient dimensions (i.e., more intra-than interrace/sex errors), but trivial cues were ignored. There was no evidence of inhibition. In addition, consistent with the notion that dominance effects emerge when individual differences heighten the salience of a dimension (Brewer et al., 1987), Stangor et al. (1992, Study 3) found that high-prejudiced people differentiated targets on the basis of race, but low-prejudiced participants did not. Although these findings were not as reliable as the situational dominance effects, they provide additional evidence that categorization on the basis of a dominant dimension, without corresponding inhibition, characterizes situations in which a single dimension is salient.

Subgroup categorization

Category dominance has frequently been assumed to be the default impression formation outcome (e.g., Bodenhausen and Macrae, in press; Brewer, 1988; Macrae et al., 1995; Fiske and Neuberg, 1990), but it is not the only potential outcome. Subgroup categorization would be expected to the extent that subgroup classification provides perceivers with more information than classification on broad dimensions (Brewer, Dull, and Lui, 1981; Deaux, Winton, Crowley, and Lewis, 1985; Hamilton, 1981; Pendry and Macrae, 1996; Taylor, 1981). This is particularly likely when crossed contexts involve commonly occurring category conjunctions (e.g., black male, black female, white male, white female) for which people may have well-defined beliefs. As Bodenhausen and Macrae note, such subgroup beliefs may have unique stereotypic characteristics (see Smith and Osherson, 1984) and "come to function as autonomous categories in their own right," in that they "compete with other possible categorizations ... for impressional dominance."

Of particular relevance to crossed-categorization predictions, Stangor et al. (1992) crossed target race and sex in the context of the name-matching paradigm to create common subgroups (e.g., black women, black men, white women, white men). This allowed for tests of two potential categorization outcomes. On the one hand, targets may be categorized independently in terms of both their race and sex group membership (e.g., black women categorized as both black and female). If this is the case, two main effects (more intra-than interrace *and* sex errors) would be expected and manipulations of category salience (e.g., accessibility) should alter the use of the dimensions. On the other hand, if perceivers have well-developed beliefs about frequently encountered category conjunctions, subgroup categorization should ensue (i.e., more intra- than intersubgroup errors). In addition, to the extent to which subgroup beliefs function as autonomous categories, manipulations that heighten the salience of a single broad dimension (e.g., race over sex) should not influence categorization.

Stangor et al. (1992) found evidence of subgroup categorization. Although targets were differentiated on the basis of both race and sex (i.e., more intra-than interrace/sex errors), these effects were subsumed by subgrouping effects (i.e., more intra-than intersubgroup errors). Importantly, subgroup categorization was greater than would be estimated based on the strength of categorization along broad individual dimensions (see Stangor et al., 1992). Manipulations of broad dimensional salience (race or sex) also did not influence categorization. Furthermore, consistent with the notion that subgroup categorization occurs when perceivers have well-developed subgroup beliefs (Bodenhausen and Macrae, in press), subgrouping effects only emerged in the perception of commonly encountered subgroups (see Studies 4 and 5).

Categorization on broad independent dimensions

There is also evidence that targets are categorized in terms of broad independent dimensions. These findings emerge when (1) available dimensions are equally salient, (2) dimensions are mutually informative, and (3) perceivers do not have well-developed subgroup beliefs. For example, when target race (black or white) was crossed with attitude stance on a race-relevant issue (i.e., pro- or anti-White Student Union; WSU), Biernat and Vescio (1993) found that categorization occurred along both race and attitude dimensions. First, category differentiation was greater when the two dimensions were confounded (i.e., all black targets were anti-WSU and white targets were pro-WSU; superimposed condition) than when a single dimension was available (i.e., simple conditions). Second, within crossed conditions, targets were categorized independently on the basis of race *and* attitude, as well as at the subgroup level. However, subgroup categorization effects (i.e., more intra-than intersubgroup confusions) were not independent of the categorization on the individual dimensions.

In sum, different categorization effects emerge in different crossed contexts. Both the salience of and compatibility among available dimensions determine the specific categorization outcomes. When dimensions are equally salient and mutually informative, categorization occurs along both broad dimensions. Categorization along independent dimensions also combines to produce subgroup differentiation. In the presence of commonly occurring subgroups (e.g., black men, black women, white men, white women), however, categorization occurs at the level of the relatively more informative subgroup level (see also Pendry and Macrae, 1996). Presumably, beliefs about familiar subgroups come to function as independent categories. Finally, in situations of unequal categorization dimension salience, one of two category dominance effects emerges. When a single dimension is salient, categorization occurs on the salient dimension and the nonsalient dimension is ignored (i.e., no inhibition). However, when multiple salient dimensions differ in terms of relative salience, activation of the dominant dimension requires the simultaneous inhibition of the competing dimension. We now turn attention to a consideration of the fit among these four categorization processes and the four viable predicted patterns of intergroup bias.

Comparing social cognition findings and crossed-categorization predictions

In comparing relevant social cognition findings and crossed-categorization predictions we are interested in issues of relative compatibility. That is, to what extent could the categorization effects emerging from social cognition research support the patterns of intergroup bias predicted by crossed-categorization perspectives? In answering this question we consider the situational constraints and/

or cognitive bases implied by each viable crossed-categorization perspective. We then turn attention to relevant social cognition findings that (1) emerge from the situations to which particular crossed-categorization perspectives speak and/or (2) produce the particular patterns of category differentiation implied by crossed-categorization perspectives. In comparing these two literatures it is our goal to generate testable hypotheses regarding both the situations to which various crossed-categorization predictions speak and the cognitive bases of inter-group bias.

Social identity and category differentiation (reduction) patterns of intergroup bias

Although the original statements of social identity (Brown and Turner, 1979) and category differentiation (Deschamps, 1977; Deschamps and Doise, 1978; see also Vanbeselaere, 1987, 1991) perspectives were in conflict (i.e., predicted different patterns of bias resulting from different mechanisms), revised state-ments of these two perspectives are largely compatible. Social identity theorists (e.g., Turner, 1981) have since discussed the category differentiation processes underlying social identity-based intergroup bias effects. Likewise, category dif-ferentiation theorists (e.g., Vanbeselaere, 1991) have modified predictions and discussed the importance of social comparison processes. More recent revised statements of these two perspectives predict the same patterns of inter-group bias (i.e., double ingroups rated more positively than partial outgroups, who are rated more positively than double outgroups) as a result of the opera-tion of both critical category differentiation and social comparison processes.

Consistent with the notion that the perspectives are more compatible than conflicting, findings from the name-matching paradigm support the cognitive predictions of both perspectives. When available categorization dimensions were equally salient, targets were differentiated on the basis of both broad dimensions, which combined to produce subgroup differentiation (Biernat and Vescio, 1993) as predicted by the social identity perspective. However, the specific pattern of subgroup differentiation emerging from crossed conditions was consistent with the category differentiation (reduction) predictions. Subgroups that did not share ingroup status (e.g., diagonally opposite subgroups; see figure 5.1) were more strongly differentiated from one another than subgroups that shared ingroup status on one dimension but not the other (e.g., adjacent subgroups, within row or column comparisons; see figure 5.1). In addition, as predicted by the category differentiation (reduction) perspective, differentiation on broad dimensions was weaker in crossed compared to simple conditions. Specifically, Biernat and Vescio (1993) found that categorization on the basis of attitude stance and race was weaker in crossed than simple and superimposed conditions, res-pectively (there was no simple comparison race condition; see also Marcus-Newhall et al., 1993).[2] These findings are consistent with the notion that competing category differentiation processes (i.e., accentuation of similarities within and differences between categories) cancel one another in the perception of adjacent subgroups of crossed conditions (Vanbeselaere, 1991).

Such subgroup differentiation would be expected to support patterns of intergroup bias predicted by the social identity and category differentiation (reduction) perspectives; differentiation between diagonally opposite subgroups is greater than differentiation between adjacent subgroups. However, this pattern of subgroup differentiation only emerged when (1) categorization dimensions were equally salient and (2) the subgroups created by crossing dimensions were not highly familiar. This suggests that an additional situational constraint is necessary. Namely, social identity and category differentiation (reduction) patterns of intergroup bias would be expected when crossed-categorization dimensions are equally salient, but the subgroups of crossed conditions are not commonly occurring (i.e., perceivers do not have developed subgroup beliefs).

Category conjunction patterns of intergroup bias

The category conjunction (dissimilarity) perspective predicts that targets will be classified as ingroup members only if they share ingroup membership on both available dimensions. This implies that categorization occurs at the level of the subgroup and that the patterns of predicted intergroup bias represent a simple ingroup–outgroup pattern. Ingroups (i.e., double ingroups) are rated more positively than outgroups (i.e., partial and double outgroups). Although the category differentiation (dissimilarity) predictions imply subgroup categorization, the situations under which predicted patterns of intergroup bias would be expected have not been discussed. We consider (1) the extent to which categorization at the subgroup level could potentially support category conjunction (dissimilarity) patterns of intergroup bias and (2) the specific situations under which such social cognition findings emerge. This provides a basis for drawing inferences regarding the situations under which category conjunction (dissimilarity) effects would be expected to hold.

Subgroup differentiation is evidenced by more intra- than inter-subgroup confusions, which are independent of the differentiation on broad dimensions. In addition, if subgroup categorization processes underlie category conjunction (dissimilarity) intergroup bias effects, confusions between targets belonging to adjacent subgroups (e.g., subgroups that share ingroup status on one but not the other dimension) should be similar to and as infrequent as confusions between targets belonging to diagonally opposite subgroups (e.g., subgroups who are outgroups on both dimensions). In other words, subgroups should be equally differentiated from one another, supporting the notion that category conjunction (dissimilarity) patterns of intergroup bias represent typical ingroup–outgroup effects. Consistently, Stangor et al. (1992) found that within-subgroup confusions were significantly greater than any kind of between-subgroup confusions. There were also no significant differences between kinds of subgroup confusions; confusions among adjacent subgroups and diagonally opposing subgroups (see figure 5.1) were similarly infrequent. Importantly, subgroup categorization effects only emerged in the case of commonly occurring category conjunctions, which are the conditions under which perceivers are likely to have well-developed subgroup beliefs. It can be inferred that patterns of ingroup–outgroup bias predicted by the category conjunction (dissimilarity) perspective should emerge when perceivers have well-developed subgroup beliefs (i.e., subgroup stereotypes). Consistent with this notion, category conjunction (dissimilarity) intergroup bias effects have been found only in contexts in which perceivers are likely to have well-developed beliefs about the crossed-category conjunctions (e.g., desegregated schools, Rogers, Miller, and Hennigan, 1981; Schofield and Sagar, 1977).

Category dominance and hierarchical patterns of intergroup bias

There are two crossed-categorization perspectives that speak to situations of unequal dimension salience. Category dominance predictions suggest that a single categorization dimension influences responding, such that dominant ingroups are rated more positively than dominant outgroups. In contrast, hierarchical ordering predictions assume that both dimensions influence responding, but differ with respect to impressional importance. The implication is that category dominance patterns of intergroup bias would be expected in situations in which a single dimension dominates perceptions (e.g., race is crossed with clothing color; Stangor et al., 1992), whereas hierarchical patterns of intergroup bias would be expected when multiple meaningful dimensions differ in terms of relative salience. Two different categorization outcomes characterize these situations. When a single dimension (of multiply available dimensions) is meaningful, targets are categorized in terms of the dominant dimension with no corresponding inhibition (e.g., Stangor et al., 1992). However, when multiple meaningful dimensions differ in terms of relative salience, targets are categorized in terms of the situationally dominant dimension and competing salient dimensions are inhibited (e.g., Macrae et al., 1995; Stroessner, 1996). The obvious question concerns the potential relationship between these two categorization outcomes and crossed-categorization predictions that speak to situations of unequal dimensional salience.

Considering the relationship between dominance intergroup bias effects and dominance categorization processes (without inhibition) is straightforward. Dominance patterns of intergroup bias (i.e., dominant ingroup–outgroup biases) necessitate the differentiation of groups on the basis of the dominant category and have been suggested to emerge when categorization dimensions differ in terms of relative salience (e.g., Brewer et al., 1987; Hewstone et al., 1993; Migdal et al., 1998). Consistent with this notion, when a single categorization dimension is salient groups are differentiated on the basis of the dominant dimension (i.e., more intra-than intercategory confusions) and not the nonsalient dimension (e.g., Stangor et al., 1992, Study 5). However, such categorization effects only emerge in situations in which a single dimension (of multiple available dimensions) is salient. This suggests a slight revision to category dominance predictions; dominance patterns of intergroup bias would be expected when a single dimension is salient (i.e., absolute rather than relative salience is important).

As noted, simultaneous excitatory and inhibitory cognitive mechanisms operate in the situations under which hierarchical predictions would be expected to hold. Although a consideration of the potential fit among dominance and inhibition categorization processes and hierarchical intergroup bias effects is more speculative, there is an additional similarity among the situations under which the two effects emerge that suggests their potential compatibility. Namely, dominance and inhibition categorization outcomes only emerge to the extent that perceivers have preexisting cognitive representations for the groups defined by available dimensions. Inhibition refers to the inhibition of cognitive representations, not the inhibition of attention to cues. Therefore, excitatory and inhibitory mechanisms are only aroused in the perception of meaningful social categories. Similarly, hierarchical intergroup biases have been found only in situations in which highly meaningful social dimensions have been crossed. For example, Brewer et al. (1987) found evidence of hierarchical intergroup biases when nationality and gender were crossed. Nationality was dominant, but not surprisingly, gender also influenced the responding of their seventh-grade participants (see also Hewstone et al., 1993), who would be expected to have well-developed cognitive representations and affect associated with gender.

We suggest that excitatory and inhibitory cognitive mechanisms could potentially support hierarchical patterns of intergroup bias. This is based on the following logic. Because mutual excitatory and inhibitory mechanisms are aroused only when perceivers have cognitive representations of salient categorization dimensions (i.e., dimensions define meaningful social categories), it is logical to assume the existence of related intergroup affect. Categorization along dominant dimensions, then, should result in strong ingroup–outgroup bias as a result of both the differentiation of targets according to meaningful social categories and the arousal of related intergroup affect. Competing salient dimensions, the cognitive representations for which are inhibited, might also be expected to exert a weaker influence on ingroup–outgroup biases to the extent that there is a dissociation between cognitive representations and intergroup affect. As all theories of emotion suggest (e.g., cognitive theories, Lazarus, 1966; Mandler, 1975; Schachter and Singer, 1962; somatic theories, Ekman and Friesen, 1975; Izard, 1977; Leventhal, 1980; Tomkins, 1962, 1963; see also Zajonc and Markus, 1984), affect is represented in terms of abstract associative structures that cannot be directly accessed. Therefore, the inhibition of categorical information would not necessarily render intergroup affect uninfluential. Specifically, in situations in which salient dimensions differ in terms of relative salience (e.g., situational salience), categorization along the dominant dimension involves the simultaneous inhibition of the competing salient dimension. Categorization of targets in terms of the dominant dimension would be expected to result in a strong ingroup–outgroup bias main effect. Although the competing dimension is inhibited, intergroup affect could potentially produce a weak ingroup–outgroup main effect. The additive combination of the strong dominant category main effect, the weak inhibited category main effect, as well as the interaction between the two, would render hierarchical intergroup bias effects.

The suggestion that categorization mechanisms of dominance and inhibition may provide the basis for hierarchical patterns of intergroup bias is admittedly speculative. However, as we have noted, generating testable hypotheses regarding both the situations to which predictions speak and the potential cognitive bases of each crossed-categorization pattern of intergroup bias was the primary goal of this chapter. Given a consideration of both the situations to which hierarchical predictions speak and the category differentiation required to support such intergroup biases, we believe that our predictions regarding the potential excitatory and inhibitory cognitive bases of hierarchical patterns of intergroup bias provide a viable possibility in light of the existing data. Importantly, the viability of these predictions is strengthened given the absence of other emergent categorization processes that could support hierarchical patterns of intergroup bias.

Summary and Conclusions

Our primary goal in this chapter was to redirect attention to both the categorization processes involved in the perception of crossed contexts and consequential intergroup bias. To this point, crossed-categorization researchers have paid little attention to mediational questions in general or attempts to test critical cognitive mechanisms in particular. This lack of mediational focus is, at least in part, due to the lack of specificity with which various crossed-categorization predictions have been articulated; predictions have typically been vague with respect to situational constraints and/or critical cognitive mechanisms. In reviewing relevant findings, we were interested in the extent to which the four categorization processes emerging from social cognition research could potentially support the four patterns of intergroup bias predicted by the viable crossed-categorization perspectives. We suggested that a consideration of the compatibility among findings emerging from these two literatures provides a basis for inferring the cognitive mechanism and/or situational constraints that determine patterns of intergroup bias.

Our analysis of the relationship between these two literatures renders testable hypotheses regarding both (1) the cognitive mechanisms underlying each crossed-categorization perspective and (2) the situations under which various crossed-categorization patterns of intergroup bias would be expected. Rather than conceptualizing crossed-categorization perspectives as competing models (e.g., Hewstone et al., 1993; Migdal et al., 1998), we suggest that different patterns of intergroup bias would be expected in different crossed contexts. In particular, the specific pattern of intergroup bias would be expected to be determined by the salience of, and compatibility among, available categorization dimensions. More specifically, we presented the following hypotheses:

1 *Category differentiation/social identity predictions.* When categorization dimensions are equally salient and mutually informative, targets will be differentiated on the basis of both broad dimensions as well as at the level of subgroups (Brown and Turner, 1979). Specifically, categorization along broad dimensions will combine such that differentiation between diagonally opposite subgroups (i.e., double outgroups) is greater than differentiation between adjacent subgroups (i.e., partial outgroups). Presumably, category accentuation processes operating across competing dimensions in the perception of adjacent subgroups (or partial outgroups) cancel one another out, such that adjacent subgroups are less differentiated from one another than diagonally opposite subgroups (Vanbeselaere, 1991). As a result, double ingroups are rated more positively than partial outgroups, who are rated more positively than double outgroups. However, these patterns would only be expected to hold to the extent that perceivers do not have well-developed subgroup beliefs.

2 *Category conjunction (dissimilarity) predictions.* When perceivers have cognitive representations for the subgroups created by category conjunctions (e.g., subgroup stereotypes), subgroups should function as autonomous categories. Categorization, then, occurs at the relatively more informative subgroup level, resulting in subgroup differentiation. As a result, ingroups (i.e., double ingroups) are rated more positively than outgroups (i.e., partial and double outgroups).

3 *Category dominance predictions.* In situations in which one available dimension is salient, categories are differentiated on the basis of the salient dimension and nonsalient categories are ignored. Differentiation along the dominant dimension provides the basis for ingroup–outgroup bias. Dominant ingroups should be rated more positively than dominant outgroups, resulting in a single main effect.

4 *Hierarchical predictions.* When multiple salient dimensions differ in terms of relative salience, categorization on the dominant dimension requires the simultaneous inhibition of the competing salient dimension. A strong ingroup–outgroup bias main effect would be expected to emerge on the dominant dimension. Although the nondominant dimension is inhibited, a weak ingroup–outgroup bias main effect may emerge on the inhibited dimension as a result of associated category affect (i.e., intergroup affect). The strong main effect on the dominant dimension, the weak main effect on the inhibited dimension, as well as the interaction between the two, are predicted

to combine additively to produce hierarchical intergroup bias effects. Double ingroups should be rated more positively than partial outgroups that share ingroup status on the dominant dimension, which are rated more positively than both partial outgroups that are outgroup members on the dominant dimension *and* double outgroups (see table 5.1). Because inhibition occurs only when perceivers have cognitive representations for the groups defined by available dimensions, hierarchical intergroup biases should only emerge in the perception of meaningful groups.

All four sets of predictions specify the situations under which predicted patterns of intergroup bias would be expected to hold and the cognitive bases of such effects. However, the degree to which our predictions are similar to, or different from, the original statements of each perspective differs. To the extent that crossed-categorization theorists have previously articulated the cognitive bases of particular patterns of predicted intergroup bias effects and the social cognition findings supported those cognitive mechanisms, the revisions to predictions included slight modifications of statements concerning situational constraints. For example, the category dominance predictions remain as originally stated, but we have modified the situations under which such patterns might be expected to emerge. Whereas the original statement of category dominance predictions implied that relative differences in the salience of available categorization dimensions mediate category dominance effects, the social cognition findings suggest that categorization on the basis of a single dimension occurs in situations in which a single dimension is meaningful or attention grabbing (e.g., only one dimension salient in an absolute sense). Although this represents a minor alteration of predictions, it is an important difference, particularly in light of the categorization processes (i.e., dominance and inhibition) that characterize situations involving multiple salient dimensions, which differ in terms of relative salience.

Our articulation of category differentiation (reduction)/social identity predictions generally restates the category differentiation (reduction) perspective, while adding mention of the fact that such effects would only be expected when dimensions are mutually informative and when perceivers do not have well-developed subgroup beliefs. However, our statement of these predictions also implies that we are taking a stance in favor of the category differentiation (reduction) perspective over the social identity perspective. On the one hand, this is true. The subgroup differentiation could potentially support the predicted pattern of intergroup bias in the absence of instantiated social comparison motives. For example, the social cognition findings are consistent with the category differentiation (reduction) predictions in terms of (1) the specific patterns of subgroup differentiation, (2) the stronger category differentiation along individual dimensions in superimposed as compared to simple conditions, and (3) the weakening of differentiation on individual dimensions in the crossed as compared to simple conditions. In addition, Marcus-Newhall et al. (1993, Study

1) found evidence that category differentiation (see table 2), as well as behavioral discrimination (i.e., reward allocation), was reduced in crossed as compared to superimposed conditions. They also provided evidence that category differentiation mediated behavioral discrimination. This suggests that category differentiation mechanisms may provide both the necessary and sufficient conditions for intergroup bias effects. On the other hand, category differentiation did not perfectly mediate behavioral discrimination (see Marcus-Newhall et al., 1993) and the categorization findings also support the predictions of the social identity perspective, which suggest that independent categorization effects combine to produce subgroup differentiation. Therefore, although we do state the predictions in terms of cognitive mechanisms, we consider the question of the relative importance of cognitive and motivational mechanisms to be an empirical problem. Given that both perspectives posit the importance of underlying category differentiation processes, predictions regarding critical cognitive mechanisms need not imply support for one perspective over the other.

This chapter undoubtedly raises more questions than it answers but, as intended, the questions raised are empirical questions that have answers. Just as an integrated consideration of social cognition and crossed-categorization theorizing and findings provided the basis for generating hypotheses, a mutual consideration of the methods the two literatures rely upon provides the tools for addressing the empirical questions raised. Testing the viability of the predictions presented requires both the demonstration of predicted patterns of ingroup bias *and* their mediation by critical theoretical mechanisms.

Notes

1　Research that collapsed across mean evaluations of partial and/or double outgroups to create indexes of outgroup evaluation (e.g., Commins and Lockwood, 1978; Deschamps and Doise, 1978; Diehl, 1990; Marcus-Newhall et al., 1993; Rehm, Lilli, and van Eimeren, 1988) effectively prevented an examination of key predictions and was excluded from the meta-analysis. In addition, only studies that measured intergroup bias as the relative positivity of ingroup vs. outgroup evaluations (i.e., affective measures), which is the most common operationalization of intergroup bias (e.g., Mullen, Brown, and Smith, 1992), were included.

2　Arcuri (1982) also suggested that his findings support category differentiation predictions. However, his data are difficult to interpret for two reasons. First, as previously discussed, category differentiation along the sex dimension in crossed conditions is less meaningful as the categorization dimension appears to have been inhibited. Second, the academic status categorization effects in the crossed conditions were compared to the strength of the sex categorization effects in the simple condition. As Arcuri noted, the *a priori* assumption was that academic status would be relatively less salient. The differences in the magnitude of the effects in crossed vs. simple conditions may be due to preexisting differences in the relative salience of available categorization dimensions in the two conditions, rather than the fact that category accentuation processes operating across competing dimensions canceled one another out.

References

Abrams, D. and Hogg, M.A. (1988). Comments on the motivational status of self-esteem in social identity and intergroup discrimination. *European Journal of Social Psychology*, 18, 317–34.

Arcuri, L. (1982). Three patterns of social categorization in attribution memory. *European Journal of Social Psychology*, 12, 271–82.

Batson, C.D., Shaw, L.L., and Oleson, K.C. (1992). Differentiating affect, mood, and emotion: Toward functionality based conceptual distinctions. In M.S. Clark (ed.), *Emotion: Review of personality and social psychology*, Vol. 13. Newbury Park, CA: Sage, pp. 294–326.

Biernat, M. and Vescio, T.K. (1993). Categorization and stereotyping: Effects of group context on memory and social judgment. *Journal of Experimental Social Psychology*, 29, 166–202.

Biernat, M., Vescio, T.K., and Manis, M. (1998). Judging and behaving toward members of stereotyped groups: A shifting standards perspective. To appear in C. Sedikides, J. Schopler, and C. Insko (eds), *Intergroup Cognition and Intergroup Behavior*. Hillsdale, NJ: Erlbaum.

Bodenhausen, G.V. and Macrae, C.N. (in press). Stereotype activation and inhibition. In R.S. Wyer, Jr, (ed), *Advances in Social Cognition*, Vol. 11, *Stereotype Activation and Inhibition*. Mahwah, NJ: Erlbaum.

Brewer, M.B. (1988). A dual process model of impression formation. In T.K. Srull and R.S. Wyer, Jr (eds), *Advances in Social Cognition*, Vol. 1. Hillsdale, NJ: Lawrence Erlbaum, pp. 65–76.

Brewer, M. B. and Campbell, D. T. (1976). *Ethnocentrism and Intergroup Attitudes: East African evidence*. New York: Sage.

Brewer, M.B., Dull, L., and Lui, L. (1981). Perceptions of the elderly: Stereotypes as prototypes. *Journal of Personality and Social Psychology*, 41, 656–70.

Brewer, M.B., Ho, H.-K., Lee, J.-Y., and Miller, N. (1987). Social identity and social distance among Hong Kong schoolchildren. *Personality and Social Psychology Bulletin*, 13, 156–65.

Brewer, M.B. and Kramer, R.M. (1985). The psychology of intergroup attitudes and behavior. *Annual Review of Psychology*, 36, 219–43.

Brewer, M.B. and Silver, M. (1978). Ingroup bias as a function of task characteristics. *Journal of Social Psychology*, 8, 393–400.

Brown, R.J. and Turner, J.C. (1979). The criss-cross categorization effect in intergroup discrimination. *British Journal of Social and Clinical Psychology*, 18, 371–83.

Commins, B. and Lockwood, J. (1978). The effects of intergroup relations of mixing Roman Catholics and Protestants: An experimental investigation. *European Journal of Social Psychology*, 8, 383–6.

Deaux, K., Winton, W., Crowley, M., and Lewis, L.L. (1985). Level of categorization and content of gender stereotypes. *Social Cognition*, 3, 145–67.

Deschamps, J.-C. (1977). Effect of crossing category membership on quantitative judgement. *European Journal of Social Psychology*, 7, 517–21.

Deschamps, J.-C. and Doise, W. (1978). Crossed category membership in intergroup relations. In H. Tajfel (ed.), *Differentiation between Social Groups*. Cambridge: Cambridge University Press, pp. 141–58.

Diehl, M. (1989). Dichotomie und Diskriminierung: Die Auswirkungen von Kreuzkategorisierungen auf die Diskriminierung im Pradigma der minimalen Gruppen [Dichotomy and discrimination: The effect of crossed categorizations on discrimination in the minimal group paradigm]. *Zeitschrift für Sozialpsychologie*, 20, 92–102.

Diehl, M. (1990). The minimal group paradigm: Theoretical explanations and empirical findings. In W. Stroebe and M. Hewstone (eds), *European Review of Social Psychology*, Vol. 1. Chichester: Wiley, pp. 263–92.

Doise, W. (1978). *Groups and Individuals: Explanations in social psychology*. Cambridge: Cambridge University Press.

Doise, W., Deschamps, J.-C., and Meyer, G. (1978). The accentuation of intracategory similarities. In H. Tajfel (ed.), *Differentiation between Social Groups: Studies in the social psychology of intergroup relations*. New York: Academic Press, pp. 136–46.

Ekman, P. and Friesen, W.V. (1975). *Unmasking the Face*. Englewood Cliffs, NJ: Prentice-Hall.

Eurich-Fulcer, R. and Schofield, J.W. (1995). Correlated versus uncorrelated social categorizations: The effect of intergroup bias. *Personality and Social Psychology Bulletin*, 21, 149–59.

Evans-Pritchard, E.E. (1940). *The Nuer*. London: Oxford University Press.

Fiske, S.T. and Neuberg, S.L. (1990). A continuum of impression formation, from category-based to individuating processes: Influences of information and motivation on attention and interpretation. In M.P. Zanna (ed.), *Advances in Experimental Social Psychology*, Vol. 23. New York: Academic Press, pp. 1–74.

Hagendoorn, L. and Henke, R. (1991). The effect of multiple category membership on intergroup evaluations in a north Indian context: Class, caste, and religion. *British Journal of Social Psychology*, 30, 247–60.

Hamilton, D.L. (1981). *Cognitive Processes in Stereotyping and Intergroup Behavior*. Hillsdale, NJ: Erlbaum.

Hewstone, M., Islam, M.R., and Judd, C.M. (1993). Models of crossed categorization and intergroup relations. *Journal of Personality and Social Psychology*, 64, 779–93.

Hogg, M.A. and Abrams, D. (1988). *Social Identifications: A social psychology of intergroup relations and group processes*. London: Routledge.

Islam, M.R. and Hewstone, M. (1993). Intergroup attributions and affective consequences in majority and minority groups. *Journal of Personality and Social Psychology*, 64, 936–50.

Izard, C.E. (1977). *Human Emotions*. New York: Plemum Press.

Lazarus, R.S. (1966). *Psychological Stress and the Coping Processes*. New York: McGraw-Hill.

Leventhal, H. (1980). Toward a comprehensive theory of emotion. In L. Berkowitz (ed.), *Advances in Experimental Social Psychology*, Vol. 13. San Diego: Academic Press, pp. 139–207.

LeVine, R. A. and Campell D. T. (1972). *Ethnocentrism: Theories of conflict, ethnic attitudes, and group behavior*. New York: Wiley.

Macrae, C.N., Bodenhausen, G.V., and Milne, A.B. (1995). The dissection of selection in person perception: Inhibitory processes in social stereotyping. *Journal of Personality and Social Psychology*, 69, 397–407.

Mandler, G. (1975). *Mind and Emotion*. New York: Wiley.

Marcus-Newhall, A., Miller, N., Holtz, R., and Brewer, M.B. (1993). Cross-cutting category membership with role assignment: A means of reducing intergroup bias. *European Journal of Social Psychology*, 32, 125–46.

Messick, D.M. and Mackie, D.M. (1989). Intergroup relations. *Annual Review of Psychology*, 40, 45–81.

Migdal, M.J., Hewstone, M., and Mullen, B. (1998). The effects of crossed categorization on intergroup evaluations: A meta-analysis. *British Journal of Social Psychology*, 37, 303–24.

Miller, N. (1992). Affective and cognitive processes in intergroup relations. Unpublished manuscript, University of Southern California, Los Angeles.

Mullen, B., Brown, R.J., and Smith, C. (1992). Ingroup bias as a function of salience, relevance, and status: An integration. *European Journal of Social Psychology*, 22, 103–22.

Murphy, R.F. (1957). Intergroup hostility and social cohesion. *American Anthropologist*, 59, 1018–35.

Oakes, P.J., Haslam, S.A., and Turner, J.C. (1994). *Stereotyping and Social Reality*. Oxford: Blackwell.

Pendry, L.F. and Macrae, C.N. (1996). What the disinterested perceiver overlooks: Goal-directed social categorization. *Personality and Social Psychology Bulletin*, 22, 249–56.

Rehm, J., Lilli, W., and van Eimeren, B. (1988). Reduced intergroup differentiation as a result of self-categorization in overlapping categories: A quasi-experiment. *European Journal of Social Psychology*, 18, 375–9.

Rogers, M., Miller, N., and Hennigan, K. (1981). Cooperative games as an intervention to promote cross-racial acceptance. *American Educational Research Journal*, 18, 513–16.

Sachdev, I. and Bourhis, R.Y. (1984). Status differentials and intergroup behaviour. *European Journal of Social Psychology*, 17, 277–93.

Schachter, S. and Singer, J. (1962). Cognitive, social, and physiological determinants of emotional state. *Psychological Review*, 65, 379–99.

Schofield, J.W. and Sagar, H. (1977). Peer interaction patterns in an integrated middle school. *Sociometry*, 40, 130–8.

Simmel, G. (1908). *The Sociology of Georg Simmel*, trans. Kurt Wolff. New York: Free Press.

Smith, E.E. and Osherson, D.N. (1984). Conceptual combination with prototype concepts. *Cognitive Science*, 8, 337–61.

Smith, E.R. and Zarate, M.A. (1992). Exemplar-based model of social judgment. *Psychological Review*, 99, 3–21.

Stangor, C., Lynch, L., Duan, C., and Glass, B. (1992). Categorization of individuals on the basis of multiple social features. *Journal of Personality and Social Psychology*, 62, 207–18.

Stroessner, S.J. (1996). Social categorization by race and sex: Effects of perceived non-normalcy on response times. *Social Cognition*, 14, 247–76.

Tajfel, H. (1959). Quantitative judgment in social perception. *British Journal of Psychology*, 50, 16–29.

Tajfel, H. (1978). Social categorization, social identity and social comparison. In H. Tajfel (ed.), *Differentiation between Social Groups*. London: Academic Press, pp. 61–7.

Tajfel, H. (1982). Social psychology of intergroup relations. *Annual Review of Psychology*, 33, 1–39.

Taylor, S.E. (1981). A categorization approach to stereotyping. In D.L. Hamilton (ed.), *Cognitive Processes in Stereotyping and Intergroup Behavior*. Hillsdale, NJ: Erlbaum, pp. 83–114.

Taylor, S.E., Fiske, S.T., Etcoff, N., and Ruderman, A. (1978). The categorical and contextual bases of person memory and stereotyping. *Journal of Personality and Social Psychology*, 36, 778–93.

Tomkins, S.S. (1962). *Affect, Imagery, Consciousness*, Vol. 1. New York: Springer-Verlag.

Tomkins, S.S. (1963). Affect as amplification: Some modifications in theory. In R. Plutchik and H. Kellerman (eds), *Emotion: Theory, research, and experience*. New York: Academic Press, pp. 342–75.

Turner, J.C. (1975). Social comparison and social identity: Some prospects for intergroup behaviour. *European Journal of Social Psychology*, 5, 5–34.

Turner, J.C. (1981). The experimental social psychology of intergroup behaviour. In J.C. Turner and H. Giles (eds), *Intergroup Behaviour*. Oxford: Blackwell, pp. 5–34.

Vanbeselaere, N. (1987). The effects of dichotomous and crossed social categorizations upon intergroup discrimination. *European Journal of Social Psychology*, 17, 143–56.

Vanbeselaere, N. (1991). The different effects of simple and crossed categorizations: A result of category differentiation process or a differential category salience? In W. Stroebe and M. Hewstone (eds), *European Review of Social Psychology*, Vol. 2. Chichester: Wiley, pp. 247–78.

van Knippenberg, A.M.F. (1984). Intergroup differences in group perceptions. In H. Tajfel (ed.), *The Social Dimension*. Cambridge and Paris: Cambridge University Press and Editions de la Maison des Sciences de l'Homme.

Zajonc, R.B. and Markus, H. (1984). Affect and cognition: The hard interface. In C.E. Izard, J. Kagan, and R.B. Zajonc (eds), *Emotions, Cognition and Behavior*. Cambridge: Cambridge University Press, pp. 73–102.

Zarate, M.A. and Sandoval, P. (1995). The effects of contextual cues on making occupational and gender categorizations. *British Journal of Social Psychology*, 34, 353–62.

Zarate, M.A. and Smith, E.R. (1990). Person categorization and stereotyping. *Social Cognition*, 8, 161–85.

6

Exploring Automatic Stereotype Activation: A Challenge to the Inevitability of Prejudice

LORELLA LEPORE AND RUPERT BROWN

Over the past fifty years dominant approaches in social psychology have consistently conceptualized prejudice as grounded in normal (and inescapable) cognitive processes, and thus inevitable. This conclusion is reached from both a purely cognitive perspective and a more motivational one – both views consider categorization as a necessary substrate to prejudicial thinking. Beginning with Allport (1954), a succession of prominent models of social perception has stressed the vital adaptive role which categorization plays in ordering and simplifying our social world (e.g., Brewer, 1988; Bruner, 1957; Fiske and Neuberg, 1990; Oakes, Haslam, and Turner, 1994; Tajfel, 1969). By saying that all perception involves an act of categorization, Bruner (1957) underscored how fundamental this process is to the human cognitive system.

A second common theme in the literature is the assumption of some equivalence between categories and stereotypes, particularly when stereotypes are defined as beliefs or attributes which distinguish one category from another (e.g., McCauley and Stitt, 1978; Secord, 1959; Tajfel, 1969; see Gardner, 1994, for a review). Indeed, in Tajfel's (1969) view categorization and stereotyping are somewhat equivalent: categorization accentuates differences between groupings (intercategory differentiation) and similarities within groupings (intracategory assimilation). This process, which consists of the differential attribution of traits learned through personal and cultural experience, *is* the process of stereotyping – though Tajfel and subsequent social identity theorists are careful to trace the content, extremity, valence, and behavioral implications of stereotyping to the immediate and more distal intergroup context (e.g., Hogg and Abrams, 1988; Tajfel and Turner, 1979; also see Spears, Oakes, Ellemers and Haslam, 1997; and Oakes, Haslam, and Reynolds, chapter 3 in this volume). If

The research reported in this chapter was supported by ESRC Grant no. R000234415, awarded to both authors. The authors would like to thank Michael Hogg for his helpful comments on an earlier draft of this chapter, as well as Chuck Stangor.

perception without categorization is impossible, and category differentiation is a consequence of such perception, then stereotyping is inevitable (see also Augoustinos and Walker, 1995).

In addition to these implications of categorization, from the perspective of social identity theory (SIT, Tajfel and Turner, 1979; Tajfel, 1981) the need to maintain and enhance a positive social identity accentuates differences between groups in a way which favors the ingroup not only at the perceptual but also at the attitudinal and behavioral levels (but see Hogg and Mullin, chapter 11 in this volume, for further details). Thus, in the motivational perspective of SIT, categorization and stereotyping may be construed as equivalent and inevitable processes, resulting in prejudice via the seemingly pervasive ingroup bias (e.g., Brewer, 1979; Mullen, Brown, and Smith, 1992) observed in intergroup contexts.

In the cognitive perspective, stereotypes have often been conceptualized as categories or schemas (e.g., Hamilton and Trolier, 1986; Hilton and von Hippel, 1996). Thus, sometimes stereotypes may be viewed as *the* mental representation of a social group. More commonly, though, stereotypes are construed as the characteristics associated with the category label within the representation (Stangor and Lange, 1994). If stereotypes are seen as the mental representation of the group, stereotyping is inevitable because the process of categorization *is* the process of stereotyping. If they are seen as associated with the group label within the representation, stereotyping is inevitable as a direct consequence of categorization. In fact, based on an associationist model (e.g., Anderson, 1983; Collins and Loftus, 1975), when the category is evoked by the real or symbolic presence of a category member, the group node is activated and the excitation spreads from the category label to associated traits – i.e., the stereotypic characteristics (Carlston, 1992; Fiske, 1982; Hilton and von Hippel, 1996; Stangor and Lange, 1994; Stephan and Stephan, 1993). This excitation is thought to be an all-or-none process (see Smith, 1998) – that is, once the category node is activated, a given number of pathways to *the* set of stereotypic attributes will also become active. Some category systems – i.e., age, gender, and ethnicity – are so fundamental that they may become activated automatically in the presence of a category member (Brewer, 1988; Fiske and Neuberg, 1990), in turn activating the associated stereotype. Evidence which is often cited in support of this point of view includes research by Banaji and Hardin (1996), Perdue and Gurtman (1990), and Dovidio, Evans, and Tyler (1986) (although cf. Lepore and Brown, 1997a, for an alternative analysis of this literature).

When categories are not fundamental, or when perceptual features are not obvious, perhaps stereotypes are activated in order to categorize, by matching the prototype with the specific instance (Hamilton and Sherman, 1994). Thus, whether as a *consequence* of categorization or as *part* of the categorization process, stereotypes are activated upon perception of a category member. In the current cognitive perspective the processes of categorization and stereotyping are substantially equivalent and stereotyping is inevitable.

Once stereotypes are activated they affect judgment and behavior (Hamilton, Sherman, and Ruvolo, 1990; Hilton and von Hippel, 1996; Stangor and Ford, 1992). The consequences of stereotyping in a negatively valenced direction can be regarded as instances of prejudice (Brown, 1995). In fact, since the negativity is evaluative, it is impossible to hold a negative stereotype and not be prejudiced against that group (see Augoustinos and Walker, 1995). Because of the ambiguous distinction between categorization and stereotyping, prejudice is inevitable in the cognitive approach too.

In this chapter such a conclusion will be challenged, mainly from a cognitive perspective, although motivational issues will also be considered. A careful reading of the stereotyping literature, and the implications of associative networks models of stereotypes, suggest that the automatic cognitive processes set in train upon the perception of a category member are not uniformly specified. It is our contention that habitual patterns of stereotype endorsement as indexed, for example, by dispositional levels of prejudice or group identification can markedly influence the nature, valence, and persistence of stereotype activation consequent upon categorization. We begin with a brief theoretical critique of the "inevitability" thesis. Then we present some recent empirical findings which illustrate the force of this critique. We conclude by arguing that the link between categorization and stereotyping is more flexible than has traditionally been assumed.

Challenging the Inevitability Argument

Considering prejudice as inevitable at an automatic level has led some researchers to suggest stereotype awareness and the conscious suppression of prejudiced responses as means to reduce prejudice (e.g., Devine, 1989; Devine and Monteith, 1993; Greenwald and Banaji, 1995). Empirical evidence for the efficacy of this strategy is mixed at present. Suppression reduced stereotyping of homosexuals (Monteith, 1993), and saying "no" to stereotypes of the elderly and skinheads became faster and easier with practice (Kawakami, Dovidio, and Moll, 1997). Along similar lines, Blair and Banaji (1996) found that the formation of a counterstereotypic intention reduced automatic gender stereotyping under high constraints (a stimulus onset asynchrony (SOA) of 250 ms) and reversed it under low constraints (a SOA of 2,000 ms). However, other research has shown paradoxical rebound effects, whereby stereotyping increases as a result of stereotype suppression (Macrae, Bodenhausen, Milne, and Jetten, 1994; Macrae, Bodenhausen, Milne, and Wheeler, 1996). Some authors have concluded that suppression in general may not be a good way to control thoughts and can have unpleasant consequences, particularly when cognitive demands are high (Newman, Duff, Hedberg, and Blitstein, 1996).

A recurring theme in the stereotyping literature is that category- then stereotype-based responses are the default mode in social perception, and indeed this is reflected in two influential models of impression formation (Brewer, 1988; Fiske and Neuberg, 1990). Here, the alternative to stereotyping is not in conscious control, as in the suppression studies, but in forming an individualized impression. Research has spelled out the conditions under which stereotypes or individuating information dominate impressions (see Kunda and Thagard, 1996, for an excellent review). In particular, a motivation to attend to individuating information because of perceived interdependence (e.g., Neuberg and Fiske, 1987) or the perceiver's goals or personal relationship with the target (Brewer, 1988) may impede stereotype activation (see Brewer, 1996). The motivation to be accurate (e.g., Neuberg, 1989), or diagnostic individuating information (e.g., Jussim, Nelson, Manis, and Soffin, 1995), can tilt the balance in favor of a nonstereotypic perception. When category information alone is provided this may not be enough to stereotype. Darley and Gross (1983) found that information about social class did not affect judgments unless there was also some additional, ambiguous (and potentially individuating) information on which to "project" the category-based stereotypes. This has also been a consistent finding of Yzerbyt and his colleagues (e.g., Yzerbyt, Schadron, Leyens, and Rocher, 1994): participants felt entitled to judge – i.e. to apply the stereotype – only when they were led to believe that additional information about the target person had been provided. In other words, categorization can give meaning to an otherwise ambiguous context (e.g., Kunda and Thagard, 1996; Medin, 1989; Oakes et al., 1994; Hogg and Mullin, chapter 11 in this volume) rather than merely serving simplification functions (by reducing a large amount of complex information to more "manageable" units with stereotypic connotations).

Studies showing the direct effect of diagnostic information lend support to the idea of a possible separation between categorization and stereotyping. Locksley, Borgida, Brekke, and Hepburn (1980) found that judgments of male and female targets as "assertive" depended on the behaviors they performed and not their gender. Category-based judgments only occurred in the absence of "individuating" information (but cf. Krueger and Rothbart, 1988). A direct effect of behavioral information on trait ratings at the expense of a stereotype has been found several times and with a variety of stereotypes, including gender (e.g., Deaux and Lewis, 1984), homosexuals and heterosexuals (Jussim et al., 1995), and housewives and construction workers (Kunda and Sherman-Williams, 1993).

Some studies have shown that category and stereotypic trait information associated with a target person may have distinct effects on the impression formed of that person. Pratto and Bargh (1991) primed gender stereotypic information (conveyed through sample behaviors) and category information (implied by the target's name). The judgments that participants formed of the target were consistent with the sex-type of the behaviors. The target's gender independently affected the impression, especially when participants were cognitively overloaded. Similarly, Ford, Stangor, and Duan (1994) observed different effects on judgment due to priming of category labels or stereotypic traits.

Perhaps the clearest demonstration that category and stereotype activation are separable comes from a study by Gilbert and Hixon (1991). Here, participants who were cognitively "busy" did not show evidence of stereotypic activation when confronted with an Asian stimulus person. However, they still categorized correctly, thus showing that category activation does not always result in stereotype activation. In sum, categorization is a necessary but not sufficient condition for the occurrence of stereotyping.

If the link between categorization and stereotyping may not be as fixed as once thought, so too has the connection between stereotyping and prejudice been questioned by empirical findings. For example, Stangor, Sullivan, and Ford (1991) and Esses, Haddock, and Zanna (1993) found that emotional responses and individual stereotypic beliefs were more predictive of prejudice than cultural stereotypes. In a meta-analysis Dovidio, Brigham, Johnson, and Gaertner (1996) noted a similarly weak relationship between shared stereotypes and prejudice, whilst individual stereotypes were significantly associated with prejudice (see also Stephan, Ageyev, Coates-Shrider, Stephan, and Abalakina, 1994). Moreover, stereotypes can have both positive and negative components, and attitudes toward a group are consistently related to the tendency to attribute positive or negative characteristics to that group (e.g., Brigham, 1971; Esses et al., 1993): Eagly, Mladanic, and Otto (1994), for example, found that individual stereotypes, in particular the evaluative content of participants' beliefs, predicted attitudes toward men, women, Democrats, and Republicans (see also Eagly and Mladanic, 1989). Individual representations of a group seem to have a stronger relation with prejudice than culturally shared stereotypes. In some models of stereotypes, affect (an evaluation of the category) is associated with the category label or traits (e.g., Fiske, 1982; Stephan and Stephan, 1993), flavoring the representation of the group. Given the empirical findings which suggest a more direct link between what people endorse of a stereotype and their attitudes toward the group, the "flavor" of the category may not be the same (negative) for everyone. Individual stereotypes could denote a person's representation of the group in memory. Within this, perhaps only some parts of the (known) cultural stereotypes are endorsed.

In addition to these empirical issues, there are theoretical reasons for doubting whether categories and stereotypes should be regarded either as synonymous or even irrevocably linked. Most current models conceptualize stereotypes as associative networks consisting of a group node (category) linked to various attributes, behaviors, exemplars, and affective responses (e.g., Carlston, 1992; Fiske, 1982; Stephan and Stephan, 1993). The representation of the social group results from the associative links between discrete nodes. The elements which are shared socially are only part of all the links within such networks. Thus, stereotypes are only *a part* of the knowledge base about a group (e.g., Devine and Elliot, 1995), or, put differently, of the group representation.

Categories and stereotypes (and their processes) are distinguishable in models of group representations as associative networks. The process of categorization can be defined as accessing the group node (the category), and the process of stereotyping as the inferences drawn from such an access – the activation and attribution of stereotypic traits as a result of categorization. Distinguishing between the group node (category) and attributes (exemplars, traits, evaluations, etc.) renders clear how people could be holding different representations of social groups, where the role of stereotypic elements may differ. Varying stereotypic characteristics may be more strongly associated with the category in different people. Within such networks, in fact, some links can be stronger than others, particularly if they are activated more often (Anderson, 1983; Collins and Loftus, 1975; Rumelhart, Hinton, and McClelland, 1986). Eventually such links will become automatically activated (Bargh, 1984; Smith and Lerner, 1986; Stangor and Lange, 1994). There could then be individual differences in the degree and nature of automatic stereotype activation. If true, it is plausible to predict that people differing in, for example, their habitual levels of prejudice will generate quite different automatic responses to the same category stimulus. There is now strong evidence in support of this hypothesis. Elsewhere, we argued that the expression "automatic stereotype activation" has been used to indicate both the consequence of categorization and direct priming effects (Lepore and Brown, 1997a). In that research we found that subliminal category activation resulted in divergent stereotype activation: high-prejudice participants formed a more negative and low-prejudice respondents a more positive impression of a target person (Lepore and Brown, 1997a, Experiment 2). On the other hand, when negative stereotypic content was primed (Lepore and Brown, 1997a, Experiment 3) high- and low-prejudice participants formed comparable negative impressions of the target person. If recent stereotype priming could override the automatic divergent activation in this way, there are grounds to hypothesize that the differences between high- and low-prejudice people would reemerge over time, as we will see in the studies to be presented shortly. Such a prediction stems from theory and research on category accessibility, which provide a final line of argument against the inevitability thesis.

Conceptualized by Bruner (1957, p. 135) as "the ease or speed with which a given stimulus input is coded in terms of a given category under varying conditions of instructions, past learning, motivation etc.," accessibility depends on a person's expectancies concerning the (social) stimuli in question, and that same person's needs and goals. The function of heightened accessibility is to allow a greater economy of effort in responding to the environment. It is easy to see that accessibility can vary as a function of situation factors (e.g., stimulus novelty or current task goals) or as a function of personalistic variables (e.g., a person's prior experience with certain people or events, or his or her habitual needs and motives). Thus, accessibility can be both temporary or chronic and, in either case, it is possible to derive reasons to think of prejudice as not inevitable. In fact, contextual as well as individual difference factors can alter the accessibility of both categories and stereotypic content (Stangor and Schaller, 1996).

Evidence for situational, and hence temporary, sources of accessibility is reviewed by Higgins (1996), and by Oakes et al. (1994). More relevant to our present purposes is research which has demonstrated enduring, or chronic, variations in accessibility (Higgins, 1989, 1996). For example, Bargh and Pratto (1986) found that trait constructs which were chronically accessible for participants (as determined in a pretest) generated more interference in a Stroop[1] color-naming task than nonchronic constructs, thus resulting in longer color-naming latencies. In another experiment, Bargh, Bond, Lombardi, and Tota (1986) showed that temporary and chronic sources of accessibility combined additively by subliminally priming constructs which were (or were not) habitually used by participants. Ratings of the target person in a subsequent impression formation task were more extreme when the construct had both been primed and was chronically accessible. In an impression formation task which occurred either immediately after priming or after a delay, Bargh, Lombardi, and Higgins (1988) found that participants with a nonprimed chronically accessible construct tended to use the primed dimension in the short delay condition; with a longer delay the chronically accessible constructs predominated. As we shall see, these findings are particularly pertinent to the research we present in this chapter.

The effects of chronic accessibility have also been observed with social categories such as ethnicity and gender. Hewstone, Hantzi, and Johnston (1991) found that people's tendency to categorize by ethnicity was sufficiently deep-rooted that it resisted attempts to modify it by varying its relevance to the task at hand or the nature of some anticipated interaction. Stangor, Lynch, Duan, and Glass (1992) also found that instructions and goals did not affect the tendency to categorize by ethnicity or gender. However, they did observe a tendency for high-prejudice participants to employ ethnic categories more readily. This was an interesting result since it suggested that individual differences in prejudice level might reflect differences in chronic accessibility of ethnic categories and stereotypes. Further evidence in this direction was provided by Biernat and Vescio (1993), who recorded differences between high-and low-prejudice people in target evaluations using the name-matching paradigm (Taylor, Fiske, Etcoff, and Ruderman, 1978). More conclusively, Stangor (1988) found that chronic accessibility for gender-related traits led to more stereotype-consistent recall of behavioral information and more categorization by gender. These last three studies provide additional evidence that the use of categorical and then stereotypical information is not fixed and constant. This supports the arguments advanced earlier against the inevitability thesis: for some people, at least, encountering a member of a given ethnic group may not inexorably lead to a single stereotypical response.

New Research on Chronic Accessibility of Social Categories:
The Effects of Prejudice Level and Group Identification

In an influential study Devine (1989, Experiment 2) primed participants sub-liminally with category labels and various (negative) stereotypic attributes of African-Americans. The effects of this prime were visible in a subsequent impres-sion formation task, where a target person was judged as more hostile (another stereotypic trait for African-Americans). Such priming effects seemed to be equally evident for high-and low-prejudice people. Devine (1989) interpreted her results as demonstrating that the stereotype was sufficiently well socialized in the United States as to be automatically (and chronically) accessible for all, regardless of their consciously held personal beliefs. This study is widely quoted as showing that high-and low-prejudice people automatically activate ethnic stereotypes in the same negative way. There are, however, several reasons for doubting this interpretation of her findings (Lepore and Brown, 1997a). To begin with, it should be noted that her priming stimuli contained both category labels *and* stereotypic attributes, about half of which had clear negative connotations (e.g., "lazy," "nigger," "ghetto"). Thus, the effects she observed in the impression formation task could have been due to semantic priming from these derogatory traits, which could have cued hostility directly. Another possibility is that the absence of differences between high-and low-prejudice people could be attribut-able to temporary accessibility effects. Stereotypes are like any other cognitive constructs and can be made accessible temporarily by priming (Bargh, 1994; Higgins, 1989). Such recent activation of available knowledge usually results in assimilation effects on applicable constructs (Bargh and Pietromonaco, 1982; Erdley and D'Agostino, 1988; Higgins, Bargh, and Lombardi, 1985). In Devine's (1989) experiment the stereotype was applicable only to the hostility-related judgment dimensions and so an assimilation-type effect was likely to occur for all participants.

An interpretation of Devine's (1989) experiment in terms of the application of temporarily accessible constructs suggests an interesting development of the work she instigated. As noted in the previous section, it is important to distin-guish between temporary and chronic accessibility, not least because the effects of the latter tend to persist longer (Bargh et al., 1988). In Devine's (1989) experiment the impression formation task occurred directly after the priming experience. We have speculated that the assimilation effects she observed might have been due to temporary accessibility. What might have happened had there been a longer delay between priming and impression formation? In such a situation we hypothesize that the effects of *temporary* accessibility would decay, but that effects of *chronic* accessibility would remain. Now, if, as seems reasonable, high-prejudice people primarily endorse the negative stereotypic aspects of ethnic groups, they are likely to access and use those features more frequently than individuals who do not endorse them (low-prejudice people). Frequency of use leads to ease of activation becoming chronic (Higgins, 1989). A likely consequence of this chronic accessibility is a longer persistence of activated stereotypes in social judgments. This would lead to the reemergence of differences between high-and low-prejudice people, given a sufficient time delay between priming and application. By extension, the same prediction could be made for other variables likely to be associated with differential chronic accessibility – for example, high and low levels of group identification.

These considerations led to the design of the experiments we wish to report here. After some preliminary work to establish the appropriate parameters for the priming procedure, we carried out two experiments in which we manipulated the duration of the delay between the presentation of primes and their application in some impression formation task. Our general hypothesis was that with short delays differences between people differing in chronic accessibility (e.g., prejudice level or identification) would be attenuated; with longer delays they would become more visible. To recap, the reason for this is that the effects of temporary accessibility generated by priming decay more quickly than effects due to chronic accessibility.

Study 1: Temporary and chronic accessibility of ethnic stereotypes

Preliminary study

When we began this work Devine's (1989) Experiment 2 had never been replicated, and so it was important to establish the viability of the paradigm she had adopted. Naturally, since the research was being conducted in a different cultural context, some modifications to the methodology and materials were called for. In particular, several of the priming stimuli she had used were replaced with words more suitable for the British context. The proportion of negatively valenced attributes was the same as she had used, however. For the impression formation phase of her study Devine (1989) used an ambiguous paragraph (describing a person called Donald), first devised by Srull and Wyer (1979). This proved to be unsuitable for British participants and, while retaining the same idea, a modified stimulus paragraph was created.

The procedure was similar to that used by Devine (1989). Priming stimuli were presented parafoveally – i.e., outside the central part of the participant's visual field – (for 100 ms) via a computer. The duration and mode of presentation of these words was such that the participants were unable to report what they were. In the experimental condition 80 percent of the priming words were evocative of the category "blacks" (e.g., "blacks," "nigger," "coon," "Brixton," "athletic," "lazy"), and the remainder were neutral words (e.g., "number," "member," "people"). In the control condition all words were neutral. Immediately following this, participants read a brief description of the events in a day of a person (called Michael), and were then asked to rate him on a number of scales, including those used by Devine (1989) and some additional dimensions which pretesting had shown were part of the stereotype of black people in Britain.

Twenty-four white British students took part in the study, randomly assigned to experimental or control conditions. Analysis of their judgments confirmed that the priming procedure was having its intended effects. The target person was rated as more hostile (using identical scales to Devine, 1989) in the experimental condition than in the control condition (7.61 vs. 6.24, p < .02) and more generally stereotypic (6.61 vs. 5.80, p < .05). In sum, we had shown that subliminal presentation of categorical and stereotypical material reliably affected people's subsequent social judgments.

The temporal persistence of priming effects as a function of prejudice level

Recall our argument that the temporary accessibility of stereotypical material may have been responsible for the comparable automatic stereotype activation obtained with high- and low-prejudice people in Devine's (1989) study. By varying the time between the priming and impression formation phases of the procedure we hoped to be able to show the effects of chronic accessibility: high-prejudice participants (for whom ethnicity is assumed to be chronically accessible) would show greater persistence of stereotype activation due to the primes than would low-prejudice participants.

The experimental materials and procedure were similar to those used in the experimental condition of the preliminary study. However, for half the participants a filler task (counting backwards for 180 seconds) was introduced after priming but before the impression formation task; the remainder proceeded directly to the impression formation phase. After rating the target person, all participants filled out a prejudice measure specially developed for use in the British context (see Lepore and Brown, 1997a). On the basis of this we were subsequently able to divide the participants into high-and low-prejudice groups (top and bottom tertiles of the distribution).

Sixty-one white students took part in the experiment. Their responses to the impression formation task were analyzed by condition (long vs. short delay), prejudice level (high vs. low), and type of rating dimension (stereotypic vs. nonstereotypic). This produced the expected three-way interaction, albeit at a marginal level of significance (p < .08; see figure 6.1). However, a planned comparison between high-and low-prejudice participants on the stereotypical scales in the long delay condition revealed, as predicted, that high-prejudice participants rated the target person more stereotypically there and only there (6.36 vs. 5.77, p < .025). None of the other high-vs. low-prejudice differences was significant.

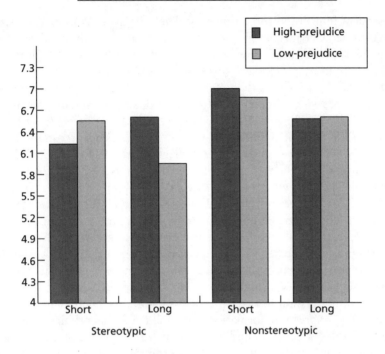

Figure 6.1 Impression of the target person as a function of delay and stereotypicality

These results are consistent with our hypothesis that the effects of primes would persist particularly for high-prejudice people on stereotypically relevant dimensions, presumably because of the greater (and chronic) stereotype accessibility for this group. They also provide more evidence that differences between high-and low-prejudice people can be detected at an automatic level and not just in controlled responses, as concluded by Devine (1989). In so doing, the argument that at this automatic level prejudice is inevitable is further jeopardized.

Study 2: Temporary and chronic accessibility of ingroup (national) stereotypes

In order to extend the argument to a different intergroup context and to show that the data were not specific to one particular experimental procedure, a second study was conducted. This differed in a number of ways from the paradigm we have just described. First of all, in place of an outgroup (ethnic) stereotype we elected to focus on an ingroup (national) stereotype. Although there may be some important differences in the evaluative flavor and complexity of ingroup and outgroup stereotypes (e.g., Judd, Ryan, and Park, 1991; Schaller and Maass, 1989; Simon, 1992), the same principles of activation and accessibility should apply to them both (Oakes et al., 1994). Thus, making ingroup stereotypical material more accessible via priming should have comparable consequences in any subsequent impression formation task. The shift in focus to ingroup stereo-types necessitated a change in our indicator of chronic accessibility. Our assumption was that those people for whom the ingroup is psychologically and habitually more important – i.e., those who identify with it strongly – should manifest greater chronic accessibility for ingroup-relevant attributes. Once again, this argument rests on the finding that frequency of activation ultimately leads to chronic accessibility (Higgins, 1989). Thus, we substituted strength of ingroup identification for level of prejudice as one of the independent variables in the design. Finally, we experimented with a different method of presenting the sub-liminal priming stimuli. Adapting a technique devised by Perdue, Dovidio, Gurt-man, and Tyler (1990), we presented category labels subliminally immediately followed by a supraliminal trait word. The category label was the word "British" and the target words were a number of traits which pretesting had established were stereotypic of British people.[2] The participants' task was simply to indicate as quickly as possible whether each word was positive or negative. It was assumed that repeated presentations of the category label and stereotypic attributes in this way would activate the appropriate ingroup stereotypes, which could then be measured in an impression formation task. As before, we manipulated the delay with which the impression formation task followed the priming activity. In addition, we added a control condition in which the priming stimuli consisted only of neutral words and no category labels. After the impression formation task we measured participants' strength of national identification using an adapted version of the scale developed by Brown, Condor, Mathews, Wade, and Williams (1986). This was subsequently used in the analysis to divide participants (at the median) into high and low identifiers.

Forty-eight British students participated in the experiment. Their judgments in the impression formation task were analyzed by condition (long delay vs. short delay vs. control, neutral prime), level of national identification (high vs. low), and stereotypic dimension (athletic vs. hardworking vs. arrogant). These dimensions had been established in pretesting as being perceived as most characteristic of British people. The analysis yielded the predicted significant three-way inter-action: condition × identification × dimension (p < .03, see table 6.1). Of particular relevance to our current concerns are the two delay conditions which also contained the "British" category label in the priming phase. Compar-ing the long and short delay cells for each stereotypic construct separately, we can note that on the "athletic" dimensions both high and low identifiers' ratings declined slightly, but in neither case significantly. However, on the "hardwork-ing" dimension it is only the low identifiers who declined significantly (p < .05) comparing the short and long delay conditions; the high identifiers changed much less (and nonsignificantly). In contrast, on the evaluatively negative dimen-sion "arrogant" exactly the opposite occurred: comparing the short and long delay conditions the high identifiers declined significantly (p < .025), whilst the low identifiers changed little, if anything increasing their negative rating after a delay. Moreover, a simple effects analysis carried out on just the two British

Table 6.1   Ratings of target person by high and low identifiers under different prime and delay conditions

Experimental condition (prime, delay)	Dimension					
	Athletic		Hardworking		Arrogant	
	High	Low	High	Low	High	Low
British short	8.04	7.76	6.48	6.81	6.78	6.67
British long	7.70	7.21	6.07	5.83	5.78	6.87
Neutral prime	7.62	8.14	6.17	7.00	7.00	6.19

prime conditions confirmed that any differences between high and low identifiers lay in the long and not the short delay conditions.

In summary, after a delay the high identifiers rated the target person less negatively, whilst the low identifiers seemed to generate a less positive impression. This is consistent with the idea that the two groups differ in their habitual stereotypic perception of the ingroup, a difference which gets obscured under the temporary accessibility effects of recent priming.

Conclusions

In this chapter we have been concerned to rebut the thesis that automatic stereotype activation is an all-or-none affair with consistent consequences regardless of people's habitually expressed social beliefs. As we have seen, that argument leads to the implication that prejudice is inevitable, at least as far as its automatic components are concerned, and can be controlled or countered only when there are sufficient cognitive resources available to do so (Devine, 1989). The findings we have presented here provide some evidence against this conclusion. The key results of the studies we have reported are interactions involving levels of prejudice or group identification and experimental conditions. If stereotyping was inevitable we would not have observed differential effects of priming delays for such groups of people; only main effects for condition should have been found. In fact, though, as we have demonstrated, automatic stereotype activation does not have the same consequences or the same time course for all people. This strongly suggests that the constituent elements and interconnections of the mental representations of various social categories can differ between different types of person.

By themselves the data reported here would hardly be conclusive. However, if we put them together with the convergent evidence from several other studies, the case against the inevitability thesis becomes much stronger. As we have seen, in some other research of ours we have shown that priming category labels (and not stereotypic material as well) can distinguish between high-and low-prejudice people (Lepore and Brown, 1997a). Moreover, Wittenbrink, Judd, and Park (1997) found that scores on an explicit modern racism measure were correlated with the degree of facilitation/inhibition in the lexical recognition of stereotype-related or unrelated words preceded by a subliminal category prime. And, in a slightly earlier study, Locke, MacLeod, and Walker (1994), using a Stroop-like paradigm, observed greater interference in naming stereotype-related words (compared with unrelated words) only for high-prejudice participants; low-prejudice participants were unaffected by word stereotypicality. All these studies were concerned in various ways with automatic stereotype activation; all revealed consistent differences between high-and low-prejudice people. Thus, the inhibition of stereotypes may not necessarily require the conscious or controlled intervention of the perceiver.

Factors other than, or interacting with, prejudice level may determine how and when stereotypes are activated, and, if activated, whether they are used in judgments (see also Brewer, 1996). For example, Gilbert and Hixon (1991) found that cognitive distraction at the point of stereotype *activation* interfered with the subsequent application of stereotypes in a social judgment task. In an elaboration of this paradigm we have observed that these effects are themselves qualified by prejudice level, reflecting once again, we believe, the different mental representations of ethnic groups held by high- and low-prejudice people (Lepore and Brown, 1997b). In another line of work we have also found that providing participants with particular processing goals – for instance, to focus on attributes relevant to a specific judgmental context – can counteract the "normal" pattern of stereotype activation consequent upon category priming (in this case by means of photographs of black people). Response latencies in a lexical decision task showed clear evidence of facilitation for task-related words (over stereotypic words) for those who had been given specific processing goals (Lepore and Brown, 1997b; see also Chartrand and Bargh, 1996; Pendry and Macrae, 1996).

All in all, the evidence from all these different strands of research seems to support a functionalist view of stereotyping in which stereotypes are regarded as useful tools, automatically activated when it is appropriate for them to be so. In this chapter we have focused on characteristics of the person (e.g., level of prejudice or group identification) that make stereotypes more or less accessible, but situation variables can also be important, as we have just noted.

In the cognitive perspective the most direct challenge to conceiving of prejudice as inevitable comes from research on automatic stereotype activation. In the motivational approach, on the other hand, evidence against the inevitability of stereotyping comes from temporary accessibility and the focus upon the comparison context. A development from SIT, self-categorization theory (SCT, Turner, Hogg, Oakes, Reicher, and Wetherell, 1987) is influenced by Bruner's (1957) view of categorization as determined by both readiness to access a category and fit of the stimulus, but also by novel approaches portraying categorization as context dependent (e.g., Medin, 1989). From this perspective, the emphasis is upon the way that categorization and stereotyping provide clarity and meaning to social situations rather than upon their self-esteem functions. Abrams and Hogg (1988; Hogg and Abrams, 1990, 1993) have argued that although self-esteem is clearly implicated in social identity processes, the way in which it is implicated is at best complicated and circumscribed (also see Long and Spears, 1997). Hogg and associates have argued from self-categorization theory that uncertainty reduction may be a more fundamental motivation behind categorization and stereotyping, and that self-esteem may be a consequence of self-categorization based on uncertainty reduction (Hogg, 1996; Hogg and Abrams, 1993; Mullin and Hogg, in press; Hogg and Mullin, chapter 11 in this volume). A series of relatively minimal group experiments shows that people only self-categorize and express intergroup behavior (including stereotyping) when categorization occurs under conditions of subjective uncertainty and when the categorization is functional in reducing uncertainty (e.g., Grieve and Hogg, in press; Mullin and Hogg, in press; see Hogg and Mullin, chapter 11 in this volume, for an overview).

The search for meaning is important in the SCT approach and the consequences of categorization depend on the context of the comparison (see Oakes, Haslam, and Reynolds, chapter 3 in this volume). The context, in fact, will affect the metacontrast ratio, i.e., the optimal way to achieve category differentiation. Research supports this prediction (e.g., Oakes and Turner, 1986). In a study conducted during the Gulf War, Haslam, Turner, Oakes, McGarty, and Hayes (1992) found that Australian participants were stereotyping Americans more negatively at the end of the war if the comparison groups were Australia and Britain; the stereotype was also more negative at the beginning of the conflict if the comparison groups included Iraq. Thus, both the specific situation (the war) and the comparison context led to variations in the stereotypic perception of Americans. The context also affected how prototypical of a category a target individual was perceived to be (Haslam, Oakes, McGarty, Turner, and Onorato, 1995). These findings, inconsistent with the idea of stereotyping and prejudice as an inevitable (and fixed) consequence of categorization, stem from procedures adopting deliberate and conscious responses.

It may be interesting to speculate on the possible links between the cognitive approach and that provided by SCT (Oakes et al., 1994). Both perspectives are strongly influenced by Bruner's (1957) conception of accessibility. Both place some emphasis on the flexibility of stereotype activation and use, depending both on the perceiver's readiness to access and use certain categorical information and the particular context in which it is to be applied (i.e., "comparative fit" in Oakes et al.'s (1994) terms). However, hitherto within SCT little research attention has been paid to the so-called "fundamental" categories of age, gender, and ethnicity. Such categories (and their associated stereotypes) may be so predominant that they may not be so much affected by temporary goals and contextual factors (e.g., Hewstone et al., 1991; Stangor et al., 1992), but more by enduring patterns of social belief (e.g., prejudice level), as we have found (see also Stangor et al., 1992). Moreover, perhaps because of the emphasis within SCT on the socially functional and strategic bases of stereotyping, its proponents have not been concerned with *automatic* cognitive processes. It is noteworthy that in Oakes et al.'s (1994) influential book there is no reference in the subject index to automaticity, neither is there any citation to the central theoretical analyses of this concept. Furthermore, few if any of the dependent measures employed in studies developing or testing SCT can be regarded as "automatic responses," at least as these are commonly defined (Bargh, 1994). However, the emphasis on the goal-directed nature of categorization and stereotyping in SCT finds parallels in current work on the automatic activation of schema by different processing goals (Chartrand and Bargh, 1996; Lepore and Brown, 1997b). This seems to be an important confluence between the cognitive and motivational approaches to stereotyping that would repay further research investment.

It would also be interesting to see whether changing the comparative context would have any effect on chronically accessible categories. Future research could implement experimental variations of comparative context with some of the fundamental categories. From the perspective we have taken here we would expect some evidence of automatic stereotype activation to occur regardless. SCT might make the opposite prediction in view of the theoretically prominent place that contextual factors occupy in the theory. In any event, such a convergence of different research traditions might do much to enrich or delimit each other's sphere of applicability.

Notes

1   In the classical Stroop paradigm color words (e.g., "red") are presented in consonant (red) or dissonant (blue) colors and the participant is required to name the color. A typical finding is that the dissonant color presentation results in longer response times than the consonant presentation, suggesting an interference between the perceptual and the semantic system.
2   There were other goals in this experiment, involving an additional condition with the label "German" as prime, with short delay. To simplify the presentation we concentrate here on the British prime conditions, with short and long delays, and the control condition.

References

Abrams, D. and Hogg, M.A. (1988). Comments on the motivational status of self-esteem in social identity and intergroup discrimination. *European Journal of Social Psychology*, 18, 317–334.
Allport, G.W. (1954). *The Nature of Prejudice*. Reading, MA: Addison-Wesley.
Anderson, J.R. (1983). *The Architecture of Cognition*. Cambridge, MA: Harvard University Press.

Augoustinos, M. and Walker, I. (1995). *Social Cognition. An integrated introduction.* London: Sage.

Banaji, M.R. and Greenwald, A.G. (1995). Implicit gender stereotyping in judgments of fame. *Journal of Personality and Social Psychology,* 68, 181–98.

Banaji, M.R. and Hardin, C. (1996). Automatic stereotyping. *Psychological Science,* 7, 136–41.

Banaji, M.R., Hardin, C., and Rothman, A.J. (1993). Implicit stereotyping in person judgment. *Journal of Personality and Social Psychology,* 65, 272–81.

Bargh, J.A. (1984). Automatic and conscious processing of social information. In R.S. Wyer, Jr and T.K. Srull (eds), *Handbook of Social Cognition,* Vol. 3. Hillsdale, NJ: Erlbaum, pp. 1–43.

Bargh, J.A. (1989). Conditional automaticity: Varieties of automatic influence in social perception and cognition. In J.S. Uleman and J.A. Bargh (eds), *Unintended Thought.* New York: Guilford, pp. 3–51.

Bargh, J.A. (1994). The four horsemen of automaticity: Awareness, intention, efficiency, and control in social cognition. In R.S. Wyer, Jr and T.K. Srull (eds), *Handbook of Social Cognition,* 2nd edn, Vol. 1. Hillsdale, NJ: Erlbaum, pp. 1–40.

Bargh, J.A. (1996). Automaticity in social psychology. In E.T. Higgins and A. Kruglanski (eds), *Social Psychology: Handbook of basic principles.* New York: Guilford, pp. 169–83.

Bargh, J.A., Bond, R.N., Lombardi, W.J., and Tota, M.E. (1986). The additive nature of chronic and temporary sources of construct accessibility. *Journal of Personality and Social Psychology,* 50, 869–78.

Bargh, J.A., Lombardi, W.J. and Higgins, E.T. (1988). Automaticity of chronically accessible constructs in person x situation effects on person perception: It's just a matter of time. *Journal of Personality and Social Psychology,* 55, 4, 599–605.

Bargh, J.A. and Pietromonaco, P. (1982). Automatic information processing and social perception: The influence of trait information presented outside of conscious awareness on impression formation. *Journal of Personality and Social Psychology,* 43, 437–49.

Bargh, J.A. and Pratto, F. (1986). Individual construct accessibility and perceptual selection. *Journal of Experimental Social Psychology,* 22, 293–311.

Biernat, M. and Vescio, T.K. (1993). Categorization and stereotyping: Effects of group context on memory and social judgement. *Journal of Experimental Social Psychology,* 29, 166–202.

Blair, I.V. and Banaji, M.R. (1996). Automatic and controlled processes in gender stereotyping. *Journal of Personality and Social Psychology,* 70, 1142–63.

Brewer, M.B. (1979). Ingroup bias and the minimal group paradigm: A cognitive–motivational analysis. *Psychological Bulletin,* 86, 307–24.

Brewer, M.B. (1988). A dual process model of impression formation. In T.K. Srull and R.S. Wyer, Jr (eds), *Advances in Social Cognition,* Vol. 1. Hillsdale, NJ: Erlbaum, pp. 1–36.

Brewer, M.B. (1996). When stereotypes lead to stereotyping: The use of stereotypes in person perception. In C.N. Macrae, C. Stangor, and M. Hewstone (eds), *Stereotypes and Stereotyping.* New York: Guilford, pp. 254–75.

Brigham, J.C. (1971). Ethnic stereotypes. *Psychological Bulletin,* 76, 15–38.

Brown, R. (1995). *Prejudice: Its social psychology.* Oxford: Blackwell.

Brown, R., Condor, S., Mathews, A., Wade, G., and Williams, J. (1986). Explaining intergroup differentiation in an industrial organization. *Journal of Occupational Psychology,* 59, 273–86.

Bruner, J.S. (1957). On perceptual readiness. *Psychological Review*, 64, 123–52.

Carlston, D.E. (1992). Impression formation and the modular mind: The Associated Systems Theory. In L.L. Martin and A. Tesser (eds), *The Construction of Social Judgments*. Hillsdale, NJ: Lawrence Erlbaum Associates, pp. 301–41.

Chartrand, T.L. and Bargh, J.A. (1996). Automatic activation of impression formation and memorization goals: Nonconscious goal priming reproduces effects of explicit task instructions. *Journal of Personality and Social Psychology*, 71, 464–78.

Collins, A.M. and Loftus, E.F. (1975). A spreading-activation theory of semantic processing. *Psychological Review*, 82, 407–28.

Darley, J.M. and Gross, P.H. (1983). A hypothesis-confirming bias in labeling effects. *Journal of Personality and Social Psychology*, 44, 20–33.

Deaux, K. and Lewis, L.L. (1984). Structure of gender stereotypes: Interrelationships among components and gender label. *Journal of Personality and Social Psychology*, 46, 991–1004.

Devine, P.G. (1989). Stereotypes and prejudice: Their automatic and controlled components. *Journal of Personality and Social Psychology*, 56, 1, 5–18.

Devine, P.G. and Elliot, A.J. (1995). Are racial stereotypes *really* fading? The Princeton Trilogy revisited. *Personality and Social Psychology Bulletin*, 21, 1139–50.

Devine, P.G. and Monteith, M.J. (1993). The role of discrepancy-associated affect in prejudice reduction. In D.M. Mackie and D.L. Hamilton (eds), *Affect, Cognition, and Stereotyping: Interactive processes in group perception*. San Diego: Academic Press, pp. 317–44.

Dovidio, J.F., Brigham, J.C., Johnson, B.T., and Gaertner, S.L. (1996). Stereotyping, prejudice, and discrimination: Another look. Part IV: Undermining stereotypes and stereotyping. In C. N. Macrae, C. Stangor, and M. Hewstone (eds), *Foundations of Stereotypes and Stereotyping*. New York: Guilford, pp. 276–318.

Dovidio, J.L., Evans, N., and Tyler, R.B. (1986). Racial stereotypes: The contents of their cognitive representations. *Journal of Experimental Social Psychology*, 22, 22–37.

Eagly, A.H. and Mladanic, A. (1989). Gender stereotypes and attitudes toward men and women. *Personality and Social Psychology Bulletin*, 15, 543–58.

Eagly, A.H., Mladanic, A. and Otto, S. (1994). Cognitive and affective bases of attitudes toward social groups and social policies. *Journal of Experimental Social Psychology*, 30, 113–37.

Erdley, C.A. and D'Agostino, P.R. (1988). Cognitive and affective components of automatic priming effects. *Journal of Personality and Social Psychology*, 54, 741–7.

Esses, V.M., Haddock, G., and Zanna, M.P. (1993). Values, stereotypes, and emotions as determinants of intergroup attitudes. In D.M. Mackie and D.L. Hamilton (eds), *Affect, Cognition, and Stereotyping: Interactive processes in group perception*. San Diego: Academic Press, pp. 137–66.

Fazio, R.H., Jackson, J.R., Dunton, B.C., and Williams, C.J. (1995). Variability in automatic activation as an unobtrusive measure of racial attitudes: A bona fide pipeline? *Journal of Personality and Social Psychology*, 69, 1013–27.

Fiske, S.T. (1982). Schema-triggered affect: Applications to social perception. In M.S. Clark and S.T. Fiske (eds), *Affect and Cognition*. Hillsdale, NJ: Erlbaum, pp. 55–78.

Fiske, S.T. and Neuberg, S.L. (1990). A continuum of impression formation, from category-based to individuating processes: Influences of information and motivation on attention and interpretation. In M.P. Zanna (ed.), *Advances in Experimental Social Psychology*, Vol. 23. New York: Academic Press, pp. 1–74.

Ford, T.E., Stangor, C., and Duan, C. (1994). Influence of social category accessibility and category-associated trait accessibility on judgments of individuals. *Social Cognition*, 12, 149–68.

Gardner, R.C. (1994). Stereotypes as consensual beliefs. In M.P. Zanna and J.M. Olson (eds), *The Psychology of Prejudice: The Ontario symposium*, Vol. 7. Hillsdale, NJ: Erlbaum, pp. 1–31.

Gaertner, S.L. and Dovidio, J.F. (1986). The aversive form of racism. In J.F. Dovidio and S.L. Gaertner (eds), *Prejudice, Discrimination and Racism*. New York: Academic Press, pp. 61–89.

Gilbert, D.T. and Hixon, J.G. (1991). The trouble of thinking: Activation and application of stereotypic beliefs. *Journal of Personality and Social Psychology*, 60, 509–17.

Greenwald, A.G. and Banaji, M.R. (1995). Implicit social cognition: Attitudes, self-esteem, and stereotypes. *Psychological Review*, 102, 4–27.

Grieve, P. and Hogg, M.A. (in press). Subjective uncertainty and intergroup discrimination in the minimal group situation. *Personality and Social Psychology Bulletin*.

Hamilton, D.L. and Sherman, J.W. (1994). Stereotypes. In R.S. Wyer, Jr and T.K. Srull (eds), *Handbook of Social Cognition*, 2nd edn, Vol. 2. Hillsdale, NJ: Erlbaum, pp. 1–68.

Hamilton, D.L., Sherman, S.J., and Ruvolo, C.M. (1990). Stereotype-based expectancies: Effects on information processing and social behavior. *Journal of Social Issues*, 46, 35–60.

Hamilton, D.L. and Trolier, T.K. (1986). Stereotypes and stereotyping: An overview of the cognitive approach. In J.F. Dovidio and S.L. Gaertner (eds), *Prejudice, Discrimination and Racism*. New York: Academic Press, pp. 127–63.

Haslam, S.A., Oakes, P.J., McGarty, C., Turner, J.C., and Onorato, R.S. (1995). Contextual changes in the prototypicality of extreme and moderate outgroup members. *European Journal of Social Psychology*, 25, 509–30.

Haslam, S.A., Turner, J.C., Oakes, P.J., McGarty, C., and Hayes, B.K. (1992). Context-dependent variation in social stereotyping 1: The effects of intergroup relations as mediated by social change and frame reference. *European Journal of Social Psychology*, 22, 3–20.

Hewstone, M., Hantzi, A., and Johnston, L. (1991). Social categorization and person memory: The pervasiveness of race as an organizing principle. *European Journal of Social Psychology*, 21, 517–28.

Higgins, T.E. (1989). Knowledge accessibility and activation: Subjectivity and suffering from unconscious sources. In J.S. Uleman and J.A. Bargh (eds), *Unintended Thought*. New York: Guilford, pp. 75–123.

Higgins, T.E. (1996). Knowledge activation: Accessibility, applicability, and salience. In E.T. Higgins and A.W. Kruglanski (eds), *Social Psychology: Handbook of basic principles*. New York: Guilford, pp. 133–68.

Higgins, E.T., Bargh, J.A., and Lombardi, W. (1985). Nature of priming effects on categorization. *Journal of Experimental Psychology: Learning, Memory, and Cognition*, 11, 58–69.

Hilton, J.L. and von Hippel, W. (1996). Stereotypes. *Annual Review of Psychology*, 47, 237–71.

Hogg, M.A. (1996). Intragroup processes, group structure and social identity. In W.P. Robinson (ed.), *Social Groups and Identities: Developing the legacy of Henri Tajfel*. Oxford: Butterworth-Heinemann, pp. 65–93.

Hogg, M.A. and Abrams, D. (1988). *Social Identification: A social psychology of inter-group relations and group processes*. London: Routledge.

Hogg, M.A. and Abrams, D. (1990). Social motivation, self-esteem, and social identity. In D. Abrams and M.A. Hogg (eds) *Social Identity Theory: Constructive and critical advances*. Hemel Hempstead: Harvester Wheatsheaf, pp. 28–47.

Hogg, M.A. and Abrams, D. (1993). Towards a single-process uncertainty-reduction model of social motivation in groups. In M.A. Hogg and D. Abrams (eds), *Group Motivation: Social psychological perspectives*. Hemel Hempstead: Harvester Wheat-sheaf, pp. 173–90.

Judd, C.M., Ryan, C.S., and Park, B. (1991). Accuracy in the judgement of in-group and out-group variability. *Journal of Personality and Social Psychology*, 61, 366–79.

Jussim, L., Nelson, T.E., Manis, M., and Soffin, S. (1995). Prejudice, stereotypes, and labeling effects: Sources of bias in person perception. *Journal of Personality and Social Psychology*, 68, pp. 228–46.

Kawakami, K., Dovidio, J.F., and Moll, J. (1997). Stereotyping: Automatically activated! Automatically suppressed? Poster presented at the 9th APS Convention, Washington, DC, May.

Krueger, J. and Rothbart, M. (1988). The use of categorical and individuating information in making inferences about personality. *Journal of Personality and Social Psychology*, 55, 187–95.

Kunda, Z. and Sherman-Williams, B. (1993). Stereotypes and the construal of individuat-ing information. *Personality and Social Psychology Bulletin*, 19, 90–9.

Kunda, Z. and Thagard, P. (1996). Forming impression from stereotypes, traits, and behaviors: A parallel constraint satisfaction theory. *Psychological Review*, 103, 284–308.

Lepore, L. and Brown, R. (1997a). Category and stereotype activation: Is prejudice inevitable? *Journal of Personality and Social Psychology*, 72, 2, 275–87.

Lepore, L. and Brown, R. (1997b). *Automatic Stereotype Activation: Towards a model*. Final report to ESRC.

Locke, V., MacLeod, C., and Walker, I. (1994). Automatic and controlled activation of stereotypes: Individual differences associated with prejudice. *British Journal of Social Psychology*, 33, 29–46.

Locksley, A., Borgida, E., Brekke, N.C., and Hepburn, C. (1980). Sex stereotypes and social judgment. *Journal of Personality and Social Psychology*, 39, 821–31.

Lombardi, W.J., Higgins, E.T., and Bargh, J.A. (1987). The role of consciousness in priming effects on categorization: Assimilation versus contrast as a function of aware-ness of priming task. *Personality and Social Psychology Bulletin*, 13, 411–29.

Long, K. and Spears, R. (1997). The self-esteem hypothesis revisited: Differentiation and the disaffected. In R. Spears, P.J. Oakes, N. Ellemers, and S.A. Haslam (eds), *The Social Psychology of Stereotyping and Group Life*. Oxford: Blackwell, pp. 216–317.

McCauley, C. and Stitt, C.L. (1978). An individual and quantitative measure of stereo-types. *Journal of Personality and Social Psychology*, 39, 929–40.

McConahay, J.G. (1986). Modern racism, ambivalence, and the modern racism scale. In J.F. Dovidio and S.L. Gaertner (eds), *Prejudice, Discrimination and Racism*. New York: Academic Press, pp. 91–125.

Macrae, C.N., Bodenhausen, G.V., Milne, A.B., and Jetten, J. (1994). Out of mind but back in sight: Stereotypes on the rebound. *Journal of Personality and Social Psychology*, 67, 808–17.

Macrae, C.N., Bodenhausen, G.V., Milne, A.B., and Wheeler, V. (1996). On resisting the temptation for simplification: Counterintentional effects of stereotype suppression on social memory. *Social Cognition*, 14, 1–20.

Macrae, C.N., Milne, A.B., and Bodenhausen, G.V. (1994). Stereotypes as energy-saving devices: A peek inside the cognitive toolbox. *Journal of Personality and Social Psychology*, 66, 37–47.

Medin, D.L. (1989). Concepts and conceptual structure. *American Psychologist*, 44, 1469–81.

Monteith, M.J. (1993). Self-regulation of prejudiced responses: Implications for progress in prejudice-reduction efforts. *Journal of Personality and Social Psychology*, 65, 469–85.

Mullen, B., Brown, R., and Smith, C. (1992). Ingroup bias as a function of salience, relevance, and status: An integration. *European Journal of Social Psychology*, 22, 103–22.

Mullin, B.A. and Hogg, M.A (in press). Dimensions of subjective uncertainty in social identification and minimal intergroup discrimination. *British Journal of Social Psychology*.

Neuberg, S.L. (1989). The goal of forming accurate impressions during social interactions: Attenuating the impact of negative expectancies. *Journal of Personality and Social Psychology*, 56, 374–86.

Neuberg, S.L. and Fiske, S.T. (1987). Motivational influences on impression formation: Outcome dependency, accuracy-driven attention, and individuating processes. *Journal of Personality and Social Psychology*, 53, 431–44.

Newman, L.S., Duff, K.J., Hedberg, D.A., and Blitstein, J. (1996). Rebound effects in impression formation: Assimilation and contrast effects following thought suppression. *Journal of Experimental Social Psychology*, 32, 460–83.

Oakes, P.J., Haslam, S.A., and Turner, J.C. (1994). *Stereotypes and Social Reality*. Oxford: Blackwell.

Oakes, P.J. and Turner, J.C. (1986). Distinctiveness and the salience of social category membership: Is there an automatic perceptual bias towards novelty? *European Journal of Social Psychology*, 16, 325–44.

Pendry, L.F. and Macrae, C.N. (1996). What the disinterested perceiver overlooks: Goal-directed social categorization. *Personality and Social Psychology Bulletin*, 22, 249–56.

Perdue, C.W., Dovidio, J.F., Gurtman, M.B., and Tyler, R.B. (1990). Us and them: Social categorization and the process of intergroup bias. *Journal of Personality and Social Psychology*, 59, 475–86.

Perdue, C.W. and Gurtman, M.B. (1990). Evidence for the automaticity of ageism. *Journal of Experimental Social Psychology*, 26, 199–216.

Pettigrew, T.F. and Meertens, R.W. (1995). Subtle and blatant prejudice in western Europe. *European Journal of Social Psychology*, 25, 57–75.

Pratto, F. and Bargh, J.A. (1991). Stereotyping based on apparently individuating information: Trait and global components of sex stereotypes under attention overload. *Journal of Experimental Social Psychology*, 27, 26–47.

Rumelhart, D.E., Hinton, G.E., and McClelland, J.L. (1986). A general framework for parallel distributed processing. In D.E. Rumelhart, J.L. McClelland, and the PDP research group (eds), *Parallel Distributed Processing*. Cambridge, MA: MIT Press, pp. 45–76.

Schaller, M. and Maass, A. (1989). Illusory correlation and social categorization: Toward an integration of motivational and cognitive factors in stereotype formation. *Journal of Personality and Social Psychology*, 56, 709–21.

Secord, P.F. (1959). Stereotyping and favorableness in the perception of Negro faces. *Journal of Abnormal and Social Psychology*, 59, 309–15.

Simon, B. (1992). Intragroup differentiation in terms of ingroup and outgroup attributes. *European Journal of Social Psychology*, 22, 407–13.

Skowronski, J.J., Carlston, D.E., and Isham, J.T. (1993). Implicit versus explicit impression formation: The differing effects of overt labelling and covert priming on memory and impressions. *Journal of Experimental Social Psychology*, 29, 17–41.

Smith, E.R. (1998). Mental representation and memory. In D. Gilbert, S.T. Fiske, and G. Lindzey (eds), *Handbook of Social Psychology*, 4th edn, Vol. 1. New York: McGraw-Hill, pp. 391–445.

Smith, E.R. and Lerner, M. (1986). Development of automatism of social judgments. *Journal of Personality and Social Psychology*, 50, 246–59.

Snyder, M. and Miene, P. (1994). On the functions of stereotypes and prejudice. In M.P. Zanna, and J.M. Olson (eds), *The Psychology of Prejudice: The Ontario symposium*, vol 7. Hillsdale, NJ: Erlbaum, pp. 33–54.

Spears, R., Oakes, P.J., Ellemers, N., and Haslam, S.A. (eds) (1997). *The Social Psychology of Stereotyping and Group Life*. Oxford: Blackwell.

Srull, T.K. and Wyer, R.S., Jr (1979). The role of category accessibility in the interpretation of information about persons: Some determinants and implications. *Journal of Personality and Social Psychology*, 37, 1660–72.

Srull, T.K. and Wyer, R.S., Jr (1989). Person memory and judgment. *Psychological Review*, 96, 58–83.

Stangor, C. (1988). Stereotype accessibility and information processing. *Personality and Social Psychology Bulletin*, 14, 694–708.

Stangor, C. and Ford, T.E. (1992). Accuracy and expectancy-confirming processing orientations and the development of stereotypes and prejudice. In W. Stroebe and M. Hewstone (eds), *European Review of Social Psychology*, Vol. 3. New York: Wiley, pp. 57–89.

Stangor, C. and Lange, J.E. (1994). Mental representations of social groups: Advances in understanding stereotypes and stereotyping. In M.P. Zanna (ed.), *Advances in Experimental Social Psychology*, Vol. 26. San Francisco: Academic Press, pp. 357–416.

Stangor, C., Lynch, L., Duan, C., and Glass, B. (1992). Categorization of individuals on the basis of multiple social features. *Journal of Personality and Social Psychology*, 62, 207–18.

Stangor, C. and Schaller, M. (1996). Stereotypes as individual and collective representations. In C.N. Macrae, C. Stangor, and M. Hewstone (eds), *Stereotypes and Stereotyping*. New York: Guilford, pp. 3–37.

Stangor, C., Sullivan L.A., and Ford, T.E. (1991). Affective and cognitive determinants of prejudice. *Social Cognition*, 9, 359–80.

Stephan, W.G., Ageyev, V., Coates-Shrider, L., Stephan, C.W., and Abalakina, M. (1994). On the relationship between stereotypes and prejudice: An international study. *Personality and Social Psychology Bulletin*, 20, 277–84.

Stephan, W.G. and Stephan, C.W. (1993). Cognition and affect in stereotyping: Parallel interactive networks. In D.M. Mackie and D.L. Hamilton (eds), *Affect, Cognition, and Stereotyping: Interactive processes in group perception*. San Diego: Academic Press, pp. 111–36.

Tajfel, H. (1969). Cognitive aspects of prejudice. *Journal of Social Issues*, 23, 79–97.

Tajfel, H. (1981). *Human Groups and Social Categories*. Cambridge: Cambridge University Press.

Tajfel, H. and Turner, J.C. (1979). An integrative theory of intergroup relations. In W.G. Austin and S. Worchel (eds), *Psychology of Intergroup Relations*. Monterey, CA: Brooks-Cole, pp. 33–48.

Taylor, S.E., Fiske, S.T., Etcoff, N.L., and Ruderman, A.J. (1978). Categorical and contextual bases of person memory and stereotyping. *Journal of Personality and Social Psychology*, 36, 778–93.

Turner, J.C., Hogg, M.A., Oakes, P.J., Reicher, S.D., and Wetherell, M.S. (1987). *Rediscovering the Social Group: A self-categorization theory*. Oxford: Blackwell.

Wegner, D.M. and Erber, R. (1992). The hyperaccessibility of suppressed thoughts. *Journal of Personality and Social Psychology*, 63, 903–12.

Wittenbrink, B., Judd, C.M., and Park, B. (1997). Evidence for racial prejudice at the implicit level and its relationship with questionnaire measures. *Journal of Personality and Social Psychology*, 72, 2, pp. 262–74.

Yzerbyt, V.Y., Schadron, G., Leyens, J.-Ph., and Rocher, S. (1994). Social judgeability: The impact of meta-informational cues on the use of stereotypes. *Journal of Personality and Social Psychology*, 66, 48–55.

Zarate, M.A. and Smith, E.R. (1990). Person categorization and stereotyping. *Social Cognition*, 8, 2, 161–85.

7

Stereotyping, Processing Goals, and Social Identity: Inveterate and Fugacious Characteristics of Stereotypes

Vance Locke and Iain Walker

Stereotypes

The dominant approach in contemporary social psychology to the study of stereotypes and prejudice, and to intergroup relations generally, is based on a social cognitive orientation. In this orientation, stereotypes are viewed as mental representations of social groups. Stereotypes exist cognitively as schemas, or cognitive structures, in memory, and facilitate cognitive processing by directing attention, guiding encoding and retrieval, and conserving cognitive resources (see Augoustinos and Walker, 1995; Fiske, in press; Hamilton and Sherman, 1994; Hilton and von Hippel, 1996; and Stangor and Lange, 1994, for recent reviews of the social cognition approach). A distinction is made between *individual* and *social* stereotypes: the former are the schemas contained within particular individuals; the latter are widely accepted, public expressions of the character of a group and its members (Stangor and Schaller, 1996). Prejudice is typically defined as an evaluation, usually negative, of a group and its members (Brown, 1995; Fiske, in press). Prejudice is often tacitly assumed to follow, or at least be closely related to, stereotypes. In the social cognition approach, the most significant recent model of the relationship between stereotypes and prejudice is that of Devine (1989). In this chapter, we will briefly summarize Devine's model and consider some conceptual and empirical limitations of, and challenges to, the model. We will present some research which suggests both stability and transience in stereotype activation. These dual, and apparently contradictory, characteristics of stereotypes provide points of commonality and difference

The studies presented in this chapter are from Vance Locke's Ph.D. thesis, submitted to the Psychology Department at the University of Western Australia. Iain Walker's contribution to the chapter was supported by grants from the Australian Research Council and from Murdoch University.

between social identity and social cognitive approaches to stereotyping. Finally, we will consider briefly how social identity and other processes can affect the activation of stereotypes through the definition of processing goals. Processing goals provide an important avenue for the integration of intra- and interindividual social cognitive processes and interpersonal and intergroup processes. Accepting James's dictum that "thinking is for doing" (Fiske, 1992), we suggest that the "doing" of stereotypic thinking lies in the evaluation of groups and their members, in the search for positive intergroup differentiation.

Devine's dissociation model

Devine's (1989) dissociation model posits that the social stereotypes of major groups in society are well known by all members of society. Everyone, regardless of their own beliefs and prejudices, can identify the contents of the stereotypes of major groups – that is, such stereotypes are consensually known. In the process of acquiring knowledge of the social world in which they live, all people are sufficiently often exposed to these social stereotypes, and rehearse the stereotypes sufficiently often, that the stereotypes not only become internalized as memory structures, but become automatized (Bargh, 1989). According to Devine's model, these stereotypes become so strongly associated with the target group and its members in the memories of individuals that the stereotypes are automatically activated whenever someone is in the presence of that group, or a group member, or even a symbolic representation of the group.

However, although all people know the stereotype of a group, and that stereotype is automatized in all people, not all people accept the stereotype. Some people have personal beliefs, values, or attitudes which conflict with the stereotype, or, more generally, with the process of stereotyping. These people – labeled "low prejudice" – must consciously and actively inhibit whatever stereotype-related information is automatically activated to ensure that this information will not continue "on-line," influencing future information processing and conflicting with their belief systems. The use of intentional or consciously controlled processes to inhibit the automatic stereotype activation takes time, however. Other people – "high-prejudice" people – experience no such conflict between the activated stereotype and their own personal beliefs, and consequently are not motivated to inhibit stereotype activation.

To support her model, Devine (1989) presents data from three different studies with white American undergraduate subjects. In the first study, subjects were asked to list all the aspects of the stereotype of black Americans that they could think of, regardless of whether they personally endorsed the things they thought of. Subjects then completed a measure of prejudice (the modern racism scale (MRS) of McConahay, 1986). Scores on this scale were used to classify subjects into either high- or low-prejudice groups. Responses from the thought-listing task were sorted into one of 15 categories (e.g., poor, aggressive, criminal). The low-and high-prejudice groups did not differ in the frequency with which they generated responses in the different categories. In Study 2 subjects judged whether each of 100 stimulus words, presented parafoveally and for just 80 ms, was on the left or the right of the computer screen. Either 80 percent or 20 percent of the words were related to the stereotype of black Americans, and the remainder were stereotype-neutral. Subjects then took part in ostensibly a separate experiment, in which they read a description of a character's behavior and then rated that behavior on several dimensions. The behavior was deliberately described ambiguously, and the character's race was not mentioned. The character's behavior was rated as more hostile by subjects in the condition where 80 percent of the stimulus words were related to the stereotype of blacks than by subjects in the 20 percent condition. This effect did not depend on the subjects' own level of prejudice. Finally, in her third study, Devine had subjects list their thoughts in response to the social group "black Americans," so, unlike Study 1, subjects were providing their own personal beliefs. High-prejudice subjects used more trait terms, and listed more negative thoughts, than did low-prejudice subjects.

Devine concludes from her three studies that low- and high-prejudice white subjects do not differ in how well they know the social stereotype of black Americans; that they do not differ in how automatically activated stereotypical information affects their subsequent judgments of ambiguous behavior; but low- and high-prejudice white subjects *do* differ when they are asked to list their own thoughts related to blacks. Devine takes these three conclusions as evidence for her model relating stereotypes to prejudice, through the mediating influence of personal beliefs.

Devine's dissociation model is now largely accepted in the social cognition literature as the most adequate account of the links between stereotypes and prejudice (e.g., Fiske, in press; Hamilton and Sherman, 1994). Many limitations in the model and its empirical support can be identified, though.

Criticisms of Devine's model

We present first some limitations in the dissociation model, and in the support Devine's data lends the model. Then we review some recent evidence which challenges the model and which suggests ways of improving our understanding of the links between stereotypes and prejudice. Finally, we speculate on ways in which the results of these studies may help identify the types of social identity processes implicated in the link between stereotypes and prejudice.

Limitations in Devine's data

Although the data from Devine's (1989) three studies may be consistent with the model, they cannot be accepted as incontrovertible evidence for the model. Several limitations have been identified (Augoustinos and Walker, 1995; Lepore

and Brown, 1997; Locke, MacLeod, and Walker, 1994). First, the model specifies information processing links between stereotype activation and expressed
prejudice as they occur on-line, within a single individual. Yet the data Devine
relies on come from different studies of different individuals, and cannot be
taken to indicate with any certainty anything about on-line processing within
individuals.

Second, the third study, in which participants completed a thought-listing task,
is used to claim that subjects high and low in prejudice differ in the extent to
which negative stereotypical information remains activated once it is amenable
to strategic processing. This is hardly convincing, since it is just as likely that the
association between prejudice level and self-reported endorsement of the stereotype of blacks is due to a common social desirability response bias affecting both
the stereotype and the prejudice measures (Locke et al., 1994). It is perhaps
unlikely that a self-report measure of stereotype endorsement could *ever* provide
a satisfactory measure of stereotype activation (Fazio, Jackson, Dunton, and
Williams, 1995).

Third, the priming effect observed in Study 2 could simply be due to the
valence of the stimuli, rather than their stereotypicality. To be able to conclude
confidently that subjects' subsequent ratings of ambiguous behaviors were due to
the previously activated stereotype, the earlier priming stimuli must be controlled
for both stereotypicality *and* valence. Related to this, Devine assumes that
positive and negative stereotype elements are bipolar unidimensional opposites
of one another. However, some studies (e.g., Katz and Hass, 1988; Walker and
Pedersen, 1997) suggest that positive and negative dimensions of stereotypes are
orthogonal to one another. So not only must valence be operationalized separately from stereotypicality, but positive and negative stimuli ought to be operationalized independently of one another.

Challenges to Devine's model

Several recent studies empirically challenge Devine's model. Lepore and Brown
(1997) showed that priming a group category (e.g., blacks) does not induce
stereotype activation in everybody. Indeed, only high-prejudice participants
were likely to show evidence of stereotype activation when presented with
category labels. In contrast, when primed with elements of the stereotype (e.g.,
hostile), both high-and low-prejudice individuals showed evidence of stereotype
activation. Augoustinos, Ahrens, and Innes (1994) presented two studies. In the
first, high-and low-prejudice participants did not differ in their ability to list the
aspects of the stereotype of Aboriginal Australians (though they did differ in
their *style* of response). This supports the dissociation model. However, in Study
2, participants had to judge whether words (either positive or negative, and
either stereotype-related or unrelated) presented on a computer screen described
the stereotype of Aboriginal Australians, and then had to endorse or not each
word. All participants were faster at judging stereotypic words than

nonstereotypic words, but high-prejudice participants were quicker than low-prejudice participants at judging negative words, whether those words were stereotypic or not. Low-prejudice participants judged positive words faster than negative words. Finally, low-prejudice participants endorsed more positive elements of the stereotype than did high-prejudice participants, who in turn endorsed more negative elements than did their low-prejudice counterparts.

Fazio et al. (1995) showed that subjects could be classified as either high or low in prejudice according to the extent to which group primes (pictures of faces) facilitated judgments of words as either connotatively good or bad, and these individual differences in automatic activation predicted prejudice-related behaviors (although they failed to predict modern racism scale scores).

To sum up, then, the apparent appeal of Devine's dissociation model appears to extend well beyond the extent to which the model is supported by her own data. Several recent studies have challenged aspects of the model, but these studies have their own limitations. The study by Lepore and Brown (1997) contained no on-line measures of stereotype activation (as with Devine's original studies). Augoustinos et al. (1994) do not examine the automatic activation of stereotypes, monitoring stereotype activation only once it has been on-line long enough to be susceptible to controlled processing. And Fazio et al. (1995) examine only the valence of the information activated, and not its stereotypicality. Together, then, these studies point to limitations in the dissociation model, but cannot address the whole model linking stereotypes to prejudice.

We turn now to consider a series of experiments designed to examine more closely the automatic and controlled activation of stereotypes, using a novel experimental procedure which allows activated information to be tracked on-line within individuals as it passes from automatic into controlled processing. These experiments also disentangle any effects of valence from stereotypicality effects.

Some recent studies

Before summarizing our recent research, we describe briefly the experimental paradigm used. In a typical experimental session, subjects are asked to make judgments about a target group category. Each experimental trial starts with a target label presented on a computer screen, indicating which category is to be judged on that trial. In all our experiments apart from the first one, the category to be judged on any particular trial was either a group ("Aborigines" or "women") or "yourself." After a stimulus onset asynchrony (SOA) of either 240 ms or 2,000 ms, a colored trait word appears, and after a further 20 ms this is masked by a pattern of letter fragments in the same color as the word. Subjects are required to name the color of the display as quickly as possible. After this response is detected, the pattern mask is replaced by the trait word, this time presented in white, and subjects are required to indicate whether the word describes the previously mentioned target. Previous research suggests that the greater the degree to which information has been activated the longer the color-naming latency will be for that information (e.g., MacLeod and Rutherford, 1994; Warren, 1972). Manipulating SOA allows a dissociation between information that is automatically activated (the 240 ms SOA) and that which remains activated once strategic or conscious processes are able to modify the activation of this information (the 2,000 ms SOA: Neely, 1977).

To confirm that the method does serve to measure the activation of categories, our first experiment asked subjects to judge whether each of a series of words was a member of one of two nonsocial categories – vegetables or animals. On the color-naming task, which fell between the category label and the final judgment task, subjects did indeed take longer to color-name exemplars of the category they were preparing to judge.

A second experiment examined differences in stereotype activation between groups high and low in prejudice against Aborigines (see Locke et al., 1994). High-prejudice subjects automatically activated only stereotype-related information, but low-prejudice subjects appeared to activate a range of information, both related and unrelated, positive and negative. In the controlled processing stage, neither high-nor low-prejudice subjects appeared to inhibit any information. Thus, differences between high- and low-prejudice subjects at the controlled level are due not, as Devine's model claims, to inhibition by low-prejudice subjects of stereotypic information but to differences in what is initially activated automatically. In a second part of the study, Singaporean students recently arrived in Australia were tested. These subjects should not have rehearsed the stereotype of Aborigines often enough for it to have become automatized, yet high-prejudice Singaporean subjects were found to automatically activate a generic set of negative information, whether or not it was related to the stereotype. This suggests that high-prejudice people perhaps automatically activate a negative evaluation of an outgroup, whether or not they have a detailed knowledge of the relevant cultural (social) stereotype.

This experiment provides evidence that prejudice level *is* associated with differences in the information which is activated when judging a group, and that people high in prejudice tend to automatically activate stereotypic information, regardless of its emotional tone when judging the stereotyped group. These results contrast starkly with Devine's model.

It is possible that the results obtained in Study 2 are the product of something idiosyncratic about the stereotype of Aborigines. It is plausible, for example, that the overwhelmingly negative content of the stereotype of Aborigines makes processing of the stereotype different from processing of the stereotypes of other groups, which may be ambivalent or even overwhelmingly positive. So a third experiment was conducted, using "women" as the social category to be judged, and using only male subjects either high or low in prejudice against women (as assessed by the Women in Society Questionnaire of Lewis, 1988). Consistent with the results from the second experiment, high-prejudice subjects alone produced longer color-naming latencies for stereotypic traits (relative to nonstereotypic traits) at the short SOA when judging the target group. Low-prejudice subjects did not differ in the length of time it took them to color-name stereotypic and nonstereotypic traits when judging the target group. However, in contrast with the second experiment, high-prejudice subjects continued to display longer color-naming latencies at the long SOA for only the negative stereotypic traits. Latencies for the positive stereotypic traits at the long SOA were no longer than those obtained for the positive nonstereotypic traits (see figure 7.1 for an illustration of these results). These results again support the idea that when high-prejudice subjects judge a group, they automatically activate the stereotype of that group. The fact that the activation of the positive components of the stereotype was modified at the long SOA, when strategic processes would have had the opportunity to modify the activation of information, is, we think, due to the fact that the stereotype of women, unlike that of Aborigines, contains fairly similar proportions of positive and negative information (Williams and Best, 1982). As such, the strategic modification of the automatically activated stereotype may pare the available information to leave only that which drives those negative judgments of the target group which led to these subjects being classified as high prejudice in the first place.

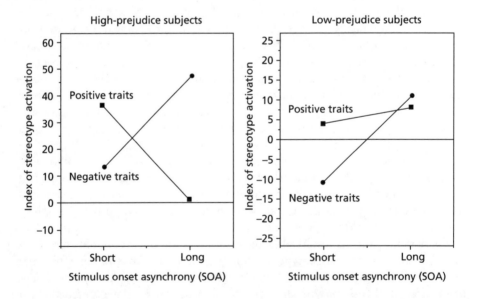

Figure 7.1   Mean stereotype activation index (calculated by taking color-naming latencies for stereotype-unrelated words from the color-naming latencies for stereotype-related words) for the high- and low-prejudice males at the short and long SOAs when judging the positive and negative traits. The resulting index is positive when there are longer color-naming latencies for the stereotype-related traits.

The second and third experiments produced a consistent pattern of results at the short SOA, with high-prejudice subjects producing longer color-naming latencies for stereotypic traits when judging the target group. These results clearly contradict the predictions derived from Devine's dissociation model and suggest that prejudice-linked differences in the activation of stereotypic information, relative to nonstereotypic information, are apparent at an automatic level of processing.

One potentially important difference between our method and Devine's is that our subjects are required to make a *judgment* of the target group. The importance of this feature is evaluated in Study 4. In this study, subjects were presented with a label (either "women" or "yourself") and asked simply to indicate whether a second label presented shortly afterward was the same as, or different from, the first label. Either 240 ms or 2,000 ms after the presentation of the first label, a trait was presented for 20 ms before being masked by a colored pattern. The time taken to color-name this stimulus was taken as an index of the activation of the trait presented. Once subjects had named the color of the mask, the second label was presented and subjects were required to indicate whether it was the same as, or different from, that presented at the beginning of the trial. Although exactly the same stimuli were employed in this experiment as in Study 3, which required subjects to judge women, and although subjects were selected to match those in Study 3 in terms of age and prejudice level, there was no evidence in this experiment of any prejudice-linked differences in color-naming latencies for stereotypic traits, relative to nonstereotypic traits, at either a short or a long SOA. While this supports the notion that prejudice-linked differences in stereotype activation occur only when subjects are required to make evaluative judgments about the target group, it is difficult to draw conclusions based on null results. So a fifth experiment was conducted, in part to compare, among other things, subjects' responses when they had to make a judgment and when they did not.

Study 5 was designed with two other purposes in mind also. First, it tests a hypothesis proposed by von Hippel, Sekaquaptewa, and Vargas (1995) that prejudice-linked differences in the activation of stereotypic information lead to biases in the *encoding* of stereotypic information about the target group. Because high-prejudice individuals activate stereotypes, they should find stereotype-congruent information easier to encode. In contrast, because low-prejudice subjects do not activate these stereotypes, they should show no encoding biases favoring stereotypic information. To address these predictions, a reading-time task was developed which assessed the time it took high-and low-prejudice subjects to read sentences describing women performing stereotype-congruent or stereotype-incongruent actions. The second purpose of this experiment was to confirm the importance of evaluative judgments in producing prejudice-linked differences in stereotype activation. To this end, male subjects completed the reading-time task under instructions that directed them either to evaluate, or else simply to remember, information concerning target group members.

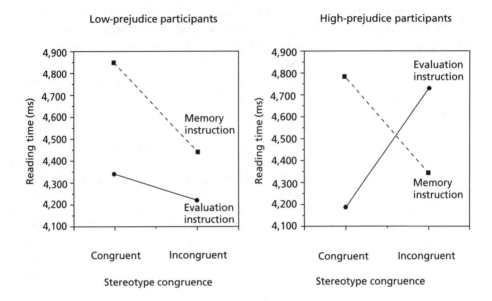

Figure 7.2 High- and low-prejudice males' mean reading times for sentences either congruent or incongruent with the stereotype of women, under instructions to either evaluate or remember the sentences.

As figure 7.2 illustrates, the high-prejudice subjects displayed shorter reading times for stereotype-congruent sentences, relative to stereotype-incongruent sentences, but did so only when they were instructed to make evaluative judgments of the group members' actions rather than simply to remember those actions. However, this trend was reversed when they were asked simply to remember the information. Here, high-prejudice subjects took longer to read stereotype-congruent information. Low-prejudice subjects showed no evidence of faster reading times for stereotypic information under either instruction condition. Indeed, they produced longer reading times for stereotype-congruent information irrespective of the instruction condition. The high-prejudice participants' results suggest that their disproportionate automatic activation of stereotypic information does indeed translate into an encoding advantage for stereotype-congruent information.

The fact that all participants found it harder to encode stereotype-incongruent information when they were under the memory instructions may help to explain the role of processing goals in memory biases observed by Stangor and MacMillan (1992). They observed that when subjects are required to judge or evaluate target groups or their members, they show a small but reliable memory advantage for stereotype-congruent information. In contrast, when subjects are required simply to remember information, they show a memory advantage for stereotype-incongruent information. The results obtained in Study 5 suggest that both high- and low-prejudice subjects find it harder to encode stereotype-congruent information when required simply to remember information about target group members. However, when required to judge the target group, high-prejudice subjects alone produced results suggesting they found it easier to encode stereotype-congruent information. This finding suggests that prejudice-linked differences in the ease of encoding of stereotype-congruent and incongruent information may be the mechanism underlying differences in memory for stereotypic information.

Summary

The studies reported here, along with the studies by Lepore and Brown (1997), Locke et al. (1994), and Fazio et al. (1995), provide strong evidence that there *are* differences between high- and low-prejudice groups in their tendency to automatically activate stereotypes, even though prejudice level is unrelated to knowledge of the social stereotype. Furthermore, our results show that stereotypes are *not* activated automatically merely by the presence of a stereotyped outgroup, or outgroup member, or symbolic representation of the outgroup, as Devine and others claim, but rather are activated only when certain processing goals are in place. We turn now to consider the nature of processing goals, since they provide a major avenue for the articulation of social identity processes with the social cognitive work we have considered so far in this chapter.

Stereotypes and Processing Goals

The studies described above demonstrate that stereotypes are activated when high-prejudice subjects are required to *judge* the stereotyped group, but not merely by the presentation of the group, or a group member, or a symbolic representation of the group. In Bargh's (1989) terms, automatic stereotype activation is goal dependent: stereotype content is activated only when high-prejudice subjects are preparing to judge the stereotyped group. This may reflect prior stereotype learning and usage, with this goal representing the condition under which stereotypic information has routinely been accessed by high-prejudice subjects in the past. If stereotypic information is repeatedly accessed by these subjects to make judgments of the stereotyped group, then this process may become proceduralized such that, once an individual prepares to judge the stereotyped group, the process is automatically engaged, with the result that the stereotypic information becomes disproportionately available. It should also be remembered that participants in our experiments were asked to make judgments about the outgroup and about themselves. This may have served to highlight, for the high-prejudice participants at least, their own group identities as well.

Recently researchers have begun to detail the role of processing goals in stereotype activation. Gilbert and Hixon (1991) suggest that linguistic representations of groups and individuals engender stereotype activation only if the social context or processing goals imbue the linguistic representation with some social relevance to the subject. In their own research, they demonstrated that subjects watching an Asian target holding cards containing word fragments such as a s_y are no more likely than subjects watching a white target to complete the stems as stereotypic words (e.g., sly) rather than nonstereotypic words (e.g., sky). Gilbert and Hixon argue that when the target persons assumed the status of "furniture," and subjects saw no purpose in judging or forming an impression of them, the relevant stereotype was not activated. The results in Studies 4 and 5 support this view that processing goals play an important role in mediating prejudice-linked differences in stereotype activation.

Other evidence has also recently emerged detailing the role processing goals may play in mediating the automatic activation of stereotypes. Pratto, Shih, and Orton (1997) adapted a procedure from Perdue, Dovidio, Gurtman, and Tyler (1990), which shows that using generic ingroup or outgroup designators (e.g., "us" and "them") as primes facilitates subsequent judgments of positive and negative words, respectively. In their first experiment, Pratto et al. (1997) selected participants high or low in social dominance orientation (SDO: Pratto, Sidanius, Stallworth, and Malle, 1994), and subjected them to the Perdue et al. (1990) procedure. SDO is a general orientation toward group relations, with those high on SDO favoring intergroup inequality and dominance, and those low in SDO favoring equality. Although ingroup primes facilitated judgments about positive words, and outgroup primes facilitated judgments about negative words, there was no difference between high and low SDO subjects in the priming effect. In a second study, the same experimental procedure was followed, but was preceded by a threat to group status – the subjects, who were all Stanford University undergraduates, read an article claiming that "Stanford students are neither as mature, prosocial, hardworking, or smart as they are reported to be and therefore fewer people who are accepted by Stanford are choosing to enroll. The essay thus symbolically attacked the participants' group along dimensions that legitimize their elite status and define their group's status" (Pratto et al., 1997, p. 15). In this experiment, high SDO subjects reproduced the priming effect from Study 1. Low SDO subjects, though, showed no evidence of the priming effect. The behavior of the low SDO subjects counters most theories of intergroup behavior, which would predict increases in ingroup favoritism and/or outgroup derogation under conditions of group threat. Social identity theory could handle these subjects' behavior only if low and high SDO subjects differed in the perceived stability and legitimacy of the dimensions of group threat. Regardless, though, the Pratto et al. (1997) results suggest that the social context can either facilitate or inhibit the automatic activation of evaluative orientations toward the ingroup and outgroup in different groups of people.

In another recent study, Fazio et al. (1995) briefly presented participants with pictures of white or black individuals before they were given a trait term (e.g., poor) and were asked to decide whether it was a "good" or "bad" word. In a series of studies they showed that more prejudiced participants were faster to evaluate negative terms following black faces, suggesting that negative information was automatically primed in memory when participants were asked to *evaluate* the trait terms that were presented. Importantly, this pattern of results was obtained even though the SOA between the presentation of the faces and the trait terms allowed only automatic processes to be mapped. Finally, Blair and Banaji (1996) employed a priming task in which participants were presented with primes that were traits stereotypic of either males or females, or were nonstereotypic. Following a short SOA which allowed only automatic processing, or a longer SOA which permitted the strategic modification of any activation, participants were presented with a name and were instructed to indicate whether it was a male or female name. Both male and female participants were faster to identify names when they were representative of the stereotypic category identified by the prime, at both an automatic and strategic level of processing. In a final experiment, participants were instructed to avoid assuming that a term that is stereotypic of, for example, women (e.g., perfume), would be followed by a female name. Indeed, participants were instructed to anticipate that a male name would be presented following a stereotypically female trait prime, and vice versa. Under these instruction conditions participants were indeed able to modify their expectations and the degree to which stereotypic expectations were activated at both strategic *and* automatic levels of processing.

Although Bargh (1994) has suggested that stereotype activation may be goal dependent, he also has suggested that stereotypes may be automatically activated preconsciously. That is, he claims that stereotypes can be activated by the mere presence of the triggering stimulus without any particular goal, or even conscious awareness of the stimulus, being needed for stereotype activation to occur. Our results, and those outlined above, suggest, though, that the mere presentation of a label identifying the stereotyped group is *not* enough to trigger automatic stereotype operation in either high-or low-prejudice subjects. However, both Lepore and Brown's (1997) and Blair and Banaji's (1996) results suggest that stereotypes may be automatically preconsciously primed by the presentation of traits which represent elements of the stereotype. When the representations of these traits are primed in memory then activation may spread to related elements within the stereotype, irrespective of the individual's personal beliefs. Importantly of course, none of these other studies contained a condition in which participants were asked to judge themselves. It may be that, at least for high-prejudice participants, self-categorizations, and not just the categorization of others, are important in determining whether stereotypes are activated.

Summary

Stereotypes (and other forms of automated "thought") have often been used to illustrate the metaphor of the "cognitive miser" – stereotypes provide a mental shortcut for the overtaxed but slothful social perceiver. A simple application of the metaphor suggests that all people all of the time should (automatically) activate the stereotype of a group whenever they are confronted by that group, or by a member of that group, or even by a symbolic representation of that group. But that would be too simple, and indeed would counter the presumed efficiency of miserly thought. Why activate the stereotype in situations where the stereotype is irrelevant to the task at hand? And especially, why activate the stereotype if it is only going to be inhibited because it conflicts with personal beliefs? A more useful metaphor is that of the "motivated tactician" (Fiske and Taylor, 1991). In this metaphor, stereotypes are activated in a more pragmatic fashion only when they provide the kinds of information useful for the judgments that have to be made according to particular situational contexts. This view sits better with the research reviewed in this section, too. Stereotypes are automatically activated when people have to make judgments about a group, but not when they have to remember information about the group. Stereotype activation can be inhibited by instructing people to expect nonstereotypic information. And stereotype activation can be inhibited in some people by manipulating the intergroup context in which they find themselves. Other areas of research suggest other kinds of processing goals which may be pertinent to stereotype activation, but which remain to be examined in this area. For example, deep or elaborate processing can be induced by instruction or context, and improves recall of information and induces longer-lasting attitude change (Petty and Cacioppo, 1981). Empathizing is a processing goal which alters how information about others is processed, and again can be induced experimentally (Batson, Polycarpou, Harmon-Jones, Imhoff, Mitchener, Bednar, Klein, and Highberger, 1997). Similarly for self-referencing processing goals, which might require a subject to compare the target object to self, or to contemplate an actual or future interaction (see Fiske and Taylor, 1991, pp. 330–9, for a general discussion of processing goals in person memory).

Stereotypes, Processing Goals, and Social Identity

Contemporary social cognitive accounts of stereotypes (e.g., Devine, 1989) view them as schemas about groups, automatically activated by the presence of the target group, a group member, or a symbolic representation of the group. However, as Bargh (1994) has pointed out, automatic processes are by no means inevitable. Research on the most basic and well-practiced tasks, such as reading, has found that reading a word primes the concept denoted by the word, and also primes related concepts automatically (i.e., it is fast and does not consume cognitive resources). However, the context surrounding the word influences the activation of the concept (e.g., MacKay, 1973). The important point here is that activation of meaning is context dependent. Different people in different contexts will activate different sets of information with which to make judgments. What sort of information – if any – is activated by a particular stimulus depends on the immediate context and on the goals (forming an impression, making a judgment, empathizing, etc.) of the person in that context.

To understand the activation of stereotypes and their link to prejudice, then, we must also understand the immediate context of the person, and the goals of that person in that context. Which goals lead to stereotype activation, and which do not? And in which contexts? These are questions which cannot readily be answered by current social cognition research. We want to end this chapter, though, by speculating about some answers, suggesting that micro-level processing goals interact with more meso-level factors such as social identity and the immediate intergroup context.

It is clear from our own research that stereotypes are activated only when subjects are motivated to evaluate or judge a group; when the motivation is to remember information, the stereotype is not activated. In "real life," when is it that people are motivated to evaluate or judge a group and its members? Social identity theory suggests that such motivations follow from conditions of real or imagined group threat, conditions in which social identity is both salient and challenged.

We briefly mentioned earlier that one difference between our method and the methods of Lepore and Brown (1997) and Blair and Banaji (1996) is that we require participants to judge other groups *and* themselves. This procedural difference may change the nature of the immediate comparative context for participants (at least for high-prejudice participants). Both social identity and self-categorization theories would predict that having participants judge both self and an outgroup forces upon those participants not only the categories of self and outgroup (and the attendant identities), but also the relationship between those two categories. This then requires an analysis of the functions played by stereotypes in the immediate social context. Stereotypes do not just "light up" *in vacuo*, but rather are purposeful, tactical, and functional. They are for doing.

The suggestion that stereotypes are context dependent is nothing extraordinary for either social identity theory (SIT) or self-categorization theory (SCT). Indeed, for both these theories, the fugacity of stereotypes, their dependence on the particulars of the intergroup setting, is their most important feature. For SIT, a stereotype of an outgroup will vary with the varying functional relationship between the ingroup and the outgroup (Condor, 1990; Tajfel, 1981). For SCT, a stereotype of any social category (self, ingroup, outgroup) is even more transient, varying in strength and content with the vagaries of the immediate comparative context (e.g., the presence of one or another third group in the setting), the

salience of the categorization, and generally serving to maximize the psychological disparity between categories in order to maximize the informativeness of the
set of categories (e.g., Oakes, Haslam, and Turner, 1994).

Social cognitive accounts of stereotypes also tend to emphasize the transience
of stereotype activation (but not content), by tying activation to the context-
dependent meaning of categories and stimuli (Bargh, 1994; MacKay, 1973) and
to the processing goals directing attention (our studies above; Gilbert and Hixon,
1991). The relative transience of stereotypes is therefore a point in common
between SIT and SCT, on the one hand, and social cognitive approaches such as
Devine's, on the other, and both theoretical approaches stand to gain by integrating the work of the other.

SCT provides perhaps the most detailed account of the context-dependent
nature of stereotypes (e.g., Haslam and Turner, 1992; Oakes et al., 1994; Wilder
and Shapiro, 1991), but it fails to provide the cognitive mechanisms which allow
some, but not other, aspects of consensually held knowledge of a social category
(self, ingroup, outgroup) to be represented as *the* stereotype of that category in
any given social context. We suggest that processing goals are one such mechanism. Processing goals also provide a means whereby intraindividual cognitive
processes operate within a social context. Processing goals obviously influence
whether a stereotype is activated or not. But processing goals are not themselves
part of the stereotype, or determinable from the stereotype or any other intraindividual process or content. They are determined in a social context by the
nature of the relationship between self and the other social categories evident in
that context. Thus, the same processing goal (for example, evaluating Cathy
Freeman, a well-known Aboriginal Australian sprinter) may activate different
stereotypes depending on whether she is categorized as belonging to an ethnic
group (Aboriginal), a national group (Australian), a gender group (female), or
some other group (athlete). The same context and the same processing goal may
also produce different stereotypes with different consequences depending on the
category memberships of the evaluator (Aboriginal or not, Australian or not,
female or male, athlete or not, prejudiced or not). Thus, the gay and straight men
in a study by Simon, Glassner-Bayerl, and Stratenwerth (1991) could equally
well document the stereotypes of gay and straight men, but since the negative
nature of the stereotype of gay men led gay men to be dissatisfied (but highly
identified) with the category "gay," they were led to engage in strategies of social
competition and creativity to make their social identity more positive.

The general, integrative point we are making, then, is that the nature of
relations between social categories in a particular social context determines
(and is determined by) the mental representations of those categories. Processing
goals are one mechanism which allows for this interplay between contextual
factors and cognitive factors.

The immediate social context can serve to inhibit, as well as activate, stereotypes. Blair and Banaji (1996) demonstrate how simple instructions to avoid
stereotypic expectancies can modify the type of information that is automatically

activated. Pratto et al. (1997) show how manipulating social context (inducing group threat) interacts with stable individual differences in social dominance orientation to inhibit generic outgroup stereotype activation in those people committed to social equality (i.e., low in SDO). Our own research suggests that prejudice level is a similar stable individual difference which serves to motivate the activation or inhibition of particular types of information. The common thread through these different studies is that particular people (low SDO, low prejudice) have an identity in which it is important for them not to stereotype (or be seen to stereotype) and that the immediate social context (provision of a group threat, instructions to avoid stereotypic expectancies) provides processing goals which allow them not to stereotype.

Finally, we want to consider briefly the unexpected results obtained from the sample of Singaporean subjects in our Study 2, which suggest that subjects unfamiliar with the social stereotype of a group nonetheless automatically activate negative information (whether related to the stereotype or not) when preparing to judge that group. This could reflect a different form of prejudice from that observed in the Australian subjects in the experiment, or this may be typical of all prejudiced individuals who have not had enough exposure to the stereotype to automatically activate it when preparing to judge the target group. Importantly, this finding suggests a possible individual difference in the predisposition for prejudice toward any group, or at least a predisposition to notice "groupness." As we have noted elsewhere (Locke et al., 1994), it is possible to imagine a "group-awareness" schema which would predispose an individual's attention to certain group markers (if they are schematic) or away from group markers (if they are aschematic or opposed to "groupness"). Such a mechanism could function theoretically in ways similar to Hinkle and Brown's (1990) use of the dimensions of individualism–collectivism and relational orientation, to make certain group identities more salient and more important for the individual. Another possibility is that these are individuals whose ego, or self-esteem, is more easily threatened. Hence, when confronted by our experimental procedure which requires them to judge themselves, on the one hand, and Aborigines, on the other, they are motivated to automatically activate negative information about the outgroup with which to judge them. As a result, their own social groups are, relatively, better off and their self-esteem is protected or enhanced. This explanation is clearly testable with our experimental paradigm outlined earlier.

A major commonality between social identity approaches and social cognitive approaches to the study of stereotypes is an emphasis on the fluid, transient nature of stereotypes. However, the research presented in this chapter also points to the *stability* of individual differences in stereotype activation. This conflicts with the dissociation model's view that stereotypes are automatically activated in all people when confronted with a group, a group member, or a symbolic representation of the group, and is a point which must be considered in revising the model linking stereotypes to prejudice. The stable individual differences reported in our studies, and in the studies by Pratto et al. (1997) and Fazio et al. (1995), also conflict with SIT and SCT. SIT, and especially SCT, posit a caducity in the mental representation of groups which does not accord with the data. Some representations of groups *are* reasonably consistent across situational contexts; people *do* consistently differ in the information they activate when judging a group. This indicates an inveterateness beyond that posited by SIT and SCT, and also conflicts with Devine's dissociation model.

Conclusions

Our results suggest that the role of processing goals may be to initiate prejudice-linked differences in automatic stereotype activation which, in turn, lead to differences in the encoding of stereotype-congruent and stereotype-incongruent information. These findings highlight the role of the social perceiver as a motivated tactician who activates a stereotype only if it is needed, and when it is appropriate. Importantly, research has, to date, only outlined a few of the many possible motivations and processing goals that may influence the activation of stereotypes. While some research has suggested that identity and group context may be important issues in determining whether stereotypes are automatically activated, little systematic research has been carried out. Given that simple instructions in a laboratory (e.g., Blair and Banaji, 1996), along with long-standing differences in personal beliefs (e.g., Lepore and Brown, 1997; Locke et al., 1994), can change the nature of the information that is activated automatically when judging someone, then it remains to be seen what other group-based motivations, such as ingroup coherence and identity, may have on the automatic activation of stereotypic information. Examining both the stable and the transitory aspects of stereotypes and stereotyping, and considering contributions of both social cognitive approaches to processes of stereotyping and social identity approaches to the content and context of stereotypes and stereotyping, can only lead to a fuller and better understanding of stereotyping and prejudice.

References

Augoustinos, M., Ahrens, C., and Innes, J.M. (1994). Stereotypes and prejudice: The Australian experience. *British Journal of Social Psychology*, 33, 125–41.

Augoustinos, M. and Walker, I. (1995). *Social Cognition: An integrated introduction*. London: Sage.

Bargh, J.A. (1989). Conditional automaticity: Varieties of automatic influence in social perception and cognition. In J.S. Uleman and J.A. Bargh (eds), *Unintended Thought*. New York: Guilford, pp. 3–51.

Bargh, J.A. (1994). The four horsemen of automaticity: Awareness, intention, efficiency, and control in social cognition. In R.S. Wyer, Jr and T.K. Srull (eds), *Handbook of Social Cognition*, 2nd edn, Vol. 1. Hillsdale, NJ: Erlbaum, pp. 1–40.

Batson, C.D., Polycarpou, M.P., Harmon-Jones, E., Imhoff, H.J., Mitchener, E.C., Bednar, L.L., Klein, T.R., and Highberger, L. (1997). Empathy and attitudes: Can feeling for a member of a stigmatized group improve feelings toward the group? *Journal of Personality and Social Psychology*, 72, 105–18.

Blair, I.V. and Banaji, M.R. (1996). Automatic and controlled processes in stereotype priming. *Journal of Personality and Social Psychology*, 70, 1142–63.

Brown, R.J. (1995). *Prejudice: Its social psychology*. Oxford: Blackwell.

Condor, S. (1990). Social stereotypes and social identity. In D. Abrams and M.A. Hogg (eds), *Social Identity Theory: Constructive and critical advances*. London: Harvester Wheatsheaf, pp. 230–49.

Devine, P.G. (1989). Stereotypes and prejudice: Their automatic and controlled components. *Journal of Personality and Social Psychology*, 56, 5–18.

Fazio, R.H., Jackson, J.R., Dunton, B.C., and Williams, C.J. (1995). Variability in automatic activation as an unobtrusive measure of racial attitudes: A bona fide pipeline? *Journal of Personality and Social Psychology*, 69, 1013–27.

Fiske, S.T. (1992). Thinking is for doing: Portraits of social cognition from daguerreotype to laserphoto. *Journal of Personality and Social Psychology*, 63, 877–89.

Fiske, S.T. (in press). Stereotyping, prejudice, and discrimination. In D.T. Gilbert, S.T. Fiske, and G. Lindzey (eds), *Handbook of Social Psychology*, 4th edn. New York: McGraw-Hill.

Fiske, S.T. and Taylor, S.E. (1991). *Social Cognition*, 2nd edn. New York: McGraw-Hill.

Gilbert, D.T. and Hixon, J.G. (1991). The trouble of thinking: Activation and application of stereotypic beliefs. *Journal of Personality and Social Psychology*, 60, 509–17.

Hamilton, D.L. and Sherman, J.W. (1994). Stereotypes. In R.S. Wyer, Jr and T.K. Srull (eds), *Handbook of Social Cognition*, 2nd edn. Vol. 2. Hillsdale, NJ: Erlbaum, pp. 1–68.

Haslam, S.A. and Turner, J.C. (1992). Context-dependent variation in social stereotyping 2: The relationship between frame of reference, self-categorization and accentuation. *European Journal of Social Psychology*, 22, 251–77.

Hilton, J.L. and von Hippel, W. (1996). Stereotypes. *Annual Review of Psychology*, 47, 237–71.

Hinkle, S. and Brown, R.J. (1990). Intergroup comparisons and social identity: Some links and lacunae. In D. Abrams and M.A. Hogg (eds), *Social Identity Theory: Constructive and critical advances*. London: Harvester Wheatsheaf, pp. 48–70.

Katz, I. and Hass, R.G. (1988). Racial ambivalence and American value conflict: Correlational and priming studies of dual cognitive structures. *Journal of Personality and Social Psychology*, 55, 893–905.

Lepore, L. and Brown, R.J. (1997). Category activation and stereotype accessibility: Is prejudice inevitable? *Journal of Personality and Social Psychology*, 72, 275–87.

Lewis, V. (1988). Measuring attitudes to women: Development of the Women in Society Questionnaire. Unpublished Master's thesis, University of Melbourne.

Locke, V., MacLeod, C., and Walker, I. (1994). Automatic and controlled activation of stereotypes: Individual differences associated with prejudice. *British Journal of Social Psychology*, 33, 29–46.

McConahay, J.B. (1986). Modern racism, ambivalence, and the modern racism scale. In J.F. Dovidio and S.L. Gaertner (eds), *Prejudice, Discrimination, and Racism*. Orlando, FL: Academic Press, pp. 91–125.

MacKay, D.G. (1973). Aspects of the theory of comprehension, memory, and attention. *Quarterly Journal of Experimental Psychology*, 25, 22–40.

MacLeod, C. and Rutherford, E. (1994). Anxiety and the selective processing of emotional information: Mediating roles of awareness, trait and state variables, and personal relevance of the stimulus materials. *Behaviour Research and Therapy*, 30, 479–91.

Neely, J.H. (1977). Semantic priming and retrieval from lexical memory: Roles of inhibitionless spreading activation and limited capacity attention. *Journal of Experimental Psychology*, 106, 226–54.

Oakes, P.J., Haslam, S.A., and Turner, J.C. (1994). *Stereotyping and Social Reality*. Oxford: Blackwell.

Perdue, C.W., Dovidio, J.F., Gurtman, M.B., and Tyler, R.B. (1990). Us and them: Social categorization and the process of intergroup bias. *Journal of Personality and Social Psychology*, 59, 475–86.

Petty, R.E. and Cacioppo, J.T. (1981). *Attitudes and Persuasion: Classic and contemporary approaches*. Dubuque, IA: W.C. Brown.

Pratto, F., Shih, M., and Orton, J. (1997). Social dominance orientation and group threat in implicit and explicit group discrimination. Manuscript in submission.

Pratto, F., Sidanius, J., Stallworth, L.M., and Malle, B.F. (1994). Social dominance orientation: A personality variable relevant to social roles and intergroup relations. *Journal of Personality and Social Psychology*, 67, 741–63.

Simon, B., Glassner-Bayerl, B., and Stratenwerth, I. (1991). Stereotyping and self-stereotyping in a natural intergroup context: The case of heterosexual and homosexual men. *Social Psychology Quarterly*, 54, 252–66.

Stangor, C. and Lange, J.E. (1994). Mental representations of social groups: Advances in understanding stereotypes and stereotyping. *Advances in Experimental Social Psychology*, 26, 357–416.

Stangor, C. and MacMillan, D. (1992). Memory for expectancy-congruent and expectancy-incongruent information: A review of the social and social-developmental literatures. *Psychological Bulletin*, 111, 42–61.

Stangor, C. and Schaller, M. (1996). Stereotypes as individual and collective representations. In C.N. Macrae, C. Stangor, and M. Hewstone (eds), *Stereotypes and Stereotyping*. New York: Guilford, pp. 3–37.

Tajfel, H. (1981). Social stereotypes and social groups. In J.C. Turner and H. Giles (eds), *Intergroup Behaviour*. Oxford: Blackwell, pp. 144–67.

von Hippel, W., Sekaquaptewa, D., and Vargas, P. (1995). On the role of encoding processes in stereotype maintenance. *Advances in Experimental Social Psychology*, 27, 177–253.

Walker, I. and Pedersen, A. (1997). Relative deprivation and prejudice: Some Australian evidence. Unpublished manuscript, Murdoch University.

Warren, R.E. (1972). Stimulus encoding in memory. *Journal of Experimental Psychology*, 94, 90–100.

Wilder, D.A. and Shapiro, P. (1991). Facilitation of outgroup stereotypes by enhanced ingroup identity. *Journal of Experimental Social Psychology*, 27, 431–52.

Williams, J.E. and Best, D.L. (1982). *Measuring Sex Stereotypes: A thirty nation study*. Beverly Hills, CA: Sage.

8

Affective and Cognitive Implications of a Group Becoming Part of the Self: New Models of Prejudice and of the Self-concept

Eliot R. Smith

The core insight of social identity theory and self-categorization theory is that a social group can "become part of" the self. What does this idea mean? Is it just a metaphor, or does it postulate a real and concrete link between the social group and individual cognitive levels? How is this idea different from saying that a person can "identify with" or "see the self as similar to" or "like" an ingroup?

When I first became interested in social identity and self-categorization theories, I was fascinated by these ideas and by their breadth of implications for such issues as social influence, deindividuation, and intergroup relations. However, I was initially put off by the frequent appearance of rhetoric that opposed social identity to social cognition approaches. With my own background solidly in social cognition, I was at first prepared to reject any viewpoint some of whose proponents seemed to brand me and my entire research tradition as the enemy. However, in thinking more deeply about the issues, I became convinced not only that social cognition and social identity approaches are compatible, but that they fit neatly together. For example, the seminal presentation of self-categorization theory in Turner, Hogg, Oakes, Reicher, and Wetherell (1987, ch. 3) draws on the basic principles of accessibility, which have been elaborated in social cognition research (Higgins, 1996), though often using different terminology. Determined to explore the implications of combining the insights of social identity and social cognition, I returned to the core idea of the former. If an ingroup can become part of the self, several predictions follow that could be readily tested by applying methods of social cognition.

Preparation of this chapter was supported by National Institute of Mental Health grants R01 MH46840 and K02 MH01178. Thanks to Art Aron, Susan Henry, Diane Mackie, and Thomas Pettigrew for various forms of assistance in this work.

This chapter describes some of the directions in which this line of thought has taken me to date. First, it follows up the idea that if a group becomes part of the self, group membership develops affective and motivational significance, just as other self-aspects do. This chapter describes a new conceptualization of prejudice that combines the idea of group membership as part of the self with appraisal theories of emotion. Initial evidence supporting this conceptualization is also presented. Second, if group membership becomes part of the self-concept, standard theories in social cognition would suggest that in certain types of task, group and individual attributes can be confused or create interference. Research testing this notion is also described. The overall goal of this chapter is to demonstrate how combining ideas from social identity theory and related perspectives with ideas and research methods from social cognition can lead to deeper insights and new approaches to core issues in social psychology.

New Conceptualization of Prejudice

Prejudice as group-based emotion

Social identity theory, and the basic idea that group membership can become part of the self, is one of the two foundation stones for the new conceptualization of prejudice that I have advanced (Smith, 1993). The other foundation is appraisal theories of emotion (Frijda, 1986; Roseman, 1984; Scherer, 1988; C.A. Smith and Ellsworth, 1985). These models hold that people experience specific emotions based on their interpretations and perceptions of objects, situations, or events. In these models, a discrete emotion is defined as a complex syndrome (including subjective feelings, cognitions, physiological reactions, and behavioral action tendencies) caused by a configuration of beliefs or appraisals of an object or situation in relation to the self. For example, the emotion of anger and associated feelings, physiological reactions, and action tendencies can be triggered by appraisals that someone else has harmed one unjustly (Frijda, Kuipers, and ter Schure, 1989; Roseman, 1984).

Appraisal theories of emotion, all the way back to the pioneering work of Arnold (1960), assume that appraisals involve the *individual* self. For example, "To arouse an emotion, the object must be appraised as affecting me in some way, affecting me personally as an individual" (Arnold, 1960, p. 171). Other influential theorists such as Lazarus and Folkman (1984) similarly suggested that an appraisal involves the question "Does this situation affect me personally?" (p. 31). Departing from this individualistic emphasis, my basic argument is that emotions can be based on appraisals that refer to the socially extended self (i.e., an ingroup) as well as the individual self (Smith, 1993). It is already well known that positive and negative moods can be based upon an ingroup's successes or failures, as when people "bask in reflected glory" of a victorious sports team

(Cialdini, Border, Thorne, Walker, Freeman, and Sloan, 1976). My model goes beyond simple positive and negative feelings to hold that a host of specific emotions can similarly be based on group membership as well as the individual person.

Relations to other theories of prejudice

This view of prejudice as group-based emotion contrasts with the now-standard one, which conceptualizes prejudice within the framework of attitude theory. This approach has many advantages, including the robust and well-tested theories and measurement tools that are available within that framework. This approach also conceptually links prejudice to related concepts, stereotypes and discrimination. Specifically, the traditional attitude-based approach identifies a group *stereotype* as beliefs about an outgroup's positive or (usually) negative attributes, *prejudice* as the resulting positive or negative attitude toward the outgroup, and *discrimination* as attitude-driven behavior toward the group. These three concepts thus fall neatly within an overall framework like that of Fishbein and Ajzen (1975): attitudes are based on beliefs about the attitude object, and in turn affect behavior (via the mediation of behavioral intentions). This conceptualization, in explicit or implicit form, lies behind much research and has been fruitful in providing many insights into the nature, causes, and consequences of prejudice.

The new conceptualization of prejudice as group-based emotion relates these three key concepts in a somewhat different way. A *stereotype* is a set of appraisals of the outgroup in relation to the ingroup in the current situation. *Prejudice* is an emotional reaction to the outgroup triggered by its relevance to the perceiver's ingroup. Finally, *discrimination* is behavior driven by an emotional action tendency.

Smith (1993) describes several advantages of this new approach over the traditional attitude-based picture. One point is that under the traditional approach, if prejudice is assumed to stem from a perceiver's stereotypic beliefs about the outgroup's characteristics, it should be relatively constant across situations or contexts. However, empirically, prejudice is often found to be markedly situation-specific (e.g., Minard, 1952). For example, an old-line racist may hate and discriminate against ethnic minorities in many contexts, but accept them in traditional, menial roles such as laborers or servants. If prejudice is considered as a group-based emotional reaction, this situation specificity becomes easier to understand. Prejudice depends on the appraisal of the outgroup in relation to the ingroup (for example, how much it threatens the ingroup). The degree of threat posed by outgroup members, and therefore the amount of prejudice felt and the amount of discriminatory behavior expressed, can vary from situation to situation. An outgroup member in a subordinate position who accepts his or her role poses little threat and may excite no negative emotions. Of course, if an outgroup is viewed as homogeneous, most or all individual members of the group may come to excite a similar range of emotions regardless of their personal qualities.

The model of prejudice as group-based emotion should also be distinguished from two other types of conceptualizations that link prejudice to the self or to affect. First, initial formulations of social identity theory (Tajfel and Turner, 1979) postulated that self-esteem maintenance or defense was one motivator of intergroup behavior, especially for members of negatively evaluated groups. However, empirical evidence on this point has been mixed. Some recent models (e.g., Turner et al., 1987; Hogg and Abrams, 1993) generally deemphasize the importance of self-esteem-related motives, while others (Crocker, Blaine, and Luhtanen, 1993) still argue that self-esteem is important, though not in a simple or straightforward way. Whatever the eventual resolution of this debate, the model I advance is substantially different from a self-esteem-based model of prejudice. I see prejudice as a group-based emotional reaction to an outgroup that is appraised as having some implications for the ingroup (for example, by threatening the ingroup). This is conceptually distinct from self-esteem, which is an evaluation that targets the self (either personal or collective) rather than an outgroup, and which is bipolar in nature (ranging from positive to negative) rather than involving a variety of distinct emotions (fear, anger, resentment, etc.).

Particularly in the first half of this century, a number of related theories of prejudice that emphasized the role of affect were prominent in social psychology. Frustration–aggression models (Dollard, Doob, Miller, Mowrer, and Sears, 1939), the authoritarian personality model (Adorno, Frenkel-Brunswik, Levinson, and Sanford, 1950), and "scapegoat" theories of prejudice (see Rothbart and Lewis, 1994), share a common core of ideas. Negative affect stemming from a variety of potential causes (economic disadvantage, deep-seated personality conflicts, etc.) was displaced onto vulnerable outgroups, motivating dislike and aggression against them. Though these models (like mine) assume that affect is a prominent part of prejudice, they also differ in many ways. First, though these models treat prejudice as an essentially abnormal reaction, my model (in common with modern cognitive models of stereotyping and social categorization) sees it as a deplorable result of more or less normal and typical processes. Second, in the older affect-based models the characteristics of the outgroup were hardly important; only the group's weakness and vulnerability were important for it to be selected as a scapegoat. In contrast, my model holds that perceptions of the outgroup's situation in relation to the ingroup, such as the threat it poses, are central in generating group-based emotions and prejudices. (Of course, these perceptions may or may not be objectively realistic.) Third, the older models postulated that only one type of affect and resulting action tendency (frustration and aggression) was relevant for understanding intergroup prejudice, while I believe that a variety of group-based emotions may come into play in various circumstances. Finally, the older models shared a common individualistic stance: it is individual frustration or psychopathology that results in prejudice. In contrast, the novel point of my model is that group-based emotions (experienced by individuals, but with respect to their social identity as group members) are what drive prejudice. These and other distinctions between the model of prejudice as group-based emotion and the earlier affective theories of prejudice seem quite central.

Examples of possible group-based emotions

Several specific emotions may be particularly likely to arise in intergroup situations. If an outgroup is appraised as threatening or as more powerful than an ingroup, the resulting emotion will be fear. The related action tendency is a motive to escape or to attack the outgroup. Direct, hostile actions against outgroups, such as lynchings or moves to take away groups' citizenship or civil rights, presumably reflect this type of emotional prejudice. Appraisals, emotions, and actions of this sort should frequently arise in situations of realistic intergroup conflicts (Campbell, 1965).

An outgroup that is appraised as violating the ingroup's norms of conduct may give rise to a different set of emotions, such as disgust. For example, outgroups (such as gays and lesbians) that violate norms of sexual conduct of some ingroups may elicit this sort of feeling, as may outgroups who violate ingroup dietary norms (e.g., some Southeast Asian cultures whose members eat dogs or cats). The related emotional action tendency is a motive to avoid the group, which might be expressed in policies of segregation or exclusion of immigrants.

Another possible emotion may be elicited by an outgroup that is appraised as attaining undeserved benefits that are not shared by, or are disproportional to, those attained by the ingroup. Resentment or envy is the resulting emotion, leading to a motive to remove the benefit or demand a similar one for the ingroup. Reactions to outgroups that are perceived as relying heavily on welfare, food stamps, or other government benefits often seem tinged with these emotions.

Note that in all these examples, the relevant appraisals refer to the position of the outgroup *in relation to* the ingroup, just as, in emotion theories, the appraisals that trigger emotions by definition refer to an object's or situation's implications for the self. The relational nature of these appraisals stands in contrast to the picture painted by the standard attitude-based conception of prejudice, in which reactions are driven by the outgroup's own inherent attributes (hostile, dirty, clannish, etc.). These attributes, though of course they may be assumed to be perceived in incorrect and biased fashion, are understood to characterize the outgroup itself, rather than to flow from the *relation* and *interaction* of the outgroup with the ingroup.

Implications of the new view of prejudice

The new view of prejudice as emotion helps us understand the hot, affectively charged quality that prejudice often has. Clearly, intergroup prejudice and discrimination can fall at various points along a continuum, from cool and calm to hot and emotional. For example, members of an outgroup may be passed over in hiring and promotion decisions because of stereotypical assumptions that they lack job-related qualifications, without much if any emotion being involved. Yet prejudice sometimes involves heat, even hate, as when people who are prejudiced against homosexuals move from simple avoidance to gay-baiting, physical aggression, and outright murder. A picture of prejudice as based on *emotions* rather than mere *negative evaluations* of an outgroup can give us some sense of why prejudice is sometimes hot.

A second implication of the new view of prejudice is that fear, disgust, resentment, and the like are distinct emotions, following from distinct configurations of intergroup relations and possibly leading to different actions. Groups that are appraised in ways that lead to these different emotions will therefore elicit specific types of subjective feelings, as well as different patterns of behavioral discrimination. In contrast, in the model of prejudice as attitude, reactions to these different outgroups would all be classified simply as evaluatively negative. This view fails to capture qualitative differences among different types of prejudice. Kovel (1970), Kluegel and Smith (1986), Katz and Hass (1988), Sachdev and Bourhis (1987), and others, have identified such qualitative differences in different intergroup situations and contexts.

The definition of prejudice as group-based emotion does not discount the importance of emotional reactions to individual outgroup members (as well as to the outgroup as a whole). People may appraise an entire group in ways that trigger emotions (e.g., "They always get more than they deserve from these government programs, while I have to work hard for everything I get"), and also experience emotional reactions to individual group members (e.g., seeing a group member using food stamps in the grocery store). In many cases, these reactions at the group and individual exemplar levels will be consistent with each other, and as Smith and Zarate (1992) emphasize, mental representations of individual group members are functionally part of the perceiver's representation of the group as a whole. Research by Zanna, Haddock, and Esses (1990) and Dijker (1987) shows, consistent with this idea, that people's reports of emotions they had experienced in intergroup encounters were correlated with their group prejudice. In fact, Stangor, Sullivan, and Ford (1991) found that emotional responses were better predictive of intergroup attitudes than were stereotypical beliefs about the outgroup. Sometimes, however, emotional reactions to groups and individuals may conflict. Conflicting views of a group vs. individual group members are traditionally considered as a major cause of stereotype change and prejudice reduction, particularly when driven by friendly and egalitarian individual contacts with outgroup members (Amir, 1976). In general, we must assume that emotional reactions to individual outgroup members and the outgroup as an entity both contribute to overall levels of prejudice and discriminatory behavior.

Initial Evidence for the Importance of Group-based Emotions

The model described here is new, and little research has yet been devised directly to test its assumptions. Still, several existing studies suggest its validity. One type of evidence for the importance of social emotions in intergroup relations stems from the literature on what is termed "symbolic racism." Numerous studies (e.g., Kinder and Sears, 1981; McConahay, 1982) have shown that measures of symbolic racism are stronger predictors of intergroup attitudes and behaviors (such as willingness to vote for outgroup members in an election) than are measures of individual-level self-interest. For example, whites' symbolic attitudes toward blacks are better predictors of attitudes toward busing for school desegregation than are such seemingly important self-interest-related variables as whether the white respondent actually has children in public school or lives in a district that might be affected. The question is what is "symbolic racism" at a conceptual level? Bobo (1983) and others have argued compellingly that it is a measure of the perceived group-based interests of the respondent. This position remains under debate (Sears and Kinder, 1985; Sniderman and Tetlock, 1986; Weigel and Howes, 1985), but if it is accepted, the various studies on symbolic racism can be seen as showing not that self-interest is unimportant, but that group more than individual interests are politically relevant.

A second line of evidence for the importance of emotional reactions based in the perceiver's group identification in intergroup relations comes from studies of relative deprivation. As is well known (Runciman, 1966), relative deprivation can be assessed at the individual level (perception that the individual respondent is not doing as well as other individuals) or the group level (perception that the respondent's ingroup is not doing as well as an outgroup). A meta-analysis reported by Pettigrew (in press) examines effects of different types of relative deprivation on various measures of prejudice. The effects of group-level deprivation are systematically larger than those of individual-level deprivation, averaging about twice the size. The largest effects are found, as the model of prejudice as group-based emotion predicts, for group-based relative deprivation comparisons that include an affective component rather than only a cognitive assessment of difference. These findings, based on aggregated results from over a dozen independent studies, point clearly to the role of affect based on perceptions of an intergroup situation.

Yet another line of evidence comes from studies that have assessed group-based pride – feelings of patriotism and glorification of an ingroup – in relation to prejudice against outgroups. Pettigrew (in press) draws on data from surveys conducted in 1988 in France, the Netherlands, Britain, and West Germany. Across all these countries, measures of pride in ingroup membership (asking how proud the respondent is to be French, Dutch, etc.) are correlated with measures of prejudice against salient ethnic minority groups in each country.

The correlations remain significant when controlling for other important variables that also affect prejudice (age, city size, education, and general political conservatism). Thus, those people who are most likely to identify with the ingroup in an emotional sense – as indicated by their readiness to report feeling pride in the ingroup – are also most likely to be prejudiced against outgroups. This pattern is conceptually interesting, for we usually tend to regard feelings of patriotism, group loyalty, and pride in an ingroup as benign and positive. Yet the negative implications of these feelings are perfectly understandable and predictable from the perspective of the model of prejudice as group-based emotion.

A conceptually similar finding emphasizing the importance of emotional identification with an ingroup comes from a survey by Clore and Rahn (1994). These researchers asked a national sample in the United States how important their national identity was, and over 80 percent of the respondents said that being an American was "extremely" or "very" important to them personally. Other questions inquired about how frequently they felt various emotions (hope, excitement, fear, anger, etc.) "when thinking about the United States." Factor analyses identified two factors of positive and negative emotions. These in turn correlated with trust in government, worry about group conflict, feelings of collective efficacy, and other important and consequential political attitudes. Thus, group-based emotions have correlates that go beyond intergroup relations (prejudice and discrimination), to political attitudes and behavior more generally. Kite and Rahn (1997) replicated these basic results in Sweden and in a second US sample.

Several types of evidence, though not arising from studies specifically designed for the purpose, thus support the basic proposition that group-based attitudes are a central component of intergroup phenomena such as prejudice and discrimination. Such attitudes may even have an importance beyond the intergroup realm, in such areas as trust in government and feelings of political efficacy, which are related to voting and other forms of political participation. Further research using measures specifically developed to reflect the hypotheses of the prejudice-as-group-emotion model should build on and refine these results.

Mental Representation of the Self-concept and the Ingroup

Laboratory studies of self–ingroup overlap

To complement survey methods, it is also possible to test basic assumptions of the new model of prejudice using laboratory approaches. Specifically, Smith and Henry (1996) used a method inspired by the work of Aron and his colleagues (1991) to examine the assumption that mental representations of the ingroup and the self can effectively merge. The reasoning behind this method is that if the self and another person or group are incorporated within the same mental representation, then matches between their attributes will speed and facilitate reports about the self. In contrast, mismatches between the self and other will slow these self-reports. The logic of this prediction is similar to the logic of Stroop interference. As is well known, reporting the color of the ink in which a word is printed is speeded if the meaning of the word matches the color: for example, the word "blue" printed in blue. On the other hand, the report of the color is slowed if the word mismatches the color, such as "blue" printed in red. Different attributes of the same object (such as the meaning and the ink color of a word) can create facilitation or interference when someone tries to report on one of the attributes. In the same way, if mental representations of two persons or groups overlap so that they are effectively a single representation, reports on attributes of one will be facilitated or inhibited by matches and mismatches with the second.

Aron and his colleagues (1991) applied this logic to determine whether people's mental representations of self and close relationship partners overlapped. Subjects filled out three questionnaires regarding themselves, their spouse, and a stranger. Each questionnaire listed 90 traits and subjects indicated the extent to which the person had the trait. Next, subjects completed a self-description task on the computer. The same 90 traits appeared on the computer screen, and subjects pressed a "yes" or "no" key to indicate whether or not they possessed the trait. Analyses indicated, as predicted, that responses on the computer task were speeded for traits on which the subject believed they matched their spouse, compared to traits involving mismatches. These findings are consistent with the assumption that mental representations of self and partner overlap, so that Stroop-like interference or facilitation occurs when the attributes match or mismatch.

Smith and Henry (1996) applied the same method to determine whether an ingroup is included within the mental representation of the self, i.e., the self-concept. They gave subjects questionnaires asking about the self, the ingroup, and a relevant outgroup. The groups used were fraternity/sorority members vs. nonmembers, and liberal arts vs. engineering majors. Subjects then participated in the same computer self-descriptiveness task. Analyses showed that ingroup traits that matched the self gave rise to fast responses on the computer, compared to ingroup traits that mismatched the self. Interestingly, the traits believed to characterize the outgroup made no difference. For example, traits on which the ingroup was particularly distinctive (different from the outgroup) showed results that were identical to traits the ingroup shared with the outgroup. The size of the effect of matching vs. mismatching the ingroup was virtually the same as the size of the effect of matching or mismatching the spouse in the study by Aron et al. (1991). This suggests that people use not only close relationship partners but also an ingroup in constructing and making judgments about the self.

In a more recent study, Smith, Coats, and Walling (in press) tested and confirmed a further prediction derived from the idea that self and ingroup representations overlap. While Smith and Henry (1996) showed that perceptions of the ingroup on various traits influence the speed with which people can report on the self, this new study showed the reverse: response time for reporting an ingroup's traits depended on the individual's perception of his or her own standing on the traits. This bidirectional pattern of facilitation and inhibition is exactly what would be expected if mental representations of the self and ingroups overlap.

How can we understand mental representations of the self, other persons, and social groups as flexible, on-line constructions, instead of as static memory structures? Actually, much recent research has pointed in this direction. Markus and Wurf (1987) argued that the self could be considered as flexible and dynamic, changing with social situations and the person's current goals. Turner, Oakes, Haslam, and McGarty (1994) wrote "the concept of the self as a separate mental structure does not seem necessary, because we can assume that any and all cognitive resources – long-term knowledge, implicit theories, . . . and so forth – are recruited, used, and deployed when necessary" to construct a self-representation appropriate for the situation. New connectionist models of mental representation, now being developed within social cognition, allow the conceptualization of the self as well as other structures as flexibly reconstructed (Smith, 1996). These models of representation assume that all cognitions are reconstructed rather than retrieved from memory in static form. Thus, thinking of the self in one context (such as a personal relationship) may result in the construction of a representation with one set of attributes, while in another context (say, an intergroup situation) the self-representation may include quite different, even opposite, attributes. This can occur because all stored knowledge (not just a stable, discrete self-concept representation) contributes simultaneously to the reconstruction process (Smith and DeCoster, 1998). Clark (1993, chs 2 and 5) provides further discussion of the implications of connectionist models of representation.

Indirect effects of intergroup friendship on prejudice

One further implication of these ideas should be mentioned. If a close relationship partner is part of the self, and the partner's ingroup is part of his or her self, then having an outgroup friend indirectly incorporates the friend's group membership in one's own self. It should therefore reduce prejudice! In fact, there is evidence that friendships across group lines reduce prejudice. Pettigrew (1997) has obtained evidence from surveys in four European nations that intergroup friendships are correlated with lower prejudice. Of course, the causal direction in this correlational relationship might go either way, but Pettigrew presents evidence from nonhierarchical causal modeling that the stronger effect is from friendship to lower prejudice, in three of the four nations. Prejudice is reduced not only for the friend's own group, but for other disliked outgroups as well. Pettigrew (1997) concludes that the long-studied effects of intergroup contact on prejudice actually depend on the formation of friendships, and "relate . . . closely to the study of long-term close relationships" (p. 182). This is, of course, the same position taken in this chapter.

In fact, not only having an outgroup friend, but having an ingroup friend who in turn has an outgroup friend, ought to reduce intergroup prejudice by the same logic. An experimental study by Wright, Aron, McLaughlin-Volpe, and Ropp (1997) supports this conclusion. In this study, after a series of events built up intergroup conflict in a laboratory setting, a member of each group was chosen to participate in a relationship-building exercise with a member of the outgroup. After these individuals returned to their groups, the general climate of intergroup hostility was found to improve. The key result is that this was true not only for the specific individuals involved in the dyadic relationship, but for the other group members as well. Because of the experimental nature of this design, it is easier to conclude that the effect of friendship on prejudice is a causal one. Thus, the conceptualization of friendship and group membership as involving the incorporation of others within the self proves powerful and predictive.

Conclusions

Social psychology as a discipline is uniquely positioned at the interface between the individual and the social/cultural environment. Social perception and social influence (which import aspects of the external environment into the individual) and social behavior (which allows the individual to actively modify the external environment) are thus key areas within our field. As Turner et al. (1987) and others have cogently argued, the incorporation of group membership as the self is a major part of the interface-spanning process, for example as a major source of social influence. I have argued that when group membership becomes part of the self, appraisals and emotions, which are parts of an individual-level self-regulatory system, can take on the new function of tying us psychologically to an ingroup's situation and fortunes. We respond emotionally and behaviorally not only to events or situations that impinge on the personal self, but also to intergroup situations that affect our important groups. As this chapter has discussed, prejudice and intergroup discrimination are among the potential consequences of this process. Better understanding of these links between the social and the cognitive will be achieved only through theoretically integrative efforts, for they link the traditional areas of concern of the social identity and social cognition approaches.

References

Adorno, T.W., Frenkel-Brunswik, E., Levinson, D.J., and Sanford, R.N. (1950). *The Authoritarian Personality*. New York: Harper.

Amir, Y. (1976). The role of intergroup contact in change of prejudice and race relations. In P. Katz (ed.), *Toward the Elimination of Racism*. New York: Pergamon, pp. 245–380.

Arnold, M.B. (1960). *Emotion and Personality*, Vol. I, *Psychological Aspects*. New York: Columbia University Press.

Aron, A., Aron, E.N., Tudor, M., and Nelson, G. (1991). Close relationships as including other in the self. *Journal of Personality and Social Psychology*, 60, 241–53.

Bobo, L. (1983). Whites' opposition to busing: Symbolic racism or realistic group conflict? *Journal of Personality and Social Psychology*, 45, 1196–1210.

Campbell, D.T. (1965). Ethnocentric and other altruistic motives. In D. Levine (ed.), *Nebraska Symposium on Motivation*, Vol. 13. Lincoln, NB: University of Nebraska Press, pp. 283–312.

Cialdini, R.B., Borden, R.J., Thorne, A., Walker, M.R., Freeman, S., and Sloan, L.R. (1976). Basking in reflected glory: Three (football) field studies. *Journal of Personality and Social Psychology*, 34, 366–75.

Clark, A. (1993). *Associative Engines*. Cambridge, MA: MIT Press.

Clore, G. and Rahn, W. (1994). American national identity, public mood, and political judgment: The informative function of social emotion. Unpublished paper, Department of Psychology, University of Illinois.

Crocker, J., Blaine, B., and Luhtanen, R. (1993). Prejudice, intergroup behavior and self-esteem: Enhancement and protection motives. In M.A. Hogg and D. Abrams (eds), *Group Motivation: Social psychological perspectives*. New York: Harvester Wheatsheaf, pp. 52–67.

Dijker, A.J.M. (1987). Emotional reactions to ethnic minorities. *European Journal of Social Psychology*, 17, 305–25.

Dollard, J., Doob, L.W., Miller, N.E., Mowrer, O.H., and Sears, R.R. (1939). *Frustration and Aggression*. New Haven: Yale University Press.

Fishbein, M.P. and Ajzen, I. (1975). *Belief, Attitude, Intention, and Behavior*. Reading, MA: Addison-Wesley.

Frijda, N.H. (1986). *The Emotions*. Cambridge: Cambridge University Press.

Frijda, N.H., Kuipers, P., and ter Schure, E. (1989). Relations among emotion, appraisal, and emotional action readiness. *Journal of Personality and Social Psychology*, 57, 212–28.

Higgins, E.T. (1996). Knowledge activation: Accessibility, applicability, and salience. In E.T. Higgins and A.W. Kruglanski (eds), *Social Psychology: Handbook of basic principles*. New York: Guilford, pp. 133–68.

Hogg, M. and Abrams, D. (1993). Towards a single-process uncertainty-reduction model of social motivation in groups. In M.A. Hogg and D. Abrams (eds), *Group Motivation: Social psychological perspectives*. New York: Harvester Wheatsheaf, pp. 173–90.

Katz, I. and Hass, R.G. (1988). Racial ambivalence and American value conflict: Correlational and priming studies of dual cognitive structures. *Journal of Personality and Social Psychology*, 55, 893–905.

Kinder, D.R. and Sears, D.O. (1981). Prejudice and politics: Symbolic racism versus racial threats to the good life. *Journal of Personality and Social Psychology*, 40, 414–31.

Kite, C. and Rahn, W.M. (1997). Public community and public mood: A comparison of the U.S. and Swedish cases. Unpublished manuscript, University of Umea, Sweden.

Kluegel, J.R. and Smith, E.R. (1986). *Beliefs about Inequality: Americans' views of what is and what ought to be*. Hawthorne, NY: Aldine de Gruyter.

Kovel, J. (1970). *White Racism: A psychohistory*. New York: Pantheon.

Lazarus, R.S. and Folkman, S. (1984). *Stress, Appraisal, and Coping*. New York: Springer-Verlag.

McConahay, J.B. (1982). Self-interest versus racial attitudes as correlates of anti-busing attitudes in Louisville: Is it the buses or the blacks? *Journal of Politics*, 44, 692–720.

Markus, H. and Wurf, E. (1987). The dynamic self-concept: A social psychological perspective. *Annual Review of Psychology*, 38, 299–337.

Minard, R.D. (1952). Race relations in the Pocahontas Coal Field. *Journal of Social Issues*, 8, 29–44.

Pettigrew, T.F. (1997). Generalized intergroup contact effects on prejudice. *Personality and Social Psychology Bulletin*, 23, 173–85.

Pettigrew, T.F. (in press). The affective component of prejudice: Empirical support for the new view. In S.A. Tuch and J.K. Martin (eds), *Racial Attitudes in the 1990s: Continuity and change*. Westport, CT: Praeger.

Roseman, I.J. (1984). Cognitive determinants of emotion: A structural theory. In P. Shaver (ed.), *Review of Personality and Social Psychology*, Vol. 5. Beverly Hills, CA: Sage, pp. 11–36.

Rothbart, M. and Lewis, S. (1994). Cognitive processes and intergroup relations: A historical perspective. In D.L. Hamilton, P.G. Devine, and T.M. Ostrom (eds), *Social Cognition: Its impact on social psychology*. Orlando, FL: Academic Press, pp. 347–82.

Runciman, W.G. (1966). *Relative Deprivation and Social Justice*. London: Routledge and Kegan Paul.

Sachdev, I. and Bourhis, R.Y. (1987). Status differentials and intergroup behaviour. *European Journal of Social Psychology*, 17, 277–93.

Scherer, K.R. (1988). Cognitive antecedents of emotion. In V. Hamilton, G.H. Bower, and N.H. Frijda (eds), *Cognitive Perspectives on Emotion and Motivation*. Dordrecht: Kluwer, pp. 89–126.

Sears, D.O. and Kinder, D.R. (1985). Whites' opposition to busing: On conceptualizing and operationalizing group conflict. *Journal of Personality and Social Psychology*, 48, 1141–7.

Smith, C.A. and Ellsworth, P.C. (1985). Patterns of cognitive appraisal in emotion. *Journal of Personality and Social Psychology*, 48, 813–38.

Smith, E.R. (1993). Social identity and social emotions: Toward new conceptualizations of prejudice. In D.M. Mackie and D.L. Hamilton (eds), *Affect, Cognition, and Stereotyping: Interactive processes in group perception*. San Diego: Academic Press, pp. 297–315.

Smith, E.R. (1996). What do connectionism and social psychology offer each other? *Journal of Personality and Social Psychology*, 70, 893–912.

Smith, E.R., Coats, S., and Walling, D. (in press). Overlapping mental representations of self, ingroup, and partner: Further response time evidence and a connectionist model. *Personality and Social Psychology Bulletin*.

Smith, E.R. and DeCoster, J. (1998). Knowledge acquisition, accessibility, and use in person perception and stereotyping: Simulation with a recurrent connectionist network. *Journal of Personality and Social Psychology*, 74, 21–35.

Smith, E.R. and Henry, S. (1996). An ingroup becomes part of the self: Response time evidence. *Personality and Social Psychology Bulletin*, 22, 635–42.

Smith, E.R. and Zarate, M.A. (1992). Exemplar-based model of social judgment. *Psychological Review*, 99, 3–21.

Sniderman, P.M. and Tetlock, P.E. (1986). Symbolic racism: Problems of motive attribution in political analysis. *Journal of Social Issues*, 42, 2, 129–50.

Stangor, C., Sullivan, L.A., and Ford, T.E. (1991). Affective and cognitive determinants of prejudice. *Social Cognition*, 9, 359–80.

Tajfel, H. and Turner, J.C. (1979). An integrative theory of intergroup conflict. In W.G. Austin and S. Worchel (eds), *The Social Psychology of Intergroup Relations*. Monterey, CA: Brooks-Cole, pp. 33–47.

Turner, J.C., Hogg, M.A., Oakes, P.J., Reicher, S.D., and Wetherell, M.S. (1987). *Rediscovering the Social Group: A self-categorization theory*. Oxford: Blackwell.

Turner, J.C., Oakes, P.J., Haslam, S.A., and McGarty, C. (1994). Self and collective: Cognition and social context. *Personality and Social Psychology Bulletin*, 20, 454–63.

Weigel, R.H. and Howes, P.W. (1985). Conceptions of racial prejudice: Symbolic racism reconsidered. *Journal of Social Issues*, 41, 3, 117–38.

Wright, S.C., Aron, A., McLaughlin-Volpe, T., and Ropp, S.A. (1997). The extended contact effect: Knowledge of cross-group friendships and prejudice. *Journal of Personality and Social Psychology*, 73, 73–90.

Zanna, M.P., Haddock, G., and Esses, V.M. (1990). The determinants of prejudice. Presented at Society of Experimental Social Psychology, Buffalo, NY.

9

Social Identity, Social Cognition, and the Self: The Flexibility and Stability of Self-categorization

DOMINIC ABRAMS

Social identity theory was explicitly advanced as a nonreductionist approach, which transcended the usual individualistic assumptions that pervade traditional research theories and paradigms (see Tajfel, 1981a). A crucial insight, according to the social identity approach, is that people relate to one another as members of social groups and categories. Traditional theory had seemingly missed this point, preferring to analyze phenomena such as social protest, prejudice, discrimination, stereotyping, as well as conformity, bargaining, and negotiation, as individual-level processes. Typically, the theories would invoke psychodynamic or behavioral processes (e.g., frustration–aggression hypothesis, the authoritarian personality), purely cognitive processes (e.g., theories of impression formation), or would extend only as far as interpersonal comparison (e.g., traditional theories of relative deprivation). Even realistic group conflict theory was castigated for accounting for intergroup relations in terms of functional interdependence. Social identity theory offered an alternative. First, the cognitive (i.e., purely psychological) process of categorization seemed to generate intergroup differentiation. Second, and at least as important, the social processes of intergroup comparison and the motivation to gain positive distinctiveness for the ingroup seemed to provide some account for ingroup bias, and for the coordination of intergroup behavior (see Abrams and Hogg, 1990; Hogg and Abrams, 1988, for more detailed coverage of the social identity approach).

The growth of social cognition research provided further grounds for critical comment from social identity theorists. Social identity theory and social cognition have often been depicted as falling at opposite ends of a continuum in social psychology (see Oakes, Haslam, and Reynolds, chapter 3 in this volume; Turner, Oakes, Haslam, and McGarty, 1994). Social psychology seemed to be repeating all the same mistakes of the past. Intraindividual, generally cognitive, processes were once again being hailed as a useful explanation for social phenomena. For example, illusory correlations were thought to provide a useful account for some aspects of stereotyping (Hamilton, 1981), stereotypes were considered to be simplifying structures that resided in the individual's head (Fiske and Neuberg, 1990), prejudice was considered largely as automatic (Devine, 1989). Some commentators have even accused social cognition of perpetuating racism through its unquestioning use of extant social categories in judgment tasks (Hopkins, Reicher, and Levine, 1997). Aside from the cognitive emphasis in stereotype research, other areas continued to disregard social or even group-level analysis. For example, theories of attitude change and persuasion (Eagly and Chaiken, 1993; Petty and Cacioppo, 1986) concentrated on intraindividual processes, while theories of prejudice and identity often concentrated on individual difference variables (e.g., McConahay, 1986; Pratto, Sidanius, Stallworth, and Malle, 1994; Sidanius, Pratto, and Mitchell, 1994).

On the other hand, social identity research itself adopted many of the same methodological approaches as the individualistic work it was supposed to supersede. The emergence of self-categorization theory (SCT, Turner, Hogg, Oakes, Reicher, and Wetherell, 1987) was, in some ways, a move toward an intraindividual level of analysis. Social cognition researchers might rightly question what was so different about the SCT model. Farr (1996) also commented on this apparent transition from a social to a purely cognitive framework (see also Hogg and Abrams, chapter 1 in this volume). Moreover, intergroup relations researchers increasingly became interested in operationalizing social identity as an individual difference variable (Brown, Hinkle, Ely, Fox-Cardamone, and Maras, 1992; Ellemers, Spears, and Doosje, 1997; Hinkle, Taylor, Fox-Cardanone, and Cook, 1989; Smith and Tyler, 1997), which may be seen as a further shift towards individualistic theorizing (Abrams, 1992a).

What, then, is left of the nonreductionist ambitions of the social identity approach? In this chapter I want to suggest that the essence of the social identity (SI) approach is that it always relates the phenomena under investigation to the social structure in which they arise. Social structure may be conceived of as a set of intercategory relationships, a set of apparent or material conditions (e.g., famine, poverty) that are perceived to affect people because of their shared or different social category memberships. It can be operationalized in different ways, including economic, historical, sociological, and psychological. Perhaps unlike traditional social cognition theories, the SI approach explicitly locates the *content* of what is observed in the social context. That is to say, although the SI approach considers intergroup and group processes to be mediated psychologically, it does not regard intraindividual processes as providing a sufficient account for what is perceived, said, or done. The psychological processes acquire and develop meaning in relation to the social context in which they arise.

The chapter starts by reviewing some effects of social context on stereotyping, prejudice, and the self-concept. In the SI approach these phenomena are necessarily interrelated. But this interrelationship might reveal something about the particularly psychological nature of social context effects. The next section considers some questions about the structure and process of the self. To what extent is it possible to reconcile an approach such as self-categorization theory

(SCT), which assumes considerable flexibility in self-conception, with research suggesting a high degree of consistency and continuity in the self-concept? The third section draws connections between the SCT approach and other models that emerge from cognitive neuropsychology and connectionism. I suggest that there is considerable convergence in the implications of the two approaches, particularly if one broadens the conception of what provides input to a network. The fourth section considers how and why intergroup behavior is regulated. A key problem is whether stereotypes form a cognitive substrate for perception, or whether they operate at a higher level as a set of comparators that are used only in some circumstances. I suggest that stereotypes may often simply provide norms against which to compare initial perceptual judgments. Finally, I propose that both social identity and social cognition research will benefit by emphasizing a process approach that always builds the context into theory.

Effects of Category Context

Context and stereotyping

Despite the prevalence of stereotypes in general, the context affects both which stereotypes are applied and to which categories (Oakes, 1996; Oakes, Turner, and Haslam, 1991). If stereotypes are well-ingrained images of social groups, it might seem strange that they can be easily switched on and off. One explanation is that people often opt to engage in individuated processing to form impressions of others. Thus, with sufficient motivation, opportunity, and the right goals, they will eschew the stereotype in favor of a more accurate, or at least more specific, judgment (Brewer, 1988; Fiske and Neuberg, 1990). When people try to inhibit stereotypical perception, their suppressed judgments sometimes carry over to affect judgments of other targets (e.g., Macrae, Bodenhausen, and Milne, 1995; Macrae, Milne, and Bodenhausen, 1994).

Research in this area suggests that context affects stereotyping by affecting the probability that (1) a stereotype will be activated, (2) other information about the target will be perceptually available, or (3) bottom-up processing about the specific attributes of individual targets will commence. However, an alternative perspective, provided by the SI approach, is that the content of perceptions will be strongly determined by category *contrasts* (Tajfel, 1969). When a particular contrast is salient, features that best distinguish between categories will be those that contribute most to stereotypical perceptions. Importantly, then, neither the dimensions nor individuals' standing on those dimensions are fixed. The stereotype associated with a category is necessarily indeterminate. It must emerge as a result of a comparison with a contrasting category (cf. Turner, 1985).

This set of assumptions generally creates no difficulty for most findings from social cognition research. In a large proportion of studies, the category memberships of targets, as well as the contrasting categories, are either obvious or probably take a default value. For a research study conducted in the United States, in which the research participants are white and the targets are black vs. white, with few other distinguishing features, it is likely that participants will attempt to relate the black/white categorization to the judgment dimension they are asked to use. In the absence of other information they will probably fall back on social stereotypes, because highly accessible social categories dominate perceptions when other bases for perception are not salient or meaningful (Smith, Fazio, and Cejka, 1996). So, when the context is relatively constant and the connection between category memberships and attributes is relatively direct (i.e., the task requires that they be aligned in some way), it is unsurprising that psychologists find support for a model that contrasts category-based processing with individuated processing. But, as is argued later, the notion of individuated vs. category-based processing is problematic if we accept SCT's line that all processing involves category contrasts at some level (Abrams, 1996; Oakes, Haslam, and Turner, 1998).

Context and prejudice

There is evidence that when social categories are activated they may automatically generate stereotypical images that are negative, and thus that prejudice may be inevitable (e.g., Devine, 1989). However, recent studies suggest a more interesting picture. Categorization does not evoke the same stereotype for all people (Lepore and Brown, 1997, chapter 6 in this volume), raising the question of whether it is wise to assume that stereotypes are widely shared and well learned. Moreover, some categorizations, such as gender, are associated with numerous, often contradictory, stereotypes (cf. Condor, 1986; Glick and Fiske, 1996; Masser and Abrams, in press). Thus, the attributes people associate with categories show some flexibility and variability, and may not be locked into a particular knowledge structure.

Research also shows that people will exhibit ingroup bias even when there is no 1979 stereotypic content associated with the categories (Tajfel and Turner, 1979; Perdue, Dovidio, Gurtman, and Tyler, 1990). It is therefore unsurprising that people use attributes in the service of their ingroup preference – the ingroup has more positive attributes than the outgroup *because* they are ingroup and outgroup, rather than vice versa. One consequence of this phenomenon is that people are "socially attracted" to ingroup members, assuming they have more positive traits even without any evidence of interpersonal similarity at the trait level (see Hogg, 1992).

Some studies have manipulated the intergroup frame of reference to show how the same category members may be evaluated quite differently depending on the comparison category. For example, Abrams and Hogg (1987) asked people from Dundee (in Scotland) to evaluate pairs of speakers. In one condition the speakers both had Scottish accents, one from Dundee and the other from Glasgow. In another condition the speakers had either a Glaswegian accent or a standard English accent. Of interest was how the Glaswegian-accented speakers would be perceived. As predicted there were highly significant shifts in the ratings, such that the Glaswegian was perceived positively (on traits reflecting social attractiveness and social status) in comparison with the English speaker, but negatively in comparison with the Dundee speaker. Similarly, a study which asked Hong Kong Chinese people to consider a story either from a Japanese or a Chinese perspective successfully manipulated whether participants identified themselves as Hongkongers vs. Chinese, which in turn affected the attributes they associated with Chinese and Japanese people (Fu, Lee, Chiu, and Hong, in press). Gaertner and Dovidio's research on the common ingroup identity model also demonstrates the point clearly (Anastasio, Bachman, Gaertner, and Dovidio, 1997; Gaertner, Rust, Dovidio, Bachman, and Anastasio, 1994). Images of and bias towards others depends on their category relationship to the perceiver. In summary, stereotype content and prejudice may be quite heavily dependent on the particular category comparisons as well as on possibly some more basic motivational processes to favor ingroups over outgroups.

Context and self-description

A third area in which context clearly has substantial effects is in the content of self-perception, or at least self-description. The McGuires' research on distinctiveness illustrated how people are more likely to describe themselves in terms of contextually distinct features (e.g., McGuire, McGuire, and Cheever, 1986). One question rarely asked of that research is why being in a minority might be particularly relevant. A social identity perspective would suggest that being in a numerical minority could in some cases confer an insecure social identity, which is perpetually under threat from the majority group. However, social identity and self-categorization theory do not accord special significance to numerical minority/majority status. Minority status is simply one of an array of factors which could make a particular categorization more meaningful as a basis for perceiving self and others (Oakes and Turner, 1986; Oakes et al., 1998). For example, Abrams, Thomas, and Hogg (1985) showed how the simple presence of outgroup category members (regardless of majority/minority status) was sufficient to make the ingroup gender category salient in the self-concept. When only the ingroup was present people tended to concentrate on distinguishing among ingroup members, but did not refer to the category label. A similar point is made by Brewer (1991), who argues that countervailing needs for distinctiveness and assimilation lead people to align themselves with groups that confer a meaningful identity in contrast to other groups, but with a strong sense of similarity or solidarity with a set of ingroup members. This process appears to operate in a context-relevant way, whether it be in a minimal group experiment or in terms of identification with larger-scale social trends and groups (Abrams, 1992b).

Smith and Henry (1996) have shown that when social categorizations are made salient, the ingroup becomes psychologically merged with, or linked to, the self. Similarly, research on more general social perceptions, such as consensus estimation, suggests strongly that people assume greater similarity with the opinions or personality of others if they share a categorization with self than when they are categorized as outgroup members (Krueger and Clement, 1994). Taken together, these findings suggest that judgments about self and others are flexibly influenced by contextually bounded comparisons. This conclusion jars with the person-centered focus of social psychology, which assumes the self is a stable and enduring entity, that stereotypes are well-learned derogatory images of social groups, and that prejudice and discrimination are inevitable consequences of biased information processing or biased motivational processes. The context dependence of self-perception is explored in more detail below.

Self as Structure and Self as Process

Theoretical orientations to the self differ in emphasis along a continuum from structure to process (Abrams, 1996). At one extreme, structure theorists are concerned primarily with the organization of self-knowledge in memory, whether as dynamically related elements or simply as components of a personality structure. At the other extreme, process theorists focus more on issues such as self-regulation and self-efficacy. Most theories involve a mixture of both structure and process, but these are normally conceived of as distinct features of the self, thus perpetuating a general model that treats process and structure as separable issues.

Structural approaches

Structural approaches assume that the self is well represented as an entity in memory. For example, Markus (1977) illustrated that some aspects of self are represented schematically. There is debate over the way information about the self is represented and retrieved (Srull and Wyer, 1993). For example Keenan (1993) suggests that we make trait inferences about ourselves using autobiographical behavioral exemplars. According to this view, our ability to make summary descriptions of ourselves depends on the number of instances of relevant behaviors we can retrieve from memory. Evidence regarding exemplar models has found some support in accounting for group categorization judgments (Judd and Park, 1988; Smith and Zarate, 1990), trait inferences about others (Kahneman and Miller, 1986), and stereotyping (Rothbart and John, 1985). Associative network models seem to be useful in accounts of impression formation (Hamilton, 1981) and the cognitive structure of social stereotypes (Andersen and Klatzky, 1987). However, in relation to self-judgments Bellezza (1984, 1993) rejects the exemplar view as being unwieldy, and as involving an infinite regress to ever more restrictive categorizations.

More recently, theory seems to be moving towards the idea that trait judgments of self are based on some combination of behavioral exemplars and abstracted trait summaries. This position is consistent with models emphasizing depth of processing (e.g., the dual exemplar/summary view espoused by Kihlstrom and Cantor, 1984) or quantity of information (the mixed-model view espoused by Klein and Loftus, 1993) to account for transitions from exemplar to trait representation. For example, Klein and Loftus (1993) suggest that, for judgments of self, trait representation can be functionally independent of autobiographical behavioral exemplars. Experimental judgmental tasks involving others tend to be made with little contextual information and usually involve retrieval of material very shortly after learning. In contrast, self-judgments are usually made with extensive information, acquired across contexts, and involving long retention intervals. These factors facilitate abstraction to summary traits more for the self than for others.

The various models support the idea of self as a relatively stable, enduring, and quite abstractly represented structure. However, the idea that summary or abstract representations of self tend to be dissociated from behavioral exemplars has interesting implications for structural and process models of self, raising the question of how behavior or other items of information retain links to a stable self-concept.

At first glance motivational models of self would appear to emphasize process rather than theory. However, the motivations are often linked to a very specific type of structure, and different components of the self-structure are usually assumed to combine to embody differing goals. Theories differ in the level at which they describe structures of the self. For example, Higgins (1987) explores discrepancies between different "self-guides." Markus and Nurius (1986) outline the impact of people's conceptions of their "possible selves," and Cantor (1990) focuses on how individuals set different life tasks for themselves (see Knowles and Sibicky, 1990, for an overview of different perspectives on the self). At a more general level, Markus and Kitayama (1991) describe cross-cultural differences in the content of self-definition, with associated motivational implications. In the United States the self is conceptualized as an independent entity, whereas in Japan it is more likely to be conceptualized as interdependent with other people. According to Markus and Kitayama, one consequence of this difference is that self-esteem is gained and sustained differently in the two cultures.

A number of structural models have distinguished between the more social and the more personal aspects of self. For example, Fenigstein, Scheier, and Buss (1975) (see also Buss, 1980; Scheier and Carver, 1981) distinguished between the private and public self. Crocker and Luhtanen (1990) distinguish between a generalized collective self and personal self (cf. Greenwald and Pratkanis, 1984). Brewer and Gardner (1996) propose that there are three distinct levels of self-representation, the collective, relational, and personal self. Breckler and Green-wald (1986) further suggest that the public, private, and collective selves emerge in a developmental sequence, each setting different ego tasks. In common with many other theorists (e.g., Cheek and Briggs, 1982), Breckler and Greenwald equate the public self with interpersonally oriented issues, the private self with "internal standards," and the collective self with cognitions about group memberships. Whether these "motivational facets" of self are structurally independent is sometimes left implicit, but this is an operating assumption shared by many researchers in areas ranging from self-presentation and self-awareness to cross-cultural differences (Triandis, 1989).

Collective and private selves

Trafimow, Triandis, and Goto (1991) proposed an explicit structural model in which cognitions about the self are divided into two distinct components or "baskets." The private self contains knowledge of one's own attitudes, traits, feelings, and behavior. The collective self contains affiliations, group memberships, and connections to collectives of all types. To demonstrate the discontinuity between the private and collective selves, Trafimow et al. (1991) conducted two experiments involving North American and Chinese students at the University of Illinois. Participants were exposed to a prime and after a short delay were asked to complete a Twenty Statements Test (TST, Kuhn and McPartland, 1954). In the first experiment the prime for private self asked subjects to think about "what makes you different from your family and friends. What do you expect yourself to do?" The prime for collective self asked them to think of "what you have in common with your family and friends. What do they expect you to do?" In the second experiment, the prime was more indirect. Participants read a story about a warrior who appointed a general either to increase his personal glory and power (private prime), or for the glory of his family (collective prime). Subsequent self-descriptions on the TST were classified as reflecting personal self-descriptions (such as traits) or social self-descriptions (such as common fate categories).

According to the structural model the two types of self are represented in separate "baskets," so priming one should facilitate access to that but not the other part of the self. Moreover, accessibility of traits within a part of the self should be greater than accessibility of traits between different parts. Retrieval of one aspect of collective self should result in greater accessibility of other aspects of the collective, but not the private self.

In the first experiment, Chinese participants (from a collectivist culture) and participants in the collective prime condition, respectively, mentioned a higher proportion of social self-descriptions than other participants. Self-descriptions tended to cluster within type (social followed by social, personal followed by personal) at a higher than chance level. The results of the second experiment were consistent with this pattern of findings. However, it is interesting to note that the total number of social self-descriptions was small in all cases.

Hierarchical structure model

Deaux (1993) and Breakwell (e.g., 1986) argued that self-images involving both social *and* personal features can be meaningful or salient in a social situation, and that many self-images cannot sensibly be described at a single level of abstraction. This perspective is rooted in more sociological approaches to the self (e.g., Stryker, 1987), while maintaining the idea that the self has considerable stability and is represented as a psychological structure. This structure has a unique meaning for each person and is not restricted to a normative framework. For example, being a psychologist can mean different things to different psychologists. Deaux (e.g., Reid and Deaux, 1996) extends Rosenberg's (1988) hierarchical classification approach, suggesting that self-classifications (be they roles or social categories) correspond to social identity while self-descriptions in terms of traits correspond to personal features of identity. The traits and categories are each structured hierarchically, and traits and categories are linked, but the particular structure is different for each individual. The chronic accessibility of particular self-images (cf. Higgins and King, 1981) will reflect their vertical position in the hierarchy. Deaux claims that this analysis is useful when trying to predict attitudes and behavior since it accepts that meanings of identity can change although the category label may remain constant. Deaux, Reid, Mizrahi, and Ethier (1995) found five types of social identity among students: personal relationships, vocations/avocations, political affiliations, ethnic/religious groups, and stigmatized groups. These differed along various descriptive dimensions. Deaux et al. (1995) suggest that the interchangeability of identities may depend on their proximity in terms of defining dimensions. Deaux et al. (1995) contrast the idea from social identity theory that social identifications are "collective and relational" with their evidence that few social identities were relational, and only ethnic, religious, some stigmatized, and some political identities were seen as collective. Occupational identities, in contrast, were perceived to be more individualistic.

A hierarchical process model

Social identity theory and self-categorization theory both describe personal and social identifications as being *functionally* antagonistic. At first glance, this would appear to be consistent with the Trafimow et al. (1991) approach, but in contrast to the Deaux (1993) approach. Early writings on social identity (e.g., Turner and Giles, 1981; Hogg and Abrams, 1988) described social and personal identity broadly as consisting of category memberships and traits, respectively. However, more recently, particularly with the development of self-categorization theory, this view has been modified and developed; personal and social identities are representations of self at different levels of abstraction relative to both one another and the social frame of reference (e.g., Abrams and Hogg, 1990; Turner et al., 1987).

Theoretically, only one self-image can be salient at any particular time. There is no requirement to specify the content of personal and social identifications, and indeed it is impossible to do so without knowledge of the subjective context (i.e., contrasting categories and stimulus set). It is, however, possible to specify the conditions under which different self-images will be made salient, and the kinds of information that might determine the central or criterial attributes of different category memberships. In fact, one of the theoretical advantages of the social identity approach is that apparent inconsistencies in individuals' behavior can be interpreted as reflecting activation of self-images framed by different social comparisons (Turner et al., 1994). In self-categorization theory the self is *potentially* multi-leveled and multi-faceted, but at any particular moment, the self is a specific product of a context-dependent comparison (cf. Markus and Nurius, 1986; Fiske and von Hendy, 1992). One way that self-conception may gain stability is when particular social comparisons are made relatively frequently and with richness of meaning. This would increase the relative accessibility of the relevant self-categorizations. The basic process underlying this model is depicted in figure 9.1.

Despite superficial similarities between the social/personal identity distinction and Trafimow et al.'s (1991) distinction between private and collective selves, there are some important differences (Abrams, 1996). In the Trafimow et al. model the strongest associative connections are horizontal (within private or within collective self). In contrast, self-categorization theory would not predict that different collective selves (self-categorizations) imply one another, but that each should be most strongly associated with the attributes for that particular categorization (Abrams, 1993, 1996). If self as "female" is salient, the collective (stereotypical) attributes of females should be more likely to be ascribed to the self. These attributes will appear as traits, behaviors, attitudes, etc. (Abrams,

Figure 9.1 Hierarchical process model of self.

Sparkes, and Hogg, 1985; Hogg and Turner, 1987; Lorenzi-Cioldi, 1991; Oakes et al., 1991). Trafimow et al. would regard these attributes as content of the private self. In other words, the largest number of associative linkages will be vertical, from categorizations to category features. This category–attribute linkage is well described in the literature on category-based perception (cf. Rosch, 1978). In applying it to the self, it is convenient to describe it as a hierarchical process model, because the process generates cascades from categories to subcategories.

As reviewed by Abrams (1996), there are often difficulties in interpreting available evidence for self-stereotyping. Some research has examined the activation of an already existing self-schema, but has not explicitly examined the generation of new material in self-descriptions (e.g., Abrams et al., 1990; Hogg and Turner, 1987; Simon and Hamilton, 1994; Trafimow et al., 1991). Nonetheless, there is quite a lot of evidence that people report that ingroup category memberships are more self-descriptive when intergroup contrasts raise the salience of those memberships (Lorenzi-Cioldi, 1991; Simon, Glassner-Bayerl, and Stratenwerth, 1991).

Abrams, Au, Waterman, Garst, and Mallett (in preparation) conducted a series of studies to examine whether self-descriptive content could be generated by changes in self-categorization. They first reconsidered the Trafimow et al. (1991) studies. In these studies it is conceivable that the "collective" primes simply activated self-categorization at a higher level of abstraction than the "private" primes. Specifically, the collective primes asked people to consider (directly or indirectly) what they had in common with their families. Because family members are normally differentiated as individuals, the only features they have in common tend to be social category memberships such as race, religion, nationality, and locality. If this were true the prime would create a self-categorization which, uniquely perhaps, generated other categories as attributes (like traits). In contrast, the private prime asked people to emphasize distinctions among family members, and thus the attributes generated were traits. We tested this idea by adding an explicit intergroup prime (differences between own family vs. others). We hypothesized that the explicit intergroup prime would generate more "social" self-descriptions than the implicit prime, and that there would be more linkages from category to trait level than between category-level self-descriptions. Both hypotheses were supported, lending greater support for the hierarchical process model than the structure model advanced by Trafimow et al.

In a second study we tried to push self-descriptions in a specific direction by having people consider intergroup differences between British and Italian people, prior to giving their self-descriptions. In that condition and in the implicit prime (commonality with family) condition, people generated more trait-level self-descriptions than in the "private" prime condition. This is consistent with the idea that social categorizations link to associated trait-level attributes. More importantly, the specific prime did result in a higher proportion of British–Italian relevant self-descriptions at the trait level. In addition, once again social self-descriptions were associated more strongly with "private" self-descriptions than other social self-descriptions (see Abrams, 1996, for more details).

Mutable self-categories: Extending the self-stereotyping hypothesis

In some respects, the hierarchical process model would seem likely to predict the same self-conception as the hierarchical structure model, since both describe a set of links from categories to attributes. However, the two differ substantially in their assumptions about the functioning of the self-concept. The structure models allow that different category memberships and individual features can be parallel in subjective importance, and that the self is represented as an interrelated *set* of categories and attributes. In contrast, the process model emphasizes that only one level of categorization is functionally salient at any one time.

It seems fair to accept that people do experience continuity and stability in their self-concepts. This structural consistency needs to be explained, and presents a potential challenge to the SCT approach. Previously (Abrams, 1990, 1992a, 1996) I have suggested that structural accounts of self can be accommodated by characterizing temporal and individual differences in self-conception as arising from variations in the particular social comparisons and particular social frames of reference (Cinnarella, 1998). Given that people spend much of their time in stable social environments, it is reasonable to expect structural stability in their self-conceptions. However, it would be extremely difficult to navigate life if the meaning and importance of categories and attributes were invariant or inflexible. For example, consider a psychologist who self-categorizes as "Doctor x." In the context of a meeting with a student this self-category confers high status, expertise, and authority. Suppose the same person turns up for an appointment with a medical consultant who subsequently notes, "oh, so you aren't a *medical* doctor?" In this context the category label confers low status, lack of expertise, and perhaps even causes embarrassment (see figure 9.2a).

Some categorizations, such as "parent" can be subjectively defined equally as a broad social category membership (e.g., at a Parent–Teachers' Association meeting) or as a uniquely individuating categorization of self (e.g., as parent to one's child). The meaning, level, and content of self-categorizations are determined not by the self-category label but by the comparison categories in the particular context (see figure 9.2b). There is evidence that this is true of ingroup and outgroup perceptions (Abrams and Hogg, 1987; Haslam and Turner, 1992; Haslam, Turner, Oakes, McGarty, and Hayes, 1992; Oakes, Haslam, and Turner, 1994).

The distinction between categories and attributes may itself be highly mutable (Abrams, 1993, 1996). First, a category at one level of abstraction can constitute an attribute in relation to a higher level of abstraction (Bellezza, 1993). Second, and more critically, the determination of which features are categorical and which are attributes is potentially indeterminate. For example, whether a person is an artistic (attribute) athlete (category) or an athletic (attribute) artist (category) depends on the comparative context (see figure 9.2c, and Abrams, 1996, for other examples).

It follows that collective and private self-conceptions cannot have a structure that is defined by content alone. If we can readily reorganize the relationship between categories and attributes in our self-concepts, any model that depends primarily on structure will inevitably miss much of the action. A critical difference between structure and process models concerns the presumed flexibility in the relationship between different components of the self. In structural models a self-conception is defined *a priori* as collective, private, or public on the basis of its content. Thus, college membership is always collective, being an intelligent

Figures 9.2a–9.2c   The flexibility of category–attribute relationships.

Self	Other	Comparison context	
		Psychology department	Hospital
"Dr" (Ph. D. Psychology)	Dr (MD)	+++	– – – –
"Dr"	Psychology student	+++++	+

(+ = positive self-evaluation, – = negative self-evaluation)

Figure 9.2a   Category contrasts influence self-evaluations.

Context	Comparison	Self-categorization	Attributes
Home in vacation	Self–Child	Parent	Loving Fun Responsible Kind Good cook etc.
School report meeting	Self–Teachers	Parent	Concerned Strict Ambitious Cooperative Intellectual etc.

Figure 9.2b   Different comparative contexts invoke different attributes for the same self-categories.

Category	Artist	Athlete	Charity worker
Attributes	Athletic Musical Charitable	Artistic Musical Charitable	Artistic Athletic Musical

Figure 9.2c   Category–attribute relationship is mutable.

person is always private. In contrast, a self-categorization approach allows for flexibility in the definition of whether a characteristic is private (attribute) or collective (category). The research problem for SCT is not to determine the structure of self, but to reveal the process by which self becomes structured.

Self and Stereotyping as Convergent, Interdependent Processes

The preceding evidence and theory emphasize that the content of self-perception and the content of social perceptions are both affected by changes in social context. In this section it will be argued that self-perception and social perception are interdependent because they both arise from self-categorizations. Both reflect the nature of the relationship between the perceiver and the perceived. It follows that, if targets of perceptions are judged primarily in terms of a category such as gender, then self is also perceived in terms of gender. That is not to say people only distinguish among others at the same level as they distinguish themselves from others. On the contrary, subgroup distinctions are made, but that happens within the context of the primary categorization. For example, a teacher may choose to ask two sets of children to engage in different activities. Even though the teacher distinguishes between the two subgroups, the primary distinction remains that between teachers and pupils. Part of the difficulty for self-categorization theory is to determine which level(s) of categorization will be salient.

The answer is provided in terms of the normative and comparative fit between the categories and the attributes observed (Oakes et al., chapter 3 in this volume). Comparative fit refers to the extent to which individuals are easily and simply divisible into memberships of different categories. For example, the comparative fit of people into gender is usually high because there are many observable attributes that unambiguously link a person to their gender. Likewise, one's own gender category maintains a stable relationship to that of other people, making it unsurprising that gender constitutes a core part of identity (Deaux, 1993). Normative fit refers to the extent to which the behaviors of category members adhere to those that are expected, or prescribed. Normative fit may often be quite low, such as when a man behaves in a feminine way, or a woman behaves in a masculine way. If normative and comparative components are sharply at odds, people will begin to seek more meaningful categories that can improve their match. At a sports venue, the crowd includes males and females, but the more meaningful categorization is between "home" and "away" supporters. The normative fit of behavior to categories is likely to be much higher for the home/away distinction than the male/female distinction.

Self-categorization theory proposes that on-line information is integrated with prior expectancies to establish meaningful and functional perceptions of self and others. From this it could follow that category-based processing does not have any special status *vis à vis* individuated or other types of processing, because categorization can occur at any level and because the attributes associated with categories are flexible. In this respect SCT provides a very similar model of social cognitive perception as emerges from connectionist approaches (cf. Smith, 1996).

Parallel constraint satisfaction

Kunda and Thagard (1996) propose that social perceivers' task in making sense of incoming information is much like text comprehension. New information is integrated on the basis of preexisting representations of social constructs such as traits, stereotypes, and behaviors, as well as knowledge about the interrelationships among those constructs. According to Kunda and Thagard's parallel constraint satisfaction (PCS) model, perception depends on the parallel operation of excitatory and inhibitory links in a network. When given only category labels as a basis for judgment, the category activates a stereotype, which activates traits and behaviors in the network. However, category information is usually given in combination with other information, such as an instance of behavior. When this happens, the information becomes integrated and may result in different perceptual outcomes.

Kunda and Thagard give an example of how an elbow nudge may be perceived as aggressive when performed by a black person but jovial when performed by a white person. Although the black/white categorization is sufficient to change the perception in this case, categorization generally is accorded no special status in the Kunda and Thagard model. In principle, a piece of information about traits, behaviors, or perhaps moods (e.g., angry vs. cheerful) could have just as strong an effect. In contrast to the Brewer (1988) or Fiske and Neuberg (1990) models, it is not assumed that stereotypes will tend to dominate perceptions. Indeed, Kunda and Thagard argue that traits are more strongly associated with behaviors than with stereotypes. The important determinant of the perceptual outcome is the relative strengths of positive and negative associations among different characteristics.

In the PCS model, observed information is a node that is always active in the network. This has links to other nodes, in the form of stereotypes, traits, and behaviors, which themselves share inhibitory and excitatory links. The network as a whole undergoes repeated cycles of parallel activation and adjustment until it becomes stable. This represents the final "output" of perception. Stereotypes can have links directly to behavior and to traits, and traits and behavior can also be linked both directly and indirectly through stereotypes. Moreover, the same stereotype may activate different traits, some of which may be consistent (excitatory links) and some inconsistent (inhibitory links) with a particular behavior. Equally, the same trait can imply different behaviors when applied to members of different groups. For example, Kunda, Sinclair, and Griffin (1997) found that perceivers expected lawyers and construction workers to manifest their aggressiveness in quite different ways. This was because the interpretation of aggressiveness was conditioned by other features associated with the two categories, such as expectations about social class membership or being "refined."

Because individuated information is accorded equal status with stereotype information, Kunda and Thagard's model allows single items of stereotype-inconsistent information to be used as a basis for subtyping. When a man behaves in a feminine way, a subtype of "homosexual" is likely to be activated (Deaux and Lewis, 1984), but other subtypes (e.g., body-builder, athlete) are likely to be inhibited. When individuating information is diagnostic of a specific trait it overrides stereotype information (e.g., Jussim, Nelson, Manis, and Soffin, 1995; Krueger and Rothbart, 1988). Thus a person who behaves aggressively is perceived as aggressive regardless of whether the stereotype for their category implies aggressiveness. In contrast, when individuating behavioral information is nondiagnostic or is ambiguous, the stereotype appears to continue to influence trait inferences from that behavior. In other words, those links in the network with stronger associations carry more weight than those with weaker associations. Moreover, stereotypes continue to affect inferences about behavior related to traits other than that for which diagnostic information has been provided (Kunda et al., 1997). This allows people to accept exceptions to the rule (e.g., this construction worker did not behave aggressively and is not aggressive), but sustain the broader stereotype because the rest of the links in the network remain activated (e.g., this construction worker is working class, unrefined, and hence is likely to engage in aggressive behavior for other reasons).

A further interesting phenomenon that can be accommodated within the parallel constraint satisfaction framework is that stereotypes can combine either to create specific subtypes with novel attributes or to inhibit attributes of either stereotype. It would seem, though, that these "new" images require controlled thought processes and reasoning. The generation of new impressions from multiple categorizations and individuating information is something which the serial models proposed by Brewer (1988) and Fiske and Neuberg (1990) may have some difficulty in accommodating. Like the self-categorization model, the parallel constraint satisfaction model does not make strong *a priori* assumptions about whether particular features will serve as categories or as traits: "many attributes that are typically viewed as individuating information appear indistinguishable from stereotypes, both structurally and in terms of reference class" (Kunda and Thagard, 1996, p. 301). Indeed, Kunda and Thagard (1996) found no evidence that stereotypes have any particular primacy over individuating information in general. They conclude that stereotype-based processing is not a default option, in fact reporting a meta-analytic effect size of .69 for the effects of individuating information against an effect size of .19 for stereotype information across 40 studies that orthogonally manipulated the two types of information.

Many questions are left unanswered by this model. For example, the question of what people notice in the first place is left to ideas about contextual salience (cf. Taylor, 1981), accessibility (Higgins and King, 1981), or perceiver goals (Brewer, 1988; Fiske and Neuberg, 1990). Similarly, the questions of how or why people seek to make judgments about others, or indeed the role of the immediate social context, are left open. Thus the model is entirely cognitive, requiring no reference to comparisons between target persons and any other external frame of reference. Such a model would at first appear to epitomize the most reductionistic tendencies in social cognition. Since the perceptual output of a person can be simulated by a computer (a computer that does not have *relationships* with other people, only knowledge about them), social perception is reduced to an algorithm that simply minimizes inconsistencies and maximizes consistencies between units of knowledge.

Context as constraints

Such models could very usefully be extended to intergroup processes by extending the scope of what people perceive. If, in addition to associations between the category memberships, traits, and behaviors of a target individual, the model were to include associations *between targets*, it would begin to accommodate the insights of self-categorization theory. To the extent that targets are assumed to share traits or descriptive features with one subset of others, but not with a different subset, a categorization will become salient (comparative fit). To the extent that behaviors exhibited by category members are also similar, a stereotype will be generated. If there is weak correspondence between behaviors and the descriptive category membership, the perceiver will generate a new basis for categorization, determined by the behavioral similarity among subsets of individuals. This is quite analogous to Kunda and Thagard's tenet that individual behavioral information can override prior categorization, and can generate novel categories (be they subtypes or new types). The meta-contrast process in self-categorization theory thus bears numerous similarities with parallel constraint satisfaction predictions, because both invoke processes that maximize the fit of the stimuli to an optimally meaningful model. Moreover, both assume that this process results in stereotype-based inferences so that perceivers orient towards an image of the target that is beyond the data given. In self-categorization theory this is portrayed as a prototype, often an extremetized perception of the group norm (Oakes, 1996). In the parallel constraint satisfaction model, it is an image that derives from a combination of the stimulus information together with its associations with other knowledge. Both approaches emphasize that the perceiver creates meaning on-line, though the Kunda and Thagard approach assumes greater priority for previously learned or established stereotypes. This is inevitable given that it chooses to focus on perceptions of individual targets rather than of targets in explicitly comparative contexts.

The self as a product of parallel constraint satisfaction

The PCS model could usefully be extended to include self-perception. We can ask whether the self should be accorded very special status, and, if so, what? Does it seem reasonable that self-perception can be maneuvered as easily as other-perception, simply by altering the connections between self and other nodes in the information structure? I would suggest that the answer is a qualified "yes." As reviewed above, the self clearly manifests considerable stability, at least as a knowledge structure. This can be located partly in the stability of the social environment in which self-knowledge is embedded. Dramatic changes in the enduring self-environment are not very common because people tend to remain linked to their locality, roles, families, personal experiences, occupations, and material circumstances. Moreover, their gender, ethnicity, nationality, and often religious background are all highly stable, both objectively and in relation to others in their environment. Thus the associative links among features of the self are likely to be extensive and strong.

In contrast, dramatic changes in the social (interpersonal or intercategory) environment are quite common. At one moment we may be among family members, at another with colleagues, at another in a shopping mall or at a football match. It is therefore possible that the meaning of self-knowledge can vary as a function of the other nodes being activated at the time. For example, a link from self to "musically able" could become positively weighted in the context of teaching a child to play its first instrument, but negatively weighted in the context of one's first attempt to play in an orchestra. In other words, category, trait, or behavioral knowledge about oneself may be well organized as networks of information, but the way those are linked to other, more contextually fluid, information should have significant effects on self-perception (Kunda, Fong, Sanitoso, and Reber, 1993). This view of the self does not go as far as Oakes et al. (chapter 3 in this volume) in embracing a social constructionist view. It assumes that self-knowledge has a great deal of temporal stability comprising well-established links between features. However, the particular relevance and evaluation of self-knowledge is strongly affected by other information in the social context.

Self-categorization theory would hold that this crucial "other information" emerges from social comparisons. These comparisons allow us to build links *to* other individuals through shared social categories. In turn we can make new inferences about ourselves from these emergent categorizations. Indeed, we use these categorizations to provide a framework for our future behavior and self-evaluations. Establishing one's group membership or category alignment can often come prior to adopting the groups' values and norms, for example in voting decisions, in pursuing organizational goals, when setting targets for achievement, or when evaluating group members (see Abrams, 1992a; Marques, Abrams, Paez, and Taboada, in press).

Regulation of Stereotyping and Behavior

Recently, Bodenhausen and Macrae (1998) elaborated a model of the way stereotypes affect interpersonal impressions, judgments, and behaviors. Their model proposes that two processes operate when we perceive others. First, there is a relatively automatic activation and inhibition of category-consistent and category-inconsistent stereotypical information. Second, there is a more effortful suppression of unwanted or undesirable stereotypical thoughts. Causal or controlled reasoning seems to occur for attributional tasks (e.g., Deaux and Emswiller, 1974), tasks in which the information is ambiguous or contradictory (e.g., Jussim, Coleman, and Lerch, 1987), when perceivers are motivated to reach a deep understanding (Fiske and Neuberg, 1990), or when they are required to construct new stereotypes or impressions to account for discrepant information (e.g., Weber and Crocker, 1983).

The Bodenhausen–Macrae model makes fairly strong assumptions about the presence of preexisting well-structured stereotypes in memory. Abrams and Masser (1998) argue that this set of assumptions would impose severe restrictions on people's capacity to reach context-dependent conclusions about others. Dependence on memory-based stereotypes would mean that these have to be inhibited or suppressed when contextual information implies alternative judgments of the targets. Even though category-based expectancies may serve to provide probabilistic weights for judging targets, the potential for huge numbers of alternative bases of categorization could demand that cognitive resources would have to be devoted to a massive inhibitory task to rule out the inappropriate ones. It would seem more efficient if there was simply a lack of activation of alternative categorizations (and perhaps inhibition of information negatively correlated with the activated category).

Because contextual information is so critical in determining the meaning of category memberships, Abrams and Masser argue that it is difficult to establish *a priori* any particular content that should be suppressed. Stereotypes are conceptualized as the "best-fitting" psychological model of the data given certain goals and perceiver characteristics (Oakes et al., 1994; Oakes et al., 1998; Oakes et al., chapter 3 in this volume). Perceivers can be expected to seek the most appropriate (in the sense of being diagnostic, useful, and meaningful) judgments of targets. Abrams and Masser suggest that stereotypes are usually generated on-line using, but not being determined by, information in memory. This degree of flexibility in stereotyping may not characterize the situation in a typical laboratory experiment, but we think it does characterize stereotype use in more complex social contexts (cf. Kunda and Thagard, 1996). Generally, inappropriate or ill-fitting stereotypes should not be applied in the first place, and hence should not have to be inhibited. In this view, stereotypes do not constitute erroneous or biased perceptions, and hence there should be no requirement to modify the impression unless something changes in the actor's goals or in their environment.

If one accepts that there is some indeterminacy in stereotype content, it becomes less easy to be sure of the relationship between stereotype activation and the everyday reasoning and interpersonal judgments that may follow. Perhaps Bodenhausen and Macrae's model holds particularly well for predominantly negative and incontestable stereotypes (e.g., stereotypes of the lowest-status, most undesirable, and distinctive groups in society). Their model may become less appropriate when stereotypes are applied in a more flexible and task-specific way.

Functionality of stereotypes

The SCT perspective raises the question of when people might perceive the application of a stereotype as a "failure to match to standard." Abrams and Masser proposed that perceivers regard only certain types of stereotype as undesirable, and only in particular circumstances. Ingroup stereotypes are usually positive (Tajfel, 1981b). Stereotypes may also contain much evaluatively neutral content (e.g., that people from New York live in skyscrapers). In addition, many stereotypical features of potential outgroups are potentially positive (e.g., white Americans may perceive Asians as mathematically talented, the French as cultured, or Germans as efficient). These make up part of the overall image of social categories and groups. If perceivers were to find the application of negative judgments undesirable *per se* this would disrupt stereotypical judgment as a whole, and it could become difficult to make *any* coherent judgments of targets.

From the standpoint that stereotypes are subjectively "reasonable" expectations about group members, situations that call for stereotype suppression are psychologically problematic. Much of the recent research on ironic thought processes (e.g., Wegner, 1994) reveals how conscious suppression of "unwanted" thoughts tends to generate rebound effects. In stereotype suppression studies perceivers' goals are manipulated so that the functionally appropriate stereotypes alter. For example, in the Macrae et al. (1994a) skinhead experiments participants were asked either to write an impressionistic "day in the life of" diary of a skinhead or were also told *not* to use stereotypes in this task. The latter group subsequently applied the skinhead stereotype more in their written descriptions when presented with an ostensibly unrelated second target, sat further from a skinhead, or responded faster to skinhead-related words.

Such effects would appear to demonstrate rebounding stereotypes, but an SCT interpretation might be that in the first phase the stereotype is supplanted because participants infer from the "not to stereotype" instruction that the category "skinhead" is too general to be diagnostic for their descriptions.

Given that the only information about the target is a photograph, this presents a challenging task. Once the requirement not to stereotype is removed, the category skinhead once again becomes the "default" basis for judging the target, and so, in phase two, the target is stereotyped more strongly. Undoubtedly the phase one instructions prime the categorization, making it more available and salient. Participants are being asked to engage in additional effort to find alternative meaningful categories with which to make a judgment. Perhaps this is simply unrealistic given the stimulus. The "rebound" effect, then, may be particularly likely when the thoughts that the participants are asked to suppress are in fact functionally appropriate to the situation.

Abrams and Masser (1998) concluded that stereotype suppression is likely to be a relatively unusual event, and that suppression would be unlikely to arise for cognitive or personal reasons. We considered that pressure for stereotype suppression is likely to arise when the personal stereotype is at variance with social norms. Thus, we see stereotypes as a part of the "cognitive success" of the perceiver, but as eliciting responses that might be construed as "social failure," because people may be concerned not to appear "unreasonable" or out of line. A social failure such as inappropriately expressing a stereotypical judgment may be a source of embarrassment, and likely to provoke admonishment from others. There is extensive documentation of prevalent cultural values and norms that shape people's sense of right and wrong (e.g., Lerner and Miller, 1978; Seligman, Olson, and Zanna, 1996; Triandis, 1995). Guilt does seem to be associated with awareness of having made unreasonably negative judgments of others (Devine, Monteith, Zuwerink, and Elliott, 1991; Monteith, 1993; Monteith, Devine, and Zuwerink, 1993). Even people with strong prejudices might attempt to justify these in some way (e.g., McConahay, 1983; Sears and Kinder, 1971), at least to themselves (cf. Adorno, Frenkel-Brunswik, Levinson, and Sanford, 1950; Billig, 1988; Potter and Wetherell, 1987). However, people may not be vigilant for such judgments unless the context demands that they are so (Monteith, 1996).

Social self-regulation

The process by which overt behavior is regulated now seems well documented as a comparison–reference value feedback loop (Powers, 1973). The conscious comparison of one's thoughts, intentions, or actions with a reference standard seems to depend on self-focused attention (Bodenhausen and Macrae 1998; Carver and Scheier, 1981; Gibbons, 1990; Wicklund, 1975). Bodenhausen and Macrae propose that stereotype suppression is more likely when people are self-aware, because they refer to personal standards to filter the output from relatively automatically activated cultural stereotypes. This incorporates the idea that stereotypes are relatively well learned, slow to change, and insensitive to people's personal experiences of different intergroup relationships. To deal with these unwieldy and poorly fitting impressions, the control system somehow locates a much more flexible personal norm or rule which facilitates or inhibits the stereotype and related behavior.

There are two problems with the Bodenhausen and Macrae model. First, it does not deal with the functional aspect of stereotyping, its flexibility and contextual fit. Second, it treats the self only as an observer. These problems are partly dealt with by the social self-regulation (SSR) model, which integrates self-awareness theory with social identity salience (self-categorization) and attentional focus as distinct contributors to behavioral regulation, as shown in figure 9.3.

Self/other categorization, and the associated stereotyping, are conceived of as generally nonconscious processes that give rise to category salience. This is distinguished from the attentional processes, which relatively consciously direct information processing and regulate behavior. Attention may be directed towards the self or towards external stimuli.

When both identity salience and self-attention are low, behavior is likely to be task-focused, routine, or inactive. In ambiguous situations or when routine is interrupted by an external event or stimulus, attention may be devoted to

Initial identity salience	Self-attention	Possible reference standard	Outcome
Low	Low	None	Routine, nonreactive, task-focus
Low	High	Search for cues to establish direction for action (through within-self and self–other comparisons)	Self-categorization influencing perceptions
High (e.g., memory-based, highly accessible, good "fit")	High	Personal stereotype	Stereotype-based action
High	High	Social stereotype Category-based	Normative stereotyping Category-serving action
		Interpersonal norm	Specific to relationship
		Personal norm, desired affect	Depends on prior goals and personal stereotype

Figure 9.3   Social self-regulation

determining the category memberships of targets, or analyzing their individual features (Abrams, 1990, 1994; Hogg and Abrams, 1993; Hogg and Mullin, chapter 11 in this volume). Increased self-attention may lower attentional capacity for processing information about others (Vallacher, 1978). Therefore, in some circumstances self-attention may increase the use of heuristics or simple assumptions, reducing differentiation among targets (Fenigstein and Abrams, 1993). This could increase the impact of stereotypical perceptions on behaviors and judgments (consistent with Bodenhausen and Macrae's findings, but not their interpretation).

The attentional process generally is oriented with respect to a particular goal. Because particular goals, standards, or motives can differ, so, too, can the consequences of self-attention. For example, when social identity is salient, enhancing attention to that identity results in increased intergroup discrimination (e.g., Abrams, 1985), perhaps in the service of a motivation to enhance a valued aspect of self. However, when interpersonal norms are used as the reference standard, self-attention may result in reduced intergroup discrimination and increased socially desirable responses (Abrams and Brown, 1989; Froming and Carver, 1981). In summary, the behavioral consequences of self-awareness depend on (1) the aspect of self which is salient, and (2) the standards being used to guide behavior. When social identity is salient self-(ingroup-) serving motives and generic social norms may represent different subsets of the potential reference values for responding. As a result it would seem hasty to expect unidirectional effects of self-attention on stereotyping or behavior.

Reference values

Abrams and Masser (1998) propose that the sequencing of personal and cultural standards in the inhibitory process could be the reverse of that proposed by Bodenhausen and Macrae (1998). Specifically, we suggest that *personal* stereotypes provide the initial output of the perceptual system (either memory-based, created on-line, or a mixture of both). The stereotype applied to a particular category can vary greatly with context and presumably with personal experience. Because it represents the best initial fit for the perceiver, it will be activated strongly, will be highly accessible and subjectively meaningful. The content of stereotypes will vary from person to person within a situation, and from situation to situation within a person. Reference values for the control processes come from cultural stereotypes in conjunction with situational norms, and these are used to modulate or compare the personal stereotype and to moderate behavior.

The context also provides normative structure for judgment and behavior. If the context invites application of a relatively simple and undifferentiated cultural stereotype, people will use that as the reference value against which to compare their personal stereotype and the behavioral options that could follow. For example, in the presence of consistent normative information from other ingroup members stereotypes and ingroup favoritism are bolstered (Haslam, Oakes,

McGarty, Turner, Reynolds, and Eggins, 1996; Marques et al., in press; Monteith, Deenan, and Tooman, 1996), a situation which Bodenhausen and Macrae refer to as "compliant" and "insincere" stereotyping. We prefer to see it as functional, adaptive, and hence "sincere," even if it is short-lived. In figure 9.3, this situation is represented in the row involving high identity salience/high self-attention/social stereotype reference value.

Imagine a situation in which a salesman ("Joe") in England is told anti-Irish jokes by a potential customer. Joe may well observe that the stereotype does not fit with his personal view of the Irish, which stems from his own experiences and time he has spent in Ireland. The context in this case provides a reference value – Joe's aim is to find common ground with his customer, which can be achieved easily by endorsing the social stereotype of the Irish. The specific content can be inferred both from his general knowledge and from the jokes told by his customer. Joe may even feel he has to tell further anti-Irish jokes, which may require that he suppresses his personally held views. Socially available norms and stereotypes are used to regulate behavior in a socially normative manner, overriding more spontaneously salient or nonconsciously based personal perceptions. The control process takes a perceptual output (from memory plus on-line inference) and compares it with a reference value (defined by a relevant social norm or standard), so that behavior can be moderated towards the norm.

This formulation of stereotype control retains the position of the self at the center of perception, consistent both with SCT and with research suggesting the relative primacy of self-related material in cognition. Given the prevalence of motives for self-enhancement and self-protection, increased self-awareness should often result in increased ingroup bias and more self–other differentiation (see also Simon, 1993, 1997), but the model also allows learned knowledge about society to provide a source of normative standards (not a default perceptual output). Thus, the self and others can be flexibly recategorized, while at the same time relatively simple and conventionalized cultural and social norms remain available to guide action. It is then possible for individuals with *different* personal knowledge (e.g., personal stereotypes) to coordinate easily with one another by referring to common social rules (e.g., social stereotypes). When situations call for personal stereotypes to be moderated in some way, self-regulation allows them either to be downplayed or expanded and exaggerated as the context requires. The same applies to behavioral choices such as whether to remain in or leave the group; the cultural or normative context provides rules for action in the light of one's salient identity. Different contexts may imply quite different rules (cf. Abrams, Ando, and Hinkle, 1998).

Conclusions

In this chapter I have stressed four points to draw the social identity and social cognition approaches closer together. First, comparative context has an important influence on the content of both stereotyping and self-stereotyping. Second, the self combines general stability of content with flexibility of meaning in relation to changing contexts. The relationship between categories and psychological attributes is often indeterminate, since they can be interchangeable. Advantages of a hierarchical process model over structure models of self were outlined. Third, there is considerable overlap between propositions derived from self-categorization theory and connectionist parallel constraint satisfaction approaches to social cognition. However, it is essential to incorporate both the self and the social context into these models in order to avoid reducing intergroup relations to purely individual-level analyses. Fouth, in social self-regulation, the initial perceptual output of social perception is likely to be a personal stereotype. Judgments and behavior are then moderated by reference to social stereotypes and situational rules or norms, as well as motives. Thus, social cognitive and social identity processes function together to produce contextually meaningful and relevant judgment and behaviors.

References

Abrams, D. (1985). Focus of attention in minimal intergroup discrimination. *British Journal of Social Psychology*, 24, 65–74.

Abrams, D. (1990). How do group members regulate their behaviour? An integration of social identity and self-awareness theories. In D. Abrams and M.A. Hogg (eds), *Social Identity Theory: Constructive and critical advances*. London and New York: Harvester Wheatsheaf and Springer-Verlag, pp. 89–112.

Abrams, D. (1992a). Processes of social identification. In G. Breakwell (ed.), *Social Psychology of Identity and the Self-concept*. San Diego: Academic Press, pp. 57–99.

Abrams, D. (1992b). Optimal Distinctiveness Theory with bells on: Music sub-culture identification among 16–20-year-olds. Paper presented at the European Association of Experimental Social Psychology Small Group Meeting on Social Cognition, Bristol, April.

Abrams, D. (1993). From social identity to action. "British Invited Speaker" presentation, British Psychological Society, Social Psychology Section Conference, Oxford, September.

Abrams, D. (1994). Social self-regulation. *Personality and Social Psychology Bulletin*, 20, 273–83.

Abrams, D. (1996). Social identity, self as structure and self as process. In W.P. Robinson (ed.), *Social Groups and Identities: Developing the legacy of Henri Tajfel*. Oxford: Butterworth-Heinemann, pp. 143–68.

Abrams, D., Ando, K., and Hinkle, S.W. (1998). Psychological attachment to the group: Cross cultural differences in organizational identification and subjective norms as predictors of workers' turnover intentions. *Personality and Social Psychology Bulletin*, 10, 1027–39.

Abrams, D., Au, W., Waterman, W., Garst, J., and Mallett, C. (in preparation). The two baskets and one process views of self: Three experiments on self-stereotyping, University of Kent.

Abrams, D. and Brown, R.J. (1989). Self-consciousness and social identity: Self-regulation as a group member. *Social Psychology Quarterly*, 52, 311–18.

Abrams, D. and Hogg, M.A. (1987). Language attitudes, frames of reference and social identity: A Scottish dimension. *Journal of Language and Social Psychology*, 6, 201–13.

Abrams, D. and Hogg, M.A. (1990). An introduction to the social identity approach. In D. Abrams and M.A. Hogg (eds), *Social Identity Theory: Constructive and critical advances*. London and New York: Harvester Wheatsheaf and Springer-Verlag, pp. 1–9.

Abrams, D. and Masser, B. (1998). Context and the social self-regulation of stereotyping: Perception, judgment and behaviour. In R.S. Wyer (ed.), *Advances in Social Cognition*, Vol. 11. Hillsdale, NJ: Erlbaum, pp. 53–68.

Abrams, D., Sparkes, K., and Hogg, M.A. (1985). Gender salience and social identity: The impact of sex of siblings on educational and occupational aspirations. *British Journal of Educational Psychology*, 55, 224–32.

Abrams, D., Thomas, J., and Hogg, M.A. (1990). Numerical distinctiveness, social identity and gender salience. *British Journal of Social Psychology*, 29, 87–92.

Adorno, T.W., Frenkel-Brunswik, E., Levinson, D.J., and Sanford, R.N. (1950). *The Authoritarian Personality*. New York: Harper.

Anastasio, P., Bachman, B., Gaertner, S., and Dovidio, J.F. (1997) Categorization, recategorization and common ingroup identity. In R. Spears, P.J. Oakes, N. Ellemers, and A. Haslam (eds), *The Social Psychology of Stereotyping and Group Life*. Oxford: Blackwell, pp. 236–56.

Andersen, S.M. and Klatzky, R.L. (1987). Traits and social stereotypes: Levels of categorization in person perception. *Journal of Personality and Social Psychology*, 53, 235–46.

Bellezza, F.S. (1984). The self as a mnemonic device: The role of internal cues. *Journal of Personality and Social Psychology*, 47, 506–16.

Bellezza, F.S. (1993). Does "perplexing" describe the self-reference effect? Yes! In T.K. Srull and R.S. Wyer, Jr (eds), *The Mental Representation of Trait and Autobiographical Knowledge about the Self: Advances in social cognition*, Vol. 5. Hillsdale, NJ: Lawrence Erlbaum Associates, pp. 51–60.

Billig, M. (1988). The notion of "prejudice": Some rhetorical and ideological aspects. *Text*, 8, 91–111.

Bodenhausen, G. and Macrae, C.N. (1998). Stereotype activation and inhibition. In R.S. Wyer (ed.), *Advances in Social Cognition*, (vol. 11). Hillsdale, NJ: Erlbaum, pp. 1–52.

Breakwell, G. (1986). *Coping with Threatened Identities*. London: Methuen.

Breckler, S. and Greenwald, A. (1986). Motivational facets of the self. In R. Sorrentino and T. Higgins (eds), *Handbook of Motivation and Cognition*. New York: Guilford, pp. 145–64.

Brewer, M.B. (1988). A dual process model of impression formation. In T.K. Srull and R.S. Wyer (eds) *Advances in Social Cognition*. Hillsdale, NJ: Erlbaum, pp. 1–36.

Brewer, M.B. (1991). The social self: On being the same and different at the same time. *Personality and Social Psychology Bulletin*, 17, 475–82.

Brewer, M.B. and Gardner, W. (1996). Who is this "We"? Levels of collective identity and self representations. *Journal of Personality and Social Psychology*, 71, 83–93.

Brown, R.J., Hinkle, S., Ely, P.G., Fox-Cardamone, D.L., and Maras, P. (1992). Recognizing group diversity: Individualist–collectivist and autonomous–relational social orientations and their implications for intergroup processes. *British Journal of Social Psychology*, 31, 327–42.

Buss, A.H. (1980). *Self-consciousness and Social Anxiety*. Glencoe: Free Press.

Cantor, N. (1990). From thought to behaviour: "Having" and "doing" in the study of personality and cognition. *American Psychologist*, 45, 735–50.

Carver, C.S. and Humphries, C. (1981). Havana daydreaming: A study of self-consciousness and the negative reference group among Cuban Americans. *Journal of Personality and Social Psychology*, 40, 545–52.

Carver, C.S. and Scheier, M.F. (1981). *Attention and Self-regulation: A control theory approach to human behaviour*. New York: Springer-Verlag.

Cheek, J.M. and Briggs, S.R. (1982). Self-consciousness and aspects of identity. *Journal of Research in Personality*, 16, 401–8.

Cinnarella, M. (1998). Exploring temporal aspects of social identity: The concept of possible social identities. *European Journal of Social Psychology*, 28, 227–48.

Condor, S.G. (1986). Sex role beliefs and "traditional" women: Feminist and intergroup perspectives. In S. Wilkinson (ed.), *Feminist Social Psychology*. Milton Keynes: Open University Press, pp. 97–118.

Crocker, J. and Luhtanen, R. (1990). Collective self-esteem and ingroup bias. *Journal of Personality and Social Psychology*, 58, 60–7.

Crosby, F., Cordova, D., and Jaskar, K. (1993). On the failure to see oneself as disadvantaged: Cognitive and emotional components. In M.A. Hogg and D. Abrams (eds), *Group Motivation: Social psychological perspectives*. London: Harvester Wheatsheaf, pp. 87–104.

Deaux, K. (1993). Reconstructing social identity. *Personality and Social Psychology Bulletin*, 19, 4–12.

Deaux, K. and Emswiller, T. (1974). Explanations of successful performance on sex-linked tasks: What is skill for the male is luck for the female. *Journal of Personality and Social Psychology*, 29, 80–5.

Deaux, K. and Lewis, L.L. (1984). Structure of gender stereotypes: Interrelationships among components and gender label. *Journal of Personality and Social Psychology*, 46, 991–1004.

Deaux, K., Reid, A., Mizrahi, K., and Ethier, K.A. (1995). Parameters of social identity. *Journal of Personality and Social Psychology*, 68, 280–91.

Devine, P.G. (1989). Stereotypes and prejudice: Their automatic and controlled components. *Journal of Personality and Social Psychology*, 56, 5–18.

Devine, P.G., Monteith, M.J., Zuwerink, J.R., and Elliot, A.J. (1991). Prejudice with and without compunction. *Journal of Personality and Social Psychology*, 60, 817–30.

Eagly, A. and Chaiken, S. (1993). *The Psychology of Attitudes*. New York: Harcourt Brace Jovanovich.

Ellemers, N., Spears, R., and Doosje, B. (1997). Sticking together or falling apart: Ingroup identification as a psychological determinant of group commitment versus individual mobility. *Journal of Personality and Social Psychology*, 72, 617–26.

Ethier, K.A. and Deaux, K. (1994). Negotiating social identity when contexts change: Maintaining identification and responding to threat. *Journal of Personality and Social Psychology*, 67, 243–51.

Farr, R.M. (1996). *The Roots of Modern Social Psychology: 1872–1954*. Oxford: Blackwell.

Fenigstein, A. and Abrams, D. (1993). Self-attention and the egocentric assumption of shared perspectives. *Journal of Experimental Social Psychology*, 29, 287–303.

Fenigstein, A., Scheier, M.F., and Buss, A.H. (1975). Public and private self-consciousness: Assessment and theory. *Journal of Consulting and Clinical Psychology*, 43, 522–7.

Fiske, S.T. and Neuberg, S.L. (1990). A continuum of impression formation, from category-based to individuating processes: Influences of information and motivation on attention and interpretation. In M.P. Zanna (ed.), *Advances in Experimental Social Psychology*, Vol. 23. New York: Academic Press, pp. 1–74.

Fiske, S.T. and von Hendy, H.M. (1992). Personality feedback and situational norms can control stereotyping processes. *Journal of Personality and Social Psychology*, 62, 577–96.

Froming, W.J. and Carver, C.S. (1981). Divergent influences of private and public self-consciousness in a compliance paradigm. *Journal of Research in Personality*, 15, 159–71.

Fu, H., Lee, S., Chiu, C., and Hong, Y. (in press). Setting the frame of mind for social identity. *International Journal of Intercultural Relations*.

Gaertner, S.L., Rust, M.C., Dovidio, J.F., Bachman, B., and Anastasio, P. (1994). The contact hypothesis: The role of a common ingroup identity on reducing intergroup bias. *Small Group Research*, 25, 224–49.

Gibbons, F.X. (1990). Self-attention and behaviour: A review and theoretical update. In L. Berkowitz (ed.), Advances in Experimental Social Psychology, Vol. 17. New York: Academic Press, pp. 249–303.

Glick, P. and Fiske, S.T. (1996). The ambivalent sexism inventory: Differentiating hostile and benevolent sexism. *Journal of Personality and Social Psychology*, 70, 491–512.

Greenwald, A.G. and Pratkanis, A.R. (1984). The self. In R.S. Wyer and T.K. Srull (eds), *Handbook of Social Cognition*, Vol. 3. Hillsdale, NJ: Erlbaum, pp. 129–78.

Hamilton, D.L. (1981). Illusory correlation as a basis for stereotyping. In D.L. Hamilton (ed.), *Cognitive Processes in Stereotyping and Intergroup Behaviour*. Hillsdale, NJ: Erlbaum.

Haslam, S.A., Oakes, P.J., McGarty, C., Turner, J.C., Reynolds, K.J., and Eggins, R.A. (1996). Stereotyping and social influence: The mediation of stereotype applicability and sharedness by the views of in-group and out-group members. *British Journal of Social Psychology*, 35, 369–97.

Haslam, S.A. and Turner, J.C. (1992). Context-dependent variation in social stereotyping 2: The relationship between frame of reference, self-categorization and accentuation. *European Journal of Social Psychology*, 22, 251–77.

Haslam, S.A., Turner, J.C., Oakes, P.J., McGarty, C. and Hayes, B.K. (1992). Context-dependent variation in social stereotyping 1: The effects of intergroup relations as mediated by social change and frame of reference. *European Journal of Social Psychology*, 22, 3–20.

Higgins, E.T. (1987). Self-discrepancy: A theory relating self and affect. *Psychological Review*, 94, 319–40.

Higgins, E.T. and King, G.A. (1981). Accessibility of social constructs: Information processing consequences of individual and contextual variability. In N. Cantor and J.F. Kihlstrom (eds), *Personality, Cognition, and Social interaction*. Hillsdale, NJ: Erlbaum, pp. 69–122.

Hinkle, S.W., Taylor, D., Fox-Cardamone, L., and Cook, K. (1989). Intragroup identification and intergroup differentiation: A multi-component approach. *British Journal of Social Psychology*, 28, 305–17.

Hogg, M.A. (1992). *The Social Psychology of Group Cohesiveness*. Hemel Hempstead: Harvester Wheatsheaf.

Hogg, M.A. and Abrams, D. (1988). *Social Identifications: A social psychology of intergroup relations and group processes*. London: Routledge.

Hogg, M.A. and Abrams, D. (1993). Towards a single-process uncertainty-reduction model of social motivation in groups. In M.A. Hogg and D. Abrams (eds), *Group Motivation: Social psychological perspectives*. London: Harvester Wheatsheaf, pp. 173–90.

Hogg, M.A. and Turner, J.C. (1985). Interpersonal attraction, social identification and psychological group formation. *European Journal of Social Psychology*, 15, 51–66.

Hogg, M.A. and Turner, J.C. (1987). Intergroup behaviour, self-stereotyping and the salience of social categories. *British Journal of Social Psychology*, 26, 325–40.

Hopkins, N., Reicher, S.D. and Levine, M. (1997). On the parallels between social cognition and the "new racism." *British Journal of Social Psychology*, 36, 305–30.

Judd, C.M. and Park, B. (1988). Outgroup homogeneity: Judgements of variability at the individual and group levels. *Journal of Personality and Social Psychology*, 54, 778–88.

Jussim, L., Coleman, L.M., and Lerch, L. (1987). The nature of stereotypes: A comparison and integration of three theories. *Journal of Personality and Social Psychology*, 52, 536–46.

Jussim, L., Nelson, T.E., Manis, M., and Soffin, S. (1995). Prejudice, stereotypes and labelling effects: Sources of bias in person perception. *Journal of Personality and Social Psychology*, 68, 228–46.

Kahneman, D. and Miller, D.T. (1986). Norm theory: Comparing reality to its alternatives. *Psychological Review*, 93, 136–53.

Keenan, J.M. (1993). An exemplar model can explain Klein and Loftus's results. In T.K. Srull and R.S. Wyer, Jr (eds), *The Mental Representation of Trait and Autobiographical Knowledge about the Self: Advances in social cognition*, Vol. 5. Hillsdale, NJ: Lawrence Erlbaum Associates, pp. 69–78.

Kihlstrom, J.F. and Cantor, N. (1984). Mental representation of the self. In L. Berkowitz (ed.), *Advances in Experimental Social Psychology*, Vol. 17. New York: Academic Press.

Klein, S.B. and Loftus, J. (1993). The mental representation of trait and autobiographical knowledge about the self. In T.K. Srull and R.S. Wyer, Jr (eds), *The Mental Representation of Trait and Autobiographical Knowledge about the Self: Advances in social cognition*, Vol. 5. Hillsdale, NJ: Lawrence Erlbaum Associates, pp. 1–50.

Knowles, E.S. and Sibicky, M.E. (1990). Continuity and diversity in the stream of selves: Metaphorical resolutions of William James's one-in-many-selves paradox. *Personality and Social Psychology Bulletin*, 16, 676–87.

Krueger, J. and Clement, R.W. (1994). The truly false consensus effect: An ineradicable and egocentric bias in social perception. *Journal of Personality and Social Psychology*, 67, 596–610.

Krueger, J. and Rothbart, M. (1988). Use of categorical and individuating information in making inferences about personality. *Journal of Personality and Social Psychology*, 55, 187–95.

Kuhn, M.H. and McPartland, T.S. (1954). An empirical investigation of self-attitudes. *American Sociological Review*, 19, 68–76.

Kunda, Z., Fong, G.T., Sanitoso, R., and Reber, E. (1993). Directional questions direct self-conceptions. *Journal of Experimental Social Psychology*, 29, 63–86.

Kunda, Z., Sinclair, L., and Griffin, D. (1997). Equal ratings but separate meanings: Stereotypes and the construal of traits. *Journal of Personality and Social Psychology*, 72, 720–34.

Kunda, Z. and Thagard, P. (1996). Forming impressions from stereotypes, traits, and behaviors: A parallel-constraint-satisfaction theory. *Psychological Review*, 103, 284–308.

Lepore, L. and Brown, R.J. (1997). Automatic stereotype activation: Is prejudice inevitable? *Journal of Personality and Social Psychology*, 72, 275–87.

Lerner, M.J. and Miller, D.T. (1978). Just-world research and the attribution process: Looking back and ahead. *Psychological Bulletin*, 85, 1030–51.

Lorenzi-Cioldi, F. (1991). Self-stereotyping and self-enhancement in gender groups. *European Journal of Social Psychology*, 21, 403–17.

McConahay, J.B. (1983). Modern racism and modern discrimination: The effects of race, racial attitudes and context on simulated hiring decisions. *Personality and Social Psychology Bulletin*, 9, 551–8.

McConahay, J.B. (1986). Modern racism, ambivalence and the modern racism scale. In J.F. Dovidio and S.L. Gaertner (eds), *Prejudice, Discrimination and Racism*. London: Academic Press.

McGuire, W.J., McGuire, C.V., and Cheever, J. (1986). The self in society: Effects of social contexts on the sense of self. *British Journal of Social Psychology*, 25, 259–70.

Macrae, C.N., Bodenhausen, G.V., and Milne, A.B. (1995). The dissection of selection in person perception: Inhibitory processes in social stereotyping. *Journal of Personality and Social Psychology*, 69, 397–407.

Macrae, C.N., Bodenhausen, G.V., Milne, A.B., and Jetten, J. (1994a). Out of mind but back in sight: Stereotypes on the rebound. *Journal of Personality and Social Psychology*, 67, 808–17.

Macrae, C.N., Milne, A.B., and Bodenhausen, G.V. (1994b). Stereotypes as energy-saving devices: A peek inside the cognitive toolbox. *Journal of Personality and Social Psychology*, 66, 37–47.

Markus, H. (1977). Self-schemata and processing information about the self. *Journal of Personality and Social Psychology*, 35, 63–78.

Markus, H. and Kitayama, S. (1991). Culture and the self: Implications for cognition, emotion, and motivation. *Psychological Bulletin*, 98, 224–53.

Markus, H. and Nurius, P. (1986). Possible selves. *American Psychologist*, 41, 954–69.

Marques, J.M., Abrams, D., Paez, D., and Taboada, C.M. (in press). The role of categorization and ingroup norms in judgments of groups and their members. *Journal of Personality and Social Psychology*.

Masser, B. and Abrams, D. (in press). Contemporary sexism: The relationship between hostile, benevolent and neosexism. *Psychology of Women Quarterly*.

Monteith, M.J. (1993). Self-regulation of prejudiced responses: Implications for progress in prejudice-reduction efforts. *Journal of Personality and Social Psychology Bulletin*, 65, 3, 469–85.

Monteith, M.J. (1996). Affective reactions to prejudice-related discrepant responses: The impact of standard salience. *Personality and Social Psychology Bulletin*, 22, 1, 48–59.

Monteith, M.J., Deenan, N.E., and Tooman, G.D. (1996). The effect of social norm activation on the expression of opinion concerning gay men and blacks. *Basic and Applied Social Psychology*, 18, 267–88.

Monteith, M.J., Devine, P.G., and Zuwerink, J.R. (1993). Self-directed versus other directed affect as a consequence of prejudice-related discrepancies. *Journal of Personality and Social Psychology*, 64, 2, 198–210.

Oakes, P.J. (1996). The categorization process: Cognition and the group in the social psychology of stereotyping. In P. Robinson (ed.), *Social groups and Identity: Developing the legacy of Henri Tajfel*. Oxford: Butterworth-Heinemann, pp. 95–120.

Oakes, P.J., Haslam, S.A., and Turner, J.C. (1994). *Stereotyping and Social Reality*. Oxford: Blackwell.

Oakes, P.J., Haslam, S.A., and Turner, J.C. (1998). The role of prototypicality in group influence and cohesion: Contextual variation in the graded structure of social categories. In S. Worchel, J.F. Morales, D. Paez, and J.C. Deschamps (eds), *Social Identity: International perspectives*. London: Sage, pp. 75–92.

Oakes, P.J. and Turner, J.C. (1986). Distinctiveness and the salience of social category memberships: Is there an automatic perceptual bias towards novelty? *European Journal of Social Psychology*, 16, 325–44.

Oakes, P.J., Turner, J.C., and Haslam, S.A. (1991). Perceiving people as group members: The role of fit in the salience of social categorizations. *British Journal of Social Psychology*, 30, 125–44.

Perdue, C.W., Dovidio, J.F., Gurtman, M.B., and Tyler, R.B. (1990). "Us" and "Them": Social categorization and the process of intergroup bias. *Journal of Personality and Social Psychology*, 59, 475–86.

Petty, R.E. and Cacioppo, J.T. (1986). The elaboration likelihood model of persuasion. In L. Berkowitz (ed.), *Advances in Experimental Social Psychology*, Vol. 19. Orlando, FL: Academic Press, pp. 124–205.

Potter, J. and Wetherell, M. (1987). *Discourse and Social Psychology: Beyond attitudes and behaviour*. London: Sage.

Powers, W.T. (1973). *Behaviour: The control of perception*. Chicago: Aldine.

Pratto, F., Sidanius, J., Stallworth, L.M., and Malle, B.F. (1994). Social dominance orientation: A personality variable predicting social and political attitudes. *Journal of Personality and Social Psychology*, 67, 741–63.

Reid, A. and Deaux, K. (1996). Relationship between social and personal identities: Segregation or integration. *Journal of Personality and Social Psychology*, 71, 1084–91.

Rosch, E.E. (1978). Principles of categorization. In E.E. Rosch and B.B. Lloyd (eds), *Cognition and Categorization*. Hillsdale, NJ: Erlbaum, pp. 87–116.

Rosenberg, S. (1988). Self and others: Studies in social personality and autobiography. In L. Berkowitz (ed.), *Advances in Experimental Social Psychology*, Vol. 21. New York: Academic Press, pp. 57–95.

Rothbart, M. and John, O.P. (1985). Social categorization and behavioral episodes: A cognitive analysis of the effects of intergroup contact. *Journal of Social Issues*, 41, 81–104.

Scheier, M.F. and Carver, C.S. (1981). Private and public aspects of self. In L. Wheeler (ed.), *Review of Personality and Social Psychology*, Vol. 2. London: Sage, pp. 189–216.

Sears, D.O. and Kinder, D.R. (1971). Racial tensions and voting in Los Angeles. In W.Z. Hirsch (ed.), *Los Angeles: Viability and prospects for metropolitan leadership*. New York: Praeger, pp. 51–88.

Seligman, C., Olson, J.M., and Zanna, M.P. (eds) (1996). *The Psychology of Values: The Ontario symposium*, Vol. 8. Mahwah, NJ: Erlbaum.

Sidanius, J., Pratto, F., and Mitchell, M. (1994). In-group identification, social dominance orientation, and differential intergroup social allocation. *Journal of Social Psychology*, 134, 151–67.

Simon, B. (1993). On the asymmetry in the cognitive construal of ingroup and outgroup: A model of egocentric social categorization. *European Journal of Social Psychology*, 23, 131–47.

Simon, B. (1997). Self and group in modern society: Ten theses on the individual self and the collective self. In R. Spears, P.J. Oakes, N. Ellemers, and S.A. Haslam (eds), *The Social Psychology of Stereotyping and Group Life*. Oxford: Blackwell, pp. 318–35.

Simon, B., Glassner-Bayerl, B., and Stratenwerth, I. (1991). Stereotyping and self-stereotyping in a natural intergroup context: The case of heterosexual and homosexual men. *Social Psychology Quarterly*, 54, 252–66.

Simon, B. and Hamilton, D.L. (1994). Self-stereotyping and social context: The effects of relative in-group size and in-group status. *Journal of Personality and Social Psychology*, 66, 699–711.

Simon, B., Pantaleo, G., and Mummendey, A. (1995). Unique individual or interchangeable group member? The accentuation of intragroup differences versus similarities as an indicator of the individual self versus the collective self. *Journal of Personality and Social Psychology*, 69, 106–19.

Smith, E.R. (1996). What do connectionism and social psychology offer each other? *Journal of Personality and Social Psychology*, 70, 893–912.

Smith, E.R., Fazio, R.H., and Cejka, M.A. (1996). Accessible attitudes influence categorization of multiply categorizable objects. *Journal of Personality and Social Psychology*, 71, 888–98.

Smith, E.R. and Henry, S. (1996). An in-group becomes part of the self: Response time evidence. *Personality and Social Psychology Bulletin*, 22, 635–42.

Smith, E.R. and Zarate, M.A. (1990). Exemplar and prototype use in social categorization. *Social Cognition*, 8, 243–62.

Smith, H.J. and Tyler, T.R. (1997). Choosing the right pond: The impact of group membership on self-esteem and group-oriented behaviour. *Journal of Experimental Social Psychology*, 33, 146–70.

Srull, T.K. and Wyer, Jr, R.S. (eds), (1993). *The Mental Representation of Trait and Autobiographical Knowledge about the Self: Advances in social cognition*, Vol. 5. Hillsdale, NJ: Lawrence Erlbaum Associates.

Stryker, S. (1987). Identity theory: Developments and extensions. In K. Yardley and T. Honess (eds), *Self and Identity: Psychosocial perspectives*. New York: Wiley, pp. 83–103.

Tajfel, H. (1969). Cognitive aspects of prejudice. *Journal of Social Issues*, 25, 79–97.

Tajfel, H. (1974). Social identity and intergroup behaviour. *Social Sciences Information*, 13, 65–93.

Tajfel, H. (1981a). *Human Groups and Social Categories: Studies in social psychology*. Cambridge: Cambridge University Press.

Tajfel, H. (1981b). Social stereotypes and social groups. In J. Turner and H. Giles (eds), *Intergroup Behaviour*. Oxford: Blackwell, pp. 144–67.

Tajfel, H. and Turner, J.C. (1979). An integrative theory of intergroup conflict. In W.G. Austin and S. Worchel (eds), *The Social Psychology of Intergroup Relations*. Monterey, CA: Brooks-Cole, pp. 7–24.

Taylor, S.E. (1981). A categorization approach to stereotyping. In D.L. Hamilton (ed.), *Cognitive Processes in Stereotyping and Intergroup Behaviour*. Hillsdale, NJ: Erlbaum, pp. 88–114.

Trafimow, D., Triandis, H.C., and Goto, S.G. (1991). Some tests of the distinction between the private self and the collective self. *Journal of Personality and Social Psychology*, 60, 649–55.

Triandis, H.C. (1989). The self and social behaviour in differing cultural contexts. *Psychological Review*, 96, 506–20.

Triandis, H.C. (1995). *Individualism and Collectivism*. Boulder, CO: Westview Press.

Turner, J. (1985). Social categorisation and the self-concept: A social cognitive theory of group behaviour. In J. Lawler (ed.), *Advances in Group Processes*, Vol. 2. Greenwich: JAI Press, pp. 77–122.

Turner, J.C. (1992). *Social Influence*. Milton Keynes: Open University Press.

Turner, J.C. and Giles, H. (eds), (1981). *Intergroup Behaviour*. Oxford: Blackwell.

Turner, J.C., Hogg, M.A., Oakes, P.J., Reicher, S.D., and Wetherell, M. (1987). *Rediscovering the Social Group: A self-categorization theory*. Oxford and New York: Blackwell.

Turner, J.C., Oakes, P.J., Haslam, S.A., and McGarty, C. (1994). Self and collective: Cognition and social context. *Personality and Social Psychology Bulletin*, 20, 454–63.

Vallacher, R.R. (1978). Objective self-awareness and the perception of others. *Personality and Social Psychology Bulletin*, 4, 63–7.

Weber, R. and Crocker, J. (1983). Cognitive processes in the revision of stereotypic beliefs. *Journal of Personality and Social Psychology*, 45, 961–77.

Wegner, D.M. (1994). Ironic processes of mental control. *Psychological Review*, 101, 35–52.

Wetherell, M. and Potter, J. (1992). *Mapping the Language of Racism: Discourse and the legitimation of exploitation*. Hemel Hempstead: Harvester Wheatsheaf.

Wicklund, R.A. (1975). Objective self-awareness. In L. Berkowitz (ed.), *Advances in Experimental Social Psychology*, Vol. 8. New York: Academic Press, pp. 233–75.

10

Implicit Self-esteem

SHELLY D. FARNHAM, ANTHONY G. GREENWALD, AND
MAHZARIN R. BANAJI

Implicit Self-esteem and Social Identity

People tend to be biased in favor of their ingroup even when ingroups are minimally defined (Tajfel and Turner, 1979). Tajfel and Turner (1986) argued that such an ingroup bias arises out of people's motivation to achieve a satisfactory image of the self through a positive social identity, leading to behaviors that enhance the ingroup and derogate the outgroup. As such, how one evaluates the self, and how one evaluates important social identities, should be related. In self-report measures positivity of the self-concept, or personal self-esteem, is correlated with evaluations of social identity, or collective self-esteem (Crocker, Luhtanen, Blaine, and Broadnax, 1994; Luhtanen and Crocker, 1992). However, the level of stigmatization of one's social identity has no effect on personal self-esteem (Crocker and Major, 1989), and the relationship between self-esteem and ingroup favoritism is unclear (Abrams and Hogg, 1988). A source of such ambiguity may be the unreliability of self-report measures of self-esteem. While self-report measures of personal self-esteem seek to assess affective self-regard, they also manage to capture constructs such as impression management and self-deception. We propose that an *indirect* measure of self-esteem, similar to indirect measures developed in attitude research, has the potential of shedding light on the relationship between personal self-esteem and ingroup favoritism.

A potential indirect measure is provided by the Implicit Association Test (IAT; Greenwald, McGhee, and Schwartz, 1998), which assesses automatic (and not necessarily consciously reportable) concept–attribute associations. The IAT has already been used to measure automatic associations of ethnic groups with evaluation (implicit prejudice, or implicit ingroup favoritism), and of gender

This research was supported by grants from National Science Foundation, SBR-9422242, SBR-9710172, SBR-9422241, and SBR-9709924, and from National Institute of Mental Health, MH-41328 and MH-001533.

with traits (implicit stereotypes; Rudman, Greenwald, and McGhee, 1998). This chapter (1) reviews the construct validity of self-report measures of self-esteem; (2) describes how the IAT can provide an indirect measure of self-esteem; and (3) discusses how the IAT may be used to further understanding between personal self-esteem and evaluation of social identity.

Self-esteem and questions of construct validity

William James (1890) defined self-esteem as a self-feeling that is determined by a comparison between the actual self and the ideal self. Following James's definition of self-esteem, standard self-report measures of self-esteem ask respondents either to rate themselves on a variety of specific traits (Marsh, 1986; Pelham and Swann, 1989; Wells and Marwell, 1976), or to indicate how they feel about themselves globally (Rosenberg, 1979). However, research has not supported James's formulation because self-esteem does not appear to be the product of honest appraisal of one's traits and abilities (Rosenberg, 1979) or one's social identity (Crocker and Major, 1989). Rather, research indicates that the higher one's self-esteem, the greater the self-enhancing bias (see Brown, 1991, for review). Consequently, psychologists have debated extensively whether self-esteem causes self-appraisals or vice versa (Brown, 1993; Pelham and Swann, 1989), whether self-esteem leads to discriminatory behavior or vice versa (Abrams and Hogg, 1988), whether people are motivated towards accuracy or positivity in their self-concepts (Brown, 1991; Shrauger, 1975; Swann, 1990), and why, if having high self-esteem is not based on accurate self-appraisals, anyone would have low self-esteem (Baumeister, 1993).

What psychologists have only recently considered is that the correspondence between self-esteem measures and self-enhancing behaviors suggests that self-esteem measures may be capturing the wrong construct (Baumeister, Tice, and Hutton, 1989): the motive to present a positive attitude toward self rather than genuine self-esteem.

A *positivity bias* provides no threat to the construct validity of self-esteem measures (i.e., their ability to measure the self-esteem construct). Whether such biases arise from positive feelings toward the self (Brown, 1993) or cognitive beliefs about the self (Markus and Wurf, 1986), they are a reflection of the level of positive self-regard. Such an automatic positivity bias can be interpreted as a manifestation of *implicit self-esteem*. Greenwald and Banaji defined implicit self-esteem as "the introspectively unidentified (or inaccurately identified) effect of the self-attitude on evaluation of self-associated and self-dissociated objects" (1995, p. 11). This tendency to overestimate one's traits and abilities is understood as a spillover of positive affect from the self to objects associated with the self. Because most people have positive self-affect (Banaji and Prentice, 1994; Greenwald, 1980; Taylor and Brown, 1988), implicit self-esteem effects usually involve a positivity bias in processing information about the self (see Greenwald and Banaji, 1995, for review). In the realm of social identity, an individual's tendency to exalt any group by virtue of its association with self is an implicit self-esteem effect (Greenwald and Banaji, 1995).

Whereas a positivity bias provides no threat to the construct validity of self-report measures of self-esteem, *self-enhancing self-presentation strategies* provide a great threat to construct validity (Paulhus, 1986). As a consequence of self-presentation strategies, explicit measures may assess strategies of associating self with positive traits and dissociating self from negative traits. These self-presentation strategies are not necessarily to be identified with the construct of self-esteem (i.e., affective self-regard).

Paulhus (1986) defined the self-presentation strategies of impression management and self-deception as follows:

> I will use *impression management* to refer to conscious dissimilation of test responses designed to create a favorable impression in some audience. In contrast, the term *self-deception* will refer to any positively biased response that the respondent actually believes to be true. (p. 144)

Impression management and self-deception can be conceived as two ends of a continuum of self-presentation, ranging from self-presentation to others to self-presentation to self (Greenwald and Breckler, 1985). Impression management is directed toward an outward audience (Goffman, 1959; Schlenker, 1980) and self-deception is directed inwardly.

Paulhus (1986) argues that while researchers should control for impression management in self-report self-esteem measures, self-deception should be allowed to emerge. Self-deception indicates high self-esteem, and thus psychologists *want* self-esteem scales to capture self-deception. However, this assertion is debatable. According to Sackeim and Gur (1978), self-deception could involve holding positive explicit beliefs and negative implicit beliefs simultaneously. Explicit measures may therefore not distinguish self-deception (explicit positivity with implicit negativity) from genuine high self-esteem (positivity at both explicit and implicit levels).

Self-report self-esteem measures have questionable construct validity

We propose that explicit (self-report) measures of self-esteem capture self-presentation in addition to affective self-regard. The support for this assertion follows.

The discriminant validity of self-reported self-esteem.   In order for a measure to have high construct validity, it should discriminate its target construct from other constructs. Therefore, it is disconcerting that self-report measures of self-esteem correlate highly with measures of self-presentation style, suggesting a discriminant validity problem (Wells and Marwell, 1976). A correlation between a tendency toward self-presentation, as a personality trait (Crowne and Marlowe, 1964), and self-esteem indicates that self-esteem measures are biased by self-presentation. Both self-deception and impression management measures correlate with self-esteem measures (Lindeman and Verkasalo, 1995), with self-deception having a higher correlation (around .6) than impression management (around .3; Raskin, Novacek, and Hogan, 1991). That people with high self-deception and impression management scores also have high self-reported self-esteem suggests they are denying or defending against threatening negative information in the items of the self-esteem questionnaires (Cohen, 1959; Coopersmith, 1959; Schneider and Turkat, 1975). Self-report measures of self-esteem do not appear to discriminate well between self-presentation and self-esteem.

The convergent validity of self-reported self-esteem.   In order for a measure to have high construct validity, it should correlate with theoretically related constructs. Although self-report measures of self-esteem tend to correlate highly with each other and other related self-reported constructs such as anxiety and depression (Blascovich and Tomaka, 1991; Fleming and Courtney, 1984; Wells and Marwell, 1976), they do not correlate as well with peer or observer reports of self-esteem (Demo, 1985). To some extent the low correlations between self-report measures and peer measures may be due to differences in kind of measures. However, using confirmatory factor analyses, Demo (1985) found that self-reported self-esteem and observer ratings of self-esteem are best considered two distinct, moderately correlated factors. Whereas Demo assumes the self-reported self-esteem more accurately represents genuine, experienced self-esteem, one might as easily argue that the observer ratings are more accurate representations, given people's tendencies toward self-presentation.

The predictive validity of self-reported self-esteem.   In order for a measure to have high construct validity, it should predict the behaviors that are theoretically related to the construct in question. However, self-esteem measures are low in predictive validity for the following reasons:

1   *Self-esteem measures inconsistently predict sensitivity to feedback.* One of James's (1890) assumptions is that a person with genuine high self-esteem should be able to receive negative feedback without finding it too painful. However, some people with self-reported high self-esteem are highly sensitive to negative feedback (Baumeister, Heatherton, and Tice, 1993). In particular, people classified as having "defensive self-esteem" (high self-reported self-esteem and high need for approval) appear to find negative feedback painful: they do not like others who give them negative feedback (Hewitt and Goldman, 1974); they increase in their need for approval following failure (Schneider and Turkat, 1975); they cheat to do well on a task (Lobel and

Levanon, 1988); and they lower their levels of aspiration following failure (Lobel and Teiber, 1994).

2 *Self-esteem scores inconsistently predict quality of relationship with parents.* Contrary to predictions of developmental psychologists, some people who have high self-esteem scores have histories of negative interactions with parents. Developmental psychologists generally assume that self-esteem is acquired through parent–child relationships, with positive self-regard being a reflection, or internal model, of the parents' regard for the child (Bretherton, 1985; Cassidy, 1988). However, on occasion a child is placed in an extremely distressing situation when the parent has negative regard for the child, and the child responds to the situation by distancing from the parent (Bretherton, 1985). Both Mikulincer (1995) and Cassidy (1988) found that persons who showed such distant, negative relations with their parents had idealized, perfectly positive self-images. Such an effect, Mikulincer (1995) argues, "may imply that their self-esteem is so low and fragile that they cannot tolerate discovery of the slightest flaw. This idealization of the self seems to be a defense against the experience of rejection by others on the recognition of one's imperfections" (p. 1213).

3 *Self-esteem measures predict behaviors that are more theoretically related to self-presentation strategies than self-esteem.* Self-reported high self-esteem scores predict a wide variety of self-enhancing behaviors (Brown, 1991) that involve self-deceptive or impression management strategies. For example, when faced with negative feedback, the high self-esteem scorer turns attention to other positive traits (Baumeister, 1982; Baumeister and Jones, 1978), inflates the self by deflating others (Brown, Collins, and Schmidt, 1988), and exaggerates estimates of how many others share a negative trait (Campbell, 1986). Baumeister et al. (1989; Tice, 1991) suggest that self-esteem scales measure differences in self-presentational styles: either self-enhancing, or self-protecting. That self-esteem measures predict the tendency to use self-presentation strategies suggests they may measure the construct "favorable self-presentation" rather than "positive self-regard."

4 *Self-esteem measurements predict self-enhancing behaviors mainly in situations where self-presentational demands are high.* The self-enhancing behaviors of those with self-reported high self-esteem become augmented in public situations, and the self-protective behaviors of those with low self-esteem increase in public situations (see Baumeister et al., 1989, for review). That self-esteem scores have a greater probability of predicting self-enhancing behaviors when they occur in public again suggests that self-esteem scores measure self-presentational tendencies.

5 *Self-esteem measurements do not predict behaviors considered implicit self-esteem effects.* Many of the behaviors considered implicit self-esteem effects, resulting from a positivity bias, are not predicted by self-esteem measures. For example, the degree to which an ingroup bias occurs in a minimal group paradigm (where self becomes associated with a group formed at random) is

unrelated to level of self-reported self-esteem (Crocker and Schwartz, 1985; Crocker et al., 1987).

6   *Self-esteem measures' ability to predict mental health may be due to its association with self-enhancing behaviors.* Self-esteem measures do a fair job of predicting mental health (Kaplan, 1975; Rosenberg, 1965). However, self-reported self-esteem's relation to self-enhancing behaviors has led a few to theorize that self-esteem leads to mental health because it plays a buffering role against the stressors of life (Greenberg, Solomon, Pyszczynski, Rosenblatt, Burling, Lyon, Simon, and Pinel, 1992; Taylor and Brown, 1988). According to this view, people with high self-esteem have a proclivity towards self-deception and self-enhancement, and are thus able to respond to stressful situations with a minimum of anxiety. In other words, self-deception and self-enhancement buffer the self against anxiety, rather than level of self-esteem.

In conclusion, self-report measures of self-esteem have questionable discriminant, convergent, and predictive validity. In particular, self-report measures of self-esteem correlate with measures of self-presentation, and predict self-presentational behaviors, suggesting that these measures capture a construct of self-presentation more than affective self-regard. In order to measure genuine self-esteem, self-presentation must be avoided altogether through indirect measures of self-esteem. Another area of measurement in social cognition that has been beleaguered by self-presentation biases is that of socially sensitive attitudes related to prejudice and discrimination. Recent developments in measures that indirectly assess attitudes (Dovidio and Fazio, 1992; Greenwald et al., 1998) provide the necessary methodology allowing the indirect measure of self-regard.

A Different Approach – Indirect Measure of Self-esteem

Recent developments in the indirect measurement of attitudes borrow extensively from a neural network model of the brain developed in cognitive psychology (see Schneider and Shiffrin, 1977; Shiffrin and Schneider, 1977, for review), where information is conceived as stored at sites in a vast tangle of neural links (Collins and Loftus, 1975) that are organized hierarchically according to semantic relationships. In essence, the relationship between any two concepts can be measured by determining how far one must travel to get from one to the other across such links.

Indirect measures of attitude use two cognitive phenomena to its advantage: the automatic activation of attitudes effect, and spreading activation. Research has shown that the evaluative as well as the semantic content of words are processed automatically upon sight (Greenwald, Klinger, and Liu, 1989; Murphy and Zajonc, 1993). In other words, affective reactions such as liking, disliking, preference, and evaluations are processed instantaneously, or *automatically activated* (Fazio, Sanbonmatsu, Powell, and Kardes, 1986; Zajonc, 1980). Research has also shown that any piece of information, once activated, makes it easier to process subsequent, similar information because of the *spread of activation* that crosses the short distance between two neighboring links (Collins and Loftus, 1975; Neely, 1977).

Using these two cognitive phenomena, Fazio et al. (1986) argued that the strength of an attitude can be measured by the ease with which a person judges the valence of one concept after being presented with another concept. For example, if a person found it very easy to judge the word "sunshine" as pleasant immediately after seeing the word "democrat," then he or she has a positive attitude towards democrats. What has occurred is that the affective information in the word "democrat" has been automatically activated, making it easier to recognize the affective information in "sunshine" through spreading activation. Fazio, Jackson, Durton, and Williams (1995) found that images of black faces facilitated categorization of negative words for white subjects, and that images of white faces facilitated categorization of negative words for black subjects.

Whether the automatic activation of attitudes effect can measure the self-concept and self-esteem depends on whether the self is an attitude object that is automatically processed (see Greenwald and Pratkanis, 1984, for discussion of the self as an attitude object). Psychologists have argued that the self-concept is a schema, a rich and highly organized cluster of ideas surrounding the central concept of self (see Kihlstrom and Cantor, 1984; or Markus and Wurf, 1986, for review). Like other schemas, the self-schema affects information processing. For example, self-consistent information is more efficiently processed than inconsistent information, and self-relevant information is easily recalled and recognized (see Markus and Wurf, 1986, for review). Most importantly for our discussion, research shows that the content of the self-concept influences how quickly self-relevant information is processed. For example, Markus (1977) found that in categorizing adjectives as "me" or "not me," people were able to make faster judgments for words for which they had well-developed self-schemas.

If the self-schema is a well-integrated whole, it ought to have an affective, *attitudinal* component that influence processing of self-relevant information (Fiske and Pavelchak, 1986; Greenwald and Pratkanis, 1984). Research suggests that affective information about the self is automatically processed just as is the affective information of any attitude object. A number of studies have found that people are quicker to judge words as "me" or "not me" if they are positive or negative than if they are neutral (Markus, 1977; Mueller and Grove, 1991; Ross, Jurek, and Oliver, 1996). More importantly, automatic processing of affective information may be used to examine individual differences in self-concept. For example, Bargh and Tota (1988) showed that individual differences may be measured by assessing how much increasing cognitive load affects reaction times. They found that nondepressed subjects had a harder time categorizing negative self-related concepts under conditions of increased cognitive load than did depressed subjects.

In sum, individual differences in level of self-esteem may be assessed using the automatic activation of attitudes effect, because the self-concept is a well-integrated schema with an affective, attitudinal component that influences how self-relevant information is processed. In particular, individual differences in levels of self-esteem may be assessed using a procedure in which individuals perform a task that they can complete more efficiently using automatic processing if they have high implicit self-esteem. The Implicit Association Test, adapted for the self-concept, is just such a procedure.

The Implicit Association Test (IAT)

Greenwald et al. (1998) developed the Implicit Association Test (IAT) to measure automatic concept–attribute associations. An assumption of the test is that strongly associated (compatible) attribute–concept pairs should be easier to classify together than are weakly associated or opposed (incompatible) attribute–concept pairs. Ease of classifying is measured by the response times and errors in performing such categorizations.

To get an idea of the IAT procedure, imagine sorting a deck of cards. Your first task is to judge if a card is a spade or a heart. You put the spades in a pile on the left, and the hearts in a pile on the right. Next, diamonds and clubs are added to the deck, and you are asked to put both spades and clubs on the left, and diamonds and hearts on the right. If spades and clubs can be cognitively grouped according to some shared feature, the task will be relatively simple. For example, by keeping the simple instruction "only black to left" in mind, the cards can easily be sorted into the left and right piles.

What happens if color cannot be used as a grouping cue? If one's task is to place clubs and hearts on the left and spades and diamonds on the right, the simple black–left, red–right strategy does not work, necessitating a more cognitively demanding strategy.

Greenwald et al. (1998) presented subjects with a series of words on a computer screen and had them categorize each word as quickly as possible by pressing a left or right key on a keyboard (see figure 10.1). The automatic association between a concept (for example, *flower*) and the attribute of evaluative pleasantness is measured by the difference in speed between the condition in which *flower* and *pleasant* were mapped together and the condition in which *flower* and *unpleasant* were mapped together (see Compatible and Incompatible screens in figure 10.1).

Using the IAT to measure implicit ingroup bias

Applying the IAT to social attitudes, Greenwald et al. (1998) assessed Korean and Japanese subjects' attitudes towards one another. Both groups found it easier

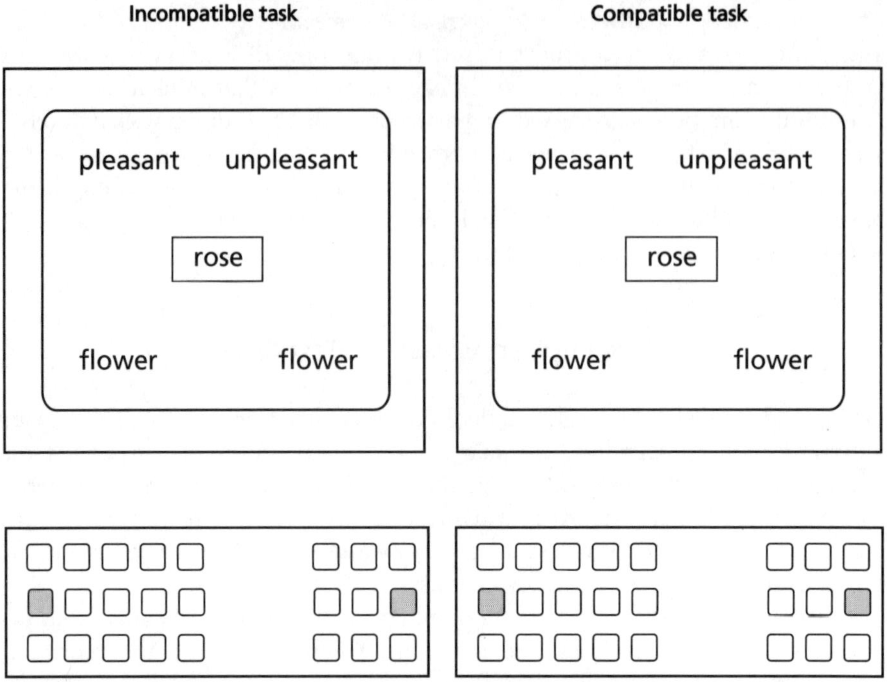

Incompatible task	Compatible task

Figure 10.1   The display screen for the computer Implicit Association Test (IAT). Individuals are presented with a word in the middle of the screen ("rose"), and must categorize it into one of the categories displayed to the left and right of the word by pressing the left or right key. The categorization task is compatible when the categories are easily associated (e.g., "pleasant" and "flower"), and incompatible when the categories are associated with difficulty (e.g., "pleasant" and "insect").

to associate pleasant words with names from their own group than pleasant words with names from the other group. The IAT had a larger effect size for the difference in attitudes towards Japanese and Koreans than did the explicit measures of attitudes towards these groups. In addition, Greenwald et al. (1997) found that white subjects more easily associated white names with pleasant words and black names with unpleasant words than vice versa. Again, the effect size of the difference in attitude towards blacks and whites proved to be greater for the IAT than for the explicit measures of attitudes. Importantly, the Japanese and Korean subjects were much more willing to explicitly show ingroup bias in their attitudes towards one another than white subjects were willing to show negative attitudes towards blacks. As a consequence, the correlations between the implicit and explicit measures were higher for the Japanese/Korean experiment than those for the white/black experiment.

Using the IAT to measure implicit self-esteem

A measure of implicit self-esteem using the IAT examines the extent to which people are faster at categorizing self words and pleasant words together than categorizing self words and unpleasant words together. To apply the IAT to measuring self-esteem, we developed a computer program that allowed subjects to provide idiosyncratic information such as first and last names, home town, and telephone number. After providing such me-objects, subjects then chose from lists of similar, not-me objects. During the IAT subjects were presented with a series of words to categorize. We measured how long it took the subject to categorize each word from the moment it appeared on the screen to the moment the correct key was pressed.

For a demonstration of the steps of the self-esteem IAT adapted to pen and paper, see figure 10.2. First subjects practiced categorizing words as being either

Step 1			Step 2			Step 3		
unpleasant		pleasant	not-me		me	unpleasant or not-me		pleasant or me
●	joy	●	●	self	●	●	self	●
●	vomit	●	●	other	●	●	joy	●
●	agony	●	●	they	●	●	them	●
●	peace	●	●	them	●	●	death	●
●	death	●	●	I	●	●	other	●
●	sunrise	●	●	mine	●	●	sunrise	●
●	warmth	●	●	it	●	●	my	●
●	corpse	●	●	me	●	●	warmth	●
●	gold	●	●	their	●	●	me	●
●	slime	●	●	myself	●	●	corpse	●

Step 4			Step 5		
me		not-me	unpleasant or me		pleasant or not-me
●	myself	●	●	they	●
●	their	●	●	vomit	●
●	me	●	●	I	●
●	self	●	●	agony	●
●	them	●	●	their	●
●	I	●	●	gold	●
●	they	●	●	it	●
●	other	●	●	peace	●
●	mine	●	●	mine	●
●	it	●	●	slime	●

Figure 10.2   Demonstration of the self-esteem IAT. Read each word in the list, and with the back of a pen tap the black circle under the category to which the word belongs. Complete each list of words as quickly as possible, without skipping any words. You will probably find Step 5 more challenging than Step 3.

pleasant or unpleasant (figure 10.2, Step 1). Second, subjects practiced categor-izing words as being me or not-me. Third, half the subjects categorized words as either me/pleasant or not-me/unpleasant, while the other half categorized words as either me/unpleasant or not-me/pleasant. Fourth, the me and not-me subca-tegories were switched and practiced. Finally, if initially me and pleasant were together, me and unpleasant were together, and vice versa. Implicit self-esteem was calculated by measuring the difference in reaction times, or latencies, between the two conditions where me words were categorized with pleasant words, and me words were categorized with unpleasant words (i.e., the differ-ence in mean latency between Steps 3 and 5).

Our results indicated that people made faster judgments when me words were categorized with pleasant words than when me words were categorized with unpleasant words (see figure 10.3, which shows the latencies for each step of the IAT). The pattern of data indicates that combining the me/not-me and pleasant/unpleasant discriminations was about as easy for subjects to do as was perform-ing either of these discriminations alone, *when* the me and pleasant items shared the same response. By contrast, the combination of two discriminations added an

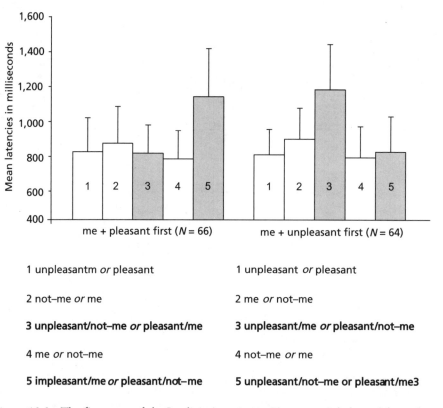

1 unpleasantm *or* pleasant   1 unpleasant *or* pleasant

2 not–me *or* me   2 me *or* not–me

3 unpleasant/not–me *or* pleasant/me   **3 unpleasant/me *or* pleasant/not–me**

4 me *or* not–me   4 not–me *or* me

5 impleasant/me *or* pleasant/not–me   **5 unpleasant/not–me or pleasant/me3**

Figure 10.3 The five steps of the Implicit Association Test, counterbalanced for order.

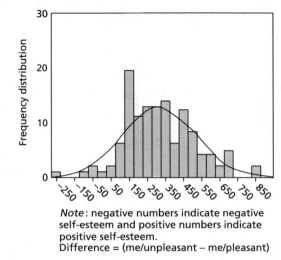

Mean = 3.17
Stand. dev. = 192
N = 127
Skewness = .28, ns

Note: negative numbers indicate negative
self-esteem and positive numbers indicate
positive self-esteem.
Difference = (me/unpleasant – me/pleasant)

Figure 10.4   IAT effect, with raw latency score, is almost normally distributed.

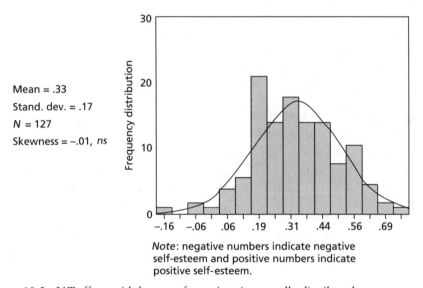

Mean = .33
Stand. dev. = .17
N = 127
Skewness = –.01, ns

Note: negative numbers indicate negative
self-esteem and positive numbers indicate
positive self-esteem.

Figure 10.5   IAT effect, with log transformation, is normally distributed.

average of about 327 ms to mean latencies when, instead, the me and unpleasant items shared the same response. This mean difference in difficulty between the two combinations, called the IAT effect, corresponded to almost two times the standard deviation of the me + pleasant condition (i.e., the effect-size measure of Cohen's $d = 1.86$, and $F(1, 119) = 439$, $p \cong 10^{41}$). Analyses were performed on log transformations of the latencies, because raw scores tend to be positively skewed (although not as skewed as those of explicit measures). See figures 10.4, 10.5 and 10.6.

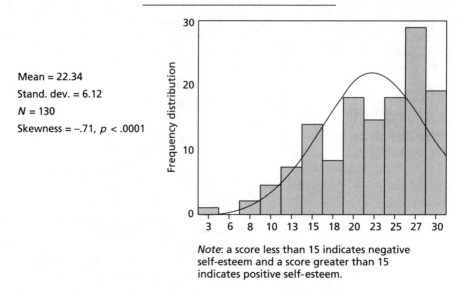

Mean = 22.34
Stand. dev. = 6.12
N = 130
Skewness = −.71, *p* < .0001

Note: a score less than 15 indicates negative
self-esteem and a score greater than 15
indicates positive self-esteem.

Figure 10.6   Rosenberg SES, raw scores are not normally distributed.

In addition to completing the IAT, subjects responded to seven explicit measures (see table 10.1). The IAT measure of self-positivity had only weak positive
correlations with these other measures (see first row of table 10.1). These low
correlations indicate that the IAT does not measure the same construct that is
represented by shared variance among the set of explicit measures. Although it is
not the only explanation of such low correlations, this conclusion is consistent
with the supposition that the explicit measures are more sensitive to self-presentation strategies than to self-esteem.

The IAT's sensitivity to the self-positivity bias, or *implicit self-esteem*,
described by Greenwald and Banaji (1995) is encouraging. Implicit self-esteem
is conceived as a transfer of affect from one's self-attitude to the concepts or
objects associated with the self. If, as we suspect, self-report measures of self-
esteem are highly sensitive to self-presentation, then assessment of the construct
validity of the IAT's self-esteem measure cannot rely on correlations with the
self-report measures. Consequently, our program of research is pursuing alternative construct validation strategies.

Using the IAT to measure the relationship between implicit ingroup bias, implicit self-esteem, and social identity

If the IAT is really measuring implicit self-esteem, then it ought to correlate
positively with ingroup bias. In addition, the level of this correlation should
depend on the level of identification with that group. To test this prediction, we
had female subjects complete three IATs measuring implicit self-esteem, implicit

Table 10.1   Intercorrelations between the IAT, measures of self-esteem, self-deception, and impression management

	IAT	Rosenberg SES	Thermometer scale	Self-affect scale	Semantic differential	Trait agreement scale	Self-attributes	Self-deception	Impression management
IAT	1	.05	.04	.26	.26	.23	.24	.18	.17
Rosenberg SES		1	.44	.84*	−.07	.74*	.41*	.48*	.07
Thermometer scale, self–other[a]			1	.41	.18	.22	.13	.22	−.23
Self-affect scale[a]				1	−.06	79*	.38	.52*	.08
Semantic differential, self–other[a]					1	−.06	−.06	.13	−.10
Trait agreement scale[a]						1	.52*	.52*	.09
Self-attributes questionnaire							1	.50*	.09
Self-deception (BIDR)								1	.37*
Impression management (BIDR)									1

[a]N = 54, otherwise N = 125; **bold** = p < .05, *italics* = p < .005, * = p < .0005

The first six measures are self-esteem measures. IAT = log latency for task with me/pleasant minus log latency for task with me/unpleasant. The Rosenberg SES (Rosenberg, 1979), self-attributes questionnaire (Pelham and Swann, 1989), trait agreement scale (Brown, 1993), self-deception scale and impression management scale (BIDR; Paulhus, 1991) were developed in previous research. All other measures (the thermometer scale, semantic differential, and self-affect scale) were developed for the current research.

ingroup bias (favoring females over males), and implicit identification with being female (Farnham and Greenwald, 1997). We measured self-esteem combining pleasant/unpleasant words with me/not-me words, as described above. Positivity towards females was measured combining female/male words (such as female, girl, woman, male, boy, and man) with pleasant/unpleasant words. Identification with female was measured by combining me/not-me words with male/female words.

In general, the 62 female subjects strongly favored females over males (IAT effect = 303 ms, d = 2.34), had positive implicit self-esteem (IAT effect = 303 ms, d = 2.06), and identified with being female (IAT effect = 204 ms, d = 1.34). More importantly, we did find that implicit self-esteem was correlated with implicit ingroup bias (r = .34, $p < .05$), and that the relationship between self-esteem and bias towards females depended on level of identification with being female, $F(1,55)$ = 3.48, p = .03, one-tailed (see figure 10.7). Thus ingroup favoritism at least to some extent is an implicit self-esteem effect, one that depends on the person's level of association between the group and the self. A promising study

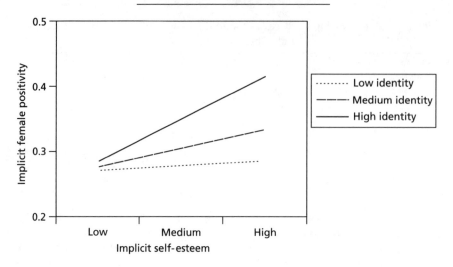

Figure 10.7 Relationship between implicit self-esteem and gender positivity depends on gender identity.

for the future is to examine whether the IAT may be able to predict people's behaviors in the minimal group paradigm.

Conclusions

The construct validity of self-reported self-esteem is questionable, because both (1) responses to these measures can be deliberately managed (i.e., they are sensitive to self-presentation and impression management strategies) and (2) the target construct of affective self-regard may be unavailable to introspection. The Implicit Association Test (IAT) provides a potential avenue around these threats to validity. As expected, the IAT reveals (1) a strong positivity bias in favor of the ingroup, or *implicit ingroup favoritism*, and (2) a strong positivity bias in favor of the self, or *implicit self-esteem*. Low correlations between the self-esteem IAT and explicit measures of self-esteem demand the conclusion that the IAT and the explicit measures assess different constructs that are no more than moderately related.

We also found that identification with group moderated the relationship between personal self-esteem and attitudes toward the ingroup. That this effect was found using measures of implicit self-esteem, implicit identification with the group, and implicit evaluation of the group, suggests that Tajfel and Turner's (1979) minimal group effect does occur on the automatic, implicit level. A person's self-affect either transfers to the ingroup as soon as the person has made the association between the self and the group, or the person dissociates the self and group if the group is perceived to be negative. Ironically, our research examining the relationship between self-esteem and social identity suggests that the field of social identity needs to take another look at balance theory explanations of ingroup favoritism (Heider, 1958), rather than focusing entirely on self-esteem theories of ingroup favoritism. Heider's balance theory, much like Festinger's cognitive dissonance theory (1957), argues that people seek balanced relationships among their attitudes and identities. Thus, the closer one identifies the self with one's social identity, the greater is the imperative to keep feelings for the self and group consistent. The IAT shows that at least on an automatic level, the relationship between the self and gender identity adheres to a balanced pattern.

References

Abrams, D. and Hogg, M.A. (1988). Comments on the motivational status of self-esteem in social identity and intergroup discrimination. *European Journal of Social Psychology*, 18, 317–34.

Banaji, M.R. and Prentice, D.A. (1994). The self in social contexts. *Annual Review of Psychology*, 45, 297–332.

Bargh, J.A. and Tota, M.E. (1988). Context-dependent automatic processing in depression: Accessibility of negative constructs with regard to self but not others. *Journal of Personality and Social Psychology*, 54, 925–39.

Baumeister, R.F. (1982). Self-esteem, self-presentation, and future interaction: A dilemma of reputation. *Journal of Personality*, 50, 29–45.

Baumeister, R.F. (ed.) (1993). *Self-esteem: The puzzle of low self-regard*. New York: Plenum Press.

Baumeister, R.F., Heatherton, T.F., and Tice, D.M. (1993). When ego threats lead to self-regulation failure: Negative consequences of high self-esteem. *Journal of Personality and Social Psychology*, 64, 141–56.

Baumeister, R.F. and Jones, E.E. (1978). When self-presentation is constrained by the target's knowledge: Consistency and compensation. *Journal of Personality and Social Psychology*, 36, 608–18.

Baumeister, R.F., Tice, D.M., and Hutton, D.G. (1989). Self-presentational motivations and personality differences in self-esteem. *Journal of Personality*, 57, 547–79.

Blascovich, J. and Tomaka, J. (1991). Measures of self-esteem. In J.P. Robinson, P.R. Shaver, and L.S. Wrightman (eds), *Measures of Personality and Social Psychological Attitudes*, Vol. 1. San Diego: Academic Press, pp. 115–60.

Bretherton, I. (1985). Attachment theory: Retrospect and prospect. *Monographs of the Society for Research in Child Development*, 50, 3–35.

Brown, J.D. (1991). Accuracy and bias in self-knowledge. In C.R. Snyder and D.F. Forsyth (eds), *Handbook of Social and Clinical Psychology: The health perspective*. New York: Pergamon Press, pp. 158–78.

Brown, J.D. (1993). Self-esteem and self-evaluation: Feeling is believing. In J. Suls (ed.), *Psychological Perspectives on the Self*, Vol. 4. Hillsdale, NJ: Erlbaum, pp. 22–58.

Brown, J.D., Collins, R.L., and Schmidt, G.W. (1988). Self-esteem and direct versus indirect forms of self-enhancement. *Journal of Personality and Social Psychology*, 55, 445–53.

Campbell, J.D. (1986). Similarity and uniqueness: The effects of attribution type, relevance, and individual differences in self-esteem and depression. *Journal of Personality and Social Psychology*, 50, 281–94.

Cassidy, J. (1988). Child–mother attachment and self in six-year-olds. *Child Development*, 59, 121–34.

Cohen, A. (1959). Some implications of self-esteem for social influence. In C. Hovland and I. Janis (eds), *Personality and Persuasibility*, Vol. 2. New Haven: Yale University Press, pp. 102–20.

Collins, A.M. and Loftus, E.F. (1975). A spreading-activation theory of semantic processing. *Psychological Review*, 82, 407–28.

Coopersmith, A. (1959). A method for determining types of self-esteem. *Journal of Abnormal and Social Psychology*, 59, 84–7.

Crocker, J., Luhtanen, R., Blaine, B., and Broadnax, S. (1994). Collective self-esteem and psychological well-being among white, black, and Asian college students. *Personality and Social Psychology Bulletin*, 20, 503–13.

Crocker, J. and Major, B. (1989). Social stigma and self-esteem. The self-protective properties of stigma. *Psychological Review*, 96, 608–30.

Crocker, J. and Schwartz, I. (1985). Prejudice and ingroup favoritism in a minimal intergroup situation: Effects of self-esteem. *Personality and Social Psychology Bulletin*, 11, 379–86.

Crocker, J., Thompson, L., McGraw, K., and Ingerman, C. (1987). Downward comparison, prejudice, and evaluation of others: Effects of self-esteem and threat. *Journal of Personality and Social Psychology*, 52, 907–16.

Crowne, D.P. and Marlowe, D. (1964). *The Approval Motive*. New York: Wiley.

Demo, D.H. (1985). The measurement of self-esteem: Refining our methods. *Journal of Personality and Social Psychology*, 48, 1490–1502.

Dovidio, J. and Fazio, R. (1992). New techniques for the direct and indirect assessment of attitudes. In J. Tanur (ed.), *Questions about Questions*. New York: Russell Sage, pp. 103–27.

Farnham, S.D. and Greenwald, A.G. (1997). Implicit balance between personal and social identity: I am female + I am good = female is good. Poster presented at the meeting of the Society of Experimental Social Psychology, Toronto, October 1997.

Fazio, R.J., Jackson, J.R., Dunton, B.C., and Williams, C.J. (1995). Variability in automatic activation as an unobtrusive measure of racial attitudes: A bona fide pipeline? *Journal of Personality and Social Psychology*, 69, 1013–27.

Fazio, R.H., Sanbonmatsu, D.M., Powell, M.C., and Kardes, F.R. (1986). On the automatic activation of attitudes. *Journal of Personality and Social Psychology*, 50, 229–38.

Festinger, L. (1957). *A Theory of Cognitive Dissonance*. Stanford, CA: Stanford University Press.

Fiske, S. and Pavelchak, M. (1986). Category-based versus piecemeal-based affective responses: Developments in schema-triggered affect. In R. Sorrentino and E. T. Higgins (eds), *Handbook of Motivation and Cognition: Foundations of social behavior*. New York: Guilford, pp. 167–203.

Fleming, J.S. and Courtney, B.E. (1984). The dimensionality of self-esteem: II. Hierarchical facet model for revised measurement scales. *Journal of Personality and Social Psychology*, 46, 404–21.

Goffman, E. (1959). *The Presentation of Self in Everyday Life*. New York: Doubleday.

Greenberg, J., Solomon, S., Pyszczynski, T., Rosenblatt, A., Burling, J., Lyon, D., Simon, L., and Pinel, E. (1992). Why do people need self-esteem? Converging evidence that self-esteem serves an anxiety-buffering function. *Journal of Personality and Social Psychology*, 63, 913–22.

Greenwald, A.G. (1980). The totalitarian ego: Fabrication and revision of personal history. *American Psychologist*, 35, 603–18.

Greenwald, A.G. and Banaji, M.R. (1995). Implicit social cognition: Attitudes, self-esteem, and stereotypes. *Psychological Review*, 102, 4–27.

Greenwald, A.G. and Breckler, S.J. (1985). To whom is the self presented? In B.R. Schlenker (ed.), *The Self and Social Life*. New York: McGraw-Hill, pp. 126–45.

Greenwald, A.G., Klinger, M.R., and Liu, T.J. (1989). Unconscious processing of dichoptically masked words. *Memory and Cognition*, 17, 35–47.

Greenwald, A.G., McGhee, D.E., and Schwartz, J.L.K. (1998). Measuring individual differences in implicit cognition: The implicit association test. *Journal of Personality and Social Psychology*, 74, 1464–80.

Greenwald, A.G. and Pratkanis, A.R. (1984). The self. In R.S. Wyer, Jr and T.K. Srull (eds), *Handbook of Social Cognition*. Hillsdale, NJ: Erlbaum, pp. 129–78.

Heider, F. (1958). *The Psychology of Interpersonal Relations*. New York: Wiley.

Hewitt, J. and Goldman, M. (1974). Self-esteem, need for approval, and reactions to personal evaluations. *Journal of Experimental Social Psychology*, 10, 201–10.

James, W. (1890). *Principles of Psychology*, Vol. 1. New York: Henry Holt.

Kaplan, H.B. (1975). *Self-attitudes and Deviant Behavior*. Pacific Palisades, CA: Goodyear Publishing Company.

Kihlstrom, J.F. and Cantor, N. (1984). Mental representations of the self. In L. Berkowitz (ed.), *Advances in Experimental Social Psychology*, Vol. 17. Orlando, FL: Academic Press, pp. 1–47.

Lindeman, M. and Verkasalo, M. (1995). Personality, situation, and positive–negative asymmetry in socially desirable responding. *European Journal of Personality*, 9, 125–34.

Lobel, T.E. and Levanon, I. (1988). Self-esteem, need for approval, and cheating behavior in children. *Journal of Educational Psychology*, 80, 122–3.

Lobel, T.E. and Teiber, A. (1994). Effects of self-esteem and need for approval on affective and cognitive reactions: Defensive and true self-esteem. *Personality and Individual Differences*, 16, 315–21.

Luhtanen, R. and Crocker, J. (1992). A collective self-esteem scale: Self-evaluation of one's social identity. *Personality and Social Psychology Bulletin*, 18, 302–18.

Markus, H. (1977). Self-schemata and processing information about the self. *Journal of Personality and Social Psychology*, 35, 63–78.

Markus, H. and Wurf, E. (1986). The dynamic self-concept: A social psychological perspective. *Annual Review of Psychology*, 38, 299–337.

Marsh, H.W. (1986). Global self-esteem: Its relation to specific facets of self-concept and importance. *Journal of Personality and Social Psychology*, 51, 1224–36.

Mikulincer, M. (1995). Attachment style and the mental representation of the self. *Journal of Personality and Social Psychology*, 69, 1203–15.

Mueller, J.H. and Grove, T.R. (1991). Trait actualization and self-reference effects. *Bulletin of the Psychonomic Society*, 29, 13–16.

Murphy, S.T. and Zajonc, R.B. (1993). Affect, cognition, and awareness: Affective priming with optimal and suboptimal stimulus exposures. *Journal of Personality and Social Psychology*, 64, 723–39.

Neely, J.H. (1977). Semantic priming and retrieval from lexical memory: Roles of inhibitionless spreading activation and limited-capacity attention. *Journal of Experimental Psychology: General*, 106, 226–54.

Paulhus, D.L. (1986). Self-deception and impression management in test responses. In A. Angleitner and J.S. Wiggins (eds), *Personality Assessment via Questionnaire* New York: Springer-Verlag, pp. 143–65.

Pelham, B. and Swann, W. (1989). From self-conceptions to self-worth: On the sources and structure of global self-esteem. *Journal of Personality and Social Psychology*, 57, 672–80.

Raskin, R., Novacek, J., and Hogan, R. (1991). Narcissism, self-esteem, and defensive self-enhancement. *Journal of Personality*, 59, 19–38.

Rosenberg, M. (1965). *Society and the Adolescent Self-image*. Princeton, NJ: Princeton University Press.

Rosenberg, M. (1979). *Conceiving the Self*. New York: Basic Books.

Ross, M.J., Jurek, A.W., and Oliver, J.M. (1996). Stimulus emotionality and processing information about the self. *Journal of Social Behavior and Personality*, 11, 43–50.

Rudman, L.A., Greenwald, A.G., and McGhee, D.E. (1998). Sex differences in gender stereotypes revealed by the implicit association test. Unpublished manuscript. Rutgers University and University of Washington.

Sackeim, H.A. and Gur, R.C. (1978). Self-deception, self-confrontation and consciousness. In G.E. Schwartz and D. Shapiro (eds), *Consciousness and Self-regulation: Advances in research*, Vol. 2. New York: Plenum Press, pp. 139–97.

Schlenker, B.R. (1980). *Impression Management*. Monterey, CA: Brooks-Cole.

Schneider, W. and Shiffrin, R.M. (1977). Control and automatic human information processing: I. Detection, search, and attention. *Psychological Review*, 84, 1–66.

Schneider, D.J. and Turkat, D. (1975). Self-presentation following success or failure: Defensive self-esteem models. *Journal of Personality*, 43, 127–35.

Shiffrin, R.M. and Schneider, W. (1977). Control and automatic human information processing: II. Perceptual learning, automatic attending, and a general theory. *Psychological Review*, 84, 127–90.

Shrauger, J.S. (1975). Responses to evaluations as function of initial self-perception. *Psychological Bulletin*, 82, 581–96.

Swann, W. B. (1990). To be adored or to be known? The interplay of self-enhancement and self-verification. In R. M. Sorrentino and E. T. Higgins (eds), *Handbook of Motivation and Cognition*, Vol. 2. New York: Guilford Press, pp. 408–48.

Tajfel, H. and Turner, J.C. (1979). An integrative theory of intergroup conflict. In W.G. Austin and S. Worchel (eds), *The Social Psychology of Intergroup Relations*. Monterey, CA: Brooks-Cole, pp. 38–48.

Tajfel, J. and Turner, J.C. (1986). The social identity theory of intergroup behaviour. In S. Worchel and W.G. Austin (eds), *Psychology of Intergroup Relations*, 2nd edn. Chicago: Nelson-Hall, pp. 7–24.

Taylor, S.E. and Brown, J. (1988). Illusion and well-being: A social psychological perspective on mental health. *Psychological Bulletin*, 103, 193–210.

Tice, D. (1991). Esteem protection or enhancement? Self-handicapping motives and attributions differ by trait self-esteem. *Journal of Personality and Social Psychology*, 60, 711–25.

Wells, L.E. and Marwell, G. (1976). *Self-esteem: Its conceptualization and measurement*. Beverly Hills, CA: Sage.

Zajonc, R.B. (1980). Feeling and thinking: Preferences need no inferences. *American Psychologist*, 35, 151–75.

11

Joining Groups to Reduce Uncertainty: Subjective Uncertainty Reduction and Group Identification

MICHAEL A. HOGG AND BARBARA-A. MULLIN

Henri Tajfel's early articulation of cognitive processes and structures with social processes and structures (e.g., Tajfel, 1969) quickly developed into social identity theory as an attempt to understand intergroup behavior (e.g., Tajfel and Turner, 1979; also see Hogg and Abrams, 1988). Although initially a distinctly European approach (cf. Tajfel, 1984), social identity theory now spans national boundaries and has had a significant impact on a revitalized social psychological interest in group processes (Abrams and Hogg, 1998; Hogg and Moreland, 1995; Moreland, Hogg, and Hains, 1994).

Social identity theory specifies how social categorization and social comparison processes work in conjunction with social belief structures to produce specific forms of group behavior. The theory has come to emphasize self-evaluation and the need for self-esteem as the principal motivational mechanism (e.g., Turner, 1982; cf. Hogg and Abrams, 1990), and as a consequence, the motivational analysis has become associated with social comparison and self-enhancement rather than social categorization. Evidence for the role of self-esteem in social identity processes is mixed – a state of affairs which may reflect methodological, operational, conceptual, or level of analysis issues, or a combination of all three (Abrams and Hogg, 1988; Hogg and Abrams, 1990, 1993; Long and Spears, 1997; Mullin, 1998; Rubin and Hewstone, 1998).

With the rapid development of contemporary social cognition in the 1980s, some social identity theorists shifted their conceptual emphasis away from social comparison and onto social categorization, to produce self-categorization theory (Turner, 1985; Turner, Hogg, Oakes, Reicher, and Wetherell, 1987). Farr (1996, see p. 10), in his historical analysis of the roots of modern social psychology, considers self-categorization theory to be the expression of modern social cognition in social identity theory. Indeed, many scholars, including advocates of social identity theory, would agree and some might lament this development (cf. the diversity of perspectives represented by chapters in Robinson, 1996). An alternative view (e.g., Hogg, 1996; Hogg, Terry, and White, 1995), however, is that self-categorization theory is part of social identity theory – it specifies the cognitive dimension of a wider social identity perspective that strives to articulate (cf. Doise, 1986; Lorenzi-Cioldi and Doise, 1990) cognitive, interpersonal, and social processes and structures to produce a properly *social* cognitive account of group behavior (cf. Levine, Resnick, and Higgins, 1993; Nye and Brower, 1996).

Self-categorization theory focuses on cognitive process rather than motivation, and thus does not further elaborate the role of self-esteem. Although it has no explicit motivational analysis, self-categorization theory does have an implicit motivational analysis which rests on meaning maximization (e.g., Abrams, 1992) or reduction of subjective uncertainty. In the present chapter we describe how self-categorization theory includes uncertainty reduction as a motivational element, describe subjective uncertainty reduction as a core social motive, and present findings from a programme of studies designed to investigate the role of subjective uncertainty in social identity/self-categorization processes (Hogg, 1996; Hogg and Abrams, 1993; Mullin, 1998).

Social Identity and Self-esteem

The minimal group paradigm (Bourhis, Sachdev, and Gagnon, 1994; Diehl, 1990; Tajfel, Billig, Bundy, and Flament, 1971) has enduring significance for social identity theory because it provides a methodology for investigating basic social cognitive mechanisms underlying group processes. Although there are alternative explanations for the minimal group effect (e.g., Rabbie, Schot, and Visser, 1989), the most widely accepted explanation is that people identify with the minimal group, and the process of identification produces behavioral intergroup differentiation (see Turner and Bourhis, 1996).

Some early explanations of why people identify with minimal groups suggested that it might be in order to impose structure on intrinsically uncertain circumstances (e.g., Tajfel and Billig, 1974). Shortly thereafter, however, investigations turned to evaluatively positive social identity as the main motivation underlying social identification, which in turn was explicated in terms of the operation of an individual motive to maintain or enhance self-esteem (e.g., Tajfel and Turner, 1979; Turner, 1982). This was described as the self-esteem hypothesis by Abrams and Hogg (1988). It was this formulation that inspired most social identity research that dealt with intergroup relations, intergroup conflict, ethnolinguistic identity, and so forth (e.g., Giles and Johnson, 1987; Hogg and Abrams, 1988; Tajfel, 1982; Taylor and McKirnan, 1984; Turner and Giles, 1981). Although unquestionably useful at the macrosocial level, it has proven difficult to establish exactly how self-esteem is related to social identification or self-categorization at a more fundamental social cognitive level (Abrams and

Hogg, 1988; Hogg and Abrams, 1990, 1993; Long and Spears, 1997; Rubin and Hewstone, 1998).

The main difficulty posed by the self-esteem hypothesis is one of "level of analysis." Social categories acquire evaluative connotations through intergroup competition ultimately for consensually valued resources or symbols. For example, schools of thought in social psychology may compete for more publications and citations as a symbol of greater prestige. Individuals represent the social evaluation of groups in terms of evaluatively weighted social identities. Identification or self-categorization leading to depersonalization is then the process through which such evaluations or social identities are internalized as an evaluation of the self – "I feel good about my group, and about myself as a member of my group." Of course, as Abrams and Hogg (1988; Hogg and Abrams, 1990) explain, this analysis logically implies that people prefer to feel good rather than bad about themselves, and are thus motivated to strive for or maintain positive self-evaluation and to avoid negative self-evaluation. There is substantial evidence for this idea (see Greenwald and Pratkanis, 1984; McReynolds, 1987). The problem arises that social identification is only one way in which a person who strives for positive self-esteem can achieve this goal, and it may therefore be important empirically to be able to distinguish between self-esteem associated with "self" as a group member (i.e., social identity) and "self" as a separate individual or "not a group member" (i.e., personal identity).

Many empirical explorations of the self-esteem hypothesis are sensitive to this issue (e.g., Hogg and Sunderland, 1991; Lemyre and Smith, 1985). Crocker and her colleagues (e.g., Crocker, Blaine, and Luhtanen, 1993; Crocker and Luhtanen, 1990; Crocker, Luhtanen, Blaine, and Broadnax, 1994) have tried to clarify matters by distinguishing between personal and collective self-esteem as traits. Early evidence suggests that high collective self-esteem is associated with intergroup discrimination, whereas later studies suggest that both high and low collective self-esteem are associated with discrimination but with different forms of discrimination. In reviewing Crocker's work, Long and Spears (1997) add further weight to Hogg and Abrams's (1990) concerns about the self-esteem hypothesis by concluding that the self-esteem hypothesis leaves unclear the relationship between self-esteem and intergroup behavior. They go on to suggest that personal self-esteem, collective self-esteem, threat to personal and social identity, and degree of identification may all interact together in complex ways to determine what people do to address self-esteem considerations.

Long and Spears's (1997) inclusion of additional variables is an important step forward, which confirms Abrams and Hogg's (1988; Hogg and Abrams, 1990) conclusion that although self-esteem is centrally involved in social identity processes, there may be other motivational mechanisms that are at least as important. In our own work we have been investigating this idea by shifting attention from motivation associated with social comparison and self-esteem to motivation associated with social categorization and uncertainty reduction (e.g., Hogg, 1996; Hogg and Abrams, 1993). The latter is the focus of this chapter.

Self-categorization

The essence of self-categorization theory is that the categorization of self and others in terms of group membership depersonalizes cognitions, behaviors, and feelings in line with contextually relevant group prototypes (Turner, 1985; Turner et al., 1987 – see recent overviews by Hogg, 1996; Hogg et al., 1995). Depersonalization explains how products of social interaction within and between groups (e.g., group norms – cf., Sherif, 1936) can be internalized by individuals through the operation of cognitive processes, and can thus influence human conduct. The depersonalization process nicely reconciles McDougall's (1920) group mind with Allport's (1924) exclamation that there is no psychology outside the head of the individual.

In contrast to social identity theory, self-categorization theory does not dwell on motivational processes. Implicitly, however, it redirects the motivational focus from evaluative to structural factors, in particular the reduction of uncertainty and the search for meaning. This surfaces primarily through discussion of the role of agreement with similar others in reducing uncertainty and in producing conformity to group norms (e.g., McGarty, Turner, Oakes, and Haslam, 1993; Turner, 1985, 1991). The more fundamental role of uncertainty reduction in motivating the initial formation and the contextual salience of groups has not been fully developed.

For example, the self-categorization analysis of the contextual salience of social categories as the basis of self-conception and conduct in a particular circumstance has thus far focused mainly on comparative fit. Drawing on early work by Bruner (1957), self-categorization theorists, mainly through the work of Oakes and her associates (e.g., Oakes, 1987, 1996; Oakes, Turner, and Haslam, 1991), have argued that social categories that are chronically accessible to us (for example, in memory) or simply accessible in the situation (for example, through priming), come into operation as the basis of self-categorization if they make good sense of the situation by accounting for similarities and differences between people and by being relevant to the situation. Salience is an interactive function of chronic accessibility and situational accessibility, on the one hand, and structural/comparative fit and normative fit on the other.

Categories may be chronically accessible if recently activated (Wyer and Srull, 1981), frequently activated (Higgins and King, 1981), or if people are motivated to use them (Klinger, Barta, and Maxeiner, 1980). Categories may be situationally accessible under conditions of direct contact (McGuire, McGuire, and Cheever, 1986; Rodriguez and Gurin, 1990), unequal group size (McGuire, McGuire, Child, and Fujioka, 1978), or even when the physical arrangement of group members draws attention to distinct categories (Gaertner and Dovidio, 1986). Research shows that chronically accessible categories (e.g., sex or race) are more readily made salient by situational primes (e.g., Hewstone, Hantzi, and

Johnston, 1991; Stangor, Lynch, Duan, and Glass, 1992; Taylor and Falcone, 1982; Walker and Antaki, 1986), but only if the categories are moderately chronically accessible (van Twuyver and van Knippenberg, 1995) rather than extremely chronically accessible (Stangor et al., 1992).

Primed categories are more salient if they are relevant to the context of the social categorization, that is, if they have good normative fit (van Knippenberg, van Twuyver, and Pepels, 1994), and if they covary closely with stimulus characteristics, that is, if they have good structural/comparative fit (Eiser, 1971; McGarty and Penny, 1988; Oakes et al., 1991; van Knippenberg et al., 1994). Although there is no formal conceptualization of motivation, it is not improbable that the motivational framework for this process involves reduction of uncertainty and the search for meaning – that is, to understand the context, to be able to predict how other people will behave, and to know how one should behave oneself.

Subjective Uncertainty Reduction

The motivational role of subjective uncertainty reduction in social identity processes developed here is based on initial ideas proposed by Hogg and Abrams (1993; also see Hogg, 1996; Mullin, 1998). People have a fundamental need to feel certain about their world and their place within it – subjective certainty renders existence meaningful and thus gives one confidence about how to behave, and what to expect from the physical and social environment within which one finds oneself. Uncertainty is aversive because it is ultimately associated with reduced control over one's life, and thus it motivates behavior that reduces subjective uncertainty.

The search for certainty is aligned more closely to Bartlett's (1932) notion of a search after meaning than James's (1890) argument that people try to simplify their experiences. This is not to say that people don't try to simplify their experiences, but rather that any simplification is merely associated with a more fundamental search for certainty. Of course, people do not strive for certainty about all aspects of life, but only those which are subjectively important. For example, one may consider art to be more important than sport, and so one would be more motivated for certainty about art rather than sport – it would matter less to feel uncertain about sport than about art.

Festinger (1950, 1954) has argued that uncertainty can be reduced by checking one's cognitions against physical reality, or, if that is not possible, against social reality – i.e., by comparing one's perceptions with those of other individuals, specifically similar others (cf. Kruglanski and Mayseless, 1990; Suls and Miller, 1977; Suls and Wills, 1991). In his original statement, Festinger considered self-evaluation and uncertainty reduction to be the primary motives for social comparison (cf. Schachter, 1959), and he was also clear that comparisons were made with individuals, not groups. Early work confirmed that, all things being equal, people prefer to make comparisons with similar rather than dissimilar others (e.g., Hakmiller, 1966; Jones and Regan, 1974; Wheeler and Koestner, 1984; Wheeler, Koestner, and Driver, 1982; Zanna, Goethals, and Hill, 1975). More recent research has focused on differences between upward and downward social comparisons (e.g., Suls and Wills, 1991) and has suggested that upward comparisons may reduce uncertainty, and that downward comparisons may satisfy self-enhancement and self-esteem motives (e.g., Wood and Taylor, 1991).

Moscovici (1976) goes further to argue that uncertainty can *only* be reduced through social comparisons because all our perceptions, and particularly the meanings attached to them, are socially constructed and are grounded in social consensus. Physical reality is taken for granted, much like behaviors which we consider "natural" or "innate," because of a wide background consensus about which we are largely unaware precisely because such consensus saturates existence (cf. Garfinkel, 1967). This is not to say that reality does not exist, but that the way we represent it is socially constructed in more or less widely shared ways.

Moscovici's perspective informs his model of social influence and has been adopted by self-categorization theory (e.g., Turner, 1985, 1991). Uncertainty arises when we discover that we disagree in our beliefs, attitudes, feelings, and behaviors with "similar" others, where similar others can be defined as people whom we categorize as members of the same group as ourselves. Uncertainty is reduced when similar others agree with us, or when we can agree with similar others (see Abrams, 1996; Abrams, Wetherell, Cochrane, Hogg, and Turner, 1990).

The self-categorization and depersonalization processes associated with social identification and group behavior are ideally suited to uncertainty reduction. Depersonalization refers to a process whereby individuality and concomitant unshared beliefs, attitudes, feelings, and behaviors are replaced by an ingroup prototype that prescribes shared beliefs, attitudes, feelings, and behaviors. Depersonalization changes people so that they appear to agree more strongly with one another. This can be a transitory effect which is tied to local situational factors, or a much more enduring effect which is tied to wider social contextual factors. Subjective certainty, then, is tied to group membership and thus to the self-concept. Things that we are certain about are linked to who we are via the prototypical features of social groups with which we identify and which form part of our self-concept – thus, certainty about attitudes, feelings, and behaviors is actually certainty about who we are. If we did not know what to think, feel, or do, then we really would not know who we are.

This link between certainty and self via social identity brings us back to our earlier comment about uncertainty mattering only if it relates to subjectively important dimensions. Perhaps we only care about uncertainties which have implications for the self-concept. Returning to the earlier art vs. sport example, it is plausible to speculate that whether one cares about uncertainty on one or the other dimension is influenced by whether one's wider or more immediate social identity is influenced by one or the other.

This analysis points to uncertainty reduction being a fundamental human motive that is satisfied, perhaps, primarily by group membership. People join or form groups to reduce uncertainty; they join or form one group rather than another group because it is more relevant to uncertainty reduction for that person in that context (e.g., in terms of the strength and the importance of the uncertainty to be reduced); and specific groups become contextually salient because they reduce uncertainty in that context (hence, the accessibility × fit mechanism operates within this motivational framework).

Because subjective uncertainty on an important (i.e., self-relevant) dimension motivates behavior, it is an aversive state which may be associated with feelings ranging from unease to fear (e.g., Fiske and Taylor, 1991; Lopes, 1987; Sorrentino and Roney, 1986). For example, it is perhaps no coincidence that the indoctrination techniques employed by orthodoxies often involve an initial stage in which dissidents or new members have their confidence in existing beliefs, perceptions, and analyses challenged or undermined (e.g., Deconchy, 1984; also see Schein's, 1961, discussion of "brainwashing") – this raises uncertainty about one's identity, causes anxiety and stress, and leaves one receptive to new attitudes and a new identity in order to reduce uncertainty. In contrast, certainty and the attainment of certainty is a positive state which makes one feel good not only about oneself, but, because it has been achieved through a group process, about the group as a whole and about the other members of the group. Thus, certainties, and those responsible for the consensus upon which certainty rests (i.e., ingroup members, including self), are imbued with positive valence.

This process helps account for: (1) positive social identity and ethnocentrism – because the ingroup has reduced one's uncertainty, it is imbued with positive valence and is evaluated more favorably than the outgroup; (2) self-esteem as a group member – because self is a depersonalized component of the ingroup, ingroup evaluation based on uncertainty reduction embraces self-evaluation; and (3) group membership-based social attraction among group members – other members of the group are also depersonalized components of the ingroup, and thus ingroup evaluation based on uncertainty reduction embraces other-evaluation (Hogg, 1992, 1993).

Commentary on Subjective Uncertainty Reduction

The idea that groups strive to achieve or maintain positive social identity has been very helpful in understanding the dynamics of intergroup relations. Close examination of self-esteem as the self-evaluative motive which may underpin positive social identity has, however, generated conceptual and empirical complexity which has led some commentators to suggest that there are boundary conditions that need to be specified (e.g., Crocker, Blaine, and Luhtanen, 1993; Long and Spears, 1997), or that there are other group membership motives which we may need to examine (Abrams and Hogg, 1988; Hogg and Abrams, 1990). The suggestion we make in this chapter is that uncertainty reduction may be one such other motivation -it may even be one of the most fundamental group motivations on which other motives, for example self-esteem, rest. This is not an entirely novel idea, even for social identity theory. Tajfel referred to dual motives for positive social identity and for a well structured and meaningful world (e.g., Tajfel, 1969).

The idea that self-esteem may be a "lesser" motive underlying *group* behaviour is shared by others. For example, Crocker et al. (1993) believe that the more primary motive underlying collective identification may be the drive for a certain self-concept rather than a positive self-concept, and Jost (1995; Jost and Banaji, 1994) believes that uncertainty reduction and the maintenance of stability may be a stronger group motive than self-enhancement. Others argue that the pursuit of self-esteem is indulged only once one has secured a certain self-concept (e.g., Sedikides and Strube, 1995; Taylor, Neter, and Wayment, 1995). Generally speaking, recent research on self-esteem is increasingly discovering that self-esteem is related to, or even contingent on, self-certainty (e.g., Banaji and Prentice, 1994; Baumgardner, 1990; Brown, Collins, and Schmidt, 1988; Campbell, 1990; Crocker et al., 1993; Gibbons and McCoy, 1991).

Finally, Stevens and Fiske conclude from their discussion of human motives involved in social survival that "the motive to belong is obviously the most important for social survival" (Stevens and Fiske, 1995, p. 205), and they consider self-esteem to be a lower-order motive. For Stevens and Fiske (1995), the need to belong is a fundamental motive because belonging facilitates interdependence in the service of survival outcomes ranging from procreation to nurturance and protection. No distinction is made between satisfaction of this need through the formation of groups or the formation of interpersonal relations – the need can be satisfied either way, and the only difference that Stevens and Fiske identify concerns the subjective importance of accuracy as a perceptual strategy. Stevens and Fiske feel that because groups protect and nurture their members, people should belong to as many groups as possible, and so they register surprise that research shows people prefer a few close friends over a large number of friends (Baumeister and Leary, 1995). These comments suggest that when Stevens and Fiske talk about belonging to groups they mainly have in mind small interactive groups and dyads rather than large-scale social categories. If this is so, it might explain the emphasis placed on interdependence. From our own perspective, belonging is a critical social motive that is satisfied by membership of social categories of all sizes, but it is a motive that is tied to an underlying need for certainty – people do not strive to belong to any and all groups, only if they seek uncertainty reduction and the specific group satisfies this need.

Subjective uncertainty is produced by contextual factors that challenge people's certainty about their cognitions, perceptions, feelings, and behaviors, and ultimately, certainty about and confidence in their sense of self. Self-certainty can be undermined because self is the critical organizing principle, referent point, or integrative framework for diverse perceptions, feelings, and behaviors. We believe that the locus of uncertainty is to be found overwhelmingly in the social context, and therefore that anyone is prone to uncertainty. However, biographical factors may have some influence on people's orientation towards uncertainty and the reduction of uncertainty.

The idea that some people are less tolerant of uncertainty than others is an old one – for example, it is captured by Adorno, Frenkel-Brunswik, Levinson, and Sanford's (1950) description of the authoritarian personality, and by Rokeach's (1948, 1960) notion of a dogmatic or closed-minded personality. More recently, Sorrentino and associates have explored the role of uncertainty orientation as an individual difference variable. Uncertainty-oriented people seek out uncertainty and work on the resolution of uncertainty in order to satisfy a self-assessment motive, whereas certainty-oriented people are more concerned with self-verification and the maintenance of existing beliefs – they avoid situations of uncertainty and if confronted by uncertainty fall back on simple heuristics rather than resolution of uncertainty (e.g., Brouwers and Sorrentino, 1993; King and Sorrentino, 1988; Roney and Sorrentino, 1995; Sorrentino, Holmes, Hanna, and Sharp, 1995; Sorrentino and Short, 1986). There is also evidence that people vary in their need for structure or closure and their fear of invalidity – people who have a high need for structure or closure are more concerned to reduce uncertainty quickly than to be correct, whereas people who have a fear of invalidity are able to tolerate greater uncertainty while they engage in a prolonged search for validity (e.g., Kruglanski, 1989; Kruglanski and Webster, 1996; Neuberg and Newson, 1993; Thompson, Naccarato, and Parker, in press; Thompson and Zanna, 1995; Webster and Kruglanski, 1994).

Finally, there are related constructs that identify individual differences in the complexity and number of explanations people have of other people (attributional complexity – Fletcher, Danilovics, Fernandez, Peterson, and Reeder, 1986), individual differences in how much people like to think deeply about things (need for cognition – Cacioppo and Petty, 1982), and individual differences in the complexity of people's cognitive processes and representations (cognitive complexity – Crockett, 1965). People also differ in self-concept clarity – the extent to which self-beliefs are clearly and confidently defined, internally consistent, and stable (e.g., Campbell, 1990; Campbell, Trapnell, Heine, Katz, Lavalle, and Lehman, 1996); self-complexity – the number of different or independent dimensions that underlie self-conception (e.g., Linville, 1987); and compartmentalization of the self (e.g., Showers, 1992).

Personality and individual difference conceptualizations of uncertainty should be treated cautiously, especially where uncertainty reduction is tied to group membership and group behavior such as intergroup discrimination. It is certainly not our intention to trace discrimination and prejudice to personality (cf. Billig, 1976) – rather, we believe that social contextual factors influence uncertainty, the resolution of uncertainty, and the way in which such resolution is expressed. If predispositions have a role to play it is a relatively minor role, and it is strongly constrained by social context (cf. Pettigrew's 1958, classic investigation of authoritarianism and prejudice).

Uncertainty reduction through social identification has direct effects on self-definition and the contextually framed self-concept. Not surprisingly, research on the self-concept describes various self-motives. The recent explosion of research on the self (see Banaji and Prentice, 1994) has energized debate over the range of different motives that may drive self-conception, and over the relationship between these motives (e.g., Sedikides and Strube, 1995; Swann and Schroeder, 1995). Self-enhancement theories propose that people are primarily motivated to construct a relatively positive sense of who they are, and that this motive is perhaps central because it rests on a fundamental human responsivenesse to pleasure and pain. Self-assessment theories propose that people strive to reduce uncertainty about their self-concept regardless of whether the uncertainty reduction process is likely to result in favorable or unfavorable implications for self (see Sedikides and Strube, 1995). Self-verification theory (e.g., Pelham and Swann, 1994; Swann, Stein-Seroussi, and Giesler, 1992) proposes that people are motivated to predict and control their social world, and therefore seek information that verifies their perceptions, including perceptions of self. Self-affirmation theory (e.g., Steele, 1988; Steele, Spencer, and Lynch, 1993) proposes that people strive for an integrated and consistent self-image, and that therefore evaluative challenges to one aspect of self motivates affirmation of another positive aspect in order to maintain the overall integrity of self. Symbolic self-completion theory (e.g., Brunstein and Gollwitzer, 1996; Wicklund and Gollwitzer, 1982) proposes that commitment to self-defining goals leads people to accumulate the symbolic trappings of the associated identity as symbols of completeness – these symbols allow others to confirm one's possession of the identity. Generally speaking, however, this research on self-motives does not explicitly tie these motives to group membership, and does not examine the possible relationship between uncertainty-based motives and group belongingness or social identification.

Studies of Uncertainty and Identification

The core idea of our model is that people identify with groups to reduce uncertainty. To investigate this idea, we have conducted a series of laboratory experiments (Grieve and Hogg, in press; Hogg and Grieve, in press; Mullin and Hogg, 1998a, 1998b, in press). The most elementary question we felt we could ask was whether subjective uncertainty motivated people in minimal group studies to identify with the explicit categorization and thus express ingroup favoritism. We suggested that minimal group studies are actually situations of high subjective uncertainty owing to the novelty of the situation and the strangeness of the resource distribution task, and therefore participants readily use the minimal categorization to reduce uncertainty about themselves and how they should behave. Social categorization *per se* does *not* produce intergroup discrimination; rather, social categorization under subjective uncertainty as opposed to subjective certainty produces identification, which in turn generates differential intergroup perceptions, feelings, and behavior (i.e., discrimination).

Based on an earlier, unsuccessful, attempt by Tajfel and Billig (1974) to test a similar idea, we conducted a conventional minimal group experiment (Hogg and Grieve, in press). Adopting a 2 (categorization) × 2 (uncertainty) design, student participants ($N = 151$) were explicitly categorized on a random basis into X-and Y-groups, or were not categorized. This was done under normal minimal group conditions, which we felt embodied relatively high subjective uncertainty, or under conditions where subjects had been given three practice trials on the matrices (low uncertainty). On a composite measure of ingroup bias (representing use of favoritism strategies on the minimal group matrices), we found significant bias only among those participants who were categorized under uncertainty ($F(1,144 = 4.55, p < .05, \eta^2 = .03$) – see figure 11.1. These people also showed significant reduction in uncertainty (uncategorized participants did not), and significantly higher self-esteem (as measured by a single item focusing on transitory and specific self-esteem) than participants who were categorized under low uncertainty. There was also some indication that these people identified more strongly with their group than other participants, as measured by a five-item identification scale.

We then went on to conduct two additional studies (Grieve and Hogg, in press). The first experiment ($N = 119$ psychology students) was a methodologically

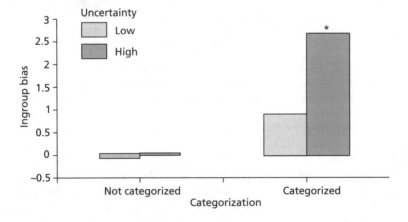

Figure 11.1   Ingroup bias (composite scale ranging from 12 to +12) as a function of categorization and uncertainty. Data from Hogg and Grieve (in press).
*significantly different to zero, $t(37) = 4.45, p < .001$.

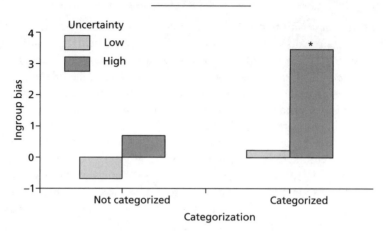

Figure 11.2 Ingroup bias (composite scale ranging from 12 to +12) as a function of categorization and uncertainty. Data from Grieve and Hogg (in press, Exp. 1). *significantly different to zero, $t(29) = 4.35$, $p < .001$.

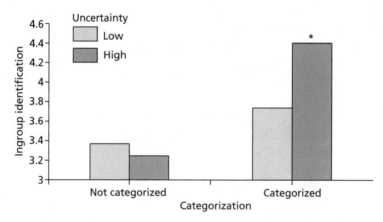

Figure 11.3 Ingroup identification (composite ten-item scale ranging from 1 to 9) as a function of categorization and uncertainty. Data from Grieve and Hogg (in press, Exp. 1). *significantly different to all other means, which did not differ from one another, by Newman-Keuls.

refined replication of Hogg and Grieve (in press). The main differences were that low-uncertainty participants completed 12 rather than only three practice matrices, and identification was measured on a ten-rather than five-item scale (taken from Hains, Hogg, and Duck, 1997; Hogg and Hains, 1996). As in Hogg and Grieve (in press), there was significant bias only among those participants who were categorized under uncertainty ($F(1,115) = 5.59$, $p < .05$, $\eta^2 = .05$) – see figure 11.2. These people also showed significantly stronger identification than

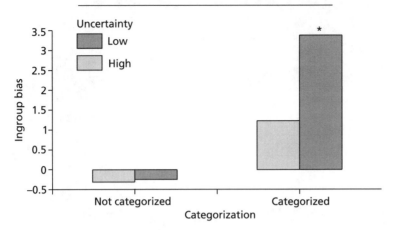

Figure 11.4 Ingroup bias (composite scale ranging from 12 to +12) as a function of categorization and uncertainty. Data from Grieve and Hogg (in press, Exp. 2). *significantly different to zero, and significantly different (by Newman-Keuls) to all other means.

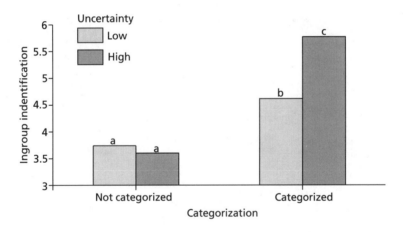

Figure 11.5 Ingroup identification (composite ten-item scale ranging from 1 to 9) as a function of categorization and uncertainty. Data from Grieve and Hogg (in press, Exp. 2). Means with unshared superscripts differ significantly by Newman-Keuls.

other participants ($F(1,115) = 3.97$, $p < .05$, $\eta^2 = .03$ – see figure 11.3) and a trend towards elevated self-esteem ($p < .10$). Unlike Hogg and Grieve (in press), measures of uncertainty reduction appeared to be insensitive to changes in uncertainty.

The second experiment was a conceptual replication of Experiment 1, but it employed a different methodology based to some extent on a modification of the affiliation paradigm used in social comparison research (e.g., Wood, 1996). In a

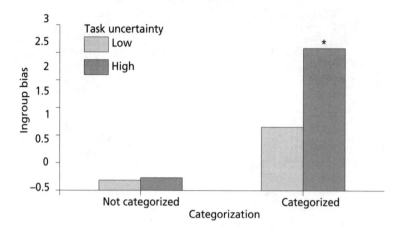

Figure 11.6 Ingroup bias (composite scale ranging from 12 to +12) as a function of categorization and task uncertainty. Data from Mullin and Hogg (1998a). *significantly different to zero.

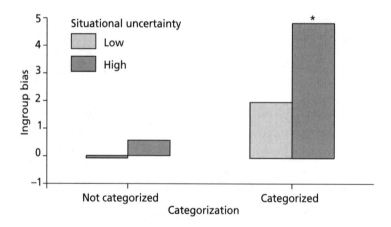

Figure 11.7 Ingroup bias (composite scale ranging from 12 to +12) as a function of categorization and situational uncertainty. Data from Mullin and Hogg (1998a). *significantly different to zero.

2 (categorization) x 2 (uncertainty) design, participants (N = 105 psychology students) had their uncertainty raised or lowered by engaging in a judgment task where the correct judgments were ambiguous or obvious. They were then explicitly categorized or not categorized, as in Experiment 1, and completed minimal group allocation matrices as well as other measures. There was significant intergroup bias only among participants who were categorized under elevated uncertainty ($F(1,104)$ = 6.21, $p < .05$, η^2 = .06 – see figure 11.4). These people also identified (ten-item composite scale) more strongly with the group ($F(1,104)$

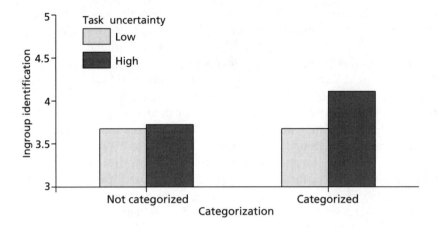

Figure 11.8   Ingroup identification (composite five-item scale ranging from 1 to 9) as a function of categorization and task uncertainty. Data from Mullin and Hogg (1998a). No means differed significantly by Newman-Keuls.

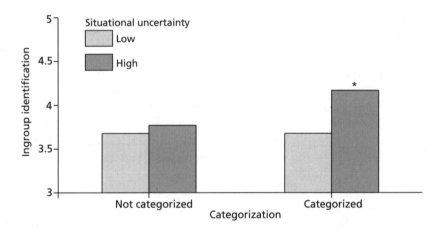

Figure 11.9   Ingroup identification (composite five-item scale ranging from 1 to 9) as a function of categorization and situational uncertainty. Data from Mullin and Hogg (1998a).
*significantly different to all other means, which did not differ from one another, by Newman-Keuls.

$= 7.61$, $p < .01$, $\eta^2 = .07$ – see figure 11.5). There was some weak evidence for higher self-esteem among these participants.

Another minimal group experiment, based closely on the Grieve and Hogg studies, was conducted by Mullin and Hogg (1998a). In this experiment we sought to distinguish between uncertainty about the task and uncertainty about the experimental setting as a whole (the two were concatenated in Grieve and

Hogg's experiments). This distinction was based on the assumption that the latter, what we called "situational uncertainty," might be more closely related to identity uncertainty because it revolved more closely around the relationship between self and other people in the social setting. Psychology students ($N = 96$) participated in a 2 (categorization) × 2 (task uncertainty) × 2 (situational uncertainty) minimal group study. Low-task uncertainty participants were given six practice matrices and told to do as many as they needed to make sure they felt completely certain about the task. Situational certainty was a subject variable – high-uncertainty participants had not yet taken part in an experiment, whereas low-uncertainty participants had already been in at least five experiments offered through the department's research participation scheme. There was significant bias only among categorized participants under high task uncertainty ($F(1,88) = 4.13$, $p < .05$, $\eta^2 = .05$ – see figure 11.6) or under high situational uncertainty ($F(1,88) = 6.58$, $p < .05$, $\eta^2 = .07$ – see figure 11.7). These effects were perfectly associated with identification: categorization interacted significantly with task uncertainty ($F(1,88) = 4.63$, $p < .05$, $\eta^2 = .05$ – see figure 11.8) and with situational uncertainty ($F(1,88) = 4.11$, $p < .05$, $\eta^2 = .05$ – see figure 11.9). There was weaker support for elevated self-esteem and reduced uncertainty associated with ingroup identification and bias.

The Grieve and Hogg (in press), Hogg and Grieve (in press) and Mullin and Hogg (1998a) experiments represent four minimal group-type studies which consistently show that categorization leads to identification and discrimination only when it occurs under conditions of task or situational uncertainty. Although there was also some support for the idea that identification would elevate self-esteem and reduce uncertainty, this aspect needs further empirical work.

Our model of uncertainty as a motivation for group identification states that for uncertainty to have motivational force it should relate to subjectively important dimensions. To test this idea we had psychology students ($N = 128$) participate in a 2 (categorization) × 2 (task uncertainty) × 2 (task importance) experiment – Mullin and Hogg (in press). They were randomly categorized as group members (Alpha- vs. Beta-group) or identified as individuals, after they had been given feedback to raise or lower subjective uncertainty about the validity of their attitudes towards low-importance or high-importance issues (e.g., trivial commodity preferences vs. important lifestyle and health preferences). As predicted, participants who were categorized under conditions of high uncertainty about important issues identified (five-item composite nine-point scale) significantly more strongly than did participants in all seven other conditions – mean of 4.91 compared with means of 2.96 through 3.97 ($F(1,120) = 9.24$, $p < .01$, $\eta^2 = .07$).

We pursued the role of dimensional importance and category relevance in two additional experiments (Mullin and Hogg, 1998b). In Experiment 1, psychology students ($N = 192$) participated in a 3 (categorization) × 2 (task certainty) × 2 (task importance) experiment employing the same paradigm as Mullin and Hogg (in press). The difference was that in one of the two categorization conditions

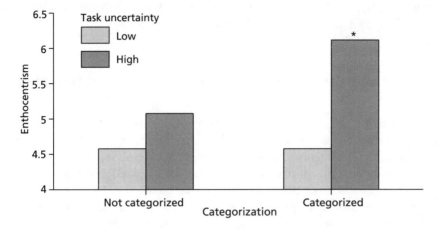

Figure 11.10 Ethnocentrism (composite four-item scale ranging from 1 to 9) as a function of category relevance and situational uncertainty. Data from Mullin and Hogg (1998b, Exp. 2).
*significantly different to all other means, which did not differ significantly (Newman-Keuls).

participants were led to infer that their category was contextually more relevant because they would later be given normative attitudinal information from their ingroup. In a replication of Mullin and Hogg (in press), participants who were categorized (high-or low-relevance groups) under conditions of high uncertainty about important issues identified (four-item composite nine-point scale) significantly more strongly than did participants in other conditions ($F(2,180) = 3.32$, $p < .05$, $\eta^2 = .04$). The category relevance manipulation was unsuccessful, and so we conducted a second experiment focusing only on category relevance and task certainty in a 2×2 design – all participants ($N = 64$) were categorized and all were given an important task. Category relevance was accentuated by relating category membership to basic personality attributes that might be useful in the experimental task (cf. Forgas and Fiedler, 1996). As predicted, participants in the high-uncertainty/high-category relevance condition showed significantly more evidence of ingroup identification than did participants in the other conditions – the effect did not attain statistical significance on the five-item identification scale ($\eta^2 = .03$), but was significant on a four-item intergroup evaluative bias scale monitoring ethnocentrism ($F(1,60) = 6.37$, $p < .05$, $\eta^2 = .10$ – see figure 11.10).

Taken together, our programme of research has provided good evidence that under relatively minimal conditions people form groups (as indicated by identification and bias/ethnocentrism measures) when they feel uncertain about the task or the situation, but only when the dimension of uncertainty is subjectively important and when the group is relevant to uncertainty reduction. Evidence that this elevates self-esteem and reduces uncertainty is less robust and clearly needs further investigation. We feel that this research provides preliminary support for our uncertainty reduction model of social identity processes.

The Larger Canvas of Uncertainty Reduction and Social Identity

That idea that uncertainty has an important role in social identity processes has substantial support. A number of scholars have argued that identification with large-scale social categories such as gender, race, and nationality seems to be strongly motivated by concerns about certain self-knowledge and psychological security (e.g., Abrams, 1990; Deaux, 1992; Mitchell, 1981). Furthermore, threats to identity that produce uncertainty (e.g., threats that arise from geographical relocation, rapidly changing status differentials, loss of membership or loss of validation of membership in a group) can have profound effects on people's self-confidence, self-esteem, and sense of who they are (Breakwell, 1986; Ethier and Deaux, 1994; Sachdev and Bourhis, 1993; van Knippenberg and Ellemers, 1993).

For example, people who relocate to a new country as immigrants or sojourners can find that everyday interactions are highly unpredictable or unfavorably stereotypical, because their self-concept does not meaningfully fit into the new social context. As a result they can redefine or adapt their social identity, retreat into a social environment that reinforces their existing identity, or show signs of acute anxiety or depression. Sudden loss of work-related identity through retrenchment or retirement can have similar effects. Uncertainty within an organizational or work context can lead to structural changes within an organization (e.g., Hickson, Hinings, Lee, Schnecker, and Pennings, 1971; Schoonhaven, 1981), and to attempts to increase organizational commitment and identification by providing an unambiguous and desirable group prototype via, for example, mission and vision statements (see Hogg and Terry, 1998).

In the case of a perceived threat to the economic or cultural security of a relatively higher-status group, there can be a "reaction" or "backlash" to try to reassert social psychological and material conditions that maintain security. For example, in 1997 in Australia, xenophobic nationalism intensified as a reaction to a perceived threat to national identity and economic security which was attributed to multiculturalism, aboriginal rights, and Asian immigration (e.g., Duck, Hogg, Lalonde, and Terry, 1997).

Related to this last point, there is also evidence that widespread social uncertainty arising from, for example, massive social reorganization and economic collapse may encourage the development and spread of rumor (Buckner, 1965; Rosnow, 1980), and can give rise to the emergence of all-consuming social ideologies (e.g., Cantril, 1941), orthodox belief systems (e.g., Deconchy, 1984), widespread social representations (e.g., Farr and Moscovici, 1984), and elaborate explanatory and justificatory belief systems (e.g., Tajfel, 1981). These cognitive structures can often be organized around conspiracy theories that attribute distressing conditions to the actions of specific social groups (e.g., Bains, 1983; Wood, 1982) – for example the world Jewish conspiracy invoked by Fascist political parties of the 1930s (see Billig, 1978; Cohn, 1966). There is good reason to believe not only that these explanatory cognitive structures reduce uncertainty, but that they are organized around social identity – they are consensual representations derived, held, and promulgated by members of a collectivity that often targets a specific outgroup. For example, Staub's (1989) theoretically eclectic and integrative analysis of the roots of genocide and other group violence considers widespread and profound social uncertainty, which he calls difficult life circumstances, to be a critical precondition for identification with totalist groups – given certain other conditions, this can then translate into genocide. Staub applies this analysis to four twentieth-century genocides: the 1915 Turkish genocide of Armenians, the holocaust of the 1940s, the Cambodian "killing fields" of the 1970s, and the Argentinian "disappearances" of the 1970s.

People may be more prone to uncertainty at particular junctures in their lives. Perhaps not surprisingly, research on cults and other "totalist" groups suggest that such groups are characterized by extreme identification, excessive devotion, and narrowly orthodox thought and behavior, and that it is adolescents (people going through a period of great subjective uncertainty) who are particularly susceptible to membership (e.g., Curtis and Curtis, 1993; Galanter, 1989).

Another source of uncertainty is intergroup contact. When members of different social groups come into enduring or short-term contact, their beliefs about the outgroup and relations between their own group and the outgroup may be challenged. Where ingroup identity is important, this may represent a serious threat to social identity (contact is often associated with intergroup anxiety – e.g., Stephan and Stephan, 1985), which can most easily be resolved by strengthened ingroup identification and accentuated outgroup hostility, particularly when ingroup attitudes are at odds with changed attitudes that may emerge through contact, and when there is implicit or overt ingroup pressures for conformity (cf. Zinkiewicz, 1997). Perhaps this is one reason why intergroup contact is such an unreliable way of improving generalized intergroup images (Brewer and Miller, 1996; Brown, 1995, 1996; Hewstone, 1994, 1996).

The link between social identification and uncertainty reduction has some oblique support in the phenomenon of groupthink (Janis, 1972, 1982; Janis and Mann, 1977). There is some evidence that when ingroup identification is extremely strong, small decision-making groups faced with difficult decisions and much uncertainty produce overwhelming social attraction and unwarranted certainty (e.g., Hogg and Hains, 1998). Research on minority influence also points to uncertainty as a key motivational factor. Active minorities have their effect on majority opinions by threatening the certainty of the majority's views at a deep cognitive level, which gradually produces cognitive reorganization to resolve uncertainty and which may lead to conversion and ultimately identity change (Moscovici, 1976; Mugny, 1982; Perez and Mugny, 1990).

Uncertainty may also be motivationally involved in the relationship between intergroup distinctiveness and group identification. Intergroup distinctiveness is reduced if there is substantial normative similarity or overlap, or intragroup normative heterogeneity. Jetten (1997) suggests that social identity theory predicts weaker identification with increasing distinctiveness (because of the motivation to differentiate categories), whereas self-categorization theory predicts the opposite (because of the more mechanical accessibility x fit mechanism), and presents evidence in support of both processes (e.g., Jetten, 1997; Jetten, Spears, Hogg, and Manstead, 1997; Jetten, Spears, and Manstead, 1996). She goes on to suggest that the self-categorization relationship may occur where identification is low, and the social identity relationship where identification is high (cf. Doosje, Ellemers, and Spears, 1995).

Another way to approach this issue is in terms of our uncertainty perspective, which would lead us to expect a U-shaped relationship between distinctiveness and identification/discrimination. Low distinctiveness would produce high uncertainty that could be resolved by boundary clarification through self-categorization, social identification, and intergroup discrimination – the ingroup and outgroup are maximally comparable and thus the availability x fit heuristic brings an ingroup–outgroup categorization into play. Extremely low distinctiveness would produce even more uncertainty, but in this case the resolution would quite probably be to recategorize ingroup and outgroup as a common ingroup (e.g., Gaertner, Dovidio, Anastasio, Bachman, and Rust, 1993; Gaertner, Rust, Dovidio, Bachman, and Anastasio, 1996) and thus reduce ingroup identification and intergroup behavior. Extremely high distinctiveness would produce little uncertainty and therefore would not engage the motivation to reduce uncertainty through social identity processes.

Finally, uncertainty reduction may help explain why minority status groups can show outgroup favoritism. Outgroup favoritism has always been a slightly tricky finding for a self-esteem motive account of social identity processes (e.g., Apfelbaum, 1979). Traditionally, it has been accounted for in terms of social belief structures that describe intergroup relations as stable and legitimate (e.g., Tajfel and Turner, 1979). This idea is extended by system justification theory (Jost, 1995; Jost and Banaji, 1994), which suggests that it can sometimes be more important for people to perceive a stable system of intergroup relations than to engage in a struggle for self-enhancement. Uncertainty is aversive and people try to justify rather than challenge an existing status quo. Jost and associates argue that this idea is consistent with a number of other notions such as failure to perceive injustice (Crosby, 1982), the just world hypothesis (Lerner, 1980), institutional loyalty (Tyler, 1990), stereotypic rationalization (Hoffman and Hurst, 1989), hierarchy enhancement (Pratto, Sidanius, Stallworth, and Malle, 1994), false consciousness (Jost, 1995), and legitimacy of inequality (Major, 1994).

Concluding Comments

Self-enhancement and evaluatively positive social identity are important motivations associated with group processes and intergroup relations. It has not been our intention in writing this chapter to contest this. Rather, we have explored the possibility that uncertainty reduction may be an equally important motive, and perhaps even a more fundamental one – a motive that is particularly closely associated with group membership and social identity.

We suggest that it is aversive to be uncertain about beliefs, attitudes, feelings, and behaviors that one feels are important to one's sense of who one is. Group identification is a particularly effective way to reduce such uncertainty, because the process of depersonalization associated with self-categorization transforms the "uncertain self" into a "certain self" governed by an ingroup prototype that is consensually validated by fellow ingroup members. In this way, group membership accentuates prototypical similarity. It also resolves uncertainty and imbues the group with positive valence that generalizes to self and fellow group members, and thus generates positive group evaluations (ethnocentrism, ingroup bias), positive self-evaluation (self-esteem), and positive evaluation of fellow members (social attraction).

In this chapter we overview some key experiments from our programme of research. These controlled laboratory studies provide some consistent support for the idea that people categorize themselves in terms of an externally designated social categorization only if they are uncertain, the dimension of uncertainty is subjectively important, and the social categorization is relevant to the uncertainty dimension. We also extend our analysis to speculate about how it may connect with and help explain naturally occurring uncertainty phenomena in wider group and intergroup contexts.

References

Abrams, D. (1990). How do group members regulate their behaviour? An integration of social identity and self-awareness behaviour. In D. Abrams and M.A. Hogg (eds), *Social Identity Theory: Constructive and critical advances*. Hemel Hempstead: Harvester Wheatsheaf, pp. 89–112.

Abrams, D. (1992). Processes of social identification. In G. Breakwell (ed.), *Social Psychology of Identity and the Self-concept*. San Diego: Academic Press, pp. 57–99.

Abrams, D. (1996). Social identity, self as structure and self as process. In W.P. Robinson (ed.), *Social Groups and Identities: Developing the legacy of Henri Tajfel*. Oxford: Butterworth-Heinemann, pp. 143–67.

Abrams, D. and Hogg, M.A. (1988). Comments on the motivational status of self-esteem in social identity and intergroup discrimination. *European Journal of Social Psychology*, 18, 317–34.

Abrams, D. and Hogg, M.A. (1998). Prospects for research in group processes and intergroup relations. *Group Processes and Intergroup Relations*, 1, 7–20.

Abrams, D., Wetherell, M.S., Cochrane, S., Hogg, M.A., and Turner, J.C. (1990). Knowing what to think by knowing who you are: Self-categorization and the nature of norm formation, conformity, and group polarization. *British Journal of Social Psychology*, 29, 97–119.

Adorno, T.W., Frenkel-Brunswik, E., Levinson, D.J., and Sanford, R.M. (1950). *The Authoritarian Personality*. New York: Harper.

Allport, F.H. (1924). *Social Psychology*. New York: Houghton Mifflin.

Apfelbaum, E. (1979). Relations of domination and movements for liberation: An analysis of power between groups. In W.G. Austin and S. Worchel (eds), *The Social Psychology of Intergroup Relations*. Monterey, CA: Brooks-Cole, pp. 188–204.

Bains, G. (1983). Explanations and the need for control. In M. Hewstone (ed.), *Attribution Theory: Social and functional extensions*. Oxford: Blackwell, pp. 126–43.

Banaji, M.R. and Prentice, D.A. (1994). The self in social contexts. *Annual Review of Psychology*, 45, 297–332.

Bartlett, F.C. (1932). *Remembering*. Cambridge: Cambridge University Press.

Baumeister, R.F. and Leary, M.R. (1995). The need to belong: Desire for interpersonal attachments as a fundamental human motive. *Psychological Bulletin*, 117, 497–529.

Baumgardner, A.H. (1990). To know oneself is to like oneself: Self-certainty and self-affect. *Journal of Personality and Social Psychology*, 58, 1062–72.

Billig, M. (1976). *Social Psychology and Intergroup Relations*. London: Academic Press.

Billig, M. (1978). *Fascists: A social psychological view of the National Front*. London: Harcourt Brace Jovanovich.

Bourhis, R.Y., Sachdev, I., and Gagnon, A. (1994). Intergroup research with the Tajfel matrices: Methodological notes. In M. Zanna and J. Olson (eds), *The Psychology of Prejudice: The Ontario Symposium*, Vol. 7. Hillsdale, NJ: Erlbaum, pp. 209–32.

Breakwell, G.M. (1986). Political and attributional responses of the young short-term unemployed. *Political Psychology*, 7, 575–86.

Brewer, M.B. and Miller, N. (1996). *Intergroup Relations*. Buckingham: Open University Press.

Brouwers, M.C. and Sorrentino, R.M. (1993). Uncertainty orientation and protection motivation theory: The role of individual differences in health compliance. *Journal of Personality and Social Psychology*, 65, 102–12.

Brown, J., Collins, R.L., and Schmidt, G.W. (1988). Self-esteem and direct vs. indirect forms of self-enhancement. *Journal of Personality and Social Psychology*, 55, 445–53.

Brown, R. (1995). *Prejudice: Its social psychology*. Oxford: Blackwell.

Brown, R. (1996). Tajfel's contribution to the reduction of intergroup conflict. In W.P. Robinson (ed.), *Social Groups and Identities: Developing the legacy of Henri Tajfel*. Oxford: Butterworth-Heinemann, pp. 169–89.

Bruner, J. (1957). On perceptual readiness. *Psychological Review*, 64, 123–51.

Brunstein, J.C. and Gollwitzer, P.M. (1996). Effects of failure on subsequent performance: The importance of self-defining goals. *Journal of Personality and Social Psychology*, 70, 395–407.

Buckner, H.T. (1965). A theory of rumor transmission. *Public Opinion Quarterly*, 29, 54–70.

Cacioppo, J.T. and Petty, R.E. (1982). The need for cognition. *Journal of Personality and Social Psychology*, 42, 116–31.

Campbell, J.D. (1990). Self-esteem and the clarity of the self-concept. *Journal of Personality and Social Psychology*, 59, 538–49.

Campbell, J.D., Trapnell, P.D., Heine, S.J., Katz, I.M., Lavalle, L.F., and Lehman, D.R. (1996). Self-concept clarity: Measurement, personality correlates, and cultural boundaries. *Journal of Personality and Social Psychology*, 70, 141–56.

Cantril, H. (1941). *The Psychology of Social Movements*. New York: Wiley.

Cohn, N. (1966). *Warrant for Genocide. The myth of the Jewish world conspiracy and the Protocol of the Elders of Zion*. New York: Harper and Row.

Crocker, J., Blaine, B., and Luhtanen, R. (1993). Prejudice, intergroup behaviour and self-esteem: Enhancement and protection motives. In M.A. Hogg and D. Abrams (eds), *Group Motivation: Social psychological perspectives*. Hemel Hempstead: Harvester Wheatsheaf, pp. 52–67.

Crocker, J. and Luhtanen, R. (1990). Collective self-esteem and ingroup bias. *Journal of Personality and Social Psychology*, 58, 60–7.

Crocker, J., Luhtanen, R., Blaine, B., and Broadnax, S. (1994). Collective self-esteem and psychological well-being among white, black, and Asian college students. *Personality and Social Psychology Bulletin*, 20, 503–14.

Crockett, W.H. (1965). Cognitive complexity and impression formation. In B.A. Maher (ed.), *Progress in Experimental Personality Research*, Vol. 2. New York: Academic Press, pp. 47–90.

Crosby, F.J. (1982). *Relative Deprivation and Working Women*. New York: Oxford University Press.

Curtis, J.M. and Curtis, M.J. (1993). Factors related to susceptibility and recruitment by cults. *Psychological Reports*, 73, 451–60.

Deaux, K. (1992). Personalizing identity and socializing self. In G. Breakwell (ed.), *Social Psychology of Identity and the Self-concept*. London: Academic Press, pp. 301–27.

Deconchy, J.P. (1984). Rationality and social control in orthodox systems. In H. Tajfel (ed.), *The Social Dimension: European developments in social psychology*, Vol. 2. Cambridge: Cambridge University Press, pp. 425–45.

Diehl, M. (1990). The minimal group paradigm: Theoretical explanations and empirical findings. *European Review of Social Psychology*, 1, 263–92.

Doise, W. (1986). *Levels of Explanation in Social Psychology*. Cambridge: Cambridge University Press.

Doosje, B., Ellemers, N., and Spears, R. (1995). Perceived intragroup variability as a function of group status and identification. *Journal of Experimental Social Psychology*, 31, 410–36.

Duck, J.M., Hogg, M.A., Lalonde, R.N., and Terry, D.J. (1997). A new legitimacy for xenophobic nationalism in Australia: A social identity analysis of media-managed "reaction." Unpublished manuscript, University of Queensland, Brisbane.

Eiser, J.R. (1971). Enhancement of contrast in the absolute judgement of attitude statements. *Journal of Personality and Social Psychology*, 17, 1–10.

Ethier, K.A. and Deaux, K. (1994). Negotiating social identity when contexts change: Maintaining identification and responding to threat. *Journal of Personality and Social Psychology*, 64, 243–51.

Farr, R.M. (1996). *The Roots of Modern Social Psychology: 1872–1954*. Oxford: Blackwell.

Farr, R.M. and Moscovici, S. (eds) (1984). *Social Representations*. Cambridge: Cambridge University Press.

Festinger, L. (1950). Informal social communication. *Psychological Review*, 57, 271–82.

Festinger, L. (1954). A theory of social comparison processes. *Human Relations*, 7, 117–40.

Fiske, S.T. and Taylor, S.E. (1991). *Social Cognition*, 2nd edn. New York: McGraw-Hill.

Fletcher, G.J.O., Danilovics, P., Fernandez, G., Peterson, D., and Reeder, G.D. (1986). Attributional complexity: An individual differences measure. *Journal of Personality and Social Psychology*, 51, 875–84.

Forgas, J.P. and Fiedler, K. (1996). Us and them: Mood effects on intergroup discrimination. *Journal of Personality and Social Psychology*, 70, 28–40.

Gaertner, S.L. and Dovidio, J.F. (1986). The aversive form of racism. In J.F. Dovidio and S.L. Gaertner (eds), *Prejudice, Discrimination, and Racism*. Orlando, FL: Academic Press, pp. 61–89.

Gaertner, S.L., Dovidio, J., Anastasio, P., Bachman, B., and Rust, M. (1993). The common ingroup identity model: Recategorization and the reduction of intergroup bias. *European Review of Social Psychology*, 4, 1–26.

Gaertner, S.L., Rust, M.C., Dovidio, J.F., Bachman, B.A., and Anastasio, P.A. (1996). The contact hypothesis: The role of a common ingroup identity on reducing intergroup bias among majority and minority group members. In J.L. Nye and A.M. Bower (eds), *What's Social about Social Cognition: Research on socially shared cognition in small groups*. Thousand Oaks, CA: Sage, pp. 230–60.

Garfinkel, H. (1967). *Studies in Ethnomethodology*. Englewood Cliffs, NJ: Prentice-Hall.

Galanter, M. (ed.) (1989). *Cults and New Religious Movements*. Washington, DC: American Psychiatric Association.

Gibbons, F.X. and McCoy, B. (1991). Self-esteem, similarity and reactions to active vs. passive downward comparison. *Journal of Personality and Social Psychology*, 60, 414–24.

Giles, H. and Johnson, P. (1987). Ethnolinguistic identity theory: A social psychological approach to language maintenance. *International Journal of the Sociology of Language*, 68, 256–69.

Greenwald, A.G. and Pratkanis, A.R. (1984). The self. In R.S. Wyer, Jr and T.K. Srull (eds), *Handbook of Social Cognition*, Vol. 3. Hillsdale, NJ: Erlbaum, pp. 129–78.

Grieve, P.G. and Hogg, M.A. (in press). Subjective uncertainty and intergroup discrimination in the minimal group situation. *Personality and Social Psychology Bulletin*.

Hains, S.C., Hogg, M.A., and Duck, J.M. (1997). Self-categorization and leadership: Effects of group prototypicality and leader stereotypicality. *Personality and Social Psychology Bulletin*, 23, 1087–99.

Hakmiller, K.L. (1966). Threat as determinant of downward comparison. *Journal of Experimental Social Psychology*, 2, 32–9.

Hewstone, M. (1994). Revision and change of stereotypic beliefs: In search of the elusive subtyping model. *European Review of Social Psychology*, 5, 69–109.

Hewstone, M. (1996). Contact and categorization: Social psychological interventions to change intergroup relations. In C.N. Macrae, C. Stangor, and M. Hewstone (eds), *Stereotypes and Stereotyping*. New York: Guilford, pp. 323–68.

Hewstone, M., Hantzi, A., and Johnston, L. (1991). Social categorization and person memory: The pervasiveness of race as an organizing principle. *European Journal of Social Psychology*, 21, 517–28.

Hickson, D.J., Hinings, C.R., Lee, C.A., Schnecker, R.E., and Pennings, J.M. (1971). A strategic contingencies' theory of intraorganizational power. *Administrative Science Quarterly*, 16, 216–29.

Higgins, E.T. and King, G.A. (1981). Individual construct accessibility and subjective impressions and recall. *Journal of Personality and Social Psychology*, 43, 35–47.

Hoffman, C. and Hurst, N. (1989). Gender stereotypes: Perception or rationalization? *Journal of Personality and Social Psychology*, 58, 197–208.

Hogg, M.A. (1992). *The Social Psychology of Group Cohesiveness: From attraction to social identity*. Hemel Hempstead and New York: Harvester Wheatsheaf and New York University Press.

Hogg, M.A. (1993). Group cohesiveness: A critical review and some new directions. *European Review of Social Psychology*, 4, 85–111.

Hogg, M.A. (1996). Intragroup processes, group structure and social identity. In W.P. Robinson (ed.), *Social Groups and Identities: Developing the legacy of Henri Tajfel*. Oxford: Butterworth-Heinemann, pp. 65–93.

Hogg, M.A. and Abrams, D. (1988). *Social Identifications: A social psychology of intergroup relations and group processes*. London and New York: Routledge.

Hogg, M.A. and Abrams, D. (1990). Social motivation, self-esteem and social identity. In D. Abrams and M.A. Hogg (eds), *Social Identity Theory: Constructive and critical advances*. Hemel Hempstead: Harvester Wheatsheaf, pp. 28–47.

Hogg, M.A. and Abrams, D. (1993). Towards a single-process uncertainty-reduction model of social motivation in groups. In M.A. Hogg and D. Abrams (eds), *Group Motivation: Social psychological perspectives*. Hemel Hempstead: Harvester Wheatsheaf, pp. 173–90.

Hogg, M. A. and Grieve, P. (in press). Social identity theory and the crisis of confidence in social psychology: A commentary and some research on uncertainty reduction. *Asian Journal of Social Psychology*.

Hogg, M.A. and Hains, S.C. (1996). Intergroup relations and group solidarity: Effects of group identification and social beliefs on depersonalized attraction. *Journal of Personality and Social Psychology*, 70, 295–309.

Hogg, M.A. and Hains, S.C. (1998). Friendship and group identification: A new look at the role of cohesiveness in groupthink. *European Journal of Social Psychology*, 28, 323–41.

Hogg, M.A. and Moreland, R.L. (1995). European and American influences in small group research. Invited paper presented at the Small Groups preconference of the joint meeting of the European Association of Experimental Social Psychology and the Society for Experimental Social Psychology, Washington, DC, October.

Hogg, M.A. and Sunderland, J. (1991). Self-esteem and intergroup discrimination in the minimal group paradigm. *British Journal of Social Psychology*, 30, 51–62.

Hogg, M.A. and Terry, D.J. (1998). Organizational identification: Social identity and self-categorization processes in organizational contexts. Manuscript submitted for publication, University of Queensland.

Hogg, M.A., Terry, D.J., and White, K.M. (1995). A tale of two theories: A critical comparison of identity theory with social identity theory. *Social Psychology Quarterly*, 58, 255–69.

James, W. (1890). *The Principles of Psychology*. New York: Holt, Rhinehart, and Winston.

Janis, I.L. (1972). *Victims of Groupthink*. Boston, MA: Houghton Mifflin.

Janis, I.L. (1982). *Groupthink: Psychological studies of policy decisions and fiascoes*, 2nd edn. Boston, MA: Houghton Mifflin.

Janis, I.L. and Mann, L. (1977). *Decision Making: A psychological analysis of conflict, choice, and commitment*. New York: Free Press.

Jetten, J. (1997). Dimensions of distinctiveness: Intergroup discrimination and social identity. Unpublished doctoral dissertation, University of Amsterdam.

Jetten, J., Spears, R., Hogg, M.A., and Manstead, A.S.R. (1997). Discrimination constrained and justified: The variable effects of group variability and ingroup identification. Manuscript submitted for publication, University of Amsterdam.

Jetten, J., Spears, R., and Manstead, A.S.R. (1996). Intergroup norms and intergroup discrimination: Distinctive self-categorization and social identity. *Journal of Personality and Social Psychology*, 71, 1222–33.

Jones, S.C. and Regan, D.T. (1974). Ability evaluation through social comparison. *Journal of Experimental Social Psychology*, 10, 133–46.

Jost, J.T. (1995). Negative illusions: Conceptual clarification and psychological evidence concerning false consciousness. *Political Psychology*, 16, 397–424.

Jost, J.T. and Banaji, M.R. (1994). The role of stereotyping in system-justification and the production of false consciousness. *British Journal of Social Psychology*, 33, 1–27.

King, G.A. and Sorrentino, R.M. (1988). Uncertainty orientation and the relationship between individual accessible constructs and person memory. *Social Cognition*, 6, 128–49.

Klinger, E., Barta, S.G., and Maxeiner, M.E. (1980). Motivational correlates of thought content frequency and commitment. *Journal of Personality and Social Psychology*, 39, 1222–37.

Kruglanski, A.W. (1989). *Lay Epistemics and Human Knowledge: Cognitive and motivational bases*. New York: Plenum Press.

Kruglanski, A.W. and Mayseless, O. (1990). Classic and current social comparison research: Expanding the perspective. *Psychology Bulletin*, 108, 195–208.

Kruglanski, A.W. and Webster, D.M. (1996). Motivated closing of the mind: "Seizing" and "freezing." *Psychological Review*, 103, 263–83.

Lemyre, L. and Smith, P.M. (1985). Intergroup discrimination and self-esteem in the minimal group paradigm. *Journal of Personality and Social Psychology*, 49, 660–70.

Lerner, M.J. (1980). *The Belief in a Just World: A fundamental delusion*. New York: Plenum Press.

Levine, J.M., Resnick, L.B., and Higgins, E.T. (1993). Social foundations of cognition. *Annual Review of Psychology*, 44, 585–612.

Linville, P.W. (1987). Self-complexity as a buffer against stress-related illness and depression. *Journal of Personality and Social Psychology*, 52, 663–76.

Long, K. and Spears, R. (1997). The self-esteem hypothesis revisited: Differentiation and the disaffected. In R. Spears, P.J. Oakes, N. Ellemers, and S.A. Haslam (eds), *The Social Psychology of Stereotyping and Group Life*. Oxford: Blackwell, pp. 296–317.

Lopes, L.L. (1987). Between hope and fear: The psychology of risk. *Advances in Experimental Psychology*, 20, 255–95.

Lorenzi-Cioldi, F. and Doise, W. (1990). Levels of analysis and social identity. In D. Abrams and M.A. Hogg (eds), *Social Identity Theory: Constructive and critical advances*. Hemel Hempstead: Harvester Wheatsheaf, and New York: Springer-Verlag, pp. 71–88.

McDougall, W. (1920). *The Group Mind*. Cambridge: Cambridge University Press.

McGarty, C. and Penny, R.E.C. (1988). Categorization, accentuation and social judgement. *British Journal of Social Psychology*, 22, 147–57.

McGarty, C., Turner, J.C., Oakes, P.J., and Haslam, S.A. (1993). The creation of uncertainty in the influence process: The roles of stimulus information and disagreement with similar others. *European Journal of Social Psychology*, 23, 17–38.

McGuire, W.J., McGuire, C.V., and Cheever, J. (1986). The self in society: Effects of social contexts on the sense of self. Special issue: The individual–society interface. *British Journal of Social Psychology*, 25, 259–70.

McGuire, W.J., McGuire, C.V., Child, P., and Fujioka, T. (1978). Salience of ethnicity in the spontaneous self-concept as a function of one's ethnic distinctiveness in the social environment. *Journal of Personality and Social Psychology*, 36, 511–20.

McReynolds, P. (1987). Self-theory, anxiety and intrapsychic conflicts. In N. Cheshire and H. Thomae (eds), *Self, Symptoms and Psychotherapy*. New York: Wiley, pp. 197–223.

Major, B. (1994). From social inequality to personal entitlement: The role of social comparisons, legitimacy appraisals, and group memberships. *Advances in Experimental Social Psychology*, 26, 293–355.

Mitchell, C.R. (1981). *The Structure of International Conflict*. London: Macmillan.

Moreland, R.L., Hogg, M.A., and Hains, S.C. (1994). Back to the future: Social psychological research on groups. *Journal of Experimental Social Psychology*, 30, 527–55.

Moscovici, S. (1976). *Social Influence and Social Change*. London: Academic Press.

Mugny, G. (1982). *The Power of Minorities*. London: Academic Press.

Mullin, B.-A. (1998). Uncertainty reduction, social identification, and group behaviour. Unpublished doctoral dissertation, University of Queensland, Brisbane.

Mullin, B.-A. and Hogg, M.A. (1998a). Dimensions of subjective uncertainty in social identification and minimal intergroup discrimination. *British Journal of Social Psychology*, 37, 345–65.

Mullin, B.-A. and Hogg, M.A. (1998b). Reducing subjective uncertainty by group identification: The role of group relevance. Manuscript submitted for publication, University of Queensland, Brisbane.

Mullin, B.-A. and Hogg, M.A. (in press). Motivations for group membership: The role of subjective importance and uncertainty reduction. *Basic and Applied Social Psychology*.

Neuberg, S.L. and Newson, J.T. (1993). Personal need for structure: Individual differences in the desire for simpler structure. *Journal of Personality and Social Psychology*, 65, 113–31.

Nye, J.L. and Brower, A.M. (eds) (1996). *What's Social about Social Cognition: Research on socially shared cognition in small groups*. Thousand Oaks, CA: Sage.

Oakes, P.J. (1987). The salience of social categories. In J.C. Turner, M.A. Hogg, P.J. Oakes, S.D. Reicher, and M.S. Wetherell, *Rediscovering the Social Group: A self-categorization theory*. Oxford and New York: Blackwell, pp. 117–41.

Oakes, P.J. (1996). The categorization process: Cognition and the group in the social psychology of stereotyping. In W.P. Robinson (ed.), *Social Groups and Identities: Developing the legacy of Henri Tajfel*. Oxford: Butterworth-Heinemann, pp. 95–119.

Oakes, P.J., Turner, J.C., and Haslam, S.A. (1991). Perceiving people as group members: The role of fit in the salience of social categorizations. *British Journal of Social Psychology*, 30, 125–44.

Pelham, B.W. and Swann, W.B. (1994). The juncture of intrapersonal and interpersonal knowledge: Self-certainty and interpersonal congruence. *Personality and Social Psychology Bulletin*, 20, 349–57.

Perez, J.A. and Mugny, G. (1990). Minority influence, manifest discrimination and latent influence. In D. Abrams and M.A. Hogg (eds), *Social Identity Theory: Constructive and critical advances*. Hemel Hempstead: Harvester Wheatsheaf, pp. 152–68.

Pettigrew, T.F. (1958). Personality and socio-cultural factors in intergroup attitudes: A cross-national comparison. *Journal of Conflict Resolution*, 2, 29–42.

Pratto, F., Sidanius, J., Stallworth, L.M., and Malle, B.F. (1994). Social dominance orientation: A personality variable predicting social and political attitudes. *Journal of Personality and Social Psychology*, 67, 741–63.

Rabbie, J.M., Schot, J.C., and Visser, L. (1989). Social identity theory: A conceptual and empirical critique from the perspective of a behavioural interaction model. *European Journal of Social Psychology*, 19, 171–202.

Robinson, W.P. (ed.) (1996). *Social Groups and Identities: Developing the legacy of Henri Tajfel*. Oxford: Butterworth-Heinemann.

Rodriguez, J. and Gurin, P. (1990). The relationships of intergroup contact to social identity and political consciousness. *Hispanic Journal of Behavioral Sciences*, 12, 235–55.

Rokeach, M. (1948). Generalized mental rigidity as a factor in ethnocentrism. *Journal of Abnormal Social Psychology*, 43, 259–78.

Rokeach, M. (1960). *The Open and Closed Mind*. New York: Basic Books.

Roney, J.R. and Sorrentino, R.M. (1995). Self-evaluation motives and uncertainty orientation: Asking the "who" question. *Personality and Social Psychology Bulletin*, 21, 1319–29.

Rosnow, R.L. (1980). Psychology of rumor reconsidered. *Psychological Bulletin*, 87, 578–91.

Rubin, M. and Hewstone, M. (1998). Social identity theory's self-esteem hypothesis: A review and some suggestions for clarification. *Personality and Social Psychology Review*, 2, 40–62.

Sachdev, I. and Bourhis, R. (1993). Ethnolinguistic vitality: Some motivational and cognitive considerations. In M.A. Hogg and D. Abrams (eds), *Group Motivation: Social psychological perspectives*. Hemel Hempstead: Harvester Wheatsheaf, pp. 33–51.

Schachter, S. (1959). *The Psychology of Affiliation: Experimental studies of the sources of gregariousness*. Stanford, CA: Stanford University Press.

Schein, E.H. (1961). *Coercive Persuasion*. New York: Norton.

Schoonhaven, C.B. (1981). Problems with contingency theory: Testing assumptions within the language of contingency "theory." *Administrative Science Quarterly*, 26, 349–77.

Sedikides, C. and Strube, M.J. (1995). The multiply motivated self. *Personality and Social Psychology Bulletin*, 21, 1330–5.

Sherif, M. (1936). *The Psychology of Social Norms*. New York: Harper and Bros.

Showers, C. (1992). Compartmentalization of positive and negative self-knowledge: Keeping bad apples out of the bunch. *Journal of Personality and Social Psychology*, 62, 1036–49.

Sorrentino, R.M., Holmes, J.G., Hanna, S.E., and Sharp, A. (1995). Uncertainty orientation and trust in close relationships: Individual differences in cognitive styles. *Journal of Personality and Social Psychology*, 68, 314–27.

Sorrentino, R.M. and Roney, C.J.R. (1986). Uncertainty orientation, achievement-related motivation and task diagnosticity as determinants of task performance. *Social Cognition*, 4, 420–36.

Sorrentino, R.M. and Short, J.C. (1986). Uncertainty orientation, motivation and cognition. In R.M. Sorrentino and E.T. Higgins (eds), *The Handbook of Motivation and Cognition: Foundations of social behavior*, Vol. 1. New York: Guilford, pp. 379–403.

Stangor, C., Lynch, L., Duan, C., and Glass, B. (1992). Categorization of individuals on the basis of multiple social features. *Journal of Personality and Social Psychology*, 62, 207–18.

Staub, E. (1989). *The Roots of Evil: The origins of genocide and other group violence*. New York: Cambridge University Press.

Steele, C.M. (1988). The psychology of self-affirmation: Sustaining the integrity of the self. *Advances in Experimental Social Psychology*, 21, 261–302.

Steele, C.M., Spencer, S.J., and Lynch, M. (1993). Self-image resilience and dissonance: The role of affirmational resources. *Journal of Personality and Social Psychology*, 64, 885–96.

Stephan, W.G. and Stephan, C.W. (1985). Intergroup anxiety. *Journal of Social Issues*, 41, 157–75.

Stevens, L.E. and Fiske, S.T. (1995). Motivation and cognition in social life: A social survival perspective. *Social Cognition*, 13, 189–214.

Suls, J.M. and Miller, R.L. (1977). *Social Comparison Processes*. Washington, DC: Hemisphere.

Suls, J. and Wills, T.A. (eds) (1991). *Social Comparison: Contemporary theory and research*. Hillsdale, NJ: Erlbaum.

Swann, W.B. and Schroeder, D.G. (1995). The search for beauty and truth: A framework for understanding reactions to evaluations. *Personality and Social Psychology Bulletin*, 21, 1307–18.

Swann, W.B., Stein-Seroussi, A., and Giesler, R.B. (1992). Why people self-verify. *Journal of Personality and Social Psychology*, 62, 392–401.

Tajfel, H. (1969). Social and cultural factors in perception. In G. Lindzey and E. Aronson (eds), *Handbook of Social Psychology*, Vol. 3. Reading, MA: Addison-Wesley, pp. 315–94.

Tajfel, H. (1981). Social stereotypes and social groups. In J.C. Turner and H. Giles (eds), *Intergroup Behaviour*. Oxford: Blackwell, pp. 144–67.

Tajfel, H. (ed.) (1982). *Social Identity and Intergroup Relations*. Cambridge: Cambridge University Press.

Tajfel, H. (ed.) (1984). *The Social Dimension: European developments in social psychology*. Cambridge: Cambridge University Press.

Tajfel, H. and Billig, M. (1974). Familiarity and categorisation in intergroup behaviour. *Journal of Experimental Social Psychology*, 10, 159–70.

Tajfel, H., Billig, M., Bundy, R.P., and Flament, C. (1971). Social categorization and intergroup behaviour. *European Journal of Social Psychology*, 1, 149–77.

Tajfel, H. and Turner, J.C. (1979). An integrative theory of intergroup conflict. In W.G. Austin and S. Worchel (eds), *The Social Psychology of Intergroup Relations*. Monterey, CA: Brooks-Cole, pp. 33–47.

Taylor, D.M. and McKirnan, D.J. (1984). A five-stage model of intergroup relations. *British Journal of Social Psychology*, 23, 291–300.

Taylor, S.E. and Falcone, H. (1982). Cognitive bases of stereotyping: The relationship between categorization and prejudice. *Personality and Social Psychology Bulletin*, 8, 426–32.

Taylor, S.E., Neter, E., and Wayment, H.A. (1995). Self-evaluation processes. *Personality and Social Psychology Bulletin*, 21, 1278–87.

Thompson, M.M., Naccarato, M.E., and Parker, K.H. (in press). The personal need for structure and personal need for invalidity scales: Historical perspectives, current applications and future directions. In G.B. Moskowitz (ed.), *Cognitive Social Psychology*. Mahwah, NJ: Erlbaum.

Thompson, M.M. and Zanna, M.P. (1995). The conflict individual: Personality-based and domain-specific antecedents of ambivalent social attitudes. *Journal of Personality*, 63, 259–88.

Turner, J.C. (1982). Towards a cognitive redefinition of the social group. In H. Tajfel (ed.), *Social Identity and Intergroup Relations*. Cambridge: Cambridge University Press, pp. 15–40.

Turner, J.C. (1985). Social categorization and the self-concept: A social cognitive theory of group behaviour. In E.J. Lawler (ed.), *Advances in Group Processes: Theory and research*, Vol. 2. Greenwich, CT: JAI Press, pp. 77–122.

Turner, J.C. (1991). *Social Influence*. Milton Keynes: Open University Press.

Turner, J.C. and Bourhis, R.Y. (1996). Social identity, interdependence and the social group: A reply to Rabbie et al. In W.P. Robinson (ed.), *Social Groups and Identities: Developing the legacy of Henri Tajfel*. Oxford: Butterworth-Heinemann, pp. 25–63.

Turner, J.C. and Giles, H. (eds) (1981). *Intergroup Behaviour*. Oxford: Blackwell.

Turner, J.C., Hogg, M.A., Oakes, P.J., Reicher, S.D., and Wetherell, M.S. (1987). *Rediscovering the Social Group: A self-categorization theory*. Oxford and New York: Blackwell.

Tyler, T.R. (1990). *Why People Obey the Law*. New Haven, CT: Yale University Press.

van Knippenberg, A. and Ellemers, N. (1993). Strategies in intergroup relations. In M.A. Hogg and D. Abrams (eds), *Group Motivation: Social psychological perspectives*. Hemel Hempstead: Harvester Wheatsheaf, pp. 17–32.

van Knippenberg, A., van Twuyver, M., and Pepels, J. (1994). Factors affecting social categorization processes in memory. *British Journal of Social Psychology*, 33, 419–32.

van Twuyver, M. and van Knippenberg, A. (1995). Social categorization as a function of priming. *European Journal of Social Psychology*, 25, 695–701.

Walker, P. and Antaki, C. (1986). Sexual orientation as a basis for categorization in recall. *British Journal of Social Psychology*, 25, 337–9.

Webster, D.M. and Kruglanski, A. (1994). Individual differences in need for cognitive closure. *Journal of Personality and Social Psychology*, 67, 1049–62.

Wheeler, L. and Koestner, R. (1984). Performance evaluation: On choosing to know the related attributes of others when we know their performance. *Journal of Experimental Social Psychology*, 20, 263–71.

Wheeler, L., Koestner, R., and Driver, R.E. (1982). Related attributes in the choice of comparison others: It's there, but it isn't all there is. *Journal of Experimental Social Psychology*, 18, 489–500.

Wicklund, R.A. and Gollwitzer, P.M. (1982). *Symbolic Self-completion*. Hillsdale, NJ: Erlbaum.

Wood, G.S. (1982). Conspiracy and the paranoid style: Causality and deceit in the eighteenth century. *William and Mary Quarterly*, 39, 401–41.

Wood, J.V. (1996). What is social comparison and how should we study it? *Personality and Social Psychology Bulletin*, 22, 520–37.

Wood, J.V. and Taylor, K.L. (1991). Serving self-relevant goals through social comparison. In J. Suls and T.A. Wills (eds), *Social Comparison: Contemporary theory and research*. Hillsdale, NJ: Erlbaum, pp. 23–49.

Wyer, R.S., Jr and Srull, T.K. (1981). Category accessibility: Some theoretical and empirical issues concerning the processing of social stimulus information. In E.T. Higgins, C.P. Herman, and M.P. Zanna (eds), *Social Cognition: The Ontario symposium*, Vol. 1. Hillsdale, NJ: Erlbaum, pp. 161–98.

Zanna, M.P., Goethals, G.R., and Hill, J.F. (1975). Evaluating a sex-related ability: Social comparison with similar others and standard setters. *Journal of Experimental Social Psychology*, 11, 86–93.

Zinkiewicz, L. (1997). A social identity approach to intergroup contact: The roles of group salience, ingroup identification, and social influence. Unpublished doctoral dissertation, University of Queensland, Brisbane.

12

Group Membership, Social Identity, and Attitudes

Deborah J. Terry, Michael A. Hogg, and Julie M. Duck

Attitude researchers have focused much of their attention on attitude–behavior relations and attitude change (see Eagly and Chaiken, 1993). A related area – the perception of the impact of persuasive communications – has also received some research attention (see Perloff, 1993, for a review). Despite the fact that such issues are embedded centrally in the realm of social psychology, the role of social influence in attitude–behavior relations and persuasion has received less attention. For the most part, an individualistic perspective has been taken – attitudes are regarded as part of people's personal belief structures – and, as a consequence, most research on attitude–behavior relations and attitude change has been conducted at this same level of abstraction. Indeed, the dominant tendency in the attitude change and persuasion literature has been to treat persuasive communication and social influence in groups as separate areas of research inquiry. Nevertheless, on the basis of social identity theory (Hogg and Abrams, 1988; Tajfel and Turner, 1979; Turner, 1982) and self-categorization theory (Turner, 1985; Turner, Hogg, Oakes, Reicher, and Wetherell, 1987), a strong theoretical case can be made for the view that attitude change and perceptions of the impact of persuasive communications cannot be well understood without reference to the wider social context of group memberships – attitudes themselves can be regarded as social products to the extent that they are likely to be influenced by social norms and expectations. Furthermore, norms of behaviorally relevant social groups and categories are likely to influence people's willingness to engage in attitudinally consistent behavior – to do so may help to validate an important social identification – and to influence their perceptions of the impact of persuasive communications.

In the present chapter, we propose that attitude–behavior consistency is influenced by both the attitudinal congruency of ingroup norms and the salience of the group membership, and, in a similar manner, that perceptions of media

Thanks are due to Jackie Wellen for her assistance in the preparation of this chapter.

influence on self and others are influenced by the social psychological relationships between self and others and by ingroup norms regarding the acknowledgment of influence. Our assertion that attitude–behavior consistency and perception of media influence cannot be understood without reference to the wider social context of group memberships is supported with the discussion of the results of our recent research in these two areas – chapters by van Knippenberg and Mackie and Hunter (chapters 13 and 14 in this volume) focus on group membership and persuasion. In our discussion of attitude–behavior consistency, we focus on the interplay between social cognitive and social normative factors. Specifically, we show that the socionormative influences (i.e., ingroup norms) on the extent to which people behave in accordance with their attitudes are independent of the corresponding effects of attitude accessibility (a central sociocognitive mechanism proposed to explain variation in attitude–behavior consistency; see Fazio, 1986, 1989; Fazio, Powell, and Herr, 1983). Furthermore, we present evidence that indicates that ingroup norms influence attitude–behavior relations under both spontaneous and deliberative decision-making conditions (cf. Fazio, 1990b). Following our discussion of attitude–behavior consistency, we focus on the socionormative influences on perceptions of the impact of persuasive communications.

Socionormative Influences and Attitude–Behavior Consistency

One of the responses to the early evidence that, contrary to expectations, people's actions are not necessarily guided by their attitudes (Wicker, 1969) was the view that there is no simple attitude–behavior relationship, and that to predict behavior accurately it is necessary to take into account other variables. The theory of reasoned action (Fishbein and Ajzen, 1975), and its recent extension, the theory of planned behavior (Ajzen, 1987, 1991; see Terry, Gallois, and McCamish, 1993, for an overview of these theories), have been particularly influential in this respect. Both theories propose that, in addition to attitudes, subjective norm – i.e., people's perception of social pressure from significant others to perform the behavior – has an independent influence on behavior, through the mediating role of behavioral intention. In the theory of planned behavior, Ajzen (1987, 1991) proposed that perceived behavioral control would emerge as an additional predictor of intentions and actual behavior – the latter effect being evident only in relation to behaviors that cannot be performed at will.

In contrast with other attitude–behavior models, the theories of reasoned action and planned behavior are noteworthy in that they do acknowledge the potential role of socionormative factors in behavioral decision-making. Support, however, for the proposed role of norms in the theories of reasoned action/ planned behavior is only weak. Across 37 tests (26 studies) of the theory of reasoned action, Farley, Lehmann, and Ryan (1981) found that the average regression weight for attitude (in the prediction of intention) dominated the average regression weight for subjective norm by a factor of 1.5, a pattern of results that did not vary as a function of type of sample (student or nonstudent), design of study (experimental or correlational), or discipline (social psychology or marketing). More recently, Ajzen (1991) summarized the results of 19 tests of the theory of planned behavior – in more than half the studies, the norm–intention relationship was nonsignificant. On the basis of consistent evidence linking attitude and perceived behavioral control to intentions, Ajzen (1991) concluded that personal factors are more influential in the prediction of behavioral outcomes than social factors.

Contrary to this view, a reconceptualization of the role of norms in attitude–behavior relations in line with recent social psychological models of group influence, specifically social identity theory (Hogg and Abrams, 1988; Tajfel and Turner, 1979; Turner, 1982) and self-categorization theory (Turner, 1985; Turner et al., 1987) may help to reemphasize the importance of socionormative factors in attitude–behavior consistency. Prior to outlining the proposed reconceptualization of the role of norms in attitude–behavior relations, we discuss the limitations in Fishbein and Ajzen's (1975) treatment of the role of social influence in attitude–behavior relations.

In our previous work, we have focused on two main problematic features of the treatment of social influence in the theories of reasoned action and planned behavior (Terry and Hogg, 1996; Terry, Hogg, and White, in press; see also Liska, 1984). First, Fishbein and Ajzen (1975) assumed that, although probably related, attitudes and subjective norms are cognitively independent, to the extent that they proposed that the constructs are based on different belief structures. People's attitudes are seen to be a function of their beliefs about the likely costs and benefits of performing a behavior, whereas subjective norms are based on people's beliefs concerning the extent to which particular others want them to perform the behavior. However, evidence that the belief-based predictors of attitudes can affect subjective norms and/or vice versa suggests that the variables are not psychologically distinct (see also Liska, 1984; Miniard and Cohen, 1981; Ryan, 1978). Recent research using structural equation modeling has indicated that such "crossover effects" are most likely to occur from normative beliefs to attitudes (Oliver and Bearden, 1985; Vallerand, Deshaies, Cuerrier, Pelletier, and Mongeau, 1992). In other words, people's attitudes are influenced not only by the perceived costs and benefits of performing the behavior, but also by their perceptions that significant others would want them to perform the behavior. This finding may reflect the fact that the consequences of performing a behavior often include pleasing others, and so "pleasing others" is a benefit of performing the behavior, thus meaning that it is a factor that influences people's attitudes (Fishbein and Ajzen, 1975; Liska, 1984). Although this is probably true, the normative belief–attitude crossover effect could reflect a more fundamental effect, namely, that people's attitudes are influenced by significant others (Hovland, Janis, and Kelley, 1953; Vallerand et al., 1992).

The second problematic feature of the manner in which social influence is conceptualized in the theory of reasoned action is that Fishbein and Ajzen (1975) assumed not only psychological independence of the constructs, but also effect independence – that is, that the effects of attitudes and norms are additive or independent of each other. People's intentions to perform a behavior are pro- posed to be influenced by both their attitude toward the behavior and the extent to which they perceive that significant others want them to perform the behavior. However, the strength of attitudinal influence is not considered to be influenced by, or dependent on, social influence. This additive model is contrary to the contingent consistency hypothesis (see Acock and DeFleur, 1972; Liska, 1984), which proposes that people are more likely to engage in behavior that is con- sistent with their attitudes if the normative climate supports the attitude. There is some support for this hypothesis (e.g., Grube and Morgan, 1990; Grube, Mor- gan, and McGree, 1986), although other studies have failed to find that norms moderate the effects of attitudes on intentions (e.g., Bagozzi and Schnedlitz, 1985), or they have found that some third variable – such as the extent of past experience at performing the target behavior – may qualify contingent consist- ency effects (Andrews and Kandel, 1979). Nevertheless, evidence of contingent consistency effects suggests further that attitudes and norms may be less inde- pendent than proposed by the theories of reasoned action and planned behavior – the perceived views of significant others may influence people's willingness to express their attitudes behaviorally.

The problems with the normative component of the theories of reasoned action/planned behavior may be attributable to the way in which social influence is viewed by these models and by the wider field of attitude–behavior relations. In their conceptualization of the role of social influence in attitude–behavior relations, Fishbein and Ajzen (1975) imply a social influence process whereby people bring their behavior into line with the behavioral expectations of import- ant others. Thus, the underlying social influence process is probably public compliance based on a need for social approval and acceptance (Miniard and Cohen, 1981; Ryan, 1982), a type of social influence that is typically referred to as normative influence (Deutsch and Gerard, 1955; Kelley, 1952). Traditionally, this type of social influence has been distinguished from informational influence, which occurs when people internalize and privately accept information from others because the information provides a basis for correct perceptions, attitudes, and beliefs (Asch, 1952; Deutsch and Gerard, 1955; Kelley, 1952). Such a dual- process model of social influence may be problematic because it conceptually compartmentalizes facets of social norms that need to be conceptualized in terms of a single process (e.g., Abrams and Hogg, 1990; Hogg and Turner, 1987; Turner, 1991). Indeed, in the theories of reasoned action/planned behavior, the lack of strong support for the role of subjective norms may reflect the concep- tualization of norms as external prescriptions that are linked to behavior to the extent that one believes that one's behavior is observable by valued others. A single-process model of social influence – which has been derived from social identity and self-categorization theory (Abrams and Hogg, 1990; Hogg and Turner, 1987; Turner, 1982, 1991) – may, therefore, form the basis for a useful reconceptualization of the role of norms in attitude–behavior relations. This reconceptualization is described below.

Social identity/self-categorization theories and attitude–behavior relations

According to social identity theory (Tajfel and Turner, 1979; Turner, 1982; see also Hogg and Abrams, 1988), an important component of the self-concept is derived from memberships in social groups and social categories. When people define and evaluate themselves in terms of a self-inclusive social category (e.g., a sex, class, team), the joint processes of categorization and self-enhancement come into play. Categorization perceptually accentuates differences between ingroup and outgroup and similarities among ingroup members (including self) on stereotypical dimensions. Because the self is defined in terms of the group membership, self-enhancement seeks behaviorally and perceptually to favor things ingroup over things outgroup. Social identity theory has been extended by Turner and his colleagues (Turner et al., 1987) to focus more specifically on the role of the categorization process – self-categorization theory.

Referent informational influence – a single-process model of social influence in groups – has been derived from these two theories (Abrams and Hogg, 1990; Hogg and Turner, 1987; Turner, 1982, 1991). The cognitive process of self-categorization underpins this process such that, when a social identity is salient, people construct a context-specific group norm from available, and usually shared, social comparative information. Subjectively, this norm is represented as a group prototype that describes and prescribes beliefs, attitudes, feelings, and behaviors that optimally minimize ingroup differences and maximize intergroup differences (the principle of meta-contrast). The process of self-categorization also means that there is an assimilation of self to the prototype and thus the self is transformed: self-perception, beliefs, attitudes, feelings, and behaviors are now defined in terms of the group prototype. In this way, group membership causes people to think, feel, behave, and define themselves in terms of group norms rather than unique properties of the self. People are influenced by norms because they prescribe the context-specific attitudes and behaviors appropriate for group members, rather than simply for social approval in a public context (as implied by the conceptualization of norms from a normative influence perspective; cf. Deutsch and Gerard, 1955; Kelley, 1952). Thus, norms are inextricable properties of groups that influence people through self-categorization.

From the perspective of referent informational influence, there are a number of factors that might explain the lack of stronger evidence for the proposed norm–intention link in the theories of reasoned action/planned behavior. First, social influence in these theories is conceptualized as being additive across all referents and reference groups that are defined by the participant as being "important" to them – in other words, the subjective norm is conceptualized as the extent of perceived social pressure from all important others to perform the behavior. However, referent informational influence links norms to specific groups, and these norms have their effect because the group is relevant to the behavioral context. Thus, researchers should focus on the norms of the reference group that is most relevant in the context under consideration. Second, individual differences in the subjective salience of a particular group membership are not specifically taken into account in the theories of reasoned action and planned behavior. Although people's motivations to comply are proposed to influence the subjective norm, this variable is not seen as having a proximal impact on intentions. Moreover, greater motivation to comply with the expectations of a reference group may not necessarily be associated with strong group identification. On the basis of a social identity/self-categorization approach, it can be proposed explicitly that behavioral outcomes are influenced by reference group norms, but only for those people for whom the group membership is a salient basis for self-definition. Third, tests of the theories of reasoned action and planned behavior tend to focus on the role of salient others rather than on salient reference groups. As such, the theory essentially focuses on how one individual influences another (interpersonal influence) rather than on how the group influences the individual through internalized social norms (group influence). It is possible that stronger and more predictable effects of norms are yielded under conditions that favor group influence.

Reconceptualizing the role of social influence in attitude–behavior relations from the perspective of referent informational influence not only suggests a number of factors that may be responsible for the relatively weak effects of subjective norm, but it can also account for the evidence that attitudes and norms may not be as independent as envisaged by Fishbein and Ajzen (1975). From this perspective, there is no reason to believe that the constructs should be independent (see also Hovland et al., 1953). Attitudes can be personal and idiosyncratic and unrelated to norms, but they can also be widely shared and normative. These shared normative attitudes are tied to specific group memberships and are part of the group prototype. Having categorized and defined themselves as members of a distinct social category, people form the context-specific stereotypic norms of the group, and these norms are internalized as their attitudes towards an issue. Thus, a social identity/self-categorization perspective would predict that psychological group membership should influence attitudes. Furthermore, this perspective would be in line with the contingent consistency hypothesis, which, as described earlier, predicts that people are more likely to behave in accordance with their attitudes if the normative climate supports the attitude – exposure to an attitudinally congruent group norm should strengthen attitude – behavior consistency because it validates the attitudinally congruent behavior as appropriate for group members. We would go further and suggest that not only must the normative climate support the attitude, but that the group membership that defines the norm should be a salient basis for self-conception. When the identity is salient, conformity to ingroup norms is likely to be enhanced because of the expectation of agreement with fellow ingroup members (Hogg and Abrams, 1988).

In our recent field research, we found that, in accord with predictions derived from social identity/self-categorization theories, the perceived norms of a specific and behaviorally relevant reference group were related to students' intentions to engage in health behaviors (regular exercise and sun-protective behavior), but only for students who identified strongly with the group (Terry and Hogg, 1996). This pattern of results was replicated in a study of recycling intentions and actions among community residents (Terry, Hogg, and White, in press). Also consistent with social identity theory was the finding that the relationship between perceived behavioral control and both intention to engage in regular exercise (Terry and Hogg, 1996) and intention to engage in household recycling (Terry, Hogg, and White, in press) was stronger for participants who did not identify strongly with the reference group than for the high identifiers. From a social identity/self-categorization perspective, the extent to which participants perceive that they are able to perform the behavior at ease – perceived behavioral control, a personal characteristic of central relevance to behavioral choice (Ajzen, 1991; Bandura, 1996) – should be related to intention more strongly for low group identifiers than for the high identifiers.

Although providing some support for the proposed reconceptualization of norms in attitude–behavior relations, Terry and Hogg (1996) failed to support the prediction derived from the contingent consistency hypothesis, namely that, for high identifiers, attitudes would be more likely to influence behavioral intentions when supported by a congruent ingroup norm rather than an incongruent norm. The notion that, as a consequence of group identification, behavior is defined in terms of the group prototype is central to the self-categorization perspective on social influence – thus it follows that attitude–behavior consistency should be most marked for high identifiers whose attitude is congruent with the group norm. In a field study, the opportunity to observe contingent consistency effects might be limited, because as a consequence of the process of referent informational influence (where the stereotypic norms of a salient ingroup are internalized as the person's own attitudes), the norms of a salient reference group are unlikely to be attitudinally incongruent. Thus, experimental research – where the attitudinal congruence of the ingroup norm can be experimentally manipulated – may be a stronger test of the proposed reconceptualization of the role of norms in attitude–behavior relations.

In the remainder of our discussion on the role of ingroup norms in attitude–behavior consistency, we describe the results of a number of experiments designed to examine – in a more controlled setting – the effects of group norms and salience of the group membership on attitude–behavior consistency. In addition to providing a further examination of the role of ingroup norms in attitude–behavior relations, these studies have been concerned explicitly with the interplay between the effects of socionormative and sociocognitive factors on attitude–behavior consistency. First, we describe the results of a number of experiments designed to examine the effects of group norms, salience of the group membership, and attitude accessibility on attitude–behavior consistency. Second, we consider the effects of group norms and group salience as a function of the mode of behavioral decision-making.

Group norms, group salience, and attitude accessibility

In addition to the field research reported above, we have conducted a number of experiments designed to examine the effects of ingroup norms and salience of group membership on attitude–behavior relations. From a social identity/self-categorization theory perspective, the central prediction tested in this research was that attitude–behavior consistency would be enhanced when people were exposed to an ingroup norm that was attitudinally congruent, but only if the group membership was a salient basis for self-conception. Group norms should have no impact on attitude–behavior consistency if the group membership is not a salient basis for self-conception. On the basis that high levels of group identification indicate that the group membership is likely to be – in an enduring sense at least – a salient basis for self-conception, measures of identification can be used to examine the moderating influence of group salience on the relationship between ingroup norms and attitude–behavior consistency. However, a stronger test of this moderating influence is to manipulate group salience experimentally, such that the group is an important and salient basis for self-conception for some participants, but only a latent category, and hence not a basis for self-definition, for others.

To examine the interplay between social identity and social cognitive variables in attitude–behavior relations, we also focused on the role of attitude accessibility. According to Fazio and colleagues (e.g., Fazio, 1986, 1989; Fazio et al., 1983), the extent of attitude–behavior consistency is determined primarily by the cognitive accessibility of the attitude or, in other words, the salience of the attitude in memory. Highly accessible attitudes are proposed to guide subsequent behavior through the mediating process of selective perception (Fazio, 1986; see also Jamieson and Zanna, 1989), which means that the perception of the attitude object is influenced by the activated attitude and, in turn, means that the behavioral response is attitudinally congruent.

There is evidence that attitude accessibility can be experimentally manipulated by asking participants to express repeatedly the relevant attitude (e.g., Downing, Judd, and Brauer, 1992; Powell and Fazio, 1984). Fazio (1986) has also argued that some attitudes are more chronically accessible than others – for instance, when attitudes are formed on the basis of direct experience with the attitude object or when people are confident in their attitude. Typically, attitude accessibility is assessed in terms of response latencies to attitudinal questions – the faster people give their response, the more accessible the attitude (e.g., Downing et al., 1992; Fazio, 1990a). In a large body of research, Fazio and colleagues have demonstrated that the more accessible the attitude is, the greater the like- lihood that it will influence behavior (e.g., Fazio, Powell, and Williams, 1989; Fazio and Williams, 1986; Houston and Fazio, 1989; see also Bassili, 1995) – this evidence has been obtained, irrespective of whether attitude accessibility is experimentally manipulated or whether an attitude is assessed as being chronic- ally more accessible.

When considering the mechanism that might account for the impact of group norms, it is possible that by making group norms salient, the relevant attitudes may also become cognitively accessible and, in this way, may influence attitude– behavior consistency (White, Hogg, and Terry, 1998). However, from a social identity/self-categorization approach, the process of activating a group prototype should go beyond simply making the relevant attitude accessible. The process makes an attitude normative, which should provide it with the prescriptive power to be reflected in action. This is because people's need for both positive self-evaluation (self-esteem) and the reduction of uncertainty (see Hogg, 1996) means that there is a strong motivational basis to behave consistently with a group prototype. Moreover, even if an attitude is made accessible, it is a relat- ively disembodied construct. A group prototype is a broader construct that embodies how one should behave as well as how one should think – it can be thought of as a networked schema with associated nodes representing the feel- ings, thoughts, and actions of a typical group member. Combined with the motivational pressures to bring behavior in line with the group prototype, the activation of this cognitive structure is likely to have a marked impact on attitude–behavior consistency because it provides detailed information on the typical characteristics of group members. Thus, it was expected that: (1) both attitude accessibility and ingroup norms would influence attitude–behavior con- sistency, and (2) the effects of attitude accessibility on attitude–behavior relations would be independent of the effects due to ingroup norms. In other words, it was proposed that the effects of ingroup normative support on attitude–behavior consistency should not be a result of simply making an attitude more cognitively accessible.

The first experiment (White, Hogg, and Terry, 1998, Experiment 1) focused on students' attitudes towards comprehensive exams. In this experiment, ingroup salience (low vs. high) and the attitudinal congruency of the ingroup norms (congruent vs. incongruent) were manipulated. Attitude accessibility was assessed in terms of attitude confidence. To manipulate ingroup salience, parti- cipants ($N=160$) were either asked to describe themselves as an individual person and to list attributes that made them unique as an individual (low salience), or to describe themselves as a University of Queensland (UQ) student and to list their similarities with other such students (high salience; see Hogg and Hardie, 1991). Participants were then exposed to bargraphs showing the percentage of opposi- tion to three issues (including the target issue) from students at UQ (ingroup) and from students at a rival university (outgroup). The graphs indicated either that the ingroup was strongly opposed to comprehensive exams and the rival campus supported them, or vice versa. To analyze the data, participants were categorized as having received either attitude-congruent ingroup support (if their attitudes and the normative information concurred) or attitude-incongruent normative support.

There were three behavioral measures – willingness to engage in behaviors in accord with initial attitude (e.g., participate or not participate in an on-campus rally opposing comprehensive university exams), willingness to sign a relevant petition, and whether or not a form letter against comprehensive exams was signed (responses to both the latter measures were coded in terms of whether they were attitude-congruent or attitude-incongruent). As expected, participants exposed to an attitudinally congruent rather than an incongruent ingroup norm behaved more consistently with their initial attitude on both the letter-signing and petition-signing measures of behavior; however, contrary to predictions, these effects did not vary as a function of ingroup salience. There was also evidence that on the measure of willingness or not to sign the petition, attitude confidence was associated positively with attitude–behavior correspondence – as expected, this effect was independent of, and weaker than, the effect due to norm congruency.

A second experiment was conducted in which attitude accessibility was manipulated and the salience manipulation was strengthened (see White, Hogg, and Terry, 1998, Experiment 2). The target issue was "separate bicycle lanes on roads," which was linked to gender identity. Under conditions of high or low gender salience, participants (N=167) were exposed to attitude-congruent or attitude-incongruent ingroup normative support (contrasted with an opposing outgroup norm). Attitude accessibility was manipulated using the repeated expression method. Three of the behavioral measures were essentially intention measures – participants indicated their willingness to engage in attitudinally congruent behaviors (e.g., whether or not to attend a seminar organized by a group supporting separate bicycle lanes), and their willingness to donate both money and time in order to implement a local student union scheme to introduce a trial system of separate bicycle lanes around campus and the surrounding residential areas. Two other measures constituted more behavioral responses. Participants responded to a ballot ostensibly conducted by the state government concerning a proposal to have separate bicycle lanes – they were also asked whether, if approached by a relevant organization, they would be prepared to sign a petition supporting separate bicycle lanes. As in Experiment 1, all responses to the behavioral measures were recoded in terms of whether the response was attitudinally congruent.

As shown in figure 12.1, there was evidence that, as expected, participants exposed to norm-congruent information were more likely to engage in attitudinally congruent behavior (in relation to willingness to donate time) under conditions of high rather than low group salience. When exposed to norm-incongruent information, there was a tendency for attitude–behavior consistency to be most

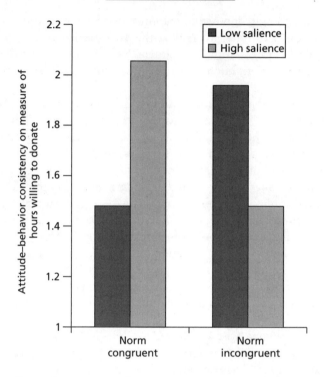

Figure 12.1   Effects of norm congruency and salience on attitude–behavior consistency on measure of hours willing to donate to a committee.

marked when the group membership was not made salient, which is consistent with the prediction that ingroup normative information has the least impact on attitude–behavior consistency when the group membership is not a salient basis for self-conception. On both the binary behavioral measures (the state transport ballot and willingness to sign a petition), there was evidence that participants were more likely to behave in accordance with their initial attitudes when: (1) they received ingroup normative support, and (2) when they were in the high attitude accessibility condition. Once again, the effects of attitude accessibility were weaker than those observed for norm congruency.

Although providing some support for the predicted effects of ingroup norms, the first two studies were limited in that an attitudinally incongruent ingroup norm was always accompanied by an attitudinally incongruent outgroup norm. Thus, it was unclear whether the effects of ingroup norms were a consequence of the fact that an explicit intergroup contrast was drawn between ingroup norms and the norms of a relevant outgroup. To examine this possibility, an additional experiment (White, Terry, and Hogg, 1998) was conducted in which ingroup norm congruency (congruent vs. incongruent) and outgroup norm congruency (congruent vs. incongruent) were independently manipulated. Ingroup salience was held constant at high levels, and attitude accessibility was measured in terms of attitude confidence. As in the previous studies, attitude accessibility was associated with stronger attitude–behavior consistency. Independent of the influence of attitude accessibility, information about ingroup norms (rather than outgroup norms) was sufficient to improve attitude–behavior consistency. These results provide further evidence that ingroups exert more influence than outgroups (see Wilder, 1990), and they also question the necessity of contrasting outgroup information for ingroup norms to influence attitude–behavior consistency. There may be a similarity between the effects of ingroup norms on attitude–behavior consistency and group polarization (e.g., Turner, 1985; Wetherell, 1987) where there does not appear to be a need to have an explicit outgroup for ingroup polarization to occur (see Hogg and Abrams, 1988).

Taken together, the results of the experiments discussed above provide strong support for the expectation that participants would be more likely to engage in attitudinally congruent behavior when they received normative support for their original attitude from a relevant reference ingroup. In the second experiment, where the manipulation of group salience was more successful than in the first experiment, we also found some evidence that, as expected, the effect of ingroup normative support was stronger under high than low group salience conditions. In both experiments, there was support for Fazio's (1986) prediction that greater attitude accessibility is associated with stronger attitude–behavior consistency. The fact that in all studies accessibility did not interact with group salience or normative support accords with the expectation that social identity and cognitive accessibility processes have independent effects on attitude–behavior consistency. People do appear to behave in accordance with their attitudes if those attitudes are cognitively accessible, but quite independently they also bring their behavior in line with their attitudes (whether they are accessible or not) when there is normative support for their attitudes from a contextually salient ingroup.

Future research needs to explore in more depth the cognitive mechanisms that underpin the effects of ingroup norms on attitude–behavior consistency. According to the process of referent informational influence, the contextual priming of a social identity makes the group prototype cognitively available, which is then acted upon in order to satisfy people's need for positive self-evaluation as well as to reduce the uncertainty of the interpretation of a social situation. Thus, any social identity effects in the context of attitude–behavior consistency should be underpinned by a process of cognitive accessibility, as are, by definition, the more traditional attitude accessibility effects. Nevertheless, in the research reviewed above, the latter effects failed to account for, or to moderate, the effects of ingroup norms, which suggests that, at a cognitive level, group-related and personal feelings and attitudes are relatively independent constructs. This suggestion is broadly consistent with the distinction that social identity theorists make between personal and social identities, although the evidence of simultaneous effects of ingroup norms and attitude accessibility is contrary to this theoretical perspective. Future research needs to explore the link between the effects of ingroup norms and attitude accessibility in more depth, given that, when attitudes are group-defining, the processes may be less independent. Indeed, under these circumstances, it is possible that the effects of ingroup norms on attitude–behavior consistency will be partially mediated through changes to the cognitive accessibility of the group-defining attitude. Nevertheless, the relatively disembodied nature of the construct of attitude accessibility means that it will not entirely explain the effect of ingroup norms – even in the context of group-defining attitudes – because it fails to take into account the motivational basis for group behavior (Hogg, 1996; Tajfel and Turner, 1979).

Group norms, group salience, and mode of behavioral decision-making

In a second body of experimental research examining the effects of social identity and social cognitive factors on attitude–behavior consistency, we manipulated – in addition to the attitudinal congruence of the ingroup norm – the mode of behavioral decision-making. In a similar vein to dual-process models of attitude change (i.e., elaboration likelihood model, Petty and Cacioppo, 1986, and heuristic-systematic model, Chaiken, Liberman, and Eagly, 1989), Fazio (1990b) distinguished two different processes through which attitudes can influence behavior – a spontaneous, theory-driven process and a deliberative, data-driven process. In this MODE model (Motivation and Oopportunity as DEterminants of mode of behavioral decision-making), Fazio hypothesized that under conditions that favor peripheral route processing of persuasive messages (i.e., low motivation and low ability; see Petty and Cacioppo, 1986), links between attitudes and behavior arise as a consequence of spontaneous processing rather than as a consequence of deliberative or reasoned processing. Specifically, when participants are making behavioral decisions via the spontaneous route, attitudes – to the extent to which they are cognitively accessible – guide behavior through the mediating process of selective perception of the situation (Fazio, 1990b; see also Jamieson and Zanna, 1989). Under deliberative processing, behavioral decisions are made in accord with the mechanism that underpins the theories of reasoned action and planned behavior – namely, as a consequence of effortful consideration of the available information, including the consequences of performing the behavior, the perceived expectations of others, and perceptions of behavioral control. Previous research has provided some support for the general predictions of the MODE model (Sanbonmatsu and Fazio, 1990; Schuette and Fazio, 1995).

Although Fazio (1990b) acknowledged that norms may influence behavioral decision-making under spontaneous processing, systematic consideration of a number of different factors – including norms – in the formation of a behavioral decision is restricted to the realm of deliberative processing. Thus, according to the MODE model, the effects of norms should be more marked under deliberative than spontaneous behavioral decision-making. In contrast, on the basis of social identity/self-categorization theory, we would predict that, irrespective of mode of behavioral decision-making, ingroup norms should influence attitude–behavior consistency. Under both processing routes, assimilation of self to the group prototype means that group norms become a central and important guide to behavioral responses. However, because people for whom the group membership is a salient basis for self-conception are motivated to consider self-relevant group norms carefully (see Mackie, Worth, and Asuncion, 1990; also Forgas and Fiedler, 1996), the effect of norms under deliberative decision-making conditions should be most marked for participants for whom the group membership is highly salient or self-relevant. When the group membership is only a latent category, the effect of the normative information should be relatively weak, because the opportunity to make the behavioral decision systematically means that the normative information is likely to be rejected because of the low personal relevance of the group membership. Thus, we anticipated that the moderating impact of group salience (or group identification) on the effects of ingroup norms would be most marked under conditions of deliberative decision-making.

To examine the effects of manipulations of ingroup norms, group salience, and mode of behavioral decision-making on attitude–behavior consistency, we used a mock jury paradigm (Terry, Hogg, and McKimmie, 1998, Experiment 2), a paradigm that has been widely employed in a range of different areas of social psychology (e.g., Davis, 1986; Davis, Stasson, Ono, and Zimmerman, 1988; Kaplan and Miller, 1978; MacCoun and Kerr, 1988; Stasser and Davis, 1977). Student participants were divided into jury groups under high or low group salience conditions, indicated their initial attitudes to a number of crimes – including the focal crime of computer hacking – and were exposed to ingroup normative information, which was congruent or incongruent with their initial attitude. They then read case notes relating to an alleged occurrence of computer hacking, and they were required to make individual decisions about guilt and punishment (behavior) under restricted or liberal time constraints (manipulation of spontaneous vs. deliberate mode of behavioral decision-making). The principal dependent variable was the extent of attitude–behavior *in*consistency.

On the absolute measure of attitude–behavior inconsistency, there was a significant main effect for norm congruency. As predicted, individuals in the norm-incongruent condition displayed greater attitude–behavior inconsistency than participants in the norm-congruent condition. Further analyses revealed that in the norm-incongruent condition, attitude–behavior inconsistency, for the most part, reflected movement towards the pole represented by the group norm – of the participants whose behavioral recommendation was inconsistent with their initial attitude, 80 percent moved in the direction of the group norm. To assess the relative importance of norms and attitudes in the prediction of the behavioral recommendation, multiple regression analyses were conducted with behavior as the criterion. Participants' perceived level of appropriate punishment and perceived ingroup norm were predictors. Analyses were performed separately for high-and low-salience participants; however, because there were no effects of mode of decision-making in the previous analyses, participants in the

Table 12.1 The prediction of behavior from attitudes and norms for high and low group salience participants

	Group salience	
	High (n = 105)	Low (n = 97)
Variable	β	β
Attitude	.38**	.39**
Norm	.28**	.19
	R² = .23**	R² = .18**

*p < .01, **p < .001

two conditions were considered together. In line with the theoretical basis for this research, norms were predictive of behavior only when group membership was highly salient (see table 12.1).

Because there was evidence that the manipulation of group salience did not have a strong effect on perceived identification with the group, a second set of analyses was performed where identification (rather than the manipulated salience variable) was used as an independent variable. These analyses revealed that for participants who did not identify strongly with the group (i.e., it was not a

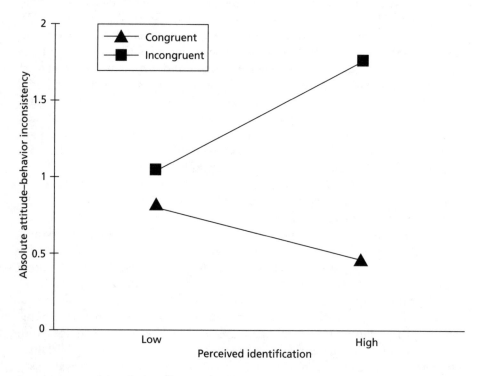

Figure 12.2 Perceived identification by norm congruency interaction on absolute attitude–behavior inconsistency.

salient basis for self-definition), norm congruency did not have a significant effect on attitude–behavior inconsistency (see figure 12.2). In contrast, participants who identified strongly with the group were influenced by the group norm. Those who received an incongruent group norm displayed greater attitude–behavior inconsistency compared to those who received a congruent norm. Among the norm-incongruent participants, there was evidence that movement towards the group norm was greatest for the high identifiers. Furthermore, norms were predictive of behavior only when individuals strongly identified with the group.

In support of the central hypothesis, the extent of attitude–behavior consistency was influenced by the attitudinal congruence of normative information. On the measure of attitude–behavior inconsistency, there was evidence that an incongruent group norm induced greater behavioral deviance from a previously expressed attitude than exposure to a congruent group norm; moreover, further analyses revealed that the attitude–behavior consistency in the norm-incongruent condition, for the most part, reflected movement towards the pole represented by the group norm. As expected, there was also some evidence that the influence of norms on the behavioral recommendation tended to be greatest when the group was a salient basis for self-definition – particularly when assessed in terms of strength of group identification. However, there was no evidence that the latter effects were most marked under deliberative decision-making conditions, a pattern of results that was also evident in a preliminary experimental study that manipulated the attitudinal congruency of ingroup norms and mode of behavioral decision-making (Terry, Hogg, and McKimmie, 1998, Experiment 1).

In a follow-up study, we varied mood to manipulate mode of behavioral decision-making rather than using an ability-based manipulation of this variable (Wellen, Hogg, and Terry, 1998), given that there is consistent evidence that mood affects mode of processing – positive mood reliably engenders spontaneous processing, whereas neutral and negative moods appear to engender deliberative processing (see Forgas, 1989; Stroessner, Hamilton, and Mackie, 1992). The focal issue for the study was whether students thought that they should be responsible for picking up litter on campus. After indicating their attitude towards this issue and a number of other student-related issues, participants had the salience of their group membership raised or lowered using the self-description task described above, were placed in a positive or negative mood (using an excerpt from either a popular comedy series or a documentary), and were provided with ingroup normative information that was congruent or incongruent with their own attitude (the normative information was presented using statements ostensibly provided by other introductory psychology students in a previous study). Behavioral measures included whether participants picked up some litter in the courtyard where they were instructed to wait prior to the second part of the study, whether – in a survey ostensibly from the Students' Union – they indicated that they would volunteer time to a project aimed at reducing litter on campus, and their willingness to engage in three litter-related behaviors (e.g., becoming a member of an action group that meets to pick up litter on campus). The focal behavioral measures were embedded in a larger questionnaire that assessed willingness to engage in a range of different student-related behaviors. In all instances, scores on the behavioral measures were recoded to be consistent or inconsistent with participants' initial attitudes.

In accord with the results of the previous experiment, there was a significant main effect of norm congruency on volunteering behavior. Overall, there was a tendency for greater attitude–behavior consistency in the norm-congruent than the norm-incongruent condition; however, this effect was qualified by a significant salience by mood by norm-congruency interaction. As expected, the effect of norm congruency was moderated by salience among the neutral mood but not the positive mood participants. For participants in the neutral mood, who had presumably engaged in deliberative processing, there was evidence that exposure to attitudinally inconsistent normative information decreased attitude–behavior consistency more for high-salience than for low-salience participants (see figure 12.3). In fact, there was also a tendency for low-salience participants in a neutral mood to show increased attitude–behavior consistency when they were provided with norm-incongruent information, possibly as a consequence of a motivation to psychologically distance themselves from a relatively unimportant group of people holding contrasting attitudes.

Additional analyses revealed a similar pattern of results when a measure of enduring identification with the group membership was used in the prediction of willingness to engage in litter-related behaviors. There was a significant identification by norm-congruency interaction in the neutral mood condition, but not in the positive mood condition. The pattern of means for high and low identifiers was similar to the means for the high-and low-salience participants shown in figure 12.3; however, a significant difference emerged when individuals were exposed to norm-congruent rather than norm-incongruent information. As expected, attitude–behavior consistency was stronger for the high identifiers who processed attitudinally congruent normative information in a neutral mood than for the low identifiers in the comparable condition.

The results of the research on the effects of ingroup norms, group salience, and mode of behavioral decision-making not only further support the proposed role of normative factors in the prediction of attitude–behavior consistency, they also provide some insight into the interplay between social identity and sociocognitive factors in this context. Contrary to Fazio's (1990b) MODE model, the results indicated that, irrespective of the cognitive conditions under which a behavioral decision is made, ingroup norms impact on attitude–behavior consistency. Nevertheless, in the second study (Wellen et al., in press), there was some evidence that, when the behavioral decision was made under deliberative conditions, normative information had the most impact on those participants for

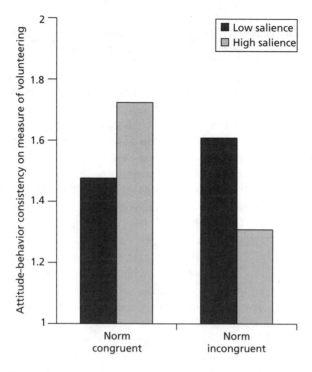

Figure 12.3   Effects of norm congruency and salience for neutral-mood participants on attitude–behavior consistency on measure of volunteering for anti-litter project.

whom the group membership was personally relevant (i.e., it was contextually salient), presumably because people are likely to accept ingroup normative information when the group from which it emanates is highly self-relevant. The converse pattern of results for the low-salience participants supports the view that, when provided with the opportunity to process the normative information systematically, such people are likely to disregard the normative information and may, in fact, be motivated to psychologically distance themselves from the group by behaving in a way that is contrary to the group norm. When participants were in a positive mood – and presumably processing the information in a spontaneous manner – there was no differential impact of the normative information as a function of group salience. Presumably, in the face of barriers to systematic processing of information, both low-and high-salience participants accept the normative information in a heuristic manner (cf. Forgas and Fiedler, 1996). Future research needs to determine whether the evidence of a moderating effect of group salience under deliberative but not spontaneous processing is specific to mood manipulations of processing mode, or whether it generalizes to other manipulations designed to engender different modes of processing.

Socionormative Influences and Perceptions of the Impact of
Persuasive Communications

In addition to the potential direct effects of persuasive messages on attitudes and behavior, people's beliefs about the impact of persuasive messages may also have a significant indirect effect. According to Davison (1983), people expect the media, and persuasive communications in general, to have a greater effect on others than on themselves (viz. the *third-person effect*) – in general, people overestimate persuasive impact on others and underestimate persuasive impact on themselves, and they act on the basis of these (distorted) perceptions. In particular, attitudinal and behavioral change may result from the belief that the opinions of others have been influenced.

In keeping with our work on attitude–behavior consistency, we argue that perceptions of the impact of persuasive messages on self and others cannot be well understood without reference to the wider social context of group member-ships. We propose that these perceptions are dependent upon salient social identities – that perceived self–other differences in media influence are affected by the social psychological relationships between self and others within varying social contexts and reflect ingroup norms regarding the acknowledgment of influence. Specifically, we emphasize an "us"–"them" or group-based distinction in perceptions of persuasive influence – a distinction that was implicit in Davi-son's (1983) original formulation of the third-person effect, but one that has been underplayed in more individualistic accounts of the phenomenon.

Evidence indicating that people perceive persuasive communications to have a greater impact on the beliefs, attitudes, and behavior of other people than on themselves comes from a range of contexts including media reports about apart-heid, news broadcasts of Middle East conflict, political advertising, defamatory newspaper articles, dramatic television series with political overtones, and prod-uct and public service advertisements (e.g., Cohen, Mutz, Price, and Gunther, 1988; Gunther, 1991; Gunther and Mundy, 1993; Gunther and Thorson, 1992; Lasorsa, 1989; Mutz, 1989; Perloff, 1989; Rucinski and Salmon, 1990; also see Perloff, 1993, for a review). There is also some evidence to show that people act on the basis of third-person perceptions. For instance, Gunther (1995) found not only that a substantial majority of American adults see others as more adversely influenced by media pornography than themselves, but also that their support for pornography restrictions parallels the discrepancy they perceive between effect on self and effect on others. In a different approach, Mutz (1989) demon-strated a link between third-person perceptions and willingness to speak out on controversial issues. She argued that people perceive that the media are biased against their point of view (i.e., *hostile media bias*, Giner-Sorolla and Chaiken, 1994; Perloff, 1989; Vallone, Ross, and Lepper, 1985): they assume that others will be influenced by "biased" coverage, and hence that public opinion is against them. Accordingly, people are reluctant to express their own view for fear of isolation (*spiral of silence*, Noelle-Neumann, 1974, 1984).

Theoretical accounts have described the third-person effect as a systematic perceptual bias or judgmental contrast arising from a combination of motivational and cognitive factors at the individual level. For instance, Perloff (1993, p. 178) concluded that the third-person effect may reflect the operation of media schemas (e.g., about the power of vivid messages, Collins, Taylor, Wood, and Thompson, 1988; and about the gullibility of the mass audience, Smith, 1986), inaccessibility of knowledge about media effects on the self (Nisbett and Wilson, 1977), and a need to assume that the self is unaffected by communications in order to preserve self-esteem or control over the social environment (cf. Weinstein, 1980). Consistent with these accounts, research suggests that factors such as personal involvement in the issue, perceived source bias and negative message content magnify third-person effects. Indeed, the evidence shows not only that third-person effects are more pronounced with respect to negative media content (e.g., violence, pornography, defamatory news articles, and product commercials) than with respect to positive media content (e.g., public service advertisements for health and safety issues; see Duck and Mullin, 1995; Gunther and Mundy, 1993; Gunther and Thorson, 1992; Innes and Zeitz, 1988), but also that the third-person effect can be eliminated, or even reversed, when the intended influence is perceived as desirable, intelligent, or beneficial. For instance, in research on the perceived impact of AIDS/HIV advertising (Duck, Terry, and Hogg, 1995), we found that respondents perceived themselves as less vulnerable than others to low-quality AIDS advertisements, but as *more* influenced than others by high-quality AIDS advertisements. Similarly, in a study on the perceived effects of commercial TV advertisements, we found that respondents perceived themselves as less influenced than others by the least-liked product ads, but as *more* influenced than others by the most-liked product ads (Duck, Hogg, and Terry, 1998). Our interpretation is that third-person perceptions reflect the motivation to deny personal persuasibility in contexts where message influence is perceived to produce negative rather than positive outcomes – the typical mass media scenario.

Another factor that is known to influence the magnitude of third-person effects is the nature of the comparison other. Most third-person research has focused on comparisons between people's judgments of media impact on self and on a single and generalized comparison other (e.g., "voters in general," Davison, 1983; "other viewers," Lasorsa, 1989; "most Americans," Rucinski and Salmon, 1990; "other people in general," Gunther, 1995). However, evidence suggests that perceived effects on others are magnified as the definition of others becomes progressively more broad or socially distant (e.g., "other Stanford students," "other Californians," "the public at large," see Cohen et al., 1988; Gibbon and Durkin, 1995; Gunther, 1991). In our own research (Duck and Mullin, 1995), we systematically varied the nature of the comparison other along two independent dimensions – vagueness and closeness. Our results indicated a pronounced third-person effect when the comparison other was both vague and distant (i.e., the average person), but no significant self–other difference when the comparison other was both specific and close (i.e., the respondent's closest friend). Theoretically it is possible to argue that vague others facilitate downward comparisons with a stereotyped image of a vulnerable or gullible person (e.g., the undiscerning "couch potato"), whereas specific others do not (Perloff and Fetzer, 1986), or that motivated self-serving biases include close friends and relatives as an extension of self (cf. Burger, 1981; Schlenker and Miller, 1977). Of more theoretical interest to us is the possibility that group processes, rather than interpersonal processes (e.g., acquaintanceship), underlie perceived self–other differences in the effects of persuasive communications.

In his original formulation of the third-person effect, Davison (1983, p. 3) argued that people believe persuasive communications will exert their greatest impact "not on 'me' or on 'you', but on 'them' – the third-persons." In doing so, he drew an implicit distinction between perceptions of media influence on first and second persons ("me" and "you" or "us") and third persons ("them"). Indeed, Davison explicitly acknowledged the role of reference groups in explaining third-person perceptions. He reasoned that people may overestimate media impact on some sections of the audience, but not on others – in particular, there might be little exaggeration of the perceived impact of a communication on members of a group that constitutes a normative reference group for the perceiver. Despite Davison's emphasis on the social psychological basis of the phenomenon, the possibility that the third-person effect reflects the nature of the social psychological relationship between self and other within varying social contexts has not been adequately explored, and has been the focus of our research. As with our work on attitude–behavior consistency, we drew on social identity theory and self-categorization theory for our theoretical framework.

Social identity/self-categorization theories and third-person perceptions

As noted earlier in this chapter, social identity/self-categorization theories recognize that an important component of the self-concept is derived from memberships in social groups and social categories. When people define and evaluate themselves in terms of a self-inclusive social category the joint processes of categorization and self-enhancement come into play. Categorization perceptually accentuates differences between ingroup and outgroup and similarities among ingroup members (including self) on stereotypical dimensions. People view themselves and others as group members rather than individuals – "I" becomes "we," and "me" vs. "you" becomes "us" vs. "them." Accordingly, group rather than individual norms prescribe the context-specific attitudes and behaviors appropriate for group members. Moreover, because the self is defined in terms of group membership, self-enhancement motives prompt the group member to seek behaviorally and perceptually to favor things ingroup over things outgroup. This process of "depersonalization" is responsive to contextual factors that influence the degree to which people identify themselves as group members rather than individuals (see Hogg, 1992). The stronger the social identification, the more pronounced the tendencies towards perceptions of similarity or equivalence between self and ingroup members (ingroup assimilation), and towards perceptions of difference between ingroup and outgroup members (intergroup contrast).

From a self-categorization perspective, we propose that third-person perceptions are sensitive to the categorization of self and other into relevant ingroup and outgroup categories, and reflect the accentuation of similarities within, and differences between, those categories. Take the typical case where a persuasive communication might be construed to have a negative impact (e.g., media violence, pornography, product advertising). To the extent that comparison others are judged as outgroup members ("them"), they will be contrasted to the perceiver's identity, evaluated negatively, and represented unfavorably – as relatively vulnerable to persuasive influence. In contrast, to the extent that comparison others are judged as ingroup members, they will be assimilated to the perceiver's identity ("us"), evaluated positively, and represented favorably, like the self – as relatively invulnerable to influence. Moreover, the tendency to categorize self and others as ingroup and outgroup members will depend on features of the social comparative context, and the extent of assimilation and contrast displayed will vary according to the perceiver's level of identification with the salient social category.

Further, we propose that perceived self–other differences in persuasibility depend not only on how we perceive others in terms of relevant group memberships (i.e., as ingroup or outgroup others), but also on the extent to which persuasibility in a given context is considered normative or desirable for the relevant ingroup. We reason that when it is socially or normatively acceptable to resist persuasion, people will see themselves and members of their ingroup as highly resistant and others as less so (a third-person effect). By contrast, when it is socially or normatively acceptable to acknowledge persuasive influence, people will see themselves and members of their ingroup as quite yielding and others as less so (a reverse third-person effect). Our proposal differs from theoretical accounts that discuss the moderating effects of outcome benefit at an individual level (e.g., "good for me" or "bad for me," Gunther and Mundy, 1993) and that focus on broad social desirability motivations (cf. Gunther and Thorson, 1992). We argue that, when social identity is salient, the social desirability of influence is defined in terms of salient group norms that prescribe the context-specific attitudes and behaviors appropriate for group members and, therefore, that perceived self–other differences in media influence reflect socionormative rather than individualistic, self-identity processes. From the perspective of referent informational influence, when social identity is salient, group members embody the norm or group prototype that optimally minimizes ingroup differences and maximizes intergroup differences.

To support our theoretical claims, we describe two studies that examined the salience of group membership and the effects of ingroup norms on the magnitude of the third-person effect. The first study is a naturalistic study conducted during the course of media campaigning for the Australian federal election in 1993. It explored the role of political identity in perceptions of media campaign impact. The second study explored the role of student identity in perceptions of the impact of AIDS/HIV advertising.

Group salience, group norms and third-person perceptions

Previous research in an election context (e.g., Davison, 1983; Rucinski and Salmon, 1990) has indicated that people perceive others as vulnerable voters, more influenced than themselves by media campaign content. Our study was designed to extend such work by focusing on political identity and the socio-normative basis of perceived self–other differences in campaign impact. Specifically, we examined the effects of political group membership on perceptions of campaign impact not only on self and on voters in general (a generalized comparison other), but also on political ingroup and political outgroup members.

In Australia voting is compulsory for Australian citizens 18 years or over. The political sphere is dominated by two major parties – the Australian Labor Party and the conservative, Liberal–National Coalition. Other political parties (e.g., the Australian Democrats) have a lower profile, with the bulk of media campaigning focusing on the relative merits of the two major parties and their policies. At the time of the 1993 election, the Labor Party was in government and the Liberal–National Coalition was in opposition. We sought to examine the perceptions of voters who identified with one of the two major parties and thus had a clearly defined political ingroup and political outgroup. Three days prior to the election, Australian university students who identified with the Labor Party or with the Liberal–National Coalition ($N = 54$) were surveyed regarding their perceptions of media campaign impact on self and on others (political ingroup members, political outgroup members, and voters in general). We examined their perceptions of the influence of two types of media campaign content – general campaign content (news reports, polls, political advertisements promoting party policies, and negative political advertisements attacking opposing candidates and their policies) and campaign content that explicitly favored the political ingroup or the political outgroup (e.g., political advertisements promoting the Labor Party).

In accordance with the notion of a third-person effect, we predicted that respondents would perceive political communications in general to have a greater influence on the voting decisions of other people than on the self. Further, in line with a socionormative perspective, we predicted that political ingroup members would be perceived, like the self, as less influenced than political outgroup members – particularly by those who identified strongly with their political ingroup. Compared with respondents who were low in political identification, we expected that those high in political identification would perceive less media influence on self and ingroup members, less difference between the level of media influence on self and on ingroup members, and more difference between the level of media influence on ingroup and outgroup members. These predictions follow from the assumption that the salience of social categorization increases perceived similarities between self and ingroup members ("us") and perceived differences between ingroup and outgroup members ("them") on dimensions relevant to the categorization, and that self-categories tend to be evaluated positively (i.e., as relatively uninfluenced). We also assumed that these perceptions might reflect, in part, a belief that media coverage of the election campaign was biased in favor of the "other" side (the hostile media phenomenon), but that these third-person perceptions would still exist after controls for the effects of perceived media bias and thus reflect an independent self-categorization dynamic.

Results indicated that respondents perceived others as more influenced by the election campaign than themselves, confirming a third-person effect in perceptions of persuasive impact. Consistent with our predictions, political ingroup members were also perceived as less influenced by campaign content than political outgroup members – that is, third-person perceptions were more pronounced with respect to the political outgroup. Compared with low identifiers, respondents who identified strongly with their preferred party (high identifiers) perceived self and political ingroup members as less influenced by campaign content and showed more evidence of positive intergroup differentiation – although, contrary to predictions, high identifiers also exaggerated self–ingroup differences. Strength of political identification made a unique contribution to prediction of third-person perceptions over and above that made by other measures of political involvement (e.g., general political interest, specific interest in the election campaign), and, although respondents perceived the media as biased against their preferred party, differences in perceived media impact according to strength of political identification were not eliminated by controls for this factor.

Further, we assumed that group-based perceptions of media influence would be more pronounced in contexts where respondents evaluated the impact of media campaign content that explicitly favored the political ingroup or the political outgroup. We reasoned that there would be strong normative pressure to reject outgroup-favoring messages and to accept ingroup-favoring messages – that is, that the norm for the acknowledgment of influence would vary with the type of campaign content. Accordingly, we predicted that respondents would perceive self and ingroup members as less influenced than outgroup members and voters in general by material favoring the political outgroup, but that self and ingroup members would be perceived as *more* influenced than outgroup members by material promoting the political ingroup.

As we predicted, results indicated that perceived similarities between self and ingroup members, and perceived differences between ingroup and outgroup members, were pronounced when respondents considered the effects of campaign material that explicitly favored one or other side. Indeed, perceived us–them distinctions in persuasive impact were most pronounced when respondents considered the impact of messages that favored the political outgroup – a context in which, theoretically, it would be particularly important for respondents to maximize intergroup differences in influence (see figure 12.4). Respondents believed that voters in general were swayed by persuasive political messages, irrespective of which party the message promoted; outgroup members were perceived to be influenced by material favoring their own party, but to be uninfluenced by material favoring the opposing party; and self and ingroup members were seen to be influenced by material favoring their own party, but to react against material favoring the opposing party – a pattern of responses that was significantly stronger for self than for members of the political ingroup. In addition, where campaign material supported the respondent's political ingroup, and influence could be construed as socially desirable, there was evidence that the self and ingroup were perceived as *more* influenced than outgroup members, although a self-serving, self–ingroup distinction was still maintained. We reasoned that the maintenance of a self–ingroup distinction, both here and with respect to the perceived impact of campaign content in general, is not

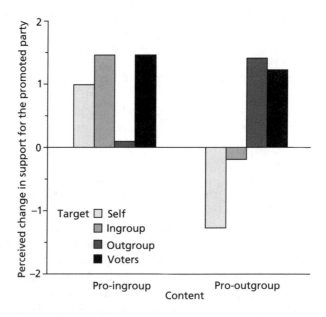

Figure 12.4 Perceived effect of pro-ingroup and pro-outgroup campaign content on support for the promoted party (for self, ingroup, outgroup, and voters in general; scale range: −4, *decreased support*; 0, *no change*; to +4, *increased support*).

incompatible with social identity theory. Rather, it might reflect the fact that political identification involves a broad and overinclusive social category that does not satisfy individual needs for distinctiveness (e.g., optimal distinctiveness theory, Brewer, 1991, 1993a, 1993b).

A second study in a different social context (Duck, Hogg, and Terry, in press) provided further evidence for our theoretical predictions. In this study we examined students' perceptions of the impact of AIDS/HIV advertisements not only on self and people in general (cf. Duck et al., 1995b), but also on students in general (ingroup others) and on nonstudents (outgroup others).

AIDS (acquired immune deficiency syndrome) is one of the most pressing current health problems and is an issue of particular relevance to university students. Research shows that students engage in sexual practices that lead to increased exposure to HIV infection (e.g., Crawford, Turtle, and Kippax, 1990; Rosenthal, Hall, and Moore, 1992; Struckman-Johnson, Gilliland, Struckman-Johnson, and North, 1990), and many of the HIV campaigns promoting safe sex have explicitly targeted people in this age bracket. The issues of AIDS and safe sex are frequently discussed in student newspapers, and student unions promote safe sex through the distribution of free condoms and information about AIDS/HIV during university orientation weeks. Accordingly, we reasoned that students who identified strongly with the student ingroup would perceive it as socially acceptable to acknowledge the impact of AIDS advertisements. However, given a general reluctance to admit personal persuasibility – especially to mass media messages – we reasoned that students who did not identify with the student community would perceive it as personally undesirable to acknowledge such influence. Thus, we proposed that the target issue of AIDS/HIV advertising presented an interesting scenario where identification with a relevant reference group might serve to reverse typical third-person perceptions.

Specifically, based on self-categorization theory, we predicted that judgments of media impact on self and on others would vary with the perceiver's level of identification with the student ingroup, that is, with the salience of student identity. We expected that respondents who did not identify strongly with the student ingroup would perceive self as less influenced than others (students, nonstudents, and people in general), whereas respondents who identified strongly with the student ingroup would perceive self and students (ingroup) as *more* influenced than nonstudents (outgroup). Compared with respondents who did not identify strongly with the student ingroup, we expected that students who identified strongly with the student ingroup would perceive more media influence on self and students (ingroup), less difference between the level of media influence on self and on students (ingroup members), and more difference between the level of media influence on students (ingroup) and nonstudents (outgroup). As in our election study, these predictions follow from the assumption that the salience of social categorization increases perceived similarities between self and ingroup members ("us") and perceived differences between ingroup and outgroup members ("them") on dimensions relevant to the categorization, and that self-categories tend to be evaluated positively (i.e., as relatively uninfluenced). We also reasoned that the effects of social identity would be clearest when there was a norm for acknowledgment of influence and, given wide variation in the quality and character of AIDS advertisements, that this norm would be stronger for some advertisements than for others. We predicted that our hypotheses would be supported more clearly when we focused on the perceived impact of a subset of AIDS advertisements which students identified as being good to be influenced by, and that this improvement in support for our predictions would be unique to this subset of advertisements and not hold for other subsets of advertisements judged as, say, the better or more informative advertisements.

To test these predictions, third year psychology students ($N = 58$) were asked to watch and evaluate 11 commercials produced by the Australian National Council on AIDS. In a later session, 40 participants from the original population were also asked to indicate the extent to which university students in general would think it is good to be influenced by each of the 11 ads. On the basis of their responses, a subset of five ads were classified as ads for which normative acceptance of influence was strongest.

As predicted, perceived self–other differences in impact varied with the salience of student identity (see figure 12.5). Respondents who did not identify

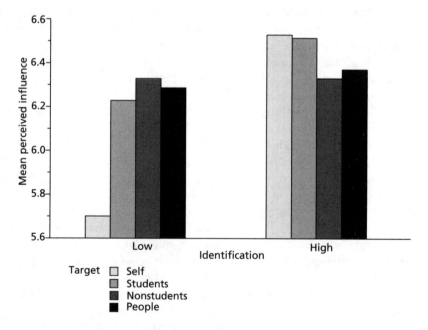

Figure 12.5 Perceived influence on self, students, nonstudents, and people in general of five AIDS commercials that students identified as being good to be influenced by (scale range: 1, *not influenced at all*, to 9, *extremely influenced*).

strongly with the student ingroups displayed the typical third-person effect, perceiving self as less influenced by AIDS advertising than others. Students who identified strongly with the student ingroup were more willing to acknowledge the impact of AIDS commercials on self and, to a lesser extent, on students in general. They differentiated less clearly between their perceptions of impact on self and students, and more clearly between their perceptions of impact on students and nonstudents, especially when considering the impact of a subset of advertisements for which influence was normatively acceptable. Moreover, in this context, they perceived self and students as somewhat *more* influenced than nonstudents – a distinction that was not apparent for subsets of ads classified as effective or emotional.

In summary, findings from these studies in two persuasive contexts – election campaigning and public service advertisements for AIDS/HIV – indicate that people's beliefs about the impact of persuasive communications on self and other are dependent upon salient group memberships. Our results suggest that when message content is related to the salient categorization, perceivers accentuate the similarities between self and ingroup others in terms of level of impact (an assimilation effect), and accentuate the differences between ingroup and outgroup others in terms of level of impact (a contrast effect), perceiving their ingroup as positively distinct from the outgroup. Further, they suggest that whether the ingroup is perceived as more or less influenced by persuasive content than the outgroup depends on group norms regarding the acknowledgment of influence – in contexts where it is normatively acceptable to deny persuasive impact, self and ingroup members are perceived as less persuaded than outgroup members (a third-person effect), but in contexts where it is normatively acceptable to acknowledge influence, self and ingroup are perceived as *more* influenced than outgroup members.

Thus, as in our work on attitude–behavior consistency, our research on third-person perceptions provides strong support for the role of group salience and group norms. It suggests that perceptions of media influence (and, presumably, behaviors based on these perceptions) cannot be understood without reference to the wider social context of group memberships. The next step for our research on the third-person effect is to examine the interplay between socionormative and sociocognitive mechanisms. What remains to be shown is how socionormative factors operate in conjunction with sociocognitive factors such as accessibility of knowledge about media effects on self and other, attributions for persuasive impact, and estimates of program or message content.

Conclusions

The research reviewed in this chapter provides support for the proposed role of norms in attitude–behavior relations along the lines suggested by social identity/

self-categorization theories. In accord with this theoretical perspective, the research also supports the expectation that perceptions of media influence on self and others are influenced by the social psychological relationships between self and others and by ingroup norms regarding the acknowledgment of influence. In sum, the research clearly supports the assertion that attitude–behavior consistency and perception of media influence cannot be understood without reference to social identity mechanisms. Whether people engage in attitudinally consistent behavior depends, in part, on whether there is ingroup normative support for their attitude. Moreover, perceptions of how much others will be influenced by persuasive communications is clearly dependent on the social psychological relationship between self and the target other.

In our discussion of attitude–behavior consistency, we showed that the socio-normative influences (i.e., ingroup norms) on the extent to which people behave in accordance with their attitudes are independent of the corresponding effects of attitude accessibility. Thus, social identity and social cognitive factors appear to impact on attitude–behavior consistency in an additive rather than an interactive manner, which suggests that group-related information (including group prototypical feelings and attitudes) and personal attitudes are separate cognitive constructs that can be primed simultaneously in the same context. In the present chapter, we also showed that, irrespective of the mode of behavioral decision-making, ingroup norms influence attitude–behavior consistency, a pattern of results that provides further evidence of the independent effects of social cognitive and social identity influences in attitude–behavior relations. Nevertheless, the suggestion that the moderating effects of group salience (on the relationship between ingroup norms and attitude–behavior consistency) may be dependent on mode of decision-making suggests a subtle interplay between social identity mechanisms and the conditions under which information is processed that should be explored in more depth in future research.

In conclusion, the present results are important in that they reflect clear support for the view that attitude phenomena cannot be well understood without reference to the broader social context in which attitudes are formed, expressed, and validated. Such results should serve to maintain an important and central role for social influence in attitude research along the lines suggested by social identity and self-categorization theories. The present results also help to elucidate the interplay between social identity and social cognitive mechanisms. In the context of attitude–behavior relations, they appear to be relatively independent of each other. Irrespective of both the cognitive conditions under which behavioral decisions are made and the cognitive accessibility of the individual attitude, ingroup norms influence attitude–behavior consistency. Thus, social identity effects in attitude research cannot be accounted for simply in terms of social cognitive processes; nevertheless, future research needs to take a more fine-grained look at the role that these two types of mechanisms play in accounting for attitude phenomena.

References

Abrams, D. and Hogg, M.A. (1990). Social identification, self-categorization, and social influence. *European Review of Social Psychology*, 1, 195–228.

Acock, A.C. and DeFleur, M.L. (1972). A configurational approach to contingent consistency in the attitude–behavior relationship. *American Sociological Review*, 37, 714–26.

Ajzen, I. (1987). Attitudes, traits, and actions: Dispositional prediction of behavior in personality and social psychology. In L. Berkowitz (ed.), *Advances in Experimental Social Psychology*, Vol. 20. New York: Academic Press, pp. 1–64.

Ajzen, I. (1991). The theory of planned behavior. *Organizational Behavior and Human Decision Processes*, 50, 179–211.

Andrews, K.H. and Kandel, D.B. (1979). Attitude and behavior: A specification of the contingent-consistency hypothesis. *American Sociological Review*, 44, 298–310.

Asch, S.E. (1952). *Social Psychology*. Englewood Cliffs, NJ: Prentice-Hall.

Bagozzi, R.P. and Schnedlitz, P. (1985). Social contingencies in the attitude model: A test of certain interaction hypotheses. *Social Psychology Quarterly*, 48, 366–73.

Bandura, A. (1996). *Social Foundations of Thought and Action: A social cognitive theory*. Englewood Cliffs, NJ: Prentice-Hall.

Bassili, J.N. (1995). Response latency and the accessibility of voting intentions: What contributes to accessibility and how it affects vote choice. *Personality and Social Psychology Bulletin*, 21, 686–95.

Brewer, M.B. (1991). The social self: On being the same and different at the same time. *Personality and Social Psychology Bulletin*, 17, 475–82.

Brewer, M.B. (1993a). Social identity, distinctiveness, and in-group homogeneity. *Social Cognition*, 11, 150–64.

Brewer, M.B. (1993b). The role of distinctiveness in social identity and group behaviour. In M. Hogg and D. Abrams (eds), *Group Motivation: Social psychological perspectives*. London: Harvester Wheatsheaf, pp. 1–16.

Burger, J.M. (1981). Motivational biases in the attribution of responsibility for an accident: A meta-analysis of the defensive-attribution hypothesis. *Psychological Bulletin*, 90, 496–512.

Chaiken, S., Liberman, A., and Eagly, A.H. (1989). Heuristic and systematic processing within and beyond the persuasion context. In J.S. Uleman and J.A. Bargh (eds), *Unintended Thought*. New York: Guilford, pp. 212–52.

Cohen, J., Mutz, D., Price, V., and Gunther, A. (1988). Perceived impact of defamation: An experiment on the third-person effects. *Public Opinion Quarterly*, 52, 161–73.

Collins, R.L., Taylor, S.E., Wood, J.V., and Thompson, S.C. (1988). The vividness effect: Elusive or illusory? *Journal of Experimental Social Psychology*, 24, 1–18.

Crawford, J., Turtle, A., and Kippax, S. (1990). Student-favoured strategies for AIDS avoidance. *Australian Journal of Psychology*, 42, 123–37.

Davis, J.H., Stasson, M.F., Ono, K., and Zimmerman, S. (1988). Effects of straw polls on group decision making: Sequential voting pattern, timing, and local majorities. *Journal of Personality and Social Psychology*, 55, 6, 918–26.

Davis, R.W. (1986). Pretrial publicity, the timing of the trial, and mock jurors' decision processes. *Journal of Applied Social Psychology*, 16, 7, 590–607.

Davison, W.P. (1983). The third-person effect in communication. *Public Opinion Quarterly*, 47, 1–15.

Deutsch, M. and Gerard, H.B. (1955). A study of normative and informational influences upon individual judgement. *Journal of Abnormal and Social Psychology*, 51, 629–36.

Downing, J.W., Judd, C.M., and Brauer, M. (1992). Effects of repeated expressions on attitude extremity. *Journal of Personality and Social Psychology*, 63, 17–29.

Duck, J.M., Hogg, M.A., and Terry, D.J. (1995a). Me, us and them: Political identification and the third-person effect in the 1993 Australian federal election. *European Journal of Social Psychology*, 25, 195–215.

Duck, J.M., Hogg, M.A., and Terry, D.J. (1998). Perceived self–other differences in persuasibility: The effects of interpersonal and group-based similarity. *European Journal of Social Psychology*, 28, 1–21.

Duck, J.M., Hogg, M.A., and Terry, D.J. (in press). Social identity and perceptions of media persuasion: Are we always less influenced than others? *Journal of Applied Social Psychology*.

Duck, J.M. and Mullin, B.-A. (1995). The perceived impact of the mass media: Reconsidering the third person effect. *European Journal of Social Psychology*, 25, 77–93.

Duck, J.M., Terry, D.J., and Hogg, M.A. (1995b). The perceived influence of AIDS advertising: Third-person effects in the context of positive media content. *Basic and Applied Social Psychology*, 17, 305–25.

Eagly, A.H. and Chaiken, S. (1993). *The Psychology of Attitudes*. Fort Worth, TX: Harcourt Brace Jovanovich.

Farley, J.U., Lehmann, D.R., and Ryan, M.J. (1981). Generalizing from "imperfect" replication. *Journal of Business*, 54, 597–610.

Fazio, R.H. (1986). How do attitudes guide behavior? In R.M. Sorrentino and E.T. Higgins (eds), *The Handbook of Motivation and Cognition: Foundations of social behavior*. New York: Guilford, pp. 204–43.

Fazio, R.H. (1989). On the power and functionality of attitudes: The role of attitude accessibility. In A.R. Pratkanis, S.J. Breckler, and A.G. Greenwald (eds), *Attitude Structure and Function*. Hillsdale, NJ: Lawrence Erlbaum Associates, pp. 153–79.

Fazio, R.H. (1990a). A practical guide to the use of response latency in social psychological research. In M.S. Clark (ed.), *Review of Personality and Social Psychology*, Vol. 11, *Research Methods in Personality and Social Psychology*. Newbury Park, CA: Sage, pp. 74–97.

Fazio, R.H. (1990b). Multiple processes by which attitudes guide behavior: The MODE model as an integrative framework. In M.P. Zanna (ed.), *Advances in Experimental Psychology*, Vol. 23. San Diego: Academic Press, pp. 75–109.

Fazio, R.H., Powell, M.C., and Herr, P.M. (1983). Toward a process model of the attitude–behavior relation: Accessing one's attitude upon mere observation of the attitude object. *Journal of Personality and Social Psychology*, 44, 723–35.

Fazio, R.H., Powell, M.C., and Williams, C.J. (1989). The role of attitude accessibility in the attitude-to-behavior process. *Journal of Consumer Research*, 16, 280–8.

Fazio, R.H. and Williams, C.J. (1986). Attitude accessibility as a moderator of the attitude–perception and attitude–behavior relations: An investigation of the 1984 presidential election. *Journal of Personality and Social Psychology*, 51, 505–14.

Fishbein, M. and Ajzen, I. (1975). *Belief, Attitude, Intention, and Behavior: An introduction to theory and research*. Reading, MA.: Addison-Wesley.

Forgas, J.P. (1989). Mood effects on decision making strategies. *Australian Journal of Psychology*, 41, 197–214.

Forgas, J.P. and Fiedler, K. (1996). Us and them: Mood effects on intergroup discrimination. *Journal of Personality and Social Psychology*, 70, 1, 28–40.

Gibbon, P. and Durkin, K. (1995). The third person effect: Social distance and perceived media bias. *European Journal of Social Psychology*, 25, 597–602.

Giner-Sorolla, R. and Chaiken, S. (1994). The causes of hostile media judgments. *Journal of Experimental Social Psychology*, 30, 165–80.

Grube, J.W. and Morgan, M. (1990). Attitude–social support interactions: Contingent consistency effects in the prediction of adolescent smoking, drinking, and drug use. *Social Psychology Quarterly*, 53, 329–39.

Grube, J.W., Morgan, M., and McGree, S.T. (1986). Attitudes and normative beliefs as predictors of smoking intentions and behaviours: A test of three models. *British Journal of Social Psychology*, 25, 81–93.

Gunther, A. (1991). What we think others think: Cause and consequence in the third-person effect. *Communication Research*, 18, 355–72.

Gunther, A. (1995). Overrating the X-rating: The third-person perception and support for censorship of pornography. *Journal of Communication*, 45, 27–38.

Gunther, A. and Mundy, P. (1993). Biased optimism and the third-person effect. *Journalism Quarterly*, 70, 58–67.

Gunther, A. and Thorson, E. (1992). Perceived persuasive effects of product commercials and public service announcements: Third-person effects in new domains. *Communication Research*, 19, 574–96.

Hogg, M.A. (1992). *The Social Psychology of Group Cohesiveness: From attraction to social identity*. London: Harvester Wheatsheaf.

Hogg, M.A. (1996). Intragroup processes, group structure and social identity. In W.P. Robinson (ed.), *Social Groups and Identities: Developing the legacy of Henri Tajfel*. Oxford: Butterworth-Heinemann, pp. 65–93.

Hogg, M.A. and Abrams, D. (1988). *Social Identifications: A social psychology of intergroup relations and group processes*. London: Routledge.

Hogg, M.A. and Hardie, E.A. (1991). Social attraction, personal attraction, and self-categorization: A field study. *Personality and Social Psychology Bulletin*, 17, 175–80.

Hogg, M.A. and Turner, J.C. (1987). Social identity and conformity: A theory of referent informational influence. In W. Doise and S. Moscovici (eds), *Current Issues in European Social Psychology*, Vol. 2. Cambridge: Cambridge University Press, pp. 139–82.

Houston, D.A. and Fazio, R.H. (1989). Biased processing as a function of attitude accessibility: Making objective judgments subjectively. *Social Cognition*, 7, 51–66.

Hovland, C.L. Janis, L., and Kelley, H.H. (1953). *Communication and Persuasion*. New Haven, CT: Yale University Press.

Innes, J.M. and Zeitz, H. (1988). The public's view of the impact of the mass media: A test of the "third person" effect. *European Journal of Social Psychology*, 18, 457–63.

Jamieson, D.W. and Zanna, M.P. (1989). Need for structure in attitude formation and persuasion. In A.R. Pratkanis, S.J. Breckler, and A.G. Greenwald (eds), *Attitude Structure and Function*. Hillsdale, NJ: Erlbaum, pp. 383–406.

Kaplan, M.F. and Miller, L.E. (1978). Reducing the effects of juror bias. *Journal of Personality and Social Psychology*, 36, 1443–55.

Kelley, H.H. (1952). Two functions of reference groups. In G.E. Swanson, T.M. New-comb, and E.L. Hartley (eds), *Readings in Social Psychology*, 2nd edn New York: Holt, Rinehart, and Winston, pp. 410–14.

Lasorsa, D.L. (1989). Real and perceived effects of "Amerika". *Journalism Quarterly*, 66, 373–8.

Liska, A. (1984). A critical examination of the causal structure of the Fishbein and Ajzen attitude–behavior model. *Social Psychology Quarterly*, 47, 61–74.

MacCoun, R.J. and Kerr, N.L. (1988). Asymmetric influence on mock jury deliberation: Jurors' bias for leniency. *Journal of Personality and Social Psychology*, 54, 21–33.

Mackie, D.M., Worth, L.T., and Asuncion, A.G. (1990). Processing of persuasive in-group messages. *Journal of Personality and Social Psychology*, 58, 812–22.

Miniard, P.W. and Cohen, J.B. (1981). An examination of the Fishbein–Ajzen behavioral-intentions model's concepts and measures. *Journal of Experimental Social Psychology*, 17, 309–39.

Mutz, D.C. (1989). The influence of perceptions of mass influence: Third person effects and the public expression of opinions. *International Journal of Public Opinion Research*, 1, 3–23.

Nisbett, R.E. and Wilson, T.D. (1977). Telling more than we can know: Verbal reports on mental processes. *Psychological Review*, 84, 231–59.

Noelle-Neumann, E. (1974). The spiral of silence: A theory of public opinion. *Journal of Communication*, 24, 43–51.

Noelle-Neumann, E. (1984). The spiral of silence: A response. In K.R. Sanders, L.L. Kaid, and E. Nimmo (eds), *Political Communication Yearbook 1984*. Carbondale, IL: Southern Illinois University Press, pp. 66–94.

Oliver, R.L. and Bearden, W.O. (1985). Crossover effects in the theory of reasoned action: A moderating influence attempt. *Journal of Consumer Research*, 12, 324–40.

Perloff, L.S. and Fetzer, B.K. (1986). Self–other judgements and perceived vulnerability to victimization. *Journal of Personality and Social Psychology*, 50, 502–10.

Perloff, R.M. (1989). Ego-involvement and the third person effect of televised news coverage. *Communication Research*, 16, 236–62.

Perloff, R.M. (1993). Third-person effect research 1983–1992: A review and synthesis. *International Journal of Public Opinion Research*, 5, 167–84.

Petty, R.E. and Cacioppo, J.T. (1986). The elaboration likelihood model of persuasion. *Advances in Experimental Social Psychology*, 19, 123–205.

Powell, M.C. and Fazio, R.H. (1984). Attitude accessibility as a function of repeated attitudinal expression. *Personality and Social Psychology Bulletin*, 10, 139–48.

Rosenthal, D.A., Hall, C., and Moore, S.M. (1992). AIDS, adolescents, and sexual risk taking: A test of the Health Belief Model. *Australian Psychologist*, 27, 166–71.

Rucinski, D. and Salmon, C.T. (1990). The "other" as the vulnerable voter: A study of the third-person effect in the 1988 U.S. presidential campaign. *International Journal of Public Opinion Research*, 2, 4, 345–68.

Ryan, M.J. (1978). An examination of the alternative form of the behavioral intention model's normative component. In H. Keith Hunt (ed.), *Advances in Consumer Research*, Vol. 5. Ann Arbor, MI: Association for Consumer Research, pp. 282–9.

Ryan, M.J. (1982). Behavioral intention formation: The interdependency of attitudinal and social influence variables. *Journal of Consumer Research*, 9, 263–78.

Sanbonmatsu, D.M. and Fazio, R.H. (1990). The role of attitudes in memory-based decision-making. *Journal of Personality and Social Psychology*, 59, 614–22.

Schlenker, B.R. and Miller, R.S. (1977). Egocentrism in groups: Self-serving bias or logical information processing? *Journal of Personality and Social Psychology*, 35, 755–64.

Schuette, R.A. and Fazio, R.H. (1995). Attitude accessibility and motivation as determinants of biased processing: A test of the MODE model. *Personality and Social Psychology*, 21, 704–10.

Smith, R. (1986). Television addiction. In J. Bryant and D. Zillman (eds), *Perspectives on Media Effects*. Hillsdale, NJ: Lawrence Erlbaum, pp. 109–28.

Stasser, G. and Davis, J.H. (1977). Opinion change during group discussion. *Personality and Social Psychology Bulletin*, 3, 252–6.

Stroessner, S.J., Hamilton, D.L., and Mackie, D.M. (1992). Affect and stereotyping: The effect of induced mood on distinctiveness-based illusory correlations. *Journal of Personality and Social Psychology*, 62, 564–76.

Struckman-Johnson, C.J., Gilliland, R.C., Struckman-Johnson, D.L., and North, T.C. (1990). The effects of fear of AIDS and gender on responses to fear-arousing condom advertisements. *Journal of Applied Social Psychology*, 20, 1396–1410.

Tajfel, H. and Turner, J.C. (1979). An integrative theory of intergroup conflict. In W.G. Austin and S. Worchel (eds), *The Social Psychology of Intergroup Relations*. Monterey, CA: Brooks-Cole, pp. 33–47.

Terry, D.J., Gallois, C., and McCamish, M. (1993). The theory of reasoned action and health behaviour. In D.J., Terry, C. Gallois, and M. McCamish (eds), *The Theory of Reasoned Action: Its application to AIDS-preventive behaviour*. Oxford: Pergamon, pp. 1–27.

Terry, D.J. and Hogg, M.A. (1996). Group norms and the attitude–behavior relationship. A role for group identification. *Personality and Social Psychology Bulletin*, 22, 776–93.

Terry, D.J., Hogg, M.A., and McKimmie, B.M. (1998). Group salience, norm congruency, and mode of behavioral decision-making: The effect of group norms on attitude–behavior relations. Manuscript submitted for publication.

Terry, D.J., Hogg, M.A., and White, K.M. (1998). The theory of planned behavior: Self-identity, social identity, and group norms. *British Journal of Social Psychology*.

Turner, J.C. (1982). Towards a cognitive redefinition of the social group. In H. Tajfel (ed.), *Social Identity and Intergroup Relations*. Cambridge: Cambridge University Press, pp. 15–40.

Turner, J.C. (1985). Social categorization and the self-concept: A social cognitive theory of group behavior. In E.J. Lawler (ed.), *Advances in Group Processes: Theory and research*, Vol. 2. Greenwich, CT: JAI Press, pp. 77–122.

Turner, J.C. (1991). *Social Influence*. Milton Keynes: Open University Press.

Turner, J.C., Hogg, M.A., Oakes, P.J., Reicher, S.D., and Wetherell, M.S. (1987). *Rediscovering the Social Group: A self-categorization theory*. Oxford and New York: Blackwell.

Vallerand, R.J., Deshaies, P., Cuerrier, J.-P., Pelletier, L.G., and Mongeau, C. (1992). Ajzen and Fishbein's theory of reasoned action as applied to moral behavior: A confirmatory analysis. *Journal of Personality and Social Psychology*, 62, 98–109.

Vallone, R.P., Ross, L., and Lepper, M.R. (1985). The hostile media phenomenon: Bias in the coverage of the Beirut massacre. *Journal of Personality and Social Psychology*, 49, 577–85.

Weinstein, N.D. (1980). Unrealistic optimism about future life events. *Journal of Personality and Social Psychology*, 39, 806–20.

Wellen, J.M., Hogg, M.A., and Terry, D.J. (1998). Group norms and attitude–behavior consistency: The role of group salience and mood. *Group Dynamics: Theory, Research, and Practice*, 1, 48–56.

Wetherell, M. (1987). Social identity and group polarisation. In J.C. Turner, M.A. Hogg, P.J. Oakes, S.D. Reicher, and M. Wetherell (eds), *Rediscovering the Social Group: A self-categorization theory*. Oxford: Blackwell, pp. 142–70.

White, K.M., Hogg, M.A., and Terry, D.J. (1998). Attitude–behavior relations: The role of ingroup norms and attitude accessibility. Manuscript submitted for publication.

White, K.M., Terry, D.J., and Hogg, M.A. (1998). The role of normative support in attitude–behavior correspondence and attitude change: Ingroup versus outgroup norms. Manuscript submitted for publication.

Wicker, A.W. (1969). Attitudes versus actions: The relationship of verbal and overt responses to attitude objects. *Journal of Social Issues*, 25, 41–78.

Wilder, D.A. (1990). Some determinants of the persuasive power of ingroups and outgroups: Organization of information and attribution of independence. *Journal of Personality and Social Psychology*, 59, 1202–13.

13

Social Identity and Persuasion: Reconsidering the Role of Group Membership

DAAN VAN KNIPPENBERG

It is impossible to go through life, or, for that matter, through a day, without being influenced by what others say and do. Not surprisingly, such influence processes have been of central concern to social psychology. Research into the cognitive processes underlying attitude change elicited by persuasive communication in particular has greatly enhanced our understanding of persuasion processes. Yet, cognitive theories of persuasion generally tend to neglect the social context in which persuasion typically takes place (cf. Eagly and Chaiken, 1993). Approaches to influence that are more sensitive to the interpersonal and group dynamics of influence processes, on the other hand, tend to be mute where the cognitive processes underlying persuasion are concerned. Hence, it would seem that the study of persuasion and social influence has much to gain by integrating social cognitive and group dynamical approaches to influence. The present chapter aims to contribute to this integration by introducing theoretical notions from the social identity approach to social influence into cognitive models of persuasion. Specifically, it will argue that theories of persuasion tend to downplay the role the source of information may play in determining both the extent and mode of information processing, and the subjective validity and persuasiveness of information and arguments presented in a persuasive message. First, however, the major cognitive models of persuasive communication and the social identity approach to social influence will be discussed.

The Social Cognition Perspective on Influence: The Processing of Persuasive Communication

Current research on persuasion is dominated by two roughly similar models, Chaiken's (1987; Chaiken, Liberman, and Eagly, 1989) heuristic–systematic model (HSM) and Petty and Cacioppo's (1986) elaboration likelihood model

(ELM). Both models distinguish an effortful processing mode from a relatively effortless mode of processing persuasive communication. The effortful systematic (HSM) or central (ELM) processing mode implies careful consideration and elaboration of the information and arguments presented in the persuasive message. Persuasion in the systematic processing mode is mediated by cognitive responses to the message (thoughts generated in response to the message): if the responses elicited by the message are predominantly favorable towards the position advocated in the message, attitude change is likely to occur, whereas when unfavorable responses are predominant no attitude change or even a movement away from the message position will occur. As a consequence of this mediating role of the cognitive responses to the message contents, the main determinant of persuasion is the perceived validity and relevance of the information and arguments presented. Because attitude change that results from systematic processing is based on careful consideration of relevant information and arguments, persuasion through systematic processing is assumed to be relatively stable over time, resistant to change, and predictive of behavior.

Systematic processing involves both time and effort. Therefore, recipients of a message are expected to engage in this effortful processing mode only when they are both motivated and able to do so. If they are not sufficiently motivated and able, they will follow the relatively effortless heuristic (HSM) or peripheral (ELM) processing mode. Although peripheral processing actually refers to a broader set of persuasion processes than heuristic processing (see, e.g., Chaiken and Stangor, 1987), for the present discussion it suffices to note that both refer to persuasion processes independent of the actual message contents. Instead, persuasion in this mode is based on persuasion cues, noncontent information (e.g., source attractiveness, source expertise, number of arguments in the message) that may be used to base message-related judgments on. On the basis of these persuasion cues recipients may determine the message's validity in a relatively effortless fashion. In contrast to change resulting from systematic/central processing, attitude change resulting from heuristic/peripheral processing is relatively unstable in time and easy to reverse.

Support for the HSM and the ELM is abundant (see, e.g., Chaiken, Wood, and Eagly, 1996; Eagly and Chaiken, 1993; Petty, Priester, and Wegener, 1994, for recent reviews). The typical finding of studies within the ELM/HSM framework is that when a message presumably is processed systematically (owing to, for example, the personal relevance of the message), cognitive responses to the message mediate attitude change, while noncontent persuasion cues have no or very little effect on attitudes, whereas under conditions conducive of heuristic processing (e.g., low personal relevance), attitudes are mainly affected by persuasion cues such as source characteristics (e.g., source expertise). Roughly speaking, this body of research suggests that persuasion will be based either on elaborate information processing, in which case persuasion is a function of the perceived validity and objectivity of the information, or on quick-and-dirty responses to noncontent persuasion cues such as source characteristics, in which case the actual argumentation in the message is of little consequence. When processing systematically, that is, when persuasion is contingent on the subjective validity of the message, recipients are assumed to determine the message's validity on the basis of its contents alone, independent of social context information such as the source of the message, the medium of communication, or the specific communication setting. That is, this approach implicitly assumes that the validity and persuasiveness of information and arguments is nonsocially determined. Validity appears to be considered to be an objectively determinable property of information, arguments, and opinions. This view may be contrasted with social identity approaches to social influence, which propose a social basis of message validity and persuasiveness.

The Social Identity Perspective on Influence: Validity as a Function of Ingroup Consensus

Approaches to influence that are more concerned with the interpersonal or group context of persuasion processes typically are less concerned with the cognitive underpinnings of these processes. Yet, most models of social influence share the ELM's and HSM's assumption that influence is based either on the objective validity of information or on noncontent factors (e.g., Deutsch and Gerard, 1955; French and Raven, 1959; Kelman, 1961). That is, although these models take social bases of influence into account, they nevertheless assume that the validity of information is nonsocially determined. The more recent social identity, or self-categorizational, approach to social influence (Abrams and Hogg, 1990; Turner, 1991; Turner, Hogg, Oakes, Reicher, and Wetherell, 1987) argues against this conceptualization of informational influence as essentially nonsocial in nature. Instead, it proposes that, although the validity of some statements or beliefs may be relatively objectively determined (e.g., by a direct physical test of the statement), in general social attitudes and behaviors tend to be based on beliefs and values of which no objective, physical test is available. Rather, the validity of many such beliefs is determined by social or cultural consensus. That is, what we deem to be true tends to be determined by what is considered to be true within the groups to which we belong. Depending on context and issue, this may be a large, broad-scale group (e.g., western society, the scientific community) or a small local group (e.g., a streetgang, a work unit). Either way, however, it is social identification that mediates this socially defined validity. Only if we are a member of a group and we share its social reality will its reality become our "objective" reality. In other words, it is not any group's consensus or any group's norms that provide subjective validity, but rather *ingroup* consensus and *ingroup* norms. For many social values, beliefs, and attitudes, it is ingroup consensus that renders a belief or opinion subjectively valid, not fulfillment of some objective, nonsocial criterion. This approach implies that, because we rely on ingroup to determine what is valid and true, the perceived validity of an attitude statement is at least in part source-determined. Whereas ingroup statements and messages are prone to be perceived as valid, outgroup statements and messages are not. Therefore, because ingroup messages are more likely to be subjectively valid than outgroup messages, people should be more influenced by ingroup than by outgroup sources. This was shown to be the case (e.g., Abrams, Wetherell, Cochrane, Hogg, and Turner, 1990; Hogg and Turner, 1987; Mackie, 1986).

In reference to the HSM and the ELM, the obvious question would seem to be what processes underlie this greater influence of ingroup sources. It is in this question that the social cognition approach to persuasion and the social identity approach to influence meet. Whereas the social identity approach is essentially mute were information processing is concerned, the social cognition answer to the question is pretty straightforward. Within the HSM and the ELM persuasion induced by source characteristics is by definition placed in the heuristic or peripheral route to persuasion, because source is not part of the actual message contents. In other words, these social cognitive models propose that social identification-induced influence is based on heuristic or peripheral mechanisms (cf. Chaiken et al., 1996; Petty et al., 1994). To a certain extent, theoretical analyses of influence based on shared group membership corroborate this view. The peripheral mechanism of self-stereotyping is proposed as one way in which group membership may affect attitudes (see, e.g., Abrams and Hogg, 1990; Hogg and Turner, 1987): once we categorize ourselves as members of a certain group, we tend to assign relevant ingroup characteristics, including attitudes and beliefs, to ourselves, which may result in attitude change. Yet, it is important to note that although these analyses suggest a peripheral mechanism for social identification-induced attitude change, they do not preclude that influence based on social identification may result from systematic processing. In fact, based on the notion that the subjective validity of attitude and opinion statements will be in part source-determined, it may be expected that recipients are more motivated to process ingroup than outgroup messages. If people tend to treat ingroup as a more valid source of information than outgroup, would it not follow that recipients will be more motivated to process ingroup, that is, valid, messages than outgroup, i.e., less valid, messages? A couple of studies have tested this prediction, using the research framework provided by the ELM and the HSM.

Source as Motivator of Systematic Processing

The ELM and HSM frameworks suggest that indications of recipients' processing mode may be found both in the cognitive responses elicited by the message and in postexposure attitudes. First, the number of issue-relevant thoughts reported on a thought-listing task is indicative of systematic processing, because more issue-relevant thoughts imply more thinking about the message contents.

Second, only when a message is processed systematically will persuasion be mediated by the favorability of issue-relevant cognitive responses. Therefore, the strength of the relationship between favorability of responses and postexposure attitudes is indicative of the extent to which recipients have engaged in systematic processing. Third, effects of the experimental manipulation of message quality may be informative about processing mode, because only when a message is processed systematically will message quality affect the favorability of cognitive responses. As a consequence, more favorable responses and more attitude change after exposure to a strong message as compared with exposure to a weak message is an indication of systematic processing.

Adopting this research framework, Mackie, Worth, and Asuncion (1990), van Knippenberg and Wilke (1991, 1992, Exp. 2), Mackie, Gastardo-Conaco, and Skelly (1992), and McGarty, Haslam, Hutchinson, and Turner (1994) presented participants with a persuasive message from either an ingroup or an outgroup source and assessed cognitive responses to the message, postexposure attitudes, and argument recall. Results of these studies generally support the prediction that ingroup sources motivate systematic processing.

First, if ingroup sources instigate systematic processing whereas outgroup sources do not, a persuasive message should elicit more message-related cognitive responses when the source is ingroup than when the source is outgroup. In support of this prediction, van Knippenberg and Wilke (1991, Exp. 1) observed more issue-relevant cognitive responses in reaction to an ingroup message than in reaction to an outgroup message. Second, if ingroup sources instigate systematic processing whereas outgroup sources do not, the favorability of the cognitive responses to the message should be predictive of postexposure attitudes when the source of the message is ingroup but not when it is outgroup. Mackie et al. (1990) and van Knippenberg and Wilke (1992, Exp. 2) found just that. Third, if ingroup sources instigate systematic processing whereas outgroup sources do not, manipulations of message quality should affect responses to ingroup but not to outgroup messages. Both Mackie et al. (1990) and van Knippenberg and Wilke (1992, Exp. 2) found that strong ingroup messages elicited more favorable responses than weak ingroup messages, whereas no such difference was found for outgroup messages. Moreover, Mackie et al. (1990), van Knippenberg and Wilke (1991), and Mackie et al. (1992) observed more attitude change after exposure to a strong ingroup message than after exposure to a weak ingroup message, while attitudes were unaffected by message quality when the source was outgroup. (McGarty et al., 1994, did not vary message quality.)

In addition, more systematic processing might also result in better message recall, but recall is a less reliable indicator of processing mode, because recall can be relatively independent of the way a message is processed. Nevertheless, more extensive processing of ingroup as compared with outgroup messages may result in better recall of ingroup messages. Indeed, corroborating the prediction that only ingroup sources would elicit systematic processing, Mackie et al. (1990), van Knippenberg and Wilke (1991, Exp. 1), and McGarty et al. (1994) found better recall of ingroup arguments than of outgroup arguments.

Further evidence in general support of the hypothesis that ingroup sources motivate systematic processing is found in studies of source and message proto-typicality as determinant of systematic processing (van Knippenberg and Wilke, 1992; van Knippenberg, Lossie, and Wilke, 1994). The concept of prototypical-ity refers to the degree of ingroup-representativeness, prototypicality being the extent to which a category instance is representative of within-category similar-ities and between-category differences (cf. Rosch, 1978; Turner et al., 1987). Van Knippenberg and Wilke argued that, if it is ingroup consensus that renders attitude statements valid, the extent to which a message or attitude statement is representative of ingroup consensus or ingroup norms, that is, the extent to which it is ingroup prototypical, should affect the perceived validity of the message and, therefore, the motivation to process the message. To test this prediction van Knippenberg and Wilke (1992, Exp. 1) exposed participants to both a prototypical and a nonprototypical ingroup message (prototypicality was manipulated by introducing one message as being representative of the source group's attitudes and the other as being nonrepresentative), and found that only the favorability of cognitive responses to the prototypical message was predictive of postexposure attitudes (but only when the prototypical message was counter-attitudinal) and that argument recall was better for the prototypical than for the nonprototypical message. In a second study van Knippenberg and Wilke (1992, Exp. 2) replicated the finding that the favorability of cognitive responses was predictive of attitudes when the message was ingroup prototypical, but not when the ingroup message was nonprototypical, and in addition found that neither prototypical nor nonprototypical outgroup messages elicited systematic process-ing. Similar results were observed by van Knippenberg et al. (1994), who exposed subjects to an ingroup message from either a prototypical source or a nonprototypical source (manipulated by information suggesting that the source, a fellow student, held either typical or atypical student attitudes towards other issues). In this study, a message from the prototypical source elicited more issue-relevant responses than a message from the nonprototypical source, and attitudes and favorability of cognitive responses were only related after exposure to the message of the prototypical source (but both only when the source's position was not known beforehand – see below). Because prototypicality in essence repres-ents the degree of "ingroupness," these studies also corroborate the notion of systematic processing motivated by social categorization of the message source as ingroup.

The above studies have also yielded some evidence as to the limiting condi-tions for the processing-motivating effect of ingroup sources. First, and perhaps most important, ingroup sources are more likely to instigate systematic process-ing to the extent that they are prototypical, that is, may be considered to represent ingroup normative attitudes and ingroup consensus (van Knippenberg and Wilke, 1992; van Knippenberg et al., 1994). In addition, Mackie et al.

(1990, Exp. 2) found that an ingroup source elicits systematic processing only when the message is group-relevant (i.e., pertaining to a topic of relative importance to ingroup), and both Mackie et al. (1992) and van Knippenberg et al. (1994) found that ingroup vs. outgroup respectively prototypical vs. nonprototypical sources instigated systematic processing only if the source's position is not known beforehand. Furthermore, there is some evidence in the van Knippenberg and Wilke (1992) study that the processing-motivating effect may be stronger when the message is counterattitudinal, possibly because a counterattitudinal ingroup message is unexpected (cf. van Knippenberg and van Knippenberg, 1994) and this expectancy-violation instigated more extensive processing (cf. Maheswaran and Chaiken, 1991), or because disagreement with ingroup may elicit uncertainty (McGarty, Turner, Oakes, and Haslam, 1993) and thus motivates processing (cf. Chaiken et al., 1989). Finally, results of the McGarty et al. (1994) study suggest that the salience of the intergroup context (induced by a prior statement of (dis)agreement with the source's opinion) moderates the memory advantage of ingroup arguments. Under the circumstances described above, when an ingroup source does not instigate systematic processing, categorization of the source as (prototypically) ingroup may be expected to function as a persuasion cue, eliciting a willingness to accept the position advocated in the message (see below after next section).

Source as Determinant of Message Persuasiveness in Systematic Processing

As argued above, message validity is codetermined by the source of the message. Therefore, recipients should respond relatively favorably to ingroup as compared to outgroup messages. That is, the very same message should be perceived to be more valid when originating from ingroup than when originating from outgroup and should elicit more favorable cognitive responses when the source is ingroup as compared with outgroup. Evidence for this source-dependent subjective quality of the message was obtained in the van Knippenberg and Wilke (1991, 1992) studies. Van Knippenberg and Wilke (1992, Exp. 2) found that ingroup messages elicited more favorable issue-relevant cognitive responses than outgroup messages. A similar result was observed in van Knippenberg and Wilke's (1992) first study, in which the prototypical (ingroup) message elicited more favorable cognitive responses than the nonprototypical message (when proattitudinal). In addition, van Knippenberg and Wilke (1992, Exp. 1) and van Knippenberg et al. (1994) found that the quality of the prototypical (ingroup) message was rated higher than that of the nonprototypical message. The finding that social categorization of the source affects responses to the actual contents of the message is especially important, because it indicates that source characteristics affect processing when a message is processed systematically. In this, it supports the social identity approach's proposition that the subjective validity of a message is socially dependent. That is, this finding in particular argues against a conceptualization of social identification-induced persuasion as (solely) rooted in heuristic or peripheral processing.

Source Categorization as Persuasion Cue in Heuristic/Peripheral Processing

As noted above, although ingroup messages may motivate systematic processing, circumstances may render heuristic processing more likely (e.g., when the message is not group-relevant or the source's position is known beforehand). In that case, social categorization of the source may be expected to function as a heuristic cue affecting the willingness to accept the advocated position independent of message contents in such a way that ingroup messages will have more impact than outgroup messages. In support of this hypothesis, Mackie et al. (1990, Exp. 2) and Mackie et al. (1992) report evidence of more persuasion by ingroup than by outgroup messages under conditions conducive of heuristic processing. Corroborating these findings, in the van Knippenberg et al. (1994) study ingroup prototypical messages caused more attitude change than nonprototypical messages irrespective of whether or not the source's position was known beforehand. Taken together, the findings discussed in this and the previous sections show that ingroup sources may persuade both through systematic and through heuristic processing.

Reconsidering the Position of Social Identification-based Persuasion in the ELM and HSM

The studies discussed above show that social categorization of the source of a persuasive message may fulfill multiple roles. Source categorization tends to affect the motivation for systematic processing and the favorability of the cognitive responses to the message when it is processed systematically, but when circumstances are less conducive to systematic processing source categorization functions as a persuasion cue eliciting acceptance of ingroup message positions. Although the latter observation does not contradict Chaiken et al.'s (1996) and Petty et al.'s (1994) proposition that persuasion based on social identification is rooted in the heuristic or peripheral processing mode, the finding that ingroup sources motivate systematic processing, and especially the finding that social categorization of the source affects the subjective validity of the message when systematically processed, directly opposes this proposition and instead suggests that greater persuasiveness of ingroup sources may have its origin in systematic processing.

Yet, although these results contradict the conception of social identification-based influence common in the social cognitive persuasion literature, the ELM and the HSM do in principle allow for multiple roles of variables in the persuasion process, and hence do not preclude the multiple role of source. Even so, the ELM and the HSM, or rather, the main researchers working within their frameworks, propose that source will only motivate processing or affect responses to a message in a specific subset of circumstances.

Specifically, based on unexpected findings of processing-motivating effects of expert (Heesacker, Petty, and Cacioppo, 1983) and attractive sources (Puckett, Petty, Cacioppo, and Fisher, 1983), Petty and Cacioppo (1984) propose that source characteristics may affect the motivation to process a message when the elaboration likelihood is moderate, that is, when the motivation to process is not clearly high or low owing to other factors (e.g., when the message is not of obvious high respectively low personal relevance). Aside from the fact that the moderate elaboration likelihood interpretation constitutes an unproven post hoc explanation of the Heesacker et al. (1983) and Puckett et al. (1983) findings, it would seem a bit odd to reserve the moderate elaboration likelihood assumption just for source effects. Any potentially motivating factor will affect the motivation to process only if elaboration likelihood is not already high or low owing to other factors. For instance, issue involvement (i.e., personal relevance of the message topic) may elicit systematic processing (Petty and Cacioppo, 1979), but one would not expect issue involvement to affect processing mode if motivation to process is already sky high owing to the prospect of a 10,000 dollar reward for correctly reproducing the gist of the message. Conversely, I for one could not, and hence would not, systematically process a message in Mandarin if my life depended on it. In other words, a potentially processing-motivating factor arguably effects processing mode only under conditions of moderate elaboration likelihood and not in the upper or lower extremes of the elaboration likelihood continuum. That is, Petty and Cacioppo's (1984) moderate elaboration likelihood assumption is most likely correct, but probably holds for any potential instigator of systematic processing and not just for source. Therefore, the processing-motivating potential of ingroup sources need not be restricted to a limited subset of situations any more than any other factor's motivating potential.

The source categorization effect on the favorability of cognitive responses in the systematic mode constitutes an instance of what both the ELM and the HSM would coin "biased processing" (e.g., Chaiken et al., 1989; Petty and Cacioppo, 1986). A recent study by Chaiken and Maheswaran (1994) links this biased processing notion to source characteristics and therefore is particularly relevant to the present discussion. On the basis of the HSM's bias assumption, which states that heuristic cues may affect the subjective validity of a systematically processed message, Chaiken and Maheswaran argue that when the validity or invalidity of a message is not obvious and self-evident, heuristic cues such as information about source expertise or source credibility may be used to determine the validity of the information and arguments presented in the message (i.e., when you are unsure whether or not to believe a particular statement, you may either accept or reject the claim depending on the extent to which you consider the source credible or knowledgeable). Supporting this prediction, Chaiken and Maheswaran found that, under conditions conducive to systematic processing, credibility of the source affected the favorability of the cognitive responses to the message, but only when the message was ambiguous and not when it was unambiguously strong or weak. In other words, Chaiken and Maheswaran found that the biasing effect of source on systematic processing occurred only for information of which the validity is not self-evident. These findings imply that the "biased processing" effect obtained by van Knippenberg and Wilke (1992; van Knippenberg et al., 1994) might be attributable to the apparent ambiguity of the messages presented in these studies. This interpretation is corroborated by the fact that effects of message quality were rather weak in these studies, even in conditions where results for other measures indicated that the message was processed systematically (conversely, Mackie et al., 1990, found reliable message quality effects and no indications of biased processing). These considerations suggest that source categorization effects on the favorability of cognitive responses may be more likely in case of an ambiguous message.

To summarize, because the ELM and the HSM allow for the multiple roles of social categorization of the source of persuasive communication, the research findings discussed in this chapter do not fundamentally challenge the ELM or the HSM. Nevertheless, the finding that ingroup sources may instigate and bias systematic processing contradicts the notion prevailing within the persuasion field that social identification-induced persuasion is always a peripheral or heuristic process. The biased processing effect might arguably be limited to ambiguous messages, but the above analysis suggests that the processing-motivating effect of ingroup sources may be just as common as the effects of other factors that have been shown to affect processing mode.

Implications for the Role of Source in the Persuasion Process

Common sense tells us that people are extremely source-minded, deciding which newspaper to read, which colleague to consult for a particular problem, "who to believe," etc. A lot of the time people consciously or unconsciously decide which source they are willing to expose themselves to, and to what extent. In view of this common-sense notion, it is surprising that so few persuasion studies yield evidence of source effects on processing mode. Aside from the studies on social identification-induced attitude change discussed in this chapter, there are virtually no reports of the processing-motivating potential of the source of a message. Given the large body of persuasion studies incorporating a manipulation of source characteristics, the fact that so little evidence of source effects on systematic processing is reported is, at least from the present point of view, a bit troublesome. One might, of course, propose that, apparently, such source effects are restricted to ingroup sources and leave it at that, but both common sense and findings like those reported by Heesacker et al. (1983), Puckett et al. (1983), and Chaiken and Maheswaran (1994) suggest there might be a little more to it. Hence, it would seem worthwhile to consider the circumstances under which source effects on systematic processing are likely to occur.

The lack of research findings pertaining to source effects on systematic processing might in part be the result of the fact that the typical persuasion experiment is not designed to test predictions regarding such effects. As Chaiken et al. (1989) note, one reason for the virtual absence of studies supporting the HSM's bias assumption may be that the typical persuasion study presents an unambiguously strong (or weak) message, rendering circumstances less conducive to biased processing. Hence, one might argue that the fact that biased processing appears to be the exception rather than the rule is a result of the use of a rather restricted subset of message types (i.e., messages that are cut out to be self-evidently valid or invalid). In the same vein, more or less echoing Petty and Cacioppo's (1984) moderate elaboration likelihood interpretation, one may point out that studies in which source characteristics are varied typically are designed to test the effects of other factors on processing mode (and not of source characteristics). It is possible that, as a consequence, the design of these studies tends to be such that other manipulations dominate the potential processing effects of source. Yet, whereas the limited support for the HSM's bias assumption might be attributed to the absence of ambiguous messages in the typical persuasion study, the suggestion that in the typical persuasion study source effects might be dominated by other effects would seem to be rather unsatisfactory, unless we are also able to specify the circumstances under which source characteristics may be expected to motivate processing.

One factor of major importance in this respect may be the "fit" between the source's characteristics and the message topic. Simply put, it may not be the particular source that motivates processing or the particular topic that motivates processing, but rather that particular source communicating about that particular topic. To illustrate this proposition, let us consider a hypothetical colleague at the psychology department, X. Colleague X is an expert on methodological and statistical issues, knows roughly everything there is to know about gardening, but knows very little about your own field of research, persuasion. Let us further assume that you do take your work seriously, but do not like gardening. Chances are that you will be more interested in what colleague X has to say about methodological issues than in her opinion about either gardening or persuasion. X being an expert is not enough: you are not interested in gardening. X talking about your favorite field of research is not enough: you do not care that much for a layperson's ideas about persuasion. But when X talks about an issue you care about and she knows a lot about, you are definitely interested. In other words, the specific expertise of your hypothetical colleague X in combination with the topic she is talking about determines your willingness to attend to her "message". That is, it is not the source's characteristics in themselves that motivate processing, it is the combination of source and message topic that will (or will not) motivate. Indeed, this is just what Mackie et al. (1990, Exp. 2) found. Mackie et al. presented a message about either a group-relevant or nonrelevant issue; only when the message was group-relevant was the message processed systematically, *but only when the source was ingroup and not when it was outgroup*. The latter is particularly important, because it demonstrates that it is not the group-relevance of the message topic in itself, but the combination of source and topic that motivates processing. That is, it is the fit between message source and message topic that gives processing-motivating potential.

In addition, processing-eliciting effects of source may be more likely for some issues than for others. Just as the degree of ambiguity of the contents of a message may make recipients more or less dependent on the source of the message to determine the message's validity (as in the Chaiken and Maheswaran, 1994, study), some issues may be more "ambiguous" than others and hence render recipients more dependent on the source of the message. At the one extreme of this hypothetical "issues ambiguity continuum" might be factual issues about which the recipient knows everything, and is able to judge the way the factual information presented in the message is combined to argue for a particular position without having to rely on anything but the line of reasoning in the message itself. In this case, source characteristics such as source expertise or the source's group membership will have virtually no influence on message processing. At the other, possibly far more common, end we might have issues about which attitudes are based more on beliefs and values than on facts. In those cases, what is valid and true is essentially socially defined and both motivation to process and favorability of responses to the message may be expected to be partially source-dependent. In other words, the extent to which an issue relates to facts (contingent on the recipient's expertise) or to beliefs and values may codetermine the extent to which a recipient will rely on others' opinions, and thus the extent to which source characteristics may affect message processing. Thus, elaborating on the above proposition regarding fit of message and source, it may be expected that the more "ambiguous" an issue is, the more likely sources that fit the message topic will be to engender systematic processing.

Some Future Directions for the Study of Social Identity and Persuasion

Even though the study of the cognitive processes underlying persuasion based on social identification suggests that a more general reconsideration of the role of source in the persuasion process might be in order (e.g., by focusing on the fit of source and message topic and the ambiguity of the issue), the social identity analysis of social influence suggests that group membership is the primary characteristic in determining the extent to which a source will engender message processing, because the motivation to process is contingent on the perception that the source's opinion will reflect a shared social reality. That is, although, for example, an expert source may fit a message more than a nonexpert source, recipients of the message may still be more interested in ingroup opinions on the issue than in the views of an outgroup expert. In other words, all kinds of sources may fit messages and motivate processing, but ingroup sources are more likely to do so than other sources. Hence, the next question might be: what issues fit ingroup?

Mackie et al.'s (1990) study suggests that the group relevance of an issue determines the extent to which ingroup sources fit a message. In the Mackie et al. study, group relevance was manipulated by presenting participants from a university on the west coast of the United States with a message concerning either oil drilling on the west coast or acid rain problems in the northeastern United States, thus implicitly defining group relevance as the extent to which something may affect the group (cf. Petty and Cacioppo's, 1979, notion of personal relevance). Notwithstanding the fact that this would indeed seem a factor that determines the group relevance of an issue, another factor may be even more directly related to group relevance: the extent to which the issue discussed in the message is group-defining. Just as some traits and characteristics may be typical of a group (e.g., rich, hardworking), some attitude issues may be typically associated with the group (e.g., income taxes). Indeed, for groups like political parties and activist groups certain attitudes are their very *raison d'être*. Messages concerning these core, group-defining attitude issues may be assumed to strongly attract attention from the members of such groups, especially when originating from ingroup. In other words, it may be proposed that ingroup sources are more likely to motivate and bias processing the more central to the group's identity the message issue is. Considering that attitudes may be more central to some groups' identity (e.g., political parties) than to other groups' identity (e.g., gender groups), we may assume that the above proposition holds stronger for groups for which attitude issues are more central to the group's identity, that is, for groups for which the core defining characteristics are attitudes rather than, for example, traits or behaviors.

People are members of more than one group simultaneously (e.g., at the same time being a psychologist, a woman, and English). Therefore, in addition to the question of what issues fit ingroup, the question of what ingroup best fits an issue is equally relevant. Given the fact that a recipient of a message has multiple potential ingroups, which of these group memberships will be most relevant where a particular message topic is concerned? It seems reasonable to assume that a message topic can make a particular group membership salient, rendering that group the ingroup that best fits the message topic. In reference to the notion of group relevance discussed above, we may propose that the membership group to which the issue is most group-defining – if any – will be the most salient ingroup. For instance, for a female student, other students may be the salient ingroup where messages concerning student issues (e.g., comprehensive examinations) are concerned, whereas for gender-related issues (e.g., affirmative action) a female source might be the relevant ingroup source. This implies not only that the social identification that is most influential may differ from issue to issue, but also that what may be an ingroup for one issue might be an outgroup for another topic. For instance, in the above example a male student might be an ingroup source where student issues are concerned and an outgroup source where gender-related issues are concerned.

Even though people hold multiple group memberships and the topic of a message may determine which of these group memberships is most salient, not all of these group memberships are equally likely to play a role in the persuasion process. Obviously, some group memberships are more important to people and more central to their identity than others. It may be assumed that the more strongly an individual identifies with a group (i.e., the more the group is identity-defining for the individual), the more the group will reflect the individual's social reality, and hence the more likely the group will be to be a salient ingroup for a number of attitude issues. On the one hand, this means that the degree of identification with a group determines to what extent membership of the group may motivate and bias message processing; on the other, that social identification may determine the range of message topics which the group subjectively fits.

To summarize, building on the finding that social identification may engender and bias systematic processing, we may further explore the role of social identity in the persuasion process by focusing on the group-defining aspects of attitude issues and on the relative importance of the recipient's multiple group memberships (e.g., as affected by the message topic and the extent to which the recipient identifies with these membership groups). The study of these tentative suggestions and other implications that may be derived from the finding that social identity may play multiple roles in the persuasion process may enhance our understanding of both influence based on group membership and of the social dynamics of the persuasion process in general.

Conclusion

As this chapter hopes to demonstrate, the social cognition approach to social identity issues, or the social identity approach to social cognition issues, enriches both research traditions. Specifically, a closer examination of the social identity account of group-mediated influence leads to a reconsideration of the position of social identification-induced attitude change in social cognitive models of persuasion. Conversely, the social cognition approach to group-mediated influence has, aside from providing the framework that inspired and facilitated the study of the cognitive processes underlying influence induced by social identification, shown that the persuasive power of ingroup sources will at least to some extent be contingent on the strength with which those sources present their case. Moreover, from this reconsideration of the role of ingroup sources follows a more general (re)appreciation of the social basis of message validity and of the role of the message's source in the persuasion process. These considerations, in turn, suggest future directions for research that may enlarge our understanding of both influence based on group membership and of the social dynamics of the persuasion process.

References

Abrams, D. and Hogg, M.A. (1990). Social identification, self-categorization and social influence. In W. Stroebe and M. Hewstone (eds), *European Review of Social Psychology*, Vol. 1. Chichester: John Wiley and Sons, pp. 195–228.

Abrams, D., Wetherell, M., Cochrane, S., Hogg, M.A., and Turner, J.C. (1990). Knowing what to think by knowing who you are: Self-categorization and the nature of norm formation, conformity and group polarization. *British Journal of Social Psychology*, 29, 97–119.

Chaiken, S. (1987). The heuristic model of persuasion. In M.P. Zanna, J.M. Olsen, and C.P. Herman (eds), *Social Influence: The Ontario Symposium*, Vol. 5. Hillsdale, NJ: Erlbaum, pp. 3–39.

Chaiken, S., Liberman, A., and Eagly, A.H. (1989). Heuristic and systematic information processing within and beyond the persuasion context. In J.S. Uleman and J.A. Bargh (eds), *Unintended Thought*. New York: Guilford, pp. 212–52.

Chaiken, S. and Maheswaran, D. (1994). Heuristic processing can bias systematic processing: Effects of source credibility, argument ambiguity, and task importance on attitude judgment. *Journal of Personality and Social Psychology*, 66, 460–73.

Chaiken, S. and Stangor, C. (1987). Attitudes and attitude change. *Annual Review of Psychology*, 38, 575–630.

Chaiken, S., Wood, W., and Eagly, A.H. (1996). Principles of persuasion. In E.T. Higgins and A.W. Kruglanski (eds), *Social Psychology: Handbook of basic principles*. New York: Guilford, pp. 702–42.

Deutsch, M. and Gerard, H.B. (1955). A study of normative and informational influences upon individual judgment. *Journal of Abnormal and Social Psychology*, 51, 629–36.

Eagly, A.H. and Chaiken, S. (1993). *The Psychology of Attitudes*. Orlando, FL: Harcourt Brace Jovanovich.

French, J.R.P. and Raven, B. (1959). The bases of social power. In D. Cartwright (ed.), *Studies in Social Power*. Ann Arbor: University of Michigan Press, pp. 150–67.

Heesacker, M., Petty, R.E., and Cacioppo, J.T. (1983). Field dependence and attitude change: Source credibility can alter persuasion by affecting message-relevant thinking. *Journal of Personality*, 51, 653–66.

Hogg, M.A. and Turner, J.C. (1987). Social identity and conformity: A theory of referent informational influence. In W. Doise and S. Moscovici (eds), *Current Issues in European Social Psychology*, Vol. 2. Cambridge: Cambridge University Press, pp. 139–82.

Kelman, H.C. (1961). Processes of opinion change. *Public Opinion Quarterly*, 25, 57–78. McGarty, G., Haslam, S.A., Hutchinson, K.J., and Turner, J.C. (1994). The effects of salient group membership on persuasion. *Small Group Research*, 25, 267–93.

McGarty, C., Turner, J.C., Oakes, P.J., and Haslam, S.A. (1993). The creation of uncertainty in the influence process: The roles of stimulus information and disagreement with similar others. *European Journal of Social Psychology*, 23, 17–38.

Mackie, D.M. (1986). Social identification effects in group polarization. *Journal of Personality and Social Psychology*, 50, 720–8.

Mackie, D.M., Gastardo-Conaco, M.C., and Skelly, J.J. (1992). Knowledge of the advocated position and the processing of in-group and out-group persuasive messages. *Personality and Social Psychology Bulletin*, 18, 145–51.

Mackie, D.M., Worth, L.T., and Asuncion, A.G. (1990). Processing of persuasive in-group messages. *Journal of Personality and Social Psychology*, 58, 812–22.

Maheswaran, D. and Chaiken, S. (1991). Promoting systematic processing in low motivation settings: Effects of incongruent information on processing and judgment. *Journal of Personality and Social Psychology*, 61, 13–25.

Petty, R.E. and Cacioppo, J.T. (1979). Issue involvement can increase or decrease persuasion by enhancing message-relevant cognitive responses. *Journal of Personality and Social Psychology*, 37, 1915–26.

Petty, R.E. and Cacioppo, J.T. (1984). Source factors and the elaboration likelihood model of persuasion. *Advances in Consumer Research*, 11, 668–72.

Petty, R.E. and Cacioppo, J.T. (1986). The elaboration likelihood model of persuasion. In L. Berkowitz (ed.), *Advances in Experimental Social Psychology*, Vol. 19. New York: Academic Press, pp. 123–205.

Petty, R.E., Priester, J.R., and Wegener, D.T. (1994). Cognitive processes in attitude change. In R.S. Wyer, J., and T.K. Srull (eds), *Handbook of Social Cognition*, 2nd edn, Vol. 2. Hillsdale, NJ: Erlbaum, pp. 69–142.

Puckett, J.M., Petty, R.E., Cacioppo, J.T., and Fisher, D.L. (1983). The relative impact of age and attractiveness stereotypes in persuasion. *Journal of Gerontology*, 38, 340–3.

Rosch, E. (1978). Principles of categorization. In E. Rosch and B.B. Lloyd (eds), *Cognition and Categorization*. Hillsdale, NJ: Erlbaum, pp. 27–48.

Turner, J.C. (1991). *Social Influence*. Milton Keynes: Open University Press.

Turner, J.C., Hogg, M.A., Oakes, P.J., Reicher, S.D., and Wetherell, M.S. (1987). *Rediscovering the Social Group. A self-categorization theory*. Oxford: Blackwell.

van Knippenberg, D. and van Knippenberg, A. (1994). Social categorization, focus of attention and judgements of group opinions. *British Journal of Social Psychology*, 33, 477–89.

van Knippenberg, D., Lossie, N., and Wilke, H. (1994). In-group prototypicality and persuasion: Determinants of heuristic and systematic message processing. *British Journal of Social Psychology*, 33, 289–300.

van Knippenberg, D. and Wilke, H. (1991). Sociale categorisatie, verwerking van argumenten en attitudeverandering. In J. van der Pligt, W. van der Kloot, A. van Knippenberg, and M. Poppe (eds), *Fundamentele Sociale Psychologie*, Vol. 5. Tilburg: Tilburg University Press, pp. 96–111.

van Knippenberg, D. and Wilke, H. (1992). Prototypicality of arguments and conformity to ingroup norms. *European Journal of Social Psychology*, 22, 141–55.

14

Majority and Minority Influence: The Interactions of Social Identity and Social Cognition Mediators

Diane M. Mackie and Sarah B. Hunter

Introduction

The chapters in this volume attest to the theoretical and empirical progress that can be made by a more systematic merging of social identity and social cognition approaches to understanding social phenomena. No topic seems quite so amenable to analysis from such a perspective as social influence, and particularly majority and minority influence. By definition, influence from a majority or minority source has identity implications – acceptance and rejection of minority messages, and thus of the majority or minority itself, is not a socially neutral activity. The centrality of these implications to a majority or minority's goal of bringing about attitude change was recognized by Moscovici (1980, 1985) and receives extensive treatment by Turner (1991; David and Turner, 1996), Wood (Wood, Lundgren, Ouellette, Busceme, and Blackstone, 1994), Clark and Maass (Clark, 1990; Clark and Maass, 1988; Maass and Clark, 1983, 1984). Understanding why and when majorities and minorities exercise influence thus depends on a careful analysis of the social identity aspects of the situation.

If our understanding of social influence benefits from a social identity analysis because identity is so central to influence, it benefits from a social cognition perspective because of relative neglect. Despite the popularity of cognitive analyses of attitude change in the past ten to twenty years, social influence phenomena were largely immune from such an approach until much more recently. Moscovici (1980) helped change this too, by suggesting radically different processes by which influence was brought about by majority and minority sources. The differences he suggested mapped on to distinctions about information processing that characterized persuasion research at the time, and triggered attempts

Preparation of the manuscript was supported in part by National Science Foundation Grant SBR–9209995 to Diane M. Mackie. We thank Karen Neddermeyer and Lynn Hastings for their assistance in the data collection.

to demonstrate whether and when majority or minority messages would be processed in a rather superficial manner or in a more thoughtful and thorough manner (Chaiken, 1980; Petty and Cacioppo, 1986). Although aligning the majority or minority origins of a message with a particular form of processing has proven too simplistic (Alvaro and Crano, 1996; Baker and Petty, 1996; Kruglanski and Mackie, 1990; Mackie, 1987; Mackie and Queller, in press), it is clear that the kind of processing that such messages receive is an important cognitive mediator of their short-term and long-term effectiveness.

In this chapter, we describe research focused on another social cognition mechanism by which the social identity concerns accompanying majority and minority influence may be mediated. Specifically, we suggest that the mental representations formed of majority and minority arguments may differ in ways that promote or prevent effective social influence. That is, representations of messages provide another means through which the social influence of a particular source may be enhanced or impeded. We first briefly review some of the social identity and social cognition mechanisms already known to impact majority and minority influence. Next, we discuss research that suggests that mental representations of arguments have important persuasive implications. We then describe two studies that investigate how majority and minority messages are mentally represented, and if and how that representation impacts acceptance. Finally, we discuss some of the implications, as well as the shortcomings, of this research and other research directions that need to be explored.

Social Identity Aspects of Majority and Minority Influence

Most of us recognize that the opinions we hold reflect not only our relevant knowledge about an issue, they also reflect something about ourselves. In this sense, attitudes are an aspect of identity, as the functional theorists have long understood (Katz, 1960; Smith, Bruner, and White, 1956). Issues of identity are particularly salient when it comes to adopting a position advocated by a majority or a minority, because in some sense to accept a group's position is to accept their identity. Both Asch and Moscovici recognized the identity issue as one that was largely problematic for minorities. For example, Asch (1956) demonstrated that people were willing to express obviously incorrect judgments in order to maintain an opinion in line with a numerical majority. Asch suggested that public compliance with a majority group reduces the stress associated with maintaining an opposing viewpoint. In addition, people apparently view majority groups as more attractive, prestigious, and desirable than minority groups (Kelman, 1958; Schachter, 1951), making messages advocated by social majorities more influential than messages advocated by social minorities (Clark and Maass, 1988). Moscovici (1980) argued that minorities had to have an impact at an indirect rather than a direct level because they produce a disruptive, unpleasant social conflict, and direct acceptance of their views would contribute to this social disruption. In these views, the social identity concerns that attend acceptance of the majority or minority position drive the social cognition mediators that we discuss in more depth later.

Turner and his colleagues (Tajfel and Turner, 1986; Turner, McGarty, Oakes, and Haslam, 1993) provided the most exhaustive analysis of the identity implications of majority and minority influence. In pointing out the somewhat paradoxical nature of Moscovici's views, Turner argues that identification is a prerequisite to influence (Back, Festinger, Hymovitch, Kelley, and others, 1950; Festinger and Thibaut, 1951; Schachter, 1951), and that even minorities must be seen as sharing commonalties with the recipient if they are to be effective change agents. According to this view, it is the disagreement with similar others that produces the uncertainty that opens the way for influence (or, alternatively, triggers recategorization processes to highlight differences between oneself and those with whom one disagrees; Hogg and Abrams, 1993; Turner, 1991). It is the recognition of similarity and identity with a group that is most likely to result in polarization of attitudes toward what is considered the normative, or prototypical, stance of the group. In contrast, a group that is perceived as dissimilar may move one's attitude to a more extreme position, away from this group. In this view, identity issues are not so much a potential concern in whether or not to accept influence; rather, shared identity is a requirement for influence to occur.

In support of this idea, David and Turner (1996) demonstrated that both majority and minority groups that are perceived as similar (i.e., ingroups) were effective persuasive agents, whereas both dissimilar majority and minority groups (i.e., outgroups) were not effective in producing any kind of influence (see also Martin, 1988). These results lend support to the idea that perceived similarity between target and source plays an important role in persuasion and that such identification might be particularly important in the case of minority influence (Mugny, 1984; Mugny and Papstamou, 1982). That is, because perceived similarity is such an important precursor of influence, and because one is unlikely to spontaneously perceive outgroups (especially minorities) as similar, social identity processes become critical for minorities attempting to be persuasive.

The social identity approach also helps explain the particular problem faced by double as opposed to single minorities. Maass (Maass and Clark, 1984; Maass, Clark, and Haberkorn, 1982) has found that single minorities (groups that differ from the recipient in only one way, perhaps just the difference of opinion) tend to be more persuasive than double minorities (who differ from recipients on more than one dimension). This persuasive differential has been found to depend on perceived similarity: single minorities are perceived to have more shared common identity with the target of the persuasive message than double minorities, opening the way, as Turner suggested, for increased persuasion.

In a recent meta-review of minority influence, Wood et al. (1994) also concluded that concerns about social acceptance and rejection were crucial considerations for targets of social influence. Messages emanating from a valued social group evoke normative pressures to align with the group, suggesting that both majorities and minorities might have persuasive power if they are viewed positively. However, a recipient's aversion to aligning with a deviant minority source often prevents minorities from being effective change agents. Thus, social identity factors play an important role in whether or not majority and minority influence is successful. This is why the study of majority and minority influence is such a promising vehicle for articulation of social identity and social cognition processes.

Social Cognitive Processing Approaches

Moscovici's (1980) classic statement on minority conversion rejuvenated research in social influence not only because it argued that minorities were particularly effective agents of social change, but also because it proposed mechanisms by which such effectiveness might come about. According to this view, when a minority source is perceived as consistent, confident, and committed, recipients of its appeal engage in a validation process. Validation consists of a careful consideration of the merits and content of the message, the kind of consideration that typically produces long-lasting, private attitude change, which Moscovici called conversion. Influence from the majority, on the other hand, is mediated by comparison processes. Faced with disagreement from a majority, recipients seek to change their own opinions to avoid conflict with the majority. No validation of message content is necessary because the motivation for change is directed solely through social comparison. Therefore, a majority is likely to produce unthinking and superficial influence, which Moscovici characterizes as compliance.

In addition to the controversial nature of some of these arguments (majorities have been demonstrated to produce private attitude change, for example, Baker and Petty, 1996; Clark and Maass; 1988; Mackie, 1987; Mackie and Queller, in press; for reviews of related research see Turner, 1991), these propositions generated research activity because they mapped onto distinctions that were currently under intense research scrutiny in the persuasion domain. Both the elaboration likelihood model (ELM; Petty and Cacioppo, 1986) and the heuristic–systematic model (HSM; Chaiken, 1980) of persuasion had made popular distinctions between careful consideration of message content that resulted in long-lasting internalized attitude change, and more superficial evaluation of the merits of an appeal based on factors other than the validity of the evidentiary base. Extensive evaluation of message content – termed systematic processing or central route in persuasion approaches – resulting in long-lasting change was similar to the validation–conversion process. At the same time, superficial (heuristic or peripheral) processing of information unrelated to the message (such as source status, for example), resulting, if not in compliance, at least in superficial acceptance, had much in common with what Moscovici termed majority-induced comparison processes.

Research was quickly directed toward assessing whether majority or minority appeals induced systematic or more superficial processing. The results of this body of work suggest a more complicated picture. First, some studies have demonstrated differences in the processing that majority and minority messages receive, but these differences do not always map clearly onto Moscovici's distinction. Maass and Clark (1983) found that arguments presented by majorities and minorities elicited similar amounts of cognitive activity and that the sheer amount of thoughts generated by such messages did not predict direct attitude change. However, majority and minority sources generated different types of cognitive responses. Specifically, the minority triggered more favorable cognitive responses and few counterarguments than the majority. Moreover, the kind of arguments that were generated was shown to be a good predictor of private attitude change. Trost, Maass, and Kenrick (1992) also found that majority and minority messages did not generate different amounts of cognitive responses but that the quality of cognitive activity triggered by majority and minority sources differed. These data support Nemeth's (1986) idea that minorities are more likely to produce divergent thinking than majorities. These results suggest that both majorities and minorities receive considerable processing, but of different types. However, the direction of the thoughts triggered were also found to depend upon the target's involvement with the issue. Targets who are highly involved with an issue may generate negative thoughts in reaction to a counterattitudinal proposal presented by a minority. In contrast, targets who are relatively uninvolved with an issue may generate positive thoughts in reaction to a minority's counterattitudinal message (Trost et al., 1992).

Second, majorities have been found to differentially evoke systematic processing compared to minorities (Mackie, 1987), especially because disagreement from a majority can violate recipients' expectancies (Hastie and Kumar, 1979; Pyszczynski and Greenberg, 1981; Ross, Greene, and House, 1977). In fact, Baker and Petty (1996) argue that messages that evoke surprise or curiosity because they violate recipient expectancies will lead to greater message scrutiny regardless of whether they emanate from a majority or minority. Thus, counterattitudinal messages advocated by a majority and proattitudinal messages from a minority evoke surprise because they suggest to the target that his or her views are not popular or widely endorsed, perhaps undermining subjective certainty (Hogg and Abrams, 1993). Such messages receive increased scrutiny. On the other hand, proattitudinal messages advocated by a majority and counterattitudinal messages advocated by a minority do not evoke surprise because they suggest that the target's views are widely accepted. These kind of messages are not likely to evoke further processing about the message or source. In sum, Baker and Petty's (1996) findings suggest that both the group status of the source and the source's position in relation to the target are important determinants of message processing.

As a whole, these studies suggest that any issues of social identification that are aroused by recognition of the majority or minority status of the source work together with cognitive mediating processes to produce influence. Although early research focused on whether or not there were privileged interactions between source status and processing mode, it is probably the case that different identity implications with differing – or even conflicting – cognitive consequences are all possible outcomes. For example, concerns about disagreement with the majority translate into increased processing, but lack of concern about adopting a majority (and thus presumably socially acceptable) position may motivate rather careless adoption of a position. At the same time, the positive identity usually conferred by majority status can sometimes accrue to minority sources (who may seem innovative, avantgarde, or creative; see Nemeth, 1986), and minorities (as Baker and Petty, 1996, showed) can elicit surprise and extensive processing with a proattitudinal advocacy just as majorities can with a counterattitudinal one. The bottom line is that social identity concerns can often be expressed through social cognition processes.

The Mental Representation of Persuasive Messages

Processing of message content has dominated the literature as the prime cognitive mediator of persuasive success. However, there are also reasons to believe that the manner in which persuasive messages are stored in memory also contributes to any influence that prevails. Why might the mental representation of persuasive messages be particularly important in the case of majority and minority influence?

First, there is considerable evidence that mental representations of groups differ, and to the extent that majorities and minorities are psychological groups, these differences might affect how information – including information about persuasive messages – about them is stored. The mental representation of social groups has been a widely investigated topic. Mullen and his colleagues (Mullen, 1991; Mullen and Johnson, 1993) have suggested that the size of a group is related to the cognitive complexity of the mental representation of the group. For example, they argue that small groups are more likely to be represented by a prototypical, and thus less differentiated, representation than are larger groups. Research evidence bears this idea out. Cognitive representations of small groups are relatively nondifferentiated, and this exaggeration of prototypicality in smaller groups occurs for both members and nonmembers. Not surprisingly, then, minorities tend to be perceived as relatively homogeneous by both majority and minority members (Simon and Brown, 1987; Simon and Hamilton, 1994). In contrast, majorities are more likely to be perceived as heterogeneous by both majority and minority group members. Thus mental representations of majorities are more likely to be differentiated than minority groups.

Majorities may also be more differentiated because mechanisms like false consensus (Ross et al., 1977) and desire for positive social identity (Tajfel and Turner, 1986) promote feelings of ingroup membership regarding majorities. That is, people tend to assume that they are part of the majority, given that they assume that most others share their opinions and views. At the same time, given the largely positive identity of majority groups, the motivation to belong to positively regarded groups increases identification with the majority. For these reasons, majority groups are more likely to function psychologically as ingroups, and research has repeatedly demonstrated that ingroups are perceived as being more heterogeneous than outgroups (Jones, Wood, and Quattrone, 1981; Park and Rothbart, 1982). For both these reasons, then, we might expect a greater degree of differentiation in the mental representations of majorities compared to minorities.

The clearest evidence that majorities are, in fact, better individuated than minorities comes from Brewer, Weber, and Carini (1995, Experiment 3). In this study, three speakers described as representing a numerical majority among students and three speakers described as representing a minority talked about their views on the United States and Russia. Participants were later presented with all the statements and asked to match each statement with the speaker who had advocated it. Results showed that participants were better able to correctly match the statements presented by majority group members than statements presented by minority group members. In other words, statements presented by minority group members were more likely to be mismatched with other members of the group than statements presented by majority group members. These findings indicate that information presented by majority group members may be better individuated in memory than information presented by minority group members.

Second, we know that arguments presented by a group perceived to be heterogeneous are more persuasive than those same arguments presented by a group perceived to be homogeneous. Both Wilder (1977) and Harkins and Petty (1987) have suggested that the perception of independence of views in the group plays an important role in persuasion. Both have demonstrated that groups that are mentally represented as having independent members are more influential than groups that are mentally represented as being less independent. For example, Harkins and Petty (1981, 1983, 1987) found that messages delivered by three individuals described as part of a committee were less persuasive than messages delivered by three unrelated individuals. These researchers concluded that the differential impact of the messages was mediated by the differential perception of the message and its source. Even though arguments were identical, representation of those arguments as coming from three independent sources made them more persuasive than when they were perceived as coming from a single homogeneous source.

The most definitive evidence of the link between mental representations of source arguments and persuasion was provided by Wilder (1990). To examine mental representations of arguments, Wilder also employed a recognition task which asked participants to match individual speakers to the particular arguments they had advanced. Results revealed that participants were able to match speakers and arguments from heterogeneous groups more accurately than they were able to match speakers and arguments from homogeneous groups. In addition, heterogeneous groups were more influential than homogeneous groups. Most convincingly, the accurate individuation of arguments and speakers mediated the persuasive impact of the influence attempt. Thus, it appears that arguments from homogeneous groups may be stored in memory tagged only with a group category, whereas arguments from heterogeneous groups may be tagged with the individual group member who presented the argument. Individuation of arguments from multiple communicators increases the perception of group members' independence, and makes the agreement of multiple independent others particularly compelling. These findings suggest that majorities may in part be more persuasive to the extent that they are perceived as heterogeneous, whereas minorities may be less persuasive to the extent that they are perceived as homogeneous.

Taken together, these considerations suggest that differential representations of persuasive messages in memory might, at least in part, mediate majority and minority influence. Messages advocated by a majority may be stored with each individual speaker, whereas messages advocated by a minority may be stored together at the level of the group. This, in turn, may impact the effectiveness of the persuasive attempt because messages that are advocated by multiple independent speakers are more compelling than messages advocated by a homogeneous group. Thus, messages advocated by a majority would have a representational advantage over messages advocated by a minority.

Our purpose in the studies described here was to assess the extent to which majority and minority arguments were individuated, and the extent to which any differences in such individuation contributed to majority and minority influence. The literature indicating that majorities are perceived to be more heterogeneous than minorities led us to predict that participants exposed to the majority position would be better able to remember the individual speaker who presented each argument than would participants exposed to a minority position. Further, we expected that this superior ability to individuate the arguments in the majority condition would lead to greater attitude change in the direction of the message advocated by the majority.

Experiment 1

To investigate these ideas, we first asked male and female undergraduates at the University of California, Santa Barbara (UCSB), to participate in a study of people's perceptions of speakers' personalities. Subjects reported their attitudes on a number of different social issues before participation in the study. Thirty-eight students who opposed the introduction of a comprehensive exam requirement for graduation at UCSB were told that they would evaluate four members of a student committee brought together to discuss whether such an exam should be instituted at UCSB in the coming year. Sixty students who opposed the legalization of marijuana were told they would listen to four members of a student committee organized to discuss this issue. Thus we were able to look at the impact of experimental manipulations on mental representations of arguments on two different topics.

Before participants heard the committee's opinions, they read the results of a poll on the relevant issue allegedly taken by the university newspaper during the previous quarter. Participants were told that over 3,000 UCSB students had responded. According to the poll, either a minority (22 percent) or a majority (78 percent) of the students polled supported either the comprehensive exam requirement or the legalization of marijuana, depending on condition. Participants then heard four speakers give arguments in support of the relevant issue. In the context of the student opinion poll, then, the speakers represented either the minority or the majority position on campus.

Participants heard two male and two female speakers each deliver two arguments on the issue that pretesting had shown to be strong and compelling. Each speaker presented just one argument at a time. As each person spoke, a head-and-shoulders photo of the speaker was projected onto a screen at the front of the experimental room so that it was possible to match an individual speaker with his or her views.

To assess the differentiation of the mental representation of the arguments presented and the possible effect this might have on persuasion, we had participants complete two key dependent measures. First, participants indicated their attitudes on the issue for a second time, allowing us to gauge the persuasive impact of hearing arguments from a majority or minority source. Second, participants were asked to match the arguments presented with the speaker who had presented them. Pictures of the four speakers were simultaneously projected at the front of the room and labeled 1, 2, 3, and 4. Participants were given a written list of the eight presented arguments, along with distracter arguments (i.e., foils) that had not been mentioned. Participants were asked to indicate which speaker, if any, had presented each argument. Comparison of the number of correct matches of speaker to statement allowed us to gauge the extent to which participants' mental representation of the majority and minority arguments was differentiated.

After ascertaining that the source manipulation had been successful, we first examined the degree of attitude change that had occurred. Comparison of participants' premessage and postmessage attitudes toward comprehensive exams and legalization of marijuana in the majority and minority conditions revealed a main effect for influence source, $F(1,95) = 14.45$, $p = .0003$, indicating that initial attitudes were significantly more affected by exposure to the majority source (M = 3.20) than the minority source (M = 1.81), as can be seen in the top panel of figure 14.1. Minority influence produced significant acceptance of the legalization of marijuana issue, but not the comprehensive exam issue. Majority influence elicited significant attitude change toward the advocated position on both issues and, in addition, majority influence was such that average attitudes toward the issues were changed from opposing the issues (M = 3.17) to supporting them (M = 6.37). Messages from the majority were thus significantly more successful in changing attitudes than exposure to minority arguments on both issues.

Having established that the majority source produced more attitude change, we then examined individuation of the arguments in the persuasive message to see whether the majority or minority message was more differentiated in

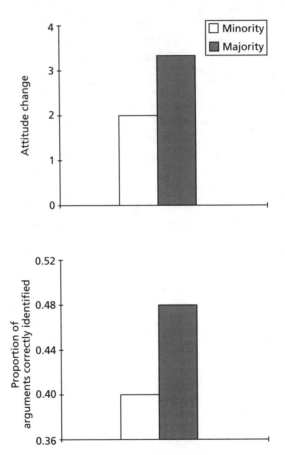

Figure 14.1 Attitude change on the comprehensive exam and marijuana issues after exposure to persuasive arguments from majority or minority communicators (Panel 1). Proportion of arguments correctly identified from majority or minority communicators (Panel 2).

memory. The proportion of the presented arguments correctly matched and the proportion of foils correctly rejected were calculated and analyzed. Participants assigned a greater proportion of arguments to the correct source in the majority condition ($M = .48$) than in the minority condition ($M = .40$), $F(1,95) = 3.68$, $p = .057$, as can be seen in the bottom panel of figure 14.1. Consistent with Brewer et al. (1995), this provided evidence that majority arguments are more closely stored with their individual source than are minority arguments.

Subjects who heard either majority or minority arguments were equally accurate in their ability to recognize foils, $F(1,95) < 1.0$. The average proportion correct in both conditions was .63, indicating that participants were able to distinguish between statements that had previously been presented and those that had not.

These first results thus suggested that the majority arguments were stored in a more differentiated fashion with each speaker than were minority arguments. In addition, exposure to the majority rather than the minority position resulted in greater attitude change. We initiated this line of research with the idea that differentiation of arguments would be responsible, at least partially, for this increased persuasion. To directly test the mediating impact of argument differentiation on attitude change, we compared the attitude change induced by the majority and minority sources in an ANCOVA, with the proportion of statements correctly attributed to speakers serving as the covariate. If the extent to which arguments are differentiated in memory mediates attitude change, then holding the level of differentiation constant should eradicate the difference in attitude change between the majority and minority conditions. This analysis revealed argument differentiation to be significantly related to attitude change, $F(1,94) = 19.30$, $p < .001$. In addition, inclusion of the proportion of arguments correctly attributed to speakers as a covariate significantly reduced the impact of message source on attitude change, although it did not erase it, $F(1,94) = 10.61$, $p < .002$. This suggests that differentiation of arguments, and in particular the greater differentiation of majority arguments that occurred, played an important role in promoting the greater attitude change initiated by the majority source. Also as expected, however, and consistent with existing research on other important mediators of social influence, argument differentiation was clearly not the only mediator of such influence.

The results of the first experiment were thus quite consistent with our theoretical predictions. Exposure to a majority point of view resulted in a more differentiated mental representation of presented arguments on two different topics, and this representation apparently helped produce the greater direct social influence elicited by the majority source on each of these issues. Our findings are thus consistent with earlier demonstrations (Wilder, 1990) indicating a persuasive advantage for messages that are presented by differentiated sources.

We are assuming that these results came about because majorities initiate the kind of processing that results in a more differentiated mental representation, and that this differentiated representation then in some way increases persuasion. In our experiment, it appeared that exposure to a majority source spontaneously resulted in more differentiated representations of the speakers and their arguments than did exposure to minority sources. Such differentiated representations may well be produced by the kind of intensive scrutiny that majority messages have received in prior research (Mackie, 1987), especially when advocating a counterattitudinal and therefore somewhat unexpected (Baker and Petty, 1996) or uncertainty-inducing position (Hogg and Abrams, 1993; Turner et al., 1993). In this regard, our findings are incompatible with suggestions that minorities show a persuasive advantage over majorities because their distinctiveness elicits increased processing (Moscovici, 1980, 1985; Mugny, 1984; Nemeth, 1986). In the context of this experiment, however, minority messages produced neither a differentiated mental representation nor persuasive effectiveness.

This is not to say that minority messages might never receive intensive processing of the kind leading to differentiated representations. In fact, our findings from Experiment 1 suggest that differentiation of minority members and their arguments might increase minority influence, where as nonindividuating majority members and their arguments might decrease majority influence. For example, the inclusion of individuating information about minority communicators should force the perception of heterogeneity that appeared, at least in this context, to naturally occur for majority communicators. This should allow the minority arguments to be stored with the individual communicators, as majority arguments appeared to be. Further, if individuation of arguments increases persuasiveness, individuated minority communicators should be as persuasive as majority communicators. Given these assumptions, we attempted in a second study to manipulate individuation independently of majority and minority status of the source, and to see if we could also increase and decrease attitude change in a related fashion. We also included in our second study some other measures to better understand the role of differentiation. Although results of accuracy on foil recognition in the first study indicated that the differentiation advantage held specifically for presented arguments, we wanted to assess the possibility that majority messages just received more scrutiny overall. In addition to continuing to measure foil recognition in the second study, we also assessed free recall of arguments before the recognition/matching task. At the same time, to see if differential impressions of majority and minority sources might be producing either differential representations or increased persuasion, we gathered information about participants' ratings of the speakers.

Experiment 2

In this study, participants who opposed a comprehensive exam requirement were exposed to arguments favoring the requirement from a majority or minority source in exactly the same way as in the first experiment. The conceptually important manipulation that was new to this experiment represented an attempt to either increase or decrease individuation of the speakers (regardless of their majority or minority status). In the nonindividuation condition, participants were given information about the composition of the committee that suggested that the speakers were similar to one another in several ways. For example, participants were told that all the committee members chosen were juniors (so that they could serve a longer term), and that they were all leaders of student groups who were brought together because they were all interested in university policies, and so forth. We expected this information to decrease individuation of speakers and thus the participants' ability to also correctly individuate their arguments. In contrast, we provided extra information about speakers in the individuation condition which was designed to make each speaker appear to be a unique individual, and thus to make it easier to keep track of each speaker's arguments. For example, one speaker was described as majoring in biology and working at the library, whereas another was described as a film studies major who also played lacrosse, and so forth.

After receiving the nonindividuating or individuating information about the speakers, participants heard the speakers voice their opinions and arguments about the comprehensive exam requirement, following the same procedure as used in the first study. They then indicated their own opinion on the issue and, after recalling as many of the presented arguments as possible, completed the task of matching the eight presented and eight foil arguments with the four speakers (or indicating that they had not heard the argument before). In this experiment we also measured perceptions of the speakers and to assess their impact on persuasion in addition to the influence of argument individuation.

After checking to see that participants had correctly recognized that either a majority or minority of UCSB students supported the examination requirement, we gauged the impact of exposure to the arguments on participants' opinions. Exposure to a majority source once again elicited significantly more attitude change ($M = 2.89$) than exposure to the minority's views ($M = 2.18$), $F(1,169) = 5.86$, $p = .02$. As can be seen in the top panel of figure 14.2, however, the extent to which the majority was more persuasive than the minority depended on whether or not individuating information was received, $F(1,169) = 3.19$, $p = .075$. Whereas the majority source ($M = 3.10$) was clearly more compelling than the minority source ($M = 1.81$) in the nonindividuated condition, $F(1,83) = 8.51$, $p < .005$, majorities and minorities produced equal amounts of persuasion in the individuated condition (Ms = 2.48 and 2.67 for the minority and majority, respectively, $F(1,86) < 1$). Thus, whereas the results of the nonindividuated condition appeared to replicate our findings from the first study, the provision of individuating information appeared to increase the persuasiveness of the minority source, while having little impact on the persuasiveness of the majority source.

We next examined the proportion of presented arguments that participants were able to attribute to the correct speaker in the majority and minority

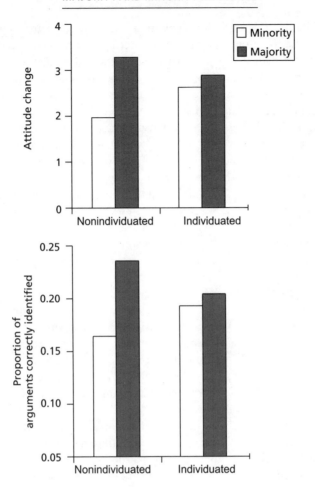

Figure 14.2 Attitude change on the comprehensive exam issue after exposure to persuasive arguments from individuated or nonindividuated, majority or minority communicators (Panel 1).
Proportion of arguments correctly identified from individuated or nonindividuated,
majority or minority communicators (Panel 2).

conditions (see lower panel of figure 14.2). This analysis revealed a marginal
interaction between message source and individuating condition, $F(1,69) = 2.46$,
$p = .11$. Further examination of the means indicated that participants were
marginally more accurate in correctly assigning arguments to speakers to the
majority ($M = .24$) than to the minority ($M = .17$) source in the nonindividuated
condition, $F(1,83) = 2.95$, $p = .09$, again paralleling, although not so strongly, the
results obtained in the first study. In the individuated condition, in contrast,
participants were equally correct in the majority ($M = .20$) and minority ($M =
.19$) source conditions, $F(1,86) < 1$. Note that argument differentiation in general

was considerably lower in this experiment than in the first. Other analyses revealed that neither foil recognition nor recall was superior for the majority (Ms = .62 and 4.57 for the proportion accurate and recall, respectively) compared to the minority (Ms = .56 and 4.16, respectively).

Participants' responses indicating both influence effectiveness and differentiation of argument representation were thus consistent. When participants were not provided with individuating information, their attitude change and argument representation responses replicated the pattern found in the first study, with greater attitude change and greater individuation of arguments accruing in the majority as compared to the minority condition. This suggests that participants may have assumed the kinds of nonindividuating information about committee make-up in Experiment 1 as we told them in Experiment 2. Even in the presence of this (either assumed or given) nonindividuating information, exposure to a counterattitudinal appeal from a majority source apparently resulted in the kind of processing that allowed recipients to better individuate arguments and speakers. That better-individuated group also produced more attitude change, again replicating results from the first experiment. To test the mediating role of argument differentiation on persuasion in the nonindividuated conditions, we again performed an ANCOVA, with correct assignment of arguments as the covariate and attitude change as the dependent measure. Again replicating the results of Experiment 1, argument differentiation covaried with attitude change, $F(1,82) = 3.40, p = .068$. In addition, and consistent with our expectations, controlling for accurate differentiation of arguments again significantly reduced the impact of the message source on attitude change, $F(1,82) = 6.94, p < .01$, but did not eliminate it. Thus, better differentiation of arguments appeared to contribute to persuasive effectiveness. As before, increased differentiation of arguments and its consequent persuasiveness appeared to accrue spontaneously to the majority source, even when somewhat nondifferentiated information was presented.

Results were quite different when participants were provided with some individuating information about the speakers. Provision of this information had no effect on individuation of or response to the majority source and message, suggesting that the majority position was spontaneously individuated at least to this extent in the nonindividuated condition. Provision of the information did have an impact on individuation of and reaction to the minority message, however, with both increasing in the presence of individuation, as predicted. To see if the increased argument individuation was responsible for the increased attitude change that occurred, we again performed an ANCOVA with argument assignment accuracy as the covariate. This analysis revealed that in the individuation condition, argument differentiation and attitude change were not related and controlling for argument differentiation had no impact on attitude change (all $Fs < 1$). Although we had expected a relationship between these two values, the success of our experimental manipulation may have hindered our ability to find it. Addition of the individuating information produced both argument differentiation and attitude change that were virtually identical in the individuating conditions, and thus reduced variance within this cell may have depressed correlations. Because argument differentiation in general was very low in Experiment 2, there was also less variance in the differentiation index. In the absence of evidence of such a clear relationship between attitude change and argument differentiation, we can conclude only that the provision of individuating information increased both argument differentiation and persuasiveness in the minority source condition, perhaps independently.

We also examined perceptions of the speakers on a number of dimensions (e.g., sociability, liking, and intelligence) to see if perceptions of majority and minority sources differed and if such impressions related to argument differentiation on attitude change. This analysis revealed no differences, with minority sources if anything being viewed slightly more positively than majority sources. We also examined participants' impressions of the speakers' independence. Participants saw speakers in the individuated condition as slightly ($M = 4.78$) but not significantly more independent than speakers in the nonindividuated condition ($M = 4.44$; $F(1,169) = 1.90$, $p = .17$). None of these measures predicted argument differentiation or attitude change in either condition.

General Discussion

The results of these two studies provide support for the idea that differentiation of message arguments can contribute to the differential persuasive capacities of majority and minority sources. In both studies, and regardless of the social issue advocated, majority support led to both greater differentiation of arguments and greater attitude change. That is, subjects were more likely to remember the individual communicator who delivered the arguments when that individual represented the majority viewpoint, and this greater differentiation of arguments contributed to the majority's persuasive advantage in Experiment 1. Further evidence for the important role of argument differentiation was obtained in Experiment 2, where presentation of individualizing information about the minority group increased differentiation of its arguments and eliminated the majority's persuasive advantage.

In this sense our results confirm earlier demonstrations that differentiated mental representations of arguments promote persuasiveness (Harkins and Petty, 1987; Wilder, 1990). Our findings offer new perspectives on the processes of majority and minority influence, however, because they demonstrated that, in two of the three conditions studied (Experiment 1 and the nonindividuated condition of Experiment 2), greater differentiation of the majority than the minority viewpoint spontaneously occurred (see also Brewer et al., 1995). Because our studies were lacking certain methodological niceties (such as complete counterbalancing in stimulus material presentations), because they are the first findings on this issue to appear, and because some of the results were not as strong as we would have liked, replication is clearly necessary before any firm conclusions can be drawn. However, these findings raise interesting questions, both about the nature of processing that led to these effects and the conditions under which such effects occur.

We assume that, under certain conditions (discussed in more detail next), majority messages are processed in such a way as to lead to more differentiated representations of their constituent arguments. Although we did not include measures that allowed us to perform cognitive response analysis, recall analysis and analysis of foil recognition showed no general processing advantage for majority messages. This is consistent with other research indicating that it is the quality of processing, rather than the quantity of processing, that is more important in producing persuasion (Maass and Clark, 1983; Trost et al., 1992). If majority messages are subject to extensive scrutiny of argument quality, this may well produce more differentiated representations (to our knowledge, no persuasion studies have included cognitive response analyses and mental representational assessments in the same procedure). At the same time, it is possible that, regardless of processing differences, majorities may have a differentiation advantage for some of the reasons proposed in the introduction. That is, majorities, and especially majorities that are perceived as ingroups, may be naturally perceived as more diverse and heterogeneous, facilitating accurate assignment of arguments to speakers and thus promoting argument differentiation. The role of these factors in enhancing differentiation gains support from the results of Experiment 2, where providing information designed to individuate group members increased argument differentiation and persuasiveness for the minority source (although there was no evidence for the direct causal effect of argument differentiation).

Although the lack of direct measures again makes any conclusions that can be drawn tentative, the impact of this individuation appears to have been mediated through argument differentiation rather than directly. In discussing the role of argument differentiation, Wilder (1990) concluded that when arguments are stored in an individuated manner, each source appears to have acquired his or her attitude independently, and this makes them more convincing because their opinions provide consensus information about the validity of the attitude. In contrast, when the sources of persuasive arguments are confused in memory, this validity is lost. Thus, argument differentiation promotes the perception of independence, which in turn promotes persuasion. Recall that in our experiments, however, neither majority nor individuated sources appeared significantly more independent than minority or nonindividuated sources, and independence ratings did not predict attitude change. On the one hand, this may be a sign that our manipulation was not particularly strong or successful. On the other hand, it could suggest that individuation increased argument differentiation and persuasion without those effects depending on increased perceptions of independence. A third possibility is that something specific about our manipulation of individuation caused these effects. In our studies, we used extra demographic information about our speakers in order to individuate them and thus their arguments. We know little about how other kinds of information about the speakers or other processing motivations might influence mental representations, or whether source individuation or argument differentiation is more important. More extensive research and replication is necessary before any firm conclusions can be drawn about these issues.

Careful consideration of the conditions under which we found both greater differentiation and greater persuasiveness for the majority source suggests certain limits on these effects that need to be borne in mind. First, both our studies focused on the consequences of receiving counterattitudinal persuasive appeals. The increased motivation and the subsequent increased processing that occurs when people are faced with a counterattitudinal persuasive message from a majority has been well established (Baker and Petty, 1996; Mackie, 1987; Trost et al., 1992). As Baker and Petty (1996) have pointed out, such processing differences might be triggered not by the majority status of the source alone, but because that particular source advocates a counterattitudinal position. Because people believe that their opinions are widely held (Ross et al., 1977), disagreement with a majority could be surprising or create subjective uncertainty about the cause of the discrepancy, creating the motivation to carefully process the message. In contrast, disagreement with a minority does not activate this increased processing. Thus, it may be counterattitudinal majority messages rather than majority messages that are spontaneously better differentiated. From this perspective, we might expect to find greater argument differentiation when a minority source advocates a proattitudinal position, as long as the recipient found that surprising or unexpected.

A second cautionary note needs to be sounded about the fact that these studies focused only on direct measures of attitude change. Although research findings differ, there is some consensus that minority sources can have enhanced indirect influence – persuasion on related issues, in absolutely private settings, in ways that do not align recipients openly with the minority. Because we had no measures of this kind, we were not able to explore the impact of individuation on indirect influence. It may be, for example, that whereas in our studies majorities were more influential than minorities at the direct level, minorities were having some indirect impact that might also have been changed by increased differentiation.

Third, we examined only majority and minority groups that were perceived as ingroups by our participants. All speakers were described as UCSB students. As Turner (1991) has pointed out, people are motivated to engage in increased cognitive activity only when they find themselves disagreeing with a source – majority or minority – with whom they did not expect to differ in any relevant way. More recently, Crano (Alvaro and Crano, 1996; Crano and Hannula-Bral, 1994) has demonstrated that task requirements mediate the attention and processing received by majority and minority positions, presumably because different tasks make salient different others with whom appropriate comparisons need to be made (Turner, 1991; Turner et al., 1993). Participants engaged in a sub-jective (no one right answer) task were more influenced by majorities, whereas those given an objective task were more vulnerable to minority influence. Thus our production of greater spontaneous argument differentiation and persuasion might be limited not only to counterattitudinal majority messages but to counter-attitudinal messages on certain issues from ingroup majorities. This point also underscores the fact that our understanding of influence processes in this study is limited to reactions to numerical majorities and minorities. Because of their associated stereotypical and social identity implications, social majorities and minorities might induce different kinds of processing and thus different kinds of persuasion (Moskowitz, 1996).

Finally, it is important to keep in mind that although differentiation of argu-ments was related to attitude change, it was by no means the only mediator. We make no claims that this cognitive mechanism is solely responsible for differ-ences in the persuasive effect of majority and minorities, regardless of the circumstances. Indeed, the results of mediational analyses of findings in Experi-ment 1 and in the nonindividuated condition in Experiment 2 tell a very clear story: although controlling for argument differentiation reduced the impact of source status on persuasion, it did not eliminate it. Thus many other social and cognitive mechanisms no doubt contribute to the persuasiveness of majority and minority sources. Given that argument differentiation has been found to play a contributing role in both majority and minority influence and ingroup and out-group influence (Wilder, 1990), however, its role in other forms and occurrences of influence and persuasion is worthy of increased scrutiny.

Our findings provide another example of the interaction between social iden-tity factors and cognitive processing mechanisms that contribute to social beha-vior (Moreland, Hogg, and Hains, 1994). Bringing the social identity and cognitive perspectives together is particularly important in the case of majority and minority influence, because examination of this phenomenon has tended to be quite different on either side of the Atlantic. Only when these perspectives are brought together does the contribution that each approach offers to the other become apparent. Note, for example, how the distinctions raised by Moscovici map nicely onto the models of attitude change developed by Chaiken (1980) and Petty and Cacioppo (1986), or how Turner's views about people's expectations about who they should agree with, have been borne out in Petty and Baker's research on minority and majority influence on pro-and counterattitudinal issues, and Crano's work on subjective and objective tasks. By examining mental representations and how they are influenced by the status of majority and minority sources, we hope to have contributed to further demonstrating the intertwining functioning of social identity and social cognition mechanisms underlying this important domain of social behavior.

References

Alvaro, E.M. and Crano, W.D. (1996). Cognitive responses to minority- or majority-based communications: Factors that underlie minority influence. *British Journal of Social Psychology*, 35, 105–21.

Asch, S.E. (1956). Studies of independence and conformity: I. A minority of one against a unanimous majority. *Psychology Monographs*, 70.

Back, K., Festinger, L., Hymovitch, B., Kelley, H., and others (1950). The methodology of studying rumor transmission. *Human Relations*, 3, 307–12.

Baker, S.M. and Petty, R.E. (1996). Majority and minority influence: Source advocacy as a determinant of message scrutiny. *Journal of Personality and Social Psychology*, 67, 5–19.

Brewer, M.B., Weber, J.G., and Carini, B. (1995). Person memory in intergroup contexts: Categorization versus individuation. *Journal of Personality and Social Psychology*, 69, 29–40.

Chaiken, S. (1980). Heuristic versus systematic information processing and the use of source versus message cues in persuasion. *Journal of Personality and Social Psychology*, 39, 752–66.

Clark, R.D., III (1990). Minority influence: The role of argument refutation of the majority position and social support for the minority position. *European Journal of Social Psychology*, 20, 489–97.

Clark, R.D., III and Maass, A. (1988). The role of social categorization and perceived source credibility in minority influence. *European Journal of Social Psychology*, 18, 381–94.

Crano, W.D. and Hannula-Bral, K.A. (1994). Context/categorization model of social influence: Minority and majority influence in the formation of a novel response norm. *Journal of Experimental Social Psychology*, 30, 247–76.

David, B. and Turner, J.C. (1996). Studies in self-categorization and minority conversion: Is being a member of the out-group an advantage? *British Journal of Social Psychology*, 35, 179–99.

Festinger, L. and Thibaut, J. (1951). Interpersonal communication in small groups. *Journal of Abnormal and Social Psychology*, 46, 92–9.

Harkins, S.G. and Petty, R.E. (1981). The multiple source effect in persuasion: The effects of distraction. *Personality and Social Psychology Bulletin*, 7, 627–35.

Harkins, S.G. and Petty, R.E. (1983). Social context effects in persuasion: The effects of multiple sources and multiple targets. In P. Paulus (ed.), *Basic Group Processes*. New York: Springer-Verlag, pp. 149–75.

Harkins, S.G. and Petty, R.E. (1987). Information utility and the multiple source effect. *Journal of Personality and Social Psychology*, 59, 1202–13.

Hastie, R. and Kumar, P.A. (1979). Person memory: Personality traits as organizing principles in memory for behaviors. *Journal of Personality and Social Psychology*, 37, 25–38.

Hogg, M.A. and Abrams, D. (1993). Towards a single-process uncertainty-reduction model of social motivation in groups. In M.A. Hogg and D. Abrams (eds), *Group Motivation: Social psychological perspectives*. Hemel Hempstead and New York: Harvester Wheatsheaf and Prentice-Hall, pp. 173–90.

Jones, E.E., Wood, G.C., and Quattrone, G.A. (1981). Perceived variability of personal characteristics in ingroups and outgroups: The role of knowledge and evaluation. *Personality and Social Psychology Bulletin*, 7, 523–8.

Katz, D. (1960). The functional approach to the study of attitudes. *Public Opinion Quarterly*, 24, 163–204.

Kelman, H.C. (1958). Compliance, identification, and internalization: Three processes of attitude change. *Journal of Conflict Resolution*, 2, 51–60.

Kruglanski, A. and Mackie, D.M. (1990). Majority and minority influence: A judgmental process analysis. In W. Stroebe and M. Hewstone (eds), *Advances in European Social Psychology*, Vol. 1. Chichester: Wiley, pp. 229–62.

Maass, A. and Clark, R.D., III (1983). Internalization versus compliance: Differential processes underlying minority influence and conformity. *European Journal of Social Psychology*, 13, 197–215.

Maass, A. and Clark, R.D., III (1984). Hidden impact of minorities: Fifteen years of minority influence research. *Psychological Bulletin*, 95, 428–50.

Maass, A., Clark, R.D., III, and Haberkorn, G. (1982). The effects of differential ascribed category membership and norms on minority influence. *European Journal of Social Psychology*, 57, 981–93.

Mackie, D.M. (1987). Systematic and nonsystematic processing of majority and minority persuasive communications. *Journal of Personality and Social Psychology*, 53, 41–52.

Mackie, D.M. and Queller, S.Q. (in press). The impact of group membership on persuasion: Revisiting "Who says what to whom with what effect." In D. Terry and M.A. Hogg (eds), *Social Identity, Social Cognition, and Social Influence*. London: Blackwell.

Martin, R. (1988). Minority influence and social categorization: A replication. *European Journal of Social Psychology*, 18, 369–73.

Moreland, R.L., Hogg, M.A., and Hains, S.C. (1994). Back to the future: Social psychological research on groups. *Journal of Experimental Social Psychology*, 30, 527–55.

Moscovici, S. (1980). Toward a theory of conversion behavior. In L. Berkowitz (ed.), *Advances in Experimental Social Psychology*, Vol. 13. New York: Academic Press, pp. 209–39.

Moscovici, S. (1985). Social influence and conformity. In G. Lindzey and E. Aronson (eds), *The Handbook of Social Psychology*, Vol. 2. New York: Random House, pp. 347–412.

Moskowitz, G. (1996). The mediational effects of attributions and information processing in minority social influence. *British Journal of Social Psychology*, 35, 47–66.

Mugny, G. (1984). Compliance, conversion and the Asch paradigm. *European Journal of Social Psychology*, 14, 353–68.

Mugny, G. and Papstamou, S. (1982). Minority influence and psycho-social identity. *European Journal of Social Psychology*, 12, 379–94.

Mullen, B. (1991). Group composition, salience, and cognitive representations: The phenomenology of being in a group. *Journal of Experimental Social Psychology*, 27, 297–323.

Mullin, B. and Hogg, M.A. (in press). Dimensions of subjective uncertainty in social identification and minimal intergroup discrimination. *British Journal of Social Psychology*.

Mullen, B. and Johnson, C. (1993). Cognitive representation in ethnophaulisms as a function of group size: The phenomenology of being in a group. *Personality and Social Psychology Bulletin*, 19, 296–304.

Nemeth, C. (1986). Differential contributions of majority and minority influence. *Psychological Review*, 93, 23–32.

Park, B. and Rothbart, M. (1982). Perception of outgroup homogeneity and levels of social categorization: Memory for the subordinate attributes of ingroup and outgroup members. *Journal of Personality and Social Psychology*, 42, 1051–68.

Petty, R.E. and Cacioppo, J.T. (1986). *Attitudes and Persuasion: Classic and contemporary approaches*. Dubuque, IA: Brown.

Pyszczynski, T.A. and Greenberg, J. (1981). Role of disconfirmed expectancies in the instigation of attributional processing. *Journal of Personality and Social Psychology*, 40, 31–8.

Ross, L., Greene, D., and House, P. (1977). The "false consensus effect": An egocentric bias in social perception and attribution processes. *Journal of Experimental Social Psychology*, 13, 279–301.

Schachter, S. (1951). Deviation, rejection, and communication. *Journal of Abnormal and Social Psychology*, 46, 190–207.

Simon, B. and Brown, R. (1987). Perceived intragroup homogeneity in minority–majority contexts. *Journal of Personality and Social Psychology*, 53, 703–11.

Simon, B. and Hamilton, D.L. (1994). Self-stereotyping and social context: The effects of relative in-group size and in-group status. *Journal of Personality and Social Psychology*, 66, 699–711.

Smith, M.B., Bruner, J.S., and White, R.W. (1956). *Opinions and Personality*. New York: Wiley.

Tajfel, H. and Turner, J.C. (1986). The social identity theory of intergroup behavior. In S. Worchel and W.G. Austin (eds), *Psychology of Intergroup Relations*, 2nd edn. Chicago: Nelson-Hall, pp. 7–24.

Trost, M.R., Maass, A., and Kenrick, D.T. (1992). Minority influence: Personal relevance biases cognitive processes and reverses private acceptance. *Journal of Experimental Social Psychology*, 28, 234–54.

Turner, J.C. (1991). *Social Influence*. Pacific Grove, CA: Brooks-Cole.

Turner, J.C., McGarty, C., Oakes, P.J., and Haslam, S.A. (1993). The creation of uncertainty in the influence process: The roles of stimulus information and disagreement with similar others. *European Journal of Social Psychology*, 23, 17–38.

Wilder, D.A. (1977). Perception of groups, size of opposition, and social influence. *Journal of Experimental Social Psychology*, 13, 253–68.

Wilder, D.A. (1990). Some determinants of the persuasive power of in-groups and out-groups: Organization of information and attribution of independence. *Journal of Personality and Social Psychology*, 59, 1202–13.

Wood, W., Lundgren, S., Ouellette, J.A., Busceme, S., and Blackstone, T. (1994). Minority influence: A meta-analytic review of social influence processes. *Psychological Bulletin*, 115, 323–45.

References

Abelson, R.P. (1994). A personal perspective on social cognition. In P.G. Devine, D.L. Hamilton, T.M. Ostrom (eds), *Social Cognition: Impact on social psychology*. San Diego: Academic Press, pp. 15–37.

Abelson, R.P., Dasgupta, N., Park, J., and Banaji, M.R. (1994). Ingroup perceptions of the collective other. Paper presented at American Psychological Society.

Abrams, D. (1985). Focus of attention in minimal intergroup discrimination. *British Journal of Social Psychology*, 24, 65–74.

Abrams, D. (1990). How do group members regulate their behaviour? An integration of social identity and self-awareness theories. In D. Abrams and M.A. Hogg (eds), *Social Identity Theory: Constructive and critical advances*. London and New York: Harvester Wheatsheaf and Springer-Verlag, pp. 89–112.

Abrams, D. (1992a). Optimal Distinctiveness Theory with bells on: Music sub-culture identification among 16–20-year-olds. Paper presented at the European Association of Experimental Social Psychology Small Group Meeting on Social Cognition, Bristol, April.

Abrams, D. (1992b). Processes of social identification. In G. Breakwell (ed.), *Social Psychology of Identity and the Self-concept*. San Diego: Academic Press, pp. 57–99.

Abrams, D. (1993). From social identity to action. "British Invited Speaker" presentation, British Psychological Society, Social Psychology Section Conference, Oxford, September.

Abrams, D. (1994). Social self-regulation. *Personality and Social Psychology Bulletin*, 20, 473–83.

Abrams, D. (1996). Social identity, self as structure and self as process. In W.P. Robinson (ed.), *Social Groups and Identities: Developing the legacy of Henri Tajfel*. Oxford: Butterworth-Heinemann, pp. 143–67.

Abrams, D. and Brown, R.J. (1989). Self-consciousness and social identity: Self-regulation as a group member. *Social Psychology Quarterly*, 52, 311–18.

Abrams, D. and Hogg, M.A. (1987). Language attitudes, frames of reference and social identity: A Scottish dimension. *Journal of Language and Social Psychology*, 6, 201–13.

Abrams, D. and Hogg, M.A. (1988). Comments on the motivational status of self-esteem in social identity and intergroup discrimination. *European Journal of Social Psychology*, 18, 317–34.

Abrams, D. and Hogg, M.A. (1990a). An introduction to the social identity approach. In D. Abrams and M.A. Hogg (eds), *Social Identity Theory: Constructive and critical advances*. London and New York: Harvester Wheatsheaf and Springer-Verlag, pp. 1–9.

Abrams, D. and Hogg, M.A. (1990b). Social identification, self- categorization, and social influence. *European Review of Social Psychology*, 1, 195–228.

Abrams, D. and Hogg, M.A. (1998). Prospects for research in group processes and intergroup relations. *Group Processes and Intergroup Relations*, 1, 7–20.

Abrams, D. and Hogg, M.A. (eds) (1990a). *Social Identity Theory: Constructive and critical advances*. London: Harvester Wheatsheaf.

Abrams, D. and Hogg, M.A. (in press). Self, group and identity: A dynamic model. In M.A. Hogg and R.S. Tindale (eds), *Blackwell Handbook in Social Psychology*, vol. 3, *Group Processes*. Oxford: Blackwell.

Abrams, D. and Masser, B. (1998). Context and the social self- regulation of stereotyping: Perception, judgment and behaviour. In R.S. Wyer (ed.), *Advances in Social Cognition*, Vol. 11. Hillsdale, NJ: Erlbaum, pp. 53–68.

Abrams, D., Ando, K., and Hinkle, S.W. (1998). Psychological attachment to the group: Cross cultural differences in organizational identification and subjective norms as predictors of workers' turnover intentions. *Personality and Social Psychology Bulletin*, 10, 1027–39.

Abrams, D., Au, W., Waterman, W., Garst, J., and Mallett, C. (in preparation). The two baskets and one process views of self: Three experiments on self-stereotyping, University of Kent.

Abrams, D., Sparkes, K., and Hogg, M.A. (1985). Gender salience and social identity: The impact of sex of siblings on educational and occupational aspirations. *British Journal of Educational Psychology*, 55, 224–32.

Abrams, D., Thomas, J., and Hogg, M.A. (1990). Numerical distinctiveness, social identity and gender salience. *British Journal of Social Psychology*, 29, 87–92.

Abrams, D., Wetherell, M., Cochrane, S., Hogg, M.A., and Turner, J.C. (1990). Knowing what to think by knowing who you are: Self- categorization and the nature of norm formation, conformity and group polarization. *British Journal of Social Psychology*, 29, 97–119.

Acock, A.C. and DeFleur, M.L. (1972). A configurational approach to contingent consistency in the attitude–behavior relationship. *American Sociological Review*, 37, 714–26.

Adorno, T.W., Frenkel-Brunswik, E., Levinson, D.J., and Sanford, R.N. (1950). *The Authoritarian Personality*. New York: Harper.

Ajzen, I. (1987). Attitudes, traits, and actions: Dispositional prediction of behavior in personality and social psychology. In L. Berkowitz (ed.), *Advances in Experimental Social Psychology*, vol. 20. New York: Academic Press, pp. 1–64.

Ajzen, I. (1991). The theory of planned behavior. *Organizational Behavior and Human Decision Processes*, 50, 179–211.

Allport, F.H. (1924). *Social Psychology*. New York: Houghton Mifflin.

Allport, F.H. (1962). A structuronomic conception of behaviour: Individual and collective. *Journal of Abnormal and Social Psychology*, 64, 3–30.

Allport, G.W. (1954). *The Nature of Prejudice*. Cambridge, MA: Addison-Wesley.

Allport, G.W. (1961). *Pattern and Growth in Personality*. New York: Holt, Rinehart, and Winston.

Amir, Y. (1976). The role of intergroup contact in change of prejudice and race relations. In P. Katz (ed.), *Toward the Elimination of Racism*. New York: Pergamon, pp. 245–380.

Anastasio, P., Bachman, B., Gaertner, S., and Dovidio, J.F. (1997) Categorization, recategorization and common ingroup identity. In R. Spears, P.J. Oakes, N. Ellemers, and A. Haslam (eds), *The Social Psychology of Stereotyping and Group Life*. Oxford: Blackwell, pp. 236–56.

Andersen, S.M. and Klatzky, R.L. (1987). Traits and social stereotypes: Levels of categorization in person perception. *Journal of Personality and Social Psychology*, 53, 235–46.

Anderson, C.A. and Sedikides, C. (1991). Thinking about people: Contributions of a typological alternative to associationistic and dimensional models of person perception. *Journal of Personality and Social Psychology*, 60, 203–17.

Anderson, J.R. (1983). *The Architecture of Cognition*. Cambridge, MA: Harvard University Press.

Andrews, K.H. and Kandel, D.B. (1979). Attitude and behavior: A specification of the contingent-consistency hypothesis. *American Sociological Review*, 44, 298–310.

Apfelbaum, E. (1979). Relations of domination and movements for liberation: An analysis of power between groups. In W.G. Austin and S. Worchel (eds), *The Social Psychology of Intergroup Relations*. Monterey, CA: Brooks-Cole, pp. 188–204.

Arcuri, L. (1982). Three patterns of social categorization in attribution memory. *European Journal of Social Psychology*, 12, 271–82.

Arnold, M.B. (1960). *Emotion and Personality*, vol. I, *Psychological Aspects*. New York: Columbia University Press.

Aron, A., Aron, E.N., Tudor, M., and Nelson, G. (1991). Close relationships as including other in the self. *Journal of Personality and Social Psychology*, 60, 241–53.

Asch, S.E. (1946). Forming impressions of personality. *Journal of Abnormal and Social Psychology*, 41, 258–90.

Asch, S.E. (1952). *Social Psychology*. Englewood Cliffs, NJ: Prentice-Hall.

Augoustinos, M. and Walker, I. (1995). *Social Cognition. An integrated introduction*. London: Sage.

Augoustinos, M., Ahrens, C., and Innes, J.M. (1994). Stereotypes and prejudice: The Australian experience. *British Journal of Social Psychology*, 33, 125–41.

Bagozzi, R.P. and Schnedlitz, P. (1985). Social contingencies in the attitude model: A test of certain interaction hypotheses. *Social Psychology Quarterly*, 48, 366–73.

Bains, G. (1983). Explanations and the need for control. In M. Hewstone (ed.), *Attribution Theory: Social and functional extensions*. Oxford: Blackwell, pp. 126–43.

Banaji, M. and Hardin, C. (1996). Automatic stereotyping. *Psychological Science*, 7, 136–41.

Banaji, M.R. and Greenwald, A.G. (1993). Implicit stereotyping and prejudice. In M.P. Zanna and J.M. Olson (eds), *The Psychology of Prejudice: The Ontario symposium*, vol. 7. Hillsdale, NJ: Erlbaum, pp. 55–76.

Banaji, M.R. and Greenwald, A.G. (1995). Implicit gender stereotyping in judgments of fame. *Journal of Personality and Social Psychology*, 68, 181–98.

Banaji, M.R. and Hardin, C. (1996). Automatic stereotyping. *Psychological Science*, 7, 136–41.

Banaji, M.R. and Prentice, D.A. (1994). The self in social contexts. *Annual Review of Psychology*, 45, 297–332.

Banaji, M.R., Hardin, C., and Rothman, A.J. (1993). Implicit stereotyping in person judgment. *Journal of Personality and Social Psychology*, 65, 272–81.

Bandura, A. (1996). *Social Foundations of Thought and Action: A social cognitive theory*. Englewood Cliffs, NJ: Prentice-Hall.

Bargh, J.A. (1984). Automatic and conscious processing of social information. In R.S. Wyer, Jr and T.K. Srull (eds), *Handbook of Social Cognition*, vol. 3. Hillsdale, NJ: Erlbaum, pp. 1–43.

Bargh, J.A. (1989). Conditional automaticity: Varieties of automatic influence in social perception and cognition. In J.S. Uleman and J.A. Bargh (eds), *Unintended Thought*. New York: Guilford, pp. 3–51.

Bargh, J.A. (1994). The four horsemen of automaticity: Awareness, intention, efficiency, and control in social cognition. In R.S. Wyer, Jr and T.K. Srull (eds), *Handbook of Social Cognition*, 2nd edn, vol. 1. Hillsdale, NJ: Erlbaum, pp. 1–40.

Bargh, J.A. (1996). Automaticity in social psychology. In E.T. Higgins and A. Kruglanski (eds), *Social Psychology: Handbook of basic principles*. New York: Guilford, pp. 169–83.

Bargh, J.A. (1997). The automaticity of everyday life. In R.S. Wyer (ed.), *Advances in Social Cognition*, vol. 10. Mahwah, NJ: Erlbaum, pp. 1–61.

Bargh, J.A. and Pietromonaco, P. (1982). Automatic information processing and social perception: The influence of trait information presented outside of conscious awareness on impression formation. *Journal of Personality and Social Psychology*, 43, 437–49.

Bargh, J.A. and Pratto, F. (1986). Individual construct accessibility and perceptual selection. *Journal of Experimental Social Psychology*, 22, 293–311.

Bargh, J.A. and Tota, M.E. (1988). Context-dependent automatic processing in depression: Accessibility of negative constructs with regard to self but not others. *Journal of Personality and Social Psychology*, 54, 925–39.

Bargh, J.A., Bond, R.N., Lombardi, W.J., and Tota, M.E. (1986). The additive nature of chronic and temporary sources of construct accessibility. *Journal of Personality and Social Psychology*, 50, 869–78.

Bargh, J.A., Lombardi, W.J. and Higgins, E.T. (1988). Automaticity of chronically accessible constructs in person x situation effects on person perception: It's just a matter of time. *Journal of Personality and Social Psychology*, 55, 4, 599–605.

Barsalou, L.W. (1987). The instability of graded structure: Implications for the nature of concepts. In U. Neisser (ed.), *Concepts and Conceptual Development: Ecological and intellectual factors in categorization*. Cambridge: Cambridge University Press, pp. 101–40.

Bartlett, F.C. (1932). *Remembering*. Cambridge: Cambridge University Press.

Bassili, J.N. (1995). Response latency and the accessibility of voting intentions: What contributes to accessibility and how it affects vote choice. *Personality and Social Psychology Bulletin*, 21, 686–95.

Batson, C.D., Polycarpou, M.P., Harmon-Jones, E., Imhoff, H.J., Mitchener, E.C., Bednar, L.L., Klein, T.R., and Highberger, L. (1997). Empathy and attitudes: Can feeling for a member of a stigmatized group improve feelings toward the group? *Journal of Personality and Social Psychology*, 72, 105–18.

Batson, C.D., Shaw, L.L., and Oleson, K.C. (1992). Differentiating affect, mood, and emotion: Toward functionality based conceptual distinctions. In M.S. Clark (ed.), *Emotion: Review of personality and social psychology*, vol. 13. Newbury Park, CA: Sage, pp. 294–326.

Baumeister, R.F. (1982). Self-esteem, self-presentation, and future interaction: A dilemma of reputation. *Journal of Personality*, 50, 29–45.

Baumeister, R.F. (ed.) (1993). *Self-esteem: The puzzle of low self-regard*. New York: Plenum Press.

Baumeister, R.F. and Jones, E.E. (1978). When self-presentation is constrained by the target's knowledge: Consistency and compensation. *Journal of Personality and Social Psychology*, 36, 608–18.

Baumeister, R.F. and Leary, M.R. (1995). The need to belong: Desire for interpersonal attachments as a fundamental human motivation. *Psychological Bulletin*, 117, 497–529.

Baumeister, R.F., Heatherton, T.F., and Tice, D.M. (1993). When ego threats lead to self-regulation failure: Negative consequences of high self-esteem. *Journal of Personality and Social Psychology*, 64, 141–56.

Baumeister, R.F., Tice, D.M., and Hutton, D.G. (1989). Self- presentational motivations and personality differences in self- esteem. *Journal of Personality*, 57, 547–79.

Baumgardner, A.H. (1990). To know oneself is to like oneself: Self-certainty and self-affect. *Journal of Personality and Social Psychology*, 58, 1062–72.

Bellezza, F.S. (1984). The self as a mnemonic device: The role of internal cues. *Journal of Personality and Social Psychology*, 47, 506–16.

Bellezza, F.S. (1993). Does "perplexing" describe the self- reference effect? Yes! In T.K. Srull and R.S. Wyer, Jr (eds), *The Mental Representation of Trait and Autobiographical Knowledge about the Self: Advances in social cognition*, vol. 5. Hillsdale, NJ: Lawrence Erlbaum Associates, pp. 51–60.

Bem, D.J. (1967). Self-perception: An alternative interpretation of cognitive dissonance phenomena. *Psychological Review*, 74, 183–200.

Berscheid, E. (1992). A glance back at a quarter century of social psychology. *Journal of Personality and Social Psychology*, 63, 525–33.

Bettenhausen, K.L. (1991). Five years of groups research: What we have learned and what needs to be addressed. *Journal of Management*, 17, 345–81.

Biernat, M. and Vescio, T.K. (1993). Categorization and stereotyping: Effects of group context on memory and social judgment. *Journal of Experimental Social Psychology*, 29, 166–202.

Biernat, M., Vescio, T.K., and Manis, M. (1998). Judging and behaving toward members of stereotyped groups: A shifting standards perspective. To appear in C. Sedikides, J. Schopler, and C. Insko (eds), *Intergroup Cognition and Intergroup Behavior*. Hillsdale, NJ: Erlbaum.

Billig, M. (1976). *Social Psychology and Intergroup Relations*. London: Academic Press.

Billig, M. (1978). *Fascists: A social psychological view of the National Front*. London: Harcourt Brace Jovanovich.

Billig, M. (1988). The notion of "prejudice": Some rhetorical and ideological aspects. *Text*, 8, 91–111.

Billig, M. and Tajfel, H. (1973). Social categorization and similarity in intergroup behavior. *European Journal of Social Psychology*, 3, 27–52.

Blair, I.V. and Banaji, M.R. (1996). Automatic and controlled processes in gender stereotyping. *Journal of Personality and Social Psychology*, 70, 1142–63.

Blascovich, J. and Tomaka, J. (1991). Measures of self-esteem. In J.P. Robinson, P.R. Shaver, and L.S. Wrightman (eds), *Measures of Personality and Social Psychological Attitudes*, vol. 1. San Diego: Academic Press.

Bobo, L. (1983). Whites' opposition to busing: Symbolic racism or realistic group conflict? *Journal of Personality and Social Psychology*, 45, 1196–1210.

Bodenhausen, G. and Macrae, C.N. (1998). Stereotype activation and inhibition. In R.S. Wyer (ed.), *Advances in Social Cognition*, (vol. 11). Hillsdale, NJ: Erlbaum, pp. 1–52.

Bodenhausen, G.V. and Macrae, C.N. (in press). Stereotype activation and inhibition. In R.S. Wyer, Jr, (ed), *Advances in Social Cognition*, vol. 11, *Stereotype Activation and Inhibition*. Mahwah, NJ: Erlbaum.

Bourhis, R.Y., Sachdev, I., and Gagnon, A. (1994). Intergroup research with the Tajfel matrices: Methodological notes. In M. Zanna and J. Olson (eds), *The Psychology of Prejudice: The Ontario symposium*, vol. 7. Hillsdale, NJ: Erlbaum, pp. 209–22.

Breakwell, G. (1986). *Coping with Threatened Identities*. London: Methuen.

Breakwell, G.M. (1986). Political and attributional responses of the young short-term unemployed. *Political Psychology*, 7, 575–86.

Breckler, S. and Greenwald, A. (1986). Motivational facets of the self. In R. Sorrentino and T. Higgins (eds), *Handbook of Motivation and Cognition*. New York: Guilford, pp. 145–64.

Bretherton, I. (1985). Attachment theory: Retrospect and prospect. *Monographs of the Society for Research in Child Development*, 50, 3–35.

Brewer, M.B. (1979). Ingroup bias and the minimal group paradigm: A cognitive–motivational analysis. *Psychological Bulletin*, 86, 307–24.

Brewer, M.B. (1988). A dual process model of impression formation. In T.K. Srull and R.S. Wyer, Jr (eds), *Advances in Social Cognition*, vol. 1. Hillsdale, NJ: Erlbaum, pp. 1–36.

Brewer, M.B. (1991). The social self: On being the same and different at the same time. *Personality and Social Psychology Bulletin*, 17, 475–82.

Brewer, M.B. (1993a). Social identity, distinctiveness, and in- group homogeneity. *Social Cognition*, 11, 150–64.

Brewer, M.B. (1993b). The role of distinctiveness in social identity and group behaviour. In M. Hogg and D. Abrams (eds), *Group Motivation: Social psychological perspectives*. London: Harvester Wheatsheaf, pp. 1–16.

Brewer, M.B. (1996). When stereotypes lead to stereotyping: The use of stereotypes in person perception. In C.N. Macrae, C. Stangor and M. Hewstone (eds), *Stereotypes and Stereotyping*. New York: Guilford, pp. 254–75.

Brewer, M.B. (1997). On the social origins of human nature. In C. McGarty and S.A. Haslam (eds), *The Message of Social Psychology*. Cambridge, MA: Blackwell, pp. 54–62.

Brewer, M.B. and Brown, R.J. (1998). Intergroup relations. In D.T. Gilbert, S.T. Fiske, and G. Lindzey (eds), *The Handbook of Social Psychology*, 4th edn New York: McGraw-Hill, pp. 554–94.

Brewer, M.B., and Camphell, D.T. (1976). *Ethrocentsism and Intergroup Attitudes: East African evidence*. New York: Sage.

Brewer, M.B. and Gardner, W. (1996). Who is this "we"? Levels of collective identity self representations. *Journal of Personality and Social Psychology*, 71, 83–93.

Brewer, M.B. and Harasty, A.S. (1996). Seeing groups as entities: The role of perceiver motivation. In R. Sorrentino and E.T. Higgins (eds), *Handbook of Motivation and Cognition*, vol. 3, *The Interpersonal Context*. New York: Guilford, pp. 347–70.

Brewer, M.B. and Kramer, R.M. (1985). The psychology of intergroup attitudes and behavior. *Annual Review of Psychology*, 36, 219–43.

Brewer, M.B. and Kramer, R.M. (1986). Choice behavior in social dilemmas: Effects of social identity, group size, and decision framing. *Journal of Personality and Social Psychology*, 50, 543–9.

Brewer, M.B. and Miller, N. (1996). *Intergroup Relations*. Buckingham: Open University Press.

Brewer, M.B. and Pickett, C.L. (in press). Distinctiveness motives as a source of the social self. In T. Tyler, R. Kramer, and O. John (eds), *The Psychology of the Social Self*. Hillsdale, NJ: Erlbaum.

Brewer, M.B. and Silver, M. (1978). Ingroup bias as a function of task characteristics. *Journal of Social Psychology*, 8, 393–400.

Brewer, M.B. and Weber, J.G. (1994). Self-evaluation effects of interpersonal versus intergroup social comparison. *Journal of Personality and Social Psychology*, 66, 268–75.

Brewer, M.B., Dull, L., and Lui, L. (1981). Perceptions of the elderly: Stereotypes as prototypes. *Journal of Personality and Social Psychology*, 41, 656–70.

Brewer, M.B., Ho, H.-K., Lee, J.-Y., and Miller, N. (1987). Social identity and social distance among Hong Kong schoolchildren. *Personality and Social Psychology Bulletin*, 13, 156–65.

Brewer, M.B., Manzi, J.M., and Shaw, J.S. (1993). In-group identification as a function of depersonalization, distinctiveness, and status. *Psychological Science*, 4, 88–92.

Brewer, M.B., Weber, J.G., and Carini, B. (1995). Person memory in intergroup contexts: Categorization versus individuation. *Journal of Personality and Social Psychology*, 69, 29–40.

Brigham, J.C. (1971). Ethnic stereotypes. *Psychological Bulletin*, 76, 15–38.

Brouwers, M.C. and Sorrentino, R.M. (1993). Uncertainty orientation and protection motivation theory: The role of individual differences in health compliance. *Journal of Personality and Social Psychology*, 65, 102–12.

Brown, J., Collins, R.L., and Schmidt, G.W. (1988). Self-esteem and direct vs. indirect forms of self-enhancement. *Journal of Personality and Social Psychology*, 55, 445–53.

Brown, J.D. (1991). Accuracy and bias in self-knowledge. In C.R. Snyder and D.F. Forsyth (eds), *Handbook of Social and Clinical Psychology: The health perspective*. New York: Pergamon Press, pp. 158–78.

Brown, J.D. (1993). Self-esteem and self-evaluation: Feeling is believing. In J. Suls (ed.), *Psychological Perspectives on the Self*, vol. 4. Hillsdale, NJ: Erlbaum.

Brown, J.D., Collins, R.L., and Schmidt, G.W. (1988). Self-esteem and direct versus indirect forms of self-enhancement. *Journal of Personality and Social Psychology*, 55, 445–53.

Brown, R. (1995). *Prejudice: Its social psychology*. Oxford: Blackwell.

Brown, R. (1996). Tajfel's contribution to the reduction of intergroup conflict. In W.P. Robinson (ed.), *Social Groups and Identities: Developing the legacy of Henri Tajfel*. Oxford: Butterworth-Heinemann, pp. 169–89.

Brown, R., Condor, S., Mathews, A., Wade, G., and Williams, J. (1986). Explaining intergroup differentiation in an industrial organization. *Journal of Occupational Psychology*, 59, 273–86.

Brown, R.J. and Abrams, D. (1986). The effects of intergroup similarity and goal interdependence on intergroup attitudes and task performance. *Journal of Experimental Social Psychology*, 22, 78–92.

Brown, R.J. and Turner, J.C. (1979). The criss-cross categorization effect in intergroup discrimination. *British Journal of Social and Clinical Psychology*, 18, 371–83.

Brown, R.J. and Turner, J.C. (1981). Interpersonal and intergroup behaviour. In J.C. Turner and H. Giles (eds), *Intergroup Behaviour*. Oxford and Chicago: Blackwell and University of Chicago Press, pp. 33–65.

Brown, R.J., Hinkle, S., Ely, P.G., Fox-Cardamone, D.L., and Maras, P. (1992). Recognizing group diversity: Individualist–collectivist and autonomous–relational social orientations and their implications for intergroup processes. *British Journal of Social Psychology*, 31, 327–42.

Bruner, J.S. (1957). On perceptual readiness. *Psychological Review*, 64, 123–52.

Brunstein, J.C. and Gollwitzer, P.M. (1996). Effects of failure on subsequent performance: The importance of self-defining goals. *Journal of Personality and Social Psychology*, 70, 395–407.

Buchanan, W. (1951). Stereotypes and tensions as revealed by the UNESCO International Poll. *International Social Science Bulletin*, 3, 515–28.

Buckner, H.T. (1965). A theory of rumor transmission. *Public Opinion Quarterly*, 29, 54–70.

Burger, J.M. (1981). Motivational biases in the attribution of responsibility for an accident: A meta-analysis of the defensive- attribution hypothesis. *Psychological Bulletin*, 90, 496–512.

Buss, A.H. (1980). *Self-consciousness and Social Anxiety*. Glencoe: Free Press.

Buss, D.M. and Schmidt, D.P. (1993). Sexual Strategies Theory: A contextual evolutionary analysis of human mating. *Psychological Review*, 100, 204–32.

Cacioppo, J.T. and Petty, R.E. (1982). The need for cognition. *Journal of Personality and Social Psychology*, 42, 116–31.

Campbell, D.T. (1958). Common Fate, Similarity, and other indices of the status of aggregates of persons as social entities. *Behavioral Science*, 3, 14–25.

Campbell, D.T. (1965). Ethnocentric and other altruistic motives. In D. Levine (ed.), *Nebraska Symposium on Motivation*, vol. 13. Lincoln, NB: University of Nebraska Press, pp. 283–312.

Campbell, D.T. (1974). "Downward causation" in hierarchically organized biological systems. In F. Ayala and T. Dobzhansky (eds), *Studies in the Philosophy of Biology*. London: Macmillan, pp. 179–86.

Campbell, D.T. (1983). Two distinct routes beyond kin selection to ultrasociality: Implications for the humanities and social sciences. In D. Bridgeman (ed.), *The Nature of Prosocial Development: Theories and strategies*. New York: Academic Press, pp. 11–41.

Campbell, J.D. (1986). Similarity and uniqueness: The effects of attribution type, relevance, and individual differences in self- esteem and depression. *Journal of Personality and Social Psychology*, 50, 281–94.

Campbell, J.D. (1990). Self-esteem and the clarity of the self- concept. *Journal of Personality and Social Psychology*, 59, 538–49.

Campbell, J.D., Trapnell, P.D., Heine, S.J., Katz, I.M., Lavalle, L.F., and Lehman, D.R. (1996). Self-concept clarity: Measurement, personality correlates, and cultural boundaries. *Journal of Personality and Social Psychology*, 70, 141–56.

Cantor, N. (1990). From thought to behaviour: "Having" and "doing" in the study of personality and cognition. *American Psychologist*, 45, 735–50.

Cantril, H. (1941). *The Psychology of Social Movements*. New York: Wiley.

Caporael, L.R. (1997). The evolution of truly social cognition: The core configurations model. *Personality and Social Psychology Review*, 1, 276–98.

Caporael, L.R. and Brewer, M.B. (1991). Reviving evolutionary psychology: Biology meets society. *Journal of Social Issues*, 47, 187–95.

Caporael, L.R. and Brewer, M.B. (1995). Hierarchical evolutionary theory: There is an alternative, and it's not creationism. *Psychological Inquiry*, 6, 31–4.

Carlston, D.E. (1992). Impression formation and the modular mind: The Associated Systems Theory. In L.L. Martin and A. Tesser (eds), *The Construction of Social Judgments*. Hillsdale, NJ: Lawrence Erlbaum Associates, pp. 301–41.

Carroll, J.S. and Payne, J.W. (eds) (1981). *Cognition and Social Behavior.* Hillsdale, NJ: Erlbaum.

Cartwright, D. and Zander, D. (eds) (1953). *Group Dynamics: Research and theory.* New York: Harper and Row.

Carver, C.S. and Humphries, C. (1981). Havana daydreaming: A study of self-consciousness and the negative reference group among Cuban Americans. *Journal of Personality and Social Psychology,* 40, 545–52.

Carver, C.S. and Scheier, M.F. (1981). *Attention and Self- regulation: A control theory approach to human behaviour.* New York: Springer-Verlag.

Cassidy, J. (1988). Child–mother attachment and self in six- year-olds. *Child Development,* 59, 121–34.

Chaiken, S. (1987). The heuristic model of persuasion. In M.P. Zanna, J.M. Olson, and C.P. Herman (eds), *Social Influence: The Ontario symposium,* vol. 5. Hillsdale, NJ: Erlbaum, pp. 3–39.

Chaiken, S. and Maheswaran, D. (1994). Heuristic processing can bias systematic processing: Effects of source credibility, argument ambiguity, and task importance on attitude judgment. *Journal of Personality and Social Psychology,* 66, 460–73.

Chaiken, S. and Stangor, C. (1987). Attitudes and attitude change. *Annual Review of Psychology,* 38, 575–630.

Chaiken, S. and Trope, Y. (eds) (in press). *Dual Process Theories in Social Psychology.* New York: Guilford.

Chaiken, S., Liberman, A., and Eagly, A.H. (1989). Heuristic and systematic processing within and beyond the persuasion context. In J.S. Uleman and J.A. Bargh (eds), *Unintended Thought.* New York: Guilford, pp. 212–52.

Chaiken, S., Wood, W., and Eagly, A.H. (1996). Principles of persuasion. In E.T. Higgins and A.W. Kruglanski (eds), *Social Psychology: Handbook of basic principles.* New York: Guilford, pp. 702–42.

Chartrand, T.L. and Bargh, J.A. (1996). Automatic activation of impression formation and memorization goals: Nonconscious goal priming reproduces effects of explicit task instructions. *Journal of Personality and Social Psychology,* 71, 464–78.

Cheek, J.M. and Briggs, S.R. (1982). Self-consciousness and aspects of identity. *Journal of Research in Personality,* 16, 401–8.

Cialdini, R.B., Borden, R.J., Thorne, A., Walker, M.R., Freeman, S., and Sloan, L.R. (1976). Basking in reflected glory: Three (football) field studies. *Journal of Personality and Social Psychology,* 34, 366–75.

Cinnarella, M. (1998). Exploring temporal aspects of social identity: The concept of possible social identities. *European Journal of Social Psychology,* 28, 227–48.

Clark, A. (1993). *Associative Engines.* Cambridge, MA: MIT Press.

Clore, G. and Rahn, W. (1994). American national identity, public mood, and political judgment: The informative function of social emotion. Unpublished paper, Department of Psychology, University of Illinois.

Cohen, A. (1959). Some implications of self-esteem for social influence. In C. Hovland and I. Janis (eds), *Personality and Persuasibility,* vol. 2. New Haven: Yale University Press, pp. 102–20.

Cohen, J., Mutz, D., Price, V., and Gunther, A. (1988). Perceived impact of defamation: An experiment on the third-person effects. *Public Opinion Quarterly,* 52, 161–73.

Cohn, N. (1966). *Warrant for Genocide. The myth of the Jewish world conspiracy and the Protocol of the Elders of Zion.* New York: Harper and Row.

Collins, A.M. and Loftus, E.F. (1975). A spreading-activation theory of semantic processing. *Psychological Review,* 82, 407–28.

Collins, R.L., Taylor, S.E., Wood, J.V., and Thompson, S.C. (1988). The vividness effect: Elusive or illusory? *Journal of Experimental Social Psychology,* 24, 1–18.

Commins, B. and Lockwood, J. (1978). The effects of intergroup relations of mixing Roman Catholics and Protestants: An experimental investigation. *European Journal of Social Psychology*, 8, 383–6.

Condor, S. (1990). Social stereotypes and social identity. In D. Abrams and M.A. Hogg (eds), *Social Identity Theory: Constructive and critical advances*. London: Harvester Wheatsheaf, pp. 230–49.

Condor, S.G. (1986). Sex role beliefs and "traditional" women: Feminist and intergroup perspectives. In S. Wilkinson (ed.), *Feminist Social Psychology*. Milton Keynes: Open University Press, pp. 97–118.

Coopersmith, A. (1959). A method for determining types of self- esteem. *Journal of Abnormal and Social Psychology*, 59, 84–7.

Coovert, M.D. and Reeder, G.D. (1990). Negativity effects in impression formation: The role of unit formation and schematic expectations. *Journal of Experimental Social Psychology*, 26, 49–62.

Crawford, J., Turtle, A., and Kippax, S. (1990). Student-favoured strategies for AIDS avoidance. *Australian Journal of Psychology*, 42, 123–37.

Crocker, J. and Luhtanen, R. (1990). Collective self-esteem and ingroup bias. *Journal of Personality and Social Psychology*, 58, 60–7.

Crocker, J. and Major, B. (1989). Social stigma and self-esteem. The self-protective properties of stigma. *Psychological Review*, 96, 608–30.

Crocker, J. and Schwartz, I. (1985). Prejudice and ingroup favoritism in a minimal intergroup situation: Effects of self-esteem. *Personality and Social Psychology Bulletin*, 11, 379–86.

Crocker, J., Blaine, B., and Luhtanen, R. (1993). Prejudice, intergroup behavior and self-esteem: Enhancement and protection motives. In M.A. Hogg and D. Abrams (eds), *Group Motivation: Social psychological perspectives*. New York: Harvester Wheatsheaf, pp. 52–67.

Crocker, J., Luhtanen, R., Blaine, B., and Broadnax, S. (1994). Collective self-esteem and psychological well-being among white, black, and Asian college students. *Personality and Social Psychology Bulletin*, 20, 503–13.

Crocker, J., Thompson, L., McGraw, K., and Ingerman, C. (1987). Downward comparison, prejudice, and evaluation of others: Effects of self-esteem and threat. *Journal of Personality and Social Psychology*, 52, 907–16.

Crockett, W.H. (1965). Cognitive complexity and impression formation. In B.A. Maher (ed.), *Progress in Experimental Personality Research*, vol. 2. New York: Academic Press, pp. 47–90.

Crosby, F., Cordova, D., and Jaskar, K. (1993). On the failure to see oneself as disadvantaged: Cognitive and emotional components. In M.A. Hogg and D. Abrams (eds), *Group Motivation: Social psychological perspectives*. London: Harvester Wheatsheaf, pp. 87–104.

Crosby, F.J. (1982). *Relative Deprivation and Working Women*. New York: Oxford University Press.

Crowne, D.P. and Marlowe, D. (1964). *The Approval Motive*. New York: Wiley.

Curtis, J.M. and Curtis, M.J. (1993). Factors related to susceptibility and recruitment by cults. *Psychological Reports*, 73, 451–60.

Daniel, H.-D. and Fisch, R. (1978). Forschungstrends in der Sozialpsychologie: Themenanalyse der *Zeitschrift für Sozialpsychologie*. *Zeitschrift für Sozialpsychologie*, 9, 265–80.

Darley, J.M. and Gross, P.H. (1983). A hypothesis-confirming bias in labeling effects. *Journal of Personality and Social Psychology*, 44, 20–33.

Dasgupta, N., Banaji, M.R., and Abelson, R.P. (1997). Beliefs and attitudes toward cohesive groups. Paper presented at Midwest Psychological Association, Chicago.

David, B. and Turner, J.C. (1996). Studies on self-categorization and minority conversion: Is being a member of the out-group an advantage? *British Journal of Social Psychology*, 35, 179–99.

Davis, J.H. (1996). Small group research and the Steiner question: The once and future thing. In E. Witte and J.H. Davis (eds), *Understanding Group Behavior*, vol. 1. Mahwah, NJ: Erlbaum, pp. 4–16.

Davis, J.H., Stasson, M.F., Ono, K., and Zimmerman, S. (1988). Effects of straw polls on group decision making: Sequential voting pattern, timing, and local majorities. *Journal of Personality and Social Psychology*, 55, 6, 918–26.

Davis, R.W. (1986). Pretrial publicity, the timing of the trial, and mock jurors' decision processes. *Journal of Applied Social Psychology*, 16, 7, 590–607.

Davison, W.P. (1983). The third-person effect in communication. *Public Opinion Quarterly*, 47, 1–15.

Deaux, K. (1992). Personalizing identity and socializing self. In G. Breakwell (ed.), *Social Psychology of Identity and the Self-concept*. London: Academic Press, pp. 301–27.

Deaux, K. (1993). Reconstructing social identity. *Personality and Social Psychology Bulletin*, 19, 4–12.

Deaux, K. (1996). Social identification. In E.T. Higgins and A.W. Kruglanski (eds), *Social Psychology: Handbook of basic principles*. New York: Guilford, pp. 777–98.

Deaux, K. and Emswiller, T. (1974). Explanations of successful performance on sex-linked tasks: What is skill for the male is luck for the female. *Journal of Personality and Social Psychology*, 29, 80–5.

Deaux, K. and Lewis, L.L. (1984). Structure of gender stereotypes: Interrelationships among components and gender label. *Journal of Personality and Social Psychology*, 46, 991–1004.

Deaux, K., Reid, A., Mizrahi, K., and Ethier, K.A. (1995). Parameters of social identity. *Journal of Personality and Social Psychology*, 68, 280–91.

Deaux, K., Winton, W., Crowley, M., and Lewis, L.L. (1985). Level of categorization and content of gender stereotypes. *Social Cognition*, 3, 145–67.

Deconchy, J.P. (1984). Rationality and social control in orthodox systems. In H. Tajfel (ed.), *The Social Dimension: European developments in social psychology*, vol. 2. Cambridge: Cambridge University Press, pp. 425–45.

Demo, D.H. (1985). The measurement of self-esteem: Refining our methods. *Journal of Personality and Social Psychology*, 48, 1490–1502.

Deschamps, J.-C. (1977). Effect of crossing category membership on quantitative judgement. *European Journal of Social Psychology*, 7, 517–21.

Deschamps, J.-C. and Doise, W. (1978). Crossed category membership in intergroup relations. In H. Tajfel (ed.), *Differentiation between Social Groups*. Cambridge: Cambridge University Press, pp. 141–58.

Deutsch, M. and Gerard, H.B. (1955). A study of normative and informational influences upon individual judgement. *Journal of Abnormal and Social Psychology*, 51, 629–36.

Devine, P.G. (1989). Stereotypes and prejudice: Their automatic and controlled components. *Journal of Personality and Social Psychology*, 56, 5–18.

Devine, P.G. and Elliot, A.J. (1995). Are racial stereotypes *really* fading? The Princeton Trilogy revisited. *Personality and Social Psychology Bulletin*, 21, 1139–50.

Devine, P.G. and Monteith, M.J. (1993). The role of discrepancy-associated affect in prejudice reduction. In D.M. Mackie and D.L. Hamilton (eds), *Affect, Cognition, and Stereotyping: Interactive processes in group perception*. San Diego: Academic Press, pp. 317–44.

Devine, P.G., Hamilton, D.L. and Ostrom, T.M. (eds) (1994). *Social Cognition: Impact on social psychology*. San Diego: Academic Press.

Devine, P.G., Monteith, M.J., Zuwerink, J.R., and Elliot, A.J. (1991). Prejudice with and without compunction. *Journal of Personality and Social Psychology*, 60, 817–30.

Diab, L.N. (1963). Factors determining group stereotypes. *Journal of Social Psychology*, 61, 3–10.

Diehl, M. (1989). Dichotomie und Diskriminierung: Die Auswirkungen von Kreuzkategorisierungen auf die Diskriminierung im Pradigma der minimalen Gruppen [Dichotomy and discrimination: The effect of crossed categorizations on discrimination in the minimal group paradigm]. *Zeitschrift für Sozialpsychologie*, 20, 92–102.

Diehl, M. (1990). The minimal group paradigm: Theoretical explanations and empirical findings. *European Review of Social Psychology*, 1, 263–92.

Dijker, A.J.M. (1987). Emotional reactions to ethnic minorities. *European Journal of Social Psychology*, 17, 305–25.

Doise, W. (1978). *Groups and Individuals: Explanations in social psychology*. Cambridge: Cambridge University Press.

Doise, W. (1982). Report on the European Association of Experimental Social Psychology. *European Journal of Social Psychology*, 12, 105–11.

Doise, W. (1986). *Levels of Explanation in Social Psychology*. Cambridge: Cambridge University Press.

Doise, W., Deschamps, J.-C., and Meyer, G. (1978). The accentuation of intracategory similarities. In H. Tajfel (ed.), *Differentiation between Social Groups Studies in the social psychology of intergroup relations*. New York: Academic Press pp. 136–46.

Dollard, J., Doob, L.W., Miller, N.E., Mowrer, O.H., and Sears, R.R. (1939). *Frustration and Aggression*. New Haven: Yale University Press.

Doosje, B., Ellemers, N., and Spears, R. (1995). Perceived intragroup variability as a function of group status and identification. *Journal of Experimental Social Psychology*, 31, 410–36.

Dovidio, J. and Fazio, R. (1992). New techniques for the direct and indirect assessment of attitudes. In J. Tanur (ed.), *Questions about Questions*. New York: Russel Sage, pp. 103–27.

Dovidio, J.F., Brigham, J.C., Johnson, B.T., and Gaertner, S.L. (1996). Stereotyping, prejudice, and discrimination: Another look. Part IV: Undermining stereotypes and stereotyping. In N. Macrae, C. Stangor, and M. Hewstone (eds), *Foundations of Stereotypes and Stereotyping*. New York: Guilford, pp. 276–318.

Dovidio, J.L., Evans, N., and Tyler, R.B. (1986). Racial stereotypes: The contents of their cognitive representations. *Journal of Experimental Social Psychology*, 22, 22–37.

Downing, J.W., Judd, C.M., and Brauer, M. (1992). Effects of repeated expressions on attitude extremity. *Journal of Personality and Social Psychology*, 63, 17–29.

Duck, J.M. and Mullin, B.-A. (1995). The perceived impact of the mass media: Reconsidering the third person effect. *European Journal of Social Psychology*, 25, 77–93.

Duck, J.M., Hogg, M.A., and Terry, D.J. (1995a). Me, us and them: Political identification and the third-person effect in the 1993 Australian federal election. *European Journal of Social Psychology*, 25, 195–215.

Duck, J.M., Hogg, M.A., and Terry, D.J. (1998). Perceived self–other differences in persuasibility: The effects of interpersonal and group-based similarity. *European Journal of Social Psychology*, 28, 1–21.

Duck, J.M., Hogg, M.A., and Terry, D.J. (in press). Social identity and perceptions of media persuasion: Are we always less influenced than others? *Journal of Applied Social Psychology*.

Duck, J.M., Hogg, M.A., Lalonde, R.N., and Terry, D.J. (1997). A new legitimacy for xenophobic nationalism in Australia: A social identity analysis of media-managed "reaction." Unpublished manuscript, University of Queensland, Brisbane.

Duck, J.M., Terry, D.J., and Hogg, M.A. (1995b). The perceived influence of AIDS advertising: Third-person effects in the context of positive media content. *Basic and Applied Social Psychology*, 17, 305–25.

Duckitt, J.H. (1992). *The Social Psychology of Prejudice*. New York: Praeger.

Eagly, A. and Chaiken, S. (1993). *The Psychology of Attitudes*. New York: Harcourt Brace Jovanovich.

Eagly, A.H. and Mladanic, A. (1989). Gender stereotypes and attitudes toward men and women. *Personality and Social Psychology Bulletin*, 15, 543–58.

Eagly, A.H., Mladanic, A. and Otto, S. (1994). Cognitive and affective bases of attitudes toward social groups and social policies. *Journal of Experimental Social Psychology*, 30, 113–37.

Eiser, J.R. (1971). Enhancement of contrast in the absolute judgement of attitude statements. *Journal of Personality and Social Psychology*, 17, 1–10.

Ekman, P. and Friesen, W.V. (1975). *Unmasking the Face*. Englewood Cliffs, NJ: Prentice-Hall. Ellemers, N., Doosje, B.J., van Knippenberg, A., and Wilke, J. (1992). Status protection in high status minority groups. *European Journal of Social Psychology*, 22, 123–40.

Ellemers, N., Spears, R., and Doosje, B. (1997). Sticking together or falling apart: In-group identification as a psychological determinant of group commitment versus individual mobility. *Journal of Personality and Social Psychology*, 72, 617–26.

Elms, A.C. (1975). The crisis of confidence in social psychology. *American Psychologist*, 30, 967–76.

Emler, N. and Reicher, S.D. (1995). *Adolescence and Delinquency: The collective management of reputation*. Oxford: Blackwell.

Epstein, S. and Pacini, R.E. (in press). Some basic issues regarding dual-process theories from the perspective of cognitive-experiential self-theory. In S. Chaiken and Y. Trope (eds), *Dual Process Theories in Social Psychology*. New York: Guilford.

Erdley, C.A. and D'Agostino, P.R. (1988). Cognitive and affective components of automatic priming effects. *Journal of Personality and Social Psychology*, 54, 741–7.

Esses, V.M., Haddock, G., and Zanna, M.P. (1993). Values, stereotypes, and emotions as determinants of intergroup attitudes. In D.M. Mackie and D.L. Hamilton (eds), *Affect, Cognition, and Stereotyping: Interactive processes in group perception*. San Diego: Academic Press, pp. 137–66.

Ethier, K.A. and Deaux, K. (1994). Negotiating social identity when contexts change: Maintaining identification and responding to threat. *Journal of Personality and Social Psychology*, 67, 243–51.

Eurich-Fulcer, R. and Schofield, J.W. (1995). Correlated versus uncorrelated social categorizations: The effect of intergroup bias. *Personality and Social Psychology Bulletin*, 21, 149–59.

Evans-Pritchard, E.E. (1940). *The Nuer*. London: Oxford University Press.

Farley, J.U., Lehmann, D.R., and Ryan, M.J. (1981). Generalizing from "imperfect" replication. *Journal of Business*, 54, 597–610.

Farnham, S.D. and Greenwald, A.G. (1997). Implicit balance between personal and social identity: I am female + I am good = female is good. Poster presented at the meeting of the Society of Experimental Social Psychology, Toronto, October 1997.

Farr, R.M. (1996). *The Roots of Modern Social Psychology: 1872–1954*. Oxford: Blackwell.

Farr, R.M. and Moscovici, S. (eds) (1984). *Social Representations*. Cambridge: Cambridge University Press.

Fazio, R.H. (1986). How do attitudes guide behavior? In R.M. Sorrentino and E.T. Higgins (eds), *The Handbook of Motivation and Cognition: Foundations of social behavior*. New York: Guilford, pp. 204–43.

Fazio, R.H. (1989). On the power and functionality of attitudes: The role of attitude accessibility. In A.R. Pratkanis, S.J. Breckler, and A.G. Greenwald (eds), *Attitude Structure and Function*. Hillsdale, NJ: Lawrence Erlbaum Associates, pp. 153–79.

Fazio, R.H. (1990a). A practical guide to the use of response latency in social psychological research. In M.S. Clark (ed.), *Review of Personality and Social Psychology*, vol. 11, *Research Methods in Personality and Social Psychology*. Newbury Park, CA: Sage, pp. 74–97.

Fazio, R.H. (1990b). Multiple processes by which attitudes guide behavior: The MODE model as an integrative framework. In M.P. Zanna (ed.), *Advances in Experimental Psychology*, vol. 23. San Diego: Academic Press, pp. 75–109.

Fazio, R.H. and Williams, C.J. (1986). Attitude accessibility as a moderator of the attitude–perception and attitude–behavior relations: An investigation of the 1984 presidential election. *Journal of Personality and Social Psychology*, 51, 505–14.

Fazio, R.H., Jackson, J.R., Dunton, B.C., and Williams, C.J. (1995). Variability in automatic activation as an unobtrusive measure of racial attitudes: A bona fide pipeline? *Journal of Personality and Social Psychology*, 69, 1013–27.

Fazio, R.H., Powell, M.C., and Herr, P.M. (1983). Toward a process model of the attitude–behavior relation: Accessing one's attitude upon mere observation of the attitude object. *Journal of Personality and Social Psychology*, 44, 723–35.

Fazio, R.H., Powell, M.C., and Williams, C.J. (1989). The role of attitude accessibility in the attitude-to-behavior process. *Journal of Consumer Research*, 16, 280–8.

Fazio, R.H., Sanbonmatsu, D.M., Powell, M.C., and Kardes, F.R. (1986). On the automatic activation of attitudes. *Journal of Personality and Social Psychology*, 50, 229–38.

Fazio, R.J., Jackson, J.R., Dunton, B.C., and Williams, C.J. (1995). Variability in automatic activation as an unobtrusive measure of racial attitudes: A bona fide pipeline? *Journal of Personality and Social Psychology*, 69, 1013–27.

Fenigstein, A. and Abrams, D. (1993). Self-attention and the egocentric assumption of shared perspectives. *Journal of Experimental Social Psychology*, 29, 287–303.

Fenigstein, A., Scheier, M.F., and Buss, A.H. (1975). Public and private self-consciousness: Assessment and theory. *Journal of Consulting and Clinical Psychology*, 43, 522–7.

Festinger, L. (1950). Informal social communication. *Psychological Review*, 57, 271–82.

Festinger, L. (1954). A theory of social comparison processes. *Human Relations*, 7, 117–40.

Festinger, L. (1957). *A Theory of Cognitive Dissonance*. Stanford, CA: Stanford University Press.

Fisch, R. and Daniel, H.-D. (1982). Research and publication trends in experimental social psychology: 1971–1980 – A thematic analysis of the *Journal of Experimental Social Psychology*, the *European Journal of Social Psychology*, and the *Zeitschrift für Sozial Psychologie*. *European Journal of Social Psychology*, 12, 395–412.

Fishbein, M. and Ajzen, I. (1975). *Belief, Attitude, Intention, and Behavior: An introduction to theory and research*. Reading, MA.: Addison-Wesley.

Fishman, J.A. (1956). An examination of the process and function of social stereotyping. *Journal of Personality and Social Psychology*, 43, 27–64.

Fiske, A.P., Kitayama, S., Markus, H.R., and Nisbett, R.E. (1998). The cultural matrix of social psychology. In D.T. Gilbert, S.T. Fiske, and G. Lindzey (eds), *The Handbook of Social Psychology*, 4th edn. New York: McGraw-Hill, pp. 915–81.

Fiske, S.T. (1982). Schema-triggered affect: Applications to social perception. In M.S. Clark and S.T. Fiske (eds), *Affect and Cognition*. Hillsdale, NJ: Erlbaum, pp. 55–78.

Fiske, S.T. (1992). Thinking is for doing: Portraits of social cognition from daguerreotype to laserphoto. *Journal of Personality and Social Psychology*, 63, 877–89.

Fiske, S.T. (1993). Social cognition and social perception. In M.R. Rosenzweig and L.W. Porter (eds), *Annual Review of Psychology*, vol. 44. Palo Alto, CA: Annual Reviews Inc., pp. 155–94.

Fiske, S.T. (in press). Stereotyping, prejudice, and discrimination. In D.T. Gilbert, S.T. Fiske, and G. Lindzey (eds), *Handbook of Social Psychology*, 4th edn. New York: McGraw-Hill.

Fiske, S.T. and Leyens, J.-P. (1997). Let social psychology be faddish or, at least, heterogeneous. In C. McGarty and S.A. Haslam (eds), *The Message of Social Psychology*. Oxford: Blackwell, pp. 92–112.

Fiske, S.T. and Linville, P.W. (1980). What does the schema concept buy us? *Personality and Social Psychology Bulletin*, 6, 543–57.

Fiske, S.T. and Neuberg, S.L. (1990). A continuum of impression formation, from category-based to individuating processes: Influences of information and motivation on attention and interpretation. In M.P. Zanna (ed.), *Advances in Experimental Social Psychology*, vol. 23. San Diego: Academic Press, pp. 1–74.

Fiske, S.T. and Pavelchak, M. (1986). Category-based versus piecemeal-based affective responses: Developments in schema-triggered affect. In R. Sorrentino and E.T. Higgins (eds), *Handbook of Motivation and Cognition: Foundations of social behavior*. New York: Guilford, pp. 167–203.

Fiske, S.T. and Taylor, S.E. (1984). *Social Cognition*. New York: Random House.

Fiske, S.T. and von Hendy, H.M. (1992). Personality feedback and situational norms can control stereotyping processes. *Journal of Personality and Social Psychology*, 62, 577–96.

Fleming, J.S. and Courtney, B.E. (1984). The dimensionality of self-esteem: II. Hierarchical facet model for revised measurement scales. *Journal of Personality and Social Psychology*, 46, 404–21.

Fletcher, G.J.O., Danilovics, P., Fernandez, G., Peterson, D., and Reeder, G.D. (1986). Attributional complexity: An individual differences measure. *Journal of Personality and Social Psychology*, 51, 875–84.

Ford, T.E., Stangor, C., and Duan, C. (1994). Influence of social category accessibility and category-associated trait accessibility on judgments of individuals. *Social Cognition*, 12, 149–68.

Forgas, J.P. (1989). Mood effects on decision making strategies. *Australian Journal of Psychology*, 41, 197–214.

Forgas, J.P. (1995). Mood and judgment: The affect infusion model. *Psychological Bulletin*, 117, 39–66.

Forgas, J.P. and Fiedler, K. (1996). Us and them: Mood effects on intergroup discrimination. *Journal of Personality and Social Psychology*, 70, 28–40.

French, J.R.P. and Raven, B. (1959). The bases of social power. In D. Cartwright (ed.), *Studies in Social Power*. Ann Arbor: University of Michigan Press, pp. 150–67.

Frijda, N.H. (1986). *The Emotions*. Cambridge: Cambridge University Press.

Frijda, N.H., Kuipers, P., and ter Schure, E. (1989). Relations among emotion, appraisal, and emotional action readiness. *Journal of Personality and Social Psychology*, 57, 212–28.

Froming, W.J. and Carver, C.S. (1981). Divergent influences of private and public self-consciousness in a compliance paradigm. *Journal of Research in Personality*, 15, 159–71.

Fu, H., Lee, S., Chiu, C., and Hong, Y. (in press). Setting the frame of mind for social identity. *International Journal of Intercultural Relations*.

Gaertner, S.L. and Dovidio, J.F. (1986). The aversive form of racism. In J.F. Dovidio and S.L. Gaertner (eds), *Prejudice, Discrimination and Racism*. New York: Academic Press, pp. 61–89.

Gaertner, S.L., Dovidio, J., Anastasio, P., Bachman, B., and Rust, M. (1993). The common ingroup identity model: Recategorization and the reduction of intergroup bias. *European Review of Social Psychology*, 4, 1–26.

Gaertner, S.L., Mann, J., Murrell, A., and Dovidio, J.F. (1989). Reducing intergroup bias: The benefits of recategorization. *Journal of Personality and Social Psychology*, 57, 239–49.

Gaertner, S.L., Rust, M.C., Dovidio, J.F., Bachman, B., and Anastasio, P. (1994). The contact hypothesis: The role of a common ingroup identity on reducing intergroup bias. *Small Group Research*, 25, 224–49.

Gaertner, S.L., Rust, M.C., Dovidio, J.F., Bachman, B.A., and Anastasio, P.A. (1996). The contact hypothesis: The role of a common ingroup identity on reducing intergroup bias among majority and minority group members. In J.L. Nye and A.M. Bower (eds), *What's Social about Social Cognition: Research on socially shared cognition in small groups*. Thousand Oaks, CA: Sage, pp. 230–60.

Galanter, M. (ed.) (1989). *Cults and New Religious Movements*. Washington, DC: American Psychiatric Association.

Gardner, R.C. (1994). Stereotypes as consensual beliefs. In M.P. Zanna and J.M. Olson (eds), *The Psychology of Prejudice: The Ontario symposium*, Vol. 7. Hillsdale, NJ: Erlbaum, pp. 1–31.

Garfinkel, H. (1967). *Studies in Ethnomethodology*. Englewood Cliffs, NJ: Prentice-Hall.

Gergen, K.J. (1973). Social psychology as history. *Journal of Personality and Social Psychology*, 26, 309–20.

Gergen, K.J. (1997). Social psychology as social construction: The emerging vision. In C. McGarty and S.A. Haslam (eds), *The Message of Social Psychology*. Cambridge, MA: Blackwell, pp. 113–28.

Gibbon, P. and Durkin, K. (1995). The third person effect: Social distance and perceived media bias. *European Journal of Social Psychology*, 25, 597–602.

Gibbons, F.X. (1990). Self-attention and behaviour: A review and theoretical update. In L. Berkowitz (ed.), Advances in Experimental Social Psychology, vol. 17. New York: Academic Press, pp. 249–303.

Gibbons, F.X. and McCoy, B. (1991). Self-esteem, similarity and reactions to active vs. passive downward comparison. *Journal of Personality and Social Psychology*, 60, 414–24.

Gilbert, D.T. and Hixon, J.G. (1991). The trouble of thinking: Activation and application of stereotypic beliefs. *Journal of Personality and Social Psychology*, 60, 509–17.

Giles, H. and Johnson, P. (1987). Ethnolinguistic identity theory: A social psychological approach to language maintenance. *International Journal of the Sociology of Language*, 68, 256–69.

Giner-Sorolla, R. and Chaiken, S. (1994). The causes of hostile media judgments. *Journal of Experimental Social Psychology*, 30, 165–80.

Glick, P. and Fiske, S.T. (1996). The ambivalent sexism inventory: Differentiating hostile and benevolent sexism. *Journal of Personality and Social Psychology*, 70, 491–512.

Goffman, E. (1959). *The Presentation of Self in Everyday Life*. New York: Doubleday.

Gollwitzer, P.M. and Bargh, J.A. (eds) (1996). *The Psychology of Action: Linking cognition and motivation to behavior*. New York: Guilford.

Greenberg, J., Solomon, S., Pyszczynski, T., Rosenblatt, A., Burling, J., Lyon, D., Simon, L., and Pinel, E. (1992). Why do people need self-esteem? Converging evidence that self-esteem serves an anxiety-buffering function. *Journal of Personality and Social Psychology*, 63, 913–22.

Greenwald, A.G. (1980). The totalitarian ego: Fabrication an revision of personal history. *American Psychologist*, 35, 603–1

Greenwald, A.G. and Banaji, M.R. (1995). Implicit social cognition: Attitudes, self-esteem, and stereotypes. *Psychological Review*, 102, 4–27.

Greenwald, A.G. and Breckler, S.J. (1985). To whom is the self presented? In B.R. Schlenker (ed.), *The Self and Social Life*. New York: McGraw-Hill, pp. 126–45.

Greenwald, A.G. and Pratkanis, A.R. (1984). The self. In R.S. Wyer and T.K. Srull (eds), *Handbook of Social Cognition*, vol. 3. Hillsdale, NJ: Erlbaum, pp. 129–78.

Greenwald, A.G., Klinger, M.R., and Liu, T.J. (1989). Unconscious processing of dichoptically masked words. *Memory and Cognition*, 17, 35–47.

Greenwald, A.G., McGhee, D.E., and Schwartz, J.L.K. (1998). Measuring individual differences in implicit cognition: The implicit association test. *Journal of Personality and Social Psychology*, 74, 1464–80.

Grieve, P.G. and Hogg, M.A. (in press). Subjective uncertainty and intergroup discrimination in the minimal group situation. *Personality and Social Psychology Bulletin*.

Grube, J.W. and Morgan, M. (1990). Attitude–social support interactions: Contingent consistency effects in the prediction of adolescent smoking, drinking, and drug use. *Social Psychology Quarterly*, 53, 329–39.

Grube, J.W., Morgan, M., and McGree, S.T. (1986). Attitudes and normative beliefs as predictors of smoking intentions and behaviours: A test of three models. *British Journal of Social Psychology*, 25, 81–93.

Gunther, A. (1991). What we think others think: Cause and consequence in the third-person effect. *Communication Research*, 18, 355–72.

Gunther, A. (1995). Overrating the X-rating: The third-person perception and support for censorship of pornography. *Journal of Communication*, 45, 27–38.

Gunther, A. and Mundy, P. (1993). Biased optimism and the third- person effect. *Journalism Quarterly*, 70, 58–67.

Gunther, A. and Thorson, E. (1992). Perceived persuasive effects of product commercials and public service announcements: Third- person effects in new domains. *Communication Research*, 19, 574–96.

Hagendoorn, L. and Henke, R. (1991). The effect of multiple category membership on inter-group evaluations in a north Indian context: Class, caste, and religion. *British Journal of Social Psychology*, 30, 247–60.

Hains, S.C., Hogg, M.A., and Duck, J.M. (1997). Self- categorization and leadership: Effects of group prototypicality and leader stereotypicality. *Personality and Social Psychology Bulletin*, 23, 1087–99.

Hakmiller, K.L. (1966). Threat as determinant of downward comparison. *Journal of Experimental Social Psychology*, 2, 32–9.

Hamilton, D.L. (1981). *Cognitive Processes in Stereotyping and Intergroup Behavior*. Hillsdale, NJ: Erlbaum.

Hamilton, D.L. (1981). Illusory correlation as a basis for stereotyping. In D.L. Hamilton (ed.), *Cognitive Processes in Stereotyping and Intergroup Behaviour*. Hillsdale, NJ: Erlbaum.

Hamilton, D.L. (ed.) (1981). *Cognitive Processes in Stereotyping and Intergroup Behavior*. Hillsdale, NJ: Erlbaum.

Hamilton, D.L. and Gifford, R.K. (1976). Illusory correlation in interpersonal personal perception: A cognitive basis of stereotypic judgments. *Journal of Experimental Social Psychology*, 12, 392–407.

Hamilton, D.L. and Sherman, J.W. (1994). Stereotypes. In R.S. Wyer, Jr and T.K. Srull (eds), *Handbook of Social Cognition*, 2nd edn, vol. 2. Hillsdale, NJ: Erlbaum, pp. 1–68.

Hamilton, D.L. and Sherman, S.J. (1996). Perceiving persons and groups. *Psychological Review*, 103, 336–55.

Hamilton, D.L. and Trolier, T.K. (1986). Stereotypes and stereotyping: An overview of the cognitive approach. In J.F. Dovidio and S.L. Gaertner (eds), *Prejudice, Discrimination and Racism*. New York: Academic Press, pp. 127–63.

Hamilton, D.L., Sherman, S.J., and Lickel, B. (1998). Perceiving social groups: The importance of the Entitativity Continuum. In C. Sedikides, J. Schopler, and C.A. Insko (eds), *Intergroup Cognition and Intergroup Behavior*. Mahwah, NJ: Erlbaum, pp. 47–74.

Hamilton, D.L., Sherman, S.J., and Maddox, K.B. (in press). Dualities and continua: Implications for understanding perceptions of persons and groups. In S. Chaiken and Y. Trope (eds), *Dual Process Theories in Social Psychology*. New York: Guilford.

Hamilton, D.L., Sherman, S.J., and Ruvolo, C.M. (1990). Stereotype-based expectancies: Effects on information processing and social behavior. *Journal of Social Issues*, 46, 35–60.

Hantzi, A. (1995). Change in stereotypic perceptions of familiar and unfamiliar groups: The pervasiveness of the subtyping model. *British Journal of Social Psychology*, 34, 463–77.

Haslam, S.A. (1997). Stereotyping and social influence: Foundations of stereotype sharedness. In R. Spears, P.J. Oakes, N. Ellemers, and S.A. Haslam (eds), *The Social Psychology of Stereotyping and Group Life*. Oxford and Cambridge, MA: Blackwell, pp. 119–43.

Haslam, S.A. and Turner, J.C. (1992). Context-dependent variation in social stereotyping 2: The relationship between frame of reference, self-categorization and accentuation. *European Journal of Social Psychology*, 22, 251–77.

Haslam, S.A. and Turner, J.C. (1995). Extremism as a self-categorical basis for polarized judgement. *European Journal of Social Psychology*, 25, 341–71.

Haslam, S.A., Oakes, P.J., McGarty, C., Turner, J.C., and Onorato, R. (1995). Contextual changes in the prototypicality of extreme and moderate outgroup members. *European Journal of Social Psychology*, 25, 509–30.

Haslam, S.A., Oakes, P.J., McGarty, C., Turner, J.C., Reynolds, K., and Eggins, R. (1996a). Stereotyping and social influence: The mediation of stereotype applicability and sharedness by the views of ingroup and outgroup members. *British Journal of Social Psychology*, 35, 369–97.

Haslam, S.A., Oakes, P.J., Turner, J.C., and McGarty, C. (1996b). Social identity, self-categorization and the perceived homogeneity of ingroups and outgroups: The interaction between social motivation and cognition. In R.M. Sorrentino and E.T. Higgins (eds), *Handbook of Motivation and Cognition*, vol. 3, *The Interpersonal Context*. New York: Guilford, pp. 182–222.

Haslam, S.A., Turner, J.C., Oakes, P.J., McGarty, C. and Hayes, B.K. (1992). Context-dependent variation in social stereotyping 1: The effects of intergroup relations as mediated by social change and frame of reference. *European Journal of Social Psychology*, 22, 3–20.

Hastie, R., Ostrom, T.M., Ebbesen, E.B., Wyer, R.S., Jr, Hamilton, D.L., and Carlston, D.E. (eds) (1980). *Person Memory: The cognitive basis of social perception*. Hillsdale, NJ: Erlbaum.

Heesacker, M., Petty, R.E., and Cacioppo, J.T. (1983). Field dependence and attitude change: Source credibility can alter persuasion by affecting message-relevant thinking. *Journal of Personality*, 51, 653–66.

Heider, F. (1958). *The Psychology of Interpersonal Relations*. New York: Wiley.

Heider, F. (1958a). Perceiving the other person. In R. Tagiuri and L. Petrullo (eds), *Person Perception and Interpersonal Behavior*. Palo Alto, CA: Stanford University Press, pp. 22–6.

Heider, F. (1958b). *The Psychology of Interpersonal Relations*. New York: Wiley.

Hewitt, J. and Goldman, M. (1974). Self-esteem, need for approval, and reactions to personal evaluations. *Journal of Experimental Social Psychology*, 10, 201–10.

Hewstone, M. (1989). *Causal Attribution: From cognitive processes to cognitive beliefs*. Oxford: Blackwell.

Hewstone, M. (1989). Changing stereotypes with disconfirming information. In D. Bar-Tal, C.F. Graumann, A. Kruglanski, and W. Stroebe (eds), *Stereotyping and Prejudice: Changing conceptions*. New York and London: Springer-Verlag, pp. 207–23.

Hewstone, M. (1994). Revision and change of stereotypic beliefs: In search of the elusive subtyping model. *European Review of Social Psychology*, 5, 69–109.

Hewstone, M. (1996). Contact and categorization: Social psychological interventions to change intergroup relations. In C.N. Macrae, C. Stangor, and M. Hewstone (eds), *Stereotypes and Stereotyping*. New York: Guilford, pp. 323–68.

Hewstone, M. and Brown, R.J. (eds) (1986). *Contact and Conflict in Intergroup Encounters*. Oxford: Blackwell.

Hewstone, M., Hantzi, A., and Johnston, L. (1991). Social categorization and person memory: The pervasiveness of race as an organizing principle. *European Journal of Social Psychology*, 21, 517–28.

Hewstone, M., Hopkins, N., and Routh, D.A. (1992). Cognitive models of stereotype change: (1) Generalization and subtyping in young people's views of the police. *European Journal of Social Psychology*, 22, 219–34.

Hewstone, M., Islam, M.R., and Judd, C.M. (1993). Models of crossed categorization and intergroup relations. *Journal of Personality and Social Psychology*, 64, 779–93.

Hewstone, M.R.C. (1989). *Causal Attribution: From cognitive processes to collective beliefs*. Oxford: Blackwell.

Hewstone, M.R.C., Stroebe, W. and Stephenson, G.M. (1996) (eds). *Introduction to Social Psychology*, 2nd edn. Oxford: Blackwell.

Hickson, D.J., Hinings, C.R., Lee, C.A., Schnecker, R.E., and Pennings, J.M. (1971). A strategic contingencies' theory of intraorganizational power. *Administrative Science Quarterly*, 16, 216–29.

Higgins, E.T. (1987). Self-discrepancy: A theory relating self and affect. *Psychological Review*, 94, 319–40.

Higgins, E.T. (1992). Achieving "shared realities" in the communication game: A social action that creates meaning. *Journal of Language and Social Psychology*, 11, 107–31.

Higgins, E.T. (1996). Knowledge activation: Accessibility, applicability, and salience. In E.T. Higgins and A.W. Kruglanski (eds), *Social Psychology: Handbook of basic principles*. New York: Guilford, pp. 133–68.

Higgins, E.T. and King, G.A. (1981). Accessibility of social constructs: Information processing consequences of individual and contextual variability. In N. Cantor and J.F. Kihlstrom (eds), *Personality, Cognition, and Social interaction*. Hillsdale, NJ: Erlbaum, pp. 69–122.

Higgins, E.T. and King, G.A. (1981). Individual construct accessibility and subjective impressions and recall. *Journal of Personality and Social Psychology*, 43, 35–47.

Higgins, E.T. and Sorrentino, R.M. (eds) (1990). *Handbook of Motivation and Cognition: Foundations of social behavior*, 2 vols. New York: Guilford.

Higgins, E.T., Bargh, J.A., and Lombardi, W. (1985). Nature of priming effects on categorization. *Journal of Experimental Psychology: Learning, Memory, and Cognition*, 11, 58–69.

Higgins, E.T., Herman, P.C., and Zanna, M.P. (eds) (1981). *Social Cognition: The Ontario symposium*. Hillsdale, NJ: Erlbaum.

Higgins, E.T., King, G.A., and Mavin, G.H. (1982). Individual construct accessibility and subjective impressions and recall. *Journal of Personality and Social Psychology*, 43, 35–47.

Higgins, E.T., Kuiper, N.A., and Olson, J.M. (1981). Social cognition: The need to get personal. In E.T. Higgins, P.C. Herman and M.P. Zanna (eds), *Social Cognition: The Ontario symposium*, vol. 1. Hillsdale, NJ: Erlbaum, pp. 395–420.

Higgins, T.E. (1989). Knowledge accessibility and activation: Subjectivity and suffering from unconscious sources. In J.S. Uleman and J.A. Bargh (eds), *Unintended Thought*. New York: Guilford, pp. 75–123.

Higgins, T.E. (1996). Knowledge activation: Accessibility, applicability, and salience. In E.T. Higgins and A.W. Kruglanski (eds), *Social Psychology: Handbook of basic principles*. New York: Guilford, pp. 133–68.

Hilton, J.L. and von Hippel, W. (1990). The role of consistency in the judgment of stereotype-relevant behaviors. *Personality and Social Psychology Bulletin*, 16, 430–48.

Hilton, J.L. and von Hippel, W. (1996). Stereotypes. *Annual Review of Psychology*, 47, 237–71.

Hinkle, S. and Brown, R.J. (1990). Intergroup comparisons and social identity: Some links and lacunae. In D. Abrams and M.A. Hogg (eds), *Social Identity Theory: Constructive and critical advances*. London: Harvester Wheatsheaf, pp. 48–70.

Hinkle, S.W., Taylor, D., Fox-Cardamone, L., and Cook, K. (1989). Intragroup identification and intergroup differentiation: A multi-component approach. *British Journal of Social Psychology*, 28, 305–17.

Hoffman, C. and Hurst, N. (1989). Gender stereotypes: Perception or rationalization? *Journal of Personality and Social Psychology*, 58, 197–208.

Hogg, M.A. (1992). *The Social Psychology of Group Cohesiveness: From attraction to social identity*. Hemel Hempstead and New York: Harvester Wheatsheaf and New York University Press.

Hogg, M.A. (1993). Group cohesiveness: A critical review and some new directions. *European Review of Social Psychology*, 4, 85–111.

Hogg, M.A. (1996a). Intragroup processes, group structure and social identity. In W.P. Robinson (ed.), *Social Groups and Identities: Developing the legacy of Henri Tajfel*. Oxford: Butterworth-Heinemann, pp. 65–93.

Hogg, M.A. (1996b). Identity, cognition, and language in intergroup context. *Journal of Language and Social Psychology*, 15, 372–84.

Hogg, M.A. (1996c). Social identity, self-categorization, and the small group. In E.H. Witte and J.H. Davis (eds), *Understanding Group Behavior*, vol. 2, *Small Group Processes and Interpersonal Relations*. Mahwah, NJ: Erlbaum, pp. 227–53.

Hogg, M.A. and Abrams, D. (1988). *Social Identification: A social psychology of intergroup relations and group processes*. London: Routledge.

Hogg, M.A. and Abrams, D. (1990). Social motivation, self-esteem and social identity. In D. Abrams and M.A. Hogg (eds), *Social Identity Theory: Constructive and critical advances*. New York: Springer-Verlag, pp. 28–47.

Hogg, M.A. and Abrams, D. (1993). Towards a single-process uncertainty-reduction model of social motivation in groups. In M.A. Hogg and D. Abrams (eds), *Group Motivation: Social psychological perspectives*. Hemel Hempstead: Harvester Wheatsheaf, pp. 173–90.

Hogg, M.A. and Abrams, D. (eds) (1993). *Group Motivation: Social psychological perspectives*. Hemel Hempstead and New York: Harvester Wheatsheaf and Prentice-Hall.

Hogg, M.A. and Abrams, D. (in press). Social categorization, depersonalization and group behavior. In M.A. Hogg and R.S. Tindale (eds), *Blackwell Handbook in Social Psychology*, vol. 3, *Group Processes*. Oxford: Blackwell.

Hogg, M.A. and Crieve, P. (in press). Social identity theory and the crisis of confidence in social psychology: A commentary and some research on uncertainty reduction. *Asian Journal of Social Psychology*.

Hogg, M.A. and Hains, S.C. (1996). Intergroup relations and group solidarity: Effects of group identification and social beliefs on depersonalized attraction. *Journal of Personality and Social Psychology*, 70, 295–309.

Hogg, M.A. and Hains, S.C. (1998). Friendship and group identification: A new look at the role of cohesiveness in groupthink. *European Journal of Social Psychology*, 28, 323–41.

Hogg, M.A. and Hardie, E.A. (1991). Social attraction, personal attraction, and self-categorization: A field study. *Personality and Social Psychology Bulletin*, 17, 175–80.< Hogg, M.A. and McGarty, C. (1990). Self-categorization and social identity. In D. Abrams and M.A. Hogg (eds), *Social Identity Theory: Constructive and critical advances*. Hemel Hempstead and New York: Harvester Wheatsheaf and Springer-Verlag, pp. 10–27.

Hogg, M.A. and Moreland, R.L. (1995). European and American Influences on small group research. Invited paper presented at the Small Groups Preconference of the joint meeting of the European Association of Experimental Social Psychology and the Society for Experimental Social Psychology, Washington, DC, October.

Hogg, M.A. and Sunderland, J. (1991). Self-esteem and intergroup discrimination in the minimal group paradigm. *British Journal of Social Psychology*, 30, 51–62.

Hogg, M.A. and Terry, D.J. (1998). Organizational identification: Social identity and self-categorization processes in organizational contexts. Manuscript under editorial review.

Hogg, M.A. and Turner, J.C. (1985). Interpersonal attraction, social identification and psychological group formation. *European Journal of Social Psychology*, 15, 51–66.

Hogg, M.A. and Turner, J.C. (1987). Intergroup behaviour, self- stereotyping and the salience of social categories. *British Journal of Social Psychology*, 26, 325–40.

Hogg, M.A. and Turner, J.C. (1987). Social identity and conformity: A theory of referent informational influence. In W. Doise and S. Moscovici (eds), *Current Issues in European Social Psychology*, vol. 2. Cambridge and Paris: Cambridge University Press and Editions de la Maison des Sciences de l'Homme, pp. 139–82.

Hogg, M.A. and Vaughan, G.M. (1998). *Social Psychology*, 2nd edn. Hemel Hempstead: Prentice-Hall.

Hogg, M.A., Hardie, E.A., and Reynolds, K.J. (1995). Prototypical similarity, self-categorization, and depersonalized attraction: A perspective on group cohesiveness. *European Journal of Social Psychology*, 25, 159–77.

Hogg, M.A., Terry, D.J. and White, K.M. (1995). A tale of two theories: A critical comparison of identity theory with social identity theory. *Social Psychology Quarterly, 58*, 255–69.

Hopkins, N., Reicher, S.D. and Levine, M. (1997). On the parallels between social cognition and the "new racism." *British Journal of Social Psychology, 36*, 305–30.

Houston, D.A. and Fazio, R.H. (1989). Biased processing as a function of attitude accessibility: Making objective judgments subjectively. *Social Cognition, 7*, 51–66.

Hovland, C.L. Janis, L., and Kelley, H.H. (1953). *Communication and Persuasion.* New Haven, CT: Yale University Press.

Innes, J.M. and Zeitz, H. (1988). The public's view of the impact of the mass media: A test of the "third person" effect. *European Journal of Social Psychology, 18*, 457–63.

Islam, M.R. and Hewstone, M. (1993). Intergroup attributions and affective consequences in majority and minority groups. *Journal of Personality and Social Psychology, 64*, 936–50.

Izard, C.E. (1977). *Human Emotions.* New York: Plemum Press.

James, W. (1890). *The Principles of Psychology.* Cambridge, MA: Harvard University Press (repr. 1950, New York: Dover Publications).

James, W. (1907). *Popular Lectures on Philosophy.* New York: Longmans, Green, and Co., pp. 43–81.

Jamieson, D.W. and Zanna, M.P. (1989). Need for structure in attitude formation and persuasion. In A.R. Pratkanis, S.J. Breckler, and A.G. Greenwald (eds), *Attitude Structure and Function.* Hillsdale, NJ: Erlbaum, pp. 383–406.

Janis, I.L. (1972). *Victims of Groupthink.* Boston, MA: Houghton Mifflin.

Janis, I.L. (1982). *Groupthink: Psychological studies of policy decisions and fiascoes,* 2nd edn. Boston, MA: Houghton Mifflin.

Janis, I.L. and Mann, L. (1977). *Decision Making: A psychological analysis of conflict, choice, and commitment.* New York: Free Press.

Jaspars, J.M.F. (1980). The coming of age of social psychology in Europe. *European Journal of Social Psychology, 10*, 421–8.

Jaspars, J.M.F. (1986). Forum and focus: A personal view of European social psychology. *European Journal of Social Psychology, 16*, 3–15.

Jetten, J. (1997). Dimensions of distinctiveness: Intergroup discrimination and social identity. Unpublished doctoral dissertation, University of Amsterdam.

Jetten, J., Spears, R., and Manstead, A.S.R. (1996). Intergroup norms and intergroup discrimination: Distinctive self- categorization and social identity. *Journal of Personality and Social Psychology, 71*, 1222–33.

Jetten, J., Spears, R., Hogg, M.A., and Manstead, A.S.R. (1997). Discrimination constrained and justified: The variable effects of group variability and ingroup identification. Manuscript submitted for publication, University of Amsterdam.

Johnston, L. and Hewstone, M. (1992). Cognitive models of stereotype change: (3) Subtyping and the perceived typicality of disconfirming group members. *Journal of Experimental Social Psychology, 28*, 360–86.

Johnston, L., Hewstone, M., Pendry, L., and Frankish, C. (1994). Cognitive models of stereotype change: (4) Motivational and cognitive influences. *European Journal of Social Psychology, 24*, 237–65.

Jones, E.E. (1985). Major developments in social psychology during the past five decades. In G. Lindzey and E. Aronson (eds), *The Handbook of Social Psychology,* 3rd edn. New York: McGraw-Hill, pp. 47–108.

Jones, E.E. (1998). Major developments in five decades of social psychology. In D.T. Gilbert, S.T. Fiske, and G. Lindzey (eds), *The Handbook of Social Psychology,* 4th edn, vol. 1. New York: McGraw-Hill, pp. 3–57.

Jones, E.E. and Davis, K.E. (1965). From acts to dispositions: The attribution process in person perception. In L. Berkowitz (ed.), *Advances in Experimental Social Psychology,* vol. 2. New York: Academic Press, pp. 219–66.

Jones, S.C. and Regan, D.T. (1974). Ability evaluation through social comparison. *Journal of Experimental Social Psychology*, 10, 133–46.

Jost, J.T. (1995). Negative illusions: Conceptual clarification and psychological evidence concerning false consciousness. *Political Psychology*, 16, 397–424.

Jost, J.T. and Banaji, M.R. (1994). The role of stereotyping in system-justification and the production of false consciousness. *British Journal of Social Psychology*, 33, 1–27.

Judd, C.M. and Park, B. (1988). Outgroup homogeneity: Judgements of variability at the individual and group levels. *Journal of Personality and Social Psychology*, 54, 778–88.

Judd, C.M. and Park, B. (1993). Definition and assessment of accuracy in social stereotypes. *Psychological Review*, 100, 109–28.

Judd, C.M., Ryan, C.S., and Park, B. (1991). Accuracy in the judgement of in-group and outgroup variability. *Journal of Personality and Social Psychology*, 61, 366–79.

Jussim, L., Coleman, L.M., and Lerch, L. (1987). The nature of stereotypes: A comparison and integration of three theories. *Journal of Personality and Social Psychology*, 52, 536–46.

Jussim, L., Nelson, T.E., Manis, M., and Soffin, S. (1995). Prejudice, stereotypes, and labeling effects: Sources of bias in person perception. *Journal of Personality and Social Psychology*, 68, pp. 228–46.

Kahneman, D. and Miller, D.T. (1986). Norm theory: Comparing reality to its alternatives. *Psychological Review*, 93, 136–53.

Kaplan, H.B. (1975). *Self-attitudes and Deviant Behavior*. Pacific Palisades, CA: Goodyear Publishing Company.

Kaplan, M.F. (1993). Group decisions are cognitive and social events. Paper presented at the meetings of the Midwestern Psychological Association, Chicago.

Kaplan, M.F. and Miller, L.E. (1978). Reducing the effects of juror bias. *Journal of Personality and Social Psychology*, 36, 1443–55.

Katz, D. and Braly, K. (1933). Racial stereotypes of one hundred college students. *Journal of Abnormal and Social Psychology*, 28, 280–90.

Katz, I. and Hass, R.G. (1988). Racial ambivalence and American value conflict: Correlational and priming studies of dual cognitive structures. *Journal of Personality and Social Psychology*, 55, 893–905.

Kawakami, K., Dovidio, J.F., and Moll, J. (1997). Stereotyping: Automatically activated! Automatically suppressed? Poster presented at the 9th APS Convention, Washington, DC, May.

Keenan, J.M. (1993). An exemplar model can explain Klein and Loftus's results. In T.K. Srull and R.S. Wyer, Jr (eds), *The Mental Representation of Trait and Autobiographical Knowledge about the Self: Advances in social cognition*, vol. 5. Hillsdale, NJ: Lawrence Erlbaum Associates, pp. 69–78.

Kelley, H.H. (1952). Two functions of reference groups. In G.E. Swanson, T.M. Newcomb, and E.L. Hartley (eds), *Readings in Social Psychology*, 2nd edn New York: Holt, Rinehart, and Winston, pp. 410–14.

Kelley, H.H. (1967). Attribution theory in social psychology. In D. Levine (ed.), *Nebraska Symposium on Motivation*. Lincoln, NB: University of Nebraska Press, pp. 192–238.

Kelly, C. (1993). Group identification, intergroup perceptions and collective action. *European Review of Social Psychology*, 4, 59–83.

Kelman, H.C. (1961). Processes of opinion change. *Public Opinion Quarterly*, 25, 57–78.

Kenrick, D.T., Groth, G.E., Trost, M.R., and Sadalla, E.K. (1993). Integrating evolutionary and social exchange perspectives on relationships: Effects of gender, self-appraisal, and involvement on level of mate selection. *Journal of Personality and Social Psychology*, 64, 951–69.

Kerr, M. (1943). An experimental investigation of national stereotypes. *Sociological Review*, 35, 37–43.

Kihlstrom, J.F. and Cantor, N. (1984). Mental representation of the self. In L. Berkowitz (ed.), *Advances in Experimental Social Psychology*, vol. 17. New York: Academic Press.

Kihlstrom, J.F. and Cantor, N. (1984). Mental representations of the self. In L. Berkowitz (ed.), *Advances in Experimental Social Psychology*, vol. 17. Orlando, FL: Academic Press, pp. 1–47.

Kinder, D.R. and Sears, D.O. (1981). Prejudice and politics: Symbolic racism versus racial threats to the good life. *Journal of Personality and Social Psychology*, 40, 414–31.

Kinder, D.R. and Sears, D.O. (1985). Public opinion and political action. In G. Lindzey and E. Aronson (eds), *Handbook of Political Psychology*, 3rd edn. New York: Random House, pp. 659–741.

King, G.A. and Sorrentino, R.M. (1988). Uncertainty orientation and the relationship between individual accessible constructs and person memory. *Social Cognition*, 6, 128–49.

Kite, C. and Rahn, W.M. (1997). Public community and public mood: A comparison of the U.S. and Swedish cases. Unpublished manuscript, University of Umea, Sweden.

Klein, S.B. and Loftus, J. (1993). The mental representation of trait and autobiographical knowledge about the self. In T.K. Srull and R.S. Wyer, Jr (eds), *The Mental Representation of Trait and Autobiographical Knowledge about the Self: Advances in social cognition*, vol. 5. Hillsdale, NJ: Lawrence Erlbaum Associates, pp. 1–50.

Klinger, E., Barta, S.G., and Maxeiner, M.E. (1980). Motivational correlates of thought content frequency and commitment. *Journal of Personality and Social Psychology*, 39, 1222–37.

Kluegel, J.R. and Smith, E.R. (1986). *Beliefs about Inequality: Americans' views of what is and what ought to be*. Hawthorne, NY: Aldine de Gruyter.

Knowles, E.S. and Bassett, R.L. (1976). Groups and crowds as social entities: Effects of activity size, and member similarity on nonmembers. *Journal of Personality and Social Psychology*, 34, 773–83.

Knowles, E.S. and Sibicky, M.E. (1990). Continuity and diversity in the stream of selves: Metaphorical resolutions of William James's one-in-many-selves paradox. *Personality and Social Psychology Bulletin*, 16, 676–87.

Kovel, J. (1970). *White Racism: A psychohistory*. New York: Pantheon.

Kraut, R.E. and Higgins, E.T. (1984). Communication and social cognition. In R.S. Wyer, Jr and T.K. Srull (eds), *Handbook of Social Cognition*, vol. 3. Hillsdale, NJ: Erlbaum, pp. 87–127.

Krueger, J. and Clement, R.W. (1994). The truly false consensus effect: An ineradicable and egocentric bias in social perception. *Journal of Personality and Social Psychology*, 67, 596–610.

Krueger, J. and Rothbart, M. (1988). The use of categorical and individuating information in making inferences about personality. *Journal of Personality and Social Psychology*, 55, 187–95.

Kruglanski, A.W. (1989). *Lay Epistemics and Human Knowledge: Cognitive and motivational bases*. New York: Plenum Press.

Kruglanski, A.W. and Mayseless, O. (1990). Classic and current social comparison research: Expanding the perspective. *Psychology Bulletin*, 108, 195–208.

Kruglanski, A.W. and Webster, D.M. (1996). Motivated closing of the mind: "Seizing" and "freezing." *Psychological Review*, 103, 263–83.

Kuhn, M.H. and McPartland, T.S. (1954). An empirical investigation of self-attitudes. *American Sociological Review*, 19, 68–76.

Kunda, Z. and Sherman-Williams, B. (1993). Stereotypes and the construal of individuating information. *Personality and Social Psychology Bulletin*, 19, 90–9.

Kunda, Z. and Thagard, P. (1996). Forming impressions from stereotypes, traits, and behaviors: A parallel-constraint-satisfaction theory. *Psychological Review*, 103, 284–308.

Kunda, Z., Fong, G.T., Sanitoso, R., and Reber, E. (1993). Directional questions direct self-conceptions. *Journal of Experimental Social Psychology*, 29, 63–86.

Kunda, Z., Sinclair, L., and Griffin, D. (1997). Equal ratings but separate meanings: Stereotypes and the construal of traits. *Journal of Personality and Social Psychology*, 72, 720–34.

Langer, E.J. (1989). Minding matters. In L. Berkowitz (ed.), *Advances in Experimental Social Psychology*, vol. 22. New York: Academic Press, pp. 137–73.

Lasorsa, D.L. (1989). Real and perceived effects of "Amerika". *Journalism Quarterly*, 66, 373–8.

Lazarus, R.S. (1966). *Psychological Stress and the Coping Processes*. New York: McGraw-Hill.

Lazarus, R.S. and Folkman, S. (1984). *Stress, Appraisal, and Coping*. New York: Springer-Verlag.

Le Bon, G. (1896). *The Crowd: A study of the popular mind*. London: Unwin.

Lemyre, L. and Smith, P.M. (1985). Intergroup discrimination and self-esteem in the minimal group paradigm. *Journal of Personality and Social Psychology*, 49, 660–70.

Lepore, L. and Brown, R. (1997a). *Automatic Stereotype Activation: Towards a model*. Final report to ESRC.

Lepore, L. and Brown, R.J. (1997b). Category activation and stereotype accessibility: Is prejudice inevitable? *Journal of Personality and Social Psychology*, 72, 275–87.

Lerner, M.J. (1980). *The Belief in a Just World: A fundamental delusion*. New York: Plenum Press.

Lerner, M.J. and Miller, D.T. (1978). Just-world research and the attribution process: Looking back and ahead. *Psychological Bulletin*, 85, 1030–51.

Leventhal, H. (1980). Toward a comprehensive theory of emotion. In L. Berkowitz (ed.), *Advances in Experimental Social Psychology* San Diego: Academic Press, vol. 13. pp. 139–207.

Levine, J.M. and Moreland, R.L. (1990). Progress in small group research. *Annual Review of Psychology*, 41, 585–634.

Levine, J.M. and Moreland, R.L. (1995). Group processes. In A. Tesser (ed.), *Advanced Social Psychology*. New York: McGraw- Hill, pp. 419–65.

Levine, J.M., Resnick, L.B., and Higgins, E.T. (1993). Social foundations of cognition. *Annual Review of Psychology*, 44, 585–612.

LeVine, R.A. and Campbell, D.T. (1972). *Ethnocentrism: Theories of conflict, ethnic attitudes, and group behavior*. New York: Wiley.

Lewin, K. (1936). *Principles of Topological Psychology*. New York: McGraw-Hill.

Lewin, K. (1952). *Field Theory in Social Science*. New York: Harper and Row.

Lewis, V. (1988). Measuring attitudes to women: Development of the Women in Society Questionnaire. Unpublished Master's thesis, University of Melbourne.

Leyens, J.-P., Yzerbyt, V., and Schadron, G. (1994). *Stereotypes and Social Cognition*. London: Sage.

Leyens, J.-Ph., Yzerbyt, V., and Schadron, G. (1992). The social judgeability approach to stereotypes. *European Review of Social Psychology*, 45, 92–120.

Lickel, B., Hamilton, D.L., Wieczorkowska, G., Lewis, A., Sherman, S.J., and Uhles, A.N. (1998). Varieties of social groups: Differing bases of perceived entitativity. Unpublished manuscript, University of California, Santa Barbara.

Lindeman, M. and Verkasalo, M. (1995). Personality, situation, and positive–negative asymmetry in socially desirable responding. *European Journal of Personality*, 9, 125–34.

Linville, P.W. (1987). Self-complexity as a buffer against stress-related illness and depression. *Journal of Personality and Social Psychology*, 52, 663–76.

Linville, P.W. and Fischer, G.W. (1993). Exemplar and abstraction models of perceived group variability and stereotypicality. *Social Cognition*, 11, 92–125.

Linville, P.W. and Jones, E.E. (1980). Polarized appraisals of outgroup members. *Journal of Personality and Social Psychology*, 38, 689–703.

Lippmann, W. (1922). *Public Opinion*. New York: Harcourt Brace Jovanovich.

Liska, A. (1984). A critical examination of the causal structure of the Fishbein and Ajzen attitude–behavior model. *Social Psychology Quarterly*, 47, 61–74.

Lobel, T.E. and Levanon, I. (1988). Self-esteem, need for approval, and cheating behavior in children. *Journal of Educational Psychology*, 80, 122–3.

Lobel, T.E. and Teiber, A. (1994). Effects of self-esteem and need for approval on affective and cognitive reactions: Defensive and true self-esteem. *Personality and Individual Differences*, 16, 315–21.

Locke, V., MacLeod, C., and Walker, I. (1994). Automatic and controlled activation of stereotypes: Individual differences associated with prejudice. *British Journal of Social Psychology*, 33, 29–46.

Locksley, A., Borgida, E., Brekke, N.C., and Hepburn, C. (1980). Sex stereotypes and social judgment. *Journal of Personality and Social Psychology*, 39, 821–31.

Lombardi, W.J., Higgins, E.T., and Bargh, J.A. (1987). The role of consciousness in priming effects on categorization: Assimilation versus contrast as a function of awareness of priming task. *Personality and Social Psychology Bulletin*, 13, 411–29.

Long, K. and Spears, R. (1996). The self-esteem hypothesis revisited: Differentiation and the disaffected. In R. Spears, P.J. Oakes, N. Ellemers, and S.A. Haslam (eds), *The Social Psychology of Stereotyping and Group Life*. Oxford: Blackwell, pp. 296–317.

Long, K.M., Spears, R., and Manstead, A.S.R. (1994). The influence of personal and collective self-esteem on strategies of social differentiation. *British Journal of Social Psychology*, 23, 313–29.

Lopes, L.L. (1987). Between hope and fear: The psychology of risk. *Advances in Experimental Psychology*, 20, 255–95.

Lorenzi-Cioldi, F. (1991). Self-stereotyping and self-enhancement in gender groups. *European Journal of Social Psychology*, 21, 403–17.

Lorenzi-Cioldi, F. and Doise, W. (1990). Levels of analysis and social identity. In D. Abrams and M.A. Hogg (eds), *Social Identity Theory: Constructive and critical advances*. Hemel Hempstead: Harvester Wheatsheaf, and New York: Springer-Verlag, pp. 71–88.

Luhtanen, R. and Crocker, J. (1992). A collective self-esteem scale: Self-evaluation of one's social identity. *Personality and Social Psychology Bulletin*, 18, 302–18.

Maass, A. and Arcuri, L. (1992). The role of language in the persistence of stereotypes. In G. Semin and K. Fiedler (eds), *Language, Interaction, and Social Cognition*. London: Sage, pp. 129–43.

Maass, A. and Arcuri, L. (1996). Language and stereotyping. In C.N. Macrae, C. Stangor, and M. Hewstone (eds), *Stereotypes and Stereotyping*. New York: Guilford, pp. 193–226.

Maass, A., Salvi, D., Arcuri, L., and Semin, G. (1989). Language use in intergroup contexts: The linguistic intergroup bias. *Journal of Personality and Social Psychology*, 57, 981–93.

MacCoun, R.J. and Kerr, N.L. (1988). Asymmetric influence on mock jury deliberation: Jurors' bias for leniency. *Journal of Personality and Social Psychology*, 54, 21–33.

MacKay, D.G. (1973). Aspects of the theory of comprehension, memory, and attention. *Quarterly Journal of Experimental Psychology*, 25, 22–40.

Mackie, D.M. (1986). Social identification effects in group polarization. *Journal of Personality and Social Psychology*, 50, 720–8.

Mackie, D.M., Gastardo-Conaco, M.C., and Skelly, J.J. (1992). Knowledge of the advocated position and the processing of in- group and out-group persuasive messages. *Personality and Social Psychology Bulletin*, 18, 145–51.

Mackie, D.M., Worth, L.T., and Asuncion, A.G. (1990). Processing of persuasive in-group messages. *Journal of Personality and Social Psychology*, 58, 812–22.

MacLeod, C. and Rutherford, E. (1994). Anxiety and the selective processing of emotional information: Mediating roles of awareness, trait and state variables, and personal relevance of the stimulus materials. *Behaviour Research and Therapy*, 30, 479–91.

Macrae, C.N., Bodenhausen, G.V., and Milne, A.B. (1995). The dissection of selection in person perception: Inhibitory processes in social stereotyping. *Journal of Personality and Social Psychology*, 69, 397–407.

Macrae, C.N., Bodenhausen, G.V., Milne, A.B., and Jetten, J. (1994). Out of mind but back in sight: Stereotypes on the rebound. *Journal of Personality and Social Psychology*, 67, 37–47.

Macrae, C.N., Bodenhausen, G.V., Milne, A.B., and Wheeler, V. (1996). On resisting the temptation for simplification: Counterintentional effects of stereotype suppression on social memory. *Social Cognition*, 14, 1–20.

Macrae, C.N., Milne, A.B., and Bodenhausen, G.V. (1994). Stereotypes as energy-saving devices: A peek inside the cognitive toolbox. *Journal of Personality and Social Psychology*, 66, 37–47.

Macrae, C.N., Stangor, C., and Hewstone, M. (eds) (1996). *Stereotypes and Stereotyping*. New York: Guilford.

Maheswaran, D. and Chaiken, S. (1991). Promoting systematic processing in low motivation settings: Effects of incongruent information on processing and judgment. *Journal of Personality and Social Psychology*, 61, 13–25.

Major, B. (1994). From social inequality to personal entitlement: The role of social comparisons, legitimacy appraisals, and group memberships. *Advances in Experimental Social Psychology*, 26, 293–355.

Mandler, G. (1975). *Mind and Emotion*. New York: Wiley.

Manstead, A.S.R. (1990). Developments to be expected in European social psychology in the 1990s. In P.J.D. Drenth, J.A. Sergeant, and R.J. Takens (eds), *European Perspectives in Psychology*, vol. 3. Chichester: Wiley, pp. 183–203.

Marcus-Newhall, A., Miller, N., Holtz, R., and Brewer, M.B. (1993). Cross-cutting category membership with role assignment: A means of reducing intergroup bias. *European Journal of Social Psychology*, 32, 125–46.

Markus, H. (1977). Self-schemata and processing information about the self. *Journal of Personality and Social Psychology*, 35, 63–78.

Markus, H. and Kitayama, S. (1991). Culture and the self: Implications for cognition, emotion, and motivation. *Psychological Bulletin*, 98, 224–53.

Markus, H. and Nurius, P. (1986). Possible selves. *American Psychologist*, 41, 954–69.

Markus, H. and Wurf, E. (1986). The dynamic self-concept: A social psychological perspective. *Annual Review of Psychology*, 38, 299–337.

Markus, H. and Zajonc, R.B. (1985). The cognitive perspective in social psychology. In G. Lindzey and E. Aronson (eds), *The Handbook of Social Psychology*, 3rd edn, vol. 1. New York: Random House, pp. 137–230.

Markus, H.R. and Kitayama, S. (1991). Culture and the self: Implications for cognition, emotion, and motivation. *Psychological Review*, 98, 224–53.

Markus, H.R., Kitayama, S., and Heiman, R.J. (1996). Culture and "basic" psychological principles. In E.T. Higgins and A.W. Kruglanski (eds), *Social Psychology: Handbook of basic principles*. New York: Guilford, pp. 857–913.

Marques, J.M., Abrams, D., Paez, D., and Taboada, C.M. (in press). The role of categorization and ingroup norms in judgments of groups and their members. *Journal of Personality and Social Psychology*.

Marsh, H.W. (1986). Global self-esteem: Its relation to specific facets of self-concept and importance. *Journal of Personality and Social Psychology*, 51, 1224–36.

Masser, B. and Abrams, D. (in press). Contemporary sexism: The relationship between hostile, benevolent and neosexism. *Psychology of Women Quarterly*.

McCann, C.D. and Higgins, E.T. (1990). Social cognition and communication. In H. Giles and W.P. Robinson (eds), *Handbook of Language and Social Psychology*. Chichester: Wiley, pp. 13–32.

McCauley, C. and Stitt, C.L. (1978). An individual and quantitative measure of stereotypes. *Journal of Personality and Social Psychology*, 39, 929–40.

McConahay, J.B. (1982). Self-interest versus racial attitudes as correlates of anti-busing attitudes in Louisville: Is it the buses or the blacks? *Journal of Politics*, 44, 692–720.

McConahay, J.B. (1983). Modern racism and modern discrimination: The effects of race, racial attitudes and context on simulated hiring decisions. *Personality and Social Psychology Bulletin*, 9, 551–8.

McConahay, J.B. (1986). Modern racism, ambivalence, and the modern racism scale. In J.F. Dovidio and S.L. Gaertner (eds), *Prejudice, Discrimination, and Racism*. Orlando, FL: Academic Press, pp. 91–125.

McConnell, A.R., Sherman, S.J., and Hamilton, D.L. (1994). The on-line and memory-based aspects of individual and group target judgments. *Journal of Personality and Social Psychology*, 67, 173–85.

McConnell, A.R., Sherman, S.J., and Hamilton, D.L. (1997). Target cohesiveness: Implications for information processing about individual and group targets. *Journal of Personality and Social Psychology*, 72, 750–62.

McDougall, W. (1920). *The Group Mind*. Cambridge: Cambridge University Press.

McGarty, C. and Penny, R.E.C. (1988). Categorization, accentuation and social judgement. *British Journal of Social Psychology*, 22, 147–57.

McGarty, C., Haslam, S.A., Hutchinson, K.J., and Grace, D.M. (1995). Determinants of perceived consistency: The relationship between group entitativity and the meaningfulness of categories. *British Journal of Social Psychology*, 34, 237–56.

McGarty, C., Turner, J.C., Hogg, M.A., David, B., and Wetherell, M.S. (1992). Group polarization as conformity to the most prototypical group member. *British Journal of Social Psychology*, 31, 1–20.

McGarty, C., Turner, J.C., Oakes, P.J., and Haslam, S.A. (1993). The creation of uncertainty in the influence process: The roles of stimulus information and disagreement with similar others. *European Journal of Social Psychology*, 23, 17–38.

McGarty, G., Haslam, S.A., Hutchinson, K.J., and Turner, J.C. (1994). The effects of salient group membership on persuasion. *Small Group Research*, 25, 267–93.

McGrath, J.E. (1978). Small group research. *American Behavioral Scientist*, 21, 651–74.

McGrath, J.E. (1997). Small group research, that once and future field: An interpretation of the past with an eye to the future. *Group Dynamics: Theory, Research, and Practice*, 1, 7–27.

McGrath, J.E. and Altman, I. (1966). *Small Group Research: A synthesis and critique of the field*. New York: Holt, Rinehart, and Winston.

McGrath, J.E. and Kravitz, D. (1982). Group research. *Annual Review of Psychology*, 33, 195–230.

McGuire, W.J., McGuire, C.V., and Cheever, J. (1986). The self in society: Effects of social contexts on the sense of self. Special issue: The individual–society interface. *British Journal of Social Psychology*, 25, 259–70.

McGuire, W.J., McGuire, C.V., Child, P., and Fujioka, T. (1978). Salience of ethnicity in the spontaneous self-concept as a function of one's ethnic distinctiveness in the social environment. *Journal of Personality and Social Psychology*, 36, 511–20.

McReynolds, P. (1987). Self-theory, anxiety and intrapsychic conflicts. In N. Cheshire and H. Thomae (eds), *Self, Symptoms and Psychotherapy*. New York: Wiley, pp. 197–223.

Medin, D.L. (1989). Concepts and conceptual structure. *American Psychologist*, 44, 1469–81.

Medin, D.L., Goldstone, R.L., and Gentner, D. (1993). Respects for similarity. *Psychological Review*, 100, 254–78.

Meenes, M. (1943). A comparison of racial stereotypes of 1935 and 1942. *Journal of Social Psychology*, 17, 327–36.

Messick, D.M. and Mackie, D.M. (1989). Intergroup relations. *Annual Review of Psychology*, 40, 45–51.

Migdal, M.J., Hewstone, M., and Mullen, B. (1998). The effects of crossed categorization on intergroup evaluations: A meta-analysis. *British Journal of Social Psychology*, 37, 303–24.

Mikulincer, M. (1995). Attachment style and the mental representation of the self. *Journal of Personality and Social Psychology*, 69, 1203–15.

Miller, J. (1984). Culture and the development of everyday social explanation. *Journal of Personality and Social Psychology*, 46, 961–78.

Miller, N. (1992). Affective and cognitive processes in intergroup relations. Unpublished manuscript, University of Southern California, Los Angeles.

Minard, R.D. (1952). Race relations in the Pocahontas Coal Field. *Journal of Social Issues*, 8, 29–44.

Miniard, P.W. and Cohen, J.B. (1981). An examination of the Fishbein–Ajzen behavioral-intentions model's concepts and measures. *Journal of Experimental Social Psychology*, 17, 309–39.

Mitchell, C.R. (1981). *The Structure of International Conflict*. London: Macmillan.

Moghaddam, F.M., Taylor, D.M., and Wright, S.C. (1993). *Social Psychology in Cross-cultural Perspective*. New York: Freeman.

Monteith, M.J. (1993). Self-regulation of prejudiced responses: Implications for progress in prejudice-reduction efforts. *Journal of Personality and Social Psychology*, 65, 469–85.

Monteith, M.J. (1996). Affective reactions to prejudice-related discrepant responses: The impact of standard salience. *Personality and Social Psychology Bulletin*, 22, 1, 48–59.

Monteith, M.J., Deenan, N.E., and Tooman, G.D. (1996). The effect of social norm activation on the expression of opinion concerning gay men and blacks. *Basic and Applied Social Psychology*, 18, 267–88.

Monteith, M.J., Devine, P.G., and Zuwerink, J.R. (1993). Self- directed versus other directed affect as a consequence of prejudice-related discrepancies. *Journal of Personality and Social Psychology*, 64, 2, 198–210.

Moreland, R.L., Hogg, M.A., and Hains, S.C. (1994). Back to the future: Social psychological research on groups. *Journal of Experimental Social Psychology*, 30, 527–55.

Morris, M.W. and Peng, K. (1994). Culture and cause: American and Chinese attributions for social and physical events. *Journal of Personality and Social Psychology*, 67, 949–71.

Morrison, B.E. (1997). Social co-operation: Redefining the self in self-interest. Unpublished Ph.D. thesis, The Australian National University, Canberra.

Moscovici, S. (1976). *Social Influence and Social Change*. London: Academic Press.

Moscovici, S. (1982). The coming era of representations. In J.-P. Codol and J.-P. Leyens (eds), *Cognitive Analysis of Social Behaviour*. The Hague: Martinus Nijhoff, pp. 115–50.

Moscovici, S. and Doise, W. (1994). *Conflict and Consensus: A general theory of collective decisions*. London: Sage.

Moskowitz, G. (ed.) (forthcoming). *Future Directions in Social Cognition*. New York: Cambridge University Press.

Mueller, J.H. and Grove, T.R. (1991). Trait actualization and self-reference effects. *Bulletin of the Psychonomic Society*, 29, 13–16.

Mugny, G. (1982). *The Power of Minorities*. London: Academic Press.

Mullen, B. (1991). Group composition, salience, and cognitive representations: The phenomenology of being in a group. *Journal of Experimental Social Psychology*, 27, 297–323.

Mullen, B. and Hu, L. (1989). Perceptions of ingroup and outgroup variability: A meta-analysis integration. *Basic and Applied Social Psychology*, 10, 233–52.

Mullen, B., Brown, R., and Smith, C. (1992). Ingroup bias as a function of salience, relevance, and status: An integration. *European Journal of Social Psychology*, 22, 103–22.

Mullin, B.-A. (1998). Uncertainty reduction, social identification, and group behaviour. Unpublished doctoral dissertation, University of Queensland, Brisbane.

Mullin, B.-A. and Hogg, M.A. (1998a). Dimensions of subjective uncertainty in social identification and minimal intergroup discrimination. *British Journal of Social Psychology*, 37, 345–65.

Mullin, B.-A. and Hogg, M.A. (1998b). Reducing subjective uncertainty by group identification: The role of group relevance. Manuscript submitted for publication, University of Queensland, Brisbane.

Mullin, B.-A. and Hogg, M.A. (in press). Motivations for group membership: The role of subjective importance and uncertainty reduction. *Basic and Applied Social Psychology*.

Murphy, R.F. (1957). Intergroup hostility and social cohesion. *American Anthropologist*, 59, 1018–35.

Murphy, S. T. and Zajonc, R.B. (1993). Affect, cognition, and awareness: Affective priming with optimal and suboptimal stimulus exposures. *Journal of Personality and Social Psychology*, 64, 723–39.

Mutz, D.C. (1989). The influence of perceptions of mass influence: Third person effects and the public expression of opinions. *International Journal of Public Opinion Research*, 1, 3–23.

Neely, J.H. (1977). Semantic priming and retrieval from lexical memory: Roles of inhibitionless spreading activation and limited-capacity attention. *Journal of Experimental Psychology: General*, 106, 226–54.

Neisser, U. (1967). *Cognitive Psychology*. New York: Appleton-Century-Crofts.

Neisser, U. (1976). *Cognition and Reality*. San Francisco: W.H. Freeman.

Neuberg, S.L. (1989). The goal of forming accurate impressions during social interactions: Attenuating the impact of negative expectancies. *Journal of Personality and Social Psychology*, 56, 374–86.

Neuberg, S.L. and Fiske, S.T. (1987). Motivational influences on impression formation: Outcome dependency, accuracy-driven attention, and individuating processes. *Journal of Personality and Social Psychology*, 53, 431–44.

Neuberg, S.L. and Newson, J.T. (1993). Personal need for structure: Individual differences in the desire for simpler structure. *Journal of Personality and Social Psychology*, 65, 113–31.

Newman, L.S., Duff, K.J., Hedberg, D.A., and Blitstein, J. (1996). Rebound effects in impression formation: Assimilation and contrast effects following thought suppression. *Journal of Experimental Social Psychology*, 32, 460–83.

Nisbett, R.E. and Ross, L. (1980). *Human Inference: Strategies and shortcomings of social judgment*. Englewood Cliffs, NJ: Prentice-Hall.

Nisbett, R.E. and Wilson, T.D. (1977). Telling more than we can know: Verbal reports on mental processes. *Psychological Review*, 84, 231–59.

Noelle-Neumann, E. (1974). The spiral of silence: A theory of public opinion. *Journal of Communication*, 24, 43–51.

Noelle-Neumann, E. (1984). The spiral of silence: A response. In K.R. Sanders, L.L. Kaid, and E. Nimmo (eds), *Political Communication Yearbook 1984*. Carbondale, IL: Southern Illinois University Press, pp. 66–94.

Nolan, M.A., Haslam, S.A., Spears, R., and Oakes, P.J. (1997). Testing between resource-based and fit-based theories of stereotyping. Manuscript submitted for publication.

Nye, J.L. and Brower, A.M. (eds) (1996). *What's Social about Social Cognition: Research on socially shared cognition in small groups*. Thousand Oaks, CA: Sage.

Oakes, P.J. (1987). The salience of social categories. In J.C. Turner, M.A. Hogg, P.J. Oakes, S.D. Reicher, and M.S. Wetherell, *Rediscovering the Social Group: A self-categorization theory*. Oxford: Blackwell, pp. 117–41.

Oakes, P.J. (1994). The effects of fit versus novelty on the salience of social categories: A response to Biernat and Vescio (1993). *Journal of Experimental Social Psychology*, 30, 390–8.

Oakes, P.J. (1996). The categorization process: Cognition and the group in the social psychology of stereotyping. In W.P. Robinson (ed.), *Social Groups and Identity: Developing the legacy of Henri Tajfel*. Oxford: Butterworth-Heinemann, pp. 95–120.

Oakes, P.J. and Dempster, A.A. (1996). Views of the categorization process, with an example from stereotype change. Paper presented at the General Meeting of the European Association of Experimental Social Psychology, Gmunden, Austria, July.

Oakes, P.J. and Reynolds, K.J. (1997). Asking the accuracy question: Is measurement the answer? In R. Spears, P.J. Oakes, N. Ellemers, and S.A. Haslam (eds), *The Social Psychology of Stereotyping and Group Life*. Oxford and Cambridge, MA: Blackwell, pp. 51–71.

Oakes, P.J. and Turner, J.C. (1986). Distinctiveness and the salience of social category membership: Is there an automatic perceptual bias towards novelty? *European Journal of Social Psychology*, 16, 325–44.

Oakes, P.J. and Turner, J.C. (1990). Is limited information processing the cause of social stereotyping? In W. Stroebe and M. Hewstone (eds), *European Review of Social Psychology*, vol. 1. Chichester: Wiley, pp. 111–35.

Oakes, P.J., Haslam, S.A., and Turner, J.C. (1994). *Stereotypes and Social Reality*. Oxford: Blackwell.

Oakes, P.J., Haslam, S.A., and Turner, J.C. (1998). The role of prototypicality in group influence and cohesion: Contextual variation in the graded structure of social categories. In S. Worchel, J.F. Morales, D. Paez and J.C. Deschanps (eds), *Social Identity: International perspectives*. London: Sage, pp. 75–92.

Oakes, P.J., Haslam, S.A., Reynolds, K.J., Nolan, M.A., Eggins, R.A., Dempster, A.A., and Tweedie, J. (1997). Relative prototypicality and stereotype change: Effects of comparative context. Manuscript submitted for publication.

Oakes, P.J., Turner, J.C., and Haslam, S.A. (1991). Perceiving people as group members: The role of fit in the salience of social categorizations. *British Journal of Social Psychology*, 30, 125–44.

Oliver, R.L. and Bearden, W.O. (1985). Crossover effects in the theory of reasoned action: A moderating influence attempt. *Journal of Consumer Research*, 12, 324–40.

Operario, D. and Fiske, S.T. (1998). Racism equals power plus prejudice: A social psychological equation for racial oppression. In J.L. Eberhardt and S.T. Fiske (eds), *Confronting Racism: The problem and the response*. Thousand Oaks, CA: Sage, pp. 33–53.

Operario, D., Goodwin, S.A., and Fiske, S.T. (1998). Power is everywhere: Social control and personal control both operate at stereotype activation, interpretation, and response. In R.S. Wyer (ed.), *Advances in Social Cognition*, vol. 11. Mahwah, NJ: Erlbaum, pp. 163–75.

Ostrom, T.M. and Sedikides, C. (1992). Out-group homogeneity effects in natural and minimal groups. *Psychological Bulletin*, 112, 536–52.

Park, B., DeKay, M., and Kraus, S. (1994). Aggregating social behavior into person models: Perceiver-induced consistency. *Journal of Personality and Social Psychology*, 66, 437–59.

Park, B., Ryan, C.S., and Judd, C.M. (1992). Role of meaningful subgroups in explaining differences in perceived variability for ingroups and outgroups. *Journal of Personality and Social Psychology*, 63, 553–67.

Parker, I. (1989). *The Crisis in Social Psychology – and How to End It*. New York: Routledge.

Paulhus, D.L. (1986). Self-deception and impression management in test responses. In A. Angleitner and J.S. Wiggins (eds), *Personality Assessment via Questionnaire* New York: Springer-Verlag, pp. 143–65.

Pelham, B.W. and Swann, W.B. (1994). The juncture of intrapersonal and interpersonal knowledge: Self-certainty and interpersonal congruence. *Personality and Social Psychology Bulletin*, 20, 349–57.

Pelham, B.W. and Swann, W. (1989). From self-conceptions to self-worth: On the sources and structure of global self-esteem. *Journal of Personality and Social Psychology*, 57, 672–80.

Pendry, L.F. and Macrae, C.N. (1996). What the disinterested perceiver overlooks: Goal-directed social categorization. *Personality and Social Psychology Bulletin*, 22, 249–56.

Pepitone, A. (1981). Lessons from the history of social psychology. *American Psychologist*, 36, 972–85.

Perdue, C.W. and Gurtman, M.B. (1990). Evidence for the automaticity of ageism. *Journal of Experimental Social Psychology*, 26, 199–216.

Perdue, C.W., Dovidio, J.F., Gurtman, M.B., and Tyler, R.B. (1990). Us and them: Social categorization and the process of intergroup bias. *Journal of Personality and Social Psychology*, 59, 475–86.

Perez, J.A. and Mugny, G. (1990). Minority influence, manifest discrimination and latent influence. In D. Abrams and M.A. Hogg (eds), *Social Identity Theory: Constructive and critical advances*. Hemel Hempstead: Harvester Wheatsheaf, pp. 152–68.

Perloff, L.S. and Fetzer, B.K. (1986). Self–other judgements and perceived vulnerability to victimization. *Journal of Personality and Social Psychology*, 50, 502–10.

Perloff, R.M. (1989). Ego-involvement and the third person effect of televised news coverage. *Communication Research*, 16, 236–62.

Perloff, R.M. (1993). Third-person effect research 1983–1992: A review and synthesis. *International Journal of Public Opinion Research*, 5, 167–84.

Pettigrew, T.F. (1958). Personality and socio-cultural factors in intergroup attitudes: A cross-national comparison. *Journal of Conflict Resolution*, 2, 29–42.

Pettigrew, T.F. (1979). The ultimate attribution error: Extending Allport's cognitive analysis of prejudice. *Personality and Social Psychology Bulletin*, 5, 461–76.

Pettigrew, T.F. (1997). Generalized intergroup contact effects on prejudice. *Personality and Social Psychology Bulletin*, 23, 173–85.

Pettigrew, T.F. (in press). The affective component of prejudice: Empirical support for the new view. In S.A. Tuch and J.K. Martin (eds), *Racial Attitudes in the 1990s: Continuity and change*. Westport, CT: Praeger.

Pettigrew, T.F. and Meertens, R.W. (1995). Subtle and blatant prejudice in western Europe. *European Journal of Social Psychology*, 25, 57–75.

Petty, R.E. and Cacioppo, J.T. (1979). Issue involvement can increase or decrease persuasion by enhancing message-relevant cognitive responses. *Journal of Personality and Social Psychology*, 37, 1915–26.

Petty, R.E. and Cacioppo, J.T. (1981). *Attitudes and Persuasion: Classic and contemporary approaches*. Dubuque, IA: W.C. Brown.

Petty, R.E. and Cacioppo, J.T. (1984). Source factors and the elaboration likelihood model of persuasion. *Advances in Consumer Research*, 11, 668–72.

Petty, R.E. and Cacioppo, J.T. (1986). The elaboration likelihood model of persuasion. In L. Berkowitz (ed.), *Advances in Experimental Social Psychology*, vol. 19. San Diego: Academic Press, pp. 123–205.

Petty, R.E. and Cacioppo, J.T. (1986). The elaboration likelihood model of persuasion. In L. Berkowitz (ed.), *Advances in Experimental Social Psychology*, vol. 19. New York: Academic Press, pp. 123–205.

Petty, R.E., Priester, J.R., and Wegener, D.T. (1994). Cognitive processes in attitude change. In R.S. Wyer, J., and T.K. Srull (eds), *Handbook of Social Cognition*, 2nd edn, vol. 2. Hillsdale, NJ: Erlbaum, pp. 69–142.

Potter, J. and Wetherell, M. (1987). *Discourse and Social Psychology: Beyond attitudes and behaviour*. London: Sage.

Powell, M.C. and Fazio, R.H. (1984). Attitude accessibility as a function of repeated attitudinal expression. *Personality and Social Psychology Bulletin*, 10, 139–48.

Powers, W.T. (1973). *Behaviour: The control of perception*. Chicago: Aldine.

Pratto, F. and Bargh, J.A. (1991). Stereotyping based on apparently individuating information: Trait and global components of sex stereotypes under attention overload. *Journal of Experimental Social Psychology*, 27, 26–47.

Pratto, F., Shih, M., and Orton, J. (1997). Social dominance orientation and group threat in implicit and explicit group discrimination. Manuscript in submission.

Pratto, F., Sidanius, J., Stallworth, L.M., and Malle, B.F. (1994). Social dominance orientation: A personality variable predicting social and political attitudes. *Journal of Personality and Social Psychology*, 67, 741–63.

Prentice, D.A., Miller, D.T., and Lightdale, J.R. (1994). Asymmetries in attachments to groups and to their members: Distinguishing between common-identity and common-bond groups. *Personality and Social Psychology Bulletin*, 20, 484–93.

Puckett, J.M., Petty, R.E., Cacioppo, J.T., and Fisher, D.L. (1983). The relative impact of age and attractiveness stereotypes in persuasion. *Journal of Gerontology*, 38, 340–3.

Rabbie, J.M. and Horwitz, M. (1969). Arousal of ingroup–outgroup bias by a chance win or loss. *Journal of Personality and Social Psychology*, 13, 269–77.

Rabbie, J.M. and Horwitz, M. (1988). Categories versus groups as explanatory concepts in intergroup relations. *European Journal of Social Psychology*, 18, 117–23.

Rabbie, J.M., Schot, J.C., and Visser, L. (1989). Social identity theory: A conceptual and empirical critique from the perspective of a behavioral interaction model. *European Journal of Social Psychology*, 19, 171–202.

Raskin, R., Novacek, J., and Hogan, R. (1991). Narcissism, self- esteem, and defensive self-enhancement. *Journal of Personality*, 59, 19–38.

Rehm, J., Lilli, W., and van Eimeren, B. (1988). Reduced intergroup differentiation as a result of self-categorization in overlapping categories: A quasi-experiment. *European Journal of Social Psychology*, 18, 375–9.

Reicher, S.D. (1987). Crowd behaviour as social action. In J.C. Turner, M.A. Hogg, P.J. Oakes, S.D. Reicher, and M.S. Wetherell, *Rediscovering the Social Group: A self-categorization theory*. Oxford: Blackwell, pp. 171–202.

Reicher, S.D. (1996). "The Battle of Westminster": Developing the social identity model of crowd behaviour in order to explain the initiation and development of collective conflict. *European Journal of Social Psychology*, 26, 115–34.

Reid, A. and Deaux, K. (1996). Relationship between social and personal identities: Segregation or integration. *Journal of Personality and Social Psychology*, 71, 1084–91.

Reis, H.T. and Stiller, J. (1992). Publication trends in JPSP: A three-decade review. *Personality and Social Psychology Bulletin*, 18, 465–72.

Reynolds, K.J. (1996). Beyond the information given: Capacity, context and the categorization process in impression formation. Unpublished Ph.D. thesis, The Australian National University, Canberra.

Robinson, W.P. (ed.) (1996). *Social Groups and Identities: Developing the legacy of Henri Tajfel*. Oxford: Butterworth-Heinemann.

Rodriguez, J. and Gurin, P. (1990). The relationships of intergroup contact to social identity and political consciousness. *Hispanic Journal of Behavioral Sciences*, 12, 235–55.

Rogers, M., Miller, N., and Hennigan, K. (1981). Cooperative games as an intervention to promote cross-racial acceptance. *American Educational Research Journal*, 18, 513–16.

Rokeach, M. (1948). Generalized mental rigidity as a factor in ethnocentrism. *Journal of Abnormal Social Psychology*, 43, 259–78.

Rokeach, M. (1960). *The Open and Closed Mind*. New York: Basic Books.

Roney, C. and Sorrentino, R.M. (1987). Uncertainty orientation and person perception: Individual differences in categorization. *Social Cognition*, 5, 369–82.

Roney, J.R. and Sorrentino, R.M. (1995). Self-evaluation motives and uncertainty orientation: Asking the "who" question. *Personality and Social Psychology Bulletin*, 21, 1319–29.

Rosch, E. (1978). Principles of categorization. In E. Rosch and B.B. Lloyd (eds), *Cognition and Categorization*. Hillsdale, NJ: Erlbaum, pp. 28–49.

Roseman, I.J. (1984). Cognitive determinants of emotion: A structural theory. In P. Shaver (ed.), *Review of Personality and Social Psychology*, vol. 5. Beverly Hills, CA: Sage, pp. 11–36.

Rosenberg, M. (1965). *Society and the Adolescent Self- image*. Princeton, NJ: Princeton University Press.

Rosenberg, M. (1979). *Conceiving the Self*. New York: Basic Books.

Rosenberg, S. (1988). Self and others: Studies in social personality and autobiography. In L. Berkowitz (ed.), *Advances in Experimental Social Psychology*, vol. 21. New York: Academic Press, pp. 57–95.

Rosenthal, D.A., Hall, C., and Moore, S.M. (1992). AIDS, adolescents, and sexual risk taking: A test of the Health Belief Model. *Australian Psychologist*, 27, 166–71.

Rosnow, R.L. (1980). Psychology of rumor reconsidered. *Psychological Bulletin*, 87, 578–91.

Ross, L.D. (1977). The intuitive psychologist and his shortcomings: Distortions in the attribution process. In L. Berkowitz (ed), *Advances in Experimental Social Psychology*, vol. 10. New York: Academic Press, pp. 173–220.

Ross, M.J., Jurek, A.W., and Oliver, J.M. (1996). Stimulus emotionality and processing information about the self. *Journal of Social Behavior and Personality*, 11, 43–50.

Rothbart, M. (1981). Memory processes and social beliefs. In D.L. Hamilton (ed.), *Cognitive Processes in Stereotyping and Intergroup Behaviour*. Hillsdale, NJ: Erlbaum, pp. 145–81.

Rothbart, M. and John, O.P. (1985). Social categorization and behavioural episodes: A cognitive analysis of the effects of intergroup contact. *Journal of Social Issues*, 41, 81–104.

Rothbart, M. and Lewis, S. (1994). Cognitive processes and intergroup relations: A historical perspective. In D.L. Hamilton, P.G. Devine, and T.M. Ostrom (eds), *Social Cognition: Its impact on social psychology*. Orlando, FL: Academic Press, pp. 347–82.

Rothbart, M. and Taylor, M. (1992). Category labels and social reality: Do we view social categories as natural kinds? In G. Semin and K. Fiedller (eds), *Language, Interaction, and Social Cognition*. London: Sage, pp. 11–36.

Rubin, M. and Hewstone, M. (1998). Social identity theory's self- esteem hypothesis: A review and some suggestions for clarification. *Personality and Social Psychology Review*, 2, 40–62.

Rucinski, D. and Salmon, C.T. (1990). The "other" as the vulnerable voter: A study of the third-person effect in the 1988 U.S. presidential campaign. *International Journal of Public Opinion Research*, 2, 4, 345–68.

Rudman, L.A., Greenwald, A.G., and McGhee, D.E. (1998). Sex differences in gender stereotype revealed by the implicit association test. Unpublished manuscript. Rutgers University and University of Washington.

Rumelhart, D.E., Hinton, G.E., and McClelland, J.L. (1986). A general framework for parallel distributed processing. In D.E. Rumelhart, J.L. McClelland, and the PDP research group (eds), *Parallel Distributed Processing*. Cambridge, MA: MIT Press, pp. 45–76.

Runciman, W.G. (1966). *Relative Deprivation and Social Justice*. London: Routledge and Kegan Paul.

Ryan, C.S. and Bogart, L.M. (1997). Development of new group members' ingroup and outgroup stereotypes: Changes in perceived group variability and ethnocentrism. *Journal of Personality and Social Psychology*, 73, 719–32.

Ryan, M.J. (1978). An examination of the alternative form of the behavioral intention model's normative component. In H. Keith Hunt (ed.), *Advances in Consumer Research*, vol. 5. Ann Arbor, MI: Association for Consumer Research, pp. 282–9.

Ryan, M.J. (1982). Behavioral intention formation: The interdependency of attitudinal and social influence variables. *Journal of Consumer Research*, 9, 263–78.

Sachdev, I. and Bourhis, R. (1993). Ethnolinguistic vitality: Some motivational and cognitive considerations. In M.A. Hogg and D. Abrams (eds), *Group Motivation: Social psychological perspectives*. Hemel Hempstead: Harvester Wheatsheaf, pp. 33–51.

Sachdev, I. and Bourhis, R.Y. (1984). Status differentials and intergroup behaviour. *European Journal of Social Psychology*, 17, 277–93.

Sachdev, I. and Bourhis, R.Y. (1987). Status differentials and intergroup behaviour. *European Journal of Social Psychology*, 17, 277–93.

Sachdev, I. and Bourhis, R.Y. (1991). Power and status differentials in minority and majority group relations. *European Journal of Social Psychology*, 21, 1–24.

Sackeim, H.A. and Gur, R.C. (1978). Self-deception, self- confrontation and consciousness. In G.E. Schwartz and D. Shapiro (eds), *Consciousness and Self-regulation: Advances in research*, vol. 2. New York: Plenum Press, pp. 139–97.

Sampson, E.E. (1977). Psychology and the American ideal. *Journal of Personality and Social Psychology*, 35, 767–82.

Sanbonmatsu, D.M. and Fazio, R.H. (1990). The role of attitudes in memory-based decision-making. *Journal of Personality and Social Psychology*, 59, 614–22.

Sanbonmatsu, D.M., Sherman, S.J., and Hamilton, D.M. (1987). Illusory correlation in the perception of individuals and groups. *Social Cognition*, 5, 1–25.

Sanna, L.J. and Parks, C.D. (1997). Group research trends in social and organizational psychology: Whatever happened to intragroup research? *Psychological Science*, 8, 261–7.

Schachter, S. (1959). *The Psychology of Affiliation: Experimental studies of the sources of gregariousness*. Stanford, CA: Stanford University Press.

Schachter, S. and Singer, J. (1962). Cognitive, social, and physiological determinants of emotional state. *Psychological Review*, 65, 379–99.

Schachter, S., Ellertson, N., McBride, D., and Gregory, D. (1951). An experimental study of cohesiveness and productivity. *Human Relations*, 4, 229–38.

Schaller, M. and Maass, A. (1989). Illusory correlation and social categorization: Toward an integration of motivational and cognitive factors in stereotype formation. *Journal of Personality and Social Psychology*, 56, 709–21.

Scheier, M.F. and Carver, C.S. (1981). Private and public aspects of self. In L. Wheeler (ed.), *Review of Personality and Social Psychology*, vol. 2. London: Sage, pp. 189–216.

Schein, E.H. (1961). *Coercive Persuasion*. New York: Norton.

Scherer, K.R. (1988). Cognitive antecedents of emotion. In V. Hamilton, G.H. Bower, and N.H. Frijda (eds), *Cognitive Perspectives on Emotion and Motivation*. Dordrecht: Kluwer, pp. 89–126.

Schlenker, B.R. (1980). *Impression Management*. Monterey, CA: Brooks-Cole.

Schlenker, B.R. and Miller, R.S. (1977). Egocentrism in groups: Self-serving bias or logical information processing? *Journal of Personality and Social Psychology*, 35, 755–64.

Schneider, D.J. and Turkat, D. (1975). Self-presentation following success or failure: Defensive self-esteem models. *Journal of Personality*, 43, 127–35.

Schneider, W. and Shiffrin, R.M. (1977). Control and automatic human information processing: I. Detection, search, and attention. *Psychological Review*, 84, 1–66.

Schofield, J.W. and Sagar, H. (1977). Peer interaction patterns in an integrated middle school. *Sociometry*, 40, 130–8.

Schoonhaven, C.B. (1981). Problems with contingency theory: Testing assumptions within the language of contingency "theory." *Administrative Science Quarterly*, 26, 349–77.

Schuette, R.A. and Fazio, R.H. (1995). Attitude accessibility and motivation as determinants of biased processing: A test of the MODE model. *Personality and Social Psychology*, 21, 704–10.

Schweder, R.A. (1991). *Thinking through Cultures: Expeditions in cultural psychology*. Cambridge, MA: Harvard University Press.

Seago, D.W. (1947). Stereotypes: Before Pearl Harbour and after. *Journal of Social Psychology*, 23, 55–63.

Sears, D.O. and Kinder, D.R. (1971). Racial tensions and voting in Los Angeles. In W.Z. Hirsch (ed.), *Los Angeles: Viability and prospects for metropolitan leadership*. New York: Praeger, pp. 51–88.

Sears, D.O. and Kinder, D.R. (1985). Whites' opposition to busing: On conceptualizing and operationalizing group conflict. *Journal of Personality and Social Psychology*, 48, 1141–7.

Secord, P.F. (1959). Stereotyping and favorableness in the perception of Negro faces. *Journal of Abnormal and Social Psychology*, 59, 309–15.

Sedikides, C. and Strube, M.J. (1995). The multiply motivated self. *Personality and Social Psychology Bulletin*, 21, 1330–5.

Seligman, C., Olson, J.M., and Zanna, M.P. (eds) (1996). *The Psychology of Values: The Ontario symposium*, vol. 8. Mahwah, NJ: Erlbaum.

Seta, C.E. and Hayes, N. (1994). The influence of impression formation goals on the accuracy of social memory. *Personality and Social Psychology Bulletin*, 20, 93–101.

Sherif, M. (1936). *The Psychology of Social Norms*. New York: Harper Bros.

Sherif, M. (1936). *The Psychology of Social Norms*. New York: Harper and Row.

Sherif, M. (1966). *Group Conflict and Co-operation: Their social psychology*. London: Routledge and Kegan Paul.

Shiffrin, R.M. and Schneider, W. (1977). Control and automatic human information processing: II. Perceptual learning, automatic attending, and a general theory. *Psychological Review*, 84, 127–90.

Showers, C. (1992). Compartmentalization of positive and negative self-knowledge: Keeping bad apples out of the bunch. *Journal of Personality and Social Psychology*, 62, 1036–49.

Shrauger, J.S. (1975). Responses to evaluations as function of initial self-perception. *Psychological Bulletin*, 82, 581–96.

Sidanius, J. (1993). The psychology of group conflict and the dynamics of social oppression: A social dominance perspective. In S. Iyengar and W. McGuire (eds), *Explorations in Political Psychology*. Durham, NC: Duke University Press, pp. 183–219.

Sidanius, J. and Pratto, F. (1993). The inevitability of oppression and the dynamics of social dominance. In P. Sniderman and P. Tetlock (eds), *Prejudice, Politics, and the American Dilemma*. Stanford, CA: Stanford University Press, pp. 173–211.

Sidanius, J., Pratto, F., and Bobo, L. (1994). Social dominance orientation and the political psychology of gender: A case of invariance? *Journal of Personality and Social Psychology*, 67, 998–1011.

Sidanius, J., Pratto, F., and Mitchell, M. (1994). In-group identification, social dominance orientation, and differential intergroup social allocation. *Journal of Social Psychology*, 134, 151–67.

Simmel, G. (1908). *The Sociology of Georg Simmel*, trans. Kurt Wolff. New York: Free Press.

Simon, B. (1992a). Intragroup differentiation in terms of ingroup and outgroup attributes. *European Journal of Social Psychology*, 22, 407–13.

Simon, B. (1992b). The perception of ingroup and outgroup homogeneity: Reintroducing the intergroup context. In W. Stroebe and M. Hewstone (eds), *European Review of Social Psychology*, vol. 3. Chichester: Wiley, pp. 1–30.

Simon, B. (1993). On the asymmetry in the cognitive construal of ingroup and outgroup: A model of egocentric social categorization. *European Journal of Social Psychology*, 23, 131–47.

Simon, B. (1997). Self and group in modern society: Ten theses on the individual self and the collective self. In R. Spears, P.J. Oakes, N. Ellemers, and S.A. Haslam (eds), *The Social Psychology of Stereotyping and Group Life*. Oxford: Blackwell, pp. 318–35.

Simon, B. (1998). Individuals, groups, and social change: On the relationship between individual and collective self- interpretations and collective action. In C. Sedikides, J. Schopler, and C. Insko (eds), *Intergroup Cognition and Intergroup Behaviour*. Hillsdale, NJ: Erlbaum, pp. 257–82.

Simon, B. and Brown, R.J. (1987). Perceived intragroup homogeneity in minority–majority contexts. *Journal of Personality and Social Psychology*, 53, 703–11.

Simon, B. and Hamilton, D.L. (1994). Self-stereotyping and social context: The effects of relative in-group size and in-group status. *Journal of Personality and Social Psychology*, 66, 699–711.

Simon, B. and Pettigrew, T.F. (1990). Social identity and perceived group homogeneity: Evidence for the ingroup homogeneity effect. *European Journal of Social Psychology*, 20, 269–86.

Simon, B., Glassner-Bayerl, B., and Stratenwerth, I. (1991). Stereotyping and self-stereotyping in a natural intergroup context: The case of heterosexual and homosexual men. *Social Psychology Quarterly*, 54, 252–66.

Simon, B., Hastedt, C., and Aufderheide, B. (in press). When self-categorization makes sense: The role of meaningful social categorization in minority and majority members' self-perception. *Journal of Personality and Social Psychology*.

Simon, B., Pantaleo, G., and Mummendey, A. (1995). Unique individual or interchangeable group member? The accentuation of intragroup differences versus similarities as an indicator of the individual self versus the collective self. *Journal of Personality and Social Psychology*, 69, 106–19.

Simpson, J.A. and Wood, W. (1992). Introduction: Where is the group in social psychology? An historical overview. In S. Worchel, W. Wood, and J.A. Simpson (eds), *Group Process and Productivity*. Newbury Park, CA: Sage, pp. 1–10.

Sinha, A.K.P. and Upadhyaya, O.P. (1960). Change and persistence in the stereotypes of university students toward different ethnic groups during the Sino-Indian border dispute. *Journal of Social Psychology*, 52, 31–9.

Skowronski, J.J., Carlston, D.E., and Isham, J.T. (1993). Implicit versus explicit impression formation: The differing effects of overt labelling and covert priming on memory and impressions. *Journal of Experimental Social Psychology*, 29, 17–41.

Smith, C.A. and Ellsworth, P.C. (1985). Patterns of cognitive appraisal in emotion. *Journal of Personality and Social Psychology*, 48, 813–38.

Smith, E.E. and Osherson, D.N. (1984). Conceptual combination with prototype concepts. *Cognitive Science*, 8, 337–61.

Smith, E.R. (1993). Social identity and social emotions: Toward new conceptualizations of prejudice. In D.M. Mackie and D.L. Hamilton (eds), *Affect, Cognition, and Stereotyping: Interactive processes in group perception*. San Diego: Academic Press, pp. 297–315.

Smith, E.R. (1994). Social cognition contributions to attribution theory and research. In P.G. Devine, D.L. Hamilton, and T.M. Ostrom (eds), *Social Cognition: Impact on social psychology*. San Diego: Academic Press, pp. 77–108.

Smith, E.R. (1996). What do connectionism and social psychology offer each other? *Journal of Personality and Social Psychology*, 70, 893–912.

Smith, E.R. (1998). Mental representation and memory. In D. Gilbert, S.T. Fiske, and G. Lindzey (eds), *Handbook of Social Psychology*, 4th edn, Vol. 1. New York: McGraw-Hill, pp. 391–445.

Smith, E.R. and DeCoster, J. (1998). Knowledge acquisition, accessibility, and use in person perception and stereotyping: Simulation with a recurrent connectionist network. *Journal of Personality and Social Psychology*, 74, 21–35.

Smith, E.R. and Henry, S. (1996). An ingroup becomes part of the self: Response time evidence. *Personality and Social Psychology Bulletin*, 22, 635–42.

Smith, E.R. and Lerner, M. (1986). Development of automatism of social judgments. *Journal of Personality and Social Psychology*, 50, 246–59.

Smith, E.R. and Zarate, M.A. (1990). Exemplar and prototype use in social categorization. *Social Cognition*, 8, 243–62.

Smith, E.R. and Zarate, M.A. (1992). Exemplar-based model of social judgment. *Psychological Review*, 99, 3–21.

Smith, E.R., Coats, S., and Walling, D. (in press). Overlapping mental representations of self, ingroup, and partner: Further response time evidence and a connectionist model. *Personality and social Psychology Bulletin*.

Smith, E.R., Fazio, R.H., and Cejka, M.A. (1996). Accessible attitudes influence categorization of multiply categorizable objects. *Journal of Personality and Social Psychology*, 71, 888–98.

Smith, H.J. and Tyler, T.R. (1997). Choosing the right pond: The impact of group membership on self-esteem and group-oriented behaviour. *Journal of Experimental Social Psychology*, 33, 146–70.

Smith, R. (1986). Television addiction. In J. Bryant and D. Zillman (eds), *Perspectives on Media Effects*. Hillsdale, NJ: Lawrence Erlbaum, pp. 109–28.

Sniderman, P.M. and Tetlock, P.E. (1986). Symbolic racism: Problems of motive attribution in political analysis. *Journal of Social Issues*, 42, 2, 129–50.

Snyder, C.R. and Fromkin, H.L. (1980). *Uniqueness: The human pursuit of difference*. New York: Plenum.

Snyder, M. and Miene, P. (1994). On the functions of stereotypes and prejudice. In M.P. Zanna, and J.M. Olson (eds), *The Psychology of Prejudice: The Ontario symposium*, vol 7. Hillsdale, NJ: Erlbaum, pp. 33–54.

Sorrentino, R.M. and Higgins, E.T. (eds) (1986). *Handbook of Motivation and Cognition: Foundations of social behavior*, vol. 1. New York: Guilford.

Sorrentino, R.M. and Roney, C.J.R. (1986). Uncertainty orientation, achievement-related motivation and task diagnosticity as determinants of task performance. *Social Cognition*, 4, 420–36.

Sorrentino, R.M. and Short, J.C. (1986). Uncertainty orientation, motivation and cognition. In R.M. Sorrentino and E.T. Higgins (eds), *The Handbook of Motivation and Cognition: Foundations of social behavior*, vol. 1. New York: Guilford, pp. 379–403.

Sorrentino, R.M., Holmes, J.G., Hanna, S.E., and Sharp, A. (1995). Uncertainty orientation and trust in close relationships: Individual differences in cognitive styles. *Journal of Personality and Social Psychology*, 68, 314–27.

Spears, R., Doosje, B., and Ellemers, N. (1997). Self- stereotyping in the face of threats to group status and distinctiveness: The role of group identification. *Personality and Social Psychology Bulletin*, 23, 538–53.

Spears, R., Oakes, P.J., Ellemers, N., and Haslam, S.A. (eds) (1997). *The Social Psychology of Stereotyping and Group Life*. Oxford: Blackwell.

Srull, T.K. (1981). Person memory: Some tests of associative storage and retrieval models. *Journal of Experimental Psychology: Human Learning and Memory*, 7, 440–62.

Srull, T.K. and Wyer, Jr, R.S. (eds), (1993). *The Mental Representation of Trait and Autobiographical Knowledge about the Self: Advances in social cognition*, vol. 5. Hillsdale, NJ: Lawrence Erlbaum Associates.

Srull, T.K. and Wyer, R.S., Jr (1979). The role of category accessibility in the interpretation of information about persons: Some determinants and implications. *Journal of Personality and Social Psychology*, 37, 1660–72.

Srull, T.K. and Wyer, R.S., Jr (1989). Person memory and judgment. *Psychological Review*, 96, 58–83.

Stangor, C. (1988). Stereotype accessibility and information processing. *Personality and Social Psychology Bulletin*, 14, 694–708.

Stangor, C. and Ford, T.E. (1992). Accuracy and expectancy- confirming processing orientations and the development of stereotypes and prejudice. In W. Stroebe and M. Hewstone (eds), *European Review of Social Psychology*, vol. 3. New York: Wiley, pp. 57–89.

Stangor, C. and Lange, J.E. (1994). Mental representations of social groups: Advances in understanding stereotypes and stereotyping. In M.P. Zanna (ed.), *Advances in Experimental Social Psychology*, vol. 26. San Francisco: Academic Press, pp. 357–416.

Stangor, C. and MacMillan, D. (1992). Memory for expectancy- congruent and expectancy-incongruent information: A review of the social and social-developmental literatures. *Psychological Bulletin*, 111, 42–61.

Stangor, C. and Schaller, M. (1996). Stereotypes as individual and collective representations. In C.N. Macrae, C. Stangor, and M. Hewstone (eds), *Stereotypes and Stereotyping*. New York: Guilford, pp. 3–37.

Stangor, C., Lynch, L., Duan, C., and Glass, B. (1992). Categorization of individuals on the basis of multiple social features. *Journal of Personality and Social Psychology*, 62, 207–18.

Stangor, C., Sullivan L.A., and Ford, T.E. (1991). Affective and cognitive determinants of prejudice. *Social Cognition*, 9, 359–80.

Stasser, G. and Davis, J.H. (1977). Opinion change during group discussion. *Personality and Social Psychology Bulletin*, 3, 252–6.

Staub, E. (1989). *The Roots of Evil: The origins of genocide and other group violence*. New York: Cambridge University Press.

Steele, C.M. (1988). The psychology of self-affirmation: Sustaining the integrity of the self. *Advances in Experimental Social Psychology*, 21, 261–302.

Steele, C.M., Spencer, S.J., and Lynch, M. (1993). Self-image resilience and dissonance: The role of affirmational resources. *Journal of Personality and Social Psychology*, 64, 885–96.

Steiner, I.D. (1974). Whatever happened to the group in social psychology? *Journal of Experimental Social Psychology*, 10, 94–108.

Steiner, I.D. (1983). Whatever happened to the touted revival of the group? In H. Blumberg, A. Hare, V. Kent, and M. Davies (eds), *Small Groups and Social Interaction*, vol. 2. New York: Wiley, pp. 539–48.

Steiner, I.D. (1986). Paradigms and groups. *Advances in Experimental Social Psychology*, 19, 251–89.

Stephan, W.G. and Stephan, C.W. (1985). Intergroup anxiety. *Journal of Social Issues*, 41, 157–75.

Stephan, W.G. and Stephan, C.W. (1993). Cognition and affect in stereotyping: Parallel interactive networks. In D.M. Mackie and D.L. Hamilton (eds), *Affect, Cognition, and Stereotyping: Interactive processes in group perception*. San Diego: Academic Press, pp. 111–36.

Stephan, W.G., Ageyev, V., Coates-Shrider, L., Stephan, C.W., and Abalakina, M. (1994). On the relationship between stereotypes and prejudice: An international study. *Personality and Social Psychology Bulletin*, 20, 277–84.

Stern, L.D., Marrs, S., Millar, M.G., and Cole, E. (1984). Processing time and the recall of inconsistent and consistent behaviors of individuals and groups. *Journal of Personality and Social Psychology*, 47, 253–62.

Stevens, L.A. and Fiske, S.T. (1995). Motivation and cognition in social life: A social survival perspective. *Social Cognition*, 13, 189–214.

Stroebe, W. and Insko, C.A. (1989). Stereotypes, prejudice, and discrimination: Changing conceptions in theory and research. In D. Bar-Tal, C.F. Graumann, A.W. Kruglanski, and W. Stroebe (eds), *Stereotypes and Prejudice: Changing conceptions*. New York: Springer-Verlag, pp. 3–34.

Stroessner, S.J. (1996). Social categorization by race and sex: Effects of perceived non-normalcy on response times. *Social Cognition*, 14, 247–76.

Stroessner, S.J., Hamilton, D.L., and Mackie, D.M. (1992). Affect and stereotyping: The effect of induced mood on distinctiveness- based illusory correlations. *Journal of Personality and Social Psychology*, 62, 564–76.

Struckman-Johnson, C.J., Gilliland, R.C., Struckman-Johnson, D.L., and North, T.C. (1990). The effects of fear of AIDS and gender on responses to fear-arousing condom advertisements. *Journal of Applied Social Psychology*, 20, 1396–1410.

Stryker, S. (1987). Identity theory: Developments and extensions. In K. Yardley and T. Honess (eds), *Self and Identity: Psychosocial perspectives*. New York: Wiley, pp. 83–103.

Stryker, S. and Statham, A. (1985). Symbolic interaction and role theory. In G. Lindzey and E. Aronson (eds), *The Handbook of Social Psychology*, 3rd edn, vol. 1. New York: Random House, pp. 311–78.

Suls, J. and Wills, T.A. (eds) (1991). *Social Comparison: Contemporary theory and research*. Hillsdale, NJ: Erlbaum.

Suls, J.M. and Miller, R.L. (1977). *Social Comparison Processes*. Washington, DC: Hemisphere.

Susskind, J., Maurer, K., Thakkar, V., Hamilton, D.L., and Sherman, J.W. (1997). Perceiving individuals and groups: Expectancies, dispositional inferences, and causal attributions. Unpublished manuscript, University of California, Santa Barbara.

Swann, W.B. (1990). To be adored or to be known? The interplay of self-enhancement and self-verification. In R.M. Sorrentino and E.T. Higgins (eds), *Handbook of Motivation and Cognition*, Vol. 2. New York: GuilFord Press, pp. 408–48.

Swann, W.B. and Schroeder, D.G. (1995). The search for beauty and truth: A framework for understanding reactions to evaluations. *Personality and Social Psychology Bulletin*, 21, 1307–18.

Swann, W.B., Stein-Seroussi, A., and Giesler, R.B. (1992). Why people self-verify. *Journal of Personality and Social Psychology*, 62, 392–401.

Tajfel, H. (1957). Value and the perceptual judgement of magnitude. *Psychological Review*, 64, 192–204.

Tajfel, H. (1959). Quantitative judgement in social perception. *British Journal of Psychology*, 50, 16–29.

Tajfel, H. (1969a). Cognitive aspects of prejudice. *Journal of Social Issues*, 25, 79–97.

Tajfel, H. (1969b). Social and cultural factors in perception. In G. Lindzey and E. Aronson (eds), *Handbook of Social Psychology*, vol. 3. Reading, MA: Addison-Wesley, pp. 315–94.

Tajfel, H. (1970). Experiments in intergroup discrimination. *Scientific American*, 223, 96–102.

Tajfel, H. (1972). Some developments in European social psychology. *European Journal of Social Psychology*, 2, 307–22.

Tajfel, H. (1974a). Intergroup behaviour, social comparison and social change. Unpublished Katz-Newcomb Lectures, University of Michigan, Ann Arbor.

Tajfel, H. (1974b). Social identity and intergroup behaviour. *Social Science Information*, 13, 65–93.

Tajfel, H. (1978a). *Differentiation between Social Groups: Studies in the social psychology of intergroup relations*. London: Academic Press.

Tajfel, H. (1978b). Social categorization, social identity and social comparison. In H. Tajfel (ed.), *Differentiation between Social Groups*. London: Academic Press, pp. 61–7.

Tajfel, H. (1979). Individuals and groups in social psychology. *British Journal of Social Psychology*, 18, 183–90.

Tajfel, H. (1981a). *Human Groups and Social Categories: Studies in social psychology*. Cambridge: Cambridge University Press.

Tajfel, H. (1981b). Social stereotypes and social groups. In J.C. Turner and H. Giles (eds), *Intergroup Behaviour*. Oxford: Blackwell, pp. 144–67.

Tajfel, H. (1982). Social psychology of intergroup relations. *Annual Review of Psychology*, 33, 1–39.

Tajfel, H. (ed.) (1982). *Social Identity and Intergroup Relations*. Cambridge: Cambridge University Press.

Tajfel, H. (ed.) (1984). *The Social Dimension: European developments in social psychology*, 2 vols. Cambridge: Cambridge University Press.

Tajfel, H. and Billig, M. (1974). Familiarity and categorisation in intergroup behaviour. *Journal of Experimental Social Psychology*, 10, 159–70.

Tajfel, H. and Turner, J.C. (1979). An integrative theory of intergroup conflict. In W.G. Austin and S. Worchel (eds), *The Social Psychology of Intergroup Relations*. Monterey, CA: Brooks-Cole, pp. 33–47.

Tajfel, H. and Turner, J.C. (1986). The social identity theory of intergroup behaviour. In S. Worschel and W.G. Austin (eds), *Psychology of Intergroup Relations*, 2nd edn., Chicago: Nelson-Hall, pp. 7–24.

Tajfel, H. and Wilkes, A.L. (1963). Classification and quantitative judgement. *British Journal of Psychology*, 54, 101–14.

Tajfel, H., Billig, M., Bundy, R.P., and Flament, C. (1971). Social categorization and intergroup behaviour. *European Journal of Social Psychology*, 1, 149–77.

Tajfel, H., Jaspars, J.M.F., and Fraser, C. (1984). The social dimension in European social psychology. In H. Tajfel (ed.), *The Social Dimension: European developments in social psychology*, vol. 1. Cambridge: Cambridge University Press, pp. 1–5.

Taylor, D.M. and McKirnan, D.J. (1984). A five-stage model of intergroup relations. *British Journal of Social Psychology*, 23, 291–300.

Taylor, D.M. and Moghaddam, F.M. (1994). *Theories of Intergroup Relations*. Westport, CT: Praeger.

Taylor, S.E. (1981). A categorization approach to stereotyping. In D.L. Hamilton (ed.), *Cognitive Processes in Stereotyping and Intergroup Behavior*. Hillsdale, NJ: Erlbaum, pp. 88–114.

Taylor, S.E. (1982). The interface of cognitive and social psychology. In J.H. Harvey (ed.), *Cognition, Social Behavior, and the Environment*. Hillsdale, NJ: Erlbaum, pp. 189–211.

Taylor, S.E. (1998). The social being in social psychology. In D.T. Gilbert, S.T. Fiske, and G. Lindzey (eds), *The Handbook of Social Psychology*, 4th edn, vol. 1. New York: McGraw-Hill, pp. 58–95.

Taylor, S.E. and Brown, J. (1988). Illusion and well-being: A social psychological perspective on mental health. *Psychological Bulletin*, 103, 193–210.

Taylor, S.E. and Falcone, H. (1982). Cognitive bases of stereotyping: The relationship between categorization and prejudice. *Personality and Social Psychology Bulletin*, 8, 426–32.

Taylor, S.E., Fiske, S.T., Etcoff, N., and Ruderman, A. (1978). The categorical and contextual bases of person memory and stereotyping. *Journal of Personality and Social Psychology*, 36, 778–93.

Taylor, S.E., Neter, E., and Wayment, H.A. (1995). Self- evaluation processes. *Personality and Social Psychology Bulletin*, 21, 1278–87.

Terry, D.J. and Hogg, M.A. (1996). Group norms and the attitude–behavior relationship. A role for group identification. *Personality and Social Psychology Bulletin*, 22, 776–93.

Terry, D.J. and Hogg, M.A. (eds) (1998). *Attitudes, Behavior, and Social Context: The role of norms and group membership*. Mahwah, NJ: Erlbaum.

Terry, D.J., Gallois, C., and McCamish, M. (1993). The theory of reasoned action and health behaviour. In D.J., Terry, C. Gallois, and M. McCamish (eds), *The Theory of Reasoned Action: Its application to AIDS-preventive behaviour*. Oxford: Pergamon, pp. 1–27.

Terry, D.J., Hogg, M.A., and McKimmie, B.M. (1998). Group salience, norm congruency, and mode of behavioral decision- making: The effect of group norms on attitude–behavior relations. Manuscript submitted for publication.

Terry, D.J., Hogg, M.A., and White, K.M. (in press). The theory of planned behavior: Self-identity, social identity, and group norms. *British Journal of Social Psychology*.

Thompson, M.M. and Zanna, M.P. (1995). The conflict individual: Personality-based and domain-specific antecedents of ambivalent social attitudes. *Journal of Personality*, 63, 259–88.

Thompson, M.M., Naccarato, M.E., and Parker, K.H. (in press). The personal need for structure and personal need for invalidity scales: Historical perspectives, current applications and future directions. In G.B. Moskowitz (ed.), *Cognitive Social Psychology*, Mahwah, NJ: Erlbaum.

Tice, D. (1991). Esteem protection or enhancement? Self- handicapping motives and attributions differ by trait self- esteem. *Journal of Personality and Social Psychology*, 60, 711–25.

Tindale, R.S. and Anderson, E.M. (1998). Small group research and applied social psychology: An introduction. In R.S. Tindale, L. Heath, J. Edwards, E.J. Posavac, F.B. Bryant, Y. Suarez-

Balcazar, E. Henderson-King, and J. Myer (eds), *Social Psychological Applications to Social Issues: Theory and research on small groups*, vol. 4. New York: Plenum Press, pp. 1–8.

Tomkins, S.S. (1962). *Affect, Imagery, Consciousness*, vol. 1. New York: Springer-Verlag.

Tomkins, S.S. (1963). Affect as amplification: Some modifications in theory. In R. Plutchik and H. Kellerman (eds), *Emotion: Theory, research, and experience*. New York: Academic Press, pp. 342–75.

Trafimow, D., Triandis, H.C., and Goto, S.G. (1991). Some tests of the distinction between the private self and the collective self. *Journal of Personality and Social Psychology*, 60, 649–55.

Triandis, H.C. (1989). The self and social behavior in differing cultural contexts. *Psychological Review*, 93, 506–20.

Triandis, H.C. (1995). *Individualism and Collectivism*. Boulder, CO: Westview Press.

Turner, J. (1985). Social categorisation and the self-concept: A social cognitive theory of group behaviour. In J. Lawler (ed.), *Advances in Group Processes*, vol. 2. Greenwich: JAI Press, pp. 77–122.

Turner, J.C. (1975). Social comparison and social identity: Some prospects for intergroup behaviour. *European Journal of Social Psychology*, 5, 5–34.

Turner, J.C. (1981). The experimental social psychology of intergroup behaviour. In J.C. Turner and H. Giles (eds), *Intergroup Behaviour*. Oxford: Blackwell, pp. 5–34.

Turner, J.C. (1982). Towards a cognitive redefinition of the social group. In H. Tajfel (ed.), *Social Identity and Intergroup Relations*. Cambridge: Cambridge University Press, pp. 15–40.

Turner, J.C. (1984). Social identification and psychological group formation. In H. Tajfel (ed.), *The Social Dimension: European developments in social psychology*. Cambridge: Cambridge University Press, pp. 518–38.

Turner, J.C. (1985). Social categorization and the self-concept: A social cognitive theory of group behaviour. In E.J. Lawler (ed.), *Advances in Group Processes: Theory and research*, vol. 2. Greenwich, CT: JAI Press, pp. 77–122.

Turner, J.C. (1987). Rediscovering the social group. In J.C. Turner, M.A. Hogg, P.J. Oakes, S.D. Reicher, and M.S. Wetherell, *Rediscovering the Social Group: A self-categorization theory*. Oxford: Blackwell, pp. 19–41.

Turner, J.C. (1991). *Social Influence*. Milton Keynes: Open University Press.

Turner, J.C. (1996). Henri Tajfel: An introduction. In W.P. Robinson (ed.), *Social Groups and Identities: Developing the legacy of Henri Tajfel*. Oxford: Butterworth-Heinemann, pp. 1–23.

Turner, J.C. and Bourhis, R. (1996). Social identity, interdependence and the social group: A reply to Rabbie et al. In W.P. Robinson (ed.), *Social Groups and Identity: Developing the legacy of Henri Tajfel*. Oxford: Butterworth-Heinemann, pp. 25–64.

Turner, J.C. and Giles, H. (eds) (1981). *Intergroup Behaviour*. Oxford: Blackwell.

Turner, J.C. and Oakes, P.J. (1986). The significance of the social identity concept for social psychology with reference to individualism, interactionism, and social influence. *British Journal of Social Psychology*, 25, 237–52.

Turner, J.C. and Oakes, P.J. (1989). Self-categorization theory and social influence. In P.B. Paulus (ed.), *The Psychology of Group Influence*. Hillsdale, NJ: Erlbaum, pp. 233–75.

Turner, J.C. and Oakes, P.J. (1997). The socially structured mind. In C. McGarty and S.A. Haslam (eds), *The Message of Social Psychology*. Oxford: Blackwell, pp. 353–73.

Turner, J.C., Hogg, M.A., Oakes, P.J., Reicher, S.D., and Wetherell, M.S. (1987). *Rediscovering the Social Group: A self-categorization theory*. Oxford: Blackwell.

Turner, J.C., Oakes, P.J., Haslam, S.A., and McGarty, C. (1994). Self and collective: Cognition and social context. *Personality and Social Psychology Bulletin*, 20, 454–63.

Tversky, A. (1977). Features of similarity. *Psychological Review*, 84, 327–52.

Tyler, T.R. (1990). *Why People Obey the Law*. New Haven, CT: Yale University Press.

Vala, J., Lima, M.L., and Caetano, A. (1996). Mapping European social psychology: Co-word analysis of the communications at the 10th general meeting of the EAESP. *European Journal of Social Psychology*, 26, 845–50.

Vallacher, R.R. (1978). Objective self-awareness and the perception of others. *Personality and Social Psychology Bulletin*, 4, 63–7.

Vallerand, R.J., Deshaies, P., Cuerrier, J.-P., Pelletier, L.G., and Mongeau, C. (1992). Ajzen and Fishbein's theory of reasoned action as applied to moral behavior: A confirmatory analysis. *Journal of Personality and Social Psychology*, 62, 98–109.

Vallone, R.P., Ross, L., and Lepper, M.R. (1985). The hostile media phenomenon: Bias in the coverage of the Beirut massacre. *Journal of Personality and Social Psychology*, 49, 577–85.

van Knippenberg, A. and Ellemers, N. (1993). Strategies in intergroup relations. In M.A. Hogg and D. Abrams (eds), *Group Motivation: Social psychological perspectives*. Hemel Hempstead: Harvester Wheatsheaf, pp. 17–32.

van Knippenberg, A., van Twuyver, M., and Pepels, J. (1994). Factors affecting social categorization processes in memory. *British Journal of Social Psychology*, 33, 419–31.

van Knippenberg, A.M.F. (1984). Intergroup differences in group perceptions. In H. Tajfel (ed.), *The Social Dimension*. Cambridge and Paris: Cambridge University Press and Editions de la Maison des Sciences de l'Homme.

van Knippenberg, D. and van Knippenberg, A. (1994). Social categorization, focus of attention and judgements of group opinions. *British Journal of Social Psychology*, 33, 477–89.

van Knippenberg, D. and Wilke, H. (1991). Sociale categorisatie, verwerking van argumenten en attitudeverandering. In J. van der Pligt, W. van der Kloot, A. van Knippenberg, and M. Poppe (eds), *Fundamentele Sociale Psychologie*, vol. 5. Tilburg: Tilburg University Press, pp. 96–111.

van Knippenberg, D. and Wilke, H. (1992). Prototypicality of arguments and conformity to ingroup norms. *European Journal of Social Psychology*, 22, 141–55.

van Knippenberg, D., Lossie, N., and Wilke, H. (1994). In-group prototypicality and persuasion: Determinants of heuristic and systematic message processing. *British Journal of Social Psychology*, 33, 289–300.

van Twuyver, M. and van Knippenberg, A. (1995). Social categorization as a function of priming. *European Journal of Social Psychology*, 25, 695–701.

Vanbeselaere, N. (1987). The effects of dichotomous and crossed social categorizations upon intergroup discrimination. *European Journal of Social Psychology*, 17, 143–56.

Vanbeselaere, N. (1991). The different effects of simple and crossed categorizations: A result of category differentiation process or a differential category salience? In W. Stroebe and M. Hewstone (eds), *European Review of Social Psychology*, vol. 2. Chichester: Wiley, pp. 247–78.

von Hippel, W., Sekaquaptewa, D., and Vargas, P. (1995). On the role of encoding processes in stereotype maintenance. *Advances in Experimental Social Psychology*, 27, 177–253.

Walker, I. and Pedersen, A. (1997). Relative deprivation and prejudice: Some Australian evidence. Unpublished manuscript, Murdoch University.

Walker, P. and Antaki, C. (1986). Sexual orientation as a basis for categorization in recall. *British Journal of Social Psychology*, 25, 337–9.

Warren, R.E. (1972). Stimulus encoding in memory. *Journal of Experimental Psychology*, 94, 90–100.

Weber, R. and Crocker, J. (1983). Cognitive processes in the revision of stereotypic beliefs. *Journal of Personality and Social Psychology*, 45, 961–77.

Webster, D.M. and Kruglanski, A. (1994). Individual differences in need for cognitive closure. *Journal of Personality and Social Psychology*, 67, 1049–62.

Wegner, D.M. (1994). Ironic processes of mental control. *Psychological Review*, 101, 35–52.

Wegner, D.M. and Erber, R. (1992). The hyperaccessibility of suppressed thoughts. *Journal of Personality and Social Psychology*, 63, 903–12.

Weigel, R.H. and Howes, P.W. (1985). Conceptions of racial prejudice: Symbolic racism reconsidered. *Journal of Social Issues*, 41, 3, 117–38.

Weinstein, N.D. (1980). Unrealistic optimism about future life events. *Journal of Personality and Social Psychology*, 39, 806–20.

Welbourne, J.L., Harasty, A.S., and Brewer, M.B. (1997). The impact of kindness and intelligence information on extremity ratings of groups and individuals. Paper presented at Midwest Psychological Association, Chicago.

Wellen, J.M., Hogg, M.A., and Terry, D.J. (1998). Group norms and attitude–behavior consistency: The role of group salience and mood. *Group Dynamics: Theory, Research, and Practice*, 1, 48–56.

Wells, L.E. and Marwell, G. (1976). *Self-esteem: Its conceptualization and measurement*. Beverly Hills, CA: Sage.

Wetherell, M. (1987). Social identity and group polarisation. In J.C. Turner, M.A. Hogg, P.J. Oakes, S.D. Reicher, and M. Wetherell (eds), *Rediscovering the Social Group: A self-categorization theory*. Oxford: Blackwell, pp. 142–70.

Wetherell, M. and Potter, J. (1992). *Mapping the Language of Racism: Discourse and the legitimation of exploitation*. Hemel Hempstead: Harvester Wheatsheaf.

Wheeler, L. and Koestner, R. (1984). Performance evaluation: On choosing to know the related attributes of others when we know their performance. *Journal of Experimental Social Psychology*, 20, 263–71.

Wheeler, L., Koestner, R., and Driver, R.E. (1982). Related attributes in the choice of comparison others: It's there, but it isn't all there is. *Journal of Experimental Social Psychology*, 18, 489–500.

White, K.M., Hogg, M.A., and Terry, D.J. (1998). Attitude–behavior relations: The role of ingroup norms and attitude accessibility. Manuscript submitted for publication.

White, K.M., Terry, D.J., and Hogg, M.A. (1998). The role of normative support in attitude–behavior correspondence and attitude change: Ingroup versus outgroup norms. Manuscript submitted for publication.

Wicker, A.W. (1969). Attitudes versus actions: The relationship of verbal and overt responses to attitude objects. *Journal of Social Issues*, 25, 41–78.

Wicklund, R.A. (1975). Objective self-awareness. In L. Berkowitz (ed.), *Advances in Experimental Social Psychology*, vol. 8. New York: Academic Press, pp. 233–75.

Wicklund, R.A. and Gollwitzer, P.M. (1982). *Symbolic Self-completion*. Hillsdale, NJ: Erlbaum.

Wilder, D. and Simon, A.F. (1998). Categorical and dynamic groups: Implications for social perceptions and intergroup behavior. In C. Sedikides, J. Schopler, and C.A. Insko (eds), *Intergroup Cognition and Intergroup Behavior*. Mahwah, NJ: Erlbaum, pp. 27–44.

Wilder, D.A. (1990). Some determinants of the persuasive power of ingroups and outgroups: Organization of information and attribution of independence. *Journal of Personality and Social Psychology*, 59, 1202–13.

Wilder, D.A. and Shapiro, P. (1991). Facilitation of outgroup stereotypes by enhanced ingroup identity. *Journal of Experimental Social Psychology*, 27, 431–52.

Wilder, D.A. and Shapiro, P.N. (1984). Role of outgroup cues in determining social identity. *Journal of Personality and Social Psychology*, 47, 342–8.

Williams, J.E. and Best, D.L. (1982). *Measuring Sex Stereotypes: A thirty nation study*. Beverly Hills, CA: Sage.

Wittenbrink, B., Judd, C.M., and Park, B. (1997). Evidence for racial prejudice at the implicit level and its relationship with questionnaire measures. *Journal of Personality and Social Psychology*, 72, 2, pp. 262–74.

Wood, G.S. (1982). Conspiracy and the paranoid style: Causality and deceit in the eighteenth century. *William and Mary Quarterly*, 39, 401–41.

Wood, J.V. (1996). What is social comparison and how should we study it? *Personality and Social Psychology Bulletin*, 22, 520–37.

Wood, J.V. and Taylor, K.L. (1991). Serving self-relevant goals through social comparison. In J. Suls and T.A. Wills (eds), *Social Comparison: Contemporary theory and research.* Hillsdale, NJ: Erlbaum, pp. 23–49.

Worchel, S., Andreoli, V.A. and Folger, R. (1977). Intergroup cooperation and intergroup attraction: The effect of previous interaction and outcome of combined effort. *Journal of Experimental Social Psychology*, 13, 131–40.

Wright, S.C., Aron, A., McLaughlin-Volpe, T., and Ropp, S.A. (1997). The extended contact effect: Knowledge of cross-group friendships and prejudice. *Journal of Personality and Social Psychology*, 73, 73–90.

Wundt, W. (1897). *Outlines of Psychology*, trans. 1907. New York: Stechert.

Wyer, R.S. (1998). *Stereotype Activation and Inhibition: Advances in social cognition*, vol. 11. Hillsdale, NJ: Erlbaum.

Wyer, R.S., Bodenhausen, G.V., and Srull, T.K. (1984). The cognitive representation of persons and groups and its effect on recall and recognition memory. *Journal of Experimental Social Psychology*, 20, 445–69.

Wyer, R.S., Jr and Srull, T.K. (1981). Category accessibility: Some theoretical and empirical issues concerning the processing of social stimulus information. In E.T. Higgins, C.P. Herman, and M.P. Zanna (eds), *Social Cognition: The Ontario symposium*, vol. 1. Hillsdale, NJ: Erlbaum, pp. 161–98.

Wyer, R.S., Jr and Srull, T.K. (1994). *Handbook of Social Cognition*, 2nd edn. Hillsdale, NJ: Erlbaum.

Wyer, R.S., Jr, and Gruenfeld, D.H. (1995). Information processing in social contexts: Implications for social memory and judgement. In L. Berkowitz (ed.), *Advances in Experimental Social Psychology*, vol. 27. New York: Academic Press, pp. 49–91.

Yzerbyt, V., Rocher, S., and Coull, A. (1996). What saves the stereotype? The role of cognitive resources in stereotype maintenance. Paper presented at the General Meeting of the European Association of Experimental Social Psychology, Gmunden, Austria, July.

Yzerbyt, V.Y., Rocher, S.J., and Schadron, G. (1997). Stereotypes as explanations: A subjective essentialistic view of group perception. In R. Spears, P. Oakes, N. Ellemers, and S.A. Haslam (eds), *The Psychology of Stereotyping and Group Life*. Oxford: Blackwell, pp. 20–50.

Yzerbyt, V.Y., Schadron, G., Leyens, J.-Ph., and Rocher, S. (1994). Social judgeability: The impact of meta-informational cues on the use of stereotypes. *Journal of Personality and Social Psychology*, 66, 48–55.

Zajonc, R.B. (1980a). Cognition and social cognition: A historical perspective. In L. Festinger (ed.), *Retrospections on Social Psychology*. New York: Oxford University Press, pp. 180–204.

Zajonc, R.B. (1980b). Feeling and thinking: Preferences need no inferences. *American Psychologist*, 35, 151–75.

Zajonc, R.B. (1989). Styles of explanation in social psychology. *European Journal of Social Psychology*, 19, 345–68.

Zajonc, R.B. and Markus, H. (1984). Affect and cognition: The hard interface. In C.E. Izard, J. Kagan, and R.B. Zajonc (eds), *Emotions, Cognition and Behavior*. Cambridge: Cambridge University Press, pp. 73–102.

Zander, A. (1979). The psychology of small group processes. *Annual Review of Psychology*, 30, 417–51.

Zanna, M.P. and Olson, J.M. (eds) (1994). *The Psychology of Prejudice: The Ontario symposium*, vol. 7. Hillsdale, NJ: Erlbaum.

Zanna, M.P., Goethals, G.R., and Hill, J.F. (1975). Evaluating a sex-related ability: Social comparison with similar others and standard setters. *Journal of Experimental Social Psychology*, 11, 86–93.

Zanna, M.P., Haddock, G., and Esses, V.M. (1990). The determinants of prejudice. Presented at Society of Experimental Social Psychology, Buffalo, NY.

Zarate, M.A. and Sandoval, P. (1995). The effects of contextual cues on making occupational and gender categorizations. *British Journal of Social Psychology*, 34, 353–62.

Zarate, M.A. and Smith, E.R. (1990). Person categorization and stereotyping. *Social Cognition*, 8, 161–85.

Zinkiewicz, L. (1997). A social identity approach to intergroup contact: The roles of group salience, ingroup identification, and social influence. Unpublished doctoral dissertation, University of Queensland, Brisbane.

Subject Index

Name Index